ARCHIVES & EXCAVATIONS

to the memory of

FRANCIS HASKELL

This volume has been published with the help of subventions from

The Dr M. Aylwin Cotton Foundation
The Late Isobel Thornley's Bequest Fund to the University of London
The Scouloudi Foundation in Association with the Institute of Historical Research

ARCHIVES & EXCAVATIONS

ESSAYS ON THE HISTORY OF ARCHAEOLOGICAL EXCAVATIONS IN ROME AND
SOUTHERN ITALY FROM THE RENAISSANCE TO THE NINETEENTH CENTURY

Edited by

ILARIA BIGNAMINI

Essays by

ILARIA BIGNAMINI, IAIN GORDON BROWN
IAN CAMPBELL, AMANDA CLARIDGE
BRIAN F. COOK, GIORGIO FILIPPI, INGO HERKLOTZ
VALENTIN KOCKEL, SUSANNA LE PERA BURANELLI
PAOLO LIVERANI, RONALD T. RIDLEY
CORNELIS SCHUDDEBOOM, RITA TURCHETTI AND
KLAUS E. WERNER

14
ARCHAEOLOGICAL MONOGRAPHS OF
THE BRITISH SCHOOL AT ROME

The British School at Rome, London
2004

© The British School at Rome, *at* The British Academy
10 Carlton House Terrace, London SW1Y 5AH

www.bsr.ac.uk

Registered Charity No. 314176

ISBN 0 904152 43 X

Cover illustration

Notes and photographs from the Thomas Ashby Collection in the archives of the British School at Rome.
(British School at Rome Archive — Notes from Ashby manuscripts R.242 (front, top left) and R.151 (front, bottom left); Ashby Collection photos nos. XI.40 (front, top right), XI.37 (front, bottom right) and 816 (back).)

Designed by SILVIA STUCKY

Typeset and printed by SOCIETÀ TIPOGRAFICA ROMANA, ROME, ITALY

CONTENTS

LIST OF FIGURES

ACKNOWLEDGMENTS

THIS BOOK originates from informal conversations with Andrew Wallace-Hadrill in the courtyard of the British School at Rome, and from the first two meetings of the workshop *Archives & Excavations* at the British School at Rome (1997) and in the Headley Lecture Theatre, Ashmolean Museum, Oxford (1998). During that period I was the Leverhulme Trust Research Fellow at the Department of the History of Art, University of Oxford, and Honorary Research Fellow of the British School at Rome. I am most grateful to Martin Kemp and the Leverhulme Trust, to Andrew Wallace-Hadrill and the staff of the British School at Rome, to Christopher Brown and the staff of the Ashmolean Museum, and to Margareta Steinby.

The workshop and this book would have hardly existed were it not for the enthusiasm, advice and help of the speakers, contributors, colleagues and friends. I am particularly grateful to Amanda Claridge and Paolo Liverani, and also to Sir Howard Colvin, Michael Crawford, Maria Fenelli, Werner Fuchs, Anna Gallina Zevi, Ian Jenkins, Simon Keay, Donna Kurtz, Maria Giuseppina Lauro, Martin Millett, Mette Moltesen, Larissa Salmina Haskell, Bert Smith, Geoffrey Waywell, Catherine Whistler and Fausto Zevi.

The meeting of the workshop in Oxford was fortunate enough to take place while Francis Haskell was still alive, and benefited enormously from his vast knowledge, genuine enthusiasm, intellectual generosity and immense love of the Antique and Italy. It is with great sadness that we can only recognize his contribution by dedicating this book to his memory.

*   *   *

THE TEXTS of the papers were gathered together by the present writer and prepared for the press by Gill Clark. I am also most grateful to Chris Wickham, Chair of the Publications Advisory Committee of the British School at Rome (1996–2000), and to the readers of this book.

*   *   *

THE PUBLICATION of *Archives & Excavations* has been made possible by generous contributions from The Dr M. Aylwin Cotton Foundation, The Late Isobel Thornley's Bequest Fund to the University of London and the Scouloudi Foundation in Association with the Institute of Historical Research.

Ilaria Bignamini
2000

Postscript
Sadly Ilaria died soon after submitting this volume, and before it could proceed to production. Much of the outstanding administrative work and the translation into English of Chapters 11–14 was undertaken by Dr Jo Berry: the School is grateful to her for her assistance.

ABBREVIATIONS

Those archives and libraries, journals, standard and other works most frequently mentioned in the footnotes to this volume have been referred to in abbreviated form.

ARCHIVES AND LIBRARIES

ASR – Archivio di Stato di Roma
ASV – Archivio Segreto Vaticano
BAV – Biblioteca Apostolica Vaticana

JOURNALS

BMusPont – *Bollettino dei Monumenti Musei e Gallerie Pontificie*
BullCom – *Bullettino della Commissione Archeologica Comunale in Roma*
BullInst – *Bullettino dell'Instituto di Corrispondenza Archeologica*
JHS – *Journal of Hellenic Studies*
JRS – *Journal of Roman Studies*
MemPontAcc – *Atti della Pontificia Accademia Romana di Archeologia. Ser. III. Memorie*
NSc – *Notizie degli Scavi di Antichità*
PBSR – *Papers of the British School at Rome*
RendPontAcc – *Atti della Pontificia Accademia Romana di Archeologia. Rendiconti*

STANDARD WORKS

AE – *L'Année Epigraphique* (1888–)
CII – A. Fabretti, *Corpus Inscriptionum Italicarum* (Turin, 1867)
CIL – *Corpus Inscriptionum Latinarum* (1863–)
CVA – *Corpus Vasorum Antiquorum* (1925–)
ICUR – *Inscriptiones Christianae Urbis Romae* (1861–)
IG – *Inscriptiones Graecae* (1873–)
IGUR – L. Moretti (ed.), *Inscriptiones Graecae Urbis Romae* (Rome, 1968–79)
NRIE – M. Buffa, *Nuova raccolta di iscrizioni etrusche* (Florence, 1935)
TLE – M. Pallottino, *Testimonia Linguae Etruscae* (Florence, 1968^2)

OTHER WORKS

DBI – *Dizionario biografico degli Italiani* (Rome, 1960–)
DBITI – J. Ingamells (ed.), *A Dictionary of British and Irish Travellers in Italy 1701–1800 compiled from the Brinsley Ford Archive* (New Haven/London, 1997)
Lanciani, *Storia* (1902–12) – Rodolfo Lanciani, *Storia degli scavi di Roma e notizie intorno le collezioni romane di antichità*, 4 vols (Rome, 1902–12)
Lanciani, *Storia* (1989–) – Rodolfo Lanciani, *Storia degli scavi di Roma e notizie intorno le collezioni romane di antichità*, reprint with additions, 7 vols (Rome, 1989–)
LIMC – *Lexikon Iconographicum Mythologiae Classicae* (Zurich/Munich, 1981–99)

PREFACE

Paolo Liverani, Martin Kemp and Andrew Wallace-Hadrill

Presentare *Archives & Excavations* non è compito facile. Non diciamo questo perché l'*excusatio* fa parte dei *topoi* più collaudati del genere 'presentazione'. La difficoltà risiede nel fatto che gli atti di questi due *workshop* (British School at Rome, 1997 e Headley Lecture Theatre, Oxford 1998) costituiscono il risultato più completo di quella strada che Ilaria Bignamini, anima e ideatrice dell'iniziativa, aveva incominciato a percorrere con tutta l'originalità e l'energia che la caratterizzavano. Al tempo stesso, però, essi rimangono solo una promessa di traguardi più ambiziosi e di una metodologia esigente, che richiede competenze di solito assai difficilmente presenti in uno stesso studioso. E non è facile individuare chi sarà all'altezza dell'impresa e avrà il coraggio di adempiere a questa promessa, visto che purtroppo Ilaria ci ha lasciato in maniera imprevedibilmente rapida e terribilmente prematura. Questo fatto aggiunge un ulteriore rimpianto di natura intellettuale a quello, già fortissimo, di natura affettiva che si portano dentro tutti gli amici e colleghi che Ilaria aveva saputo contagiare con il suo entusiasmo e convertire a questo tipo di ricerche.

Ma sforziamoci di tornare al metodo. Se lo storico dell'antichità utilizza — per esempio — Tito Livio, egli sa bene che la sua fonte va letta contemporaneamente almeno su due livelli. Il testo fornisce infatti informazioni su un determinato periodo della storia repubblicana, ma — allo stesso tempo e in maniera indissociabile — è specchio della cultura, della mentalità e delle passioni politiche dell'età di Augusto e — più in generale — del passaggio cruciale tra Repubblica e Impero. I due livelli, inoltre, interagiscono tra di loro e non si comprenderebbe il primo senza approfondire il secondo e viceversa.

Una tale coscienza, invece, non si può dire sia ancora pienamente acquisita in chi, per un motivo o per un altro, lavora utilizzando i dati degli scavi archeologici di un passato più o meno remoto. L'archeologo in genere prende quel che trova nella bibliografia corrente, magari lamentando le condizioni di scavo e la mancanza di informazioni sul contesto o la prassi disinvolta dei suoi predecessori. Difficilmente tenta di risalire fino alle fonti contemporanee, ancor più raramente ne cerca di nuove per dirimere dubbi e incertezze. Lo storico dell'età moderna, oppure più di recente lo storico dell'arte, si sforza di dare un profilo ai personaggi e alle vicende che hanno a che fare con l'archeologia del periodo che lo occupa, ma di solito il suo interesse per i risultati effettivi degli scavi e degli studi di tale periodo è secondario e serve più a dare colore e gradevolezza alla narrazione che reale sostanza al quadro storico. Se trova notizie inedite spesso non sa o non gli interessa valorizzarle dal punto di vista archeologico.

D'altronde è cosa nota: i *curricula* accademici sono separati, addirittura le biblioteche in cui si studia sono differenti, dunque un simile risultato è inevitabile. Tra le due guerre mondiali, inoltre, gli archivi hanno dormito sonni piuttosto tranquilli senza troppo disturbo, soprattutto per quel che riguarda gli archeologi, quasi avessero ormai esaurito tutti i loro tesori. Solo di recente gli antichisti hanno ripreso a frequentarli con una certa serietà.

Non si può dire che mancassero modelli illustri tra gli studiosi della fine dell'800 o dei primi del '900, personaggi come Rodolfo Lanciani o Thomas Ashby che avevano tentato una sintesi tra i vari ambiti disciplinari. Nel panorama degli studi novecenteschi, però, questa terra di confine tra storia, arte e archeologia non poteva certo dirsi affollata e anche chi la frequentava in molti casi lo faceva in maniera poco sistematica.

È qui che si colloca l'intuizione di Ilaria: mettere insieme in modo non episodico archivi, storia e scavi. Incardinare gli scavi nel periodo in cui vennero realizzati, con una puntigliosa documentazione che faccia giustizia dei luoghi comuni sempre ripetuti, può portare a risultati imprevedibili. La ricchezza e il valore dei dati, su cui si basano di solito gli studi delle varie discipline interessate al problema, possono essere scossi o rinnovati radicalmente da una seria ricerca sulle fonti, simile a quella che gli storici tedeschi chiamano la *Quellenkunde*, a patto di poter contare su una significativa competenza ed esperienza in tutti e tre i campi.

Illustrare questi risultati non è il nostro compito: i testi che sono raccolti nel volume ci riescono benissimo da soli. È invece il valore di questa idea semplice, ma estremamente feconda che vorremmo sottolineare. Un'idea che negli ultimi anni costituiva il principale scopo e la più forte passione intellettuale di Ilaria.

Come a volte succede, a questa semplice idea era arrivata per percorsi relativamente complessi. Si era inizialmente occupata di arte contemporanea, collaborando in particolare con la rivista *Flash Art*, ma poi i suoi interessi si erano indirizzati verso l'Inghilterra. La laurea, ottenuta a Milano nel 1978 *summa cum laude*, consisteva infatti in una tesi su 'William Hogarth tra 'The Battle of the Pictures' e 'Industry and Idleness'' seguita da Enrico Castelnuovo. Il Ph.D. arrivò dieci anni più tardi al Courtauld Institute of Art di Londra con una dissertazione dal titolo 'The Accompaniment to Patronage. A Study of the Origins, Rise and Development of an Institutional System for the Arts in Britain, 1692–1768', sotto la direzione di Michael Kitson. Gli anni intermedi erano stati occupati da varie collaborazioni e borse di studio ed era iniziato anche un duraturo rapporto con il Paul Mellon Centre for Studies in British Art, che l'aveva portata a sondare tutti gli archivi italiani, anche i più sperduti, alla ricerca di materiali sui *British Travellers* diretti a Roma e a Venezia nel XVIII secolo. I risultati sarebbero confluiti nella grande opera del *Dictionary of British and Irish Travellers in Italy 1701–1800* (New Haven/London, 1996).

I viaggiatori inglesi erano ormai divenuti i suoi compagni inseparabili e si può dire che l'avessero contagiata: ormai si spostava come un pendolo tra Oxford da un lato, Roma e Milano dall'altro. Il Department of the History of Art dell'Università di Oxford costituiva la sua affiliazione istituzionale, Roma l'oggetto dei suoi studi, Milano il luogo degli affetti e significava soprattutto il marito Luca, dal quale spesso si trovava distante per le vicissitudini delle sue ricerche, ma del quale — nonostante una certa riservatezza — parlava sempre con una luce particolare negli occhi, che gli amici avevano imparato a distinguere immediatamente.

Il risultato più noto di questi anni di lavoro era stata nel 1996 la grande mostra sul Grand Tour, curata assieme ad Andrew Wilton alla Tate Gallery di Londra e presentata l'anno successivo a Roma al Palazzo delle Esposizioni.

Era a questo punto che si collocava l'ultimo passo, l'ingresso deciso nel campo dell'archeologia. Lo studio e la ricerca di marmi romani da collezionare e da riportare in patria era infatti uno degli elementi essenziali del Grand Tour e inglesi erano stati anche i principali scavatori e mercanti d'arte antica della seconda metà del XVIII secolo.

Decidere di entrare in un diverso ambito accademico, quando ormai la propria identità di studioso è configurata, è un'impresa che forse si poteva ancora tentare nel XVIII secolo. Oggi, con la specializzazione delle discipline, è un salto che nessun temerario si azzarda più a fare. Eppure a Ilaria era riuscito di penetrare nel recinto degli archeologi, ostico labirinto per chi lo guarda dal di fuori. C'era entrata con il suo stile e il suo taglio, ovviamente, ma certo non vi si trovava a disagio. E la via inglese si era rivelata il percorso meno prevedibile, ma più fruttuoso, per condurre a unità un fascio di interessi solo apparentemente disparato.

Le ultime imprese che stava affrontando, logica evoluzione di queste premesse, erano una storia degli scavi di Ostia, completamente rinnovata sulla base dei ricchissimi fondi archivistici da lei esplorati, e un volume che aveva deciso di intitolare 'Digging & Dealing in the Eighteenth Century. The British Conquest of the Marbles of Ancient Rome'.

Ilaria Bignamini (bottom row, left) with some of the participants in the Oxford workshop in 1998, including some contributors to the present volume (Amanda Claridge (top row, second from right), Giorgio Filippi (top row, left), Valentin Kockel (bottom row, right), Paolo Liverani (bottom row, centre) and Cornelis Schuddeboom (top row, centre)). *(Photograph reproduced courtesy of Giorgio Filippi.)*

Dei suoi lavori su Ostia è uscita una versione preliminare nel catalogo della mostra tenutasi a Ginevra nel 2001, che dunque non fece in tempo a vedere stampata, e una seconda più ampia è in corso di stampa nella *Rivista di Archeologia e Storia dell'Arte*. Del volume, invece, a parte contributi di dettaglio e testi di conferenze, resta purtroppo una stesura sufficientemente dettagliata solo del primo capitolo. Dei successivi, chiaramente elencati nell'indice già previsto, restano tra le sue carte solo appunti, frammenti e una gran quantità di documenti destinati alle appendici e densi di annotazioni sparse, che testimoniano delle idee e ipotesi che continuavano ad affollarsi alla sua mente fino agli ultimi mesi di vita.

Una buona introduzione dovrebbe ora concludersi con un colpo d'ala e qualche bella figura retorica, ma chi — come noi — la conosceva da vicino non può rifugiarsi nelle formule a effetto. Preferiamo quindi lasciar parlare il volume, testimone non solo della vastità di prospettive e interessi di un'amica, ma ancor più della sua energia contagiosa, alla quale era impossibile resistere, tanto che inevitabilmente arrivava a coinvolgere tutti coloro che incrociava sulla sua strada. Una buona rappresentanza di essi, trascinata da Ilaria a Roma o a Oxford in indimenticabili giornate di lavoro e discussione, compare nelle pagine che seguono.

Paolo Liverani
January 2004

❖ ❖ ❖

ILARIA — A PERSONAL MEMOIR

Ilaria Bignamini was speaking at the Association of Art Historians Annual Conference in 1990 at Trinity College, Dublin, the first time the Association had ventured outside the United Kingdom. She felt at home with her colleagues in British art history, and was establishing a growing reputation amongst her peers. I was attending another section of the conference, but pulled out to hear her, because I was interested in her subject as advertised in the programme, 'The rise of an institutional system for the arts in Britain, 1692–1758'. At that time she was working on the intellectual and artistic environment of the Royal Academy and its predecessor 'academies' in London, with a particular concern for the use of the human model and anatomical instruction. The immediate fruit of her researches was the notable exhibition and catalogue, *The Artist's Model: its Role in British Art from Lely to Etty* (Nottingham, 1991), undertaken with Martin Postle and shown in 1991 at Kenwood House, London, and the University Art Gallery, Nottingham.

Arriving late, after misreading the map of conference venues, I found Ilaria already in full flow. The air of intensity in the darkened room was palpable. Dressed angularly in black, stooped over the lectern and illuminated only by light reflected from her notes, her aquiline features were sculpted into dramatic relief. Like an elegant bird of prey, she voraciously picked tasty verbal and visual morsels from her text, presenting them to her attentive audience with urgency, verve and humour. Her highly individual accent, far from stock Italian, gave her delivery a baroque timbre more like that of a native Slav. Here, clearly, was someone to reckon with.

I subsequently arranged to meet her in London to discuss, as they say, areas of mutual interest. Her knowledge and eager engagement with the role of anatomy in the artists' proto-academies in the eighteenth century was prodigious, far surpassing what I knew in an area that I thought I had researched. As anyone who encountered Ilaria will testify, no conversation was ever confined by set concerns, and I was rapidly taken on a journey across contemporary art, the Grand Tour (on which she was becoming the leading expert) and stations in between. It also became apparent that while she was adept at finding sources of funding to sustain her research, she was effectively a homeless scholar — at least in academic terms. Her real home, with Luca in Milan, was very much another matter, and was the site of a partnership that was as unorthodox as it was warming. She faced the double dilemma of having cut - herself off from the system of job patronage in Italy and of not really fitting into the career structures available in British art history departments. The topics of her research and her growing seniority counted against her in competing for junior, mainstream posts in Britain. She was fully aware of where she stood, and at some point openly took the decision to devote herself to her research, come what may, rather than trimming her activities to conform to a standard career path.

This lack of obvious 'fit' became even more obvious when she forged her new and highly personal research field on the history of archaeological excavations. Her studies of the records of the British excavators and dealers who dominated the unearthing of ancient marbles in Italy for a substantial period in the eighteenth century interacted with a number of disciplines — the history of ancient art, archaeology and its history, the history of art and dealing, the development of taste and collecting, and the social and political history of Rome. But her new discipline belonged wholly to none of them. Her findings extended from meticulous identification of the sources of 'marbles' in particular digs, and their correlation with inventories, to the illumination of some extraordinary personalities, not least those of the disreputable and exiled sons of English lords who caused less immediate embarrassment if they followed their inclinations in far-away Italy. She became extraordinarily naturalized in the society of the ex-patriate British in Rome, precisely mirroring her own naturalizing as an Italian in matters British. She took a particular relish in the way that Rome had become a magnet for an extraordinarily rich assembly of international *cognoscenti*, scholars, aristocratic rogues and sharp operators.

The originality and interest of her research was recognized in research terms, most notably by her obtaining a Leverhulme grant to work in the Centre for Visual Studies that I had newly founded in Oxford, and in the support she received from the British School at Rome under the Direction of Andrew Wallace-Hadrill. Her interests and unquenchable enthusiasm drew together scholars from diverse disciplines, acting as a catalyst for exchanges of information and ideas between people who should have known each other but didn't. The most public manifestations of this catalytic activity were the conferences 'Archives and Excavations' hosted in Oxford in 1998 and in Rome in 1997. I was able to attend only the former. Ilaria's own paper, dense with new material and illuminated by bright flashes of wit, as she paraded her notable cast of historical characters, was the undoubted highlight of one of the most effective gatherings of scholars I have attended.

Her presence in Oxford, now marked by the dedication of our visiting scholars' room to her memory, affected all who knew her. Ilaria was never mediocre of spirit or dissembling in manner. Whether unveiling her most recent discovery, persuading me that I needed to do something, interacting with students (which she did with unstinted generosity), cooking pasta with panache, or smoking one of far too many cigarettes, Ilaria never did anything by halves. She worked for recovery from her devastating last illness with her characteristic sense of the excitements that still lay ahead. I still cannot believe that she is not going to call, joyfully announcing her arrival, lifting our spirits through her unabashed vitality, taking us out of our administrative grind and transporting us into her world, historical and present. She is missed. At least the present volume gives a glimpse into the new intellectual territory she was defining. She has lit a torch that it is for others now to carry.

Martin Kemp
June 2004

❊ ❊ ❊

ILARIA BIGNAMINI AND THE 'DIGGING OF DIGGINGS'

Ilaria Bignamini's death, all too soon and all too swift, deprived us of a friend of whom the abiding memory is vivacity, energy, enthusiasm, laughter. Just short of 49, she had reached the peak of her development: she had discovered a field that was truly her own, and the more she worked on it, the richer the results and the wider the implications proved. She had a dream to create a new discipline that would span archaeology and art history. Those who listened to the ambitious proposals she was developing in the last two years of her life were easily converted by her enthusiasm, and left a little breathless by the endless fertility of her suggestions. What only emerges looking at her archive is how much she had already achieved, and how close she was to the realization of her ambitions. She relished the thought that her subject, the investigation of the eighteenth-century waves of excavations around Rome by a group of British entrepreneurs, was the excavation of an excavation, or, as she put it, the 'digging of diggings'. Perhaps she would have also relished the irony that to understand fully what she was doing, we must now excavate her own archive: the digging of digging of diggings.

In a research proposal developed in the months before she fell ill, she listed her current research projects as follows:

- *Digging and Dealing in the Eighteenth Century. The British Conquest of the Marbles of Ancient Rome*, in progress (book)
- *I 'Marmi inglesi' in Vaticano: catalogo generale*, Vatican City, in progress (catalogue)
- *Correspondence of British excavators and dealers active in Rome in the eighteenth and early nineteenth centuries. With appendices of excavation and export licences, and sales* (research in progress)
- *Ostia and Porto: excavations from the Renaissance to 'Roma capitale'* (research in progress)
- *Castelporziano and Castelfusano: excavations from the Renaissance to 'Roma capitale'* (research in progress)
- *Campo Iemini: Robert Fagan's excavations of 1794*, in progress (article).

Under normal circumstances, anybody laying claim to six concurrent research projects might expect to encounter a certain scepticism: some at least must surely prove no more than castles in the air. Yet Ilaria's archive shows that all the projects were not only in hand, but in an advanced state of progress, with substantial material collected and written up for three separate books, and half a dozen further more specific projects, some (like the contribution to the Castelporziano volume) ready for publication.

The frenetic activity ('I'm writing non-stop', she reported in December 2000) was the culmination of a decade's activity in which she progressively closed in on and defined the field she wished to create. Her energy and range are visible from her earliest work: the radical student in the '70s writing on Soviet art and dissent in the USSR, while developing the engagement with British artists in her work on William Hogarth, then moving to London to work on English Arts Academies, a theme that would occupy her through the '80s. The turning point, as Paolo Liverani suggests, was the project on the Brinsley Ford archive of British and Irish travellers in Italy for the Paul Mellon Centre (1988–92). From then on, the eighteenth-century Grand Tour became her prime focus, a commitment cemented by the major exhibition held on the Grand Tour at the Tate in 1996 and the Palazzo delle Esposizioni at Rome in 1997, on which she worked from 1990.

Focusing first on the travellers, especially the members of the Royal family, and then on the art works that reached Britain as a result of the Grand Tour, and in particular the Townley marbles at the British Museum, she developed the theme that was central to all her projects for a decade. At its core was the group of three British artists, Gavin Hamilton, Thomas Jenkins and Robert Fagan, who as diggers and dealers excavated and exported an exceptional number of Roman statues, forming the core of the Townley collection, as well as many new accessions to the Vatican. She realized that between the Townley Papers in the British Museum, and the Vatican archives, an exceptional vein of information was available, which would make it possible to provenance with considerable precision many of the Roman statues in those collections.

Emblematic was her 'rediscovery' of the 'Campo Iemini' Venus in the British Museum. As she showed in the *Burlington Magazine* in 1994, the documentation allowed her to reconstruct the entire history of the statue, from its excavation by Prince Augustus Frederick and Robert Fagan in 1794 on an estate of the Duke Sforza Cesarini, through the vain attempts of the authorities to retain it in Rome as the French Revolution caused British influence to falter, to its donation to the future King George IV, and its subsequent passage to the British Museum, and gradual falling into neglect and consignment to the basement. The Grand Tour exhibition returned it to public view for the first time in 70 years, and to Rome for the first time in 196. But the same statue illustrates how this vein of research continued to bear results. In the Spring of 1997, Ilaria unearthed in the Archivio di Stato the documentation of a legal dispute between Duke Sforza Cesarini and the tenant of Campo Iemini, with maps that revealed the precise location of Fagan's dig. It corresponded with the traces of a site of a Roman villa identified by Maria Fenelli. Thanks to the discovery, it was possible to place a 'vincolo' on the site. One day, it will be possible to 'rediscover' the precise archaeological context of the statue 'rediscovered' by Ilaria in the cellars of the British Museum. The publication of this second discovery, with Maria Fenelli, was just one of her six projects 'in progress'.

If Campo Iemini is just an example, the other projects revolved round the same set of issues, but on a vast scale. The Leverhulme Research Fellowship under Martin Kemp at Oxford between 1996 and 1999 allowed her to break the back of an enormous archival project: dedicated work and meticulous scholarship driven by passion. In this period she produced the material for an annotated edition of the correspondence of the principal excavators of Roman marbles, above all Hamilton, Jenkins and Fagan, between 1751 and 1814, in chronological order. The draft runs to 214 pages and 185,000 words. It provides one of the two essential primary sources for her work.

The object of the Leverhulme Fellowship, however, was the compilation of a site catalogue of British archaeological excavations in Italy, 1764–1802. Though incomplete and, like the Correspondence volume, still without full introduction, the main body of text was there, including the site catalogue of 63 sites, and the list of papal export licences granted to dealers, arranged alphabetically under dealer, and a list of sales by British diggers to the Vatican. The draft amounts to some 296 pages or 94,000 words, excluding numerous supplements on individual sites.

The project took Ilaria deep into her most important primary source, after the correspondence of the excavators, that is the archives of the Reverenda Camera Apostolica that granted both licences to dig and to export material so excavated. She became increasingly convinced of the wealth of this source. Between 1425 and 1870, the office of the Cardinale Camerlengo by and large controlled all excavation in the Papal States; and once the identity of the succession of Camerlenghi and other officers responsible had been established, it was possible to reconstruct nearly the whole series of licences for over four centuries.

As a scholar, Ilaria had two, complementary modes. One was the appetite for meticulous research that enabled her to assemble and edit documents, draw up lists, tables and catalogues. Alongside the dry collector was a speaker, writer and performer who was anything but dry: none present at her contribution to the Grand Tour conference at the British School at Rome in 1997 could forget the exuberant humour, the irreverent depiction of the touring British royals, the vivid evocation of place and time. Perhaps in the development of her projects in her final years one can see the reassertion of this second Ilaria, reminiscent of the bubbling conversationalist treasured by her friends, over the meticulous cataloguer.

By the end, the project had metamorphosed into an extraordinary book: *Diggers and Dealers*. The book was planned in full detail: five sections (Digging, Dealing, Displaying, Talking and Writing, and the British Conquest of the Marbles of Ancient Rome) with seventeen chapters, most planned down to the subsection. Only the first three chapters were written, stopping short before chapter 4, 'Digging of diggings'. The humour of the section and chapter titles reflects the desire to bring alive the whole world of eighteenth-century Rome, its grand visitors, enterprising artists and dealers, and their interactions with the locals. Hence the titles of chapter 2, 'The 'Cavas'' and chapter 3, 'Works at the 'cavas'', deliberately lean on the anglicized plural of an Italian word to evoke the language of English excavators; subsection 2.3 'I have now three cavos in hand' offers a variant. With one heart in Oxford, and one in Milan, Ilaria rejoiced in such linguistic code-switching.

Humorous the titles might be, but the three chapters, with their supporting appendices, are dense with detail: setting out for the first time a full analysis of the system of papal licences, the archives, the officers, the procedures of the authorities on the one hand, and the methods, motives and language of the excavators on the other. The draft, of 63 sides or 22,000 words, is an invaluable essay, which not only puts back the finds in their archaeological context, as she had done for the Campo Iemini Venus, but, most important of all, puts back the excavations in their social, historical and human context.

The implication of Ilaria's argument is that we cannot understand the objects collected in our Museums, nor indeed the formation of those Museums themselves, without understanding the historical context that generated them. This she located firmly in a world of politics and power-relations, of the flexing of muscle by Britain in Europe in the wake of the Seven Years' War, and its use of the antiquities of Italy to forge for itself a new 'imperial' identity. That theme was set out best in her Neale Lecture at University College London in 2000, 'The British conquest of the marbles of ancient Rome: aspects of the material and cultural conquests', and would of course have been developed in her section V, 'The British conquest of the marbles of ancient Rome'.

Ilaria wished to reunite disciplines that she felt were falsely separated: to restore to the history of British archaeology its vital eighteenth-century background; to reintegrate it with art history and museum studies; and to do so using the tools of the historian: on the one hand, research into documentary archives, on the other, the reconstruction of social and political contexts. What she demonstrated beyond doubt was the need to cross disciplines in order to make sense of the field; and she pioneered a vein of research, a 'cava', which will surely continue to produce abundant 'robba'. She communicated excitement in her subject, and the two conferences she organized on 'Archives and Excavations' that are represented by the present volume reflect both her desire to involve others, and her success in doing so.

Andrew Wallace-Hadrill
January 2004

INTRODUCTION

Ilaria Bignamini

I

ARCHAEOLOGISTS, art historians, historians and classicists are all aware that our knowledge of past excavations is inadequate. A broader and deeper knowledge of this material evidence is needed for undertaking new excavation, for the cataloguing of sculpture and other marble fragments, for the protection of sites, and for the cataloguing of drawings after the antique, views and plans of ruins, and maps. Furthermore, such knowledge might encourage both more scholarship on the countless artists and patrons whose activities as excavators are still largely ignored, and more study of manuscript and printed sources. More generally, it might aid the advancement of learning.

Centuries after their first discovery, many sites and remains have either disappeared, or cannot be located now. Others still exist, but knowledge of what was actually found by generations of excavators is very fragmentary. Indeed, we know little of the general or specific details of the archaeological record or of the actual processes of its exploration in the past. The same applies to the excavation provenances of countless finds; to the complete chronology of licences granted for excavations in and near Rome since the Renaissance; to the correspondence about the archaeology of any period and area, within and outside Italy (including Greece, Asia Minor, North Africa, England, Scotland, Ireland, France, Spain and Germany); and to the drawings, plans and maps originally enclosed with letters and reports written by the excavators to various officials of the Papal States or other governments and to dealers and collectors. Written documents are mostly found in archives and libraries, while visual documents illustrating them are preserved in public and private collections and are often catalogued as mere 'views with ancient ruins', or 'studies after the antique'. A longer list of shortcomings might easily be produced, but the important point is that a radical change in our attitude towards past excavations has now become a priority. 'Excavations' in archives, libraries and collections eventually should be regarded as an integral part of modern archaeology.

Archives & Excavations is the first book on the subject to appear. Its aim is to stimulate a new approach to the history of excavations by drawing attention to a vast and important area of research that has been much neglected, if not completely forgotten, for almost a century. The cause of this neglect is the institutionalization of specialized knowledge early in the twentieth century. More precisely, there was a cultural and disciplinary separation of complementary disciplines such as archaeology and art history in the period between the two World Wars. Archaeology developed into a modern intellectual discipline, art history was preoccupied with redefining its territory, and there was a decline in antiquarianism and, more recently, in documentary research and micro-analytical studies. Archaeology has gradually lost the memory of its own past, while other related disciplines, notably art history, have lost their natural links with material culture and the immense body of past and present archaeological facts and evidence. These combined factors have contributed to an increase in our ignorance of the origins of archaeology and excavations. This fact notwithstanding, and precisely because there is still insufficient awareness of the loss, prejudice against early excavators and antiquarianism has grown considerably.

The growth of archaeology and art history as modern disciplines and professions, of intellectually rigorous connoisseurship, aesthetics, stylistic studies, iconography and philology, the rise of new disciplines, methodologies and technologies and, more generally, the professionalization of archaeological scholarship and fieldwork, alongside the growth of more rigorous legislation and professional ethics, have all contributed to the gradual dismissal, if not denigration, of earlier excavators, their discoveries and the antiquarian tradition of their documentation. The strong commercial motives of early excavators are still used as arguments to dismiss their contributions, a moralistic objection that should be rejected once and for all. Gavin Hamilton, the Scottish painter and one of the greatest excavators of the eighteenth century, used to describe himself as a *cavatore* and *negoziante*, a digger and dealer. This, however, does not detract from the fact that his great discoveries (for example, the Pantanello of Hadrian's Villa, Tor Colombaro, Centocelle, Prima Porta, Monte Cagnolo, the area of Porta Marina at Ostia, Portus, Castel di Guido, Gabii, Acquatraversa) were of great significance to Roman archaeology. Nor does it mean that these discoveries were made by a man ignorant of ancient history, the classics and topography, who was unable to assess what he found. From the time of the Renaissance, countless 'diggers and dealers' made significant discoveries. Like Hamilton, most of them were digging 'for money' and needed more money to carry on digging. This, however, does not imply that they were, according to the standards of their own days, bad diggers, that they had no archaeological ideas, or that they destroyed more archaeological remains than subsequent excavators. Early in the nineteenth century, Carlo Fea, one of the forefathers of modern Roman archaeology, lamented the disorder caused by excavators like the English painter Robert Fagan at Ostia, and early in the twentieth century Rodolfo Lanciani denounced the confusion caused by past excavators at Tor Paterno (Castelporziano). Yet modern archaeologists might, in turn, criticize Fea and Lanciani themselves, and historians might point to the muddle they made of papers and visual records documenting their excavations; indeed, much of the material they published can hardly be used as such. (And within a generation or less, inevitably today's leading scholars will in turn be criticized for their methods and views.)[1]

II

Since *Archives & Excavations* aims to encourage the growth of a new approach to past excavations, particularly those carried out in and near Rome from the Renaissance to the late nineteenth century, this essay introducing it must emphasize the role of the Italian archaeologist Rodolfo Lanciani (1845–1929). Lanciani was the author of the *Storia degli scavi di Roma e notizie intorno le collezioni romane di antichità*,[2] that is to say the most comprehensive account of the history of excavations in Rome and a first-rate work that marks the end of the antiquarian tradition. A deeper understanding of this and similar contemporary works,

of their merits and defects, is a precondition for assessing how far the present volume might be regarded as a new start.

A graduate in engineering, Lanciani soon devoted himself to archaeology. In 1866 he excavated at Portus and in 1868 he published his first article.[3] A few years later, in 1872, he was appointed secretary of the newly established Commissione Archeologica Comunale and in 1876 engineer for the Ufficio Tecnico degli Scavi. In such capacities he played a particularly active role in the creation of the *Bullettino della Commissione Archeologica Comunale in Roma* (1872–) and *Notizie degli Scavi di Antichità* (1876–). In 1878 he began teaching at the Università di Roma and in 1882 was appointed to the chair of Roman Topography, which he held until 1927. In 1911, the same year as the momentous archaeological exhibition held as part of the Esposizione Universale, Lanciani was made a Senator of the Italian Republic. In 1919, he submitted the *Forma Italiae*, a project of the Accademia dei Lincei, to the Union Académique Internationale in Brussels, whose members were then discussing the broader project of the *Forma Romani Imperii*. One of the fathers of modern Roman archaeology and topography, Lanciani stands virtually alone as the great historian of excavations carried out in and near Rome. Though a number of later contributions can be mentioned, the simple fact that Lanciani's *Storia* still remains unchallenged and failed to inspire subsequent related work speaks for itself. Besides the lack of studies of the archaeological record and related analyses of remains discovered in the past, one might point to the absence of archaeological biographies, of studies of papal legislation relating to excavations and the conservation of monuments and, more generally, of studies of the institutional mechanisms governing the search for, discovery, recording, acquisition and export of antiquities. The reasons for the lack of this research should not be sought solely in the deliberate omission of such study caused by the disciplinary reorganization of archaeology and art history in the early twentieth century, but in Lanciani's *Storia* itself and in the curious destiny of its author.

While Lanciani is one of the major figures of modern cultural history, only a few lines have been devoted to him so far. These include a homage written by his English friend and admirer, Thomas Ashby, in 1929 and a few other short essays, notably by Ferdinando Castagnoli, Fausto Zevi and Antonio Giuliano.[4] Ashby devoted some lines to the *Forma Urbis Romae*,[5] the work for which Lanciani is still most remembered, but hardly commented on his *Storia*. In contrast, Castagnoli, Zevi and Giuliano focused on the latter work. Castagnoli showed that, while Lanciani's *Storia* is a typical work of late nineteenth-century antiquarian erudition, nevertheless it succeeds in making vital contributions to studies of classical art and its heritage; Zevi drew attention to the transition from *cronaca* (vol. I) to *storia* (vol. II onwards); and Giuliano remarked that Lanciani and other major scholars of his generation (Theodor Mommsen, Christian Hülsen, Adolf Michaelis, Giacomo Boni and Ashby in Rome, and Giuseppe Fiorelli and Mario Capasso in Naples) helped to forge a new approach to classical antiquity, in which the history of excavations played an important role, an approach generally abandoned after the First World War. Yet no author has tried so far to investigate the shortcomings of Lanciani's *Storia* with the aim of understanding why such a monumental work failed to meet its principal goal of stimulating the development of a real history of archaeological excavation.

In the preface to the first volume (1902), Lanciani stated that the aim of his work was to give as complete a picture as possible of archaeological discoveries in and near Rome, from the beginning of the eleventh century to 1870, when Rome became the capital of unified Italy, and to provide as many data as possible on the excavation provenance of the countless marbles that had ended up in museums and collections throughout Italy and Europe. Lanciani, it should be remembered, was writing more than a decade before countless marbles from old European collections, most of them British, were dispersed at sales, causing the rapid growth of American collections. By 1902 Lanciani had spent 25 years of his life amassing data on the devastation and destruction of ancient Rome. Information was scattered in countless publications and manuscript papers. He began collecting documentary material in or around 1877, that is to say in the same year in which the German archaeologist Adolf Michaelis visited England for the third and final time, to complete research for his seminal work, *Ancient Marbles in Great Britain*.[6] Though very different, Lanciani's and Michaelis's works are closely related to each other. Besides tracing the first comprehensive history of the taste for the antique in Britain, Michaelis consulted as many sources as possible in order to provide both the excavation and collection provenances of marbles in English private collections. Lanciani, besides making a heroic attempt at covering the whole history of Roman archaeology and collections — which inevitably

resulted in islands of enlightenment scattered throughout an ocean of fragmentary information —, produced, among other things, new information on the provenance of many of the marbles catalogued by Michaelis himself.[7] Indeed, the histories of excavations and collections can hardly be separated from each other. Their fruitful interaction was masterfully demonstrated in Lanciani's day by Michaelis's *Catalogue of the Ancient Marbles at Lansdowne House with an Appendix Containing Original Documents Relating to the Collection*. This volume was edited by Arthur Hamilton Smith,[8] who later supplemented the letters reproduced there with others written by Gavin Hamilton to the collector Charles Townley.[9] But for all Smith's efforts to delve deeply into the provenance of marbles in the British Museum's collection, his entries in the *Catalogue of Sculpture in the Department of Greek and Roman Antiquities*[10] were, from this point of view, rather disappointing. To develop this aspect of the history of British collections any further would have required a greater development of the documentary history of Roman excavations. How little this had developed half a century later is demonstrated by the fact that Seymour Rowland Pierce met with as many difficulties as Smith in editing letters from Rome by the excavator and art dealer Thomas Jenkins, now held in the library of the Society of Antiquaries.[11]

This is hardly surprising, as by that period the histories of excavations and collections had long been separated (or more accurately divorced) from each other almost everywhere, except at the Vatican Museums. Here, thanks to Carlo Pietrangeli, the old antiquarian tradition was revived and is still kept alive. Elsewhere, the history of excavations was omitted from mainstream modern archaeology and could hardly find a place within the newly-drawn boundaries of modern art history. In contrast, the history of collections developed further within the disciplinary fields of both art history and archaeology, though it still lies at the margins of university education and museum curatorial duties in most countries. The virtual death of wide-ranging research into past excavations has had a fatal impact upon the study of provenance, which gradually has lost the vitality it still had in Lanciani's days. When provenance is given at all, it is in most cases a mere ornamental addition and adds nothing to information given in old catalogues. Evidence of this is provided by comparison of Michaelis's work along with the additions and corrections to it published by Cornelius Vermeule and Dietrich von Bothmer between 1955 and 1959,[12] with recent catalogues of the collections covered by Michaelis's book. If one were to check virtually any entry in them, one would conclude that at least three important areas of research have been long neglected: biographical study of artist-excavators, such as Giovanni Volpato; truly complete biographies of key figures, such as Johann Winckelmann (who happens to be described in one of the new catalogues as an excavator, something he never was); and the excavation history of important sites, such as Ostia. Specialized modern selective dissections of the lives of artists, patrons and art writers written in the context of the institutionalization of specialized knowledge are so lacking in detail as to need little comment.[13] Despite the many contributions published in the last two decades both within and outside Germany, Winckelmann's writings, ideas, taste and even private life are still seen as separate from his records of old and contemporary excavations, his archaeological investigations and duties as Commissario delle Antichità e Cave di Roma from 1763 to 1768. The same applies to artist-excavators like Volpato, who is fairly well known as an engraver, art dealer and producer of small-scale souvenir *biscuits*, but is quite unknown as one of the most active excavators and dealers of the late 1770s and 1780s. Some of these omissions might have been filled had a real history of archaeological sites, at least of major ones like Ostia, been generated from Lanciani's *Storia*. Instead, we rely still on the fragmentary, and often incorrect, accounts published by Fea and Ludovico Paschetto,[14] on fragmented information published by Lanciani and on other similar records, most of which are secondary sources. An example of the muddle made of the provenance of marbles discovered at Ostia, Portus and their vicinities is provided by the *Relief with Volcanus*, now in the Vatican Museums.[15] Acquired in 1772, it is described in current catalogues as probably having been found by Hamilton at Ostia, which is impossible since he did not excavate there until two years later. His licence to excavate is dated 3 May 1774 though, according to his own letters, he began digging a few days earlier, on 28 April. In 1772 Hamilton excavated at Portus (licence of 22 January) and Centocelle (licence of 12 February). We know enough from his letters and other reports of his finds at Centocelle to believe that the 'Ostia' provenance of the *Relief* recorded in the Museums' early catalogues is likely to have meant 'Portus'. This example shows that even for major sites such as Ostia and for exceptionally well-documented collections such as those of the Vatican Museums, we still rely on weak evidence to ascertain provenance. The issue is more important than it might appear; important conclusions often have been drawn from dubious or wrong evidence. Several marbles that are believed to have come from public buildings in fact come from private villas; inscriptions that have been associated with certain statues were actually found next to others; and marbles such as the *Relief with Volcanus*, which are supposed to have come from Ostia, were discovered at different sites and in other archaeological contexts.

These problems are the natural outcome of many years of neglect of historical research and, more generally, of modern negative attitudes towards the 'utility' of past scholarship. Such views had already emerged in Lanciani's own day. In 1907 the German archaeologist Christian Hülsen, whose research on past excavations[16] paralleled and supplemented Lanciani's, lamented those who shared the opinion of Giovanni Battista de' Rossi. He had described the drawings by Ciriaco d'Ancona as *diagrammata plane imaginaria* ('completely imaginary diagrams'). Hülsen replied: 'We will see, however, that even these drawings, examined carefully, are not without interest for the history of the monuments of Rome, and in particular for the history of archaeological studies'.[17]

Other problems are inherent in Lanciani's own approach and, more generally, in his attitude as a historian and archaeologist. Lanciani can hardly be described as a historian, especially when compared to the approach of Michaelis in both the *Ancient Marbles* and *Storia della collezione capitolina di antichità fino all'inaugurazione del museo nel 1734*.[18] In the preface to his first volume, he stated that his *Storia* was based on no less than 96 volumes of documentary material, including 18,369 notes from documents preserved in the Archivio di Stato di Roma (9 vols); 6,352 notes from documents in the Archivio Storico Capitolino (8 vols); 6,000 cards with notes on ancient, medieval and modern topography (33 vols); notes on the history of the destruction of ancient Rome (2 vols); notes on museums, galleries and libraries (5 vols); notes on excavation and export licences (11 vols); notes on excavations at Ostia (2 vols); and documents relating to topography, epigraphy and archaeology from the Visconti and Vespignani archives and from the collection made by Pietro Pieri (26 vols). Lanciani emphasized that archival documents were his principal sources. This is only true in part, since he relied greatly on secondary sources that were not acknowledged and treated as such in his work. In his *Storia* he shows no awareness, for instance, of the complexities of using such 'politically-based' works as Vasari's *Vite* and their sources (for instance, the anti-Albertian life of Brunelleschi written by Antonio di Tuccio Manetti in the 1480s; see Ian Campbell's essay in the present volume), nor of the 'ancient' debate among antiquarians about primary and secondary sources that has been summarized masterfully and discussed by Arnaldo Momigliano.[19] Moreover, in Lanciani's *Storia* one does not find enlightening commentary on Renaissance sources such as those made by Ashby in the introductory paragraph of his study of the Bodleian Library manuscript of Pirro Ligorio:

Antiquarian research in the Renaissance period was unfortunately not always free from the reproach of deliberate falsification. It seems strange, at first sight, that the amount of genuine material discovered did not suffice to occupy the minds of archaeologists, and that they should have found it necessary to add to it by purely gratuitous inventions. But, given a certain knowledge of the subject, it was easy for a fertile brain and a facile pen to fabricate inscriptions, coins, plans of buildings, etc., whether in order to prove a favourite theory or to attain an ideal completeness which could not be attained by more prosaic, though more honest, means.[20]

But however brilliant passages like this might be, Ashby, Lanciani, Hülsen and other contemporary scholars were still rather casual in the analysis of visual sources, though certainly better informed about new attributions, dating and studies on style and iconography than their successors. Evidence of this is provided by a comparison of Ashby's pioneering study of Carlo Labruzzi's drawings of the Via Appia and later publications on the same subject.[21] The fact that for almost a century no effort was made to establish a more precise sequence of versions of such a key document of visual archaeology[22] reveals clearly that archaeology and art history, still so close in studies of classical art written along the lines of Winckelmann's work, have scarcely interacted in the visual realm for a long time. Archaeologists, for instance, still assign to Fra' Giocondo drawings that art historians have not regarded as by his hand for quite some time.

Archives & Excavations heralds the reunion of these two disciplines; a full body of evidence (written and visual) is used and discussed by contributors to this volume, taking into consideration the institutional contexts in which documents were generated and later preserved. The same cannot be said of Lanciani's *Storia*. The author claimed to have personally collected documentary material for his work in Italy, France, Belgium, Holland, Germany, Switzerland and England, while he said he relied upon authoritative correspondents for information from other countries. This is only partly true, since much material taken from the Roman archives was not recorded by him personally but by colleagues, friends and assistants, whose names and contributions are sometimes mentioned and sometimes omitted. This applies, for instance, to Federico Cerasoli, the author of a little-known study on institutional mechanisms governing excavations in Renaissance Rome.[23] The numerous licences granted by the Reverenda Camera Apostolica between 1426 and 1576 (held in the Archivio Segreto Vaticano), which were listed, discussed and partly reproduced in full by Cerasoli for the first time (though a few had already been published by Eugène Müntz[24]) are also found in Lanciani. This information Cerasoli used in order to understand the institutional mechanisms governing excavations during the period, as a tool for locating more documents, and to form a better idea of the contemporary legislation, a prerequisite for understanding how antiquities were unearthed and new finds recorded. Lanciani, on the other hand, used the same data to make his chronology of excavations more complete. It is true that he recorded information on the office of the Magistri Viarum (later Presidenza delle Strade) and the Commissariato delle Antichità, which, together with the Camerlengato and the Tesorierato, were in charge of granting excavation and export licences. However, in Lanciani's work there is no sign of a real interest in the institutional context of archaeological discoveries. In contrast, little-known authors such as Cerasoli were exploring areas of research that have been much neglected since. Andrea Emiliani's anthology of edicts and other legislative measures for the protection of antiquities and works of art in the Italian states is very useful but hardly discusses legislative mechanisms.[25] Similar remarks can be made about Ronald T. Ridley's study of the Commissari delle Antichità e Cave di Roma between 1534 and 1870[26] and Daniela Sinisi's and Orietta Verdi's coverage of licences from the Registri delle Lettere Patenti of the Presidenza delle Strade for the years 1691–1701.[27] All these contributions are of the utmost importance, but many years' neglect of research of the general institutional context of archaeological discoveries still seriously inhibits their growth and full development. The questions that need to be addressed are:

- when and why did regulated excavations originate?

- what were the precise competencies of the various individual officials of the Reverenda Camera Apostolica?
- what orders exactly did the legislation give to excavators and dealers as to licences, excavation reports and descriptions of the newly found and acquired objects?
- who were the excavators, their patrons and partners?
- what is known of reports, drawings, plans and maps sent by the excavators to the Reverenda Camera?
- is there any relationship between such reports and the information published by contemporary antiquarians and print engravers?
- what is known of the writings of excavators and commissioners?

Documents to answer these and other related questions still exist. *Archives & Excavations* does not provide answers to all of them, but it is the first book to openly address them and provide partial answers and new suggestions. More satisfactory and wide-ranging answers will come if *Archives & Excavations* succeeds in its aim of stimulating a new approach to past excavations.

The problems raised by Lanciani's *Storia* that have been addressed so far mostly relate to the author's mind-set as a historian and the merits and shortcomings of his work. What remains to be discussed is his approach as an archaeologist, namely the value he attached to historical research in the context of his fieldwork. As soon as the first volume appeared (1902), Lanciani realized that the arrangement of the material in a strict chronological order made his *Storia* difficult to consult and potentially useless from an archaeological point of view. In the preface to the second volume (1903) he announced a major change: in that and future volumes readers would find the same three basic components as in the first one (excavations, collections and exports), but, instead of finding the information arranged chronologically, they would find it arranged topographically. By adopting a more clearly defined topographical method, Lanciani laid the foundations for general and specific histories of the archaeological record. But this was more a promise than a reality. In 1903 Lanciani turned his *Storia* into a sort of topographical database; its primary function was to provide new information for the revision of his *Forma Urbis Romae* (1893–1901), a task that unfortunately has not yet been carried out along the modern lines of archaeological topography. This shift in the scope of Lanciani's *Storia* led to the neglect, or rather marginalization, of data regarding areas outside the city of Rome. Except for Ostia, those areas had been of secondary interest from the beginning for practical reasons; the *Storia* originates, above all, from Lanciani's duties as engineer of the Ufficio Tecnico degli Scavi and his awareness of the vast and irreparable loss that the chaotic and frenetic building works related to the transformation of papal Rome into the capital of modern Italy caused. From its first (1902) to its last volume (a general index, published in 2002), Lanciani's *Storia* reflects its author's anxieties about the destiny of ancient Rome in modern times and, naturally enough, it reflects his urge to record as much evidence as possible as quickly as possible, in order to preserve the memory of what had already been lost and what was about to disappear for good. Lanciani had little time to think of the historical model or to indulge in topographical completeness. His preoccupation with wider topographical coverage developed in the last few years of his life (it is shown by the recording of data on cards, the contents of which have been reproduced in the new volume VI of the *Storia*) and coincided with the inception of the *Forma Italiae* project, which was undertaken by Giuseppe Lugli and others from 1926. Despite this, when writing of individual sites (for instance, Castelporziano[28]), Lanciani scarcely made use of the documentary material relating to old excavations and confused those carried out in different centuries.[29] On the other hand, the editors and authors of the various volumes of the *Forma Italiae*, while they reproduced early maps and drawings, did not regard wide-ranging historical research into individual sites as an integral part of modern archaeological topographical study.

In conclusion, Lanciani and his contemporaries did not develop a real history of the archaeological record, nor did they attempt the actual reconstruction of past excavations comparable to Pietrangeli's *Otricoli*,[30] which still stands virtually alone above all for not having separated Etruscan and Roman archaeology. Lanciani and most of his contemporaries (notably German scholars based in Rome, such as Hülsen and Theodor Schreiber, author of 'Unedirte Römische Fundberichte'[31]) were preoccupied with the destiny of ancient Rome in modern times and did their best to record as many documents relating to past discoveries as possible. Their work as historians fits, in many respects, the definition of antiquarian studies given by Francis Bacon early in the seventeenth century; they helped to 'save and recover somewhat from the deluge of time'.[32] Lanciani went further than anybody else in that direction, and produced what Zevi has described as 'an exceptionally learned work of information and records'.[33] In fact, his *Storia* is outstanding as a work that marks the end of the antiquarian tradition. A different attitude towards the study and use of written and visual documents, less erudite and more factual, emerged at the time when Pietrangeli published his first study of the papal excavations at Otricoli[34] and Castagnoli his analysis of documents relating to excavations carried out in Rome in the years 1860–70.[35]

Archives & Excavations is the first book written by a group of scholars who, whether by profession archaeologists, historians or art historians, are aware of the urgency of developing advanced studies of the history of the archaeological record, of reconstructing properly past excavations and of good quality research into excavation provenance designed to help field archaeologists and museum curators alike.

III

This volume consists of sixteen essays divided chronologically into three parts. Part I addresses various aspects of the history and historiography of excavations from the early Renaissance to the late seventeenth century. Ian Campbell discusses the alleged origins of excavations in Rome at the very beginning of the fifteenth century when, according to Antonio di Tuccio Manetti (and thus Vasari), Brunelleschi and Donatello visited Rome and carried out some excavations in order to study ancient remains. The author directs attention to cultural values associated with first-hand knowledge of archaeological remains and compares stories (probably true but still unsubstantiated) with actual facts and evidence for the period between the 1420s (Pope Martin V's *Renovatio Romae*) and the 1550s (Ligorio's excavations at Hadrian's Villa, Tivoli). To do so, he explores primary and secondary sources, both written and visual. Cornelius Schuddeboom focuses on the formal birth of Christian archaeology in 1578 (with the accidental discovery of a catacomb then thought to be that of Priscilla). He draws attention to the nature and scope of early written and visual records of Christian remains and fragments, notably those kept by the Louvain antiquary Philips van Winghe, who visited Rome in 1589–92. Van Winghe, together with his compatriot Jean l'Heureux and the Spanish Dominican Alfonso Chacón, laid the basis for Antonio Bosio's *Roma*

sotterranea.[36] Amanda Claridge's essay considers Rome's two archaeologies, one abstract and the other on the ground, and assesses their impact upon written and visual records. Her essay reviews some of the idiosyncrasies involved and their likely influence on the nature of the key records of the late sixteenth and seventeenth centuries, such as the 'memoirs' of the sculptor Flaminio Vacca (written in 1594), of the gentleman-scholar and collector Cassiano dal Pozzo, of the dean of the Pantheon, Cipriano Cipriani, and of the artist, antiquary and Commissario delle Antichità e Cave di Roma, Pietro Santi Bartoli, whose records cover excavations carried out between 1650 and the 1690s. Ingo Herklotz's essay introduces the restless activities of excavators in and around Rome, within the context of the growth of collections. The author focuses on Leonardo Agostini, the Commissario delle Antichità e Cave di Roma from 1641 to 1674, and his records of excavations carried out during that period. Herklotz's appendix of documents, summarizing Agostini's letters and reports written to Francesco Barberini, Carlo di Tomaso Strozzi and Leopoldo de' Medici, is of great interest. It throws new light on documentary sources: the eyewitness records of Agostini can now be compared with the *memorie di scavi* tradition, notably those of Bartoli, which often overlap with them.

Part II is devoted to the eighteenth and early nineteenth centuries. The first three essays are closely related to each other; they deal with various aspects of the 'British conquest' of the marbles of ancient Rome. The essay by the present writer introduces the general theme of material and cultural conquests. It addresses the institutional mechanisms inherent in the search for, discovery, sale and export of ancient marbles, draws attention to the role played by British excavators and dealers during the second half of the eighteenth century, and discusses a few individual examples taken as documentary case-studies. These are designed to demonstrate the extent to which a variety of written and visual sources can help in identifying antiquities, clarifying their provenance, even on occasion questioning their authenticity, as well as rediscovering and protecting sites.

The establishment of the precise location of ancient sites on the basis of literary evidence was an integral part of eighteenth-century archaeology. The essay by Iain Gordon Brown is devoted to this topic; more precisely it looks into Allan Ramsay's search for Horace's Villa at Licenza between the 1750s and 1780s. While Ramsay's archaeological search was motivated by his curiosity about the natural setting of a famous ruin, excavations carried out by Thomas Jenkins, Colin Morison, Hamilton and Fagan were aimed primarily at the sale of finds to wealthy British collectors. Brian F. Cook explores written and visual records relating to the most important of those collections, that of Charles Townley, which was acquired by the British Museum in 1805. The author draws attention to the relevance of those records not only to the history of collections and the art market but also to the history of excavations. Marbles discovered by the British and their Italian colleagues during the second half of the eighteenth century were partly exported and partly acquired for the Vatican Museums, that is to say the Pio-Clementino collection. Besides marbles, since 1778 the Reverenda Camera acquired a spectacular collection of Roman mosaics, mostly from new excavations. Klaus Werner's essay focuses on the documentary evidence relating to them, their excavation provenance, their original appearance and restoration. Though wide-ranging, documents used by contributors mentioned so far are confined to written and two-dimensional visual sources relating to excavations carried out in and near Rome, that is to say in the territory of the Papal States. Valentin Kockel's essay draws attention to the Kingdom of Naples and to three-dimensional models used as records of archaeological discoveries, both to those that still exist and those that have been lost, including Domenico Padiglione's 1:48 scale model of the ruins of Pompeii. The author, besides providing a short and most useful introduction to such models, investigates the use made by model-makers of published sources.

Part III is devoted to the nineteenth century and to specific archaeological sites in Rome (the Roman Forum, the Campus Martius, the ancient baths in the area between the Scala Santa and the Lateran Palace), in the Sabina (Poggio Sommavilla) and in Etruria (notably Veii). Rita Turchetti's essay on the excavations of Giacomo Boni at the Roman Forum (1899–1911) introduces the theme of the use of photography as an 'archival document'. Thomas Ashby's photographs of the Forum taken prior to Boni's various excavations reveal not only structures that had been excavated and then buried but also, and more particularly, archaeological preconceptions of the period, monuments destroyed in the search for more ancient levels and reconstructions based on mistaken identifications of architectural fragments. Susanna Le Pera Buranelli's analysis of medieval remains under the Palazzo Le Roy (in the central area of the Campus

Martius) shows how archival research might lead to new discoveries in the topography of ancient and medieval Rome alike. Written documents, plans and photographs have allowed the reconstruction of part of the Euripus in the Campus Martius, discovered during excavations under the Museo Barracco when the Corso Vittorio Emanuele II was constructed (1886–1900). A medieval tower, which is now well documented, was also discovered in this area, within the limits of the Farnesina ai Baullari building. Paolo Liverani's reconstruction of excavations at the Scala Santa in 1852–3 shows how, after the studies of Philippe Lauer and Antonio Maria Colini, almost nothing has been added to our knowledge of the area of the Lateran, that is that of the medieval Lateran Palace demolished under Sixtus V, between the Sanctuary of the Scala Santa and the Lateran Palace. The author's study of the excavations of 1852–3 leads to the new identification of a series of sculptures (mostly in the Gregorian Museum of Pagan Antiquities) and enables one to understand better the remains of a bath-building in that area. This information, combined with unpublished finds and little-known remains under the Oratory of the Confraternity of the Holy Sacrament to the south of the Scala Santa, allows a more general understanding of the topography of the area.

The last three essays in the volume are devoted to two areas of archaeological importance outside Rome, the Sabina and Etruria. Giorgio Filippi's reconstruction of excavations carried out first by Benedetto Piacentini and then by Melchiade Fossati (1836) at the necropolis of Poggio Sommavilla is a sort of detective-story written in the literary style of a report by a police officer or Italian *carabiniere*, a style that is suited perfectly to the events. Archival documents, and especially Fossati's own writings, throw new light on the 25 years of archaeological activity in Rome, Etruria, Umbria and the Sabina of this little-known excavator and dealer. His discoveries contributed to the growth of the Vatican Museums, the Museo di Parma and the Louvre. The case of Poggio Sommavilla also throws new light on the coexistence of legal and illegal excavations and chance discoveries, and on the contrast between gifted excavators such as Fossati and the members of the Commissione Generale Consultiva di Belle Arti, who were qualified individuals but still bureaucrats, in a period when important laws (the Edict of Cardinal Pacca and the Ruling of the Commissioni Ausiliarie di Belle Arti) were issued to protect better archaeological sites and works of art. Ronald T. Ridley's essay offers both an overview of the cultural and market discovery of the Etruscans during the first three decades of the nineteenth century and provides insights into legal and illegal excavation activities carried out at key sites such as Vulci and Bomarzo. Paolo Liverani's essay on Veii provides a perfect finale to this book. Its introduction centres on Rodolfo Lanciani, and Liverani's essay deals with Lanciani's archaeological activity at Veii between 1878 and 1882 (when the so-called Chigi Tomb and a famous Greek olpe were discovered north of Veii), and again in 1889 (when excavations at the necropolis of Picazzano, to the north of the city, and also in the cemetery of Vaccareccia, to the east, were undertaken for Teresa Cristina Empress of Brazil). Thanks to unpublished records kept by Lanciani, it is now possible to add new elements to the limited information concerning the excavations of 1889, to identify many finds scattered throughout private and public collections around Europe, and to correct some hypotheses about the chronology of the cult and identification of the divinity to whom offerings were made.

Archives & Excavations does not provide a complete picture of excavations carried out in Italy from the Renaissance to the late nineteenth century, but it sketches some of the main themes of a new approach to the history of excavation during those five centuries.

NOTES

1. Paolo Liverani's comments on the first section of my introduction are so central to the subject that I shall quote them in full: 'To demonstrate the utility and necessity of this type of investigation I would propose yet another argument. The concept is expressed in a synthetic way by the German word *Quellenkunde*. Archaeologists, myself included, look at data relating to old excavations in a naive way, as if they come from an ideal and perfect world. We might complain about the lack of data, but we never address problems relating to their evaluation. This does not occur, for instance, with ancient history. Take the example of a historian, who studies the history of Rome during the Republican period by reading Livy; he will investigate Livy's sources, the context in which he lived and wrote, his political ideas and so on. There is no doubt that archaeological evidence and historical accounts are quite different; a vase will always be a vase, while a narrative is inevitably open to different interpretations. Archaeologists, or excavators, have always operated in specific contexts and, through the centuries, their discoveries have served different aims, which did not coincide necessarily with scientific progress. Take the example of the nationalist context in which excavations were carried out in the late nineteenth century; the results of these excavations cannot possibly be separated from the political passions of the period. Take the example of the scandal of the Villa Giulia, and also the polemics about the Janiculum and, more recently, about the so-called Villa of Agrippina. But for earlier periods one has to face a different set of problems. F. Delpino ('Sulla scoperta della tomba Campana di Veio: un falso dell'archeologia romantica?', *RendPontAcc* 57 (1984–5), 191–201) has shown, for instance, how the contents of the Campana Tomb at Veii, which plays a major role in the field of Etruscology, were artfully put together. But without going to such extremes, we can assess the reliability of data coming from a particular excavation if we know the contemporary context in which the research took place. We may also be able to recognize a case of exaggeration, or one where information previously discarded as untrustworthy may, indeed, be genuine'.
2. Lanciani, *Storia* (1902–12; 1989–).
3. R. Lanciani, 'Ricerche topografiche sulla città di Porto', *Annali dell'Instituto di Corrispondenza Archeologica* 40 (1868), 144–95.
4. T. Ashby, 'Scrittori contemporanei di cose romane (Rodolfo Lanciani)', *Archivio della Società Romana di Storia Patria* 51 (1928), 103–43; F. Castagnoli, 'Preface' to the reprint of R. Lanciani, *Storia degli scavi di Roma e notizie intorno le collezioni romane di antichità* (Bologna, 1975); reprinted as 'Premessa alla ristampa dell'opera di Rodolfo Lanciani's *Storia degli scavi di Roma e notizie intorno le collezioni romane di antichità*', in F. Castagnoli, *Topografia antica* I (Rome, 1993), 55–8; F. Zevi, Preface to Lanciani, *Storia* (1989–), I, 1–8; A. Giuliano, 'Rodolfo Lanciani e la 'Storia degli scavi di Roma'', *Xenia Antiqua* 1 (1992), 155–60.

5. R. Lanciani, *Forma Urbis Romae* (Rome, 1893–1901; reprinted Rome, 1989).

6. A. Michaelis, *Ancient Marbles in Great Britain* (Cambridge, 1882).

7. Lanciani died long before all the volumes of his *Storia* were finished, and volume VI supplementing Michaelis's entries has only just appeared, although it should be noted that its coverage of the eighteenth and nineteenth centuries is much thinner than that of earlier periods. Cf. C. Pietrangeli, *Scavi e scoperte di antichità sotto il pontificato di Pio VI* (Rome, 1943; Rome, 1958²); C. Pietrangeli, *The Vatican Museums: Five Centuries of History* (Rome/Vatican City, 1993) (= *I Musei Vaticani: cinque secoli di storia* (Rome, 1985)), and his articles on the provenance of the Vatican antiquities ('La provenienza delle sculture dei Musei Vaticani, I', *BMusPont* 7 (1987), 115–49; 'La provenienza delle sculture dei Musei Vaticani, II', *BMusPont* 8 (1988), 139–210; 'La provenienza delle sculture dei Musei Vaticani, III', *BMusPont* 9 (1) (1989), 85–140; 'La raccolta epigrafica vaticana nel Settecento, I', *BMusPont* 12 (1992), 21–31; 'La raccolta epigrafica vaticana nel Settecento, II', *BMusPont* 13 (1993), 49–79). These works give a more complete picture of the period, since Pietrangeli's work was based on that of Lanciani but took into account that of Michaelis.

8. A. Michaelis, *Catalogue of the Ancient Marbles at Lansdowne House with an Appendix Containing Original Documents Relating to the Collection* (ed. A.H. Smith) (London, 1889).

9. A.H. Smith, 'Gavin Hamilton's letters to Charles Townley', *JHS* 21 (1901), 306–21.

10. *Catalogue of Sculpture in the Department of Greek and Roman Antiquities*, 3 vols (London, 1892–1904).

11. S. Rowland Pierce, 'Thomas Jenkins in Rome', *The Antiquaries Journal* 45 (1965), 200–29.

12. For example, C. Vermeule and D. von Bothmer, 'Notes on a new edition of Michaelis' *Ancient Marbles in Great Britain*', *American Journal of Archaeology* 63 (1959), 139–66, 329–48.

13. N. Thomson de Grummond (ed.), *The Encyclopaedia of the History of Classical Archaeology* (London/Chicago, 1996) has gathered together for the first time a good number of those biographies, although our knowledge has increased and moved on considerably in the years since its publication.

14. In particular, C. Fea, *Relazione di un viaggio ad Ostia* (Rome, 1802); L. Paschetto, *Ostia colonia romana. Storia e monumenti* (*Dissertazioni della Pontificia Accademia Romana di Archeologia* 2.10) (Rome, 1912).

15. Sala Rotonda 14, inv. 247.

16. Notably his *Topographie der Stadt Rom im Alterthum* I.3 (Berlin, 1907).

17. C. Hülsen, *La Roma antica di Ciriaco d'Ancona* (Rome, 1907), 3: 'Vedremo però, che anche questi disegni, accuratamente esaminati, non sono privi d'interesse per la storia dei monumenti di Roma, ed in particolare per la storia degli studi archeologici'.

18. A. Michaelis, *Storia della collezione capitolina di antichità fino all'inaugurazione del museo nel 1734* (Rome, 1891).

19. A. Momigliano, 'Ancient history and the antiquarian', *Journal of the Warburg and Courtauld Institutes* 13 (1950), 285–315.

20. T. Ashby, 'The Bodleian Ms. of Pirro Ligorio', *JRS* 9 (1919), 170–201.

21. T. Ashby, 'Dessins inédits de Carlo Labruzzi relatifs aux ruines de la voie Appiane', *Mélanges d'Archéologie et d'Histoire de l'École Française de Rome* 23 (1903), 375–418.

22. I. Bignamini and A. Claridge, 'The Tomb of Claudia Semne and excavations in eighteenth-century Rome', *PBSR* 66 (1998), 215–44.

23. F. Cerasoli, 'Usi e regolamenti per gli scavi di antichità in Roma nei secoli XV e XVI', *Studi e Documenti di Storia e Diritto* 18 (1897), 133–49.

24. E. Müntz, 'Les monuments antiques de Rome à l'époque de la Renaissance, nouvelles recerches (*suite*)', *Revue Archéologique* (July–December 1884), 38–53.

25. A. Emiliani, *Leggi, bandi e provvedimenti per la tutela dei beni artistici e culturali negli antichi stati italiani 1571–1860* (Bologna, 1978).

26. R.T. Ridley, 'To protect the monuments: the papal antiquarian 1534–1870', *Xenia Antiqua* 1 (1992), 117–54.

27. D. Sinisi and O. Verdi (eds), 'I registri delle lettere patenti della Presidenza delle Strade (1691–1701)', in *Roma nel primo Settecento. Case, proprietari, strade, toponimi* (*Archivi e Cultura* 28) (Rome, 1995), 123–243.

28. R. Lanciani, 'Le antichità del territorio Laurentino nella reale tenuta di Castelporziano', *Monumenti Antichi Pubblicati per Cura della Reale Accademia dei Lincei* 13 (1903), 133–98; R. Lanciani, 'Le antichità del territorio Laurentino nella reale tenuta di Castelporziano', *Monumenti Antichi Pubblicati per Cura della Reale Accademia dei Lincei* 16 (1906), 214–72.

29. I. Bignamini, 'Scavi ottocenteschi a Tor Paterno: gli scavi Chigi del 1777–80 e gli scavi camerali del 1783', in M.G. Lauro (ed.), *Castelporziano* IV: *campagne di scavo e restauro 1992–1998* (Rome, in press).

30. C. Pietrangeli, *Otricoli* (Rome, 1978).

31. T. Schreiber, 'Unedirte Römische Fundberichte aus Italiänischen Archiven und Bibliotheken', *Berichten der Kgl. Sächs. Gesellschaft der Wissenschaften Philol.-hist. Classe* (1885).

32. F. Bacon, *Advancement of Learning* (ed. A. Johnston) (Oxford, 1974), 72.

33. A '*summa* eruditissima di informazioni e notizie', F. Zevi, preface to Lanciani, *Storia* (1989–), I, 2.

34. C. Pietrangeli, 'Lo scavo pontificio di Otricoli', *RendPontAcc* 19 (1942–3), 47–68.

35. F. Castagnoli, 'Documenti di scavi eseguiti in Roma negli anni 1860–70', *BullCom* 73 (1949–50), 123–87.

36. A. Bosio, *Roma sotterranea* (Rome, 1632).

THE RENAISSANCE AND
SEVENTEENTH CENTURY

Rescue archaeology in the Renaissance

Ian Campbell

Art historians used to believe that they knew exactly when architects began to excavate in order to find out more about ancient Roman buildings. Antonio di Tuccio Manetti tells us that Filippo Brunelleschi invented Renaissance architecture after losing the competition for the second set of bronze doors for the Baptistery in Florence in 1401: Brunelleschi and Donatello went off to Rome to study sculpture, but Brunelleschi became increasingly interested in architecture and 'decided to rediscover the fine and highly skilled method of building and the harmonious proportions of the ancients'.[1] He and Donatello:

> made rough drawings of almost all the buildings in Rome and in many places beyond the walls, with measurements of their widths and estimated the heights as far as they could ascertain by estimation, and also the lengths, etc. In many places they had excavations made in order to see the junctures of the membering of the buildings and their type ... Since they undertook excavations they had to hire porters and other labourers at no small expense which wasn't cheap. No one else tried such work or understood why they did it ... they were generally called the 'treasure hunters'.[2]

By doing this for many years, Brunelleschi learnt to understand the different styles of Roman architecture, and the characteristics of the Ionic, Doric, Tuscan and Corinthian orders: according to Manetti, this can be seen in his buildings.[3]

Unfortunately, virtually every aspect of this story has been called into question over the last 50 years: even if Brunelleschi did visit Rome (which is likely enough, despite the lack of corroborative evidence), little in his architecture can be shown to come directly from Roman antiquity. The overall forms generally come from fourteenth-century buildings, while the ornaments derive from Tuscan Romanesque examples, especially San Miniato al Monte and the Baptistery.[4] It is now suspected that Manetti invented the story when he was writing the *Life* in the 1480s, because by then it was what would have been expected of his hero.[5] So when did the various activities attributed to Brunelleschi begin? Already in 1375, we have the example of Giovanni Dondi (1318–89), the humanist friend of Petrarch, measuring monuments in Rome, with what sounds like an astrolabe, and recording the numbers of columns and orders of monuments such as the Pantheon and Colosseum.[6] During the first half of the fifteenth century, Ciriaco d'Ancona (1391–post-1453), the merchant autodidact, drew antique buildings encountered on his journeys in Italy and in the east Mediterranean, some of which have come down to us in copies, and the architect Giuliano da Sangallo (1443–1516) put the date 1465 at the front of his great sketchbook, the *Barberini Codex*.[7]

What we lack is a specific reference to the excavation of ruins, but Manetti is hardly likely to have invented the idea. The problem with excavation, as he said, was that it was not cheap to hire labourers to dig, and the average artist or humanist would not have had the financial resources to do so. However, we do have references to Leon Battista Alberti (1404–72) dredging up one of the Roman ships from Lake Nemi, in 1447, at the instigation of Cardinal Prospero Colonna.[8] If Alberti were capable of persuading a patron to finance the dredging to salvage something of no intrinsic monetary value, it seems likely that he could have done the same for the analogous activity of archaeological excavation. Ironically, Manetti may be our strongest testimony, since his determination to show that Brunelleschi was the first to do it has to be seen in the light of the markedly anti-Albertian bias of the *Life*.[9]

So what is the earliest specific reference to excavation being undertaken to understand a piece of architecture? The excavation of an Etruscan tomb near Viterbo in 1493 for the benefit of the visiting pope, Alexander VI, was not undertaken from interest in the tomb itself but for its

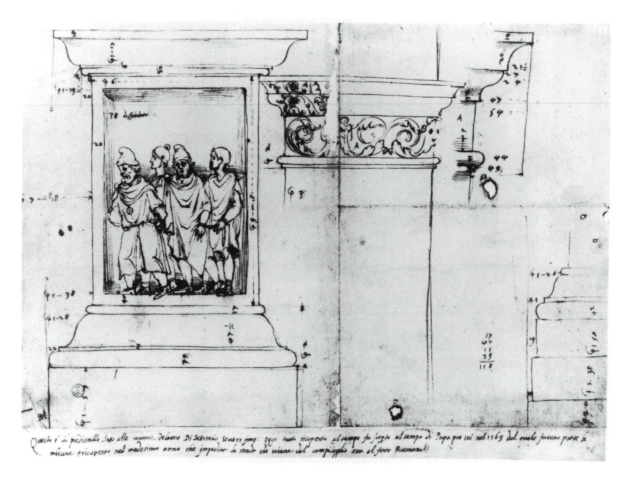

FIG. 1. Giovanni Antonio Dosio, Detail of a pedestal of the Arch of Septimius Severus, Roman Forum, excavated in 1563. Drawing. Florence, Gabinetto Disegni e Stampe, Galleria Uffizi, UA 2575. *(Reproduced courtesy of the Ministero dei Beni e le Attività Culturali. All further reproduction is prohibited.)*

purported contents, some statues that were fakes made under the guidance of Annio of Viterbo, who recorded the story.[10] A near miss was the accidental finding of the lower part of the obelisk of the Augustan Sundial during the pontificate of Julius II (1503–13), by a barber digging in his garden. Julius was petitioned to excavate the whole obelisk and to re-erect it, but he was too busy fighting wars, and the barber finally covered it up again, where it remained for another two centuries.[11] Closer comes a reference in a drawing by Giovanni Antonio Dosio (1533–1609) of a pedestal of the Arch of Septimius Severus, with a note saying that it was excavated, measured and reburied in 1563, in connection with the making of a new road from the Campidoglio to the Forum (**Fig. 1**).[12] Another drawing shows the whole arch during the partial excavation (**Fig. 2**).[13] But even here it is not clear whether the pedestal would have been uncovered in making the road anyway, or whether the digging for the road was extended to one side to undertake the excavation of the pedestal. What is

clear is that Dosio was taking the opportunity of something else happening to undertake his investigative work; and that this was the norm during the Renaissance.

The return of the united papacy to Rome in 1420, under Pope Martin V, led to the *Renovatio Romae*, the 'Renewal of Rome', with ever-increasing building activity affording lots of opportunities for staring down holes. The three chief reasons given in requests for licences to excavate were, in order of frequency:

1. to provide foundations for new buildings;
2. to salvage building materials;
3. to hunt for treasure, artistic or otherwise.[14]

In *Roma instaurata*, written 1444–6, Flavio Biondo (1392–1463) reported that, while foundations were being dug in vineyards next to the Lateran, vaults, rooms, pavements and columns of coloured marble were found eight to ten feet below the ground level.[15] However, although some antiquaries, such as Biondo, could look down holes and interpret material evidence, more preferred to stay in libraries and work with texts.

FIG. 2. Giovanni Antonio Dosio, View of the Arch of Septimius Severus during the 1563 excavation. Drawing. Florence, Gabinetto Disegni e Stampe, Galleria Uffizi, UA 2521. *(Reproduced courtesy of the Ministero dei Beni e le Attività Culturali. All further reproduction is prohibited.)*

It is architects whom we find really looking at ruins and trying to make sense of what they saw.

On a reconstruction plan of the Basilica of Constantine (**Fig. 3**), Francesco di Giorgio (1439–1501) noted that in the west apse sat a gigantic marble statue. This dates his observation to 1486, when the colossal statue of Constantine the Great was unearthed and moved to the Palazzo dei Conservatori, where it still can be seen.[16] But more interesting for us is the detail of the south portico, which agrees broadly with archaeological evidence. We do not know what was happening in the vicinity of the basilica in 1486, but it may be that the works that revealed the statue also left some remains of the portico visible for a short time and that Francesco was on hand to recognize their significance. Only one later drawing shows the portico, most draughtsmen following Giuliano da Sangallo in substituting an apse to match that on the north side, assuming that the basilica must have been symmetrical.[17]

In the sixteenth century, the volume of building work in Rome increased enormously, especially with the decision to rebuild Saint Peter's in 1506, which created a voracious appetite for building materials. This had disastrous consequences for built antiquities: Raphael's famous letter to Leo X (dating to either 1513/14 or to 1519) laments that all this new Rome, however great, however beautiful, however adorned with palaces and churches, had been built with lime made from ancient marbles. In the less than twelve years since Raphael (1483–1520) had been in Rome, so many beautiful things had been ruined — the pyramidal tomb that was in the Borgo, the arch at the entrance to the Baths of Diocletian, the Temple of Ceres on the Via Sacra, a part of the Forum Transitorium (burned and destroyed only a few days before the letter was written, and lime made from its marbles) and most of the Basilica Aemilia.[18] Leo X did give Raphael limited powers in 1515 to preserve stones bearing inscriptions and reliefs from destruction; moreover, to mitigate the loss of knowledge, Raphael was commissioned to survey all the ancient monuments and described a way of drawing monuments by

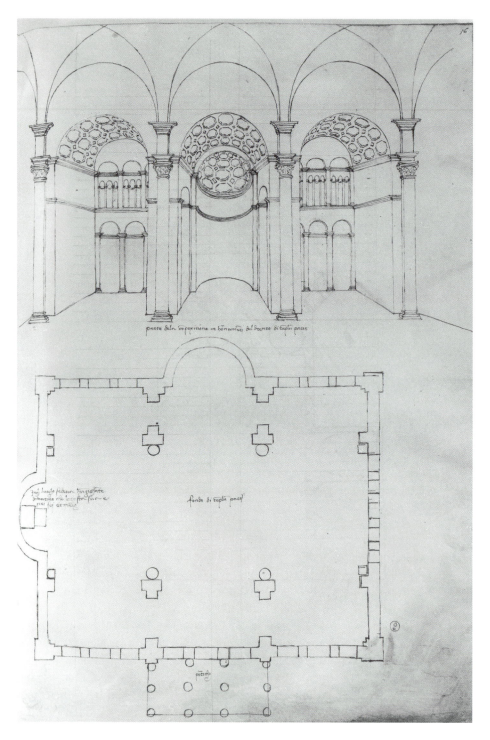

FIG. 3. Francesco di Giorgio, Reconstruction plan of the Basilica of Constantine. Drawing. Turin, Biblioteca Reale, Cod. Saluzzo 148, fol. 176r. *(Reproduced courtesy of the Ministero per i Beni e le Attività Culturali. All further reproduction is prohibited.)*

means of orthogonal projection so that at least they were recorded accurately.[19] How far the project had progressed before Raphael's premature death is unclear, but some of the most detailed drawings of the period come from Baldassare Peruzzi (1481–1536) and Antonio da Sangallo the Younger (1484–1546), both of whom assisted Raphael on Saint Peter's.[20] What is significant is that in some cases it is because they were involved in clearing sites that they were able to record evidence that might otherwise not have come to light or have been disregarded.

Sebastiano Serlio tells us that not much was known of the plan of the Theatre of Marcellus until Peruzzi was building the new Palazzo Savelli on and in its ruins from 1519 (**Fig. 4**): 'While they were excavating the foundations they found the remains of many different parts of the ornamentation of this theatre and clear traces of the ground plan. As a result he deduced the whole from that part uncovered, and thus measured it very carefully'.[21]

Only a few detail drawings by Peruzzi himself are extant (most were probably taken to France by Serlio and lost), but many by Antonio da Sangallo the Younger survive. He was drawing the adjacent temples of San Nicola in Carcere at the same time as Peruzzi was building the palace, and it is easy to imagine them crossing over to look every time one or the other found something new. In building the new palace much of this debris appears to have been destroyed, either to clear space for the new building or for reuse, so that the drawings and Serlio's woodcuts are now the best evidence for what was there.

Similarly, we have many sheets covered in details and studies of the three temples at San Nicola in Carcere by Peruzzi, by Antonio da Sangallo the Younger and by his brother, Giambattista, on which all subsequent reconstruction depends.[22] Often these are

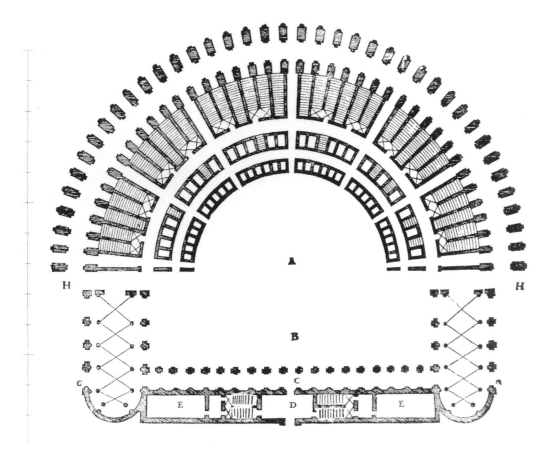

FIG. 4. Sebastiano Serlio after Baldassare Peruzzi, Reconstruction plan of the Theatre of Marcellus. Woodcut. From S. Serlio, *Il Terzo libro … nel qual si figurano e descrivono le antiquita di Roma* (Venice, 1540), XLVII.

combined with theoretical studies from Vitruvius, which provide the key to understanding the intense interest Antonio showed in these temples. Instead of following the common antiquarian tradition, based on literary sources, that identifies them as the temples of Janus, Spes and Pietas, Antonio called the southern, Doric, temple 'Jove Stator', which can come only from Vitruvius's descriptions of the canonical types of temples, where the Temple of Jove Stator by Hermodorus in the Porticus of Metellus is given as the exemplar of the peripteral type.[23] On the same drawing Antonio called the northern temple the 'Carcere', the jail, which is conventional enough (it was converted to a jail in the early Middle Ages by filling in the intercolumniations). But on another sheet he called it 'Honour and Virtue', which again is taken from the same passage in Vitruvius where the Temple of Honour and Virtue near the Monument of Marius is the exemplar of the peripteral *sine postico* type.[24]

Far more drawings of the Doric temple survive than of the two Ionic temples. In part this can be explained by the fact that in Rome examples of the Doric order were much rarer than those of the Ionic, but a note on a drawing by Giovanni Battista da Sangallo provides another reason: it says that part of the cornice of the Doric temple had been transferred to the courtyard of the Palazzo Farnese.[25] Antonio was building the palace from 1517, and it seems likely that the temple was being used as a quarry (it had been used to store hay): it was precisely because it was being destroyed that the Sangallo brothers and Peruzzi were able to record it in such forensic detail. By contrast, there are fewer record drawings of the middle and northern temples, still encased in the post-antique masonry of the church of San Nicola and the adjacent jail (**Fig. 5**). Only Peruzzi seems to have spotted an Ionic capital belonging to the northern temple, while the normally meticulous Antonio gave it Corinthian capitals.

The process of recording the Theatre of Marcellus and San Nicola temples was analogous to modern rescue archaeology in town centres, where redevelopment means the loss of historic sites: but at least archaeologists can use the opportunity of excavation and demolition for other purposes, to undertake as

FIG. 5. Girolamo Franzini, S. Nicola in Carcere in the later Cinquecento. Woodcut. From G. Franzini, *Templa Deo et Sanctis eius Romae Dicata* (Rome, 1596), pl. F4.

thorough a survey as possible, thereby sometimes gaining knowledge that might otherwise remain undiscovered. While we may regret the scale of losses of ancient remains in Renaissance Rome, we can at least be grateful that sometimes architects as perceptive as the Sangallo brothers and Peruzzi were involved, and that they left us their record drawings.

Pirro Ligorio (*c.* 1513–83), the greatest architect-antiquary of the next generation, has been credited with undertaking 'the first large-scale modern archaeological 'dig'' at Hadrian's Villa at Tivoli between 1550 and 1568.[26] However, again the excavations fail the test in that the primary motive was not to understand the site better, but principally to find building materials and statues for the new villa that Ligorio was erecting for his patron, Cardinal Ippolito d'Este, in Tivoli. The 10,000-word description of the villa and the accompanying plan, to which he referred, were by-products of the quarrying.

Having failed to answer the original question of when archaeological excavation for the sake of knowledge begins, we end by posing another: of Ligorio's plan of Hadrian's Villa only two fragments survive, one in Turin and one at Windsor, the latter formerly part of Cassiano dal Pozzo's Museo

Cartaceo in seventeenth-century Rome.[27] Both drawings are clearly preparatory in nature, and as such are extremely rare in Ligorio's *oeuvre*, since virtually every extant drawing by him is a finished work intended for one of his treatises, like the drawing of the Temple of Portunus again from the Museo Cartaceo and now at Windsor (**Fig. 6**).[28]

The Temple of Portunus drawing appears to be intended to illustrate his argument that the decagonal Licinian Garden Pavilion on the Esquiline could not be the Basilica of Gaius and Lucius, as Flavio Biondo had suggested.[29] In a manuscript of his writings in Oxford, Ligorio argued against Biondo on the grounds that Vitruvius had said that basilicas were rectangular, but he failed to suggest an alternative site.[30] The unearthing of the two inscriptions to Gaius and Lucius just in front of the Temple of Portunus in 1552 gave him just the 'evidence' he needed to argue that it was the basilica in his *Paradosse* of 1553.[31]

A clue to the fate of the thousands of record drawings and preliminary sketches Ligorio must have needed to prepare the hundreds of surviving finished reconstruction drawings is on a copy of the Windsor fragment of the plan of Hadrian's Villa, by Francesco Contini (1599–1669), again from the Museo Cartaceo (**Fig. 7**). An attached label says that the rest of Ligorio's drawings of the villa were sold by a Ferrarese dealer to a 'Monsú d'Autreville'.[32] This is corroborated by a manuscript in the Vatican Library, which contains some disjointed fragments about Cassiano dal Pozzo's attempts to obtain copies of the Ligorio manuscripts in Turin. One of the fragments is a note saying that:

A great quantity of drawings of the aforementioned Pirro Ligorio, to the number of five thousand, including large and small of every sort, and among which were very many things excavated from the antique, and others made in imitation of the antique, such as myths, histories and things of architecture, were sold in Rome in January 1632 by Giorgio Raimondi, a Ferrarese dealer in paintings and frames, to a Frenchman called Monsieur d'Autreville, who took them to Paris.[33]

The Dutch art historian, Arnold Noach, in his invaluable curatorial notes on the architectural drawings at Windsor, recorded an Autreville, who published a history of France in 1617.[34] Nothing else is known, but if we could find more we might be on the way to discovering the fate of the largest hoard of drawings of architectural antiquities outside the Uffizi.

FIG. 6. Pirro Ligorio, Reconstructional view of the Temple of Portunus, Forum Boarium. Drawing. Windsor Castle, Royal Library inv. no. RL 19258. (© HM The Queen. Reproduced by permission of Her Majesty the Queen.)

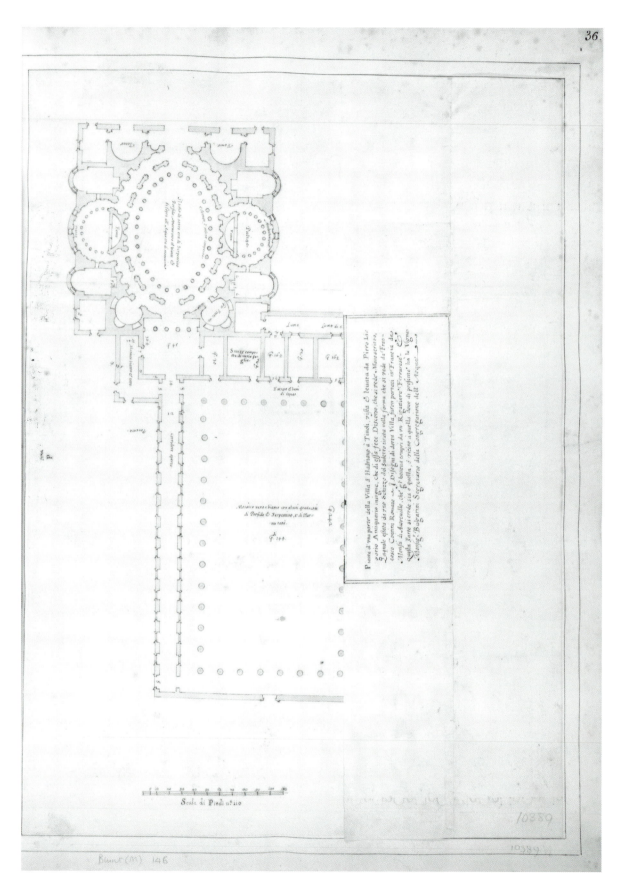

FIG. 7.   Francesco Contini after Pirro Ligorio, Plan of the 'Accademia', Hadrian's Villa, Tivoli. Drawing. Windsor Castle, Royal Library inv. no. RL 10389. (© HM The Queen. Reproduced by permission of Her Majesty the Queen.)

Notes

1. A. di Tuccio Manetti, *The Life of Brunelleschi* (ed. H. Saalman, trans. C. Engass) (London, 1970), 50.
2. Manetti, *Life* (above, n. 1), 52–4.
3. Manetti, *Life* (above, n. 1), 54.
4. See H. Burns, 'Quattrocento architecture and the antique: some problems', in R.R. Bolgar (ed.), *Classical Influences on European Culture 500–1500* (Cambridge, 1971), 269–87; J.B. Onians, 'Brunelleschi: humanist or nationalist?', *Art History* 5 (1982), 96–114.
5. Manetti, *Life* (above, n. 1), 29.
6. R. Weiss, *The Renaissance Discovery of Classical Antiquity* (Oxford, 1973), 51–3.
7. On Ciriaco, see Weiss, *Renaissance Discovery* (above, n. 6), 109–10, 137–41. On the *Barberini Codex*, see C. Hülsen (ed.), *Il libro di Giuliano da Sangallo: Codice Vaticano Barberiano Latino 4424*, 2 vols (Leipzig, 1910).
8. F. Biondo, *De Roma Triumphante Libri Decem … Romae Instauratae Libri iii … Italia Illustrata* (Basle, 1531) [hereafter *Roma instaurata*], 325–6; G. Mancini, *Vita di Leon Battista Alberti* (Rome, 1967), 278–9; Weiss, *Renaissance Discovery* (above, n. 6), 113.
9. Manetti, *Life* (above, n. 1), 28–9.
10. R. Weiss, 'Traccia per una biografia di Annio da Viterbo', *Italia Medioevale e Umanistica* 5 (1962), 434.
11. *CIL* VI (I) 702; R. Lanciani, *The Ruins and Excavations of Ancient Rome* (London, 1897), 467–8.
12. Florence, Gabinetti dei Disegni e Stampe degli Uffizi [hereafter Florence UA], inv. A. 2575; C. Acidini, 'Roma antica', in F. Borsi (ed.), *Roma antica e i disegni di architettura agli Uffizi di Giovanni Antonio Dosio* (Rome, 1976), 27–166, at p. 105 no. 95: 'Questo è jl piedistallo sotto alle colonne de l'arco di Settimio Seuero jmp. oggi tutto ricoperto al tempo fu scop[er]to al tempo di Papa Pio IIII nel 1563 dal quale furono prese le misure e ricoperto nel medesimo anno che jmpediua la strada che uiene dal campidoglio e ua al foro Romano' ('This is the pedestal under the columns of the Arch of Septimius Severus, today completely reburied. When it was discovered, at the time of Pope Pius IV in 1563, measurements were taken from it and it was reburied in the same year since it was blocking the road that comes from the Campidoglio to the Roman Forum').
13. Florence UA, inv. A. 2521; Acidini, 'Roma antica' (above, n. 12), 72 no. 52.
14. F. Cerasoli, 'Usi e regolamenti per gli scavi di antichità in Roma nei secoli XV e XVI', *Studi e Documenti di Storia e Diritto* 18 (1897), 133–49.
15. Biondo, *Roma instaurata* (above, n. 8), 238. See P. Spring, *The Topographical and Archaeological Study of the City of Rome, 1420–47* (Ph.D. thesis, Edinburgh University, 1972), 357–60.
16. T. Buddensieg, 'Die Konstantinsbasilika in einer Zeichnung Francesco di Giorgios und der Marmorkoloss Konstantins des Grossen', *Münchner Jahrbuch der Bildenden Kunst* 13 (1962), 37–8.
17. Buddensieg, 'Die Konstantinsbasilika' (above, n. 16), 42–8,

18. V. Golzio, *Raffaello nei documenti* (Vatican City, 1936), 83.
19. On Leo X's brief of 1515, see Golzio, *Raffaello* (above, n. 18), 39–40. On Raphael's recording proposals, see Golzio, *Raffaello* (above, n. 18), 87–91; A. Nesselrath, 'Raphael's archaeological method', in C.L. Frommel and M. Winner (eds), *Raffaello a Roma* (Rome, 1986), 357–62.
20. According to Marcantonio Michiel, one of Rome's fourteen ancient regions had been completed. See Nesselrath, 'Raphael's archaeological method' (above, n. 19), 363.
21. S. Serlio, *Sebastiano Serlio on Architecture* (ed./trans. V. Hart and P. Hicks) (New Haven/London, 1996), 136; Peruzzi's plan is copied on the page facing p. 137.
22. See L. Crozzoli Aite, 'I tre templi del Foro Olitorio', *MemPontAcc* 13 (1981), catalogue nos. 18–42; I. Campbell, *Reconstructions of Roman Temples made in Italy between 1450 and 1600* (D.Phil. thesis, University of Oxford, 1984), I, 213–46, and II, figs 7:15–40, for discussions of these drawings in general.
23. Vitruvius, *De Architectura* iii.2.5; Campbell, *Reconstructions* (above, n. 22), 229; P.N. Pagliara, 'Studi e pratica vitruviani di Antonio da Sangallo il Giovane e di suo fratello Giovanni Battista', in J. Guillaume (ed.), *Les traités d'architecture de la Renaissance: actes du colloque tenu à Tours du 1er au 11 juillet 1981* (Paris, 1988), 191.
24. Vitruvius, *De Architectura* iii.2.5; Campbell, *Reconstructions* (above, n. 22), 229; Pagliara, 'Studi e pratica' (above, n. 23), 191 n. 75.
25. Florence UA, inv. A. 1658v: 'Cornice de quello tempietto dove staua gia nel fieno acanto a santo niccola in carciere sta nel cortile di farnese adesso, del difizio dorico' (Cornice of that small temple that once stood in the hay [barn] next to San Nicola in Carcere, now stands in the courtyard of the [Palazzo] Farnese, from the Doric building); Crozzoli Aite, 'Tre templi' (above, n. 22), 43.
26. E. Mandowsky and C. Mitchell, *Pirro Ligorio's Roman Antiquities* (London, 1963), 7–8.
27. On the description and the plans of the villa, see W.L. MacDonald and J.A. Pinto, *Hadrian's Villa and its Legacy* (New Haven/London, 1995), 216–20, figs 261–2; the plans are Archivio di Stato di Torino, Cod. a.II.7.J.20, fol. 91r, and Windsor Castle, Royal Library, inv. no. RL 10377 r and v. On the latter, see I. Campbell, *Roman Topography and Architecture* (*The Paper Museum of Cassiano dal Pozzo: Series A — Antiquities and Architecture* 9), 3 vols (London, forthcoming), I, nos. 51–2.
28. See Campbell, *Roman Topography and Architecture* (above, n. 27), I, no. 65.
29. Biondo, *Roma instaurata* (above, n. 8), 244.
30. Bodleian Library, MS Canon. ital. 138, fol. 26r.
31. P. Ligorio, *Libro di M. Pyrrho Ligori Napolitano, delle antichità … con le paradosse del medesimo auttore* (Venice, 1553), fols 39v–40r. The inscriptions are *CIL* VI (I) 897–8.
32. Windsor Castle, Royal Library, inv. no. RL 10389; MacDonald

and Pinto, *Hadrian's Villa* (above, n. 27), 218, fig. 263; Campbell, *Roman Topography and Architecture* (above, n. 27), I, no. 53.

33. BAV, Vat. Lat. 10486, fol. 81r: 'Un quantità grande di Disegni del sud[ett]o Pirro Ligorio al n[ombr]o di cinq[ue] mila inc.a fra grandi e piccoli d'ogni sorte e tra quali erano moltissime cose cauati dall'antico, et altre fatte à immitation dell'antico tanto di fauole, de historie, e cose d'Architetture furono il 1632 di Gen[nai]o uenduta in Roma da Giorgio Raimondi Ferrarese Rigatt[ie]ro di quadri ne cornaci [sic] a un francesi detto Monsu d'Autreville chegli portò a Parigi'; F. Solinas, 'Poussin et Cassiano dal Pozzo', in A. Mérot (ed.), *Nicolas Poussin (1594–1665)*, 2 vols (Paris, 1996), I, 298.

34. Windsor Castle, Royal Library, notes on RL 10389, citing J.C.F. Hoefer, *Nouvelle biographie géneral*, 46 vols (Paris, 1852–66), III, 791; the book by d'Autreville is *État géneral des affaires de France sur tout ce qui s'est passé, tant dedans que dehors la royaume, depuis la mor déplorable de Henri IV jusqu'à présent* (Paris, 1617): I have not been able to trace a copy in the UK, and would be grateful for any further information.

RESEARCH IN THE ROMAN CATACOMBS BY THE LOUVAIN ANTIQUARIAN PHILIPS VAN WINGHE

Cornelis Schuddeboom

INTRODUCTION

'IN FLORENCE I began suffering from the third-day fever.' This short personal note was written by Philips van Winghe in his small *Notebook* on 18 August 1592.[1] This illness, malaria, turned out to be fatal; he passed away some two weeks later at the age of 32. His unexpected and untimely death caused a great stir among the learned men of the day. His fame was such that someone remarked that 'would he have lived longer, he would certainly have surpassed all the others in matters concerning antiquity'.[2]

Philips van Winghe was born in 1560 to a noble Louvain family.[3] After the death of his parents, he was placed under the guardianship of his uncle, Maximilien Morillon, bishop of Tournay and chancellor to the notorious Cardinal De Granvelle. After completing his studies at Louvain, he travelled to Paris in the company of the well-known Utrecht scholar Arent van Buchell, with the aim of carrying out research on the ancient remains of that city. They visited Fontainebleau, and admired and discussed copies of antique statues in the collection of Francis I. On their journey van Winghe eagerly copied every inscription and monument he saw, which caused van Buchell to write to a friend 'how tedious is this work, but what fun we have!'.[4] From Paris van Winghe returned to Antwerp, where he visited the collector Nicholaas Rockox and the royal cartographer Abraham Ortelius, one of his closest friends. (Philips wrote a beautiful entry in Ortelius's *Album Amicorum* to commemorate their friendship.[5]) In 1589 he departed for Rome, where he arrived in November of the same year. A cosmopolitan circle of scholars and artists greeted him. Amongst others, he made the acquaintance of Fulvio Orsini, the librarian to the Farnese family, and of Cardinal Cesare Baronio, who was to praise him in the fourth volume of his *Annales*.[6] With the Dutch painter Hendrick Goltzius he made a trip to Naples through the Campagna, which is vividly described in Carel van Mander's *Schilder-boeck*.[7] Goltzius also drew a beautiful portrait of van Winghe, which was engraved after his death by Jacob Matham (Fig. 1).

Of all the people van Winghe met in Rome, two were to play a decisive role in his work. One was his compatriot Jean l'Heureux, alias *Macarius*, the author of *Hagioglypta*, the first book on Christian iconography. The other, the Spanish Dominican Alfonso Chacón,[8] had written an extensive *History of the Popes* and had started work on a historical description of Rome that, unfortunately, was never published.[9] Both these men were well known for their vast knowledge of classical and early Christian monuments, and undoubtedly stimulated Philips's interest in the latter, which led him to document as much as possible of the remains of the early Church.

THE BRUSSELS *NOTEBOOK*

Of all the material collected by van Winghe during his stay in Rome, only one manuscript in his own hand seems to have survived, a small *Notebook* of some 180 pages, formerly in the possession of the Bollandist Society in Antwerp and now preserved in the Royal Library in Brussels.[10] This precious manuscript contains copies of hundreds of ancient inscriptions and monuments, both pagan and Christian, which are commented upon in a neat but very minute hand. Van Winghe copied most of the material *in situ*, and his topographical remarks are of the utmost value to our knowledge of their original location. At the end of the *Notebook* there is a short diary of events in Rome in which

FIG. 1. Jacob Matham after Hendrick Goltzius, *Philips van Winghe*. Engraving. *(Reproduced courtesy of the Prentenkabinet, Rijksuniversiteit Leiden.)*

one can find curious details about the four conclaves that were held between the death of Pope Sixtus V in 1590 and the election of Clement VIII in 1592. These were troublesome times for the city of Rome, and the situation was worsened by the fact that the Tiber flooded twice. Van Winghe did not have much esteem for the modern Romans and Roman society, as is quite obvious from a remark in one of his letters to Ortelius: 'I would hold him for a madman, who in times of peace would leave a city like Antwerp for the city of Rome, which has nothing special to offer and where there is nothing that has not been brought there, not even the wine!'.[11]

After his sudden death in Florence in 1592, Jean l'Heureux took care of van Winghe's belongings and sent them to Flanders, to Philips's brother Hieronymus, a canon of the cathedral in Tournay. In the years to follow Hieronymus went to great lengths to get the material published, unfortunately with little success. He bequeathed most of Philips's manuscripts to the cathedral library, but during the French Revolution all the original notes and drawings seem to have been dispersed.[12]

THE VATICAN AND PARIS CODICES

In my reconstruction of the scientific legacy of Philips van Winghe published in 1996, I tried to prove that, apart from the *Notebook*, two other manuscripts contain a large number of firsthand copies of drawings that he had made in Rome.[13] One of them is a well-known codex in the Vatican Library, formerly in the possession of Giovanni Battista de' Rossi.[14] He ascribed it to Claude-François [le] Menestrier, a French antiquarian in the household of Francesco Barberini, as a result of which the manuscript became known as the *Codex Menestrier*. I was able to prove, however, that the drawings and annotations in this manuscript were not assembled by Menestrier, but by the French humanist and scholar Claude-Nicholas Fabri de Peiresc (1580–1637). He was a close friend of Hieronymus van Winghe, who exchanged some of his brother's drawings for tulips and other botanical items, and even gave him the *Notebook* on loan for a period of nearly eleven years. From the unpublished correspondence between Peiresc and Philips's brother, Hieronymus, we know that Peiresc had copies made of the *Notebook* and also of most of the drawings by van Winghe, and that he assembled them in a volume, which has been identified with the manuscript in the Vatican Library (Vat. Lat. 10545). Hence, it should be called the *Codex van Winghe/Peiresc*.

The second manuscript was acquired at the end of the nineteenth century for the Bibliothèque Nationale in Paris and since then it has been completely forgotten.[15] This manuscript was assembled in the period 1600–20 by Dionysius de Villiers (1546–1620), the dean of the chapter of Tournay and a close friend of both Philips and Hieronymus. It contains numerous drawings of both pagan and early Christian monuments in Rome, mainly dating from the years 1589–92. A comparison between this manuscript and Vat. Lat. 10545 reveals a striking resemblance both in style and content, which clearly indicates a common archetype, namely the original drawings by Philips van Winghe, most of which are now lost. De Villiers was a close friend of Hieronymus van Winghe and thus had easy access to Philips's papers. The copies of catacomb paintings in both manuscripts were almost certainly sketched by the same artist and the annotations were written in the same hand, probably that of Hieronymus.[16]

RESEARCH IN THE CATACOMBS

From the contents of these three manuscripts, the *Notebook* in Brussels and the assembled copies in the Vatican and in Paris, one might conclude that Philips van Winghe visited at least four different catacombs during his stay in Rome. The first he explored was the complex on the Via Salaria Vecchia, in the vineyard of a certain Pietro Cortes, at the time thought to be the catacomb of Priscilla but now known as the anonymous catacomb of the Via Anapo.[17] This complex had been discovered by accident on 31 May 1578, a date that is now regarded as the birthday of Christian archaeology. The paintings decorating it were copied only twice before they became inaccessible due to the collapse of the entrance in 1592. Alfonso Chacón had hired some professional draughtsmen to copy them, and the drawings are to be found in the manuscript Vat. Lat. 5409. According to Jean l'Heureux, van Winghe was not happy with their quality and found them to be quite unfaithful to the original paintings.[18] Thus, he decided to make more accurate ones. One of his original drawings is still extant in the Bibliothèque Nationale in Paris,[19] while the others are only known through firsthand copies. He visited the catacomb several times in the company of the Roman antiquarian Angelo Breventano. On one of the walls they left their signatures as a lasting witness to their visits. Due to the collapse of the entrance to the catacomb, Bosio was to make use of the drawings of both Chacón and van Winghe for his *Roma sotterranea*.[20]

In his *Notebook*, van Winghe also described some of his many visits to the actual catacomb of Priscilla in the Via Salaria Nuova, the entrance of which was located in the vineyard of a certain Hieronymus Cupis. In February 1590 he mentioned the excavation of early Christian inscriptions and of Roman brickwork:

In the month of February 1590 in the vineyard of Hieronymus Cupis in the Via Salaria, not far from the Salarian bridge, I witnessed the excavation of the following Christian inscriptions, and of some pagan

inscriptions as well … this was once the Christian cemetery of Priscilla … amongst other remains some slabs or giant ceramic roofing-tiles were excavated, in the middle of which one could read the mutilated inscription ///OPVS DOLIAREX/// that also were found a few days ago on the Via Appia in some Christian crypts and also elsewhere in great number.[21]

There had been more excavations as 'you also can see on this spot the remains of a square structure, in which numerous inscriptions and fragments of sarcophagi have been gathered, which were found in earlier days'.[22] This passage tells us that the remains of the chapel of San Silvestro, situated above the catacomb, served in those days as a kind of storeroom for archaeological material. There, van Winghe copied several inscriptions that have since been lost.

Together with Angelo Breventano, he drew a simple ground-plan of the galleries that they explored in the southern part of the catacomb of Priscilla, and the same plan was used in *Roma sotterranea* (Fig. 2), due to the fact that Bosio found the entrance to the catacomb blocked by debris.[23] It appears to be the first archaeological plan ever made and offers a good example of van Winghe's scientific approach. He copied the paintings found in four rooms marked in his plan: four scenes from the *Cubicolo del Velatio*, one from the *Cubicolo dell'Annunziazione,* the famous painting of the wine sellers in the *Cubicolo dei Bottai*, and an *orante*.[24] A comparison between his drawings and those made for Chacón clearly shows van Winghe's greater reliability, as was pointed out by Wilpert in 1891.[25] The reason for this might be found in the different purposes of their copies. Chacón collected material in order to illustrate the early history of the Church from an apologetic point of view, to illustrate the statements made by Baronio and other champions of the Counter-Reformation. Van Winghe's interests, on the contrary, were predominantly antiquarian-scientific; they were based on the humanistic tradition of the Low Countries.

The third complex visited by van Winghe was the catacomb of Domitilla, which he could not identify as such but rather described as 'a catacomb in the Via Ardeatina where a street leads from San Paolo fuori le mura to San Sebastiano'.[26] He was among the first to visit this catacomb, probably in the company of some other Dutchmen who left their signatures on the walls from 1591 onwards.[27] In the catacomb of Domitilla, van Winghe copied paintings and inscriptions in the immediate vicinity of the entrance staircase.[28] Most of

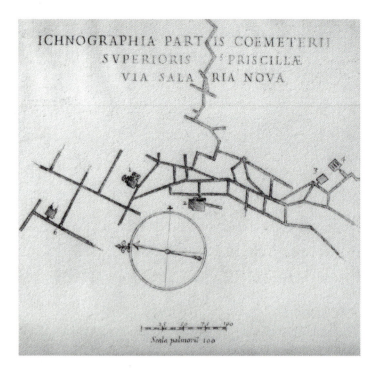

FIG. 2. After Philips van Winghe and Angelo Breventano, Plan of the first floor of the catacomb of Priscilla. From A. Bosio, *Roma sotterranea* (Rome, 1632), 591f.

the original paintings in this part of the complex were removed during the eighteenth century and are now preserved, though severely mutilated, in the Museo Comunale at Catania in Sicily. Thanks to van Winghe's drawings, it is still possible to reconstruct their original disposition.

Evidence for his visits to the catacomb of San Sebastiano on the Via Appia is found in all three manuscripts.[29] In his *Notebook* van Winghe copied the famous inscription of the priests Proclinus and Ursus (Fig. 3).[30] He also drew the fragments of the *cancelli* donated by them to the tomb of Saint Sebastian, still extant in the martyrium of the saint in the southeastern corner of the basilica. Through this chamber, which originally formed part of an underground gallery, one could easily descend into the catacomb. This is clearly indicated in a drawing by van Winghe, of which two identical copies are known (one being shown in Fig. 4).[31] These drawings are almost identical and show an elaborate ground-plan of the subterranean area below and to the northeast of the basilica of San

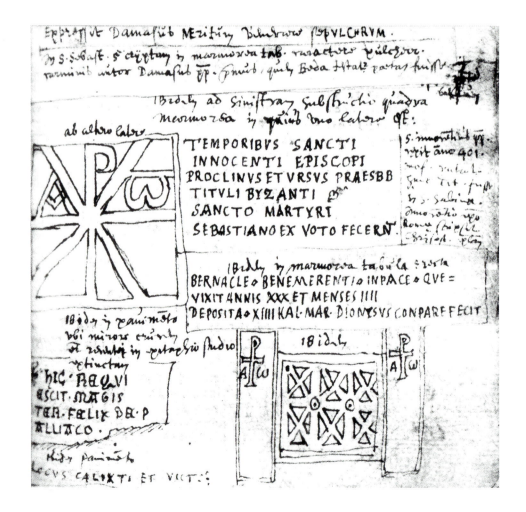

FIG. 3. Inscription in the martyrium of Saint Sebastian. From the *Notebook* of Philips van Winghe. Brussels, Royal Library Albert I, inv. no. 17.872–3, fol. 33. *(Reproduced courtesy of the Royal Library Albert I, Brussels.)*

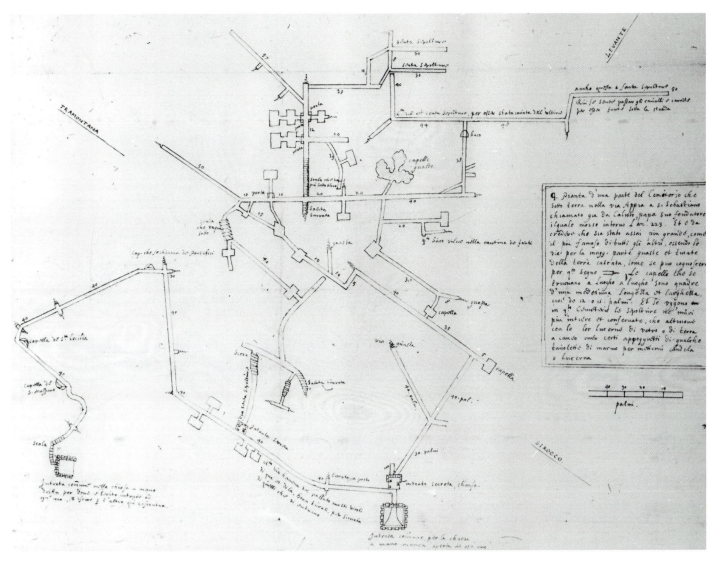

FIG. 4. **After Philips van Winghe, Ground-plan of the catacomb of San Sebastiano (copy). BAV, Vat. Lat. 10545, unnumbered folio between 183v and 184.** *(Reproduced courtesy of the Biblioteca Vaticana.)*

Sebastiano.[32] This plan has caused some confusion, because on the left-hand side of the drawing van Winghe identified three burial chambers as respectively 'the chapel of Saint Maximus', 'the chapel of Saint Cecilia' and 'the chapel that is known as that of the Popes'.[33]

At first glance one would be inclined to think that he had drawn part of the actual catacomb of San Callisto, some 600 m to the northeast of San Sebastiano. From written sources we know that the martyr Maximus was buried there, and this, indeed, is the location of the chamber of Santa Cecilia, an annexe to the so-called chapel of the popes. But this can hardly be reconciled with the two entrances in the left- and right-hand sides of the basilica of San Sebastiano and the detailed measurements in *palmi romani* in comparison to the actual distance between the basilica and the galleries of San Callisto. The cause for his confusion can be found in the character of the inscriptions he copied while visiting the underground galleries. After entering the complex through the right-hand entrance in the middle of the basilica[34] he identified the first burial chamber as that of the martyr Maximus by two inscriptions he found there (**Figs 5–6**):

SANCTO
MARTYRI
MAXIMO [35]

and:

MAXIMVS IN PACE
XII. KAL. MA.[36]

FIG. 5. *Titulus* of an *oratorium* dedicated to Maximus. BAV, Vat. Lat. 10545, fol. 199v. *(Reproduced courtesy of the Biblioteca Vaticana.)*

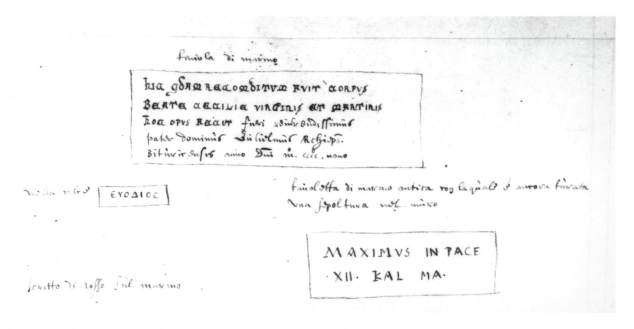

FIG. 6. After Philips van Winghe, Inscriptions from the catacomb of San Sebastiano (copy). BAV, Vat. Lat. 10545, fol. 200. *(Reproduced courtesy of the Biblioteca Vaticana.)*

The first inscription was probably a *titulus* for an *oratorium* dedicated to Maximus. He added in the margin that Maximus, Valerianus and Tiburtius were converted by Saint Cecilia and suffered martyrdom under Alexander Severus on the Via Appia.

The second inscription is undoubtedly a grave slab, as is stated in his annotation: 'a small antique marble slab with which a grave in the wall is still sealed'.[37] He obviously thought that he had identified here the tomb of the martyr Maximus, and found it to be logical that the body of the saint would have been laid to rest in the vicinity of the tomb of Cecilia, which he located some 50 m to the north. Here he copied the inscription, placed there by the bishop of Bourges in 1409 to commemorate, erroneously, the burial place of Saint Cecilia (**Fig. 6**):

HIC QDAM RECOMDITVM FVIT CORPVS
BEATE CECILIE VIRGINIS ET MARTIRIS
HOC OPVS FECIT FIERI REVERENDISSIMVS
PATER DOMINVS GVLIELMVS ARCHIEPS
BITVRICENSIS ANNO DNI M.CCCC.NONO.[38]

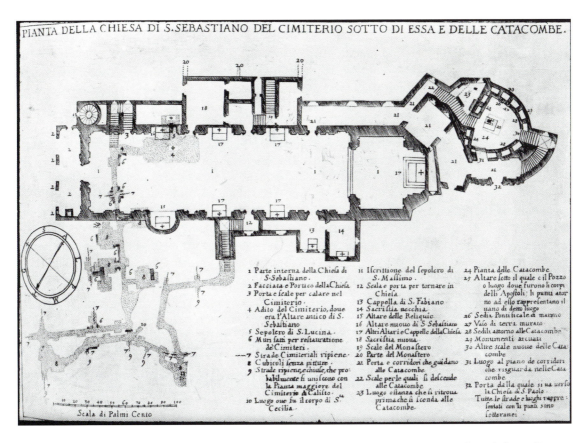

Fɪɢ. 7. Francesco Contini's plan of the subterranean area below the church of San Sebastiano. From A. Bosio, *Roma sotterranea* (Rome, 1632), 185.

In the light of secondary written sources, he must have concluded that the next chamber that he found, some 80 *palmi romani* to the northeast, was the so-called chapel of the popes, although no papal grave was found there.

Consistently with his conclusions, van Winghe drew an accurate plan of the galleries below San Sebastiano, but misinterpreted the chambers and inscriptions he actually saw and took them as solid proof that he was in the catacomb of San Callisto. This is confirmed by the title of his ground-plan: 'Plan of a part of the catacomb that lies underground on the Via Appia near the church of San Sebastiano, named after its founder Pope Callixtus, who died around the year 223'.[39] The same mistake was later made by Bosio and other contemporaries; they believed that the catacombs of San Sebastiano and those of San Callisto constituted one vast complex.

A comparison between van Winghe's drawing and the plan by Contini in Bosio's *Roma sotterranea* (**Fig. 7**) clearly shows that van Winghe had penetrated much further into the complex than Bosio did. Probably he made use of one of the two 'secret entrances' that are marked in his drawing. The first one is situated near the main entrance at the left-hand side of the church ('General entrance to the church, open to everyone'),[40] which leads through the burial chamber of Saint Sebastian. Van Winghe described it as a 'secret entrance, closed'[41] and suggested that a wall had been placed there to prevent people from entering. The second one, still accessible from the long gallery, connected the two main entrances open to the public and is also described as a 'secret entrance'. From here he could descend further down into the complex. In Bosio's days the latter 'secret entrance' was no longer accessible, as the plan in his book describes the spot as: 'blocked and inaccessible streets, which probably connect this part with that on the major plan of the catacomb of Callixtus'.[42] This explains also why van Winghe's drawing depicts much more of the complex, that is to say the northeastern region, than the other plan. But Bosio and his followers must have known that beyond those 'blocked streets' there were more galleries. This might explain why Giovanni Severano, the editor of *Roma sotterranea*, tried to obtain the drawing made by van Winghe after the death of Bosio in 1629. In a letter dated 21 July 1632, to Cassiano dal Pozzo, Severano mentioned the need for more drawings to serve as illustrations to Bosio's book, and he specifically asked for a copy of a ground-plan of the catacomb of San Callisto made by Philips van Winghe.[43] He knew of the existence of several copies (quite correct, since the original was at the time in Tournay and copies had been made for both Peiresc and De Villiers) and asked Cassiano to provide him with a copy. Obviously Cassiano did not succeed in this task, and he asked Contini to make a new plan, which was later inserted in *Roma sotterranea*.

In his plan van Winghe made annotations at the different staircases to indicate the different levels of the galleries, such as the 'stairway leading further into the ground'.[44] He also tried to explain why some galleries were without tombs: 'This road (gallery) is without tombs, because it was one of the last to have been excavated/constructed'.[45] In the far eastern area he discovered a gallery, where 'horses can be heard passing overhead, which indicates that we are under the street'[46] — indeed, for he found himself in the region directly underneath the Via Appia! According to the title in his ground-plan, he believed that he had surveyed only part of the complex:

> One must assume that this catacomb was much larger, as the most famous of all, while a great part of the roads has been disturbed and blocked by falling earth, which one can recognize though this sign ⊃〰 . The different rooms that one encounters are square and of the same length and width, that, is *c.* 12 or 15 *palmi romani*. And one can see in this catacomb the tombs more intact and better conserved than elsewhere, with their glass or earthenware lamps or gabled-top constructions made from small marble tablets to shelter candles or lamps.[47]

Most of the tombs seen by van Winghe were still intact, which is also an indication that he descended deeper into the complex than anybody else before him. Whether he did discover a connection between the complex of San Sebastiano and the catacomb beneath the Vigna ex-Chiaravaglio, which is situated between San Sebastiano and San Callisto, remains to be investigated.

It is quite remarkable that van Winghe was able to draw such an elaborate and accurate plan of the intricate patterns of the underground galleries. All the more so, if we think of the rather primitive circumstances in which these first explorations took place. It was pitch dark, and one had to tie a rope around the waist or leave chalk marks on the walls and at corners in order to be able to find one's way back. It must have been very difficult to define the direction of the galleries and to take reasonably exact measurements, especially for someone who had little experience.

CONCLUSION

The fact that van Winghe did make ground-plans of the catacombs of Priscilla and Domitilla provides solid evidence that his approach was more antiquarian-scientific than that of other pioneers of early Christian archaeology, who were interested mostly in the apologetic value of the paintings and objects. In conclusion, the material from his scientific legacy is still a reliable and useful source of knowledge about early Christian monuments and their topographical disposition at the end of the sixteenth century.

NOTES

1. 'Cepi florentiae laborare febri tertiana.' Brussels, Royal Library Albert I, inv. no. 17.872–3 [hereafter *Notebook*], unnumbered folio. For the manuscript, see below, n. 10.

2. Jean l'Heureux, *Hagioglypta* (ed. R. Garrucci) (Paris, 1856), 4.

3. G.J. Hoogewerff, 'Philips van Winghe', *Mededelingen van het Nederlands Instituut Rome* 7 (1927), 59–82; C. Schuddeboom, 'Winghe, Philips van', *Nationaal Biografisch Woordenboek* 8 (1984), xl; C. Schuddeboom, *Philips van Winghe (1560–1592) en het Ontstaan van de Christelijke Archeologie* (Haren, 1996), 26–56.

4. Utrecht University Library, inv. no. 984, fols 2–3 (A. van Buchell to A. Verduin in Douai, 12 October 1586). For a detailed description of their journey, see Utrecht University Library, inv. no. 798, part of which is reproduced in A. van Buchell, *Description de Paris* (ed./trans. A. Vidier) (Paris, 1900).

5. See J. Puraye, *Album Amicorum Abraham Ortelius* (Amsterdam, 1969); the original *Album* is preserved in the library of Pembroke College, Oxford.

6. C. Baronius, *Annales Ecclesiastici* IV (Antwerp, 1594), 46: 'Philippo Vignio, nobili Lovaniensi, juvene erudito, ac rerum antiquarum studiosissomo, quarum causa patrio solo relicto Romae versatur' ('[from] Philips van Winghe, a young and learned nobleman from Louvain, an eager student of antiquity, for which purpose he left his homeland to go to Rome').

7. C. van Mander, *Het Schilder-boeck* (Haerlem, 1604), 281–3.

8. For Chacón, see S. Grassi Fiorentino's entry in *DBI* XXIV (Rome, 1981).

9. A. Recio Veganzones, 'La 'Historica Descriptio Urbis Romae'. Obra manuscrita de fr. Alfonso Chacón, O.P. (1530–1599)', *Anthologia Annua* 16 (1968), 44–102.

10. Brussels, Royal Library Albert I, inv. no. 17.872–3. Originally, the *Notebook* (above, n. 1) consisted of two separate volumes, which were bound together at the end of the nineteenth century; it contains 182 pages partially numbered by van Winghe himself.

11. Leiden University Library, inv. no. BPL 2766 (P. van Winghe to A. Ortelius in Antwerp, Rome 24 December 1589).

12. G.J. Hoogewerff, 'De Romeinse catacomben', *Nederlands Archief voor Kerkgeschiedenis* 44 (1961), 223, mentioned the existence of a second notebook, which was in the possession of Christian Hülsen in Florence in 1935. He identified it as van Winghe's autograph, containing numerous drawings and copies of both Christian and pagan inscriptions and also biographical material. After Hülsen's death (1935) he tried to obtain it from his heirs, but it appeared to have been lost and has never been recovered.

13. Schuddeboom, *Philips van Winghe* (above, n. 3), 58–119.

14. The manuscript had been purchased on the Belgian art market by the director of the Royal Library in Brussels, C. Ruelens, who donated it to de' Rossi, the first to recognize the close relationship between the contents of the manuscript and van Winghe's *Notebook*. See *Bullettino di Archeologia Cristiana* (1865), 80. After de' Rossi's death it was acquired by the Vatican Library and catalogued as Vat. Lat. 10545.

15. It was acquired by the Bibliothèque Nationale in 1889 at the auction of the Collection Bordier in Paris, and had formerly been in the possession of a Dutch magistrate, C.A. Rethaan de Macaré (1792–1861); see Schuddeboom, *Philips van Winghe* (above, n. 3), 73–4. The only reference to it is by L. Delisle, *Manuscrits latins et français ajoutés aux fonds des nouvelle acquisitions pendant les années 1875–1891* I (Paris, 1891), 18–19; he ascribed it to an anonymous Dutch antiquarian of the early seventeenth century.

16. Peiresc visited Hieronymus van Winghe in 1606. He paid a considerable sum of money to have copies made of Philips's drawings because these could be done much more cheaply in Tournay than Paris. In their correspondence there are numerous references to those copies, which have helped to identify them as those in BAV, Vat. Lat. 10545; see Schuddeboom, *Philips van Winghe* (above, n. 3), 94–9.

17. J.G. Deckers, G. Mietke and A. Weiland, *Die Katakombe 'Anonima di Via Anap'. Repertorium der Malereien* I–III (Vatican City, 1991).

18. L'Heureux, *Hagioglypta* (above, n. 2), 3–4: 'et imagines, uti suis oculis viderat, fideliter et coloribus et figuris veris exprimebat, cum diceret in picturis Ciaconii pictores quos adhibuerat plus sibi indulsisse quam par erat, dum nimium properant, vel non satis figuras observant. Volebat autem Philippus omnia, quantum fieri poterat, archetypo respondere, et fidelis esse testis rei antiquae' ('and he copied the paintings from his own observations, faithful both to their colours and forms; in contrast he said that the draughtsmen hired by Chacón added more of their own work to their copies than was to be seen, either because they worked too hastily or because they did not observe the figures very well').

19. Bibliothèque Nationale, Fonds latin 8957–8, fol. 393; see C. Schuddeboom, 'Een onbekende tekening van Philips van Winghe (1560–1592), *Was getekend … Liber amicorum Prof. Dr. E.K.J. Reznicek* (Houten, 1988)', *Nederlands Kunsthistorisch Jaarboek* 38 (1987), 312–23.

20. A. Bosio, *Roma sotterranea* (Rome, 1632), 502.

21. 'Anno 1590 mense feb.erui vidi, in vinea Hieronymi Copijs via Salaria, non procul a Ponte Salaria seqq. Inscriptiones christianas, cum nonnullis ethnicis … Cemiterium olim fuit Christianorum Priscillae … inter cetera monumenta recenter eruta erant tegulae illae aut imbrices ingentes fictiles, in quarum medio inscriptio mutila ////OPVS DOLIAREX/// quales paucis ante diebus repertae Via Appia in crijpta christianorum et passim infinitae', *Notebook* (above, n. 1), fol. 33.

22. *Notebook* (above, n. 1), fol. 33.

23. Bosio, *Roma sotterranea* (above, n. 20), 591: 'Pianta dei una parte del Cimiterio superiore di Priscilla nella Via Salaria nuova, levata gia dal Vinghio e dal Breventano …' ('Ground-plan of the higher catacomb of Priscilla on the Via Salaria, once drawn by Van Winghe and by Breventano …').

24. Schuddeboom, *Philips van Winghe* (above, n. 3), 161–6 and catalogue nos. C30–C36.

25. J. Wilpert, *Die Katakombengemälde und ihre Alten Copien:*

eine Ikonografische Studie (Freiburg im Breisgau, 1891), 13: 'Er war ein geschickter Zeichner, aber kein Zeichner von Profession, welche, wie damals, so auch heute noch in die Copien etwas von ihrer Kunstfertigkeit hineinlegen zu müssen glauben. Er besass sodann das wissenschaftliche Verständniss, hatte also nicht allein das 'artistische' sondern auch das 'wissenschaftliche' Auge' ('He was an able draughtsman, but not a professional one, who in those days — as today — thought it necessary to display something of their own artistic ability in their copies. Thus he possessed a scientific judgement; he was, as it were, endowed with both artistic and scientific insight').

26. 'Un cimitero nella Via Ardeatina su la strada che va da S. Paulo a S. Sebastiano.' BAV, Vat. Lat. 10545, fol. 186. This road is known now as Via delle Sette Chiese.

27. A.H.L. Hensen, 'Nederlanders op het eind der zestiende eeuw in de catacombe van Domitilla', *De Katholiek* 119 (1914), 410–23.

28. Schuddeboom, *Philips van Winghe* (above, n. 3), 145–58.

29. He saw the church in a more original state than we can see it today, before the large-scale remodelling of 1609–12 commissioned by Cardinal Scipione Borghese.

30. *Notebook* (above, n. 1), fol. 43.

31. One is found in manuscript BAV, Vat. Lat. 10545 (van Winghe/Peiresc) between folios 183 and 184 (Fig. 4), the other in manuscript Bibliothèque Nationale, Nouv. Acq. Lat. 2343 (van Winghe/De Villiers), fol. 98.

32. The plan was first published in R. Krautheimer, S. Corbett and W. Frankl, *Corpus Basilicarum Christianarum Romae* IV (Vatican City, 1970), 102 and fig. 121. Krautheimer erroneously dated the drawing around 1560 and ascribed it to Menestrier.

33. The 'capella de S. Massimo', the 'capella de Sta Cecilia' and the 'Cap[ella]. che se chiama de Pontifici'. BAV, Vat. Lat. 10545, unnumbered folio between fols 183 and 184. At first I jumped to the conclusion that van Winghe had discovered a passage from San Sebastiano to San Callisto. Further research made it clear, however, that he did, in fact, misinterpret the rooms he found as being part of the catacomb of San Callisto. See Schuddeboom, *Philips van Winghe* (above, n. 3), 171–2.

34. 'Intrata com[m]une nella chiesa a mano dritta per dove e lecito intrare ad ogn'uno, et uscire per l'altra qui riscontra' ('A common entrance on the right-hand side of the church, through which everyone is permitted to enter, and one leaves by the other on the opposite side'): BAV, Vat. Lat. 10545, unnumbered folio between fols 183 and 184.

35. 'To the Holy Martyr Maximus'. BAV, Vat. Lat. 10545, fol. 199v (van Winghe/Peiresc); also Bibliothèque Nationale, Nouv. Acq. Lat. 2343 (van Winghe/De Villiers), fol. 115v. See *ICUR* III, 13189 (after van Winghe).

36. 'Maximus in Peace 12 Kalend of May'. BAV, Vat. Lat. 10545, fol. 200 (van Winghe/Peiresc); also Bibliothèque Nationale, Nouv. Acq. Lat. 2343, fol. 113 (van Winghe/De Villiers). See *ICUR* III, 13190 (after van Winghe/Peiresc).

37. A 'tavoletta di marmo antico con laquale e ancora turata una sepoltura nel muro'.

38. 'Here had been buried once the body of the Saintly virgin and martyr Cecilia. This work was done by the order of the very reverend father and Lord William bishop of Bourges in the year of our Lord 1409.' BAV, Vat. Lat. 10545, fol. 200 (van Winghe/Peiresc); also Bibliothèque Nationale, Nouv. Acq. Lat. 2343, fol. 113 (van Winghe/De Villiers).

39. 'Pianta d'una parte del Cimiterio che sotto terra nella via Appia a S. Sebastiano chiamata gia da Calisto papa suo fondatore, il quale morse intorno l'an. 223.' BAV, Vat. Lat. 10545, unnumbered folio between fols 183 and 184.

40. 'Intrata com[m]une per la chiesa a mano manca aperta ad ogn'uno': BAV, Vat. Lat. 10545, unnumbered folio between fols 183 and 184.

41. An 'intrata secreta, chiusa': BAV, Vat. Lat. 10545, unnumbered folio between fols 183 and 184.

42. 'Strade ripiene, e chiuse, che probabilmente si uniscono con la Pianta maggiore del Cimiterio di Calisto': Bosio, *Roma sotterranea* (above, n. 20), 185.

43. Accademia dei Lincei, Roma, Carteggio Puteano 4 (VI), 167r. See I. Herklotz, 'Cassiano and the Christian tradition', in *Cassiano dal Pozzo's Paper Museum (Proceedings of a Conference Convened jointly by the British Museum and the Warburg Institute on 14 and 15 December 1989)* I (*Quaderni Puteani* 2) (Milan, 1992), 32–3.

44. The 'scala che va piu sotto terra'. BAV, Vat. Lat. 10545, unnumbered folio between fols 183 and 184.

45. 'Quaesta via e senza sepolture, per esser stata cavata dell'ultime', or simply 'senza sepolture'. BAV, Vat. Lat. 10545, unnumbered folio between fols 183 and 184.

46. 'Se sente passar gli cavalli per esser forte sotto la strada.'

47. 'Et e da credere che sia stato assai piu grande, come il piu famoso di tutti gli altri, essendo le vie per la magg[ior]. Parte guaste et turate della terra cascata, come se puo cognoscere per q[ues]to segno. Le capelle che se trovano a luogho a luogho sono quadre d'una medesima longezza et larghezza, cioe de 12. o 15. palmi. Et se uggono in q[ue]sto Cemeterio le sepolture ne'muri piu intiere e conservate, che altruove con lo lor lucerne di vetro o di terra a caneo over certi appoggietti di qualche tavolette di marmo per mettervi candela o lucerna.' BAV, Vat. Lat. 10545, unnumbered folio between fols 183 and 184.

Archaeologies, antiquaries and the *memorie* of sixteenth- and seventeenth-century Rome

Amanda Claridge

Although modern archaeologists often wish that all archaeological enquiry could conform to a common pattern (hoping for universal methods if not universal answers), in practice the world is still composed — and likely to stay composed — of hundreds of individual archaeologies. At the most basic level, this is simply because no one archaeological entity can be investigated in identical fashion to another: the physical evidence is never quite the same, neither is the person of the investigator, nor for that matter is the nature of the record that is left behind. The archaeologist has been (and still is) a quite different creature from one time and one place to another. Most archaeological sites that have been under investigation for any length of time have developed their own distinct archaeological traditions, and the more complex the nature and history of a site, the more idiosyncratic the terms and conditions of its modern investigation and documentation generally have become. The city of Rome is one such; indeed, its peculiar archaeological history provides the very concept of 'Archives and Excavations' as predicated in this volume. While the discovery of unpublished records of past excavations can happen anywhere (indeed the non-publication by archaeologists of their own archaeological fieldwork is currently a major cause for concern[1]), and while the bulk of all excavations anywhere in the past was not made by archaeologists or for archaeological purposes, it has long been the case that in Rome, to a degree unknown anywhere else, many people have been expected in an official capacity — or have taken it upon themselves for a variety of reasons — to register details of finds made in the city and its environs.

ARCHAEOLOGY IN ROME

Rome has always had at least two very different archaeologies, each with its own history and its own particular documentary traditions. One is that which exists on the ground and is the equivalent of complex urban archaeologies everywhere, though more complex than most. The city is intricately stratified both above and below ground, with buildings over 2,000 years old still standing and functioning in the midst of the modern city together with remnants of every intervening age, while the upper subsoil consists of man-made deposits regularly up to 20 m deep, sometimes much deeper.[2] In addition, there is the further, very significant, complication that what lies in — or rather, can be pulled up from — the subsoil is not just of historical interest, but has long had a high commercial value. Any excavation in Rome, digging a drain or a well, levelling a vineyard or garden, sinking the foundations for a new house or church, or tunnelling for the Metropolitana underground railway, is almost guaranteed to hit something. Buildings tend to be fragmentary, or at any rate only visible in small part, and any temptation to leave them visible, if not immediately overruled by the purpose of the excavation, minimal. The holes are usually backfilled, since normal urban life has been expected to carry on above them. On the other hand, depending on the depth of the excavation and the configuration of the particular site, even now, the movable antiquities can include huge blocks of stone, columns, statues, marble and mosaic floors, and certainly a plethora of small objects from worked bone, masses of pottery, glass, and items made of iron or bronze, not to mention the ever present possibility of a hoard of silver or gold coins. For centuries it was normal to quarry all manner of reusable artefacts, as well as building materials, from beneath the city. As a consequence, for almost as long, Rome had its own local legislation concerning digging into the ground as well as demolishing standing structures, counting among the profitable activities for which licences were required not only mining for *pozzolana* sand and tufa but also the search for marble, travertine, *peperino*, statues, columns and other valuable antiquities; from 1534 it had a commissariat specifically to attempt to police the discovery and allocation of the latter.[3] The bigger items (life-size and larger statues, monolithic columns, sarcophagi, fine mosaics, exotic stone veneer) had been symbols of high status and exceptional wealth in ancient Rome, and were taken up again to express those same qualities among the hugely competitive élites of Italy and then the rest of Europe in the fourteenth to nineteenth centuries. Sculpture, ideally free-standing, in fine marble and of high artistic quality was the main target of desire and political control, followed by equally high quality figurative reliefs, and marble furniture, vases and veneer. Alongside and below all that, however, there ranged an infinitely graded scale of collectability among the smaller objects, the coins, gems, pottery, glass and metal objects that could pass into and through the hands of people in many other ranks of society, cherished for a variety of reasons — as relics, amulets, investments, heirlooms — or just for the emotive satisfaction of possessing and handling something extremely old. In the last 50 years, private ownership of any form of archaeological heritage has become an increasingly difficult issue, and from a modern ethical standpoint the past history of Rome's object-oriented archaeology is a disgrace, but it has a force all of its own.

Rome's other archaeology, though it concerns the site of Rome in a way that the object-oriented archaeology never has (at least until recently), is an essentially intellectual pursuit. It is the study of ancient Roman topography, the attempt to reconstruct the vanished city of (principally) the Roman emperors. Ottavio Falconieri wrote in the preface to the first edition of Famiano Nardini's *Roma antica*:

> If the ancient appearance of Rome were represented in its ruins as it is depicted — sometimes vividly — in the pages of ancient writers, less need there would be for someone who would satisfy the noble desire of scholars to wear themselves out in tracing the vestiges erased by time, and confused or covered by modern buildings. But seeing that she … transformed by the vicissitudes of fortune and lacerated by the frequent incursions of barbarian nations, can only be recognized for what she was by the remains that are still standing, there will always be praise for those who manage, as far as they are able, to make those remnants live again.[4]

Roman topography is thus an erudite game, mainly based on — and intended as a contextual companion to — the historical record. Interest in the ground is directed primarily at filling in the gaps between the standing monuments, seeking to fix the positions of the hundreds of places and buildings mentioned in ancient literature, inscriptions and the Regionary Catalogues of the fourth century AD, to which can be added a tantalizing selection of public monuments depicted and named on ancient coins, as well as the 'Marble Plan' — a detailed map of the city as it was in the early third century AD, incised on marble, hundreds of fragments of which were recovered in the 1560s. Then comes a whole swathe of medieval and early modern documents, including accounts of once visible remains, drawn or written about before anyone thought of Rome as a topographical puzzle. It is not necessary to be in Rome to play the topography game — a fact that accounts for much of its enduring appeal — indeed, it is better played with documents and maps, in isolation from the shortcomings, doubts and confusions of the physical reality.

THE ROMAN *ANTIQUARIO*

Not surprisingly, professional involvement with either of the two archaeologies has taken some very different forms over the centuries, and it is difficult now to appreciate some of the nuances that may have distinguished the situation in Rome in the sixteenth or seventeenth century from that in other cities, let alone other ages. In northern European circles[5] it is normal to employ the terms 'antiquary' (or its English neologism 'antiquarian') and 'antiquarian scholar' interchangeably to signify anyone with an early interest in antiquity, and to assume that that interest must connect in some way with more recent approaches to and perceptions of the past. However, further south, and especially in Rome, the profession of *antiquario* has a rather different history, in which 'antiquary' and 'scholar' are not necessarily synonymous at all.

In Rome at the end of the fifteenth century the exploration and documentation of the remains on and from the ground was the natural preserve of architects, sculptors and painters. They possessed the skills to interpret fragmentary structures, sculptures or frescoes, to draw and restore them, usually having a vested interest in recreating antiquity for their own ends. From their world there emerged the first Roman *antiquari* — experts in the practical interpretation of the models of antiquity for contemporary architectural, sculptural or painterly purposes who would also advise on the quality, rarity and thus value of ancient works of art and other collectors' items. In 1568 the Neapolitan painter and architect Pirro Ligorio (1513/14–83) was recommended as the foremost 'antiquary' of Rome and praised specifically for his knowledge of 'medals' (coins), his skill in drawing and in the workmanship of fortifications.[6] He also compiled illustrated encyclopedias of antiquities, not only drawn but also commented upon at length by himself, but in the latter he was considered by his contemporaries (and himself) to have stepped beyond the normal boundaries of his profession.[7] By the end of the sixteenth century many architects, sculptors and painters combined their profession as a matter of course with that of the *antiquario*, which could include expertise in finding as well as evaluating and dealing in movable antiquities and works of art. It is worth noting that a distinction between ancient and modern was not the overriding preoccupation it is today; 'antiquities' could signify anything old, including Old Master drawings, prints and paintings. Most serious collectors developed a preference for one or another category of object, but a collector of coins and medals, for instance, would often collect both and enjoy classifying them according to anything but chronological criteria; nor was it necessary to draw any particular distinction between original and replica.

By the early seventeenth century, *antiquario* could be a full-time occupation, to do with the phenomenon of collecting per se. It might be a paid post attached to a single wealthy Roman household, where the collection (or 'museum') was usually housed in the library, and curatorial duties might therefore include advising on the purchase of and looking after the library books as well. Or it could take a more freelance and highly commercial form, working for a wide circle of customers both in the city and abroad, buying, selling and exchanging. Such *antiquari* might be of quite modest background compared with their sixteenth-century predecessors, with limited education and poor literary skills, but they knew their markets, had good visual memories, were often good draughtsmen, and could make reliable inventories and valuations for sale or inheritance purposes. The more successful assembled their own collections.

Leonardo Agostini (1594–?1675), whose professional activities and a selection of letters are presented here in more detail by Ingo Herklotz (Chapter 5), is a good example of the new seventeenth-century breed. Originally from Siena, he was appointed *antiquario* to Cardinal Francesco Barberini in Rome in 1639, supplied antiquities to the Medici court in Florence as

well, and served during the reign of Pope Alexander VII (1655–67) as Commissario delle Antichità for Rome and its district. His latter role was to inspect and evaluate new finds according to the terms of their licences, and chase up accidental discoveries. When the Commissariato had begun in 1534 it was a post held by noblemen, but by the end of the century was being recruited from the ranks of architects, artists and soon thereafter among the *antiquari*. Agostini's predecessors as Commissario were Ludovico Compagni (served 1620–37), described as a 'leading *antiquario*', and Niccolò Menghini (served 1638–55), who was a sculptor.[8] Agostini became a skilled organizer of excavations for his wealthy patrons, the quantities of small antiquities in which he dealt came largely from his own 'quarries' (*cave*); he assembled a fine collection of gems, and paid for it to be engraved and printed.[9] Significantly, for the commentary to the latter he sought help from the much more learned Bellori (see below).

Other individuals who could be described as *antiquari* in seventeenth-century Rome are Pietro Stefanoni, Barthélémy Joly, Claude Menestrier, Francesco Angeloni, Giovanni Pietro Bellori, Fioravante Martinelli and Francesco Gualdi.[10] Stefanoni (fl. 1600–34) came from Vicenza, of obscure status, and travelled widely in pursuit of his trade, which was evidently the buying and selling of collections of coins and other small antiquities. He had a shop on the Via del Corso in Rome, which also sold paintings, drawings and prints. He was called 'antiquario della prima classe' by Lorenzo Pignoria of Padua.[11] The Frenchman Joly (dates unknown) was in Rome on several occasions between 1615 and 1623, assembling a valuable cabinet of coins, gems and small bronzes, which he sold on his return to Paris.[12] Menestrier (ob. 1639), another Frenchman, came to Rome in 1623 as protégé and agent of the French humanist scholar Nicolas Claude Fabri de Peiresc of Provence; he tried to obtain a post in the Vatican, but his handwriting was not of the required standard; he could draw, however, and did jobbing copy-work for some years, eventually joining the household of Cardinal Francesco Barberini in 1630 as 'librarian' (to be succeeded in 1639 by Agostini). He collected small antiquities himself and played the local Roman market for Barberini, Peiresc and others, apparently always with the hope of bettering his position, but died in debt.[13]

The other names show that the term could also denote a non-dealing collector, or enthusiast, should they have no other more particular claim to status or fame. Francesco Angeloni (1587–1652) came from Terni, and worked as secretary to Cardinal Ippolito Aldobrandini, assisting mainly in the composition of letters of greeting to princely contemporaries. He was also involved in the acquisition of the cardinal's collection of coins and antiquities, in the process of which he was able to assemble a 'museum' of his own, from which his particular reputation as an *antiquario* in later life derived. He wrote a history of the Roman emperors based on their coinage,[14] but his closest friends were artists, notably Domenichino and Poussin, and he also made a major collection of drawings and paintings.[15] Francesco Gualdi (1576–1657) was another whose 'museum' was his main distinguishing feature, a member of the lesser aristocracy and something of an eccentric, he spent much of his resources and energies in acquiring and donating antiquities to his favoured churches and public institutions in the city.[16] Fioravante Martinelli (1599–1667) was born in Rome in poverty, but entered the priesthood and was employed as second secretary of Hebrew and Latin in the Vatican Library, thanks to an unusually close rapport he formed with the later cardinal, Orazio Giustiniani.[17] He published earnestly on churches and church matters but on his tombstone styled himself an 'expert on antiquities' ('vir antiquitatae eruditis') and was the author of *Roma ricercata nel suo sito e nella scuola di tutti gli antiquarij*,[18] a handy pocket guide to monuments and collections in the city. Many *antiquari* were already supplementing their income by guiding visitors around the sights of Rome and Lazio.

Giovanni Pietro Bellori (1613–96) was an exceptional *antiquario* by any definition.[19] Born in Rome, he was the protégé of Angeloni, through whom he became part of the artistic circle of Poussin and a friend of the future cardinal, Camillo Massimo.[20] Talented as a painter, poet, letter-writer and numismatist, he could have obtained many different posts, but after the death of Angeloni (who had made him his heir) in 1652 was able to remain independent for many years, during which he published, among other things, an impressively scholarly study of the symbolism of bees on ancient coins, addressed to Francesco Barberini in 1658. His biography of the remarkable traveller and collector Pietro della Valle (1587–1652) appeared in 1662, a guide to the museums and collections of Rome in 1664, a theoretical work on the 'Idea of Beauty' in painting, sculpture and architecture in 1666, and the first part of *Lives of Modern Painters,*

Sculptors and Architects in 1672. By the late 1660s, however, he seems to have been in some financial need or simply bored. He had occasionally assisted the ailing Leonardo Agostini in his duties as papal Commissario (contributing much of the commentary to the catalogue of Agostini's gem collection), and in 1670 he took up the post himself, holding it for the next 24 years while undertaking an astonishing programme of further publications. These were at first sponsored by Massimo, one on the Marble Plan (1673), perhaps illustrated by himself,[21] and one on Massimo's coin collection (1676).[22] After Massimo's death in 1677, Bellori went on to catalogue rare coins in Cardinal Gaspare Carpegna's library, and then those belonging to Queen Christina of Sweden,[23] for whom he also served as *antiquario*. In collaboration with the printer De Rossi and the painter-engraver Pietro Santi Bartoli (1635–1700), who had also worked for Massimo, he produced a hugely successful series of corpora, illustrated by Bartoli's engravings. An edition of prints of ancient bas-reliefs had already appeared by 1677,[24] to be followed by the Column of Marcus Aurelius and its reliefs in 1679,[25] the paintings in the Tomb of the Nasonii on the Via Flaminia, discovered in 1674 (published 1680),[26] the triumphal arches of Rome in 1690,[27] ancient funerary lamps in 1691[28] and ancient burials in 1697.[29]

Unlike Bellori, most seventeenth-century *antiquari* published nothing, and when they did, like Agostini, it was usually a promotional catalogue of their own collection or just one or two items from it. Menestrier's one published work, a study of the image Ephesian Diana, based on examples in his own collection, appeared close to twenty years after his death, also benefiting from Bellori's ministrations.[30] On the whole, although seventeenth-century Roman *antiquari* might be very knowledgeable about the artefacts they handled, they were not (nor did they generally consider themselves) scholars. If they did presume to academic scholarship, they laid themselves open to hostility and scorn from their social superiors and professional rivals, the *curiosi*.

CURIOSI

Academic scholarship of all kinds was the jealous preserve of gentlemen scholars and scholarly churchmen. They prided themselves on reading and writing Latin fluently, and sometimes Greek, and were widely read in the classical texts. The richer among them cultivated academic interests as a desirable adjunct to their social rank; the less well-off serviced those interests, finding employment as secretaries, archivists, legal draughtsmen or university professors, identifying themselves intellectually with their patrons. They might like to keep abreast of new discoveries and often put themselves out to visit excavations and see the evidence at first hand, but they would not actually engage in the organization and direction of the digging, nor would they undertake the recording of finds. They saw their role as that of the learned commentator, explaining objects of exotic and unusual iconography, making connections between the written sources and the visible evidence in the identification of famous monuments, famous events and personages, and the particulars of Roman society, religion and manners. In this, their studies were no less topical than those of contemporary painters and architects, since the institutions and culture of ancient Rome provided the ideological models that underscored both aristocratic and ecclesiastical power in contemporary Italian, and to a remarkable degree also some European polities further afield.

The topography game was an eminently *curioso* pastime. In their hands it started as a purely literary pursuit, but each new topographical study would naturally claim to have incorporated the latest finds, parading knowledge of things the author had seen for himself or heard of from fellow enthusiasts. From Flavio Biondo's *De Roma Instauratae* of 1444–6 (first printed in Rome *c.* 1480–1) and his *De Roma Triumphante* of 1457–9, to Bartolomeo Marliani's *Antiquae Urbis Romae Topographia* (Rome, 1534), Jean Jacques Boissard's *Topographia Romae* (Frankfurt, 1597–1603), Alessandro Donati's *Roma Vetus ac Recens* (Rome, 1639; Rome, 1644[2]; Rome, 1665[3]), and Famiano Nardini's *Roma antica descritta per regioni* (Rome, 1666; Rome, 1704[2]; Rome, 1741[3]), the basic idea remained the same.[31] The city was explored on paper and mainly in words, divided into its main topographical units such as the city walls and gates, streets, hills and regions, and describing the individual monuments they held, their builders and famous inhabitants. It was the topographers who were most keen to collect every scrap of information from the *antiquari* and other eyewitnesses, and who also took an early initiative in seeking out past written records, creating for their particular purposes a subcategory that by the eighteenth century had come to be called 'memorie'.

'MEMORIE'

The earliest substantial document of the sort was written in 1594 by Flaminio Vacca (1538–1605), a sculptor, in the form of a letter addressed to one of his patrons, Anastasio Simonetti of Perugia (who was preparing a treatise on the antiquities of Rome): 'to show my thanks for the many obligations that I owe you, I am sending you this *stracciafoglio*, in which are noted all those antiquities that from my childhood to the age of 56 years I remember seeing and heard talked about being discovered in various places in Rome'. Vacca's letter circulated in manuscript copies under various titles throughout the seventeenth century,[32] being cited by Martinelli,[33] for example, well before it appeared in print in 1704, appended to the second edition of Nardini's topographical work *Roma antica*,[34] with the title *Memorie di varie antichità trovate in diversi luoghi della città di Roma*. In the preface to the third edition of Nardini in 1741 the editor observed that, since official bodies were conspicuously refusing to do so:[35]

> … it is desirable that in every age there is some individual of good taste who assumes the responsibility of leaving to posterity an accurate, succinct, and clear description of the antiquities that in his time in Rome and in Lazio have been dug up, emulating the incomparable Flaminio Vacca …

but the best he could offer in addition to reprinting those of Vacca[36] were some faux *memorie* compiled by extracting passages from Ulisse Aldrovandi's *Raccolta delle statue di Roma* of 1556,[37] and from the quite recently published works of Francesco Ficoroni (1664–1747), *antiquario romano*,[38] with some contributions by a churchman Francesco Valesio (1670–1742), an indefatigable diarist of all sorts of events in Rome in the early 1700s.[39] At the last minute the Marchese Frangipani produced a package of documents attributed to Pietro Santi Bartoli, which the editor inserted at the end of the book under the title *Memorie di varie escavazioni fatte in Roma e nei luoghi suburbani vivente Pier Santi Bartoli*.[40]

In 1790 that same corpus was expanded, re-edited and reprinted by Carlo Fea (1753–1836)[41] in the first volume of his *Miscellanea filologica, critica e antiquaria*. This contained some more pseudo-*memorie* compiled of excerpts from Ficoroni's later publications and those of Johann Joachim Winckelmann, and a range of letters and notes from the Chigi library (where Fea was employed at the time). Fea introduced numbering to all the individual passages in the various sets of *memorie* thus formulated, which greatly facilitated reference and endowed them with a general air of coherence. The second volume of Fea's *Miscellanea* appeared 46 years later, just after Fea's death. Included were one genuine *memoria*, written for him in 1790 by a painter Gasparo Scaramucci, recalling excavations in the Agro Romano during 1744–59,[42] some more material he had gathered from the Chigi library or archives about excavations in 1777–80 at Tor Paterno,[43] and a seventeenth-century document he had found in the Barberini Library, a report by Cipriano Cipriani, dean of the Pantheon, on discoveries made when digging drains in the reigns of Gregory XV and Urban VIII.[44] The rest of the volume is composed of reprints of various notices from the *Giornale de' Letterati*, the *Antologia Romana* and other eighteenth-century Roman news-sheets, lectures he had delivered to the 'Accademia Archeologica' (also known as the Instituto di Corrispondenza Archeologica) and other short discursive articles. Oddly, although Fea served as papal Commissario delle Antichità for 35 years (1801–36),[45] and was instrumental in setting up new standards of documentation and reporting, he seems to have made no attempt to search out older records of papal licences and reports of finds, to which he presumably had access.

In 1874, Giacomo Lumbroso published another manuscript telling of discoveries under Urban VIII, written in 1642 by Cassiano dal Pozzo (1588–1657), head of the household of the pope's nephew, Cardinal Francesco Barberini.[46] Lumbroso, no doubt recognizing its relationship to the other *memorie*, called it Cassiano's 'Memoriale' and appended to it a selection of other passages of antiquarian or artistic interest that he gleaned from the dal Pozzo letters.[47]

In the 1880s, the German scholar Theodor Schreiber produced corrected editions of both the Vacca and Cipriani texts, and added some more seventeenth- and eighteenth-century archival documents,[48] but Fea's editions are still the more widely used in archaeological circles in Rome today, standard sources in the archaeological literature, repeatedly cited for the information they provide on the date, location and circumstances of particular finds. The basic service they perform was codified in the course of the later nineteenth century, and eventually embodied in the 'Notiziario' of the Rome-based journals *Bullettino della Commissione Archeologica di Roma* and the *Notizie degli Scavi di Antichità*. The practice of creating new *memorie* by extracting suitable passages from other sources has

also continued — as Ingo Herklotz has done with the Agostini letters.

Appropriated by topographers for topographical purposes, the *memorie*, especially all those that appear in Fea's *Miscellanea*, have acquired a certain group identity. They have become standard sources, frequently cited in the archaeological literature for just one small item of information they provide of relevance to one particular monument, and since there is actually very little in them that is of topographical interest, the bulk of what they have to say is completely ignored; I expect that they are rarely read as continuous texts. As outlined above, however, their authors came from different circles and were arguably writing for very different purposes. It is interesting to look at the four earlier ones — Vacca, dal Pozzo, Cipriani, Bartoli — in more detail, with an eye to that diversity and the circumstances in which they were written.

FLAMINIO VACCA[49]

The *memorie* of Vacca (1538–1605) are not only the earliest but also in many respects the best. They consist of some 126 paragraphs,[50] almost every one beginning with the words 'Mi ricordo' ('I remember'). Vacca was a true Roman *antiquario* of the sixteenth century: a marble sculptor who made his living mainly by carving portraits and statues for churches, and repairing, restoring and adapting ancient sculpture, but also by dealing in marble and antiquities, sometimes digging for them himself. His family lived behind the Pantheon in a house built into another ancient monument, the Arco della Ciambella (thought then as now to be part of the Baths of Agrippa). His written style can be difficult to follow (his later Italian copyists and editors could not resist trying to improve it), but his accounts are full of practical information and useful circumstantial detail. He was well able to tell the difference between Republican, Imperial Roman, late Roman and early medieval (which he called *antico moderno* or 'early modern') walls, could judge the quality of ancient workmanship with a fellow carver's eye, and displayed a lot of good sense when it came to interpreting the subsoil. A selection is appended here in translation (Appendix 1), chosen not so much for the significance of the discoveries they refer to as for the picture they give of the variety of the archaeological experience.

Usually the first thing Vacca recalls is on whose property the find was made, not only because there was no other more precise method of describing a location (and his notes were addressed to someone interested primarily in topography), but also because remembering specific places and circumstances of discovery helped to identify which sites might be worth digging further, and which ones were likely to have been one-off occasions. His last four *memorie* recount local tales of sites of buried treasure whose potential had not yet been tested to the full (124, 126), and he promised to keep Simonetti informed of future events. At least one excavation (his own?), at the foot of the Aventine Hill, which had found evidence of ancient metalworking, he thought would be worth pursuing for curiosity's sake (119). He was a keen observer of the conditions of deposition in the ground and reckoned he could recognize land clearance (89). A mass burial in the substructures of the Baths of Constantine intrigued him: he believed it to be of late Roman date and described it in detail, calling on Simonetti, as a historian, to be able to find the answer (113).

Many finds of sculpture were made in concentrated batches, especially on the outskirts of the city. Some had evidently been gathered together in one place for safekeeping in antiquity (48); other groups consisted of fragments, collected to be burnt for lime but never fired (12). A peculiarity were the sculptures smashed into hundreds of small pieces used as building material in the foundations of late Roman walls (13).[51] Roman *antiquari* who knew their business would be prepared for such eventualities, and be able to spot likely sites to look for them, the lore growing from one generation to the next, and transmitted as part of an artist's studio training. Some group discoveries were of more recent formation, such as a collection of statuary in two rooms near Porta Portese (97). Some were very disappointing (25).

Families were quite possessive of the remains they lived amidst; Vacca described discoveries he and his father made under their own cellars (54–5). Many other finds were recounted in the same terms: careful to note where the pieces went to, who bought them, what they were used for. It was a way of life, in which ordinary people had a daily acquaintance with antiquity. Vacca was in the marble trade, buying 136 cartloads of stone from excavations in Piazza Sciarra (28), and paving slabs from the Temple of Roma and Venus (74).

The figure of the Maestro di Strade (Street Commissioner) is a recurrent and powerful one — called 'magnificent' or 'great'. They commanded considerable work forces and could order buildings demolished or huge statues transported from one place to another — influential and necessary persons to know if you were looking to fit out a sculpture garden (76).

Digging for treasure was something the rich did for pleasure (53) (which also gives an insight into the lively mythology of place-names), but the sad tales of Paolo Bianchini, a salvage operator on the Tiber (93), and another (80) show how difficult it was for the poor to profit legitimately from their chance discoveries.

CASSIANO DAL POZZO[52]

Born in Turin in 1588, graduating at Pisa in civil and ecclesiastical law in 1607, Cassiano moved to Rome in 1612 and lived there until his death in 1657. In 1623 he was appointed *gentiluomo ordinario* to Cardinal Francesco Barberini, nephew of Pope Urban VIII, becoming his *primo maestro di camera* or head of the household in 1633, independently wealthy and a prominent figure in the Republic of Letters, corresponding by virtue of his influential position in papal circles with scholars all over Europe. Together with a younger brother Carlo Antonio, who continued the project until his own death in 1689, Cassiano assembled a huge reference collection of prints and drawings of ancient reliefs and other antiquities, which he called his 'Museo Cartaceo' (Paper Museum).[53] Cassiano would definitely qualify as a *curioso*, but was primarily a courtier, and his antiquarian initiatives appear mostly to have been undertaken in cultivation of and response to a wider circle of learned and influential acquaintances, not driven by any systematic scholarly agenda of his own.

He was in his 50s when he wrote *Notizie di diversi anticaglie trovate nel mio tempo* ('Notes on various antiquities found in my time'), evidently taking his lead from Vacca's work, a copy of which he owned and is preserved in the same codex.[54] Like most of his literary efforts, the attempt was apparently abandoned unfinished. It consists of 24 paragraphs, the first sixteen very brief, skipping from one place and one topic to another, giving no dates, predominantly finds made during Barberini building operations in the city or pieces that entered their collections (see Appendix 2). Topography was the least of his concerns: he noted an ancient aqueduct on the site of Sant'Ignazio, probably only because he was given a plan of it by the architect who found it (1),[55] he reported that traces of the Circus Flaminius were found near Santa Lucia (4), and of the Circus of Domitian under San Niccolò dei Lorenesi (5), but laid no claim to such identifications, merely saying 'most believe'; the fields of ancient oil jars near San Francesco a Ripa (13) and the buildings and streets at Termini (15) get very short shrift. There is an anodyne note on bronze roof beams in the Pantheon porch and the fact that the nails became collectors' items (2).[56] He registered the finding of sculpture and other valuables with rather more enthusiasm: statues in the Barberini collection (3,[57] 7, 8), the Ludovisi battle sarcophagus (he interviewed the finder) (6), statues that went to Cardinal Mazzarino (10), some terracottas at Nemi (11) and a Priapus statuette in his own collection (14). The rest relate to finds of which he had drawings in his Museo Cartaceo: ancient frescoes in a room at San Gregorio Magno (7) (see Herklotz, Chapter 5, p. 55)[58] and the painted landscape found in the grounds of the Palazzo Barberini (9);[59] how the Nile mosaic at Palestrina had been lifted in pieces without first taking a plan or drawing of it, and other information on its later restoration with the aid of dal Pozzo drawings (12).[60] There is merely a passing reference to inlaid pavements found near Santa Susanna (16).

Towards the end, however, the paragraphs become longer and more detailed, as he described some events of recent vintage: the remains of an arch in Piazza Sciarra, including reliefs and an inscription, which were given to the Barberini (17–18), for example.[61] Cassiano now named the property owners and the director of the excavation, one Domenico L'Aquilano, as well as Cardinal Barberini's *antiquario* Leonardo Agostini, who was sent to supervise, relating what they had told him. But he gave equal weight to reporting the fact that the cardinal had given due priority to the needs of the carnival, which was about to be held, and ordered the excavation to be back-filled, to be opened up another time. *Memoria* 20 is an even longer account of an excavation near Santa Maria sopra Minerva, which was reported to Cassiano's brother Carlo Antonio (perhaps in some official capacity[62]) and they were taken to visit the site on the morning of 30 March 1642. Prompted by that particular memory, Cassiano's pen then wandered off into the realms of his real passions — natural history and court etiquette, with a tale of the 'brogiotti' fig trees of Santa Maria sopra Minerva recounted to him by the priest that day, and one he had from another priest about swallows and cuckoos — ending with a note on a portrait of Sannazzaro attributed to Raphael and an account of a battle between French and Spanish ambassadors for precedence in the procession that greeted the arrival of Cardinal Macchiavelli for his investiture on 26 March 1642.

Cassiano was in a position to hear of, and see for himself, the hundreds of new discoveries that must have been made during the many new building projects that the Barberini undertook during the papacy of Urban VIII. Yet his surviving papers contain few other records of such discoveries and the Museo Cartaceo has little or nothing beyond the drawings specifically referred to in the *Notizie di anticaglie*, which may in fact be the full measure of Cassiano's interest and knowledge on the matter. What or whom he had in mind when he began his *Notizie* is difficult to say.

CIPRIANO CIPRIANI[63]

The account 'Of the ancient remains found underground when making the new drain'[64] was originally addressed to Pope Urban VIII (reg. 1623–44), but was submitted again to Pope Alexander VII (reg. 1655–67) as part of a 'Report on some memorable things relevant to the restoration of the famous church of St Mary and the Martyrs, called the Rotunda [i.e the Pantheon]'.[65] By then Cipriani tells us he had been dean of the church for 43 years. Alexander began restoring it in late 1662 (see here, Herklotz, Chapter 5, p. 76, appendix, no. 61). Neither an *antiquario* nor a *curioso*,[66] Cipriani's real concern was the flooding of the Campus Martius, especially around the Pantheon, caused by the new aqueducts that had been led into the area without new drains having been provided. The influx had raised the local water table by over a metre, turning cellars into fishtanks, attracting toads and water snakes. Cipriani had taken part in a twelve-year campaign, initiated under Gregory XV (reg. 1621–3) and finished under Urban VIII, which had laid new drains between the river, the Pantheon and the Campus Martius, and a parallel system along the Via del Corso. His account is first and foremost a celebration of these operations, describing the ancient drains they met en route as well as the successes achieved by the new drains, but he also included details of the obstacles in the subsoil that had to be cut through or around, giving relative depths and other dimensions, which can be of rather more practical value to the topographer than most of what Cassiano had to say: a sample is translated in Appendix 3.

PIETRO SANTI BARTOLI

A copy of Vacca's *Memorie* was reportedly also among the papers left by the painter-engraver Pietro Santi Bartoli.[67] Born in Perugia in 1635 of urban middle-class parents, Bartoli was educated at home until the age of eight, then sent to Rome under the protection of a family friend, who saw to his schooling in 'humanities' (that is, classical texts) and arranged for drawing lessons.[68] His abilities evidently tended towards the latter, and in 1651 he joined the household of Pierre Lemaire, a French painter resident in Rome, first as his servant, then as apprentice in 1652–4.[69] After that he was admitted to the studio of Lemaire's own master, Nicolas Poussin, working mainly as a copyist of Raphael and ancient sculpture, until Poussin's death in 1665.[70] Subsequently, in Poussin's executor Carlo Antonio dal Pozzo and another close friend Camillo Massimo (1620–77), Bartoli found two willing patrons, for whom he was to make fine albums of coloured copies of ancient paintings and mosaics.[71] Massimo also employed him as his drawing teacher and encouraged him to develop his skills as an illustrator and engraver of antiquities. In 1667–70, taking advantage of scaffolding erected to take casts for Louis XIV, Bartoli made a new series of plates illustrating the reliefs on Trajan's Column. The series was published by Giovan Giacomo de' Rossi in 1672, dedicated to Massimo, and with a new commentary by Giovanni Pietro Bellori (1613–96).[72] Bartoli and Bellori (who had known each other since the 1640s) went on to collaborate on another six major books (see above, p. 36) and Bartoli succeeded Bellori as Commissario from 1694 until his own death in 1700.[73]

The original documents supplied by Marchese Frangipane for the first publication of Bartoli's *Memorie* in 1741 (and now lost?) were not a coherent text but a collection of notes, which the 1741 editor realized were in some disorder but in the interests of speed printed as they were. Reprinting (and numbering) the 156 entries in 1790, Carlo Fea rearranged the 1741 version and claimed also to have rewritten parts in what he considered a more elegant fashion, but his editorial interventions seem to have been minimal.[74]

Bartoli's name (and reputation as an antiquary) may be attached to them, but they are a curious mixture of information at first and second hand, the latter consisting of notes taken from Biondo[75] and Aldrovandi,[76] whilst others seemingly are based on published sources.[77] Various other inconsistencies suggest that, although they may have been found among Bartoli's papers, they were not — or not all — his own work. Most disconcertingly, he is spoken of several times in the third person, as the author of published prints.[78]

A date of 1682 is usually ascribed to the set as a whole, since four refer to 'this year 1682' or 'the present year 1682' (93, 99, 107, 153), but there are two

that refer to 1682 in the past tense (19, 75); some other entries that give a specific year, such as 1675 (74), 1679 (120), 1680/81 (49, 85), read very similarly and could belong to the same series.[79] But the great bulk, if dated at all,[80] refer only to the reigning pope, and the popes in question range back to Urban VIII (1623–44) and earlier (for an index of dated entries, see Appendix 4). In one the writer, with a different written style, declared that 'my time' was the reign of Alexander VII (1655–67) (128). In another (11), there is a reference to an accompanying plan, as if the text were part of a separate exercise.

In two of the 1682 entries the writer sounds as if he must be an official, probably the Commissario, called in to inspect and report on new discoveries (76, 93). In 1682, however, Bellori was the Commissario; Bartoli did not take over until 1694. Perhaps, given their collaboration on other projects through the 1670s and 1680s, Bartoli stood in for Bellori in earlier years, but just as likely these records could be the work of Bellori himself. In another entry, presumably referring to the 1650s or '60s (48), Agostini is said to 'have been sent' to verify a 'report'. The style of reporting and the general focus of interest, not only in those relating to the 1680s but also far into the past, is just that which one would expect from someone in the Commissario's office, with access to older records: finds of statuary, marbles, coin hoards, other movable antiquities. The writer is able to specify who had the licence (the phrase 'ad istanza' (on application) as in 53 has a definitely legal ring[81]), who directed the excavation (a stonemason/builder like Baratta (44, 139) or a painter like Grimaldi (53)[82]) and who acquired the statuary (most mention is made of Camillo Massimo[83]). There is just as much concern for what had or might have escaped the net (for example 75, 143), what was exported (139), and remarks on the scandalously low prices asked for them (63). Incidentally, the tale of a visit to Carsoli instead of Terni to escape the plague in 1656 (155), which has been taken as evidence of a return visit by a very young Bartoli to Perugia, might just as well or rather better suit Bellori, who may actually have been intending to visit Terni.[84]

Bartoli could have been privy to all the same sources as Bellori, but one may doubt whether he would normally be collecting such information. The texts for the books of his engravings of Roman monuments and antiquities were written by Bellori and presumably the reason was not only that Bartoli did not have time or inclination, but that he had nothing of the same learning and writing skills. Only after Bellori's death

(1696) would he have had to think of such things for himself. Perhaps Bellori gave him lots of notes over the years, and especially in that last year of his life. Reports of burials of one sort or another feature quite strongly,[85] and were the subject of their last book (*Gli antichi sepolcri*), for which Bartoli had to write the preface and see it through the press in 1697.

Endnote

It is interesting to observe how the professional divisions (and rivalries) of the past endured in Rome throughout the eighteenth and nineteenth centuries, and continue in only slightly modified forms today: topographical research is undertaken in a university department, the survey and analysis of (usually standing but also archaeological) monuments is taught by architectural schools, day-to-day 'rescue' fieldwork is done by the State or municipal archaeological (and architectural) services, as is the inventorying of finds and the implementation of protective legislation and management of museums and archives. Under outside influence from other archaeological traditions of more recent formation and different circumstances, the distinctions between the two main Roman camps are becoming less clear cut — university departments are excavating; members of the archaeological services (trained at university) are pursuing significant academic research — but a lot of archaeology in Rome still operates within the framework of its older traditions. (And, as legislation enters the field, some of the different traditions elsewhere are coming closer to the older Roman model.) Even the *antiquario* still exists, though he is now strictly a commercial dealer in coloured marbles and antique furniture, rather than antiquities, and rarely if ever engaged in archaeological excavations. And even now, when proper mechanisms exist to ensure that every find is officially registered and recorded, it is possible for a lot of information to evade the net, and future generations will probably still be turning to eyewitness reports in daily or periodic newspapers, in 'News from Rome'-type circulars, web-sites, personal journals, diaries and letters.

Appendix 1

EXTRACTS FROM THE *MEMORIE* OF FLAMINIO VACCA, WRITTEN 1594

12. Excavations in front of Santi Quattro Coronati in some reed-beds, found large numbers of epitaphs, among which one referring to Pontius Pilate, and nearby there was a vineyard full of fragments of figures and squared blocks stacked up together: digging further, the owner found a lot of lime made by the early moderns; and I think that said fragments were there to make lime from them, probably in the times of those popes who wished to stamp out idolatry.

13. Under the hospital of San Giovanni in Laterano runs a massive foundation, all made of pieces of excellent sculpture. I found there some knees and elbows in the Greek style — the equal of the Laocoon in the Belvedere — you can see them still. So much for a poor sculptor's labours!

25. Not far away [from Santi Pietro e Marcellino], in the vineyard of Francesco da Fabriano, were found seven nude statues of good workmanship but the 'early moderns', to destroy the appearance of antiquities, had chiselled away at many parts of them and had in their ignorance destroyed their beautiful and gracious style.

28. Piazza di Sciarra is called after Sig. Sciarra Colonna, who lives there. In the time of Pius IV [1559–65] were found fragments of the Arch of Claudius and many pieces of figurative relief with the portrait of Claudius, which were bought by Sig. Giovanni Giorgio Cesarini and are now in his garden near San Pietro in Vincoli. I bought the rest of the fragments, and there were 136 cart-loads. All were of fine white marble; only the footings were of *saligno* [a term for coarse-crystalled greyish marble].

48. Outside the Porta di San Giovanni, in Annibale Caro's vineyard, there was a large ancient structure — an encumbrance for the vineyard — which Signor Annibale resolved to level to the ground. Walled up inside he found many portraits of emperors, beyond the basic twelve, and a large sarcophagus on which were carved all the labours of Hercules and many other fragments of statues 'in the Greek manner', worked by excellent sculptors, everything was good. I don't remember what was done with the heads, but the front side of the sarcophagus was sawn off and sent to Monsignor Visconti at Nuvolara.

53. I heard tell from Gabriel Vacca, my father, that Cardinal della Valle, taking a fancy to dig for treasure, ordered an excavation in the Baths of Agrippa and there was found a great Imperial wreath in gilded bronze. The excavators called it the 'ciambella' after its resemblance to certain ring-shaped cakes sold in Rome in those days, and thereafter, I don't know how

long, an innkeeper took over the site and took said ciambella as his sign; that's how it's always been called *la Ciambella*.

54. My own houses, where I live now, are built on top of those Baths [of Agrippa]. Digging the foundations for a wall, I struck water, and making soundings with an iron rod, heard it strike marble, and wanting to see what it was, I saw it was a Corinthian capital, measuring 4 *palmi* from the horn to the flower, thus the same size as those of the Pantheon porch, but having satisfied my curiosity I decided to let the capital sleep on. When I made my cellar I found a large 'niche' all lined with box flue tiles, and floored with marble slabs, under which was a strong bedding, and under that many little piers, which held it suspended, between which passed the hot air. We also found a thick wall sheated in lead, carefully pinned in place with bronze nails, and four granite columns, but they weren't very big, and I resolved to backfill, without searching any further.

55. Under our archway [the Arco della Ciambella] when my father had been digging for a cellar, he found some pieces of cornice, one 13 palms [*c.* 2.9 m] long, 8 [*c.* 1.8 m] deep and 5 [*c.* 1.1 m] high, which he sold to a marble-carver and from which was then made the tombstone of the Duke of Melfi in Santa Maria del Popolo.

74 [73]. In the monastery [of Santa Maria Nova], towards the Colosseum, is a large niche [cella of Temple of Roma and Venus], which was excavated underneath and a platform/pavement of *saligno* marbles — an astonishing find — in slabs 13 palms [*c.* 2.9 m] long by 9 [2 m] wide, 3 [*c.* 0.6 m] thick. I bought some of them, which I had sawn up to make tombstones. There were also found many panels of *alabastro cotognino*, and although there were niches, no trace of statues was found; they must have been robbed.

76 [75]. I remember hearing tell that the magnificent Metello Vari, Street Commissioner, had carried from the Via Prenestina outside the Porta San Lorenzo, that lion in mezzo-rilievo which, restored by Giovanni Sciarano of Fiesole, now stands in the loggia of the garden of Grand Duke Ferdinand [de Medici, on the Pincian], who had me make another to accompany it, in full relief.

80 [79]. I remember, in the time of Pius IV [1559–65], Matteo da Castello took it into his head to level a vine-

yard on top of the Aventine, and digging found lead vases containing a quantity of gold coins with the image of Saint Helena, and crosses on the reverse. He took them to the pope, who said he could keep them for being so honest, but the pope's entourage grabbed all but 200 of them off him. Thus he told me himself. Each of them weighed 18–20 *giulii*, and he found about 1,800.

89 [88]. I remember that in the Piazza behind Santi Apostoli there were found many *saligno* marbles in huge blocks, all dressed masonry but damaged, thrown there by our 'early moderns' who found great ruins in their way. I have seen in many such excavations that the pieces of ruins could not have fallen naturally into the positions in which they are found; but since the ruins rose above ground level, and annoyed the citizenry, who could neither use them as they were, nor make use of them to build something else, they would dig a large hole alongside and throw the marble into it: so it is that they are found buried in such disorder.

93 [92]. I remember that a man who made his living salvaging boats and collapsed wharves from the Tiber bed, dived underwater to fish up a boat between the Porta del Popolo and the Ripetta and found a seated consul [togatus], in statuary marble, of very good workmanship; it lacked only the head, which is now in the house of the notary Palombo who lives behind Santa Maria in Via. Said excavator told me that he had found many marbles, but he did not dare excavate them without a licence. Anyway he's dead; he was called Paolo Bianchini.

97 [96]. On the Tiber bank opposite the Cesarini, near Porta Portese, so-called because it leads to Porto, in the Vittori vineyard, were found many statues, heads of philosophers and emperors hidden in two rooms, one alongside the other. Sculptors' tools were found with them, which suggests that they had been brought there to be repaired or reworked and then, because of some unexpected papal proclamation, they were hidden again. Most of them are today in the house of the Vettori, but Cardinal Farnese chose the best for himself.

105 [104]. I remember, behind the Baths of Diocletian, where the owner of a vineyard wanted to build a hut to house his hoes and vineyard tools, he saw two walls standing slightly above ground and began excavating between them, and digging down, he saw a small hole, and making it bigger, he entered it. It was shaped like a fur-

nace and stacked inside were 18 heads of philosophers, which he sold for 700 scudi to Sig. Giorgio Cesarini, and now Sig. Giuliano [Cesarini] has sold them to Cardinal Farnese, who keeps them in his *galleria*.

113 [112]. I remember that in the Baths of Constantine above Monte Cavallo in front of San Silvestro, in a place owned by Bernardo Acciajuoli, digging he found several vaulted rooms filled with earth. He decided to clear them out, and found inside many pieces of columns of statuary marble, 30 palms [6.9 m] long, and some capitals and bases. At one end these vaults were walled up with a wall that was not vertical and was badly built. Deciding to break through it, he came into two vaults that were filled with human bones. Being my friend, he sent for me; I entered with considerable difficulty, because there was but 5 palms [1.1 m] space between the vault and the bones, and wherever you stepped your foot sank up to the knee, and when you touched them they disintegrated into dust: and as far as we went we could not find the end. They could be as long as 100 palms [22 m] and 30 [6.6 m] wide. We were amazed at the number of dead. Some said they were some cruelty of Nero, since there were some buildings of Nero nearby, and they were martyrs. Others said, some great plague. I reasoned that, since the vaults were not broken through from above, they must have been fed through from the front; however, I want to believe that they all died at once, and in one day, and because of the stench were stacked up all at once, from ground to roof; and that space of 5 palms from the roof to the bones was the shrinkage that occurred as the flesh was lost. If they had been placed in there as bones, they would have filled up to the roof, and the bones would be seen thrown in confusion, but we saw them as whole bodies. This shows that they were placed there with the flesh on them, and that badly made wall, which sealed the vault, did not signify other than how those masons of a thousand years ago sought to escape the great smell of those corpses. But your Excellency, as an expert in history, will be able to discover the truth; it being a thing worthy of consideration.

119 [118]. At the foot of the Aventine Hill towards San Saba, in the vineyard now owned by Sig. Giuseppe Grillo, was discovered a seated marble faun, life-size, of excellent workmanship, with other fragments of statues; and also a copper cauldron full of bronze quattrine-sized coins, all covered in earth, though I have never been able to work out what they were; and several copper bucket handles, and a pair of iron scissors

2½ palms [0.56 m long] of the kind where one side remains fixed while the other acts as a lever, used by tinsmiths and those who cut copper; and those scissors lead me to believe that in that place there were foundries, since those tools are foundrymen's. These finds were made last year, and there is no doubt that, excavating further, other things would be found, which would clarify the matter.

123 [122]. Where today runs Via di San Carlo dei Catinari behind to the head of the Via dei Chiavari I have always heard it said that in olden times it was full of jewellers and wealth, that in the early wars, invaded by the enemies of Rome, they buried everything in the ground, since when building the house of Tomaso Valleschi they found traces of workshops and tools. But, because the builders did not have money to spend on excavations, and because the neighbours were against it, or rather, according to some documents I have seen, because relatives disagreed over the siting of the building, it was prohibited from extension by excavation. Some big reason there must have been for sure. The situation has remained so, and no one else has taken it in hand. But people are certain nevertheless that great jewels were buried at the time.

126 [125]. It is firm opinion that in Via di San Giovanni, especially behind the Scala Santa, about halfway along the line of the aqueduct, there are some notable things, because there was a princely residence, ruined in the time of the Goths and after; and little has been found since little has been dug: and at the time of the sacks of Rome there was hidden a great treasure. I heard this from a foreigner (an Oltramontano) who had note of it and wanted to organize excavations, but then came to a duel over the matter with a friend and companion; outside the Porta di San Lorenzo they shot at each other and he died.

For now I have nothing else: if it happens, I'll let you know when the occasion offers.

Appendix 2

THE *NOTIZIE* OF CASSIANO DAL POZZO, WRITTEN 1642

(1)   In excavating the foundations for the church of Sant'Ignazio they found an ancient watercourse; unable to divert it otherwise, or cut if off so as to be able to ensure stable foundations, it was led into a

drain, also ancient, running in the direction of the Pantheon. The Jesuit father Horatius Grassi from Savona, architect of the church, drew a plan of the aqueduct, of which we have a copy in house. There was also found a head generally agreed to portray Cicero, which the Jesuit fathers gave to Cardinal Ludovisi.

(2)   The beams of wood currently visible under the Pantheon porch roof were previously of bronze. These were removed and the metal in large part served to cast the spiral columns in Saint Peter's and to make pieces of artillery, and of these some were made out of the metal from the nails alone. Of those nails the Duke of Alcalà asked for one, which he sent off to Spain with his prized curiosities.

(3)   In Saint Peter's, at the confessio of the Apostles, in excavating the foundations for the spiral bronze columns, was found quite near the said confessio a statue of someone lying on a bed, larger than life, with an inscription in praise of the dishonest epicurean life, which was destroyed, and the statue was preserved and taken to the garden of Cardinal Barberini at Quattro Fontane.

(4)   When making the foundations for the new building that Cardinal S. Onofrio [Antonio Barberini] ordered for Santa Caterina ai Funari opposite the church of Santa Lucia, they found huge pieces of travertine of which many were dug out; most believe that they are the remains of the Circus Flaminius, the precise point where they were located is in the adjacent street where you see the cardinal's arms.

(5)   In rebuilding the church of San Niccolò de' Lorenesi near the Anima, digging for the foundations, were found huge pieces of travertine; they are generally judged to be the remains of the Circus of Domitian. Many of said travertine blocks were dug out and used in the façade by a certain M. du Jardin of Lorraine, architect in charge of the work.

(6)   The sarcophagus in low relief which you see in the vigna Ludovisi, believed on several grounds to be that of the emperor Volusianus, was found in a field a stone's throw beyond the Porta di San Lorenzo, or to be more precise, in an abandoned vineyard belonging to a certain Bernusconi, stonemason, and it was in 1621; and in said vineyard were found, as the same Bernusconi himself told me, in his father's day, the two

granite basins that serve as fountains in Piazza Farnese, and these were filled with statues. Moreover, the same man said that when he uncovered a buried ancient wall and destroyed it, he found contained within it infinite statues but so broken into pieces that no one could make any use of them, and I think they are those that at the time of Gregory were ordered to be destroyed so as not to encourage idolatry.

(7)   When digging in the garden of the monks of San Gregorio they found an underground room with its vault and side walls painted in fresco, the vault with arabesques or more accurately grotesques of various kinds, with two portraits of a man and a woman, and the walls with putti playing, and a scene of a Venus who plays in the water, swimming, and recorded among the drawings in house; it was then completely demolished after Cardinal Barberini in company with the Duke of Parma, who was in Rome at the time, had seen it: in the same excavation sometime earlier were found various ancient bronzes, namely a statuette like a seated Cybele, most superbly dressed a little over a *palmo* in height, a group of a centaur between an Aesculapius and Hercules, on a slightly larger scale, that for 20 scudi was brought by Cardinal Barberini, a head of Mercury with its bust, and all of exquisite skill.

(8)   In the ditches of Castello were found during digging two statues that were taken to the garden of Cardinal Barberini, one of a river in the usual reclining position, the other the torso of a Faun, equal to the Belvedere torso. There were also found I don't know how many pieces of ancient jasper, which Cardinal Barberini also has.

(9)   In excavating the ground in the Barberini garden at Quattro Fontane, previously the Horti Carpensi, in order to distance the earth from the first-floor apartment was found a room painted with a fresco of a landscape. Immediately a copy in oils was commissioned from Frangione, the Flemish painter, and from that were made various other copies.

(10)   Along the road which goes from San Giovanni Laterano to Santi Quattro in a vineyard on the left-hand side were found when excavating various statues of beautiful style, among them two of Fauns dancing with *crotali* (castanets) and I don't know what at their feet; statues truly remarkable; they were sold to M. Mazzarino. Apart from this were found stone channels for carrying water from one place to another, that made

one believe, given the care with which they were worked, that it was in antiquity a luxury resort [*luogo di delitia*].

(11) At Nemi, seat of the princes Frangipani, was found an ancient room under whose pavement were found various statuettes of a *palmo* and a *palmo*-and-a-half high [223 mm and 335 mm] and others similar, in part clothed, part nude, in other part separate elements such as heads, hands, half-busts, and all of terracotta, hollow with a hole in the back made so that they could be attached to a wall; and these statues were votives in that said place Nemi, in the famous temple of Diana Nemorese.

(12) The famous mosaic of the temple of the goddess Fortuna of Palestrina mentioned by Pliny was donated by Cardinal Andrea Peretti, who was at the time bishop of that city, to Cardinal Magalotto and lifted from there in pieces without first making a plan or drawing; Cardinal Magalotto gave it then to Cardinal Barberini, keeping only one piece for himself, which he gave to the Grand Duke [of Tuscany] on the occasion of his visit to Rome, and this was the little scene of those who are dining under a pergola; said piece, from a very exact copy in oils that was commissioned from Vincenzo and is in house, the Cardinal Barberini ordered to be remade by Gio. Battista Calandra, of Vercelli, most expert in mosaic work, who restored the other pieces of mosaic. And taken back by order of said cardinal to Palestrina, joining them together again as best one could with the aid of the drawings we had in house, he put it back to use in the floor of a room in said place at Palestrina: Calandra was able to avail himself, both in remaking said missing piece and in repairing the others, of various breccias found in the environs of Palestrina.

(13) The large ancient pottery storage jars that are in the theatre of the vigna Ludovisi were found in the public road that leads from San Francesco a Ripa, and every day in those vineyards are found both complete examples or fragmentary ones.

(14) The rather strange idol of Priapus that we have in house was found near Sant'Agnese outside Porta Pia.

(15) Having built the new granaries at Termini they set to work to dig out or empty the old granaries of Gregory XIII and they found underneath them ancient streets and rooms; and many of these were emptied, but then it was judged too costly to continue digging to recover the land, so they stopped, leaving open only some part of the streets that had been uncovered.

(16) In the extension that Cardinal Barberini ordered to the lodgings of the nuns of Santa Susanna, to the rear, were found ancient pavements of varied inlay.

(17) When building the church of San Francesco Saverio, making the cut to open the new street from Piazza di Sciarra to the Pantheon, enlarging the Casa degl'Incurabili where at present lives Monsignor Paolucci but previously the Jacovacci, in excavating the foundations of that corner were found pieces of various bas-reliefs, belonging perhaps to some arch, which being pulled out, though not all of them, were by the place of San Jacomo donated to Cardinal Barberini and were for a while deposited in the dining hall of the old residence of the Capuchins now that of the Courtiers.

(18) A few months later, digging foundations in front of the entrance to the Palazzo dei Colonnesi, previously di Palestrina and now di Carbognano in said Piazza Sciarra, and opposite the Incurabili, to erect the door of said palazzo, was found a large block which was one third of an inscription from an arch honouring Claudius after he subjugated England. Encouraged by this, on the orders of the Cardinal [Francesco Barberini], they began to extend the excavation to search further and found several other pieces of bas-relief, companions to those which had been found first under the Casa degli Incurabili and a column certainly belonging to the arch. By the excavator who directed the excavation, who was Domenico, nicknamed L'Aquilano, and by the antiquary of Cardinal Barberini who oversaw the work, who was Leonardo Agostini, I was told that on top of one of the pilasters of the arch last year was placed the corner of the house of San Giacomo, all of which was reported to his Excellency but given that over it would pass the carnival, so as not to block the road on those days, it was judged expedient to close it for the time being and make new investigations another time, and so was done. The piece of inscription, like the other pieces of bas-relief, was donated by the Duca di Carbognano to Cardinal Barberini, who had them taken to his palazzo at Quattro Fontane.

(19) Searching below the church of Santi Quattro [Coronati] in Monticello, which faces the main road to San Giovanni Laterano, in the hope of finding statues,

which did not succeed, although they did find the die for the lead seals of Innocent III or IV, if I'm not mistaken, which was given to Cardinal Antonio [Barberini].

(20) In new building at the monastery for the Dominican fathers of Santa Maria sopra Minerva, in addition to finding a statue of Isis and Serapis in Egyptian marble, excavations under the cellar floor on the side towards the church of the Bergamaschi found an ancient pavement of intaglio, all with figures and Egyptian hieroglyphs that bordered the room, leaving the space in the middle for a certain mosaic of stone, but said pavement had been turned over, with the figures inlaid, which in some part still were seen painted, towards the earth and going on to excavate them to bring them up, they were found to be burned and seriously damaged by fire: none the less they were dug out, in conformity with as they have been found underground, and were ordered by the lay-brother Vincenzo to be carried to a ground-floor room to see if it was possible to put them back together again: in addition to this was found a superb hand in Parian marble and a fragment of Lydian marble equally Egyptian, also damaged by the fire, and a piece of column worked with extravagant spiral bands: the chance to see these ancient curiosities at the Minerva I owe to Father Reginaldo Lucarino, who came to the house to report to my brother, and he took us to the place to see them all, on the morning of March 30, 1642.

Appendix 3

EXTRACTS FROM THE *RELAZIONE* OF CIPRIANO CIPRIANI, WRITTEN c. 1630–60

XXIII *Chiusino* (access shaft) of the main drain

Having described the new drain and its results from the river to the Ghetto gate beside Cenci to the Piazza del Pantheon, and from there almost as far as the Cecchini in (Piazza del) Campo Marzio and also described how from the Piazza del Pantheon the (ancient) main drain was cleared of rubbish as far as San Bartolomeo de' Bergamaschi, so that it was possible for the Jesuit fathers to lay the foundations for the church of Sant'Ignazio, it now remains to describe the new drain and all those things that were seen from said very ancient drain as far as the (Palazzo) Caetani on the Corso, and thence to the Via della Croce, to free the flooding of the cellars causing malaria in those parts.

The new drain was laid from the *chiusino* of the main

drain in the Piazza del Pantheon along the Via dei Pastini, of which no more than 4 canne [9 m] had been built than we came across a large foundation (*platea*) made of basalt (*selci*) 16 palmi [3.5 m] wide and 15 palmi [3.3 m] below ground, and shortly afterwards another foundation of the same material, and not very far on the third, of the same structure and width, which, with other subterranean remains, alongside show that there was some superb building here.

XXIV Via dei Pastini

Beyond the three foundations, passed with great difficulty, the new drain was built in the Via dei Pastini without further impediment as far as the second corner of the Orfani where, meeting an obstructing foundation, we had to change direction and having effected that, it drained dry the cellars on both sides of the street, with the Seminario Romano and the Case degli Orfani, whose cellars were lakes (*piscine*).

XXVI San Giuliano

In the street that goes to the Pazzarelli behind San Giuliano was found a piece of column in yellow (stone), 12 palmi [2.7 m] long, 3 palmi [0.67 m] in diameter, 24 palmi [5.3 m] below ground, which was taken to the Quirinal palace of our patron Cardinal Barberini by order of Monsignor Cicalotto and the Street Commissioners, who at the time were Francesco Soderini and Alessandro Caetani.

XXX Piazza di Sciarra

Digging the new one, the old drain under the Via Flaminia was found 32 palmi [7 m] below, with many outlets from which rose quantities of water, which in the past not having any way of escape flooded the cellars some 8 or 10 palmi [1.8 or 2.2 m] deep as far as those of the house of Cardinal Cornaro and Your Holiness's steward Giovanni degli Effetti, who in recognition of the great favour I did him by knowing how to liberate his cellar of 8 palmi of water gave me a gold medal commemorating Your Holiness, which I shall keep always.

XXXIV Further along the Corso

Not far from Piazza Colonna, as far as the Casa de' Letterati, was found a curtain wall of *peperino* blocks and many pieces of travertine, never used, 18 palmi [4 m] below ground; and again we found the ancient drain 10 palmi [2.2 m] under the Via Flaminia, on which the master builders built the new drain, from place to place breaking through the roof so that the water would have more escape; and obtained those results as has been said in cellars and wells as was desired by the inhabitants of those parts.

EXTRACTS FROM THE *MEMORIE* OF PIETRO SANTI BARTOLI (?), PROBABLY COMPILED c. 1670–82

11.   On the main road from the Colosseum to San Giovanni, on the right-hand side in a garden below Santi Quattro [Coronati] was found among the other ancient ruins a bath-building of beautiful layout, which you could see had been converted by the early Christians into a church, since there were some holy images painted in it, which the barbarians of excavators, so as not to be inhibited, immediately destroyed; and the lower level, which served as the heating apparatus, was reduced to a cemetery; as will be seen in the illustration, which will be shown in the plan: in that place every compartment had, in addition to the bones of the corpse, its tear-bottles, with other Christian signs, but of the early modern period [*tempi antichi moderni*].

44.   In remaking the Palazzo Pamphilj on the Corso, in the time of Innocent X, as related by Gio. Maria Baratta, stonemason and also something of an architect, for which reason he oversaw said work, was found in the large courtyard a temple of not great size but with very thick travertine walls, which could be seen to have been richly decorated, but all in stucco.

48.   In the convent of the Spirito Santo at Trajan's Column was discovered in the time of Alexander VII a column of *africano* 66 palmi [14.7 m] long; and Leonardo Agostini having been sent to see its quality, and size, it was found to agree with the report which had been received, all in perfect state. In the same place, when building, were found most beautiful columns of *giallo antico*, from which a lot of money was made.

53.   Further on, alongside that place [Villa Fonseca on the Caelian], in the garden of Francesco Morelli called the Blind (since he was), excavating in the time of Innocent X, at the request [*ad istanza*] of Marchese del Bufalo, with the assistance of Gio. Francesco Grimaldi, Bolognese painter, found statues, which were sent by the Marchese to France.

74.   In the Holy Year 1675 a ploughman in the bishopric of Portus, at the time held by Cardinal Francesco Barberini, in cultivating the land broke with his plough a piece of wall on the surface, in which he dis-covered a vase of ancient gold coins, with various heads of emperors; but it was not possible for the cardinal, despite every effort, to catch up with it, although he did get many of the coins from Morelli, to whom was paid the value of the gold; but many more were scattered around Rome in the hands of various dealers, and *curiosi*, among whom could be counted the Cardinal.

75.   In 1682 [at Portus] by chance a landslip brought on by rain exposed a great quantity of marked lead piping, from which the peasants who found it made a lot of money. There was found among other things a beautiful marble vase, all carved in figured relief; into whose hands it fell is not known. Coin hoards have been found among those ruins on endless occasions; it is likely that they were all hidden at the time that Rome was tormented by the Goths. The Ginetti made excavations here when they were decorating their chapel in Sant'Andrea della Valle [1670s], whence they shipped to Rome great quantities of *africano* marble.

76.   At this point came notice that at Trajan's Harbour have been found some subterranean rooms, which I shall certify by personal inspection. There have been found more beautiful marbles of varied breccias; and there were also worked pieces.

93.   Of the walls of Rome between the Porta San Giovanni and the Porta Latina fell a piece 8 or 10 canne in length in which could be seen a headless statue, from its drapery an Aesculapius or Jupiter … I saw the place, which will be recorded properly [*notato per l'appunto*] when I have made the necessary inspections on the side towards the city.

128.   In the period when Urban VIII constructed the Priorato Bastion [on the Aventine], there were found endless curiosities; in particular the corner of a great palace, rusticated; two walls, between which was found almost an entire silver service, decorated in low figurative relief. The marble cornice that covered said two walls was taken to the Villa Pamphilj, designed by Gio. Francesco Grimaldi of Bologna and not, as some would have it, by Cavalier Algardi. There was also found a large hoard in a pottery vase, of coins and rings; and although a commissar was sent after it with policemen by Cardinal Antonio Barberini [the Chamberlain] they could not catch it. By another gentleman from L'Aquila was equally found a lead casket, which must have contained something precious

because he took flight without waiting for the wages that he had laboured many days to earn.

After the excavation was abandoned, it was started again in my time, which was in the pontificate of Alexander VII; and there was discovered a beautiful heated bath, all intact, decorated with marbles, and *peperino*, which went to adorn the palazzo of Cavalier Bernini [near Sant'Andrea] alle Fratte.

139. In Hadrian's Villa at Tivoli, by order of Cardinal Francesco Barberini, all the buildings were traced by a certain Arcucci, architect, who made a most beautiful plan, which then put into print was a horrible thing, because of the ignorance of the engraver; and on that occasion was found the beautiful marble candelabrum, work of a distinguished sculptor, with other statues, which I don't recall, now in Palazzo Barberini at Quattro Fontane. Excavations were later made by order of Innocent X, under the direction of Giovanni Maria Baratta, which also found noble things; but particularly a staircase with steps of *alabastro orientale*, the side walls panelled with breccias; some of them with traces of gilded bronze frames. A part of the villa across the way from the Centocelle where the Praetorian guards were lodged was occupied by the Jesuits who, making demolitions, found ten Egyptian statues all in the same type of stone, but all broken, at least some of them. They were sold for a pittance to Cardinal Massimi who, having them restored, they turned out to be of inestimable value. After the cardinal's death [1677], the statues were bought by the Marchese del Carpio, the Spanish ambassador, I dare say for a lesser price than when they were in pieces. In the same place were found fragments of legs, heads, the ears of a bull, tails of other animals, which it was difficult to tell what they were.

155. At Carsoli, below Porcheria, near Acquasparta, most ancient city, and destroyed, one sees the portico of a very beautiful Corinthian temple with large, intact columns; a circus or hippodrome, with a travertine Arch. In the time of the plague of Alexander VII [1656], when I had occasion to pass through there, since the sickness was at Terni, I saw that place with great admiration. In the same period, or a little later, was found a terracotta box, full of ancient coins; but the priest of I don't know which parish church nearby had them melted down to make bells; and some that by accident survived were sold by the priest to a Roman grain merchant. From some, which were of Trajan, he made many scudi.

DATED ENTRIES IN THE BARTOLI *MEMORIE*

Note: few of the entries give dates in calendar years, most referring to the reigning pope. Some dates are (and were presumably intended to be) deducible from other internal evidence, as when the finds were made or bought by a famous purchaser, or made when digging the foundations for a named church or palazzo.

1431–47 (Eugenio IV) : 94
1446 : 148

1534–49 (Paul III) : 78

1575+ : 69
1547 : 21
1570 : 29
1590s : 34

1592–1605 (Clement VIII) : 96

1611 : 125
1612 : 39

1623–44 (Urban VIII Barberini) : 5, 31, 35–6, 45, 82, 98, 100, 116–17, 128, 139, 150
1626 : 32

1644–55 (Innocent X Pamphilj) : 6, 22, 25, 44, 53, 55, 58, 61, 71, 78–9, 90, 92, 139, 142, 144–5, 147, 154
1650 : 141
1652–4 : 1
1653 : 2

1655–67 (Alexander VII Chigi) : 4, 7–8, 12, 16–17, 23, 30, 43, 48, 50, 56–7, 65, 68, 78, 89, 113–15, 128, 132–3, 137–8, 146, 149, 151–2, 155
1656 : 155
1660–78 : 46

1667–70 (Clement IX Rospigliosi) : 18, 40, 62, 134, 144

1670–76 (Clement X Altieri) : 13, 24, 27, 37, 54–5, 59, 63, 72, 75, 81, 86, 112, 118, 130, 140, 143
1675 : 74
1675–9 : 41

1676–89 (Innocent XI Odescalchi) : 79, 108, 135
after 1677 : 139
1679 : 120
1680–1 : 49, 85
1682 : 19, 75, 93, 99, 107, 153

Undated : 3, 9–11, 14–15, 20, 26, 28, 33, 38, 42, 47, 51–2, 60, 64, 66–7, 70, 73, 76–7, 80, 83–4, 87–8, 91, 95, 97, 101–6, 109–11, 119, 121–4, 126–7, 129, 131, 136, 156

Notes

1. C. Renfrew and P. Bahn, *Archaeology. Theories, Method, Practice* (London, 2000³), 559–63.

2. For an account of some of the processes involved in the formation of Rome's archaeological subsoil, see R. Lanciani, *The Destruction of Ancient Rome* (London, 1899). The subject awaits some modern study.

3. R.T. Ridley, 'To protect the monuments: the papal antiquarian (1534–1870)', *Xenia Antiqua* 1 (1992), 117–54: the duties of the Commissario are described on pp. 118–19. For the issuing of licences by the Camerlengo and other authorities, such as the Presidenza delle Strade, see Chapters 1 and 6.

4. F. Nardini, *Roma antica descritta per regioni* (Rome, 1666), i [my translation].

5. See, for example, B. Trigger, *A History of Archaeological Thought* (Cambridge, 1989), ch. 2, 'Classical archaeology and antiquarianism'; A. Schnapp, *The Discovery of the Past. The Origins of Archaeology* (London, 1996), ch. 2, 'The Europe of the antiquaries'.

6. V. Golzio, *Raffaello nei documenti, nelle testimonianze dei contemporanei e nella letteratura del suo secolo* (Vatican City, 1936; reprinted Farnborough, 1971), 5.

7. Called the *Libri di antichità*, substantial parts of two sets are preserved in Turin and Naples: see E. Mandowsky and C. Mitchell, *Pirro Ligorio's Roman Antiquities* (London, 1963); G. Vagenheim, 'Les inscriptions ligoriennes. Notes sur la tradition manuscrite', *Italia Medioevale e Umanistica* 30 (1987), 199–309. Also C. Volpi, 'Ligorio (Pirro) (c. 1513–1583)', in C. Nativel (ed.), *Centuriae Latinae: cent une figures humanistes de la Renaissance aux Lumières offertes à Jacques Chomart* (Geneva, 1997), 497–503.

8. Ridley, 'To protect the monuments' (above, n. 3), 128–30.

9. L. Agostini, *Le gemme antiche figurate di Leonardo Agostini senese*, 2 vols (Rome, 1657, 1669).

10. These are all named in a letter from Carlo Antonio dal Pozzo in Rome to Carlo Dati in Florence in May 1659, which first lists his late brother Cassiano's favourite artists and then goes on to the *antiquari* with whom he had 'domestichezza', that is was closely acquainted (Florence, Biblioteca Nazionale Centrale, Racc. Bald. 258 V.6 no. 4: published in I. Herklotz, *Cassiano dal Pozzo und die Archäologie des 17. Jahrhunderts* (Munich, 1999), 404–5 no. 4).

11. 'antiquario di prima classe', in a letter to Paolo Gualdo 18 July 1614: *Lettere d'uomini illustri che fiorirono nel principio del secolo decimo-settimo non più stampate* (Venice, 1744), 139.

12. A. Schnapper, *Le géant, la licorne et la tulipe. Collections et collectioneurs dans la France du XVIIe siècle* I: *histoire et histoire naturelle* (Paris, 1988), 205; Herklotz, *Cassiano* (above, n. 10), 25.

13. Herklotz, *Cassiano* (above, n. 10), 42–4.

14. F. Angeloni, *La Historia Augusta da Giulio Cesare a Costantino il Magno, illustrata con la verità delle antiche medaglie* (Rome, 1641), addressed to Louis XIII of France.

15. See M. Pomponi, 'Alcune precisazioni sulla vita e produzione artistica di P.S. Bartoli', *Storia dell'Arte* 75 (1992), 195–225,

esp. pp. 198–9, and, most recently, the account of Angeloni's circle by T. Montanari, 'La politica culturale di Giovan Pietro Bellori', in E. Borea (ed.), *L'Idea del Bello. Viaggio per Roma nel Seicento con Giovan Pietro Bellori*, 2 vols (Rome, 2000), I, 39–49.

16. C. Franzoni and A. Tempesta, 'Il museo di Francesco Gualdi nella Roma del Seicento: tra raccolta privata ed esibizione pubblica', *Bollettino d'Arte* 73 (1992), 1–42.

17. He was also a close friend and staunch defender of the architect Francesco Borromini, who converted a small country villa for him: C. D'Onofrio, *Roma nel Seicento* (Rome, 1969), xiii–xviii; *sub voce* in J. Turner (ed.), *Dictionary of Art* XX (London, 1996), 495 (by Alessandra Anselmi).

18. 'Rome explored on the ground and with the advice of all the antiquaries'. The first edition was printed in 1644, a second in 1650, and a third (definitive) in 1658. He also produced a guide to Rome's churches: *Roma ethnica sacra* (Rome, 1653).

19. K. Donahue, 'The ingenious Bellori. A biographical study', *Marsyas* 3 (1943–5), 107–38; E. Borea (ed.), *L'Idea del Bello. Viaggio per Roma nel Seicento con Giovan Pietro Bellori*, 2 vols (Rome, 2000), *passim*, but esp. T. Montanari, 'La politica culturale' (above, n. 15).

20. See M. Pomponi (ed.), *Camillo Massimo collezionista di antichità: fonti e materiali* (Rome, 1996).

21. *Fragmenta Vestigii Veteris Romae ex Lapidibus Farnesianis nunc Primum in Lucem Edita cum Notis Jo. Petri Belloris ad ... Camillum Maximum* (Rome, 1673): M.P. Muzzioli, 'Bellori e la pubblicazione dei frammenti della pianta marmorea di Roma antica', in Borea (ed.), *L'Idea del Bello* (above, n. 19), II, 580–8.

22. *Selecti Nummi Duo Antoniniani, quorum Primus Anni Novi Auspicia, Alter Commodum et Annium Verum Caesares Exhibet ex Bibliotheca ... Camilli Cardinalis Maximi* (Rome, 1676). For Bellori's publications in general, see Borea (ed.), *L'Idea del Bello* (above, n. 19), II, 695.

23. *Scelta de' medaglioni più rari della biblioteca dell'Eminentiss... Gasparo Carpegna* (Rome, 1679); he used Queen Christina's cabinet for the reverses he added to a second edition of Angeloni's *Historia Augusta* (see n. 14) in 1685.

24. *Admiranda Romanarum Antiquitatum ac Veteris Sculpturae Vestigia Anagliphico Opere Elaborata ex Marmoreis Exemplaribus quae Romae adhuc Extant ...* — although the main printings date from 1691 and 1693, the inventory of Camillo Massimo's library in 1677 already included a copy: Pomponi, 'Alcune precisazioni' (above, n. 15), 222 n. 99.

25. *Columna Antoniniana Marci Aureli.. nunc Primum a Petro Sancti Bartoli Iuxta Delineationes in Bibliotheca Barberina Adservatas a se cum Antiquis Ipsius Columnae Signis Collatas ... cum Notis Excerptis et Declarationibus Io Petro Bellori* (Rome, n.d. [1679]).

26. *Le pitture antiche del sepolcro de' Nasonii nella Via Flaminia* (Rome, 1680).

27. *Veteres Arcus Augustorum Triumphis Insignes ex Reliquis quae Romae adhuc Supersunt* (Rome, 1690).

28. *Le antiche lucerne sepolcrali figurate raccolte dalle cave sot-*

terranee e grotte di Roma, nelle quali si contengono molte erudite memorie (Rome, 1691).

29. *Gli antichi sepolcri overo mausolei romani et etruschi trovati in Roma et altri luoghi celebri* (Rome, 1697).

30. C. Menestrier, *Symbolica Dianae Ephesiae Statua Exposita* (Rome, 1657).

31. And continued into the nineteenth century with Antonio Nibby's re-issue of Nardini ('checked and enlarged with the latest discoveries') in 1818–19 (F. Nardini, *Roma antica descritta per regioni* (Rome, 1818–19⁴)), to Henri Jordan's *Topographie der Stadt Rom in Alterthum* (Berlin, 1878–1907), down to Giuseppe Lugli's *I monumenti antichi di Roma e suburbio* (Rome, 1930–40), *Roma antica. Il centro monumentale* (Rome, 1946) and *Itinerario di Roma antica* (Milan, 1970). In the twentieth century a parallel branch developed in the form of topographical dictionaries: S. Platner and T. Ashby, *A Topographical Dictionary of Ancient Rome* (Oxford, 1929); L. Richardson, Jr, *A New Topographical Dictionary of Ancient Rome* (London, 1992); E.M. Steinby (ed.), *Lexicon Topographicum Urbis Romae* I–VI (Rome, 1993–2000).

32. For example, *Ricordi di antichità romane*, *Notitie di antichità diverse*: see T. Schreiber, 'Flaminio Vacca's Fundberichte', *Berichte der Phil.-hist. Classe der Königl. Sächs. Gesellschaft der Wissenschaften* (1881), 43–91, esp. p. 51.

33. *Roma ricercata* (Rome, 1658), 161, for example.

34. F. Nardini, *Roma antica descritta per regioni* (published and printed by Giovanni Andreoli; Rome, 1704²), unpaginated addendum. B. de Montfaucon, *Diarium Italicum sive Monumentum Veterum, Bibliothecarum, Musaeorum, & Notitiae Singulares in Itinerario Italico Collectae* (Paris, 1702) had used lengthy extracts, in Latin translation.

35. F. Nardini, *Roma antica descritta per regioni* (published and printed by Fausto Amidei; Rome, 1741³), xii. Schreiber, 'Vacca' (above, n. 32), 46–7, argued that the anonymous editor was Ridolfino Venuti, at the time librarian and *antiquario* to Cardinal Alessandro Albani, later papal Commissario (Ridley, 'To protect the monuments' (above, n. 3), 138–40). R.T. Ridley, *The Pope's Archaeologist. The Life and Times of Carlo Fea* (Rome, 2000) names one G.L. Barbiellini, but gives no source.

36. Nardini, *Roma antica* (above, n. 35), 214–66.

37. Nardini, *Roma antica* (above, n. 35), 195–213. Ulisse Aldrovandi (1522–1605), of Bologna, was interested principally in natural history, but at a loose end in Rome during 1549–50 amused himself by making a catalogue of the statues and other marbles he saw in the houses and on the streets of the city: see D. Gallo, 'Ulisse Aldrovandi, 'Le statue di Roma' e i marmi romani', *Mélanges de l'École Française de Rome. Italie et Méditerranée* 104 (1992), 479–90.

38. Nardini, *Roma antica* (above, n. 35), 267–92, drawing on F. Ficoroni, *Memorie più singolari di Roma e sue vicinanze notate in una lettera* (Rome, 1730); F. Ficoroni, *La bolla d'oro de' fanciulli nobili Romani e quella de' libertini, ed altre singolarità spettanti a mausolei nuovamente scopertisi* (Rome, 1732). The 1741 editor expressed the hope that Ficoroni 'would have published his own monograph on all the discov-

eries that in his long life he had been involved with personally or examined more carefully than anyone else, lamenting that the civic authorities were not given to keeping accurate records of all the statues and ancient buildings daily being uncovered in the city'. Ficoroni, an excavator and successful dealer in art and antiquities, with early pretensions to scholarship that led him into trouble (*DBI* XLVII, 395), did publish in 1744 *Le vestigie e rarità di Roma antica ricercate e spiegate*, which drew heavily on his own experiences.

39. Eleven volumes of his diaries from the years 1700–42 are preserved in the Archivio Capitolino in Rome: see T. Schreiber, 'Unedirte römische Fundberichte aus italiänischen Archiven und Bibliotheken', *Berichten der Kgl. Sächs. Gesellschaft der Wissenschaften Philol.-hist. Classe* (1885), 2–10, with some extracts relating to the 1720s.

40. Nardini, *Roma antica* (above, n. 35), 293–369.

41. Cf. Ridley, *The Pope's Archaeologist* (above, n. 35).

42. C. Fea, *Miscellanea filologica, critica e antiquaria* (Rome, 1790–1836), II, 208–12.

43. Fea, *Miscellanea* (above, n. 42), II, 213–26; see further I. Bignamini, 'Scavi ottocenteschi a Tor Paterno: gli scavi Chigi del 1777–80 e gli scavi camerali del 1783', in M.G. Lauro (ed.), *Castelporziano* IV: *campagne di scavo e restauro 1992–1998* (Rome, forthcoming 2004).

44. Fea, *Miscellanea* (above, n. 42), II, 213–26; see below, n. 64.

45. Ridley, *The Pope's Archaeologist* (above, n. 35), 79–99.

46. Naples, Biblioteca Nazionale, MS V.E.10 fols 25–30: G. Lumbroso, 'Notizie sulla vita di Cassiano dal Pozzo protettore delle belle arti, fautore della scienza dell'antichità nel secolo decimosettimo con alcuni suoi ricordi e una centuria di lettere', *Miscellanea di Storia Italiana* 15 (1874), 129–388, also available printed separately (Turin, 1875); the Naples 'Memoriale' is at pp. 175–84 (1874).

47. Lumbroso, 'Notizie sulla vita' (1874) (above, n. 46), 184–211.

48. Schreiber's edition of Vacca (see above, n. 32) was based primarily on a copy in Rome, Biblioteca Casanatense MSS Miscellanea X.V 24 fol. 346 and that in a dal Pozzo codex in Naples, Biblioteca Nazionale, MS V.E.10, fols 47–78. For his edition of Cipriani, see below, n. 65; the latter article also included extracts from the Valesio diaries (see above, n. 39), from letters between Francesco Vettori (1710–70) and Giovanni Bottari (1689–1775) and Francesco Gori (1691–1759), the 'Diarium' of Cassiano dal Pozzo in the dal Pozzo codex in Naples (see above and n. 46), and some Vatican papers including those of Joseph Marie Suarès (1599–1677).

49. Of Spanish descent, Vacca studied marble-working in Florence in 1546–60 and became a member of the Virtuosi al Pantheon in 1572. He was the president of the Accademia di San Luca in 1599. V. Martinelli, 'Flaminio Vacca, scultore e antiquario romano', *Studi Romani* 2 (1954), 154–64; for his self-portrait, carved in marble and strongly influenced by ancient Roman models, see M.L. Madonna (ed.), *Roma di Sisto V* (Rome, 1993), 438 no. 8 (by S. Lombardi).

50. The numbering added by Carlo Fea in his edition of 1790 and that given in Schreiber, 'Vacca' (above, n. 32), correspond as

far as no. 60, but at that point Fea forgot to number the next *memoria* and thereafter Schreiber's numbering is one ahead of Fea's. The numbering in Appendix 1 follows Schreiber, but since Fea's edition is still the more widely available, where the two differ Fea's number is also given in brackets.

51. For a study of this phenomenon, which apparently followed in the wake of the demolitions required to erect the Aurelianic Walls in AD 271–5, see R. Coates-Stephens, '*Muri dei bassi secoli* in Rome: observations on the re-use of statuary in walls found on the Esquiline and Caelian after 1870', *Journal of Roman Archaeology* 14 (2001), 217–38.

52. Herklotz, *Cassiano* (above, n. 10), *passim*; also F. Solinas (ed.), *Cassiano dal Pozzo. Atti del seminario internazionale di studi* (Naples, 1989); F. Solinas (ed.), *I segreti di un collezionista: le straordinarie raccolte di Cassiano dal Pozzo 1588–1657* (Rome, 2001); *DBI* XXXII, 209–13 (by G. Stumpo).

53. A substantial amount of the 'Museo' still survives, though dispersed in the Royal Library at Windsor Castle, the British Museum, Sir John Soane's Museum, and other public and private collections. A catalogue raisonné of all known drawings is in progress (see volumes cited below, nn. 55, 58, 61).

54. See above, n. 48.

55. The date is not given, but the foundation stone of the church was laid in 1626; see I. Campbell, *The Paper Museum of Cassiano dal Pozzo. Series A. Part IX. Roman Topography and Architecture* (2004), 2, cat. nos. 243–6.

56. Removed by order of Urban VIII in 1626 and the cause of much protest.

57. 4 August 1626, cf. account in a Chigi manuscript published by Fea, *Miscellanea* (above, n. 42), I, cvii.

58. Also H. Whitehouse, *The Paper Museum of Cassiano dal Pozzo. Series A. Part I. Ancient Mosaics and Wallpaintings* (London, 2001), 229–38.

59. Whitehouse, *The Paper Museum* (above, n. 58), 200–8.

60. Whitehouse, *The Paper Museum* (above, n. 58), 71–84.

61. We know from other sources that the finds were made in 1641. Cassiano had two drawings of the inscription: see W. Stenhouse, *The Paper Museum of Cassiano dal Pozzo. Series A. Part VII. Ancient Inscriptions* (London, 2002), pp. 324–5 cat. no. 189, p. 400 appendix II(b) fol. 12, fig. 19, the latter probably the work of Agostini.

62. Carlo Antonio was appointed a *capitano di fanteria* in September of that year: D. Sparti, 'Carlo Antonio dal Pozzo (1606–1689): an unknown collector', *Journal of the History of Collections* 2 (1) (1990), 7–20, esp. p. 8, n. 27.

63. Apart from what he says in his *Relazione* (see n. 65), I have no information regarding Cipriani's life.

64. *De reliquie antiche sotterranee trovate coll'occasione della nuova chiavica*, the copy published in Fea, *Miscellanea* (above, n. 42), II, on the basis of a manuscript then in the Barberini Library, 'no. 1066', is said by Schreiber to be the 'worst and shortest' version (see below, n. 65).

65. *Relazione d'alcune cose memorabili e spettanti alla restaurazione del famoso tempio di S. Maria ad Martyres, chiamato della Rotonda*, which embodied a section called *Relatione*

delle chiaviche e necessità di esse per servitio della Città. Both texts were published by Theodor Schreiber as part of his 'Unedirte römische Fundberichte' in 1885 (see above, n. 39), 50–75, on the basis of a copy in the Archivio di Stato in Rome, but he found various other versions of the manuscript, not only in the Barberini Library (Barb. Lat. XLVIII.68, XLVIII.77, LVI.107, now in the the Vatican Library, call numbers unknown), but also in the Vatican (Vat. Lat. 6424 and 9027) and Verona (Bibl. Capit. MS CCCCXLI no. VI), and he was able to correct numerous errors in the version published by Fea (see n. 64).

66. In the later version Cipriani clearly struggled to respond to 'objections' that had been levied at his findings: Schreiber, 'Unedirte römische Fundberichte' (above, n. 39), 73.

67. F. Ficoroni, *Osservazioni sopra l'antichità di Roma descritte nel diario italico dal B. de Montfaucon* (Rome, 1709), 3. On Montfaucon's edition, see above n. 34.

68. See Pomponi, 'Alcune precisazioni' (above, n. 15).

69. Pomponi, 'Alcune precisazioni' (above, n. 15), 199.

70. Pomponi, 'Alcune precisazioni' (above, n. 15), 200.

71. For Massimo's album, see C. Pace, 'Pietro Santi Bartoli: drawings in Glasgow University Library after Roman paintings and mosaics', *PBSR* 47 (1979), 117–55; cf. Borea (ed.), *L'Idea del Bello* (above, n. 19), II, 606 no. 40bis; also B. Andreae and C. Pace, 'Das Grab der Nasonier in Rom (Teil 1)', *Antike Welt* 32 (4) (2001), 369–82, and C. Pace, 'Das Grab der Nasonier in Rom (Teil II)', *Antike Welt* 32 (5) (2001), 461–73. For the dal Pozzo album, see H. Whitehouse, 'The rebirth of Adonis', *PBSR* 63 (1995), 215–43; Whitehouse, *The Paper Museum of Cassiano dal Pozzo* (above, n. 58), 48–50, 176–94, 285–97.

72. M. Pomponi, 'La Colonna Traiana nelle incisioni di P.S. Bartoli', *Rivista dell'Istituto Nazionale di Archeologia e Storia dell'Arte* 14–15 (1991–2), 347–77; V. Farinella, 'Bellori e la Colonna Traiana', in Borea (ed.), *L'Idea del Bello* (above, n. 19), II, 589–95.

73. Ridley, 'To protect the monuments' (above, n. 3), 133–4.

74. *Miscellanea* (above, n. 42), I, ccxxii–cclxxiii. Fea's numbering of the passages replaced the toponymic headings that had characterized the entries in the 1741 edition, and integrated that information with the first sentence of text. He changed their sequence in many cases, so as to group topographically related information more closely together, but the overall order still appears fortuitous.

75. 94, 95, 106, 148.

76. 67, 110.

77. For example 29 (discoveries on the Viminal in the 1570s), 38 (a tale of coins found by the builders of Sant'Andrea delle Fratte in 1612), 69–70 (marble yards found on the site of the Chiesa Nuova and sculptors' workshops on Monte Giordano — the writer cannot say exactly where), 77 (story of the different elements of the Hercules Farnese being found in three different places), 78 (more antiquities in the Farnese collection), 97 (Adonis in the Piccini collection) and 98 (finds on the Quirinal).

78. 56: 'a bas-relief of an ancient wedding, which can be seen printed in the *bassi rilievi* of Pietro Santi Bartoli'; 63: 'a series

of very rare coins, which will be printed engraved by Pietro Santi Bartoli' (possibly those in the *Giornale de' Letterati di F. Nazari* 1673 — 'Ragguaglio di due medaglie, una d'Othone e l'altra di due figlioli di Antonino, trovate ultimamente in Roma' —, which Montanari, 'Politica' (above, n. 19), 45, suggested was written by Bellori, the engravings by Bartoli); 100: (re. Santa Costanza) 'The ornament of the cupola is engraved by Pietro Santi Bartoli'; 118: 'a third (cameo) that Camillo Massimi acquired, and was engraved by Pietro Santi Bartoli'. The excavations in question, outside the Porta San Pancrazio, may have been those for which Bellori requested a licence in 1674: see Montanari, 'Politica' (above, n. 19), 44 n. 60.

79. Distinctive is the use of the word 'scassare' (to break up, demolish).

80. Thirty-eight are undated: see Appendix 4.

81. Also 16 (Francesco Barberini for an excavation by Agostini) and 21(Cardinal Trivulzio in 1547).

82. Who was also named in 128 (see Appendix 4: the claim that Grimaldi, not Algardi, designed the Villa Pamphilj could be an indication of Bartoli's authorship here, since he married one of Grimaldi's daughters: Pomponi, 'Alcune precisazioni' (above, n. 15), 200) and 154 (with reference to excavations he made for columns at Otricoli under Innocent X, reg. 1644–55).

83. Massimo became a major collector once he was made cardinal in 1670: see Pomponi, *Camillo Massimo* (above, n. 20). He is cited in the Bartoli *Memorie* as the purchaser in ten cases: 4, 13, 24, 30, 72, 118, 131, 134, 139, 140; several times he is quoted as a source of information: 6, 33, 59, 81. Christina of Sweden, Bellori's other late patron, is named as a buyer in 17, 23, 68; Francesco Barberini in 5, 16, 23, 35, 139, 145.

84. His early patron Francesco Angeloni came from Terni. He had died in 1652, but Bellori was his heir and may have inherited property in the town, to which he had first thought to retreat from the plague in Rome.

85. 11, 14, 43, 56, 63, 65–6, 80–1, 86–7, 90–2, 118–23, 132–4.

Excavations, collectors and scholars in seventeenth-century Rome

Ingo Herklotz

In May 1639, an event took place that caused considerable excitement among the interested public. An ancient funeral chamber, later known as the Sepolcro Corsini, had been discovered accidentally near the church of San Gregorio Magno, on the side facing the Circus Maximus, and was said to have outstanding pictorial decoration.[1] A certain Claudio brought the news to the papal palace, where unfortunately he was not able to gain access to Cardinal Francesco Barberini until the next day. Barberini immediately sent Cassiano dal Pozzo, one of his *gentiluomini* and a renowned expert in ancient art, to San Gregorio together with a painter, and they arrived just in time to prevent the worst. The monks of the nearby monastery had not only carelessly destroyed one of the tondi in the ceiling but also had started deliberately cutting out pieces of the wall. Soon afterwards, Cardinal Barberini himself arrived, together with his brother, Antonio, and numerous other cardinals and prelates. The old Guidi di Bagno, suffering from gout but none the less most curious to see what had been unearthed, was carried to the site in a litter. Such a gathering of high-ranking clergymen, an eyewitness tells us, could have given the impression that the papal stationary liturgy, usually celebrated at San Gregorio in November, had been brought forward to May. Upon close examination of the frescoes, with their festoons, portraits, scenes of children playing and maritime imagery, the observers agreed that they represented the height of antique painting from the period between Augustus and Antoninus Pius. Moreover, the works obviously contradicted the widespread prejudice that the ancients had surpassed the moderns in the art of sculpture but not in painting. Although it did not even appear certain that the decoration had been the work of a first-rate artist, it was doubtless a masterpiece of its genre. Later, the ceiling was drawn and the chamber closed to unauthorized visitors. However, when the Duke of Parma visited the papal court at the end of the year, he was taken to the site by Francesco Barberini.[2]

This episode seems to confirm a certain cliché in modern studies on seventeenth-century Rome, one that envisages a harmonious community of patrons — ecclesiastic or otherwise —, scholars and artists collaborating efficiently to build up collections, engage in learned discourse and protect a common cultural heritage. The reality, however, was far from this. During the first half of the seventeenth century, at least, the most ambitious antiquarian projects conceived by scholars working in Rome had come to nothing, while the number of archaeological publications was meagre when compared to those appearing in, say, contemporary Padua.[3] The lack of patronage for classical studies was certainly a decisive reason for this failure. On the other hand, this same period was characterized by a flourishing culture of collecting, and most aristocratic collectors employed their own antiquarians and agents. But what kind of collections were these?

Some years ago, Michael Vickers demonstrated that in seventeenth-century England museums of antiquities moved on two different social and intellectual levels, spheres that did not necessarily intersect.[4] The aristocratic sculpture gallery, on the one hand, and the learned cabinet, on the other, represent these two spheres. Vickers's observation can be generalized for seventeenth-century continental collecting as well, or at least for Rome, where the frequent distinction *per l'arte* (for art) and *per l'eruditione* (for learning) reflects this twofold approach even in linguistic usage. Indeed, the coins, gems, objects of ancient material culture, inscriptions and other fragments, collected by people such as Lelio Pasqualini, Claude Menestrier or Marzio Milesi, had been acquired for the sake of learned documentation on ancient life, as material for study.[5] Aristocrats and churchmen, such as Ciriaco Mattei, Vincenzo Giustiniani, Camillo and Scipione Borghese and Ludovico Ludovisi, on the other hand, coveted works by ancient sculptors — preferably sculpture in the round, but also reliefs — primarily for aesthetic pleasure, as decoration for their gardens and palaces.[6] Restoration of these works was standard practice, though such restorations were, all too often, not intended to be accurate archaeological restorations. Such a case can be seen in the Barberini inventory of 1626, regarding the torso of a cuirassed statue: 'it could serve as a Julius Caesar, or even an Augustus'.[7] In these collections, ancient works of art were a means of social display rather than a sign of erudition.

Only at this point do excavations assume a significant role. The manifold and restless activities of excavators in seventeenth-century Rome were aimed primarily at the formation of aristocratic collections. If they made a contribution to archaeological knowledge, this was at best an involuntary by-product. The present paper focuses on somebody who justifiably may be viewed as the most important organizer of excavations in and near Rome from the 1650s to the late 1660s: the papal antiquarian Leonardo Agostini (1594–1675).[8] Although not an obscure figure, the available information on Agostini's endeavours by no means has been explored exhaustively. What follows is based upon some 260 letters, for the most part unpublished, written by Agostini to the grand dukes of Tuscany, to Cardinal Leopoldo de' Medici, then in charge of Florentine cultural politics, and to various of the latter's agents, among whom the cultured Carlo di Tomaso Strozzi played a pre-eminent role.[9]

Born in Siena in 1594, Agostini came to Rome early in the pontificate of Urban VIII (Maffeo Barberini). Initially he served Cardinal Spada, but later the support of Cassiano dal Pozzo helped him to become antiquarian to Francesco Barberini in 1639. He reached the peak of his career only sixteen years later, in 1655, when Alexander VII — alias Fabio Chigi and, like Agostini, from Siena — appointed him antiquarian to the pope and Commissario delle Antichità for Rome and the Papal States.[10] It seems that he held this position until the summer of 1667, when Onofrio Cocchi became his successor.[11] After less than three years, however, the office was transferred once more, this time to Agostini's friend and former pupil Giovanni Pietro Bellori.[12] While Agostini worked for several other Roman patrons besides those mentioned, his Florentine connections proved essential for his financial and social security.

Agostini's scholarly output was modest. In 1649 he published a new edition of Filippo Paruta's work on Sicilian coins of 1612, to which he was able to contribute some 200 additional specimens.[13] In 1657

(followed by a second volume in 1669), the newly-installed papal antiquary proudly presented a book on his own gem collection illustrated with 200 engravings by Giovanni Battista Galestruzzi, for many years Agostini's closest artistic collaborator.[14] It was the plates, rather than the text — heavily laced with flattery of the Roman aristocracy —, that accounted for the book's favourable reception. Yet, as Agostini himself admitted, the accompanying explanations, short and at times trivial as they are, could not have been written without the continuous support of Bellori.[15] In essence, *Gemme antiche* represents an early example of the antiquarian coffee-table book that was to become popular later in the century, mainly through Bellori himself. Towards the end of his life, Agostini worked on a publication of Egyptian antiquities. Although some 35 plates had been engraved already, this project was never completed.[16]

Rather than a scholar, Agostini embodied a new kind of commercial or court antiquary that would play an important role in the future.[17] An excellent knowledge of the trade in antiquities and current excavations, the ability to distinguish between authentic works and fakes, particularly when dealing with coins and gems, and an eye for style and artistic quality were the main qualifications of the commercial antiquary. Historical knowledge played a minor role in his training. Acquisitions of works of art and the drawing up of inventories, together with the assessment of individual pieces or entire collections and the supervision of restorations, were among his most frequent duties.[18] In fact, the Barberini account books record that Agostini was procuring ancient reliefs and statues long before becoming a member of Cardinal Francesco's household.[19] A particular strength of Agostini, however, must have been his talent for organizing excavations.

Little is known of Agostini's activities under Urban VIII. The first excavation we know of, however, must have been the one that established his fame. It was conducted for Don Lelio Orsini, the brother of Cardinal Virginio Orsini, near the church of San Clemente and the Via Labicana in the early 1650s.[20] Here an older, unidentified, site had been used by the fifth-century prefect and consul (and for some months in 455 emperor) Petronius Maximus for the construction of his forum.[21] In fact, the association with Maximus is based to a great extent on Agostini's discovery of what appears to have been the lintel of the entrance gate, with Maximus's building inscription. Further architectural remains brought to light in this area included columns, capitals and fragments of a pavement. Moreover, rumour had it that 'within a couple of days', Agostini unearthed 42 statues.[22] Although this may have been an exaggeration, his finds were spectacular enough to attract numerous prominent visitors, including the Duke and Duchess of Bracciano and Marchese Corsini, to say nothing of other, less important, figures such as antiquaries and dealers in antiquities.[23]

As a rule, Agostini's discoveries became the property of Lelio Orsini, who had sponsored the campaign and shared in its results with great enthusiasm.[24] Nevertheless, the antiquary was able to sell some of the material he found. Thus in September 1652, Cavaliere Francesco Gualdi acquired two capitals, possibly among those he donated to the church of Trinità dei Monti (**Figs 1** and **2**) in the same year,[25] and, by agreement with Orsini, Agostini offered some of the most exquisite statues to the Florentine court.[26] Already it becomes obvious that Agostini's excavations were intimately linked with profitable interests. However, the success of their work induced Orsini and Agostini to enter upon another joint venture. For the autumn of 1654 they scheduled excavations at the alleged forum of Claudius at Lake Bracciano, which now belonged to the Orsini family, a plan that was prevented first by Agostini's illness and then, one may assume, by the new duties he faced from the next year.[27] A later campaign by Orsini, conducted in the baths of Helena close to Santa Croce in Gerusalemme, was realized without his former collaborator.[28]

The renowned excavation at the forum of Petronius Maximus may have contributed to Agostini's appointment as papal antiquary in 1655. After all, as a cardinal, Alexander himself had visited the site.[29] Agostini could, of course, flatter himself with having found a pope who was not only deeply interested in classical culture, but also was willing to open his purse for the restoration and exploration of antiquities. In addition, he made ambitious plans for the restructuring of the city.[30] Indeed, several of Agostini's commissions in

FIG. 1. **Capital, in the church of Trinità dei Monti, Rome. Bibliotheca Hertziana neg. no. U.Fi.D 377a.** *(Reproduced courtesy of the Bibliotheca Hertziana.)*

FIG. 2. **Capital, in the church of Trinità dei Monti, Rome. Bibliotheca Hertziana neg. no. U.Fi.D 377d.** *(Reproduced courtesy of the Bibliotheca Hertziana.)*

the years to come derived from this programme of urban renewal.

As early as 1655, the Chigi pope instigated the restoration of the famous pyramid of Gaius Cestius, next to the Porta San Paolo, a campaign that at times must have involved more than 100 men working simultaneously.[31] The first step was to lower the area around the building, which over the centuries had

i *Porta di* S. *Paolo*.   SEPOLCRO E PIRAMIDE DI C·CESTIO RISTAVRATA DA N·S·PAPA ALESANDRO VII.   2. *Mura di* Roma.
Per Gio. Iacomo Rossi in Roma alla Pace. cō P. del SP.

Gio·Batta Falda di et f.   34

FIG. 3. Pyramid of C. Cestius after the restoration of Alexander VII. From G. Falda, *Il nuovo teatro delle fabriche et edificii in prospettiva di Roma moderna* ([Rome], 1666). Bibliotheca Hertziana neg. no. U.Pl.D 19884. *(Reproduced courtesy of the Bibliotheca Hertziana.)*

considerably increased in height, to its ancient level (**Fig. 3**). Groundwater soon presented difficulties, but only by undertaking such work could the structure be renewed to its former monumentality. 'The height is 175 *palmi*', Agostini wrote, deeply impressed, 'and its sides measure 135 *palmi* each'. The excavators could enter the inner tomb chamber to examine its fresco decoration through an opening on the east wall, which he claimed had been broken through 'by the barbarians'. The paintings, it seems, did not meet with great approval, though they were copied and ten years later published by Ottavio Falconieri.[32] Graffiti on the walls left no doubt that previous visitors had been there in 1595, among them Antonio Bosio and the painter Andrea Commodi.[33] After these inspections, Agostini decided that access to the interior should no longer be granted. Further discoveries were made outside the building, where at least two Corinthian marble columns measuring 30 *palmi romani* in height came to light. An inscription on a pedestal and the foot of a bronze statue led to the conclusion that one of the columns formerly had held the statue of Gaius Cestius himself. Furthermore, a small brick tempietto was discovered close to the pyramid, which unfortunately was not recorded in the archaeological documentation.

Alexander's efforts to imbue the appearance of his city with modernity and splendour did not omit the core of ancient Rome itself, that is the Roman Forum. His vision called for the entire area — hitherto a pasturing ground for sheep and cows amidst some ancient ruins — to be redesigned with a park avenue flanked by double rows of mulberry trees leading from the Arch of Septimius Severus to that of Titus.[34] It must have been in relation to this project that we find Agostini repeatedly digging in the Roman Forum between 1656 and 1658.[35] Although he himself does not appear to have been too impressed by the results of his campaign, he must have unearthed an architectural structure of considerable extent — later identified as the Porticus Margaritaria — on the slope of the Palatine. Disappointingly, after extensive remodelling in late antique times, the portico seems to have lacked any sophisticated decoration.

Another excavation campaign of equal or even greater scope took place about five years later, when Alexander planned the renewal of the quarter around the Pantheon (1662).[36] At some distance down the street leading to the church of Santa Maria sopra

FIG. 4. Pantheon and Piazza Rotonda after the restoration of Alexander VII. From G. Falda, *Il nuovo teatro delle fabriche et edificii in prospettiva di Roma moderna* ([Rome], 1666). Bibliotheca Hertziana neg. no. U.Pl.D 19888. *(Reproduced courtesy of the Bibliotheca Hertziana.)*

Minerva, houses were torn down to return the circular temple to its former, free-standing, position. Enormous quantities of marble were required for the renovation of the building and its surroundings, and much of this was obtained from the ruins in and outside the city (**Fig. 4**). Since two columns were missing from the portico's left flank, Alexander commissioned an excavation in the nearby Piazza San Luigi, where the baths of Hadrian were thought to have stood. And in fact his hopes were justified: the building materials discovered on the site (the baths of Nero, not Hadrian) included two very similar granite columns corresponding to the height of the portico.

A papal order had provided for the booths and vendors' stalls in front of the Pantheon to be removed to the Piazza di Pietra, located half-way between the area now subject to renovation and the column of Marcus Aurelius, although the Piazza di Pietra itself had to be prepared for its new use. Thus the medieval church of Santo Stefano del Truglio fell victim to the requirements of space. Its destruction, however, turned out to be worthwhile, since four huge marble reliefs, two with trophies and arms and two with personifications of Roman provinces, came to light. Another four

reliefs, obviously from the same series, were discovered when the ground in front of the Pantheon was lowered to its ancient level (**Fig. 5**). Agostini thought that these sculptures had been moved from their original location in late antiquity and attributed their provenance to the basilica or temple of Antoninus, the remains of which he believed were located in the Piazza di Pietra. Needless to say, what he saw was the temple of Hadrian, and this is in fact the origin of the reliefs. Agostini was also right in associating these works with others then in the Palazzo Farnese, where they had been taken by Paul III more than a century before, and now to be found in Naples. During the restoration of the Pantheon, another relief from the same group was unearthed by the Jesuit fathers of Sant'Ignazio while working on the foundations of their seminary.

Thus Agostini's entrance into the service of Alexander VII certainly altered the scope of some of his excavations, although on occasion his activities took on a rather different purpose as well. Alexander also commissioned him to search the Roman catacombs for the relics of Christian martyrs.[37] The cemetery of San Ciriaco at the Campo Verano and the cata-

FIG. 5. Reliefs from the Temple of Hadrian. Rome, Capitoline Museums. *(Photo: Author.)*

comb of Priscilla on the Via Salaria were among the places he explored. It soon became evident, however, that Agostini did not have the ambition to become a new Bosio. Whenever we witness enthusiasm in the reports of his discoveries, it is prompted by ancient coins, metal statuettes, fragments of mosaics and other *galanterie*, such as a beautiful cup of agate, not by early Christian decorations or inscriptions. Indeed, it seems to have been the remains of pre-Christian civilization that, in his eyes, made these sites worth ransacking.

In addition to the campaigns connected with major papal restoration projects, Agostini also directed at least a dozen minor excavations during these years. Thus, in the autumn of 1656, he was digging not only in the Roman Forum, but also close to Santa Cecilia in Trastevere.[38] In the years to come, he worked next to Castel Gandolfo, at Piazza Santissimi Apostoli, on the Esquiline, at the Porta Portuensis, near San Lorenzo in Panisperna and on the Velabrum.[39] In 1662, he started at least two new campaigns, one in the vicinity of the Colosseum, the other close to Santa Maria in Domnica.[40] From 1663 onwards, extensive excavations followed in various places around the church of San Gregorio Magno.[41] In 1667, he returned to the area of the Colosseum, from which he advanced into the so-called 'Baths of Titus', an agglomeration of structures that previously was likely to have been part of the

Domus Aurea.[42] It is not always clear who sponsored these excavations. Some of them, no doubt, were papal commissions, though one suspects that the initiative came from Agostini rather than from Alexander VII. Others could have been executed for private patrons. Agostini continued to work for Barberini, at least, long after 1655.[43] Finally, in at least one case and possibly more, the antiquary claims to have financed the excavation from his personal budget.[44] However, despite the promising ancient ruins on the various sites, not all of these campaigns proved successful. Some of them were abandoned after a couple of trial digs. But, then, what constituted a successful campaign? It is at this point that we have to discuss the mentality informing seventeenth-century excavations.

Agostini's letters confirm much of what is already known about the origins of modern excavation techniques — that is to say that they did not spring from classical, but rather prehistoric, archaeology, and certainly not from Italy, but from northern Europe.[45] One of the most amazing features of his correspondence is how little he was concerned with archaeological sites as such. Whenever he hit a wall, it was torn down.[46] *Opus sectile* pavements were unearthed piece by piece in order to be put to different use.[47] Remarks of a stratigraphic nature are extremely rare. His dig in the piazza of San Gregorio Magno, however, provides one such example.[48] Here he brought to light the paving of a street 11 *palmi romani* below the seventeenth-century surface, and Agostini concluded that this street must have been laid down when Constantine erected his triumphal arch. Another 9 *palmi romani* down, he discovered huge blocks of travertine that he thought had once belonged to a portico facing the famous Septizodium of Septimius Severus at the southeast end of the Circus Maximus. The association of archaeological layers with different periods in history, however, is as exceptional in Agostini's reports as are his attempts to reconstruct a building, and one surmises that such considerations happened for lack of more spectacular news. After all, the excavation at San Gregorio was a disappointment: 'I have been excavating in the piazza of San Gregorio for three months now', he wrote in January 1664, 'and all I have found are these blocks of travertine'. His account of the work he did for the Barberini at the Villa of Domitian, near Castel Gandolfo, in 1657 is still more baffling: 'This autumn the excavation of Castello has not produced much of interest, only my discovery of the Villa Domiziana ... the residence of the emperor, the hippodrome, the stadium, the portico and the Castrum Praetorium'.[49] He did, at least, decide to commission a ground-plan of these ruins.

Agostini's disregard for architecture is equalled by his ignorance of Roman topography, which on occasion falls well below sixteenth-century standards. Agostini was certain neither of the function nor of the patron of the Hadrianeum.[50] He assumed that the Curia Hostilia, which stood next to the Comitium, was adjacent to the Colosseum instead.[51] He also erred when he located the Baths of Hadrian close to San Luigi dei Francesi, and so on.[52]

Like all excavations in seventeeth-century Rome, the primary motivation for Agostini's campaigns was the discovery of ancient sculpture. These are the finds he speaks of with greatest enthusiasm and in most detail; and sculpture in the round, full-length statues and portrait busts, certainly were preferable to relief sculpture. Agostini's approach to these works is that of an amateur, or rather an art dealer, not that of a scholar. In fact, rather than recording academic discourse, his letters read like sale catalogues, which is what many of them were intended to be. Size, materials, state of conservation and quality of execution — in terms of both the period style and the craftsmanship of the individual artist — continually come into play.

It goes without saying that the value of a statue increased with its size and good state of preservation. The sculptor Bartolomeo Cennini, a collaborator of

Bernini and Algardi and an expert in the restoration of antique sculpture, worked with Agostini for many years, so that the papal antiquary used to offer Cennini's services along with the statues he sold.[53] Regarding materials, there was a clear hierarchy. In full accord with Baroque taste, exotic stones such as green and black marble from Egypt, *giallo* and *africano* ranked highest. Alabaster was preferred to white marble, marble, of course, to travertine. As far as stylistic criteria are concerned, Agostini offered little more than the distinction between 'belissimo' ('extremely beautiful') and 'mediocremente bona' ('less good'), which correspond to the earlier empire and late antiquity. The term 'maniera greca' ('in the Greek style') was used for works of outstanding quality, but should not be taken literally. Such clichés notwithstanding, it is with regard to the aesthetic characteristics of ancient sculpture that Agostini provided the most sensitive descriptions. Thus in January 1653 he reported the discovery of a decorated sarcophagus including a nautical scene in the vineyard of Rotilio Paracciani outside the Porta San Sebastiano (the front of which is now in the Vatican Museums; **Fig. 6**), describing it as:

> a large sarcophagus with historical reliefs ... In its reliefs, one sees the most beautiful things, such as landscapes, cities, towers, figures inside galleys, boats and infinite things ... The style is not particularly rare because one can see the mastery of the Constantinian age, but its diligence is inexpressible, because both large and small figures completely stand out in the air.[54]

Modern scholars have dated this work to around the year AD 260. The same high quality seems to have been the most impressive feature of the famous archaistic statue of Minerva in Dresden (**Fig. 7**), once in the Chigi collection and unearthed close to the Baths of Caracalla in February or March 1662. The long stole hanging down to Minerva's feet, showing the gods struggling against the giants, received Agostini's utmost admiration: 'the tiny figures are no more than half a finger in height, but so well made that, even using wax, one could not match it nowadays'.[55] Similar praise was voiced early the next year when the famous figural capital, now in the Vatican Cortile della Pigna (**Fig. 8**), was unearthed at Piazza San Luigi dei Francesi during the search for two new columns for the Pantheon: he described it as 'something, in truth, never seen in my time'.[56]

No doubt there were attempts to go beyond visual admiration and to enter into archaeology. When deal-

FIG. 6. Front of a sarcophagus with mythological figures and a nautical scene. Vatican Museums. Deutsches Archäologisches Institut, Rome, neg. no. 31.1138. *(Reproduced courtesy of the Deutsches Archäologisches Institut, Rome.)*

ing with portrait iconography, Agostini can be said to be at his best, although even here we find utterances that sound remarkably amateurish. Such is the case when he reported on two heads found near the Porta San Sebastiano in 1641 and later acquired by Antonio Barberini: 'One of them I recognized as being of Cicero. Since the other one looks so similar and they were both from the same spot, I concluded that the second must be of Quintus, Cicero's brother'.[57] Later evaluations are certainly less naive. His observation that the infant *togatus* of dark marble (now in the Uffizi; **Fig. 9**) — for sale in 1651, at which time it still lacked its modern head — might represent Gaius or Lucius, one of the grandsons of Augustus, was not far off the mark.[58] Modern scholars have dated it to Augustus's later years.

Agostini's work with coins and gems provided a solid background for his study of portraits. In one instance his identification sounds both typical of the seventeenth century and, at the same time, surprisingly modern. In 1646 a statue of the goddess Cybele riding on a lion was discovered in the Antonine villa of Lorium on the Via Aurelia, and there is much to be said in favour of its identification with a sculpture in the Villa Doria Pamphili (**Fig. 10**).[59] Agostini's description,

however, did not bother overly with the goddess at issue, thus showing a lack of interest in mythological iconography rather widespread during the seventeenth century.[60] Instead, he conceived of the statue as a portrait of Faustina, probably meaning the younger Faustina, Marcus Aurelius's wife. Medals of the imperial lady, he stated, led him to this conclusion. In fact, the features and hairstyle of the statue at the Villa Doria Pamphili do resemble those of Faustina, as known from some of her coins and medals.[61] Agostini's conclusion found additional support in the fact that at least one type of Faustina's medals shows Cybele riding a lion on the reverse,[62] an iconographic association that may be due to particular veneration that the goddess enjoyed within the Antonine family, or even to a post mortem association of Faustina with Cybele. Be that as it may, a relationship between the Doria Pamphili statue and Faustina has been confirmed by modern scholars as well.[63]

The evidence of coins, of course, could also be misleading. When a statue of a general in the nude, now in the Louvre (**Fig. 11**), was discovered outside the Porta Maggiore in December 1656, Agostini hastened to identify it as the emperor Claudius Albinus (ob. 197).[64] Since modern scholarship has assigned the work unanimously to the first half of the third century — without, however, arriving at a convincing identification —, the result of Agostini's reasoning is certainly less bewildering than his arguments. The cornucopia carved on the trunk of the statue, he stated, reminded him of Claudius's *Saeculum frugiferum* medals. The *Saeculum frugiferum* iconography, as well as the symbolism of the cornucopia, however, was far too widespread to allow such a specific association, a fact that can hardly have escaped Agostini's notice. One would therefore prefer to assume that he also had a certain familiarity with portrait statuary from the decades after the Antonine dynasty. This knowledge, no doubt, put him on more secure ground than his iconographic speculations.

It seems that considerations of portrait iconography were of minor importance to the Florentine court. Beauty was what mattered here. Moreover, the question of whether a certain statue would match something already in the collection was an issue of some concern. As soon as the Medici showed interest in a work that Agostini had indicated as being on the market, he usually sent a drawing and measurements in order to give a better impression. Drawings of a beautiful head of 'Seneca' for sale in 1658 and of a Bacchic relief offered in 1666 (**Figs 12** and **13**) have survived among his letters.[65] On occasion, Florentine agents came to inspect the works under discussion. Even the painter Pietro da Cortona acted in this capacity in the early 1650s.[66] How many and which statues were actually sold to Florence through Agostini's intervention, however, is not easy to determine. The Uffizi group of Cupid and Psyche (**Fig. 14**), discovered on the Caelian by a friend of his in 1666, was certainly among them, as was the infant *togatus* (**Fig. 9**) mentioned earlier.[67] Likewise, in Agostini's letters at least eight portrait busts from excavations and other, sometimes unspecified, sources are documented as having gone through his hands before arriving in Florence. The head of an Egyptian princess, known in the seventeenth century as Berenice, the pseudo-Seneca and a presumed Clodius Pupienus, all now in the Uffizi, belonged to this group.[68] On the other hand, busts of Germanicus, Antoninus Pius, Marcus Aurelius, Septimius Severus, Cleopatra and a head of Agrippina in relief, all recorded in the correspondence, present serious problems for identification. In these cases, either no such portraits can be traced in the Uffizi — which may, of course, be due to the erroneous names under which they circulated in the seventeenth century — or the Uffizi possesses several portraits of each of these

FIG. 7. **Statue of Minerva. Dresden, Staatliche Kunstsammlungen.** *(Reproduced courtesy of the Staatliche Kunstsammlungen, Dresden.)*

personalities and those sold by Agostini cannot be distinguished.[69] A significant early Christian metal lamp in the form of a ship with Peter and Paul (**Fig. 15**) was excavated by Agostini himself on the Caelian in March 1667, at which time he reported his discovery to the Florentine court.[70] He sent a drawing in July, and the work is documented in the grand ducal collection a few years later (now in the Museo Archeologico of Florence). Towards the end of his life Agostini sold his own collection of coins and at least some of his gems to the Florentine court, and contrived and organized the most prominent acquisition of ancient sculpture

FIG. 8. Capital from the Thermae Alexandrinae. Vatican Museums. Deutsches Archäologisches Institut, Rome, neg. no.
38.1651. *(Reproduced courtesy of the Deutsches Archäologisches Institut, Rome.)*

ever made by Cardinal Leopoldo, that of fifteen statues from the Ludovisi collection.[71]

What is amazing about all of these sales is how freely Agostini disposed of the available archaeological material and how he was able to direct newly-discovered and other statues into the Florentine collections. Considering that similar deals with Roman collectors did not require extensive correspondence, we may surmise that the Medici museums were not the only ones to benefit from Agostini's activities. In fact, some of the material he either discovered or at least offered to Florence is later documented in the palaces of Cardinals Massimo and Chigi.[72] In all this, one can hardly avoid the impression that the papal antiquarian expanded the competences of his office to his own profit, occasionally even pushing the boundaries of legality. While he repeatedly pointed out that a new discovery was 'presently at my house',[73] his standard formula when offering something for sale read 'mi e capitato una testa/una statua' ('I came across a head/a

statue') and so on, leaving the provenance tellingly vague. As early as 1652, he arranged for the grand duke to grant him a storeroom situated in the garden of the Villa Medici in Rome, where he could gather all potential Medici acquisitions (and probably others) without being observed by his detractors, as he himself explained.[74] In fact, there is much to say about Agostini and his enemies. Among the latter, the Maestro di Strade and numismatic scholar Francesco Gottifredi held a place of honour. His view of Agostini's activities, although thoroughly biased, merits a brief consideration.[75]

The rivalry between Agostini and Gottifredi must have been rooted in some obscure events of the past, but the decisive stumbling-block was their common passion for ancient coins. In addition to competing to acquire the rarest specimens for their personal collections, they also tried to outdo one another when dealing with potential clients.[76] Certainly Agostini had no stature as a scholar when measured against Gottifredi,

FIG. 9. Statuette of a boy wearing a toga. Florence, Uffizi. After G.A. Mansuelli, *Galleria degli Uffizi. Le sculture* (Rome, 1958–61).

FIG. 10. Statue of Cybele riding a lion. Rome, Villa Doria Pamphili. Deutsches Archäologisches Institut, Rome, neg. no. 69.429. *(Reproduced courtesy of the Deutsches Archäologisches Institut, Rome.)*

a weakness often pointed out by the latter, who even accused his adversary of being ignorant of Latin and Greek.[77] Their hostility culminated in the early 1650s, when they were both employed as agents of the Florentine court. At that time Gottifredi also worked for the Dogana (Roman customs board).[78] Agostini feared that Gottifredi might stop his consignments to Florence, which could be seen as proof that they were exports of doubtful legality. However, his plea for absolute discretion was a constant concern in his dealings with the grand ducal court.[79] To some extent this concern was well justified, since another Florentine agent, the Englishman Peter Fitton, was on excellent terms with Gottifredi and asked him for additional judgements on the numismatic material Agostini

offered for sale, including the latter's own collection.[80]

The situation became increasingly awkward for Gottifredi after Agostini entered the papal service in 1655, especially since he himself, it seems, had hoped to be appointed to the office of Roman commissioner.[81] According to Gottifredi, it was at Agostini's instigation that his predecessor, Nicola Menghini, renewed the notorious 'Bando del Camerlengo' in the summer of 1655, thereby aggravating the restrictions established in an earlier version of 1634.[82] The new regulations stipulated that the papal antiquary was to be notified of all acquisitions valued at more than a scudo and that all sales to foreigners were categorically forbidden. Complete control of the Roman antiquities market by the papal antiquary would have been

FIG. 11. **Statue of a Roman General. Paris, Louvre AGR MA 1059.** *(Reproduced courtesy of the Louvre.)*

accused him of gathering all the most exquisite coins that came to light under pretence of presenting them to the pope (who had a right of pre-emption), but then choosing the best for his private collection.[83] As a commissioner of antiquities, Agostini was in charge of inspections of other people's excavation sites.[84] In contrast, he seems to have had an entirely free hand with his own excavations. The temptation to use such a profitable situation for non-scholarly purposes must have been considerable. The easiest way to sell ancient statues, either within the city or outside, for those who did not enjoy Agostini's privileged position, seems to have been to pass them through his hands.

Let us return to our initial point of departure. Obviously, Agostini primarily served only one of the two different types of antiquities collections. Must we then conclude that his excavations were irrelevant for the scholarship of the day? On the whole, one would have to say so. The dominant aim of seventeenth-century archaeology was the investigation of customs and institutions (*mores et instituta*), a field of study that had been re-established in the fifteenth century.[85] Within it, ancient religion, the administration of the state, private life and military antiquities represented four major areas of study. Ancient material culture — that is, objects of daily use, costume and insignia of social rank — was essential to the understanding of the various aspects of classical civilization. Whoever intended to illuminate material culture by more than textual sources alone had to investigate either the surviving objects themselves or their representations in ancient art (witness dal Pozzo's

achieved by the enforcement of such restrictions. Whether this goal was achieved is open to doubt. That Agostini abused the competences of his office, however, is a view certainly shared by Gottifredi, who

Museo Cartaceo, the most complete graphic documentation of *mores et instituta* produced in its age). Agostini, however, displayed no interest in such objects. As he put it, in 1659 when asked about some military insignia, 'This is not really my concern. I had such things in the past, but I usually gave them to Mr. Bellori in exchange for coins'.[86] On the other hand, the advocates of a scholarly approach often had expressed their disregard for the hedonistic worship of ancient sculpture. Thus the oft-quoted statement by Antonio Agustín, that enough nude statues had been excavated by his time, should not be interpreted as prudish Counter-Reformation hostility towards antiquity altogether, but rather as a plea for an intellectual, as opposed to a purely aesthetic, approach to the classical past.[87] More elegant in rhetoric, but similar in spirit, is Nicolas Claude Fabri de Peiresc's statement upon receiving the first volume of the *Galleria Giustiniana* in 1636, with the reproductions of Vincenzo Giustiniani's free-standing statues: 'If this first book already tells so much about ancient gods and their attributes', he asks, 'how much more shall scholars learn from the second part, which will also include relief sculpture?'.[88] In dal Pozzo's Museo Cartaceo free-standing statues are rare, and if they appear at all are meant to illustrate specimens of classical costume. Nude statues are completely absent.[89]

This paper should not conclude without a brief look at the excavations Agostini conducted toward the end of his life, which, it seems, were of far greater consequence than all his earlier work. The most spectacular findings from his campaign on the Esquiline in 1668 were ancient paintings, mainly of mythological characters.[90] Although this was certainly not what Agostini had hoped for, his discoveries were the cause of much interest among the interested public and scholars. Further specimens of ancient pictorial art were brought to light in the decades to come (suffice it to mention the Tomb of the Nasonii, unearthed in 1674; **Fig. 16**), and one may assume that some of the relevant fieldwork was stimulated by Agostini's success. Ancient painting was a subject that previously had been studied on the basis of Pliny and other literary descriptions. Soon after the archaeological discoveries, these new examples of ancient painting were documented in ponderous

FIG. 12.   **Bust of pseudo-Seneca (Florence, Uffizi). Archivio di Stato di Firenze, Carte Strozziane, vol. 184, 111r.** *(Reproduced courtesy of the Ministero per i Beni e le Attività Culturali. All further reproduction is prohibited.)*

volumes of copies by Camillo Massimo and Pietro Santi Bartoli.[91] Another decisive step was taken in the 1680s, when Bartoli and Bellori began publishing a series of illustrated books on ancient painting.[92] The sequel to these remarkably successful volumes may be identified in publications by George Turnbull, Anne Claude Philippe, Comte de Caylus and other eighteenth-century authorities. The archaeological significance of these works remains to be analysed. It seems certain, however, that they placed new emphasis on the study of classical mythology, which had never enjoyed much favour among the researchers of *mores et instituta*. Moreover, most seventeenth-century scholars had used statues, reliefs, paintings, coins and objects of material culture indiscriminately as historical documents. There is good reason to believe that the unprecedented concentration on painting, which made

FIG. 13. **Bacchic relief.** Archivio di Stato di Firenze, Carteggio d'artisti, vol. 17, 111v. *(Reproduced courtesy of the Ministero per i Beni e le Attività Culturali. All further reproduction is prohibited.)*

itself felt from the later seventeenth century onwards, made scholars more aware of stylistic changes, and thus contributed to the revolution in archaeological method that took place a few decades later.

APPENDIX

DISCOVERIES FROM EXCAVATIONS IN AND NEAR ROME AS DOCUMENTED BY LEONARDO AGOSTINI 1641–74

The following notes, intended to supplement older publications of seventeenth-century *memorie di scavi*, are taken from Agostini's letters to Francesco Barberini (BAV, Barb. Lat. 6455), Carlo di Tomaso Strozzi in Florence (ASF, Carte Strozziane) and Leopoldo de' Medici and his agents, including Strozzi (ASF, Carteggio d'artisti vol. 17). All letters were written from Rome. In what follows, Agostini's references to his own and others' discoveries have been recorded fully, except for coins and medals. His emphasis on inscriptions when writing to Strozzi is due to the latter's interest in

epigraphic material. The passages quoted verbatim have preserved Agostini's often incorrect and inconsistent spelling, although punctuation has been added for the sake of clarity. Another comprehensive account of Roman excavations during the third quarter of the seventeenth century was compiled by Pietro Santi Bartoli and published by Carlo Fea in his *Miscellanea* of 1790. While Bartoli may have used older notes, the final redaction of his text dates from 1682. Unlike Agostini, he does not seem to have written as an eyewitness to many of the discoveries he recorded. Hence, when speaking about the same events, Agostini's reports are often more precise than Bartoli's, whose indications have, none the less, been taken into consideration in the footnotes.

(1) **23 March 1641.** ASF, Carte Strozziane s. III, vol. 158, fol. 1r. In a vineyard at the Porta San Sebastiano, a certain Antonio had found 'alcuno cassettello' ('some small caskets') that had short funerary inscriptions (probably cinerary urns), which were bought by a Genoese gentleman.[93]

Previously two wonderful heads had been found in the

FIG. 14. Statue of Cupid and Psyche. Florence, Uffizi. Deutsches Archäologisches Institut, Rome, neg. no. 72.138. *(Reproduced courtesy of the Deutsches Archäologisches Institut, Rome.)*

FIG. 15. Metal lamp in the form of a ship with Peter and Paul (Florence, Museo Archeologico). From P.S. Bartoli and G.P. Bellori, *Le antiche lucerne sepolcrali figurate* III (Rome, 1691). *(Reproduced courtesy of the Bibliotheca Hertziana.)*

same place. Since Francesco Barberini had not wanted them, they had been acquired by Cardinal Antonio Barberini. 'Sono state riconosciute da me una per Cicerone et perche l'altra è similiss. et erono tutte in una buca ò fatto la consequenza che sia Quinto suo fratello' ('One of them I recognized as being of Cicero. Since the other one looks so similar and they were both from the same spot, I concluded that the second must be of Quintus, Cicero's brother').[94]

Two cinerary urns had been discovered at the Porta Latina. One of them had a round shape and some letters inscribed on it. On its lid an animal was sculpted, which Agostini could not identify. The other one was square and had ornamental leaves and birds. An inscription was engraved upon it.[95]

(2) **6 April 1641.** ASF, Carte Strozziane s. III, vol. 158, fol. 3r. On the previous day, Agostini had been to the excavation of M. Antonio at the Porta Latina, where he bought 'alcune scrittioncelle' ('some inscriptions').

Afterwards he had visited the excavation 'di quell sacerdote mio amico' ('of that priest, my friend') outside the

Porta Latina, where he had seen an inscription on a curved piece of marble with sculpted figures around it.

(3) **24 August 1641.** ASF, Carte Strozziane s. III, vol. 158, fol. 117r. Agostini had heard about an inscription found at an excavation at the Porta Portuensis and of another one at the riverside next to San Paolo, thus far only partially unearthed.

(4) **16 April 1646.** BAV, Barb. Lat. 6455, fols 99r–v. Discoveries of the previous week had included some iron instruments that, Agostini thought, had been used to torture early Christian martyrs.

Excavations at Piazza di Pietra had brought to light 'gran pezzi di marmi con bassi rilievi del tempio quivi vicino d'Antonino' ('large pieces of marble with bas-reliefs from the nearby Temple of Antoninus').[96]

In the garden of the hospital at San Giovanni in Laterano, where Marchese del Bufalo was in charge of an excavation, a temple with numerous columns and seven statues had been brought to light.[97]

At Castel di Guido, formerly a famous villa of Antoninus Pius known as Loria, Mons. Vaij had discovered 'una statua a cavallo sopra un leone, che à mio credere è Faustina, che si trova la medaglia in quel modo' ('a figure mounted on a lion, which I believe to be Faustina, who is found on medals in that manner').[98] At the same time, two heads, one of Commodus, the other of Lucius Verus, and three beautiful busts, one of alabaster, had been found.[99]

In an excavation outside the Porta Maggiore, Cavaliere Altieri had unearthed a startling sarcophagus with historical reliefs (an object Agostini had not yet seen).[100]

Excavations at San Lorenzo fuori le mura had led to the discovery of a Christian cemetery with wonderful relics, thus far untouched by excavators.

(5) 16 July 1646. BAV, Barb. Lat. 6455, fol. 102r. An ancient 5 lb weight had been found in an excavation at the Porta San Sebastiano on 10 July. It was inscribed: EX [two letters missing] AVC · Q IVNII / RVSTICI PRIV (not in *CIL*). A drawing of this object was given in the letter.

(6) 7 October 1649. BAV, Barb. Lat. 6455, fol. 105r. Agostini sent a drawing showing a recently discovered metal lamp: 'è curiosa per aver il segnio di Constantino et una croce che sostiene detta lucerna con tre catenelle' ('it is unusual because it has the mark of Constantine and a cross that supports the lamp by means of three chains').[101]

Two other drawings represented the heads of Saints Peter and Paul, the latter damaged when it was uncovered at Santa Priscilla. According to Agostini, the first (?) was used as the mark of a soldier whose name appears to be written upon it.

(7) 29 October 1651. ASF, Carteggio d'artisti vol. 17, fol. 5r. 'Si è trovato una belliss. figurina vestita di un putto

in abito consolare che a mio credere potrebbe esser uno de nepoti di Augusto Caio ò Lucio. Gli manca la testa, una mano et i piedi. E di altezza palmi 4, e di questa pietra nobiliss. che si chiama egittia di color verde scuro.' ('A most beautiful figurine was found, a boy in consular dress who I believe could be one of the grandsons of Augustus, Gaius or Lucius. It is missing its head, a hand and the feet. It is 4 *palmi* in height and made from a very noble stone, which is called Egyptian, and is of dark green colour.')[102]

(8) 8 September 1652. ASF, Carte Strozziane s. III, vol. 184, fol. 6v. On this morning Francesco Gualdi had gone to see Agostini at his excavation and bought two capitals, which he wanted to present to the Capitol.[103]

(9) 19 October 1652. ASF, Carte Strozziane s. III, vol. 184, fol. 10v. During his excavation, Agostini had found the torso of a nude male figure, 'di rarissima maniera' ('of a most rare style'). He was confident of making further discoveries, since more than half of the 'room' remained to be exposed.

(10) 16 November 1652. ASF, Carte Strozziane s. III, vol. 184, fol. 12v. At his excavation Agostini had discovered earlier the same day 'un pezzo di colonna di fior di persicho assai bella' ('a fragment of a very beautiful column of *fior di persico*').

Don Lelio Orsini had taken possession of the aforementioned 'torso di homo nudo di maniera greca' ('torso of a naked man in the Greek style') (see no. 9).

(11) 30 November 1652. ASF, Carte Strozziane s. III, vol. 184, fol. 13r. At Agostini's excavation a beautiful dog, missing its head and legs, and a granite column 18 *palmi* in height had been discovered. Furthermore, there were 'molti pietre minute di porfido serpentina et altri mischi che facevano pavimento di stanze' ('many minute fragments of serpentine porphyry and various other types of stone that formed the floor of rooms').

(12) 7 December 1652. ASF, Carte Strozziane s. III, vol. 184, fol. 14v. In his excavation Agostini had discovered the pavement of a room (see also no. 11), a green table slab measuring 5 x 3 *palmi*, a granite column and the marble head of a ram.

(13) 21 December 1652. ASF, Carte Strozziane s. III, vol. 184, fol. 16r. On the previous day, Agostini's excavation had brought to light the statue of a faun, 5.5 *palmi* in height, but missing its legs and half of its arms. He also had found the other half of the 'column of *fior di persico*' (see no. 10) with its Corinthian capital, measuring 14 *palmi*.

(14) 28 December 1652. ASF, Carte Strozziane s. III, vol. 184, fol. 19v. On this morning, Agostini had discovered a beautiful statuette of Mercury, measuring 1 *palmo*, at his excavation. It would enter the collection of Lelio Orsini. He also had found five fragments of coloured stone from an altar 'di metallo corintio' dedicated to Bacchus.

(15) 3 January 1653. ASF, Carte Strozziane s. III, vol. 184, fol. 27r. During the previous two days, Agostini had discovered five beautiful statues: a Minerva, 8 *palmi* high, a group of two figures of 4.5 *palmi* each, another figure of 4 *palmi* and a wonderful bull, 'tutti di rarissima maniera e beniss. conservati et di marmi' ('all in a most rare style, very well preserved and of marble'). They were to be taken to the palace of Lelio Orsini at Pasquino.

(16) 11 January 1653. ASF, Carte Strozziane s. III, vol. 184, fol. 28r. The statues mentioned in no. 15 were still at Agostini's excavation. The day before, Pietro da Cortona had gone to see them and had been much enamoured of them, in particular the statue of a 'zittella tutta ammantata, che tiene nelle mani una colomba … e intera conservation et non gli mancha solo che mezzo braccio, che spero di trovarlo in breve giorni' ('a young girl completely cloaked, who holds a dove in her hands … and completely preserved, missing only half an arm, which I hope to find in the next few days'). He also had found a fragment of a male head and the leg of a youth during the previous week.

'I pavimenti delle stanze [see no. 11] sono di porfido serpentino et giallo, et ne ho tratto la quantita che si potrebbe farne qual cosa per che ci sono de pezzi assai grandetti.' ('The floors of the rooms are of serpentine porphyry and giallo, and I have taken out such a quantity that it could be put to different use, because there are rather large pieces among it.')

(17) 18 January 1653. ASF, Carte Strozziane s. III, vol. 184, fol. 32r. At his excavation Agostini had found a pedestal with four feet.

(18) 25 January 1653. ASF, Carte Strozziane s. III, vol. 184, fols 33v–34r. 'Questa settimana e stato ritrovato fuora della Porta di santo Sebastiano un pilo di marmo storiato grandiss. nel quale sono cose belliss. di lontananze, di città torri, con figurine dentro galere, barchette con infinite cose, che per non esser ancora uscito del suo letto non ho possuto ben considerare, la maniera non e tanto rara per che si vede la maestria dei tempi di Constantino, ma la diligenza e indicibile, perche le figure grandi come piccole sono tutte staccate in aria. Sara del Sig.r Card.l Barberino, per che la vignia e di un suo servitore, il quale e fratello del Sig.r Angelo Paracciani.' ('This week a large sarcophagus with historical

reliefs was found outside the Porta San Sebastiano. In its reliefs, one sees the most beautiful things, such as landscapes, cities, towers, figures inside galleys, boats and infinite things that, since it has not yet been removed from its bedding, I have been unable to study. The style is not particularly rare because one can see the mastery of the Constantinian age, but its diligence is inexpressible, because both large and small figures completely stand out in the air. It will be given to the Sig.r Card.l Barberini since the vineyard belongs to one of his servants, the brother of Sig.r Angelo Paracciani.')[104]

(19) 15 February 1653. ASF, Carte Strozziane s. III, vol. 184, fol. 37v. In his own excavation Agostini had found half a column of *fior di persico* that belonged with a fragment he had discovered many weeks before (see nos. 10 and 13).

(20) 8 March 1653. ASF, Carte Strozziane s. III, vol. 184, fol. 41r. In his excavation a head with bust had come to light, which Agostini identified as being of L. Iunius Brutus ('quello che scacciò i Tarquini' ('the one who overthrew the Tarquins')).

(21) 10 May 1653. ASF, Carte Strozziane s. III, vol. 184, fol. 57r. In Agostini's excavation, a fragment of an architrave, 11 *palmi* long, had been discovered. On it, parts of an inscription were legible: ... ECTVS BIS CONSVL ORD SQVALORE SVMMOTO.[105] Two days previously, Agostini also had found 'una statua di donna vestita di boniss. maniera. Et era vicino à un muro dove sono due nicchie fatte con molto garbo et si vede esser stato un Ninfeo per che ci si conosce giochi di aqua et erono fatte di musaicho et incrostate di pietre miste' ('a statue of a dressed woman of the best style. And it was near a wall where there are two graceful niches and it is clear that this was a nymphaeum because water games can be recognized and they were made of mosaic and encrusted with various stones'). He intended to tear down these structures.

(22) 17 May 1653. ASF, Carte Strozziane s. III, vol. 184, fol. 58r. The female statue mentioned above (no. 21) had not required any restoration. He also had discovered a drunken Hercules leaning on a faun, a column of 'affricano' marble 20 *palmi* in height, and another fragment of the architrave (see no. 21). Meanwhile, six niches belonging to the structure (see no. 21) had been unearthed.

(23) 24 May 1653. ASF, Carte Strozziane s. III, vol. 184, fol. 59r. Additional fragments of the architrave (see nos. 21–2) had come to light. Although still incomplete, the

inscription now read: PETRONIVS MAXIMVS IIII PRAEF / ECTVS BIS CONSVL ORD SQVALORE SVMMOTO ... (*CIL* VI (1) 1197).

(24) 21 June 1653. ASF, Carte Strozziane s. III, vol. 184, fol. 61r. Agostini had found two figures of Muses, one of them a torso representing not more than half of the original statue, the other one complete and 9 *palmi* in height, holding an instrument in its hand, 'maniera rarissima' ('of an unusual style'). The previous day he had discovered 'due pezzi di cornicione intagliate mirabiliss. di marmo' ('two pieces of marvellously carved marble cornice').

(25) 5 July 1653. ASF, Carte Strozziane s. III, vol. 184, fol. 72r. In his excavation Agostini had come across a fluted column of *pavonazzo*, 22 *palmi* tall, but broken into two pieces.

(26) 20 December 1653. ASF, Carte Strozziane s. III, vol. 184, fol. 76r. Agostini was now leading a promising excavation 'in luogo di belle rovine' ('in a site of beautiful ruins'). Some subterranean chambers had been discovered on this site.[106]

(27) 20 June 1654. ASF, Carte Strozziane s. III, vol. 163, fols 33v–34r. At the site where Agostini had found the inscription of Petronius Maximus (see nos. 21–3), he kept finding 'sempre qualche curiosita' ('always another curiosity'). The previous Saturday, he had discovered 'una belliss. testa di Alessandro Magnio simigliantiss. a un belliss. intaglio che mi ritrovo in pietra ametista di singolar bellezza' ('a beautiful head of Alexander the Great, most similar to a gem of amethyst stone of particular beauty that is in my own possession').[107]

In the countryside outside the Porta San Giovanni, the inscription D.M. DASVMIAE SOTERIDI LIBERTAE ... (*CIL* VI (3) 16753) had been discovered, together with a beautiful marble sarcophagus and the head of a cupid. Since there had been indications that the spot was formerly a family tomb, excavations were to continue.

(28) 1 August 1654. ASF, Carte Strozziane s. III, vol. 163, fol. 39r. 'Alla cava nelle scale del suo palazzo [the palace of Francesco Barberini], le quale sono large 10 palmi, nelle rovine vi ho trovato li due beliss. basi rilevi d'ermafroditi e due statue intere grandi, 3 colonne di marmo canelate con capitelli d'ordine doria, una testa del magnio Alessandro, serva li altri fragmenti. Spero d'altre cose per che non sono ancora alla meta d'esse, e poi mi resta il palazzo havendo in sino à ora cavato nelle bagni e altre delitie.' ('In the excavation in the stairs of his palace, which are 10 *palmi* wide, in

the ruins there I found two beautiful bas-reliefs of hermaphrodites and two large and intact statues, three fluted marble columns with capitals of the Doric order, a head of Alexander the Great, amongst other fragments. I hope for other things because I am not yet half-way through, and then there remains the palace, having up to now excavated in the baths and other delightful things.')[108]

Inside the Porta San Sebastiano, in the second vineyard, the inscription IVLIA ELATE FECIT ZETHO … (*CIL* VI (3) 20433) had been found.

(29) 15 August 1654. ASF, Carte Strozziane s. III, vol. 163, fol. 43r. Agostini announced the discovery of 48 inscriptions, but did not indicate their provenance.

In his own excavation the torso of a small faun had been unearthed.

(30) 17 December 1654. ASF, Carte Strozziane s. III, vol. 184, fol. 79r. Agostini had found a damaged head of Minerva. Otherwise his current excavation had not produced good results, 'la terra essendo ormai tante volte crivellata' ('the earth by now having been gone over many times').

(31) 27 February 1655. ASF, Carte Strozziane s. III, vol. 163, fol. 82r. A beautiful imperial bust had been brought to light in Agostini's excavation.

(32) 22 May 1655. ASF, Carte Strozziane s. III, vol. 163, fol. 95r. Agostini recalled the 'beliss. Minerva' ('beautiful Minerva') that he had discovered the day that Alexander VII (probably before his election to the papacy) had come to see his excavation.

(33) 24 July 1655. ASF, Carte Strozziane s. III, vol. 163, fol. 106v. At the Gesù, one female statue and another missing its head and half its arms had been discovered. The pope had ordered them to be restored for his garden on the Quirinal.

(34) 14 August 1655. ASF, Carte Strozziane s. III, vol. 163, fol. 113r. In his own excavation, Agostini had found nothing for quite a while, but he intended to return soon to the site of Petronius Maximus (see no. 23).

The pope had given orders to restore the pyramid of Cestius.[109]

(35) 16 September 1655. ASF, Carte Strozziane s. III, vol. 163, fol. 124r. Agostini sent to Strozzi a copy of an inscription (see fol. 125r = *CIL* VI (2) 9405) found in a vineyard at San Cesareo close to the Porta San Sebastiano.

(36) 18 September 1655. ASF, Carte Strozziane s. III, vol. 163, fols 129r–v. The pyramid of Cestius had been unearthed down to the lower edge of its revetments. A tomb chamber with 'diverse pitture grottesce, rabeschi et altre curiosita' ('various grotesque paintings, arabesques and other curiosities') had been found inside. An outstanding Corinthian column of Carrara marble, 30 *palmi* high, had been unearthed at a distance of 10 *palmi* from the north-eastern corner of the pyramid. Agostini thought that it had served to carry the bronze statue of Gaius Cestius himself. A foot of this statue and its base had survived. A copy of the inscription on this base (M. VALERIVS MESSALLA CORVINVS … = *CIL* VI (1) 1375b) accompanied the letter (see fol. 130r).[110]

(37) 27 September 1655. ASF, Carte Strozziane s. III, vol. 163, fol. 133r. Close to the pyramid the excavators had hit a 'bel tempietto fatto tutto di mattoncini arrotati' ('a beautiful little tempietto constructed entirely in polished bricks').

In his own excavation, Agostini had discovered a 'testa di una donna di basso relievo di assai bon garbo' ('head of a woman in bas-relief of very graceful form'). Nevertheless, he was looking for a more promising site.

(38) 22 January 1656. ASF, Carte Strozziane s. III, vol. 163, fols 134r–v. Outside the Porta San Paolo an armed imperial statue, 12 *palmi* high, had been discovered. Agostini was taking care of its restoration, since the pope wanted to set it up together with those found at the pyramid.[111]

At the pyramid another column had been discovered. The tempietto (see no. 37) had been completely unearthed.

(39) 25 March 1656. ASF, Carte Strozziane s. III, vol. 184, fol. 80r. The pope had commissioned Agostini to search the catacombs for the bodies of saints, a campaign that was supposed to continue for a few weeks. Even in these holy places he had come across coins and other 'galanterie' ('beautiful objects'), in particular a precious cup of agate. All these discoveries, including the *medaglione* ('huge medal') he found, had become papal property.

The restoration of the pyramid (see nos. 36–8) was continuing.

His own excavation had not revealed anything noteworthy, but he hoped to return to the site of Petronius Maximus (see no. 23) within a few days.

(40) 27 May 1656. ASF, Carte Strozziane s. III, vol. 163, fol. 136r. Agostini had been ordered to excavate the cemetery of San Ciriaco in Agro Verano in order to find the relics of martyrs.[112]

(41) 16 September 1656. ASF, Carte Strozziane s. III, vol. 163, fol. 151r. In the preceding days, Agostini had gone to the excavation of an unnamed gentleman in order to unearth two octagonal columns of oriental alabaster, one of them entirely preserved, the other broken. The excavator had hidden them with fraudulent intentions.

An inscription copied here (see fol. 152r = *CIL* VI (2) 10701) had been found in a vineyard at San Sebastiano.

(42) 7 October 1656. ASF, Carte Strozziane s. III, vol. 163, fol. 167r. 'Ho cominciato una cava nel Foro Romano vicino alla Chiesa della Consolatione. Trovo ogni cosa incendiata con molta quantita di marmi ridotti quasi in polvere, con un belliss. pavimento di pietre africane gialli che vado pensando che ivi possi esser stato il Tempio di Augusto fatto in honore di Cesare.' ('I have started an excavation in the Roman Forum near to the Church of the Consolation. I find everything burnt and a great quantity of marble reduced almost to dust, with a beautiful pavement of yellow African stones that make me think that this may be the temple built by Augustus in honour of Caesar.')[113]

'Di questa settimana cavandosi vicino all' Anfiteatro et alla Curia Hostilia si è trovata una belliss. colonna di giallo di palmi 13.' ('Excavating near the amphitheatre and the Curia Hostilia this week a beautiful column of yellow marble was found, 13 *palmi* in height.')[114]

Another excavation took place next to the Porta San Sebastiano.

(43) 29 December 1656. ASF, Carte Strozziane s. III, vol. 163, fol. 172r. Agostini had led an excavation close to Santa Cecilia in Trastevere, where many 'curiosità di metallo' ('curiosities of metal') had been found and taken to the pope.

'Di presente si e trovata fuora di Porta Maggiore una beliss. statua di Clodio Albino di palmi undici nudo con paludamento è parazzonio nella sinistra in atto di far parlamento all' esercito. Nel tronco che si appoggia la statua vi è scolpito un bel cornucopio pieno di vari frutti, che allude alla sua medaglia con SAECVLO FRVGIFERO.' ('Up to now, outside the Porta Maggiore, a beautiful statue of Claudius Albinus has been found, 11 *palmi* high, nude except for the *paludamentum* and with a short sword in his left hand, who is about to speak to his troops. On the trunk that supports the statue there is carved a beautiful cornucopia full of different fruits, which alludes to his medal with SAECVLO FRVGIFERO.')[115] Agostini signalled this discovery to Alexander VII, who was supposed to grant the present owner a licence to sell the statue, unless Alexander wanted it for himself.

(44) 30 November 1657. ASF, Carte Strozziane s. III, vol. 184, fol. 91r. 'Quest autunno la cava di Castello non à

dato cosa di rilevo, solo che ho scoperto il teatro della Villa Domiziana con alzato di 23 scalini. Ho riconosciuto la pianta della scena, che i marmi di essa superbamente intagliate dimonstrano la magnificentia di essa, si come ancora ho riconosciuto l'habitatione dell'Imperatore, l'Ipodromo, lo Stadio, il portico et il Castro Pretorio, ogni cosa adeguata alla medesima magnificentia.' ('This autumn the excavation of Castello has not produced much of interest, only my discovery of the theatre of the Villa Domiziana with its elevation of 23 steps. I recognized the plan of the scena, the magnificence of which is demonstrated by the superbly carved marbles, just as I identified the residence of the emperor, the hippodrome, the stadium, the portico and the Castrum Praetorium, each one having the same magnificence.')[116] Agostini had commissioned a ground-plan of these structures, the final copy of which, however, had been delayed by the fact that Signor Galestruzzi (to whom the work had been entrusted) was presently employed engraving the stage sets for a comedy commissioned by Cardinal Barberini in honour of Queen Christina.[117]

(45) 1657. ASF, Carte Strozziane s. III, vol. 163, fol. 82b. This letter included a drawing of a lead pipe, inscribed IMP CAESAR DOMITIANI AVG ... (*CIL* XIV 2304), found at Castel Gandolfo in 1657.[118]

(46) 23 January 1658. ASF, Carte Strozziane s. III, vol. 184, fol. 93r. Agostini reported on the coins discovered in the catacomb of Priscilla outside the Porta Salaria.

At this time, many finds were being bought by the agents of Cardinal Massimo.

(47) 6 April 1658. ASF, Carte Strozziane s. III, vol. 184, fol. 95r. While Agostini's own excavation had brought nothing noteworthy to light, new coins had been discovered in the catacombs, where he had also found 'un basso rilevo di metallo che contiene una lupa con i gemelli, et si è trovato ancora alcuni uccelli di musaico finiss. in detti cimiteri et alcune statuette di metallo' ('a bas-relief in metal that depicts a she-wolf with the twins, and also discovered in the said cemetery have been several birds in the finest mosaic-work and several metal statuettes'). These discoveries had been taken to Agostini's own house in order to be cleaned.

In Agostini's excavation at Campo Vaccino fragments of a statue had been found in a wall. On 20 April (fol. 105r) he showed himself disappointed by the results of this dig.[119]

(48) 20 September 1659. ASF, Carte Strozziane s. III, vol. 163, fol. 186r. In an excavation close to Agostini's, two columns of *verde antico*, 16 *palmi* high, had been discovered. They were acquired by the pope and taken to San

Giovanni in Laterano, where another fourteen columns of the same type existed. Agostini had been ordered to find as many columns of the same stone as possible.[120]

(49) 4 October 1659. ASF, Carte Strozziane s. III, vol. 184, fol. 114r. At the excavation on the Esquiline Hill, where the two columns of green marble had been found previously (see no. 48), three pieces of a column of oriental alabaster had now come to light.

(50) 26 May 1660. ASF, Carte Strozziane s. III, vol. 163, fol. 216r. The fathers of San Pietro in Vincoli had been organizing an excavation at this time.[121]

Agostini had led an excavation at the Porta Portuensis where he had found a 'campanella antica … con una patera, un bacciletto et un vaso' ('ancient bell … with a patera, a small basin and a vase'). A mosaic with a club seemed to indicate that the site had once been a temple of Hercules. Indeed, three years previously a marble statue, 3 *palmi* in height and inscribed on its pedestal HERCVLI INVICTO SAC(R)VM M CLAVDIVS ESYCHVS DD (*CIL* VI (4.2) 30736), now in Agostini's collection, had been found in the same place together with an inscribed club, probably a votive offering, which he gave to Bellori.[122]

(51) 26 May 1660. ASF, Carteggio d'artisti vol. 17, fol. 34r. Agostini had sent copies of six inscriptions found 'in questi giorni nelle rovine delle Terme di Tito dove sono gli horti dei Padri di S. Pietro in Vincola nell'Esquilie' ('recently in the ruins of the Baths of Titus where the orchards of the priests of San Pietro in Vincola on the Esquiline are located').

(52) 31 July 1660. ASF, Carte Strozziane s. III, vol. 183, fol. 29r. In Agostini's excavation, a beautiful female bust, probably of Lucilla when she was a girl, had been discovered recently.

(53) 27 August 1660. ASF, Carte Strozziane s. III, vol. 184, fol. 124r. The previous Tuesday Agostini had taken a female statue, 11 *palmi* high but without its head, to the (papal) garden at Monte Cavallo. It had been found 12 miles from Rome on the Via Flaminia.

'Nel giardino del S.r Duca Mattei nel Monte Palatino contiguo a quello del Ser.mo di Parma et alla Vigna di Mons.r Roncioni, dove fu ritrovato l'Ercole che sta nel cortile di Pitti, e stato trovato due beliss. statue. Una rappresenta l'Antinoo, che sta in Belvedere a S.to Pietro, l'altra perche non ha testa non si conosce.' ('Two beautiful statues were found in the garden of S.r Duca Mattei on the Palatine Hill next to that of the Ser.mo di Parma and to the vineyard of Mons.r Roncioni,

where the Hercules that stands in the courtyard of the Palazzo Pitti was found. One represents the same Antinous, whose statue stands in the Belvedere at Saint Peter's, the other is unrecognizable because it does not have a head.')[123]

(54) 28 August 1660. ASF, Carte Strozziane s. III, vol. 183, fol. 36r. 'Delle cave ho che dirgli solo che à Porta Portuense trovo molte vetture di forma grandissima tutte rotte per causa che ne tempi posteriorici havevon fabbricato sopra. Mi e' capitato una testa di marmo ritratto incognito mediocremente bona, gli manca naso.' ('Of the excavations, I have to say only that at the Porta Portuense many large blocks of marble were found, all broken due to having been built upon in more recent times. I came across a quite good marble head of an unknown person, which is missing its nose.')

(55) 24 December 1660. ASF, Carte Strozziane s. III, vol. 184, fol. 125r. Agostini had unearthed a statue of travertine that would be set up above the colonnades of Piazza San Pietro.[124]

(56) 3 July 1661. ASF, Carte Strozziane s. III, vol. 183, fol. 55r. In the garden of the 'Moniche Barberini in capo alla valle Quirinale' ('Barberini nuns at the top of the Quirinal valley') excavations had been going on for two years. Great quantities of travertine had been discovered in this place, along with columns, either entirely preserved or broken, together with their capitals and bases. The day before Agostini had chosen fourteen beautiful columns of different orders for Cardinal Antonio Barberini. Statues had not been found, since the buildings unearthed dated from late antiquity and older ones could be seen below their ruins.[125]

(57) 17 December 1661. ASF, Carte Strozziane s. III, vol. 183, fol. 69r. At this time, Agostini was cleaning 'un belliss. toretto di metallo di N(ostro] S[ignore] ritrovato alle grotte de martiri con occasione che si cava li corpi santi' ('a beautiful metal bull, property of Our Lord [the pope] found in the grottoes of the martyrs on the occasion of the excavation of the holy bodies').

He intended to begin an excavation at the Colosseum the following Monday.

(58) 15 April 1662. ASF, Carte Strozziane s. III, vol. 183, fols 73r–v. In February, 'in un orto sopra la Suburra sito del S.r Abb. Santarelli' ('in an orchard above the Suburra site of S.r Abb. Santarelli'), a statue of Ganymede had been discovered. Except for the head of the eagle and the tip of the boy's right foot, it had been undamaged. At that time, it was being kept by the abbot.[126]

A few days later, in a vineyard belonging to the nuns of San Sisto del Monte Magnanapoli close to the Terme Antoniniane, a beautiful statue of Minerva had been unearthed. Its head was missing, but it had a long stola extending to the feet and showing her battles with Hercules — 'le figurine sono non più di mezzo dito, sono tanto ben fatte che di cera non si farebbe più questa oggi' ('the figures are not more than half a finger in height, but so well made that, even using wax, one could not match it nowadays').[127]

Agostini himself had found a beautiful head of Trajan, and a small metal statuette of a urinating Hercules, 'maniera bellissima' ('of most beautiful style'), half a *palmo* high, with its ancient base. Furthermore, he had discovered a metal statuette of Venus, eight metal lamps, two paterae, a buckle, the head of an ox, the head of a bull 'con coltello da sacrifitio' ('with sacrificial knife'), and a soldier injuring another.

At an excavation next to San Sebastiano, an inscription was said to have been found.

(59) 1 July 1662. ASF, Carte Strozziane s. III, vol. 184, fol. 127r. For six months he had been excavating around the Colosseum but had not made any significant discovery.

According to S.r Cennini, a beautiful relief with twelve figures representing the Muses [sic!] had been unearthed during preparation for the foundations for the colonnades of Piazza San Pietro.[128]

(60) 18 November 1662. ASF, Carte Strozziane s. III, vol. 183, fol. 65r. New discoveries made in the countryside had had to be inspected by Agostini for Cardinal Chigi.

Two inscriptions copied here (fol. 66r = *CIL* VI (1) 771–2) were found at San Cesareo.

(61) 8 December 1662. ASF, Carte Strozziane s. III, vol. 183, fols 62r–v. The pope now was restoring the Pantheon. All houses attached to it had been torn down 'in sino a mezza strada che conduce alla Minerva' ('up to halfway along the street that leads to the Minerva'). Since two columns had been missing from the portico, an excavation had begun in Piazza San Luigi, where in fact two columns, corresponding in material and size, though each broken into three pieces, had been discovered. They had been taken to the Pantheon, where they would be restored and put into place. It seemed obvious that for the refurbishing of the Pantheon, 250 *cassate* of marble would be insufficient. Accordingly, the pope had given orders for the ruins inside and outside the city to be searched for building materials.[129]

In Piazza San Luigi another column of *pavonazzo*, 4.5 *palmi* in diameter but broken into two pieces and lacking its collar ('colarino'), was also discovered.[130]

The church of Santo Stefano in Truglio had been demolished. Excavations at the same site had brought to light four huge marble reliefs, two of them with trophies and arms, the other two with female figures representing provinces.[131]

Another four reliefs similar to these had been unearthed in the foundations underneath the houses next to the Pantheon, which had been taken down recently. It seems that in late antiquity these reliefs had been brought here from the 'Basilica di Antonino', remains of which could still be seen in Piazza di Pietra. Further reliefs from the same group had survived in the Palazzo Farnese, where they had been placed under Paul III.[132]

At this time, excavations were taking place in the Piazza della Rotonda, the ancient travertine level of which had been discovered 10 or 12 feet below its modern surface. The old fountain was supposed to be set up in the middle of the new Piazza.

The previous week, while working on the foundations of their seminary on the side facing the 'Basilica di Antonino', the Jesuit fathers had found another marble relief similar to those mentioned, 'con un belliss. trofeo et arme di quelli re soggiogati dalli imperatori Antonino e Marco Aurelio' ('with a beautiful trophy and the arms of those kings subjugated by the Emperors Antoninus and Marcus Aurelius').[133]

The Arco di Portogallo had been destroyed and its reliefs taken to the Capitol.[134]

Further excavations in two vineyards close to San Paolo had brought to light 'belliss. marmi intagliati con varij trofei et festoni tanto divinamente fatti che e' una maraviglia' ('beautiful pieces of marble carved with different trophies and festoons so divinely made that they are a marvel'). They derived from the tomb of a noble family. Two inscriptions included here (fol. 63r), M. ULPIO AVG. LIB. PHILOTAE (*CIL* VI (2) 8553) and DORM. VERATIVS MACER … (*CIL* VI (4) 28540), had been found in the same place, as had been the beautiful statue of Minerva (see no. 58).[135]

Agostini himself had been digging close to the Navicella, next to the street leading to San Giovanni (in Laterano), where he had found the head of a philosopher and a small figure of a consul on a 'sella curulis'.

In the countryside, an Egyptian animal sculpture similar to those at the foot of the stairs leading up the Capitol had been discovered a few days earlier.[136]

(62) 27 January 1663. ASF, Carte Strozziane s. III, vol. 183, fol. 83r. In Piazza San Luigi a beautiful composite capital that belonged to the *pavonazzo* column (see no. 61) had been found. It was decorated with sixteen figures, one of them a gladiator, 'cosa in vero non più veduta al mio tempo' ('something, in truth, never seen in my time').[137]

In an excavation 'above the Colosseum' four statues and

a beautiful bust of a philosopher had been discovered the previous week. Another bust had come to light only the day before.

As for his own excavation, there was little to report.

(63) 5 January 1664. ASF, Carte Strozziane s. III, vol. 205, fol. 68r. 'Sono gia tre mesi spirati che fo cavare nella piazza di Santo Gregorio e non trovo altro che travertini assai grossi, che alla struttura si vede era un portico, che seguitava longo la strada è si conosce faceva fronte al Settizonio di Settimio Sèvero … In questa cava dico si trovo pochi giorni sono una medaglia di oro dell' Imperatore Valentiniano … quale fu data a NS. come suo tributo. Si trova una belliss. selciata sotto 11 palmi, che fu fatta in tempo di Constantino, [quando] fece derizare il suo Arco, et sotto a detta selciata altri 9 palmi si trovano le vestigii di questo portico.' ('I have been excavating in the piazza of Santo Gregorio for three months now, and I have not found anything other than very large pieces of travertine, which it is clear came from a portico that ran along the street that is known to have faced the Septizodium of Septimius Severus … In this excavation, a few days ago was found a gold medal of the Emperor Valentinian … this was given to Our Lord, as his tribute. A beautiful paving was found at a depth of 11 *palmi* that was constructed in the time of Constantine, [when] he erected his Arch, and a further 9 *palmi* beneath this paving were the remains of this portico.')[138]

Due to bad weather and too much water in the street leading from the Colosseum, Agostini had had to postpone this campaign and instead had started excavating in the garden of San Gregorio, close to the monastery. Many years before, numerous metal statuettes acquired by Agostini for Cardinal Barberini — two of which he had kept for himself — had been found in this place.[139]

(64) 20 December 1664. ASF, Carte Strozziane s. III, vol. 205, fol. 65r. In recent days, several metal objects from ancient sacrifices, two seated philosophers 1 *palmo* in height, two griffins and a lamp had been discovered in an excavation on the Caelian Hill. By authority of his office, Agostini had had this material confiscated so that some of it could be taken to the papal palace.[140]

(65) 8 August 1665. ASF, Carte Strozziane s. III, vol. 205, fol. 67r. A few days before the fathers of San Pietro in Vincoli had discovered a magnificent statue of an emperor while excavating behind the apse of their church.[141]

(66) 4 September 1665. ASF, Carteggio d'artisti vol. 17, fol. 65r. Agostini sent drawings of two metal figures of seated philosophers about 1 *palmo* high 'trovati alla cava di un gentiluomo amico mio nel Monte Celio vicino a S.to Stefano Rotondo' ('found in the excavation of a gentleman-friend of mine on the Caelian Hill near to Santo Stefano Rotondo') (see no. 64).[142] Other metal works had been discovered previously on the same site, some of which were still in Agostini's own house.

(67) 12 September 1665. ASF, Carteggio d'artisti vol. 17, fol. 66r. In the garden of Santa Maria sopra Minerva, an obelisk was about to be unearthed. To judge from what could be seen already, the hieroglyphs had been cut remarkably well and the height might have been as much as 30 *palmi*. It lay at about 20 *palmi* below ground level, with its pedestal nearby. In the same garden a beautiful statue of Osiris had been found earlier, its sparrowhawk head made of the black stone that Pliny calls basalt. By September 1665 it was in the gallery of Cardinal Antonio Barberini.[143]

(68) Undated. ASF, Carteggio d'artisti vol. 17, fol. 67r. The letter included a drawing of the semi-unearthed obelisk mentioned in no. 67. A statue of black stone, which according to Agostini represented Isis, also had been discovered. The head and parts of the arms were missing; none the less, it was 10.5 *palmi* in height.[144]

(69) 10 October 1665. ASF, Carte Strozziane s. III, vol. 205, fol. 66r. In his own excavation Agostini had found nothing noteworthy. However, he did not want to give up the site, since it was a noble one that had brought to light wonderful things three years earlier.[145]

In their garden, the fathers of Santa Maria sopra Minerva had found an obelisk, a drawing of which had been sent to Principe Leopoldo, and a statue of Isis carved of black Ethiopian stone (see no. 68).

(70) 13 October 1665. ASF, Carteggio d'artisti vol. 17, fols 74r–v. In the previous days a beautiful statue of an empress, 12 *palmi* tall and dressed in a chlamys, had been discovered. It lacked only half of one arm. It had become the property of the Barberini and at that time was being restored.[146]

In Agostini's own excavation, the torso of a nude statue had been discovered the day before.

(71) 30 January 1666. ASF, Carteggio d'artisti vol. 17, fol. 89r. The excavations in the garden of Santa Maria sopra Minerva (see nos. 67–9) had brought to light several columns and the fragment of an animal that some considered a horse, but which Agostini had identified as the 'ox of Apis', worshipped by the Egyptians.

(72) 24 July 1666. ASF, Carteggio d'artisti vol. 17, fol. 99r. The previous Tuesday, in his excavation at San Gregorio, Agostini had discovered the beautiful torso of a gladiator wounded on the right side of the body, a satyr lacking its legs and a piece of a column of 'affricano di belliss. colore' ('beautifully coloured *africano*'). He had ordered all of this to be taken to the (papal) garden at Monte Cavallo.

(73) 21 August 1666. ASF, Carteggio d'artisti vol. 17, fol. 107r. In his house Agostini kept 'un Giesu Cristo fanciullo con la croce in spalla et uno uccelletto in mano, e solo mezza figura di assai buona maniera' ('a Jesus Christ as a child with the cross on his shoulders and a small bird in his hand; it is a half-figure representation only, but of very good style'). It had been discovered in the catacomb of Priscilla on the Via Salaria.

(74) 23 October 1666. ASF, Carteggio d'artisti vol. 17, fol. 120r. The previous Saturday, in a garden on the Caelian Hill, a friend of his had discovered 'un bellissimo gruppo di due figure di 5 palmi rappresentante Amore et Psiche. Sono di maravigliosa bellezza, manca solo la meta delle gambe con la base, nel resto sono belliss. conservatosi et di marmo candidissimo Pario' ('a beautiful group consisting of two figures, 5 *palmi* in height, representing Cupid and Psyche. They have a wonderful beauty, lacking only half of the legs and the base, the rest being beautifully preserved and of pure white Parian marble').[147]

This excavation had taken place at the same site where the heads of Germanicus, Antoninus, Marcus Aurelius and Pupienus, now all in the grand duke's gallery, had been discovered previously.[148]

(75) 9 November 1666. ASF, Carteggio d'artisti vol. 17, fol. 122r. 'Alli giorni passati è stato ritrovato nel Monte Aventino un bellissimo vaso tondo di marmo pario figurato intorno di Baccanti di bellissima maniera et è andato alle mani di Mons.re Massimi Patriarca di Gerusalemme.' ('In the last days a beautiful round vase of Parian marble, adorned around with Bacchants of most beautiful style, was found on the Aventine Hill. It was given to Mons.re Massimi, Patriarch of Jerusalem.')[149]

(76) 13 November 1666. ASF, Carte Strozziane s. III, vol. 205, fol. 63r. A wonderful group of statues representing Cupid and Psyche had been discovered in a garden on the Caelian Hill, which belonged to a friend of his (see also no. 74).

Some days before, during repairs to the road leading from Rome to Velletri, an oval-shaped vessel of Egyptian basalt, 8 *palmi* in length, had been found. It was now in the palace of Cardinal Chigi at the Santi Apostoli. On 4 February 1667

(fol. 78r) Agostini informed Strozzi that, at his request, a small size alabaster copy of this vessel, 2 *palmi* long, had been made.

(77) 4 February 1667. ASF, Carte Strozziane s. III, vol. 205, fol. 78r. In his excavation close to the Colosseum, Agostini had found two columns of *bardiglio*, 16 *palmi* high.

In another excavation within the same garden, a column of *portasanta*, 22 *palmi* long and 3.5 *palmi* in diameter, had been unearthed the previous week.

(78) 25 March 1667. ASF, Carteggio d'artisti vol. 17, fol. 139r. Preparing the foundations for Piazza San Pietro, a sphinx of Egyptian stone, 8 *palmi* long, had been discovered.[150]

In his friend's excavation on the Caelian Hill (see nos. 74 and 76) a new discovery had been made, that is 'una lucerna di bronzo fatto a modo di nave con due figure, una à poppa et altra a prora con l'albero et un lavaro in cima ad esso, longo più di un palmo' ('a bronze lamp made in the shape of a ship with two figures, one in the stern and the other in the prow, with a mast and a labarum at its top longer than 1 *palmo*').[151]

(79) 18 July 1667. ASF, Carteggio d'artisti vol. 17, fol. 140r. 'Alla mia cava si è trovato una stanza di stucchi assai belli di figure è grottesche.' ('In my excavation a room with quite beautiful figures and grotesques in stucco was found.')[152]

(80) 11 September 1668. ASF, Carteggio d'artisti vol. 17, fol. 148r. Agostini announced 'un disegnio di una pittura trovata alla mia cava' ('a drawing of a picture found in my excavation').[153]

(81) 25 September 1668. ASF, Carteggio d'artisti vol. 17, fol. 150r. Agostini promised to send 'il disegnio di una pittura della mia cava, rappresenta balnea Faustina' ('the drawing of a picture from my excavation, depicting the bath of Faustina').[154]

(82) 27 October 1668. ASF, Carteggio d'artisti vol. 17, fol. 153r. Ancient wall-paintings, which were being copied at the time that Agostini wrote, had been discovered in his excavation. The representations of Aeneas leaving Dido and of three dancing women were of particular beauty.[155] 'Vi sono tra uno spartimento et l'altro alcune grottesche dove si vede varie sorti di uccelli a meraviglia belli et altri animaletti et puttini, ma quello [che] fa meravigliare è una pernice.' ('There are, between one part and the other, several

grotesques where one can see different kinds of most beautiful birds and other animals and cupids, but that which makes one gasp in wonder is a partridge.')

(83) 3 November 1668. ASF, Carteggio d'artisti vol. 17, fol. 159r. Agostini gave a detailed description of the five figural paintings belonging to the discovery mentioned in no. 82. According to him, they represented Bacchus with 'two bacchants', Aeneas and Dido, a queen who was being offered a child, three women dancing, and Pallas with two companions.[156]

(84) 10 November 1668. ASF, Carteggio d'artisti vol. 17, fol. 161r. Further paintings, albeit badly preserved, had been discovered in Agostini's excavation.

(85) 18 November 1668. ASF, Carteggio d'artisti vol. 17, fol. 152r. On the day before, new paintings had been discovered in Agostini's excavation.

(86) 1 December 1668. ASF, Carteggio d'artisti vol. 17, fol. 164r. Two herms in the form of Muses wearing laurel wreaths had come to light in Agostini's excavation.

(87) 31 March 1674. ASF, Carteggio d'artisti vol. 17, fol. 245v. Agostini soon hoped to write about a 'room' discovered on the Via Flaminia some four miles from Rome and painted 'della più degna maniera antica, che si sia veduta sino al giorno d'hoggi' ('in the most dignified ancient style that has been seen to date').[157]

(88) 7 April 1674. ASF, Carteggio d'artisti vol. 17, fol. 264r. 'La sepoltura ritrovata nella Via Flaminia [see no. 87] della Famiglia Nasonia conforme che dimostra l'inscrittione trovata nella sepoltura, si comprende che è fatta ne' i tempi de' Costantini, e tutta cavata nella pietra viva che qua si chiama tufo … Questi Signori la fanno tagliare in pezzi dà quindeci in sedici operari, per condurla al' loro Palazzo.' ('The tomb of the Nasonia family found on the Via Flaminia, identified from the inscription found inside the tomb, is understood to have been built in the age of the Constantinian dynasty, and completely excavated from living stone that here is called tufa … These men have caused it to be cut into pieces by 15 or 16 workmen, in order to transfer it to their palazzo.') In addition, he sent a discussion of these paintings written by Bellori.[158]

NOTES

1. For what follows, see Biblioteca Oliveriana di Pesaro [hereafter BOP], MS 76, fols 246r–v: letter from Francesco Gottifredi to an unnamed addressee in Pesaro, 27 June 1637; also I. Herklotz, *Cassiano dal Pozzo und die Archäologie des 17. Jahrhunderts* (Munich, 1999), 56. For other contemporary accounts of this discovery, see G. Lumbroso, *Notizie sulla vita di Cassiano dal Pozzo* (Turin, 1875), 49; T. Schreiber, 'Unedirte Römische Fundberichte aus Italiänischen Archiven und Bibliotheken', *Berichte der Kgl. Sächs. Gesellschaft der Wissenschaften. Philol.-hist. Classe* (1885), 23–4; Lanciani, *Storia* (1989–), V, 140–3. For modern studies of the paintings discovered in 1639, based on seventeenth-century drawings, see B. Andreae, *Studien zur Römischen Grabkunst* (Heidelberg, 1963), 143–53, and H. Joyce, *The Decoration of Walls, Ceilings and Floors in Italy in the Second and Third Centuries A.D.* (Rome, 1981), 88–9. Both authors dated this decoration to the second quarter of the third century.

2. Lumbroso, *Cassiano dal Pozzo* (above, n. 1), 49.

3. Herklotz, *Cassiano dal Pozzo* (above, n. 1).

4. M. Vickers, 'Greek and Roman antiquities in the seventeenth century', in O. Impey and A. MacGregor (eds), *The Origins of Museums. The Cabinet of Curiosities in Sixteenth- and Seventeenth-Century Europe* (Oxford, 1985), 223–31.

5. Some of these collections are discussed in Herklotz, *Cassiano dal Pozzo* (above, n. 1), 22–9, 42–4.

6. Surveys of such sculpture galleries are provided by P. Dent Weil, 'Introduction', in O. Boselli, *Osservazioni della scultura antica* (Florence, 1978), 69–103; C. Pietrangeli, *Le collezioni private romane attraverso i tempi* (Rome, 1985); G. Daltrop, 'Antikensammlungen und Mäzenatentum um 1600 in Rom', in H. Beck and J. Schulze (eds), *Antikenrezeption im Hochbarock* (Berlin, 1989), 37–58; C. Gasparri, 'Collezioni archeologiche', in *Enciclopedia dell'arte antica classica e orientale* (2nd suppl.; Rome, 1994), 192–225; M. van der Meulen, *Rubens Copies after the Antique* I (London, 1994–5), 46–68. Studies dedicated to the specific collections mentioned here include E. Schröter, 'Der Kolossalkopf 'Alexanders des Großen' im Cortile della Pigna und andere Antiken der Villa Mattei im Vatikan', *Pantheon* 51 (1993), 101–28; K. Kalveram, *Die Antikensammlung des Kardinals Scipione Borghese* (Worms, 1995); L. Guerrini, '"Indicazioni" giustiniane (II). Di affreschi e stucchi ritrovati e perduti', *Xenia* 12 (1986), 65–96; L. Guerrini, '"Indicazioni" giustiniane (I). Di rami e statue ritrovate e perdute', in *Studi per Laura Breglia* III. *Archeologia e storia* (Rome, 1987), 165–88.

7. 'Puo servire per un Giulio Cesare, overo Augusto.' Cf. M.A. Lavin, *Seventeenth-century Barberini Documents and Inventories of Art* (New York, 1975), 73 no. 35. The nature and extent of Baroque restorations of ancient statues has been discussed by J. Montagu, *Roman Baroque Sculpture. The Industry of Art* (New Haven/London, 1989), 151–72; Kalveram, *Die Antikensammlung* (above, n. 6), 89–137; D.L. Sparti, 'Tecnica e teoria del restauro scultoreo a Roma nel

Seicento, con una verifica sulla collezione di Flavio Chigi', *Storia dell'Arte* 92 (1998), 60–131.

8. A. Bertolotti, 'L'antiquario del Papa Alessandro VII', *Il Bibliofilo* 3 (1882), 100–1; R. Barabesi, 'L'antiquario Leonardo Agostini e la sua terra di Boccheggiano', *Maremma. Bollettino della Società Maremmana* 3 (1926–7), 149–89; M. Piacentini, 'L'epistolario di Leonardo Agostini e due notizie sul Bernini', *Archivi* s. II 7 (1940), 71–80; *DBI* I, 464–5; R.T. Ridley, 'To protect the monuments: the papal antiquarian (1534–1870)', *Xenia Antiqua* 1 (1992), 117–54, esp. pp. 130–2. Several studies have been devoted to Agostini's relationship with the Medici court. See L. Giovannini, 'Notizie sulle medaglie della collezione Agostini acquistate dal Cardinale Leopoldo de' Medici', *Rivista Italiana di Numismatica e Scienze Affini* 81 (1979), 155–76; L. Giovannini (ed.), *Lettere di Ottavio Falconieri a Leopoldo de' Medici* (Florence, 1984), 202–3 n. 3; E.L. Goldberg, *Patterns in Late Medici Art Patronage* (Princeton, 1983), 104–9; Sparti, 'Tecnica e teoria del restauro' (above, n. 7), esp. pp. 90–2. See also D.L. Sparti, *La casa di Pietro da Cortona. Architettura, accademia, atelier e officina* (Rome, 1997), 105–10. Agostini's activities from 1646 to 1648 are reported by Lucas Holstenius in his letters to Francesco Barberini; see BAV, Barb. Lat. 6489, fol. 150v; Barb. Lat. 6490, fols 2r, 42r, 45r, 72r; Barb. Lat. 6492, fols 33v, 123r. The best account of Agostini's collection is provided by Philip Skippon, who was in Rome in 1664 and 1665; see 'An account of a journey made thro' part of the Low-Countries, Germany, Italy, and France', in *A Collection of Voyages and Travels, some Now First Printed from Original Manuscripts, others Now First Published in English* VI (London, 1732), 359–736, esp. pp. 678–9.

9. For his letters addressed to Francesco Barberini, see BAV, Barb. Lat. 6455, fols 98r–108v. For his letters to the Medici court in Florence, see Archivio di Stato di Firenze [hereafter ASF], Carteggio d'artisti vol. 17; for those to Carlo di Tomaso Strozzi, see ASF, Carte Strozziane s. III, vols 158, 161, 163, 183, 184, 205. Publications of this material include E. Müntz, 'Plans et monuments de Rome antique', in *Mélanges Giovanni Battista De Rossi (Supplément aux Mélanges d'Archéologie et d'Histoire de l'Art* 12) (Paris/Rome, 1892), 137–58, esp. pp. 154–8 (four letters from Carte Strozziane s. III, vol. 158); Piacentini, 'L'epistolario' (above, n. 8), 77–80 (two letters from vols 163 and 184); D. Mahon, 'Addenda to 'Seicento Studies'', *Burlington Magazine* 92 (1950), 80–1 (one letter from vol. 184); M. Mercantini, *Due disegni inediti berniniani per Piazza S. Pietro* (Città di Castello, 1981), 26–47 (seventeen letters from Carteggio d'artisti).

10. With Barberini's protection, Agostini became a member of the papal *famiglia* in June 1655. Subsequently we find him working together with the papal antiquary Nicola Menghini. He became Menghini's successor after the latter's death on 5 December 1655. The official document of his appointment is published in Lanciani, *Storia* (1989–), V, 204; see also Ridley, 'To protect the monuments' (above, n. 8), 130. For Agostini's previous services to Alexander VII, see Agostini himself in

ASF, Carte Strozziane s. III, vol. 163, 103r, and also the letters by Francesco Gottifredi in BOP, MS 76, fols 131v–132r.

11. For Cocchi's appointment on 23 August 1667, see Lanciani, *Storia* (1989–), V, 241. This document disproves the previously suggested dates for the end of Agostini's time in office; see Goldberg, *Patterns* (above, n. 8), 104, and Ridley, 'To protect the monuments' (above, n. 8), 131.

12. Lanciani, *Storia* (1989–), V, 254.

13. F. Paruta, *La Sicilia descritta con medaglie, e ristampata con aggiunta di L. Agostini* (Rome, 1649).

14. L. Agostini, *Le gemme antiche figurate* (Rome, 1657). A second part followed in 1669. The engravings are reproduced in *The Illustrated Bartsch* 46/21 (New York, 1982), 117–256. For later editions of this book, see P. Zazoff and H. Zazoff, *Gemmensammler und Gemmenforscher. Von einer Noblen Passion zur Wissenschaft* (Munich, 1987), 37–8. A rather bewildering example of Agostini's use of the archaeological material in this book is given below in n. 102. Some of the gems from Agostini's collection have been identified in the Museo Archeologico in Florence; see A. Giuliani, *I cammei della Collezione Medicea nel Museo Archeologico di Firenze* (Milan, 1989), cat. nos. 13, 18, 34, 54, 143, 157, 162, 174, 192, 212, 259 (entries by M.E. Micheli). For Galestruzzi, see P. Bellini, *Italian Masters of the Seventeenth Century (The Illustrated Bartsch* 46 — *Commentary)* (New York, 1985), 152–295. Drawings and engravings by Galestruzzi frequently accompanied Agostini's letters to Florence. See ASF, Carteggio d'artisti vol. 17, fols 36r, 46r, 65r, 111v, 112r, 130r, 182v; Carte Strozziane s. III, vol. 184, fol. 107r; see also Mercantini, *Due disegni* (above, n. 9), figs 21–3. Further references to their collaboration may be found in Carte Strozziane s. III, vol. 205, fol. 68v, and Carteggio d'artisti vol. 17, fols 28r, 36r, 45r, 110r.

15. ASF, Carte Strozziane s. III, vol. 184, fol. 95r (6 April 1658): [Bellori] '… m'è stato di non poco aiuto nelle esplicationi delle mie gemme, che nel rimanente havevo dato materia a più d'uno di ridersi delle mie debolezze come a suo tempo S.A.S. et lei vedreranno le mie scocherie' ([Bellori] '… was of more than a little help in the explanation of my gems, for the part that I had done by myself would have given cause for more than one person to laugh at my ignorance, and in time S.A.S. and you yourself may see for yourselves my ignorance'). Such emphasis on the limits of his knowledge occurs repeatedly in Agostini's letters and is indeed more than a rhetorical conceit; see also vol. 163, fols 33v, 95r; vol. 184, fols 90r, 110r, 113r. Bellori also wrote the dedication for the second part of *Gemme antiche* (above, n. 14) published in 1669, addressed to the grand duke. See ASF, Carteggio d'artisti vol. 17, fols 207r, 211r.

16. ASF, Carteggio d'artisti vol. 17, fols 254r, 271v (19 May and 1 December 1674).

17. This type of antiquary is illustrated in Goldberg, *Patterns* (above, n. 8), 91–122.

18. Agostini's inventory of the Sannesi cabinet (prior to October 1647) has survived in Bibliothèque de l'École de Médecine, Montpellier, MS H. 267, fols 46r–47v. In 1653–4, he reorgan-

ized the cabinet of the Farnese; see ASF, Carte Strozziane s. III, vol. 163, fols 30v, 33r; vol. 184, fols 52r, 55r. At the same time he also made an inventory of the cabinet of Francesco Barberini; see vol. 163, fols 34v, 65r.

19. Lavin, *Barberini Documents* (above, n. 7), 125–9, 142.

20. See Appendix, nos. 8–17, 19–25, 29, 32.

21. For Petronius Maximus, see J.R. Martindale (ed.), *The Prosopography of the Later Roman Empire* II (Cambridge, 1980), 749–51; for his forum, F.A. Bauer, 'Einige weniger bekannte Platzanlagen im spätantiken Rom', in R.L. Colella, M.J. Gill, L.A. Jenkens and P. Lamers (eds), *Pratum Romanum. Richard Krautheimer zum 100. Geburtstag* (Wiesbaden, 1997), 27–54, esp. pp. 37–41, with further bibliography.

22. P.S. Bartoli, 'Memorie di varie escavazioni', in C. Fea (ed.), *Miscellanea filologica critica e antiquaria* I (Rome, 1790), CCXXII–CCLXXIII. A statement by Cassiano dal Pozzo does not sound quite as enthusiastic: 'Ha il sig. D. Lelio Orsini fratello del Card.le in un altra cava pur poco discosto da S. Giovanni Laterano trovato marmi molto belli, dico statue, e bassi rilievi' ('Sig. D. Lelio Orsini, brother of the Cardinal, in another excavation not far from San Giovanni in Laterano, has found many beautiful marbles, such as statues and bas-reliefs'). See Österreichische Nationalbibliothek, Vienna, MS 9431, fols 76v–77r. Elsewhere Cassiano described these findings as 'cose assai gentili, e belle, come d'inscrittioni, bassi rilievi, e simili' ('rather delicate things, and beautiful, such as inscriptions, bas-reliefs and such like') (31 October 1654). See Lumbroso, *Cassiano dal Pozzo* (above, n. 1), 73.

23. ASF, Carte Strozziane s. III, vol. 184, fols 57v, 76r.

24. See the Appendix, nos. 10, 14, 15. The 'young girl' (*zitella*) mentioned in the Appendix, no. 16, was likewise later set up in Orsini's palace; ASF, Carte Strozziane s. III, vol. 184, fol. 36r. For Orsini's constant preoccupation with this excavation, see also vol. 163, fols 48v, 82r and vol. 184, fols 5r, 10v, 12v, 57r. Regrettably, little is known as to the later whereabouts of Orsini's collection. An attempt of 1659 to sell at least parts of it to Cardinal Mazarin in Paris led to trouble with the papal export restrictions. See Lanciani, *Storia* (1902–12), I, 176.

25. See the Appendix, no. 8. According to Agostini, the works Gualdi acquired were destined for the Capitol. No such donation, however, is known, whereas three capitals and other objects were given for public display to the Trinità dei Monti in the same year of 1652; see C. Franzoni and A. Tempesti, 'Il museo di Francesco Gualdi nella Roma del Seicento tra raccolta privata ed esibizione pubblica', *Bollettino d'Arte* 73 (1992), 1–42, esp. pp. 17, 19–22, with relevant archaeological literature. The two splendid Corinthian double capitals generally are thought to derive from the gardens of the Acilii on the Pincio. See also E. Nash, *Pictorial Dictionary of Ancient Rome* I (rev. ed., London, 1981), 488–90. With regard to the possibility suggested by Agostini's letter, this provenance might be worth reconsidering.

26. ASF, Carte Strozziane s. III, vol. 184, fols 28r, 32r–v, 33v, 58r, 59r.

27. ASF, Carte Strozziane s. III, vol. 163, fols 30r, 33r, 48r, 65r.

28. Bartoli, 'Memorie' (above, n. 22), no. 12.

29. Appendix, no. 32.

30. Excellent surveys on the patronage and building activities of Alexander VII have been provided by R. Krautheimer, *The Rome of Alexander VII, 1655–1667* (Princeton, 1985), and T. Magnuson, *Rome in the Age of Bernini* II (Stockholm, 1986), 121–253. Agostini himself was pleased to have frequent discussions with Alexander concerning ancient coins and other antiquities; see ASF, Carte Strozziane s. III, vol. 163, fols 95r, 106r, 116r.

31. For what follows, see the sources quoted in the Appendix, nos. 34, 36–9.

32. O. Falconieri, *Discorso intorno alla Piramide di C. Cestio, et alle pitture, che sono in essa,* published as an appendix to F. Nardini, *Roma antica* (Rome, 1666).

33. His visits to the interior of the pyramid are attested by Bosio himself in his *Roma sotterranea* (Rome, 1632), 145.

34. Krautheimer, *The Rome of Alexander* (above, n. 30), 109–13.

35. Appendix, nos. 42, 47.

36. Appendix, nos. 61–2.

37. Appendix, nos. 39–40, 46–7, 57.

38. Appendix, no. 43.

39. Appendix, nos. 44–5 (Castel Gandolfo), 48 (Esquiline), 50, 52, 54 (Porta Portuensis), 70 (San Lorenzo in Panisperna); L. Ozzola, 'L'arte alla corte di Alessandro VII', *Archivio della Società Romana di Storia Patria* 31 (1908), 5–93, esp. p. 86 (Piazza Santissimi Apostoli in February 1657); and Agostini himself, ASF, Carte Strozziane s. III, vol. 163, fol. 198r (Velabrum in December 1659).

40. Appendix, nos. 59, 61.

41. Appendix, nos. 63, 72.

42. Appendix, nos. 77, 79–86.

43. The excavations at Castel Gandolfo and at San Lorenzo in Panisperna seem to have been Barberini commissions; see the Appendix, nos. 44–5, 70. In 1660 Agostini appears in the Barberini account books as having provided stones used to restore the famous Palestrina mosaic; see J. Merz, 'Das Fortuna-Heiligtum in Palestrina als Barberini-Villa', *Zeitschrift für Kunstgeschichte* 56 (1993), 409–50, esp. p. 415 n. 18.

44. ASF, Carte Strozziane s. III, vol. 205, fol. 68r, referring to the excavation at the monastery of San Gregorio Magno; see the Appendix, no. 63.

45. See A. Schnapp, *La conquête du passé. Aux origines de l'archéologie* (Paris, 1993), esp. pp. 36, 199–204.

46. Appendix, no. 21, for example.

47. Appendix, nos. 11, 16. Significantly, Agostini also provided stones for the restoration of mosaics; see above, n. 43.

48. Appendix, no. 63. For similar remarks see the Appendix, no. 56.

49. Appendix, no. 44.

50. Appendix, nos. 4, 61.

51. Appendix, no. 42.

52. ASF, Carte Strozziane s. III, vol. 183, fol. 62r, and the Appendix, no. 61.

53. For Cennini, see the bibliography in *Allgemeines*

Künstlerlexikon. Die Bildenden Künstler aller Zeiten und Völker XVII (Munich/Leipzig, 1997), 518–19, as well as V. Martinelli (ed.), *Le statue berniniane del Colonnato di San Pietro* (Rome, 1987), 208, and H. Tratz, 'Werkstatt und Arbeitsweise Berninis', *Römisches Jahrbuch für Kunstgeschichte* 23–4 (1988), 395–483, esp. pp. 407–41. He appears in Agostini's letters as 'un giovane mio vicinio che mi accomoda tutte le mie cose, et si porta bene venendo dalla scuola dell'Algardi' ('a young man close to me who fixes all my objects, and works well coming from Algardi's workshop'); see ASF, Carteggio d'artisti vol. 17, fol. 106r (14 August 1666). Travelling frequently between Florence and Rome, he acted as Agostini's postman. In 1660, he restored a marble head identified by Agostini as that of Lucius, grandson of Augustus; see ASF, Carte Strozziane s. III, vol. 183, fol. 7r. In those days he went to see Agostini almost daily at his excavation sites; ASF, Carte Strozziane s. III, vol. 183, fol. 29r. In April 1662, while working with Bernini on the statue of Saint Augustine for the Basilica of Saint Peter's, he restored a metal statuette of Venus. In the autumn of 1668 he was supposed to work on the group of Cupid and Psyche (Appendix, no. 74) but was kept too busy by Bernini and the statues for Ponte Sant'Angelo; ASF, Carteggio d'artisti vol. 17, fol. 149r.

54. Appendix, no. 18.
55. Appendix, no. 58.
56. Appendix, no. 62.
57. Appendix, no. 1.
58. Appendix, no. 7.
59. Appendix, no. 4.
60. Herklotz, *Cassiano dal Pozzo* (above, n. 1), 289–91.
61. For her coins, see H. Mattingly, *Coins of the Roman Empire in the British Museum* IV: *Antoninus Pius to Commodus* (London, 1940) (see index, *sub voce*); R. Stoll, *Frauen auf Römischen Münzen. Biographisches und Kulturgeschichtliches im Spiegel der Antiken Numismatik* (Trier, 1996), 96–103; for medals, see F. Gnecchi, *I medaglioni romani* (Milan, 1912), 38–42.
62. Gnecchi, *Medaglioni* (above, n. 61), 40 no. 19, with pl. 68,6.
63. R. Calza (ed.), *Antichità di Villa Doria Pamphilj* (Rome, 1977), 94.
64. Appendix, no. 43.
65. The drawing of the Bacchic relief can be attributed to Galestruzzi. It was sent to Florence on 9 September 1666 and was published by Mercantini, *Due disegni* (above, n. 9), fig. 21. See also ASF, Carteggio d'artisti vol. 17, fols 100r, 110r, 118r, 129r. It was eventually acquired by Camillo Massimo and is still in the Palazzo Massimo-Del Drago; see M. Pomponi, 'Schedatura dei disegni del taccuino', in *Camillo Massimo collezionista di antichità. Fonti e materiali* (Rome, 1996), 73–87, esp. pp. 83–4, with pl. LVI. The head of pseudo-Seneca is discussed in ASF, Carte Strozziane s. III, vol. 184, fols 98r, 105r, 106r. The drawing (= fol. 111r) was sent on 24 May 1658. This appears to represent the sculpture published in G.A. Mansuelli, *Galleria degli Uffizi. Le sculture* (Rome, 1958–61), II, no. 10. Heads of Seneca were also referred to in 1656 and 1665, although it is unclear whether the same sculp-

ture was meant. See ASF, Carte Strozziane s. III, vol. 163, fol. 167v; vol. 205, fol. 61r; and G. Capecchi, 'La collezione di antichità del Cardinale Leopoldo de' Medici: i marmi', *Atti e Memorie dell'Accademia Toscana di Scienze e Lettere La Colombaria* 44, n.s. 30 (1979), 123–45, esp. p. 137. A drawing of the Cupid and Psyche group was sent on 1 January 1667. See ASF, Carteggio d'artisti vol. 17, fol. 130r; and the Appendix, nos. 74, 76. For further drawings supplied by Galestruzzi, see also ASF, Carte Strozziane s. III, vol. 163, fol. 187r; vol. 184, fols 37r, 58r, 59r; vol. 205, fol. 78r; ASF, Carteggio d'artisti vol. 17, fols 33r, 130r, 140r.

66. ASF, Carte Strozziane s. III, vol. 184, fols 5r, 6r, 15v, 28r, 39r, 74r; ASF, Carteggio d'artisti vol. 17, fol. 2r. Elsewhere Agostini refused to offer anything to the Florentine court without first asking the advice of Cortona, Sacchi, Bernini and Algardi; ASF, Carte Strozziane s. III, vol. 184, fol. 5v (8 September 1652). For Sacchi see also ASF, Carte Strozziane s. III, vol. 184, fol. 41r. In 1663, Ciro Ferri inspected Agostini's statues for Leopoldo; see ASF, Carte Strozziane s. III, vol. 205, fol. 69r.

67. Appendix, nos. 7, 74, 76. Leopoldo's collection of ancient statues was studied by Capecchi, 'La collezione di antichità' (above, n. 65), 123–45.

68. The Berenice was sold (together with a relief portrait of Agrippina, restored on the basis of a gem, and a head of Cleopatra) in 1665; see ASF, Carte Strozziane s. III, vol. 205, fols 65r, 66r. The Pupienus is mentioned in the Appendix, no. 74. For the alleged Seneca, see n. 65 above. For an archaeological discussion of these sculptures, see Mansuelli, *Galleria degli Uffizi* (above, n. 65), II, nos. 10, 18, 152.

69. The busts of Germanicus, Antoninus Pius and Marcus Aurelius were offered by Agostini on 27 August 1651; see ASF, Carteggio d'artisti vol. 17, fol. 2r. From the source cited below (Appendix, no. 74), we know that they had been acquired by 1666. The head of Marcus Aurelius was also listed in a *Nota delle robbe piu singulari ritrovate in diversi tempi nel horto delli Morelli a S. Stefano Rotondo confinante d'una banda col'horto delli Sig.ri Fonsechi con l'occasione della cava fatta ivi nelli anni come segue* (written after 1676); see Biblioteca Angelica, Rome, MS 1678, fol. 46r. The passage reads: 'Dell'anno 1651. Una testa di statua di marmo sopra il naturale rappresentante Marco Aurelio Imperatore venduta al Sig.r Card.le de Medici, et due busti di statue d'alabastro cotagnino senza teste' ('In the year 1651. A head of a marble statue larger than life-size of Emperor Marcus Aurelius sold to Sig. Cardinal de Medici, and two busts of *cotagnino* alabaster statues without heads'). (The garden of Francesco Morelli was also mentioned by Bartoli, 'Memorie' (above n. 22), no. 54.) Agostini sold the Septimius Severus in 1652/3 after it had been inspected by Cortona; ASF, Carte Strozziane s. III, vol. 184, fols 5r, 40r. These works should be identified among the material published by Mansuelli, *Galleria degli Uffizi* (above, n. 65), II, *passim*. For Cleopatra and Agrippina, not known among the Uffizi statues today, see n. 68.

70. Appendix, no. 78; and ASF, Carteggio d'artisti vol. 17, fol. 140r.

71. For his coins, see Giovannini, 'Notizie sulle medaglie' (above, n. 8); for the gems, M.R. Casarosa, 'Collezioni di gemme e il Cardinale Leopoldo dei Medici', *Antichità Viva* 15 (4) (1976), 56–64; Giuliani, *I cammei* (above, n. 14), cat. nos. 13, 18, 34, 54, 143, 157, 162, 169, 174, 192, 212, 259 (entries by M.E. Micheli). The acquisition of the Ludovisi sculptures has been discussed by Goldberg, *Patterns* (above, n. 8), 108–9, and more thoroughly in Giovannini, *Lettere di Ottavio Falconieri* (above, n. 8), 50–62.

72. Appendix, nos. 58, 61, and n. 65 above.

73. Appendix, nos. 63, 66, 73.

74. ASF, Carteggio d'artisti vol. 17, fols 2r, 5r–v; ASF, Carte Strozziane s. III, vol. 184, fol. 5r, and Goldberg, *Patterns* (above, n. 8), 107.

75. For Gottifredi, see Goldberg, *Patterns* (above, n. 8), 98–104; M.C. Molinari, 'La collezione numismatica', in *Camillo Massimo* (above, n. 65), 159–91, esp. pp. 165–6. His numerous letters to the Florentine court are preserved in ASF, Carteggio d'artisti vol. 8. An extensive volume with drafts of his letters has survived in BOP, MS 76, a source largely ignored by modern scholars.

76. For the rivalry over the quality of their collections, see ASF, Carte Strozziane s. III, vol. 184, fols 17r, 40r. Their struggle for lucrative bargains is highlighted by an anecdote told by Agostini on 8 February 1653 (see ASF, Carte Strozziane s. III, vol. 184, fol. 38r): 'Anni sono che havevo stretta amicitia con un Prencipe in Regnio il quale si dilettava di queste materie [di medaglie] et si serviva della mia opera. Fu penetrato dal detto Sig.r Gottifredi et sotto nome finto di Francesco Susanna recapitava a quel Sig.re medaglie, dal quale poi mi fu mandato sue lettere et io le feci con rossore leggerle e fargli riconosce la sua mano. Et doppo quel Sig.re se ne andro in cielo, et avanti alla sua morte mi condono il suo studio di medaglie, delle quali molte ne riconobbi et glile feci vedere' ('For years I have had a close friendship with a prince in Regnio who delighted in this material [medallions] and made use of my work. He was approached by the said Signor Gottifredi, and, under the false name of Francesco Susanna, delivered medallions to that Signor. His letters were then sent to me, and I made him read them with embarrassment and made him identify his handwriting. And afterwards that Signor died, and before his death he gave me his study of medallions, many of which I recognized and showed to him').

77. BOP, MS 76, fol. 210r: to Pierre Seguin, 3 June 1664. According to Gottifredi, Agostini's sparse commentary was also the reason why his new edition of Paruta's *Sicilia descritta con medaglie* (above, n. 13) did not sell; BOP, MS 76, fol. 114r.

78. ASF, Carte Strozziane s. III, vol. 184, fol. 13r.

79. ASF, Carte Strozziane s. III, vol. 184, fols 13r, 14r, 37v, 61r. This plea was repeated even after he had become papal antiquary; see ASF, Carte Strozziane s. III, vol. 163, fols 192r, 198r.

80. BOP, MS 76, fols 229v–230r.

81. At least this is what Agostini assumed: 'ci sono stati personaggi qualificati che hanno domandata questa carica e il S.r Gottifredi ha fatto le ultime sue prove' ('there have been qualified individuals who have requested this office and Signor Gottifredi made his last attempts'). See ASF, Carte Strozziane s. III, vol. 163, fol. 134v.

82. BOP, MS 76, fols 131v, 134r. According to Gottifredi, the restriction of 1634 already had had fatal consequences for the Roman antiquities market. Dealers used to bury what they owned, unearthing it only after the death of Urban VIII.

83. BOP, MS 76, fol. 173r.

84. Numerous licences with references to Agostini's inspections were published by Lanciani, *Storia* (1989–), V, 204–11, 218–19, 222–30, 233, 235, 243–5, 262.

85. The history of this approach has been traced in Herklotz, *Cassiano dal Pozzo* (above, n. 1), 151–239.

86. ASF, Carte Strozziane s. III, vol. 163, fol. 186r.

87. E. Mandowsky and C. Mitchell, *Pirro Ligorio's Roman Antiquities. The Drawings in MS. XIII.B.7 in the National Library in Naples* (London, 1963), 31.

88. Quoted in E. Cropper, 'Vincenzo Giustiniani's 'Galleria'. The Pygmalion effect', in *Cassiano dal Pozzo's Paper Museum* II (Turin, 1992), 101–26, esp. p. 106 n. 19. For the archaeological significance of this and Agustín's statement, see Herklotz, *Cassiano dal Pozzo* (above, n. 1), 186.

89. Herklotz, *Cassiano dal Pozzo* (above, n. 1), 274–83.

90. Appendix, nos. 80–5.

91. Studies of these copies include C. Pace, 'Pietro Santi Bartoli. Drawings in Glasgow University Library after Roman paintings and mosaics', *PBSR* 47 (1979), 117–55; H. Joyce, 'Grasping at shadows: ancient paintings in Renaissance and Baroque Rome', *Art Bulletin* 74 (1992), 219–46; H. Whitehouse, 'The rebirth of Adonis', *PBSR* 63 (1995), 215–43; M. Pomponi, 'La collezione del Cardinale Massimo e l'inventario del 1677', in *Camillo Massimo* (above, n. 65), 91–157, esp. pp. 104–5 with notes. For the seventeenth-century study of Pliny as a source for ancient painting, see I. Herklotz, 'Poussin et Pline l'Ancien: à propos des monocromata', in O. Bonfait, C.L. Frommel, M. Hochmann and S. Schütze (eds), *Poussin et Rome. Actes du colloque à l'Académie de France à Rome et à la Bibliotheca Hertziana 16–18 novembre 1994* (Paris, 1996), 13–29.

92. See the bibliography in G.P. Bellori, *Le vite de' pittori, scultori e architetti moderni* (ed. E. Borea, with an introduction by G. Previtali) (Turin, 1976), LXXVIII–LXXXIII. An important earlier study by Bellori relevant in this context is contained in his *Nota delli musei, librerie, galerie* (Rome, 1664/5), 56–66. As already noted, the rediscovery of the paintings inside the pyramid of Gaius Cestius in 1655 prompted a brief discussion by Falconieri in his *Discorso intorno alla Piramide* (above, n. 32).

93. The first three letters cited here were published by Müntz, 'Plans' (above, n. 9), 154–8.

94. Several alleged heads of Cicero are recorded in the Barberini inventories; see Lavin, *Barberini Documents* (above, n. 7), *passim* (index: 570). Sculptural representations of Cicero's younger brother, Quintus Tullius Cicero, are unknown.

95. While the urns described cannot be traced, the two different

types mentioned are well known; see F. Sinn, *Stadtrömische Marmorurnen* (Mainz, 1987), esp. nos. 400, 555, for the circular type, which has an eagle on top. No. 555 is known to derive from the collection of Camillo Massimo in Rome; see also B. Cacciotti, 'La dispersione di alcune antichità della collezione Massimo in Spagna e in Inghilterra', in *Camillo Massimo* (above, n. 65), 213–37, esp. p. 222.

96. According to Bartoli, 'Memorie' (above, n. 22), nos. 78 and 114, this excavation was necessitated by the laying of a new water-pipe to Piazza Navona. Reliefs from the nearby *templum Hadriani*, dedicated by Antoninus Pius in AD 145, were found on numerous occasions during the seventeenth century; see also Agostini's references in this Appendix, no. 61. For the style, iconography and present location of these sculptures, see J.M.C. Toynbee, *The Hadrianic School. A Chapter in the History of Greek Art* (reprint, Rome, 1967), 152–9, with pls XXXIV–XXXVI.

97. On this excavation, see also Lucas Holstenius to Francesco Barberini, 16 September 1647, in BAV Barb. Lat. 6490, fol. 59r: 'In un'altra cava dietro a S. Giovanni fatta per il Sig.r Marchese del Bufalo nelle roine e vestigi d'un tempio di Venere si sono trovate parecchie statue, principalmente una di Adone molto stimata' ('In another excavation made for the Marchese del Bufalo behind the church of S. Giovanni in the ruins and remains of a temple dedicated to Venus quite a number of statues have been found, in particular one of Adonis that is highly esteemed'). Bartoli, 'Memorie' (above, n. 22), no. 53, refers to a 'cortile di non molta grandezza, entrovi sette bellissime statue, le quali dal detto marchese [del Bufalo] furono mandate in Francia' ('a not very large courtyard, within which there were seven beautiful statues, which were sent to France by the said Marchese [del Bufalo]').

98. The palace of Antoninus Pius at Lorium, close to modern Bottaccia and Castel di Guido, was situated some 20 km away on the Via Aurelia. The fullest account of the building and its history is given in the doctoral thesis of M. Leppert, *23 Kaiservillen. Vorarbeiten zu Archäologie und Kulturgeschichte der Villegiatur der Hohen Kaiserzeit* (University of Freiburg im Breisgau, 1974), 258–73. Previously known documents concerning excavations on this site do not go beyond the eighteenth century; see Leppert, *23 Kaiservillen*, 270–3. The statue described by Agostini must have represented the goddess Cybele, who is frequently shown riding a lion; see E. Simon's contribution in *LIMC* VIII.1, 758–9. Only one statue of the riding Cybele was well known in seventeenth-century Rome. It is preserved in the Villa Doria Pamphili (**Fig. 10**), where it is first documented through the engravings of *Villa Pamphilia, eiusque Palatium, cum suis Prospectibus, Statuae, Fontes, Vivaria, Theatra, Areolae, Plantarum, Viarumque Ordines* (Rome, n.d.), no pagination. This book, published by 'Formis Io. Iacobi de Rubeis, apud Templum S. Mariae de Pace', has no date of publication, but probably appeared after the death of Camillo Pamphili in 1666. The statue has long been held to come from Nettuno, a provenance first given by Bartoli, 'Memorie' (above, n. 22), no. 156, and nowadays generally accepted; see, for instance, Calza, *Antichità* (above,

n. 63), 93. There are, however, reasons for identifying the Pamphili Cybele with the statue noted by Agostini instead. Firstly, Bartoli mentioned the work in the same breath as the famous Borghese Gladiator, known to be from Nettuno, but brought to Rome prior to June 1611. It therefore seems unlikely that he was an eyewitness to the arrival of the Cybele in Rome. Secondly, Agostini's observation that the statue resembles (the younger?) Faustina has been confirmed by modern scholarship, and the work itself has been dated to the Antonine period; see Calza, *Antichità* (above, n. 63), 96. While Nettuno never enjoyed the special favour of the Antonine dynasty, Lorium belonged to the Antonine family legacy. Faustina herself spent much of her time there; see Leppert, *23 Kaiservillen*, 259, 266–7. It must also have had a circus (Leppert, *23 Kaiservillen*, 268–9), which is a likely provenance for this statue reproducing the famous image of Cybele in the Roman Circus Maximus. Thirdly, it seems plausible that an outstanding archaeological discovery made during the reign of Innocent X would end up in a Pamphili collection. Payments for Pamphili marble work at Castel di Guido are documented for the second half of the same year; see J. Garms (ed.), *Quellen aus dem Archiv Doria-Pamphilj zur Kunsttätigkeit in Rom unter Innozenz X* (Rome/Vienna, 1972), 214, no. 1045.

99. While none of these statues can be identified, it is not unlikely that portraits of Lucius Verus and Commodus formed part of the villa's decoration, since both rulers used to sojourn there; see Leppert, *23 Kaiservillen* (above, n. 98), 266–7.

100. This seems to be the excavation mentioned in Bartoli, 'Memorie' (above, n. 22), no. 25, as having brought to light 'quantità grande di metalli, particolarmente bellissimi vasi dell' istessa materia' ('a large number of metal objects, particularly beautiful vessels in this material'). For other excavations organized by Cavaliere Martino Altieri, see Lanciani, *Storia* (1989–), V, 227.

101. Lamps similar to the one described here were published by P. Aringhi, *Roma subterranea novissima* II (Rome, 1659), 195, and P.S. Bartoli and G.P. Bellori, *Le antiche lucerne sepolcrali figurate* III (Rome, 1691), nos. 24 and 30.

102. Size, material and damage correspond precisely to a statue in the Uffizi (**Fig. 9**), dated to the late Augustan period or to the first decades thereafter; see Mansuelli, *Galleria degli Uffizi* (above, n. 65), II, no. 51, and Capecchi, 'La collezione di antichità' (above, n. 65), 130–1. This statue seems to be the source for the engraving of a gem [!] published in Agostini's *Gemme antiche* 1 (above, n. 14), no. 172 (= *Illustrated Bartsch* 46/21 (above, n. 14), 203), as *Britannicus praetextatus*. The same *Britannico pretestato di selce verde Egittia* was documented by Bellori, *Nota* (above, n. 92), 6, as being in Agostini's own collection; see also Skippon, 'Account' (above, n. 8), 678 (a small statue of Britannicus, of green marble).

103. This and the following remarks concern Agostini's excavation at the forum of Petronius Maximus; see above nn. 21–2. For Francesco Gualdi and the two capitals, see n. 25.

104. Angelo Paracciani and his brother Rotilio were both members of the household of Francesco Barberini; see M. Völkel,

Römische Kardinalshaushalte des 17. Jahrhunderts, Borghese–Barberini–Chigi (Tübingen, 1993), 431, no. 98. The sarcophagus, however, did not become Barberini property. It was still documented as being outside the Porta San Sebastiano in 1683; see Herklotz, *Cassiano dal Pozzo* (above, n. 1), 133–4. Only the front relief has survived (**Fig. 6**) and is now in the Vatican Belvedere; see R. Amedick, *Die Sarkophage mit Darstellungen aus dem Menschenleben* IV: *Vita Privata* (Berlin, 1991), 162–3.

105. A more complete version of the inscription is quoted in Appendix, no. 23. It is identical with *CIL* VI (1) 1197. The entry there cites documents on the later whereabouts of this fragment, which was first acquired by Francesco Barberini. Its discovery was also reported by Bartoli, 'Memorie' (above, n. 22), no. 1.

106. Although Agostini did not say where this excavation took place, it seems to be a new campaign he was leading.

107. The amethyst engraving is published in Agostini's *Gemme antiche* (above, n. 14), no. 34 (= *Illustrated Bartsch* 46/21 (above, n. 14), 134).

108. The site of this excavation is not sufficiently specified. Agostini may be referring to the Barberini villa at Castel Gandolfo, built on the site of a villa of the Emperor Domitian, where Barberini excavations are documented for 1656 and 1657; see R. Krautheimer and R.B.S. Jones, 'The diary of Alexander VII. Notes on art, artists and buildings', *Römisches Jahrbuch für Kunstgeschichte* 15 (1975), 199–233, here no. 80, 138 and below, nos. 44–5. Excavations during the pontificate of Innocent X, however, were also mentioned by Bartoli, 'Memorie' (above, n. 22), no. 147. For the archaeological discoveries made on this site, see P. Liverani, *L'antiquarium di Villa Barberini a Castel Gandolfo* (Vatican City, 1989).

109. Agostini's letters prove that Alexander's famous restoration of the pyramid was begun earlier than is usually assumed and obviously was not prompted by the burial of the plague victims in 1656. A modern account of this restoration has been given by M. Pomponi, 'Il restauro della Piramide Cestia. Ricerche antiquarie e fortuna delle pitture', *Xenia Antiqua* 2 (1993), 149–74, esp. pp. 156–8; see also Krautheimer, *The Rome of Alexander* (above, n. 30), 102–4, and Lanciani, *Storia* (1989–), V, 230–2. All these studies contain incorrect dates for the individual steps of the campaign.

110. At least two columns excavated were set up again on the west side of the building. These, however, have Doric capitals rather than Corinthian; see P.S. Bartoli, *Gli antichi sepolchri overo mausolei romani et etruschi* (Rome, 1697), pl. 62, and Pomponi, 'Restauro' (above, n. 109), figs 9, 10, 13, 16; Nash, *Pictorial Dictionary* I (above, n. 25), 322. The bronze foot referred to by Agostini was reproduced in Bartoli, *Antichi sepolchri*, pl. 63. The base of the statue found in front of the building has also survived; see Nash, *Pictorial Dictionary* I (above, n. 25), 323, although the date of discovery given there (1662) has now been disproved.

111. The statue, 'trovata a Torre di valle fuor di porta S. Paolo' ('found at Torre di valle outside the Porta San Paolo') prior to 3 January 1656, was restored by the sculptor Baldassare Mari

and set up in the Vatican Belvedere garden. Agostini also organized its transport to the papal palace. See Ozzola, 'L'arte' (above, n. 39), 5–93, esp. p. 86; Lanciani, *Storia* (1989–), V, 230.

112. On 2 May 1656 relics were removed from the cemetery. Two mosaics with portrait busts, now in the Vatican Museums, were discovered during the same campaign; see K.E. Werner, *Die Sammlung Antiker Mosaiken in den Vatikanischen Museen* (Vatican City, 1998), 35–42.

113. Agostini's indication as to the site is contradictory, since the church of Santa Maria della Consolazione does not adjoin the Forum. In the seventeenth century the only church dedicated to the Virgin situated close to the Forum was Santa Maria Liberatrice on the slope of the Palatine. Agostini's excavation in front of this church might be confirmed by Bartoli, 'Memorie' (above, n. 22), no. 50. According to Bartoli, the excavation brought to light 'edifizij sotteranei in quantità tale, che non pareva, che mai vi fosse stata piazza alcuna' ('underground buildings in such numbers that it does not seem likely that a piazza could have been located here'). These structures have been identified as the so-called Porticus Margaritaria; see Lanciani, *Storia* (1989–), V, 213. For this building and its controversial dating, see also Nash, *Pictorial Dictionary* I (above, n. 25), 252–3. There is no evidence that Agostini excavated the temple of Divus Iulius. For Pope Alexander's urbanistic interest in the Forum, see Krautheimer, *The Rome of Alexander* (above, n. 30), 109–13.

114. If the *Anfiteatro* referred to is the Colosseum, Agostini must have confused the Curia Hostilia, formerly located close to the Comitium, with a structure at the east corner of the Palatine.

115. The reference is probably to Claudius Albinus (ob. AD 197), co-regent and later opponent of Septimius Severus. For his *Saeculum frugiferum* coins, see H. Mattingly, *Coins of the Roman Empire in the British Museum* V: *Pertinax to Elagabalus* (London, 1950), 37–8, 134–6. Securely identified portrait statues of Claudius are unknown. The figure described by Agostini, on the other hand, corresponds precisely to a statue in the Louvre (inv. no. MA 1059), known to have come from the Villa Albani and previously in the Palazzo Verospi in Rome (**Fig. 11**). While the head betrays certain similarities to Claudius, a convincing identification of this statue has never been achieved. For stylistic reasons, it has been dated to the time of Pupienus, emperor in 238. See K. de Kerauson, *Catalogue des portraits romains* II: *de l'année de la guerre civile (68–69 après J.-C.) à la fin de l'Empire* (Paris, 1996), 452–3.

116. Another description of this campaign is given by Agostini on 3 November 1657 in ASF, Carteggio d'artisti vol. 17, fol. 25r. In this letter, it sounds as if the excavation had been commissioned by Alexander VII ('per esser stato à Castello à servir N. S. nel cavamento alla cava della Villa Domitiana' ('to have been at Castello to help Our Lord in the excavation at the Villa Domitiana')). Alexander's own diary (Krautheimer and Jones, 'Diary' (above, n. 108), 138, no. 80) speaks rather of the 'Cava de Barberini' ('Barberini excavation'). Bartoli, 'Memorie' (above, n. 22), no. 147, likewise located this excavation 'nella

vigna del principe Barberini' ('in Prince Barberini's vineyard'). For Domitian's Villa and its decoration, see Liverani, *L'antiquarium* (above, n. 108), and the bibliography (pp. 9–10); more recently, R. Darwall-Smith, 'Albanum and the villas of Domitian', *Pallas* 40 (1994), 145–65. Seventeenth-century drawings of some of the villa's structures have been published recently; see B. Amendolea and L. Indrio, 'Monumenta Albani et locorum adiacentium, una raccolta di disegni del XVII secolo', *Palladio* 16 (July–December 1995), 107–26, esp. pp. 111–13. If they pre-date Agostini's activity there, his own report on his discoveries should be viewed as not free from exaggeration.

117. For the plan by Galestruzzi commissioned by Francesco Barberini, which does not seem to have survived, see also Lanciani, *Storia* (1989–), V, 224. For his engravings of the stage sets for Giuglio Rospigliosi's *La vita humana*, performed for Queen Christina in the Barberini theatre in 1656, see F. Petrucci Nardelli, 'Il card. Francesco Barberini Senior e la stampa a Roma', *Archivio della Società Romana di Storia Patria* 108 (1985), 138–98, esp. pp. 167–8.

118. The same object was recorded by Joseph Maria Suares as 'in agro Albano ad Castrum Gandolfi in Exc.mi Principis Praenestini [i.e. Barberini] horto, tubo plumbeo ibidem invento anno 1657' ('in the countryside of Albano at Castel Gandolfo, in the garden of his Most Excellent Prince Praenestini [Barberini], a lead pipe having been found in the same place in the year 1657'). See Schreiber, 'Unedirte Römische Fundberichte' (above, n. 1), 122.

119. Campo Vaccino is the seventeenth-century name for the Forum Romanum. Hence this excavation should be related to the one noted in no. 42. Alexander's account books record payments to Agostini for three statues and a fragment of a column found at Campo Vaccino between May and June 1658; see Bertolotti, 'L'antiquario' (above, n. 8), 101.

120. For the location of these finds, see no. 49. According to documents published by Ozzola, 'L'arte' (above, n. 39), 87, the two columns were discovered in the garden of a certain Mario Perusco, from whom Alexander bought them, 'compresoci due pezzi di pilastrelli' ('including two pieces of pilaster'), for 265 scudi. In the Lateran Basilica they were obviously used to complete the series of green marble columns formerly in the aisles of the church and later re-employed for the tabernacles in the nave.

121. A papal licence for excavations 'nell'horto de' RR. Padri di S. Pietro a Vincola posto nel monte Esquilino' ('in the garden of the holy fathers of San Pietro a Vincola located on the Esquiline Hill') dates from 8 March 1660. See Lanciani, *Storia* (1989–), V, 208, and no. 65 here.

122. The shrine of Hercules Cubans was actually situated some 500 m outside the Porta Portuensis; see Nash, *Pictorial Dictionary* I (above, n. 25), 462–70, and E.M. Steinby (ed.), *Lexicon Topographicum Urbis Romae* III (Rome, 1996), 11–12, with further bibliography.

123. Excavations in the Mattei garden on the Palatine are also recorded by Bartoli, 'Memorie' (above, n. 22), nos. 6–7. The 'Hercules that stands in the courtyard of the Palazzo Pitti'

means the statue of Hercules and Antaeus in the principal courtyard of the Palazzo Pitti in Florence, discovered prior to 1509. Its discovery on the Palatine is not otherwise documented. Its history has been discussed by F. Haskell and N. Penny, *Taste and the Antique. The Lure of Classical Sculpture 1500–1900* (New Haven/London, 1981), 232–4. For the Belvedere Antinous, cited by Agostini for iconographic comparison, see Haskell and Penny, pp. 141–3.

124. The colonnades in front of Saint Peter's were one of Alexander's major building projects; see Krautheimer, *The Rome of Alexander* (above, n. 30), 63–73. For the travertine statues placed on top, see Martinelli, *Le statue berniniane* (above, n. 53). Contrary to Agostini's suggestion, however, ancient statues do not seem to have been reused.

125. The 'Moniche Barberini' are the nuns of the monastery of the Santissima Incarnazione. Together with the church of Santa Maria dell'Annunziata, the monastery was located in Via Alta Semita, close to the Quattro Fontane. See L. Pascoli, *Vite de' pittori, scultori, ed architetti* (ed. M. Marabottini) (Perugia, 1992), 200 n. 14. An excavation licence for the garden attached to the monastery dates from 4 March 1659; see Lanciani, *Storia* (1989–), V, 211.

126. A statue of Ganymede that soon acquired fame is documented in the collection of Camillo Massimi as early as 1665, when Bellori published his *Nota* (above, n. 92), 33. This statue is now in the Prado (inv. no. 35-E). Its later history has been traced by Pomponi, 'La collezione del Cardinale Massimo' (above, n. 91), 141 n. 63 and fig. 78. For the statue itself, see A. Blanco, *Museo del Prado. Catalogo de las esculturas* (Madrid, 1957), 38, pl. XX. The parts of the statue noted as missing by Agostini are in fact restored in the Madrid sculpture. Although the latter displays further restorations, it seems reasonable to identify it as the marble found in the Santarelli garden. Additional repair could have become necessary after its transport to Spain, or Agostini could have simply exaggerated its state of preservation. For Santarelli's excavations, see also the licences in Lanciani, *Storia* (1989–), V, 210–11, 245. The location of his property is here defined as 'nel monte esquilino sopra la suburra' ('on the Esquiline Hill above the Suburra') and also 'Esquilino e di S. Maria Maggiore confinante' ('Esquiline and the neighbouring S. Maria Maggiore').

127. The reference can only be to the archaistic Minerva in Dresden (Staatliche Kunstsammlungen, inv. no. 26), which comes from the Chigi collection in Rome (**Fig. 7**). The stola displays the battles of the Olympians with the Giants, rather than Minerva's fights against Hercules. For this statue, see the bibliography in *LIMC* II.1, 133 no. 1402, 1090 no. 223; more recently M.D. Fullerton, *The Archaistic Style in Roman Statuary* (Leiden, 1990), 50–3, 70 and *passim*. Agostini speaks of this statue in no. 61 as well, indicating a somewhat different place of discovery.

128. The relief is also mentioned by Bartoli, 'Memorie' (above, n. 22), no. 56: 'fu trovata una porta, sopra della quale vi era un bellissimo bassorilievo di un matrimonio antico' ('a door was found, above which there was a beautiful bas-relief depicting an ancient wedding'). It was published in a reversed engraving

as an *Epithalamium* in P.S. Bartoli and G.P. Bellori, *Admiranda Romanarum Antiquitatum* (Rome, n.d., but 1666), pl. 76, when it had passed into the collection of Cardinal Flavio Chigi. In 1970, it was acquired for the Museo Nazionale Archeologico in Siena; see A. Talocchini's contribution to 'Nuove acquisizioni dei musei e gallerie dello stato', *Bollettino d'Arte* s. V, 57 (1972), 242–58, with fig. 17. While the iconographic type of this relief seems rather unique, Agostini's reference to the Muses certainly makes more sense than Bartoli's reading as a wedding ceremony. For Cennini, see above, n. 53.

129. The renovation of the Pantheon, together with the clearing up of the square in front of it, was one of Alexander's most ambitious urban projects; see Krautheimer, *The Rome of Alexander* (above, n. 30), 104–9; and T. Marder, 'Bernini and Alexander VII. Criticism and praise of the Pantheon in the seventeenth century', *Art Bulletin* 71 (1989), 628–45. For the two columns excavated at San Luigi dei Francesi, obviously belonging to the Baths of Nero (due to later rebuilding also known as the Thermae Alexandrinae) formerly located in this area, see also Bartoli, 'Memorie' (above, n. 22), nos. 113–14. For further remains from the same structures, see Nash, *Pictorial Dictionary* I (above, n. 25), 460–4.

130. Perhaps this is the '[colonna] scannellata a vite' ('[column] decorated with tendrils') referred to by Bartoli, 'Memorie' (above, n. 22), no. 114.

131. The church of Santo Stefano in Truglio was located close to Piazza di Pietra; see C. Huelsen, *Le chiese di Roma nel medio evo. Cataloghi ed appunti* (Florence, 1927), 485–6. Its destruction was necessitated by Alexander's order to relocate the vendors' booths formerly crowding around the Pantheon to this area. The ancient reliefs discovered on this occasion came from the nearby Temple of Hadrian; see also Bartoli, 'Memorie' (above, n. 22), nos. 78, 115, and n. 96 above.

132. The 'Basilica di Antonino' is the Temple of Hadrian. The rediscovery of parts of its relief decoration close to the Pantheon was confirmed by Bartoli, 'Memorie' (above, n. 22), no. 78, who also recognized that these sculptures are related to others, then in the Palazzo Farnese.

133. The iconography should, of course, be related to Hadrian; see the study by Toynbee, *The Hadrianic School* (above, n. 96).

134. The so-called Arco di Portogallo was removed in order to create an unimpeded vista down the Via Flaminia. Its demolition began on 7 August 1662; see Krautheimer and Jones, 'Diary' (above, n. 108), no. 598, and the documents in Lanciani, *Storia* (1989–), V, 203, 212. The reliefs from the arch are still in the Capitoline Museums; see E. La Rocca (ed.), *Rilievi storici capitolini* (Rome, 1986), esp. pp. 21–37.

135. In an earlier letter (no. 58) a somewhat different provenance is given for the Chigi Minerva. Since the other letter was written almost eight months earlier, it may be considered more reliable.

136. The Egyptianizing lions still flanking the stairs on the north side of the Capitoline have been discussed by A. Nesselrath, *Das Fossombroner Skizzenbuch* (London, 1993), 175–7.

137. This is the famous capital in the Vatican Cortile della Pigna

(Fig. 8); see E. von Mercklin, *Antike Figuralkapitelle* (Berlin, 1962), 156–8. A somewhat inaccurate note by Bartoli, 'Memorie' (above, n. 22), no. 114, might be referring to the same work.

138. Bartoli, 'Memorie' (above, n. 22), nos. 9–10, seems to recall the same campaign. For the ancient structures surrounding the monastery of San Gregorio Magno, see A.M. Colini, 'Storia e topografia del Celio nell'antichità', *MemPontAcc* 7 (1944), 199–218.

139. These earlier excavations at San Gregorio were prompted by the discovery of the Sepolcro Corsini in 1639 (above, n. 1). Some of the metal artworks that entered Barberini's collection were listed by Cassiano dal Pozzo; see Lumbroso, *Cassiano dal Pozzo* (above, n. 1), 49; also Lanciani, *Storia* (1989–), V, 142–3.

140. The same discoveries are referred to in Biblioteca Angelica, Rome, MS 1678, fol. 46r, among the findings in the Morelli garden (see above, n. 69): 'Dell'anno 1664. Due hipogrifij di metallo, et due statuette a sedere parimente di metallo rappresentante due filosofi, o vero consoli venduti poi al Sig.r Gio. Pietro Bellori' ('In the year 1664. Two metal hippogriffs, and two seated statuettes also in metal depicting two philosophers, or rather consuls, later sold to Sig.r Gio. Pietro Bellori').

141. The excavations at San Pietro in Vincoli, already referred to in no. 50, actually continued for several years; see the licences in Lanciani, *Storia* (1989–), V, 208.

142. Agostini's insistence on seated statues is due to Strozzi's support of Valerio Chimentelli's work on ancient seats as honorary distinctions, investigations that led to the publication of Chimentelli's *Marmor Pisanum de Honore Bisellii* (Bologna, 1667). See also ASF, Carteggio d'artisti vol. 17, fols 36r, 37r, 43r, 45r, 46r, 54r, 55r, 65r.

143. For the obelisk and its reinstallation by Bernini in front of the church, see C. D'Onofrio, *Gli obelischi di Roma* (Rome, 1967²), 232–7. The statue of Osiris could be the one listed in Cardinal Antonio's inventory of 1644; see Lavin, *Barberini Documents* (above, n. 7), 181 no. 652. The discovery of Egyptian sculpture close to Santa Maria sopra Minerva is due to the presence of a former sanctuary of Isis and Serapis in this area; see Nash, *Pictorial Dictionary* I (above, n. 25), 510–11.

144. This statue is also mentioned by Bartoli, 'Memorie' (above, n. 22), no. 112; he, however, dated its discovery to the pontificate of Clement X (1670–6). According to Bartoli, the statue was acquired by Camillo Massimo. Massimo's interest in Egyptian gods is well documented; see Cacciotti, 'La dispersione di alcune antichità' (above, n. 95), 213–15.

145. This appears to be at San Gregorio Magno, where Agostini is also documented in the summer of 1666; see no. 72. For his earlier excavation there, see no. 63.

146. Possibly the 'statua di Livia Augusta dell altezza di 13 palmi' ('statue of Livia Augusta 13 *palmi* high') mentioned by Bartoli, 'Memorie' (above, n. 22), no. 16. According to Bartoli, Agostini found it while digging for Francesco Barberini at San Lorenzo in Panisperna.

147. Bartoli, 'Memorie' (above, n. 22), no. 54, dated this discovery once more to the papacy of Clement X. He seems better

informed, however, on the later whereabouts of this group, which was acquired by Leopoldo de' Medici and has remained in the Uffizi ever since; see Mansuelli, *Galleria degli Uffizi* (above, n. 65), I, 90–1, Sparti, 'Tecnica e teoria del restauro' (above, n. 7), 63–4, and **Fig. 14** here. According to Bartoli, the site of this dig was in the garden of Francesco Morelli, where the Marchese del Bufalo had made an earlier excavation; see no. 4. This site is confirmed by the *Nota* in Biblioteca Angelica, Rome, MS 1678, fol. 46r, where the discovery of the Cupid and Psyche group is dated to 1667.

148. Agostini himself had sold these heads to the Florentine court; see n. 69 above.

149. An inventory of the contents of the Massimo palace drawn up in 1744 lists a 'Vaso di marmo antico istoriato con figure, cioè Baccanti, in qualche parte ristaurato, alto palmi tre e mezzo' ('ancient marble vase adorned with figures, specifically Bacchants, restored in places, 3¹/₂ *palmi* high'); see Pomponi, 'La collezione del Cardinale Massimo' (above, n. 91), 139 n. 16. While Bacchic scenes appear all too frequently on ancient marble vases, the size best corresponds to a piece now in the British Museum; see D. Grassinger, *Römische Marmorkratere* (Mainz, 1991), 172 no. 14. This identification is, however, by no means certain.

150. See also Bartoli, 'Memorie' (above, n. 22), no. 56, who specified the find as occurring 'nell'accomodarsi le scale di detta chiesa' ('during the repair of the stairs of said church'). The statue is now in the Vatican Museums; see A. Roullet, *The Egyptian and Egyptianizing Monuments of Imperial Rome* (Leiden, 1972), 134 no. 282, with a wrong date of discovery.

151. This lamp soon entered the Medici collection in Florence; see M. De la Chausse, *Romanum Museum Sive Thesaurus Eruditae Antiquitatis* IV (Rome, 1690), no. 3, and Bartoli and Bellori, *Le antiche lucerne* (above, n. 101), no. 31 (= our **Fig. 15**). Today it is in the Museo Archeologico in Florence (inv. no. 1671); see also Colini, 'Storia e topografia' (above, n. 138), 254. Biblioteca Angelica, Rome, MS 1678, fol. 46r, mentions the lamp as another discovery in the Morelli garden (1667).

152. This passage is also quoted by Giovannini, *Lettere di Ottavio Falconieri* (above, n. 8), 63, who wrongly related it to the harbour landscape discovered in 1668 (see no. 81). The present site cannot be identified, although the stucco decoration was drawn for Carlo Antonio dal Pozzo, as Agostini emphasized.

153. For the ancient paintings discovered in 1668, see the bibliography in n. 91; also Giovannini, *Lettere di Ottavio Falconieri* (above, n. 8), 62–6, 206–11, 215, 225–7. Very few of these paintings have survived: most of them, however, are known from seventeenth-century drawings. They were located in a series of rooms at the foot of the Esquiline. Although seventeenth-century antiquaries used to think of these structures as the 'Terme di Tito' or 'Palatio di Tito', they may have been part of the Domus Aurea.

154. The painted building belonged to a monumental harbour landscape; see Whitehouse, 'Rebirth' (above, n. 91), 224, 240; Giovannini, *Lettere di Ottavio Falconieri* (above, n. 8), 63,

206–11. A summary of the modern archaeological discussion has been given by S. De Maria, *Gli archi onorari di Roma e dell'Italia romana* (Rome, 1988), 257–9.

155. The paintings are discussed in the bibliography cited in n. 91.

156. The entire letter is published in Mercantini, *Due disegni* (above, n. 9), 45–6; the description of the paintings was also reproduced by Giovannini, *Lettere di Ottavio Falconieri* (above, n. 8), 64–5. Modern iconographic study has arrived at different conclusions in at least two cases. The 'Aeneas and Dido' is now thought of as 'Venus and Adonis', and Agostini's vague reference to the queen who is being offered a child has been interpreted as 'The Birth of Adonis'. While all five paintings were acquired by Camillo Massimo, only the 'Birth of Adonis' has survived, albeit heavily restored, in the Ashmolean Museum in Oxford. In this regard, see Whitehouse, 'Rebirth' (above, n. 91).

157. This was the famous Tomb of the Nasonii (see also no. 88). For a modern archaeological investigation of its paintings, see Andreae, *Studien zur Römischen Grabkunst* (above, n. 1), 88–130, who also discussed the seventeenth-century copies of them (**Fig. 16**).

158. Parts of the decoration were taken to the villa of Gaspare Altieri next to Santa Croce in Gerusalemme. They are now in the British Museum. See Lanciani, *Storia* (1989–), V, 264. Bellori's preliminary analysis of these wall-paintings seems to have survived in various manuscript versions; see BAV, Vat. Lat. 9136, fols 56r–57r; Biblioteca Angelica, Rome, MS 1678, fols 98r–v, 108r; also Filippo Baldinucci's manuscript in the Biblioteca Nazionale Centrale, Florence, II.II.110, fols 288r–289r. Since Baldinucci was a close collaborator of Cardinal Leopoldo, the latter could be the text sent by Agostini, or at least a copy of this text. Bellori devoted a more detailed study to the tomb chamber illustrated by Bartoli in his *Le pitture antiche del sepolcro de' Nasonii nella Via Flaminia* (Rome, 1680), which was reprinted and translated several times. In this work he was able to definitively date the decoration to the second century AD.

THE EIGHTEENTH AND
EARLY NINETEENTH CENTURIES

BRITISH EXCAVATIONS IN THE PAPAL STATES DURING THE EIGHTEENTH CENTURY: WRITTEN AND VISUAL SOURCES

Ilaria Bignamini

INTRODUCTION

DURING the second half of the eighteenth century, countless archaeological excavations were carried out in and around Rome, by two principal groups of excavators, the Italians and the British. Their finds were in part acquired for the Vatican Museums, in part sold on the Roman market, and in part legally exported to other Italian states, Britain and other European countries. **Figure 1** shows the dynamics of excavation licences granted between 1762 and 1802, drawing upon a provisional chronology of 739 licences granted from the fifteenth to the mid-nineteenth centuries.[1] It reveals that a high proportion of these licences was held by the British between 1769 (the date of Gavin Hamilton's discovery of the Pantanello of Hadrian's Villa, Tivoli) and 1798 (the date of the first French occupation of Rome and the establishment of the Roman Republic). This conclusion is confirmed by the percentage of marbles acquired from British diggers and dealers that are preserved in various rooms of the Pio-Clementino Museum (**Fig. 2**).[2] The 'British marbles' in the Vatican form a remarkable collection; no other European nation contributed such a large number of antiquities to this 'Grand Tour museum' *par excellence*. The same applies to the number of British excavations in the Papal States, a phenomenon requiring some introductory remarks about the 'British conquest' of the marbles of ancient Rome during the golden age of the Grand Tour, and the legal and technical mechanisms of 'digging and dealing' in those days.[3] The following remarks provide an introduction to the discussion of eleven examples that demonstrate the extent to which:

1. a stricter distinction between primary and secondary sources should be made;
2. documents may produce conflicting evidence and clash with modern archaeological knowledge and connoisseurship;
3. in many cases, despite the potential conflicts, documents help greatly in identifying antiquities and clarifying their provenance, in locating, re-discovering and protecting sites, and even reconstructing lost remains.

THE 'BRITISH CONQUEST' OF THE MARBLES OF ANCIENT ROME

Adam Smith's *Inquiry into the Nature and Causes of the Wealth of Nations*[4] and Edward Gibbon's *History of the Decline and Fall of the Roman Empire*,[5] both written in the age of the Grand Tour by scholars who had experienced the educational tour of continental Europe (Smith and Gibbon) and Italy (Gibbon), appeared at the time of the Declaration of American Independence (1776). In the following years, members of the British and Italian ruling classes appear to have reflected much upon similarities between ancient Rome and modern Britain. Their thoughts are echoed in a poem, *Voti di Pace all'Inghilterra/Sonetto*, written by an anonymous writer in *c.* 1783 or shortly before, which is preserved among the papers of John Strange (1732–99), the British Resident at Venice 1774–86:[6]

Intrepida Albion, del mar l'impéro
Véggo che il Fato, e il tuo valor ti diede,

Sò che popoli e Rè d'altro emisfero
T'offrono tributarj omaggio al piede.
Del Gallo a fronte e del possédente Ibero
Te sola, e invitta star l'océano véde,
E forse ancor l'Américano altero
Mal sicuro tremar nella sua sede.
Roma seppé così ne' dì felici
con un braccio domar civili sdegni
Vincer con l'altro e debéllar nemici.
Ma Roma cadde il sai … Cadono i régni …
Tu non cadrai? … Solo fra' voti amici
Roma la pace a non sprezzar t'insegni.

Britain was described as the new ancient Rome, that is to say the most powerful of all nations, a position she had gained for herself by the end of 1763 (the date of the Peace of Paris, which concluded the Seven Years' War). From then to the end of the century, the number of travellers who visited Italy on the British Grand Tour grew to unprecedented peaks, and their travels had a profound impact upon modern art and architecture, namely through the appreciation of Old Master paintings and the lure of the antique.[7] Nevertheless, as the author of the sonnet reminded his readers, Britain, like ancient Rome, was fragile and might make fatal mistakes. The Peace of Versailles, which recognized the independence of the American colonies, was signed in the same year, 1783.

The growth of the Grand Tour, comparisons between ancient Rome and modern Britain, and the fabulous wealth of some of its travellers and collectors were all matters of great curiosity to members of the Italian ruling class. Their curiosity towards Britain is shown in a letter written two years later by Thomas Jenkins, one of the principal excavators and dealers active in Rome, to Charles Townley (1737–1805), a Grand Tourist and one of the principal recipients of newly-excavated ancient marbles. On 12 November 1785 Jenkins wrote: 'The Secretary of State Expressed a desire to See a Work by Doctor Adam Smith on the Wealth of Nations two Vol: Quarto'.[8] A few months later, on 7 January 1786, he thanked Townley for sending the book, presumably the newly-published third edition. Cardinal Ignazio Boncompagni Ludovisi, the Segretario di Stato in 1785–9,[9] a man well informed about the Grand Tour, had asked not for Gibbon's *Decline and Fall of the Roman Empire* but for Smith's *Wealth of Nations*. He was more curious about the power and wealth of Britain, than about the decline of ancient Rome. Jenkins, who had just purchased a number of marbles from the Villa Negroni collection,

was the ideal man for Ludovisi to ask, while Townley, a Catholic capitalist who was amassing Roman antiquities in his London house, was the ideal recipient of the request from Jenkins.

Modern Britain and ancient Rome, the Grand Tour and excavations, modern politics, military power and economic growth were so inextricably linked that it is pointless to discuss which came first. It is better to concentrate on facts and evidence. During the eighteenth century, especially after 1763, Britain championed the Grand Tour to a greater extent than any other country. The British were the foremost foreign community of excavators and dealers in antiquities active in Rome, and their excavations and exports of ancient marbles and other works of art were 'politically' favoured by the governments of Clement XIV (Giovanni Vincenzo Ganganelli, pope 1769–74) and Pius VI (Gianangelo Braschi, pope 1775–99). Modern Rome, still splendid but rather weak, needed an invincible 'ally', and Britain, though defeated in America, had won on the battlefields of Europe. How powerful the British were and how Anglophile and Grand Tour-oriented the popes were during the second half of the century is demonstrated by, among other things, information about the booming market of *cave* and *robba*, two words used in those days to describe archaeological digs and ancient marbles suitable for sale.[10] British collections and the Vatican Museums were their principal recipients, but British diggers and dealers contributed to the expansion of many other European collections as well. This phenomenon can be described as the 'British conquest' of the marbles of ancient Rome.

'DIGGING AND DEALING' IN EIGHTEENTH-CENTURY ROME

Edicts issued by successive popes since the Renaissance ordered that those who wished to dig in Rome, or elsewhere in the Papal States, should send a written application to the Reverenda Camera Apostolica asking for an excavation licence.[11] Licences were written documents, signed and recorded by the Camerlengo, Tesoriere, Magister Viarum (later the Presidente delle Strade), and by *uditori* and *notai camerali*. During the period under consideration here, they were of three principal types:

1. *licenze di pozzolana*, or *tavolozza*, specifying the property in which the applicant was allowed to dig to find either building materials or antiquities,

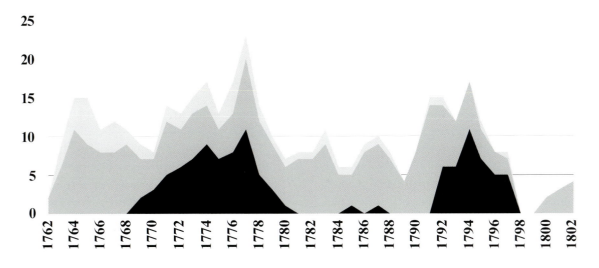

FIG. 1. Excavation licences granted by the Reverenda Camera Apostolica 1762–1802.

■ Total number of applications

■ Number of licences that were to find antiquities rather than building materials

■ Number of licences held by the British

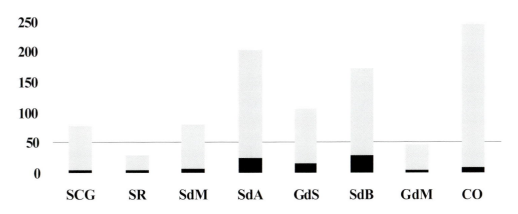

■ Total no. of marbles

■ No. of marbles unearthed or purchased and resold by the British

SCG = Sala a Croce Greca   SR = Sala Rotonda
SdM = Sala delle Muse   SdA = Sala degli Animali
GdS = Galleria delle Statue   SdB = Sala dei Busti
GdM = Gabinetto delle Maschere   CO = Cortile Ottagono

FIG. 2. 'British marbles' in the Pio-Clementino Museum.

provided that he/she was given permission to do so by the landowner;

2. *facultas/licentia effoiendi thesauros*;

3. *licenze generali di scavo archeologico*, enabling the applicant to dig within wider regions, even 'throughout the Papal States'.[12]

Thomas Jenkins (1722–98), Gavin Hamilton (1723–98) and Colin Morison (1732–1810), three of the foremost excavators of the second half of the eighteenth century, and Venceslao Pezolli (ob. *c.* 1790), Domenico De Angelis (active 1771–80), Nicola La Piccola (1727–90), Giovanni Corradi (active

1776–82) and Giovanni Volpato (c. 1755–1803), the most successful among their Italian colleagues, were usually granted *licenze di pozzolana*, or *tavolozza*.[13] General excavation licences were rarer. One of the earliest, dated to December 1591, was supposed to be granted to a noblewoman, Ginevra Salviati, who, however, never received it; a note written in the draft of her licence says 'draft copy neither finished nor sent out'.[14] Digging in Rome was a free, but well-regulated, activity, and one open to all those who, for pleasure, curiosity or profit, wished to try their luck. By profession, British and Italian diggers of the eighteenth century were usually painters, sculptors and art dealers, who undertook excavations for shorter or longer periods of time for money. Yet, since most of them lost rather than gained, clearly they were motivated also by a genuine passion for archaeological discoveries. This certainly applied to Robert Fagan (1761–1816), the foremost excavator of the 1790s who, thanks to Prince Augustus Frederick (1773–1843), later Duke of Sussex and an amateur archaeologist himself, was granted a general excavation licence in 1793, renewed in 1796.[15]

Numerous excavation licences are recorded, together with countless other licences (to install water-pipes, to produce and sell olive oil and wine, for example), in the Registri del Camerlengo preserved in the Archivio di Stato di Roma, which date from 1467 to 1831.[16] Just as many excavation licences, together with other licences relating to road works, are recorded in the Registri del Presidente delle Strade, also in the Archivio di Stato, dating from 1569 to 1825.[17] The Presidente delle Strade was in charge of checking that excavations did not interfere with public roads, aqueducts, monuments, cemeteries and so on. Licences recorded in these two sets of *registri* should be duplicates, but they seldom are; they rather seem to be complementary. Other licences are scattered among papers preserved under other headings in the Archivio di Stato, in other archives and libraries, among the papers of the Commissari delle Antichità e Cave di Roma, in the account books of landowning families, churches, monasteries and convents, and in the correspondence of the excavators. These sources, especially the papers of the Commissari who were in charge of inspecting sites and purchasing newly-discovered antiquities for the Vatican Museums,[18] should include duplicates of licences recorded in the *registri* of the Camerlengo and the Presidente delle Strade, but they very seldom do. In general, one might expect, in theory, modern archives to reflect the political struc-

ture of the old states to which they relate. However, the inconsistencies in record-keeping in all periods, the dispersal of documents, the rebinding and rearranging of *registri* and loose papers, and the introduction of new methods of cataloguing documents all mean that archives tend to reflect political structures only roughly.

The chart of excavation licences that is reproduced here (**Fig. 1**) is still provisional, but it is fairly reliable statistically, since it is based on a more complete set of data than those recorded by Rodolfo Lanciani and Carlo Pietrangeli.[19] It shows the dynamics of licences granted in the years 1762–1802, coinciding with the golden age of the Grand Tour and of excavations in Rome. The data come mostly from the *registri* of the Camerlengo and the Presidente delle Strade, in which *licenze di pozzolana*, or *tavolozza*, and general excavation licences are recorded. Light grey represents the total number of applications per year; they range from two granted in 1762 to 23 in 1777. Dark grey represents the number of licences that were to find antiquities rather than building materials, while black represents the number of them held by the British. The fact that a licence was granted does not tell one whether excavations were actually carried out; to know this, one needs other documents. Licences, however, are very important because they provide the precise location of sites, which are rarely given in other sources, and single out areas of archaeological interest.

The total number of sites excavated by Jenkins, Hamilton, Morison and Fagan over three decades currently is over 80, and includes major *cave* such as Tivoli, Ostia, Palestrina and Gabii, where excavation took place for long periods. This figure can be compared to the 70 plus sites currently attributed to Pezolli, De Angelis, La Piccola, Corradi and Volpato. Thus, the British held about half of the *cave* market. However, it should be noted that 'occasional' Italian excavators were very numerous and thus the total number of Italian digs does not bear comparison to British ones.

The chart (**Fig. 1**) shows the impact of the British Grand Tour upon excavations, and the growth of the demand for antiquities at a time when major collections were created in Britain and elsewhere in Europe (notably in Germany, Sweden and Russia). It also reveals the key role played by the Pio-Clementino Museum. During the second half of the century, Roman aristocrats and collectors were selling rather than acquiring, one of the few exceptions being Prince

Emilio Altieri, who was active as a 'digger' between the mid-1760s and the late 1770s. The chart also shows the difficulties met by the British in the late 1770s and 1780s. This was due to the growth of *cave camerali*, that is to say excavations carried out for Pius VI, the *Papa Cavatore* mentioned in many letters by Jenkins and Hamilton. Moreover, the chart shows the resumption of British excavations in the 1790s, coinciding with the growing strategic power of Britain in the Mediterranean. It was then that Prince Augustus patronized Fagan's excavations, and the ageing but indefatigable Hamilton obtained the monopoly of *cave* on the immense estates of the Borghese family. Finally, the chart shows the collapse of all licences during the period of the French occupation of Rome and the Roman Republic of 1798–9 (all pre-existing licences were annulled by Cardinal Romualdo Braschi Onesti's Edict of 21 August 1801), and their slow recovery early in the new century. By then, however, the golden age of British excavations had come to an end. Subsequently, the British were still granted licences but they never again had such a large share of them.

Most of the applications for excavation licences examined so far were successful; rejections became more frequent later. This reflects the nature of legislative measures — generally rigorous throughout the whole period from the Renaissance to the mid-nineteenth century but more liberal and flexible in the second half of the eighteenth century and more restrictive afterwards, especially after the issue of Cardinal Bartolomeo Pacca's Edict (7 April 1820), when the number of recorded illegal excavations increased considerably. There was always some illegal digging by peasants and local treasure hunters, but what strikes one most is that in the eighteenth century there is almost no evidence for real illegal excavations. Apparently there was no need for them in a period when licences were so easily obtained and the ownership of discoveries so sensibly regulated. The general rule was that one-third of the finds went to the landowner, one-third to the excavator and his partners, and one-third to the Reverenda Camera for the Vatican Museums. But rules were flexible: the landowner could sell his third, the excavator could buy thirds and smaller shares from his partners, the Commissario could renounce his third and, of course, the pope through his Commissario (who was also the Director of the Vatican Museums) had the right to claim all finds for the Museums. However, in this case, the Tesoriere had to pay cash and quickly, like all the

participants in the *cave* and *robba* market. Rules changed later in line with the needs of museums in Rome, which were left almost empty by the depredations of the occupying French army. Cardinal Giuseppe Doria-Pamphili's Edict (1 October 1802) ordered that lists of all antiquities and other works of art in private hands should be compiled, and it authorized the Commissario to purchase objects for the Vatican and other museums 'a prezzi ragionevoli' ('at reasonable prices'), that is, below market-prices. Once the museums were filled again and most of the marbles returned by the new French Government, rules changed again; Cardinal Pacca's Edict, for instance, authorized landowners and excavators to share equally all finds from a single *cava*.

In his licence, the successful applicant was reminded that he should not dig near 'Luoghi Sagri, Cemeterj, Mura di Città, Condotti di Fontane, Strade Pubbliche, ed Antichità che servono di erudizione' ('Holy Places, Cemeteries, City Walls, Fountain Conduits, Public Roads, and Antiquities that have educational value'); that, once granted the licence, he should apply for written permission from the owner of the land where he intended to dig; that were he to find antiquities of any value, he should report them to the Commissario; that once the excavation had been completed, he should restore the ground to its original state; and that in general he should conform to edicts. This implied, among other things, that he should promptly report all finds to the Commissario, a rule applying also to casual discoveries. In a land so densely filled with archaeological remains, virtually any excavation produced some discoveries. Moreover, diggers were compelled by law to list all objects (statues, busts, inscriptions, slabs, water-pipes, for example) in a report addressed to the Commissario.

The Commissario personally inspected sites, or entrusted experts of his choice with it; he and the Camerlengo were also the recipients of applications for the export of antiquities and other works of art. Moreover, it was the Commissario who selected marbles for the Vatican Museums, though it was the Tesoriere who ordered payments to be made. An understanding of this process enables one to find documents relating to exports and acquisitions; they are preserved among the *registri* and loose papers of the Commissario, Camerlengo and Tesoriere and, more generally, under the Reverenda Camera, that is to say Camerale I, Camerale II and Camerlengato in the Archivio di Stato di Roma. These papers, however, are as fragmentary and dispersed as those relating to excavation licences.

As soon as works at a *cava* were completed, all finds were listed and valued by experts, who were either *assessori* (assistants to the Commissario) or restorers and dealers such as Bartolomeo Cavaceppi (1716–99), Francesco Antonio Franzoni (1734–1818) and Vincenzo Pacetti (1746–1820).[20] During the eighteenth century, it was comparatively rare for restorers to excavate; Giovanni Battista Piranesi (1720–78) and Volpato were among the few exceptions, though no conclusion can presently be drawn because too little is known of the lives of many of the excavators, restorers and dealers.

These remarks, besides providing an introduction to the following examples of documents selected for this essay, may help the reader to understand better papal policy and its consequences. The tangible and admirable nature of its results still can be observed in the rooms of the Vatican Museums. A very high number of those marbles were acquired (at below market-price) at the apex of Pius VI's liberal policies regarding excavation and export licences, when thousands of marbles and other fragments left Rome to fill countless collections around Europe. The number of marbles acquired by the Reverenda Camera from British excavators and dealers is remarkable and unrivalled by those of other non-Italian sellers. **Figure 2** is still provisional and it only covers well-documented 'British marbles' in some rooms of the Pio-Clementino Museum. In the histogram, light grey columns represent the total number of marbles room by room, while black columns represent the number of marbles unearthed or purchased and resold by the British. Their percentage ranges from about 4% (Cortile Ottagono) to 22% (Sala Rotonda), and it includes conservative estimates such as 20% in the Sala dei Busti and 15% in the Sala degli Animali, where further identifications are still to be made.

Besides filling the Vatican Museums, the British also contributed to the expansion of several other collections in and outside Britain. How many items were actually unearthed and dealt with by Jenkins, Hamilton, Morison and Fagan is still hard to tell. Rough calculations suggest a few thousand, from which one can extrapolate the numbers from *cave* and *robba* throughout the century and draw conclusions about the age of the Grand Tour, when Britain and other countries conquered the marbles of ancient Rome, but modern Rome, in its turn, conquered the world with its antiquities and other works of art.

WRITTEN AND VISUAL DOCUMENTS AT WORK

Eleven examples have been selected for this essay, which illustrate three principal issues raised by documents relating to eighteenth-century excavations.

I. DISTINCTION BETWEEN PRIMARY AND SECONDARY SOURCES

The first two examples draw attention to secondary sources that until now have been regarded as primary sources. The cases considered are Ennio Quirino Visconti's essay on the *Monumento degli Scipioni* (Rome, 1785),[21] and Carlo Fea's *Relazione di un viaggio ad Ostia* (Rome, 1802). The rediscovery in 1780–3 of the Tomb of the Scipios at Vigna Sassi (near the Porta San Sebastiano) was one of the great events of eighteenth-century archaeology.[22] Ennio Quirino Visconti (1751–1818), then librarian to Prince Sigismondo Chigi, generally has been considered to be the sole author of the essay published in 1785, the same year in which he became director *de facto* of the municipal Capitoline Museums and a year after the death of his father Giovanni Battista Visconti (1722–84), Commissario and Director of the Vatican Museums from 1770 to 1784.[23] Newly-discovered documents question Ennio Quirino's sole authorship and throw new light on his father. According to English travellers and excavators who visited the site, it was 'the Abbé Visconti, the Pope's Antiquary' (that is, Giovanni Battista) who carried out excavations after the casual discovery of the tomb on 13 May 1780, who made interesting remarks about inscriptions and who sent a letter about the discovery and finds to the Tesoriere, Guglielmo Pallotta.[24] An unsigned and undated draft of Giovanni Battista's letter is preserved in the Biblioteca Apostolica Vaticana, while a similar but longer report, signed by him and dated 1782, is held in the Archivio di Stato di Roma.[25] Giovanni Battista's report was the source of Ennio Quirino's essay. Moreover, Giovanni Corradi was the excavator responsible for the actual excavation carried out for the Commissario and his excavation reports and lists of finds (untraceable) must have been, in turn, the sources of the Commissario's original report.

Ennio Quirino Visconti and Fea, whose works are usually regarded as primary sources for excavations, published several reports originally written by excavators and rewritten by Commissari. During this process of writing and rewriting for different purposes, some valuable information was lost and mistakes were made.

To prove this is difficult, since very few original reports survive and even fewer exemplary cases such as that of the Tomb of the Scipios can be cited. However, other documents can be used, notably excavation licences and the letters of excavators. This applies, for instance, to the chronology of eighteenth-century excavations at Ostia and Portus. According to Fea (and also Nibby and Paschetto), there were some excavations in the area of Ostia in 1775 and 1783, Hamilton excavated there in 1788, some discoveries were made at Portus in 1794 and Fagan was active at Ostia in 1794–1800.[26] In 1912 Thomas Ashby demonstrated that letters from excavators published by Arthur Hamilton Smith in 1889 and 1901 added much to Paschetto's (and Fea's) picture.[27] Moreover, from 1902, when the first volume of Lanciani's *Storia* appeared, it has been apparent that research on excavation licences provides additional information and corrects many mistakes. For all the efforts made by Lanciani and Ashby, the Fea-derived chronology of excavations at Ostia and Portus is still regarded as fairly complete and reliable. It is now possible to demonstrate that Carlo Fea (1753–1836), the Commissario and Director of the Vatican Museums (1801–36),[28] made little use of papers left in his office because his principal aim in writing his *Relazione* was not to contribute a fully documented history of excavations, but to produce a well-documented manifesto denouncing the long period of savage exploitation of Ostia and its territory, which had culminated in Fagan's activities there. Thus, a politically-motivated book has been regarded as a primary source for almost two centuries. In fact, were one to explore genuine primary sources, namely excavation licences and letters, one would produce quite a different picture:

1) Hamilton excavated at Portus in 1772 and Ostia in 1774–6 and 1778–9;
2) Prince Emilio Altieri, G.B. Cenci, Jenkins and others excavated at Ostia (possibly Portus) in 1776–8;
3) Volpato and Jenkins excavated at Ostia in 1779–80;
4) excavations near Ostia were carried out in 1783;
5) the Portuguese Minister, Don Diego Norogna, was patron of the excavations at Ostia in 1783;
6) Pezolli excavated at Ostia for the Reverenda Camera in 1788–9;
7) important discoveries were made at Portus in 1794;
8) Fagan was active at Ostia between 1794 and 1801.

Fagan's are the only excavations that are reasonably well documented by Fea. Yet, when one compares his chronology and list of finds with the actual primary sources, the picture changes. This applies, for instance, to the Vatican Museums' *Colossal statue of Abbondanza, or Fortuna* (Braccio Nuovo 79, inv. 2244), discovered by Fagan at Tor Boacciana, Ostia, in 1797, not in 1798 as stated by Fea. The latter was at that time librarian to Prince Chigi and only later Commissario, and so not an eyewitness to Fagan's excavations.[29] The precise date is given by Fagan in a letter to George Cumberland of 10 June 1797; among the marbles discovered between May and early June he mentioned 'a statue of Fortune 10 palms high'.[30] Fagan excavated at Ostia for six years and his *cave* were scattered over a vast area (the western part of the site, from Porta Marina to Tor Boacciana, down to Via della Foce). Thus the dating of individual discoveries is essential to establish where he found particular antiquities, which otherwise would form a meaningless list of no use to present archaeologists.

II. THE POSSIBILITY OF CONFLICTING EVIDENCE

The following four examples reveal the extent to which documents provide conflicting evidence. These examples include the *Chigi Head of Agrippina Minor*, illustrated in the second volume of Giuseppe Antonio Guattani's *Monumenti antichi inediti* of 1785 (**Fig. 3**), and the *Head of Agrippina Minor, also called Agrippina Major, Livia, Antonia and Drusilla*, of the Ashmolean Museum, Oxford (**Fig. 4**).[31] No Agrippina, or similar head that might be safely identified with either of these heads, is listed among marbles recovered for Prince Sigismondo Chigi at Tor Paterno in 1777–80, or in the Chigi inventory of 1793.[32] Evidence that an Agrippina was found by the Prince at Tor Paterno is provided by a letter from Ennio Quirino Visconti to Paolo Angelini of 15 April 1785:

The beautiful Empress represented in a stupendous bust has been identified as Agrippina Minor; it was found between those monuments that have been brought to light on the Campi Laurentini by the munificence of Sig. Principe Chigi. It perfectly resembles the Farnesina, although its more youthful aspect better illustrates her beauty; a beauty evident on her corpse even to her parricide son; it also could be said that, in terms of hairstyle, the famous bust could represent the daughter of Germanicus rather than the mother of Nero.[33]

FIG. 3. Head of Agrippina Minor, supposedly from Tor Paterno. Engraving by Mochetti, March 1785. From G.A. Guattani, *Monumenti antichi inediti* II (Rome, 1785), pl. II. The British School at Rome Library. *(Photo: Mauro Coen.)*

In 1958 Carlo Pietrangeli tentatively identified this head with a portrait of Agrippina at the Palazzo Chigi, Ariccia. But what about the *Agrippina* in the Ashmolean Museum? In 1798, Robert Fagan purchased most of the marbles discovered at Tor Paterno from Sigismondo's son and heir, Agostino. Shortly afterwards, the French occupation army requisitioned the marbles in Fagan's hands, including several from Tor Paterno and also a 'Bust of Agrippina'.[34] Once released, some of these marbles were exported legally by Fagan and some were acquired from him for the Vatican Museums.[35] A 'Bust of Agrippina', probably the same one requisitioned in 1798, is recorded in Fagan's export licence of 25 July 1800.[36] This bust is certainly the Hope, later Ashmolean Museum, *Agrippina*. It might be that both heads, or one of them, were discovered at Tor Paterno, but documents found so far do not allow any conclusions to be drawn.

Another example of the uncertainties of archival research is the Vatican Museums' *Colossal statue of seated Tiberius*,[37] which allegedly was found by Giuseppe Petrini at Privernum in 1796.[38] Indeed, the modern marble block on which Tiberius is seated bears the following inscription: 'Ex ruderibus Priverni / Ioseph Petrinus anno MDCCXCVI' ('from the ruins of Privernum / Ioseph Petrinus / 1796'). However, in a section of his report on the antiquities of Sicily, Fagan claimed to have discovered it.[39] Yet a letter found recently seems to undermine Fagan's statement; on 24 April 1796, Gavin Hamilton reported to Townley that 'Petrine with the other associates have been more fortunate in their Cava at Piperno Vechio'. It might be that Petrini and Fagan were both involved, but the truth is still uncertain.

The extent to which the evidence of documents might clash with modern archaeological knowledge and connoisseurship of ancient marbles is demonstrated by the *'Penelope' relief* in the Vatican Museums,[40] a marble acquired from Fagan in 1804 and long regarded as a Greek work after a lost original of the mid-fifth century BC.[41] According to the *Descrizione delle Antichità del Museo Chiaramonti*, written in 1806 by Filippo Aurelio Visconti

FIG. 4.   Bust of Agrippina Minor, or Agrippina Major, Livia, Antonia and Drusilla, possibly from Tor Paterno. Fine-grained white marble 0.66 m high, from base of neck to crown 0.34 m, from chin to crown 0.23 m. Second quarter of the first century AD. Ashmolean Museum, Oxford (formerly Hope Collection, Deepdene, no. 51), inv. 1917.67. *(Photo: Ashmolean Museum. Reproduced courtesy of the Ashmolean Museum, Oxford.)*

FIG. 5.   Bust of Sabina, allegedly from Monte Cagnolo. Fine-grained white marble 0.78 m high. Second century AD, recently catalogued as an eighteenth-century fake. Vatican Museums, Sala dei Busti 49, inv. 634. Archivio Fotografico dei Musei Vaticani, neg. no. XXXII.70.16. *(Reproduced courtesy of the Direzione Generale, Monumenti, Musei e Gallerie Pontificie.)*

(1754–1831), the Commissario and Director of the Vatican Museums in 1784–99, this 'fragment of a woman seated on a basket, or vase' was one of the 'monuments found at Ostia [sic: Via Appia] inside the sepulchral room of Claudia Semne by Mr Feghan'.[42] In 1792–3 Fagan was actually responsible for excavations at Vigna San Sebastiano (Via Appia Antica on the corner with the Appia Pignatelli), where he discovered the Tomb of Claudia Semne and other funerary monuments, and in 1804 he sold several of those finds to the Reverenda Camera. This, however, is not sufficiently strong evidence to overcome objections one might make on the basis of modern archaeological knowledge and connoisseurship; the provenance of the *Relief* is still an open question.[43]

Similar remarks can be made about the exceptional output of a truly virgin *cava*, so exceptional as to raise serious problems for the identification of originals and

fakes. The *cava* in question is Monte Cagnolo, the 'Mountain of the Dogs', between Genzano and Civita Lavinia (Lanuvio), which Hamilton believed to be the site of Antoninus Pius's villa. In 1773–4, he found there the Vatican and British Museums' groups of two dogs.[44] Comparison of them at the *Grand Tour* exhibition in 1996–7 has led some visitors to feel that one of them might be a fake. Stronger suspicions have been raised recently by the *Monte Cagnolo Sabina* (**Fig. 5**), which is now catalogued as an eighteenth-century fake.[45] Its perfect state of preservation, the surface, technique, style, neoclassical appearance and other details (the fact that it was carved out of one block of marble, the survival of the original nose, the use of the rasp, the handling of the drapery, the elaborate scroll) make it a very unusual piece of sculpture, a fact mentioned at the time of its discovery. On 21 March 1774, Hamilton described it to Townley as 'a most beautifull bust of Sabina preserved as when it came from the hands of the Sculptor not even the point of the nose broke'. A more telling description (written by the Commissario) appeared in the *Diario ordinario* of 9 April: 'At the end of the excavations of Civita Lavinia, Mr Gavin Hamilton found a Bust of Sabina Augusta, exceptional in terms of sculpture and completeness'.[46] Since one of the arguments advanced to conclude that the bust is a fake has been the implausible story of 'Sabina in cucina' (that the bust was either restored or manufactured in the kitchen of Hamilton's house in Rome), I fully investigated the documentary evidence relating to it and have come to the conclusion that it proves nothing, and might even support the opposite view. The *Monte Cagnolo Sabina* is documented in no less than fourteen unpublished letters written by Hamilton to Townley between February 1774 and July 1780. It was viewed and much admired in Hamilton's kitchen by the Tesoriere (Gianangelo Braschi, later Pope Pius VI), the Commissario (Giovanni Battista Visconti) and by various English Grand Tourists, collectors and connoisseurs (George Beaumont, Matthew Nulty, Edward Lord Clive, George Grenville). It was immediately purchased for the Vatican Museums and valued at 360 scudi, a high value for a bust (the receipt for an advance payment of 52 scudi is dated 8 March 1774), but eventually it was presented by Hamilton to the newly-elected pope, Pius VI. The bust actually entered the Vatican Museums in May 1775. One or more casts of it were made by Giovanni Crosati before it was removed from Hamilton's house. (Townley was charged 3 scudi for one of them on 7 April 1777.) Six years after its discovery, the *Monte Cagnolo Sabina* was still regarded as a paradigm of quality and perfection (Hamilton to Townley, July 1780). Sometime after 1775, one or more casts were made by Carlo Albacini, and one of them reached the Trustees' Academy in Edinburgh in a group of 255 plaster casts 'after the antique' purchased from Albacini's son Filippo in 1838. Thus, after more than half a century, the *Monte Cagnolo Sabina* was still regarded as a masterpiece of Roman Imperial portraiture and placed next to casts of the most celebrated portraits preserved in the museums of Rome, Naples and Florence. In conclusion, the *Monte Cagnolo Sabina* is either one of the most extraordinary cases in the history of forgeries of classical sculpture, or it was the victim of 'cosmetic restoration' in the 1770s.[47]

More generally, one might note that while we know much (but still not enough) about eighteenth-century integrative restorations, we know little of what might be described as 'cosmetic restorations', which ranged from light treatments with *pumice* and *aquafortis* (as Hamilton described them) to serious plastic surgery and the use of the *rota*. In spring 1776, Townley asked Hamilton's opinion about a Venus, which had been offered to him by Jenkins. On 5 May, he answered that 'it has been originally good, but being much corroded they have barbarously given it the rota all over, excepting the vase with drapery over it which is vergin, in this rotation they have spared neither muscles nor bones'. This must have been an old restoration (by della Porta), but there is plenty of evidence that the *rota* was much used on sarcophagi of the Pio Christian Museum, which were restored by Bartolomeo Cavaceppi and Giuseppe Angelini in the last quarter of the eighteenth century.[48] Finally, one might also note that we know even less about scientific experiments in the eighteenth-century conservation of ancient fragments. One curious example that can be cited is 'the magic ointment of *Medea*, with which the fresh roses of green Youthfulness are brought back to the wan faces of Decrepitude'.[49] This cosmetic remedy was one of several chemical experiments carried out by a Roman Professor of Medicine called Nicola Martelli on wall-paintings discovered by Prince Chigi at Tor Paterno in 1777–80.[50] Martelli's experiments were serious attempts to find a new glue but, as often occurs with scientific experiments, they resulted in tragedy; the Tor Paterno paintings were lost, for ever.

III. HOW ARCHIVAL DOCUMENTS CAN HELP IN THE IDENTIFICATION OF ANTIQUITIES

The following five examples demonstrate the ways in which written and visual documents can help to identify antiquities and clarify their provenance; to locate, rediscover and protect sites; and to reconstruct lost remains. The Vatican Museums' *Relief of gladiators and lions*, acquired from Hamilton in 1776,[51] shows the extent to which excavators' correspondence can provide evidence about the excavation provenance of marbles of which nothing was known previously, and can help to cast new light on the decoration of famous Roman monuments. On 10 May 1775 Hamilton wrote to Townley:

I have got a fragment of a large bassorelievo, being part of the triumphal arch of M[arcus]. Aurelius, found digging the foundation of the Nunry of St. Silvester in Capite, it represents a giostra of lions & tigres in some amphitheatre, I have got a man combating with a tigre

& another with a lion, I am told that part of this bassorelievo is in the gardens of the above nuns, & made use of to support the orange pots, in a day or two I shall get leave to rummage in every hole & corner for the rest of this capital performance, being figures as large as life & then shall send you a drawing of it.[52]

Studies published since the late nineteenth century have ascertained that the area of the convent of San Silvestro in Capite was once occupied by the Temple of the Sun.[53] Hamilton, whose letter adds new elements to our knowledge of that monument, believed that this relief was part of the triumphal arch of Marcus Aurelius. To question and discuss his views is not necessary. More generally, old documentary sources should never be corrected in the light of modern archaeological knowledge until research has been completed; otherwise one risks missing descriptions of the same piece in other contemporary records and one might be left with neither arches nor temples, nor firmly identified and located fragments.

However, provenances recorded in excavators' correspondence are occasionally misleading. This applies, for instance, to the Vatican Museums' *Bust with head of a young Claudian prince (the young Nero), originally described as Titus Claudius* and *Bust with head of Titus*.[54] Both heads were found by Hamilton in a *cava* at Palo, the ancient Alisum, in spring 1775. Their provenance is not recorded by the excavator, but is found in one of two surviving versions of his sale to the Reverenda Camera for the year 1776 recording a 'Head of Titus found at Palo … s[cudi] 100' and a 'Head of Claudius found at Anzio [sic. Alsium] … s[cudi] 80'.[55] One would hardly reach the same conclusion if one had believed what Hamilton wrote to Townley. On 16 April 1775 he announced that he was about to go 'to Palo with 30 men leaving ten at Ostia'; he had great expectations and intended to dig on a grand scale.[56] But on 10 May he lamented: 'I have thrown away 500 crowns at Palo being all dug very probably by Leo the tenth & others'. It is probable that Hamilton did not find much, but he lied to Townley; a few months later he sold the heads to the Reverenda Camera for 180 scudi. Yet he had told Townley some of the truth; Palo was not a *cava vergine* (Hamilton loved 'virgin digs');[57] it had been *profanata* (profaned) over two centuries before, and presumably more than once. This passage might actually enable us to locate Hamilton's *cava*, probably the same site where extensive excavations had been carried out for Paolo Giordano Orsini in the 1560s, not under Leo X

FIG. 6. Archaic herm-bust, with the seller identification number (15 = Francesco Antonio and Giuseppe Franzoni) painted in red varnish in the middle of the forehead. Marble, 0.33 m high. End of the first century AD. Vatican Museums, Museo Chiaramonti XIV.14, inv. 1391. Archivio Fotografico dei Musei Vaticani, neg. no. 88 VAT. 278. *(Reproduced courtesy of the Direzione Generale, Monumenti, Musei e Gallerie Pontificie.)*

but under Pius IV.[58] This example demonstrates that, for market or other reasons, excavators might hide the truth, but their lies in themselves may prove illuminating to the modern researcher; that contrary to what is generally believed, vast and deep excavations were carried out in Rome and elsewhere in Lazio from the Renaissance; that Renaissance documents might prove crucial for the location of eighteenth-century *cave* (and vice versa); and, more generally, that studies of the history of specific excavations need to be developed to a greater extent than has occurred so far.

The same applies to research on little-studied documents, both written and visual, such as the numbers painted or traced on the objects themselves. Numbers are often marked on ancient marbles — some of them are recent, others old, some are collection or museum numbers, but some do not fit into either of these categories; they are excavation and sellers' numbers. It

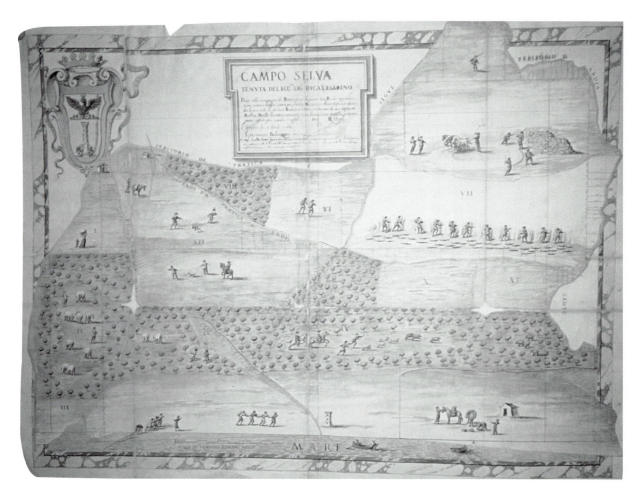

Fig. 7. G. Belenzona, The Campo Selva estate belonging to the Sforza Cesarini family, 14 April 1587. The site where the Campo Iemini villa has roughly been located is in the wood where a boar hunt is taking place. Archivio di Stato di Roma, Presidenza delle Strade 432(8) (Catasto Alessandrino). *(Photo: I. Bignamini by permission of the Archivio di Stato di Roma. Reproduced courtesy of the Ministero per i Beni e le Attività Culturali, ASR 2/2003. All further reproduction is prohibited.)*

has already been noted that excavators were compelled by law to send a list of all finds to the Commissario. Some lists still survive and objects listed there are numbered. Since important finds are mixed with other finds, it is reasonable to assume that these numbers mirror the sequence in which the objects were discovered. No excavation number actually marked on an object has been found so far, but their existence is suggested by numbers in manuscript and printed lists. Amanda Claridge and I have tested this hypothesis on the Tomb of Claudia Semne, and results have been sufficiently satisfactory to allow us to place marbles and inscriptions back in the tomb and its garden.[59] One case is not enough to be conclusive, and other list numbers need to be tested.

Numbers marked on objects, such as code numbers still painted in red varnish on many marbles acquired for the Vatican Museums in 1804, or thereabouts, might also disclose the identity of the original sellers.[60]

According to one of several versions of Fagan's *Nota degli oggetti*, as soon as marbles acquired from him entered the Museums they were 'marked with their individual numbers and the number 22'.[61] Since 22 was Fagan's identification number as a seller, that sentence could only mean that each piece sold by him was marked 22. This has proved to be true and has led to the discovery of all the surviving seller numbers in the Vatican Museums (**Fig. 6**), and also to an understanding of their function and relationship to corresponding numbers recorded in early manuscript catalogues of the Chiaramonti Museum.

How far drawings and engravings by professional artists can contribute to locating eighteenth-century digs and to reconstructing lost remains has been demonstrated by the use Amanda Claridge and I have made of Carlo Labruzzi's views of the Tomb of Claudia Semne.[62] My previous remarks about written documents apply to an even greater extent to visual

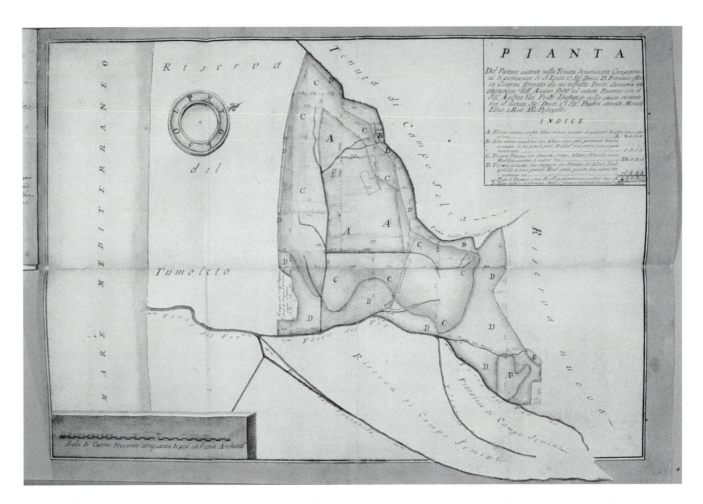

FIG. 8. G. Gabrielli, The pond in the Sforza Cesarini estate of Campo Iemini in which the 'luogo ove il Signor Feghan fece lo Scavo, e trovò varie Statue' ('the place where Mr Feghan excavated, and found several statues') is marked near the shore, next to the Fosso del Feo, 10 November 1801. Archivio di Stato di Roma, Disegni e mappe, Coll. I, cart. 92 no. 723, ff. 8014/1–30 (Campo Jemini. Relazione giudiziale fatta ad istanza dell'Eccellentissima Casa [Sforza] Cesarini contro [Giovanni Battista] Paolini intorno ai danni derivanti per l'essicagione non fatta del Pantano del Feo, 17 December 1801). (Photo: Archivio di Stato di Roma. Reproduced courtesy of the Ministero per i Beni e le Attività Culturali, ASR 2/2003. All further reproduction is prohibited.)

records; all possible versions of depictions, such as Labruzzi's exterior and interior views of the Tomb of Claudia Semne, should be traced and dated; the original sketch recording more faithfully what was actually seen by the artist on the spot needs to be identified; and later, unrealistic, additions should never be dismissed because they might carry symbolic meaning, leading, for instance, to the precise location of sites. Works such as Labruzzi's countless sketches and finished drawings for his *Via Appia Illustrata ab Urbe Roma ad Capuam* (Rome, 1794) are not mere illustrations, but proper works of art and visual documents of the utmost importance for the history of archaeology and excavations.

Maps, too, can augment written documents and produce strong evidence for the location of sites, provided that one finds the whole series of maps needed or, at least, those most useful for one's purpose.

This applies, for instance, to Campo Iemini, a Sforza Cesarini estate on the ancient coast of Lazio, where Fagan excavated in 1794. He discovered a large room, possibly a nymphaeum, belonging to a villa of the Hadrianic period, and unearthed several marbles, including a *Venus* of the Capitoline type.[63] In 1994, I tentatively located the villa near modern Torvaianica, on the basis of a 1587 map of the Campo Selva estate (Campo Iemini being part of it) (**Fig. 7**) and Fea's description of the site. But, in 1997, I discovered a more promising map, which had been made for a legal action in 1801 (**Fig. 8**). Close to the shore, next to the Fossa del Feo, one reads: 'the place where Mr Feghan excavated, and found several statues'.[64] Promising, but not enough; the site could not be located precisely. More recently, an 1878 map of the Istituto Topografico Militare was found in an old box of Thomas Ashby's research material in the Archive of the British School

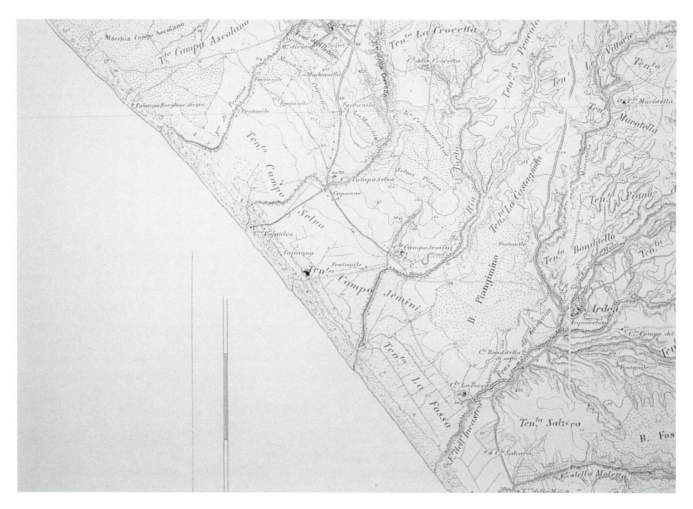

FIG. 9. Detail of the Istituto Topografico Militare 1:50,000 map of the area of Ardea (Rome, 1878). The site, near the shore and next to the Fosso del Feo, where the Campo Iemini villa has been located, is marked on it. The British School at Rome Library. *(Photo: I. Bignamini.)*

at Rome; the same peculiar shape of the Fossa del Feo as in the 1801 map was marked on it (**Fig. 9**). A visit with Maria Fenelli and Alessandro Jaia in spring 1998 to two fields miraculously left untouched between Torvaianica and Riotorto has led to the precise location of the Campo Iemini villa, and even to the location of the 'large room with niches' ('stanzone con nicchione') (9–10 x 3–4 m), a nymphaeum or similar room, where Fagan had found several statues, including four in the Vatican Museums, and the British Museum *Venus*. Campo Iemini is now a protected area, where excavations might be carried out fairly soon. This last case shows how far one can go with research on *Archives & Excavations*.

NOTES

1. These data derive from research being undertaken by the author [at the time of her premature death] on 'Licences granted by the Reverenda Camera Apostolica for archaeological excavations in Rome and elsewhere in the Papal States from the Renaissance to the mid-nineteenth century'. The author collected information on many of the licences during a three-year research project entitled 'British archaeological excavations in Italy 1764–1802' when she was a Leverhulme Trust Research Fellow at the Department of the History of Art, University of Oxford, 1996–9. The estimated total number of licences granted during the whole period is about 2,000–2,500. The data for the eighteenth and early nineteenth centuries are almost complete, and the percentage of excavations carried out by the British as compared to Italians or citizens of other European nations is fairly accurate.

2. The data are provisional and the histogram covers only a few rooms of the Pio-Clementino Museum. Total numbers room by room are inclusive of mosaics, plaster casts and modern sculptures. See I. Bignamini, 'I marmi Fagan in Vaticano. La

vendita del 1804 e altre acquisizioni', *BMusPont* 16 (1996), 331–94; I. Bignamini, 'Review of B. Andreae (ed.), *Buildkatalog der Skulpturen des Vatikanischen Museums* I: *Museo Chiaramonti*', *JHS* 118 (1998), 198–204. Work has been facilitated by the numerous identifications made by Carlo Pietrangeli ('La provenienza delle sculture dei Musei Vaticani I', *BMusPont* 7 (1987), 115–49; 'La provenienza delle sculture dei Musei Vaticani II', *BMusPont* 8 (1988), 139–210; 'La provenienza delle sculture dei Musei Vaticani III', *BMusPont* 9 (1) (1989), 85–140; 'La raccolta epigrafica vaticana nel Settecento I', *BMusPont* 12 (1992), 21–31; 'La raccolta epigrafica vaticana nel Settecento II', *BMusPont* 13 (1993), 49–79). His work has been continued by Paolo Liverani (*Museo Chiaramonti* (Rome, 1989); in B. Andreae (ed.), *Buildkatalog der Skulpturen des Vatikanischen Museums* I: *Museo Chiaramonti* (Berlin/New York, 1995)) and Giandomenico Spinola (*Il Museo Pio Clementino* I (Vatican City, 1996); *Il Museo Pio Clementino* II (Vatican City, 1999)).

3. See I. Bignamini, 'The British conquest of the marbles of ancient Rome: aspects of the material and cultural conquests', written for *Responding to the Antique* (joint seminar series, The American Academy in Rome and The British School at Rome, 1999), revised and expanded for the *Neale Colloquium in British History* (University College, London, 3–4 March 2000).

4. A. Smith, *Inquiry into the Nature and Causes of the Wealth of Nations* (London, 1776; 1784³, with additions).

5. E. Gibbon, *History of the Decline and Fall of the Roman Empire*, 6 vols (London, 1776–88).

6. For example, British Library, 1970 (Letters to John Strange II, 1778–87), fol. 237. The sonnet, unsigned and undated, was included among papers written around 1783. For Strange and other British travellers and residents mentioned in this essay, see *DBITI*.

7. For the Grand Tour, see the catalogues of the exhibitions held in London (Tate Gallery) and Rome (Palazzo delle Esposizioni): A. Wilton and I. Bignamini (eds), *Grand Tour. The Lure of Italy in the Eighteenth Century* (London, 1996); A. Wilton and I. Bignamini (eds), *Grand Tour. Il fascino dell'Italia nel XVIII secolo* (Rome, 1997). For the most admired marbles, see F. Haskell and N. Penny, *Taste and the Antique. The Lure of Classical Sculpture, 1500–1900* (New Haven/London, 1981).

8. Letters addressed to Townley are preserved in the British Museum Archive, while those addressed to other collectors, Commissari and others are dispersed in archives and libraries in and outside the United Kingdom and Rome. No change to the original spelling has been made.

9. For a list of the Segretari di Stato from 1644 to 1970, see N. Del Re, *La Curia Romana. Lineamenti storico-giuridici* (Rome, 1970), 74–6.

10. For such terminology, see I. Bignamini, 'Gli scavi archeologici a Roma nel Settecento', in A. Germano (ed.), *Pallade di Velletri: il mito, la fortuna* (Rome, 1999), 13–24.

11. For the edicts, see A. Emiliani, *Leggi, bandi e provvedimenti per la tutela dei beni artistici e culturali negli antichi stati italiani 1571–1860* (Bologna, 1978). For a list of Camerlenghi, 1188–1970, see Del Re, *Curia Romana* (above, n. 9), 307–9.

12. 'In tutto lo Stato Pontificio.' *Pozzolana* was a sand used to make cement, while *tavolozza* was used for bricks and tiles. While digging to find building materials, applicants were likely to find antiquities as well, which explains why from the Renaissance onwards all applicants had to conform to the same rules. *Facultas/licentia effoiendi thesauros*, usually granted by the Tesoriere, are met more frequently among applicants who were amateur local diggers searching for gold and silver. Other licences included *facultas/licentia effoiendi lapides*, or *marmora et lapides*, *patentes litterae effoiendi in alma Urbe* or *in agro* etc.

13. For Pezolli, see U. Schädler, 'Dallo scavo al museo. Scavi di Pio VI nella Villa dei Quintili', *BMusPont* 16 (1996), 287–30; U. Schädler, 'Scavi e scoperte nella Villa dei Quintili', in A. Ricci (ed.), *La Villa dei Quintili. Fonti scritte e fonti figurate* (Rome, 1998), 38–46. Almost nothing is known of De Angelis (apparently not the painter of the same name) and Corradi, while La Piccola and Volpato are known as artists but not as excavators. Volpato was responsible for numerous *cave* in the late 1770s and 1780s.

14. That is, 'minuta non completata né spedita'. ASR, Camerale II, Antichità e Belle Arti, b. 3, fasc. 109. Women, both Italian and foreigners, as patrons of archaeological excavations were not as numerous as men but, contrary to common belief, they existed from the Renaissance.

15. For Fagan, see I. Bignamini, 'The 'Campo Iemini Venus' rediscovered', *Burlington Magazine* 136 (1097) (August 1994), 548–52; Bignamini, 'I marmi Fagan in Vaticano' (above, n. 2); I. Bignamini and A. Claridge, 'The Tomb of Claudia Semne and excavations in eighteenth-century Rome', *PBSR* 66 (1998), 215–44.

16. ASR, Camerale I, Diversorum del Camerlengo; see inv. 112/4.

17. ASR, Presidenza delle Strade, lettere patenti; see inv. 171; also D. Sinisi and O. Verdi (eds), 'I registri delle lettere patenti della Presidenza delle Strade (1691–1701)', in *Roma nel primo Settecento. Case, proprietari, strade, toponimi* (*Archivi e Cultura* 28) (Rome, 1995), 123–243.

18. For a list of the Commissari from 1534 to 1870, see R.T. Ridley, 'To protect the monuments: the papal antiquarian (1534–1870)', *Xenia Antiqua* 1 (1992), 117–54.

19. Lanciani, *Storia* (1989–), specifically vol. VI; C. Pietrangeli, *Scavi e scoperte di antichità sotto il pontificato di Pio VI* (Rome, 1958²).

20. For Cavaceppi, see C. Gasparri and O. Ghiandoni, *Lo studio Cavaceppi e le collezioni Torlonia* (Rome, 1994). For Franzoni, see R. Carloni, 'I fratelli Franzoni e le vendite antiquarie del primo Ottocento al Museo Vaticano', *BMusPont* 13 (1993), 161–226. The publication of Pacetti's diary, edited by C. Gasparri and others, is in progress [2000].

21. Reprinted in E.Q. Visconti, *Opere varie* I (ed. G. Labus) (Milan, 1827), 1–70.

22. The tomb was discovered in 1616 and rediscovered in 1780. See Pietrangeli, *Scavi e scoperte* (above, n. 19), 16–17; F.

Coarelli, 'Il sepolcro degli Scipioni', *Dialoghi di Archeologia* 4 (1) (1972), 36–106; F. Coarelli, *Guide archeologiche Laterza: Roma* (Bari, 1995), 377–83. For inscriptions and other fragments in the Vatican Museums (Vestibolo Quadrato, Gabinetto dell'Apoxyomenos and Cortile Ottagono), see Spinola, *Il Museo Pio Clementino* I (above, n. 2).

23. For the Viscontis, see Ridley, 'To protect the monuments' (above, n. 18), 142–5 (Giovanni Battista and Filippo Aurelio); C. Pietrangeli, *The Vatican Museums: Five Centuries of History* (Rome/Vatican City, 1993) (= *I Musei Vaticani: cinque secoli di storia* (Rome, 1985)), 113; D. Gallo, 'I Visconti. Una famiglia romana al servizio dei papi, della Repubblica e di Napoleone', *Roma Moderna e Contemporanea* 2 (1) (January–April 1994), 77–90; C. Pietrangeli, 'Il taccuino di Giambattista Visconti', *BMusPont* 15 (1995), 317–34; P. Vian (ed.), *La raccolta e la miscellanea Visconti degli autografi Ferrajoli* (Vatican City, 1996), particularly the introduction.

24. Society of Antiquaries, London, Minute Books XVIII (3 April 1783), 404–12 (copy): John Ramsay to Philip, 2nd Earl Stanhope, Rome, 19 February 1783. See also, in the same volume (16 May 1782), 179–80, a letter of 2 March 1782 from the architect Thomas Hardwick, and the description of a 'Ring found in the ancient Building, called the Tomb of the Scipios', the stone representing 'a Victory, with a crown of Laurel in its hand', which Louis Dutens presented to the Society (Minute Books XX (27 May 1784), 395–6). Also T. Jenkins to C. Townley, Rome, 29 January and 23 March 1782, and 8 January 1783.

25. BAV, Vat. Lat. 10307, fols 34–36v; ASR, Camerale II, Antichità e Belle Arti, b. 4, fasc. 141 (reports dated 18 and 31 January, and 15 November 1782).

26. C. Fea, *Relazione di un viaggio ad Ostia e alla Villa di Plinio detta Laurentino* (Rome, 1802); A. Nibby, 'Viaggio antiquario a Ostia', *Atti della Pontificia Accademia Romana di Archeologia* 3 (1829), 267–347; L. Paschetto, 'Ostia colonia romana. Storia e documenti', *Dissertazioni della Pontificia Accademia Romana di Archeologia* 10 (2) (1912), esp. pp. 488–97.

27. T. Ashby, 'Recent discoveries at Ostia', *JRS* 2 (2) (1912), 154–94; A. Michaelis and A.H. Smith, *A Catalogue of the Ancient Marbles at Lansdowne House … With an Appendix Containing Original Documents Relating to the Collection* (London, 1889); A.H. Smith, 'Gavin Hamilton's letters to Charles Townley', *JHS* 21 (1901), 306–21.

28. For Fea, see R.T. Ridley's entry in *DBI*; Ridley, 'To protect the monuments' (above, n. 18), 145–9; R.T. Ridley, *The Pope's Archaeologist: the Life and Times of Carlo Fea* (Rome, 2000).

29. Fea, *Relazione* (above, n. 26), 49. Also W. Amelung, *Die Sculpturen des Vaticanischen Museums* I (Berlin, 1903), 101–3, no. 86, pl. 13; Paschetto, 'Ostia colonia romana' (above, n. 26), 493 no. 44; M.A. De Angelis, 'Il primo allestimento del Museo Chiaramonti in un manoscritto del 1808. Provenienza delle sculture, oggi dislocate fuori del Chiaramonti, nei documenti dell'Archivio Storico dei Musei Vaticani', *BMusPont* 16 (1993), 105 no. 455. For new docu-

ments, see Bignamini, 'I marmi Fagan in Vaticano' (above, n. 2), 355–6 no. 7.1.

30. British Library, Add. MS 36498 (Cumberland Papers VIII), 184–5.

31. G.A. Guattani, *Monumenti antichi inediti* II (Rome, 1785), XIX–XXIV, pl. II. Also F. Matz and F. von Duhn, *Antike Bildwerke in Rom mit Ausschluss der Grösseren Sammlungen* I (Leipzig, 1881–2; reprinted Rome, 1968), 514 no. 2020 (Palazzo Chigi, Rome); Pietrangeli, *Scavi e scoperte* (above, n. 19), 128 no. 32 n. 7 (possibly the *Agrippina Minor* at Palazzo Chigi, Ariccia). For the Ashmolean Museum head, see A. Michaelis, *Ancient Marbles in Great Britain* (Cambridge, 1882), 285–6 no. 15 (possibly Agrippina); Christie's, London (Sale, 23–4 July 1917), lot 225 (Agrippina); P. Gardener, 'A new portrait of Livia', *JRS* 12 (1922), 32, pl. VII (Livia); F. Poulsen, *Greek and Roman Portraits* (Oxford, 1923), 60 (Antonia Minor); C.C. Vermeule, 'Notes on a new edition of Michaelis: *Ancient Marbles in Great Britain*', *American Journal of Archaeology* 59 (1955), 134 *sub* Deepdene no. 15 (225) (Livia); H. Jucker, *Das Bildnis im Blätterkelch. Geschichte und Bedeutung einer Römischen Porträtform* I (Lausanne/Freiburg, 1961), 51 n. 12 *sub* no. B2 (Agrippina Major); H. Bartels, *Studien zum Frauenporträt der Augusteischen Zeit. Fulvia, Octavia, Livia, Julia* (Munich, n.d. [1963]), 70 (possibly Drusilla); K. Fittschen and P. Zanker, *Katalog der Römischen Porträts in den Capitolinischen Museen und den Anderen Kommunalen Sammlungen der Stadt Rom* III (Mainz, 1983), 6–7 *sub* no. 5, n. 4, no. III h (Agrippina Minor); G.B. Waywell, *The Lever and Hope Sculptures* (Berlin, 1986), 93–4 no. 51, pls 58–9 (either Agrippinas). For both heads, see R. Neudecker, *Die Skulpturen-Ausstattung Römischer Villen in Italien* (Mainz, 1988), 239, nos. 69.24–5.

32. I. Bignamini, 'Scavi ottocenteschi a Tor Paterno: gli scavi Chigi del 1777–80 e gli scavi camerali del 1783', in M.G. Lauro (ed.), *Castelporziano* IV: *campagne di scavo e restauro 1992–1998* (Rome, forthcoming).

33. 'Si è riconosciuta per Agrippina minore la bellissima Imperadrice rappresentata in una stupenda testa, e ritrovata fra que' monumenti che da' campi Laurentini ha richiamati alla luce la munificenza del Sig. Principe Chigi. Assomiglia questa perfettamente alla Farnesiana, sennonchè l'età più giovanile fa risaltar maggiormente la bellezza di lei; bellezza contemplata fino dal figlio parricida sul suo cadavere; onde quell'insigne busto può dirsi più acconciamente rappresentarci la figlia di Germanico che la madre di Nerone': Guattani, *Monumenti* II (above, n. 31), XXII; also Visconti, *Opere varie* I (above, n. 21), 127.

34. A. D'Este, *Memorie di Antonio Canova* (Florence, 1864), 238.

35. Bignamini, 'I marmi Fagan in Vaticano' (above, n. 2), 353–4 no. 3, 558–9 nos. 12.1–2, 359–60 no. 13, 366 no. 30, 368 no. 36, 369 no. 40, 374 no. 51, 377–8 nos. 54.1–4; Bignamini, 'Scavi archeologici a Tor Paterno' (above, n. 323).

36. ASR, Camerale II, Antichità e Belle Arti, b. 9, fasc. 225.

37. Museo Chiaramonti XXI.3, inv. 1551.

38. Amelung, *Sculpturen* I (above, n. 29), 632–3 no. 494, pl. 67; B. Andreae (ed.), *Buildkatalog der Skulpturen des*

Vatikanischen Museums I: *Museo Chiaramonti* (Berlin/New York, 1995), 19, pls 160–4.

39. British Library, Add. MS 36730, fol. 179v (R. Fagan, *A Small Account of the Island of Sicily Respecting its Antiquities*, c. 1812). Also Bignamini, 'I marmi Fagan in Vaticano' (above, n. 2), 385–6 no. 11.

40. Museo Gregoriano Profano, inv. 1558

41. Amelung, *Sculpturen* I (above, n. 29), 215–17 no. 465, pl. 65; W. Fuchs, in W. Helbig, *Führer durch die Öffentlichen Sammlungen Klassischer Altertümer in Rom* I (Tübingen, 1963), no. 341; De Angelis, 'Il primo allestimento del Museo Chiaramonti' (above, n. 29), 115 no. 517 and 116 fig. 5; Bignamini, 'I marmi Fagan in Vaticano' (above, n. 2), 378–9 no. 54.6; F. Sinn, 'Rilievo della 'Penelope'', in *Via Appia. Sulle ruine della magnificenza antica* (Rome, 1997), 44; F. Sinn, *Museo Gregoriano Profano* (forthcoming).

42. 'Frammento di donna sedente sopra canestro, o vaso'; 'monumenti trovati a Ostia [sic: Via Appia] dentro la stanza sepolcrale di Claudia Semne dal Sig. Feghan': Archivio Storico dei Musei Vaticani, b. IV, no. 21.

43. Bignamini and Claridge, 'The Tomb of Claudia Semne' (above, n. 15). The Relief has not been listed among the finds from the tomb, but it has been added only tentatively to the end of the second table.

44. Sala degli Animali 158, inv. 430; British Museum, no. 2131. Wilton and Bignamini, *Grand Tour* (1996; 1997) (above, n. 7), 250–1 nos. 204–5 and 258–9 nos. 204–5.

45. Sala dei Busti 49, inv. 634. Spinola, *Il Museo Pio Clementino* II (above, n. 2), 92 no. 49, fig. 15. Also W. Amelung, *Die Sculpturen des Vaticanischen Museums* II (Berlin, 1908), 549–50, no. 359, pl. 71; Neudecker, *Die Skulpturen-Ausstattung* (above, n. 31), 163 no. 21; Pietrangeli, 'La provenienza III' (above, n. 2), 112 no. 49 (634).

46. 'Nel terminare i scavi di Civita Lavinia, Monsieur Gavino Hamilton ha ritrovato un Busto di Sabina Augusta, per la scultura e per l'integrità singolarissimo.'

47. For a full account, see I. Bignamini, 'La Sabina del Museo Pio Clementino: scavi, restauri e calchi a Roma nel Settecento', *RendPontAcc* 71 (2001), 167–89.

48. Inv. 31532, 31481 and 31472, for instance. C. Gennaccari, 'Museo Pio Cristiano. Documenti inediti di rilavorazione e restauri settecenteschi sui sacofagi paleocristiani', *BMusPont* 16 (1996), 236, 251, 275.

49. The 'unguento magico di *Medea*, onde riconduceva sugli smorti volti della Decrepitezza le fresche rose della verde Gioventù': Nicola Martelli to Prince Sigismondo Chigi, Rome 18 January 1784, quoted in G.A. Guattani, *Monumenti antichi inediti* I (Rome, 1784), XVII.

50. Bignamini, 'Scavi archeologici a Tor Paterno' (above, n. 32).

51. Sala a Croce Greca 4, inv. 194. G. Lippold, *Die Skulpturen des Vaticanischen Museums* III (Berlin, 1956), 153 no. 127(0), pl. 65; Pietrangeli, 'La provenienza I' (above, n. 2), 144 no. 1270 (194); Spinola, *Il Museo Pio Clementino* II (above, n. 2), 217 no. 4.

52. The drawing is missing.

53. See, in particular, C. Hülsen, 'Il Tempio del Sole nella Regione

VII di Roma', *BullCom* 23 (1895), 39–59; Ministero della Pubblica Istruzione, Direzione Generale delle Antichità e Belle Arti, *Carta archeologica di Roma. Tavola II* (Florence, 1964), 170 no. 90; F. Castagnoli, 'Due disegni inediti di Pirro Ligorio e il Tempio del Sole', *RendPontAcc* 51–2 (1978–9/1979–80), 371–87, reprinted in F. Castagnoli, *Topografia antica. Un metodo di studio. I: Roma* (Rome, 1993), 573–88; L. Richardson, Jr, *A New Topographical Dictionary of Ancient Rome* (Baltimore/London, 1992), 363–4; J. Calzini Gysens and F. Coarelli, 'Sol, Templum', in E.M. Steinby (ed.), *Lexicon Topographicum Urbis Romae* IV (Rome, 1999), 331–3.

54. Sala dei Busti 3, inv. 591; Sala dei Busti 130, inv. 721, respectively. See Amelung, *Sculpturen* II (above, n. 46), 491 no. 293 (I), pl. 63, and 481 no. 280, pl. 64; Pietrangeli, 'La provenienza III' (above, n. 2), 105 no. 3 (591), and 124 no. 130 (721); Spinola, *Il Museo Pio Clementino* II (above, n. 2), 60–70 no. 3 and 142–3 no. 130.

55. 'Testa di Tito trovata a Palo … s[cudi] 100' and 'Testa di Claudio trovato ad Alzio … s[cudi] 80'. Archivio Storico dei Musei Vaticani, b. II, fasc. 8 (1776), no. 39. In another copy of the same list (ASR, Camerale II, Antichità e Belle Arti, b. 17, ins. 107) their provenance is omitted: 'Testa di Tito con poco petto e pieduccio di scultura molto superiore al busto Capitolino, e forse anche a quello della Villa Albani, creduto finora il più eccellente di Roma … s[cudi] 100' ('Head of Titus with small part of chest and sculpture base, much superior to the Capitoline bust, and perhaps also to that of the Villa Albani, until now believed to be the best in Rome … 100 s[cudi]'), and 'Testa simile di Ti[to]: Claudio, la migliore che siasi finora trovata … s[cudi] 80' ('Head similar to that of Titus: Claudius, the best that has been found so far … 80 s[cudi]').

56. On the same date Hamilton wrote along similar lines to William Petty, 2nd Earl of Shelburne and later Marquess of Lansdowne; see *Catalogue of the Celebrated Collection of Ancient Marbles the Property of the Most Honourable The Marquess of Lansdowne* (Christie's, London, 5 March 1930), 92 (also in E. Fitzmaurice, *Letters of Gavin Hamilton, edited from Mss at Lansdowne House* (Devizes, 1879), 35–6, and Michaelis and Smith, *Ancient Marbles at Lansdowne House* (above, n. 27), 73–4). Hamilton was granted an excavation licence for the 'Tenuta di Palo spettante a sua Eccellenza il Signor Conte di Potenza', on 26 September 1774 (ASR, Presidenza delle Strade, lettere patenti, b. 67, fols 282r–v), and on 16 January 1775 he announced to Townley: 'I have a palazzino at Palo that is in readiness for your reception where are all the amusements a reasonable man can desire besides a Cava Imperiale'.

57. This expression, with some variations, such as Jenkins's *terre vergini*, was much in use during the period. See Bignamini, 'Gli scavi archeologici a Roma' (above, n. 10).

58. L. Borsari, 'Notizie inedite intorno a scoperte di antichità in Roma e suo territorio', *BullCom* 25–6 (1897–8), 37–9.

59. Bignamini and Claridge, 'The Tomb of Claudia Semne' (above, n. 15). More recently, the same hypothesis has been

tested on the Imperial villa at Tor Paterno; see Bignamini, 'Scavi archeologici a Tor Paterno' (above, n. 32).

60. Bignamini, 'I marmi Fagan in Vaticano' (above, n. 2); Bignamini, 'Review' (above, n. 2).

61. 'segniati con i loro respettivi numeri e tutti 22': Archivio Storico dei Musei Vaticani, b. I, fasc. 3, fols 316–17.

62. Bignamini and Claridge, 'The Tomb of Claudia Semne' (above, n. 15).

63. British Museum, no. 1578. Bignamini, 'The 'Campo Iemini Venus'' (above, n. 15). For other Campo Iemini marbles, see Neudecker, *Die Skulpturen-Ausstattung* (above, n. 31), 134–5 no. 4; Bignamini, 'I marmi Fagan in Vaticano' (above, n. 2), 355 no. 6, 356–7 no. 8.1–2, 365 no. 25.

64. The 'luogo ove il Signor Feghan fece lo Scavo, e trovò varie Statue'.

A PAINTER IN SEARCH OF A POET: ALLAN RAMSAY AND HORACE'S VILLA, 1755–84

Iain Gordon Brown

INTRODUCTION

LATE in life, Allan Ramsay (1713–84) was encouraged by the London literary circle of which he was a prominent member to publish his observations on Horace's Sabine Villa. The work that his friends hoped soon to see in print might have been the culmination of years of active antiquarian exploration and scholarly musing. By 1778, when Sir Joshua Reynolds, Edward Gibbon, Samuel Johnson and James Boswell, among others, urged him to commit his thoughts to the press, Ramsay (**Fig. 1**), a man once Reynolds's rival for the most fashionable portrait commissions, was no longer able to paint because of an injury to his arm. He had, in any case, long wished to indulge his second career as a writer of essays on subjects ranging from politics to aesthetics; and for these pursuits he had all but abandoned his practice at the easel.[1] Roman archaeology and classical literature, old diversions, now claimed much of Ramsay's attention; and first among these interests was his quest for the Sabine farm.

This paper concerns a treatise that never, in fact, appeared in its author's lifetime. Manuscript versions of Ramsay's *Enquiry into the Situation and Circumstances of Horace's Sabine Villa*, one mainly autograph and the other largely in the hand of his wife as amanuensis, survive in the National Library of Scotland (MS 730; **Fig. 2**) and in Edinburgh University Library (MS La III.492). Both date from the later 1770s, but have significant additions dating from 1782 and 1783. A further, probably contemporary, manuscript, not autograph but perhaps Ramsay's fair copy intended for publication, has recently been found in the library of the University of California, Los Angeles (MS bound MSS, Coll. 170/376). Related drawings are bound into the National Library manuscript (below, **Figs 3–6**). Other drawings, watercolours and gouaches by Ramsay, and by Jacob More, Jakob Philipp Hackert and other artists who were associated with the project, are in the National Gallery of Scotland (below, **Figs 7–8**) and in public and private collections elsewhere. This corpus of material has now been brought together, the manuscript texts collated and edited, the drawings and maps arranged in sequence, and the whole published as a monograph in which the original treatise is accompanied by a series of essays dealing with various aspects of the work and its background.[2] The present paper focuses on the evidence for one scholar's search for a particular ancient site. However, it illustrates, in a more general way, the value that documentary sources — excavated, as it were, from the *latebriae dulces* ('the delicious lurking-places', to adapt a phrase from Horace, *Epistles* I.16) of libraries and print-rooms — have in enlarging our knowledge of antiquarian and archaeological investigation in Italy in the eighteenth century.

RAMSAY'S FOUR VISITS TO ITALY

Horace, the Prince of the Roman lyric poets, was possessed of a Villa or farm in the Sabinia, a province more remarkable for the purity of its air than the fertility of its soil; and therefore not an unfit place for the residence of a man who was both a philosopher and a poet: one who sought for health and repose, and who found in the exercise of his genius that pleasure which wealth endeavours in vain to procure for its possessors. Accordingly his fondness for this rural retreat breaks forth in many of his poems.

FIG. 1. Allan Ramsay, Self-portrait from about the time he began his search for Horace's Villa. Pastel 406 x 282 mm. Scottish National Portrait Gallery, Edinburgh, PG 727. *(Reproduced courtesy of the National Galleries of Scotland.)*

[opposite] FIG. 2. Page from the earliest of the three *Enquiry* manuscripts showing Ramsay's discussion of the naming of Roman villas after geographical locations. National Library of Scotland, Edinburgh, MS 730. *(Reproduced courtesy of the National Library of Scotland.)*

Thus does Ramsay open his *Enquiry*.[3] Behind his enterprise lies the long tradition of adulation of the poet and, in particular, the admiration of Horace and his works and way of life shared by Ramsay and his poet father, Allan Ramsay the elder (1684–1758). The poet had, as his son acknowledged, caught well the spirit of the *Odes* and had 'imitated some of them with a truly Horatian felicity'.[4] He had made Horace, as it were, speak Scots; and he had written in praise of a life of virtuous ease, contented and detached in modest sufficiency, akin to that of the Roman.[5]

For the younger Ramsay, classical scholarship and archaeological investigations complemented wider literary interests. Uniquely among British artists of the

period, he made four visits to Italy.[6] Archaeology figured to varying degrees in all of them; and the search for Horace's Villa was the central feature of the third and fourth visits. A number of important archaeological developments stemmed from his first study visit of 1736–8. Ramsay was able to purchase for Dr Richard Mead an album of Pietro Santi Bartoli's splendid watercolour copies of ancient wall-paintings from the Tomb of the Nasonii. These were in the Massimo collection, and are now in Glasgow University Library.[7] Ramsay was also instrumental in arranging to have copies made by his Neapolitan friend Camillo Paderni of other Roman paintings for the use of George Turnbull in his *Treatise on Ancient Painting, Containing Observations on the Rise, Progress, and Decline of that Art amongst the Greeks and Romans* (1740).[8] Ramsay's first publication was on an antiquarian subject: in 1740 he translated for the *Philosophical Transactions* of the Royal Society of London two letters of Paderni describing some of the first discoveries at Herculaneum.[9]

The Italian sojourn of 1736–8 alerted Ramsay to the possibilities, as well as the inherent dangers, of archaeology. Paderni's letters exposed the darker side of archaeological discovery. Ramsay's translations certainly told the learned world of the exciting developments at Herculaneum; but they also made clear Paderni's disquiet at present (and, in all probability, future) wholesale obliteration of evidence: 'Things ... of great Curiosity and Erudition which, not being copied, are gone to Destruction' in the course of digging for more exotic works of art. '... the greater Misfortune will be ours, to hear that what Time, Earthquakes, and the ravages of the Volcano have spared, are now destroyed by those who pretend to have the care of them'.[10] Such concerns would still motivate Ramsay more than 40 years later, when he was working at Horace's Villa. He remained ever conscious of the value of material and documentary evidence of all kinds; and while looking forward to the opportunities for increasing knowledge that archaeology afforded, with improved standards and new technology, he was equally troubled by the loss of precious and irreplaceable evidence through ignorance, indolence, greed or superstition.

During his second Italian visit, in the mid-1750s, Ramsay was, with Giovanni Battista Piranesi, Charles-Louis Clérisseau and Robert Adam, one of a remarkable band of brothers. They sketched and explored together monuments in Rome and the Campagna, fell in and out of friendship, influenced each other and

Impune totum per nemus] This wood is frequently mentioned in Horace's works. I shall defer my remarks upon it till I come to Book 1. Sat. 6.

orbibus ducenti hitulis. This ode appears to have been written about the beginning of harvest, at which time the letter forward in the line

Ultimusque dulci Tyndari fistula.

I,X[II]   *Valles et Ustica cubantis*

Levia personuere saxa.] This passage have very much perplexed the modern Commentators and Geographers. All of them Seem to take *Ustica* to be the name of Horace's farm, and not knowing what to make of the words *Levia Saxa*, when applied to a valley, some have Supposed them to mean the Smooth hewen Stones of which his house might have been built. But we have no instance amongst the ancient Romans of a proper name being given to any gentleman's country house, which, when not named after the proprietor, always recieved its title from some district, or known town in the neighbourhood: Such as Villa Tusculana, Villa Albana, Villa Formiana, or else such a one's Tusculanum, Albanum or Formianum. Nor can we easily conceive that the walls of a small house, such as Horace's is supposed to be, could produce any echo. The Ancient Scholiast says: *Ustica nomen montis et Vallis in Sabinis. cum autem* ~~saxositatem~~ *suaviter dixit ad resupinam regionem attendens. Sic enim in Epistolis: Continui montes nisi dissocientur opaca valle. Cubantis, depressæ: int —— Megarosque sinus, Tapsumque jacentem.* But here our Scholiast is of very little authority, as he appears to have no knowledge of the place or its made important contributions to the neoclassical movement. Sensitive drawings in the National Gallery of Scotland show how Ramsay absorbed the magic of the ruins. In 1755 and 1756 he spent time on *villeggiatura* at Tivoli, and thence made his first reconnaissance of the domestic landscape of Horace in the Licenza valley beyond Vicovaro. In 1755, too, was published Ramsay's *Dialogue on Taste*, his most important contribution to aesthetics.[11] Here Ramsay's alter ego, Colonel Freeman, describes how archaeology — in Ramsay's own day flourishing in the Campagna and around the bay of Naples — had begun in the Renaissance: 'Thus, at the same time that the Greek and Roman classics were diligently sought after, amidst the dust and scholastic nonsense of the libraries and convents; the pick-ax was every where employed among the ruins, in search of statues and bas-reliefs, which the ignorance and misery of the times had suffered to lie for ages under ground'.[12]

The high point of Ramsay's third visit to Italy (1775–7) was the summer spent at Licenza when, with his base in the Orsini palace, he worked in earnest on his treatise on the site of Horace's farm. It was a voyage not just into antiquity, but into the living past of Italy, for he came to know and respect the country people of the Sabinia and to study them for the continuity they represented with the inhabitants of Horace's day.

Five years later, Ramsay's wife died. Partly to assuage his grief he made one final journey to Italy, this time with his son to take his mother's place as amanuensis in the ultimate stages of revision of his *Enquiry*. A further season of contemplation and consideration of Horace's poetry, views and ambience (1783) brought his work as near completion as was ever to be the case; for Ramsay died in August 1784 before his essay — now very likely planned to include a map or maps and a selection of prints designed to emphasize the points of his minute discussion of literature in relation to landscape — could pass to the last stages of preparation for the press.

RAMSAY'S *ENQUIRY*

The manuscripts of the treatise on Horace's Villa, together with the drawings relating to this exercise in classical textual scholarship, topographical study and archaeological exploration, allow us to examine the methods of a man possessed of high intelligence and finely-tuned critical faculties. Ramsay's literary and physical pursuit of the precise location of Horace's farm shows him as a characteristic product of the Scottish Enlightenment, with its emphasis on empiricism and rigorous analysis of evidence. His scholarship on the whole represents a scientific approach, but one by no means entirely devoid of emotion. A very real sensibility to landscape, poetry and spirit of place was moderated by the reasoned arguments that could evolve only from close personal inspection of the topography, and from study of the available material evidence. Throughout Ramsay's *Enquiry*, personal acquaintance with the topography is matched by intimate knowledge of the Horatian texts. With these two vital requirements are combined an innate sympathy with the poet's mind and art. For Ramsay's generation, Horace's Villa had both a literary (or cerebral) and a physical existence: it was a site at once real and of the imagination, a place embedded in the Western consciousness and known to educated men since schooldays. As in Renaissance Italy, so in Augustan Britain: Roman villa life became an ideal to be imitated, and Horace was a companionable guide to that fantasy. By Ramsay's day, writing about villas, actual and imagined, had become a pursuit in itself. Ramsay was far from unmoved by the appeal of the Horatian ideal of 'Beatus ille'('happy the man') (*Epodes* II.1), and by the enduring wish 'to give to airy nothing / a local habitation and a name'. But still greater was his desire to fit the poems of Horace into their actual, rather than conjectural, landscape.

Ramsay first visited the countryside of the Licenza valley and the putative site of the villa in 1755. He was a very early visitor to the site, and quite probably the first British traveller to venture there: he may well have been the first of any grand-touring nationality.[13] His *Enquiry* is one of the earliest accounts specifically devoted to the villa, and moreover the first such dissertation in English. During that summer of 1755 Ramsay made two separate expeditions, the most significant of which he described in a letter to an Edinburgh friend, Sir Alexander Dick.[14] Here was outlined the inspiration governing all Ramsay's subsequent work on his long-term project. What began merely as a journey for holiday diversion became a scholarly obsession. From a very early stage he appreciated the need for two things: *plein-air* landscape studies from nature — initially rough sketches that might later be worked up by more accomplished topographical draughtsmen (Figs 3–6) — and accurate maps. To these he would later add graphic records of architectural and decorative features of the villa site. All mark a change: from

FIG. 3. Allan Ramsay, *Llandscape sketch*, titled in his hand, made with the illustration of his *Enquiry* in mind. Probably drawn during the 1777 campaign of work at Licenza: this, together with those reproduced as Figs 4 and 5, were to be worked up into finished watercolours by Jacob More. Pen, ink and pencil 185 x 222 mm. National Library of Scotland, Edinburgh, MS 730. *(Reproduced courtesy of the National Library of Scotland.)*

simple appreciation of literary landscapes of allusion to the methodology of scientific topographical and archaeological enquiry. This first expedition, he told Dick, was one

which you or any man of elegant taste would have been glad to have partaken of, and which we shall remember with pleasure as long as we live. This was to go in search of Horace's farm in the Sabinia. We set out early one morning [from Tivoli] each upon our ass with a sumpter ass fraught with roast meat etc., dining the first day under a poplar by the side of the Anio, and the second by a fountain which I took for the Fons Blandusiae, but was afterwards led by a countryman to one that still better answered the description of Horace. But the particulars of this jaunt and my observations upon the ground compared with the passages

that relate to it in the poet I will defer till I can communicate to you at the same time the plan of the situation and some of the principal views, without which any description by words must remain obscure and defective.[15]

In this last sentence we have the essence of Ramsay's inspiration — to compare the topography with the poetry in order to prove the essential truthfulness to nature of Horace's descriptions — and of his method: personal inspection and minute acquaintance with the landscape, which he would record in observations illustrated and made clear by drawings, maps and plans. All that followed until 1783 stems from that expression of object and means of attainment. Ramsay was indeed inspired by love of Horace and by the sentimental call of a landscape of association: but know-

FIG. 4. Allan Ramsay, *Llandscape sketch*, titled in his hand, made with the illustration of his *Enquiry* in mind. Probably drawn during the 1777 campaign of work at Licenza. Pen, ink and pencil 185 x 222 mm. National Library of Scotland, Edinburgh, MS 730. *(Reproduced courtesy of the National Library of Scotland.)*

ledge of a specific monument, achieved through the application of scientific method, was his goal. Self-promotion, by the identification of a site that might yield treasures and confer fame upon its discoverer, played no part.

Conscious, perhaps, that his investigation was but the most recent in a line of similar published and unpublished reports over some centuries on the likely location of the villa, Ramsay early offered this defence of his undertaking:

> But the enquiry into the situation of Horace's country house has something more to claim in its favour than a bare indulgence: as it will be found that its true situation being known, new lights will be from thence reflected upon his poetry, which has long been the delight of men of the best understandings, and will

always be held in the highest esteem, while there are charms in the truest pictures of nature, and the most exalted sentiments of morality, conveyed in the best chosen and happiest words.[16]

More prosaically, Ramsay's work was, as he put it, an essay in the 'illustration of the ancient geography of Italy'.[17] It embraces also classical textual scholarship, topographical exploration, archaeology (excavation, epigraphy and museology of a kind), romantic sensibility (as, for example, in his attitude to the country people of his own day and their primitive subsistence and way of life) and an element of anthropological observation and feeling for the picturesque, combined with awareness to those elements of landscape scenery as might appeal to a painter's eye.

Ramsay shows familiarity with the work of scholars

FIG. 5. Allan Ramsay, *Llandscape sketch*, titled in his hand, made with the illustration of his *Enquiry* in mind. Probably drawn during the 1777 campaign of work at Licenza. Pen, ink and pencil 185 × 222 mm. National Library of Scotland, Edinburgh, MS 730. *(Reproduced courtesy of the National Library of Scotland.)*

from the mid-fifteenth century to his own day: from Flavio Biondo through Philipp Clüver and Lucas Holstenius, to Giuseppe Rocco Volpi and the Abbés Bertrand Capmartin de Chaupy and Domenico De Sanctis.[18] For most of these he has but scanty praise. He delivers himself of excoriating criticism of Volpi in particular, whom he dismisses as either 'lazy', 'stupid' or slow on the uptake of the obvious,[19] and he seems to take more than ordinary pleasure in pointing out the faults and misconceptions of his predecessors in the field: Holstenius alone escapes with credit. Some crumbs of comfort are occasionally flung in the direction of de Chaupy, whom Ramsay once goes so far as to praise for his 'zeal and activity … which merit the grateful acknowledgements of all true lovers of antiquity'; but we are left in little doubt, from the subtle phrasing, that this is an isolated instance of such

magnanimity.[20] One might cynically observe that, in Ramsay's view, he and his wife and their asses learned more about the site of Horace's *Sabinum* on a day's picnicking followed by a little light fieldwork than all the scholars of Europe since the revival of letters had done in the rarefied seclusion of their book-filled studies. In Ramsay's opinion, the learned de Chaupy did himself no service by allowing his argument to become swamped by the digressions of a three-volume work that was not really about the subject that it purported to treat. Ramsay was determined not to produce something so overblown and diffuse. That he was tempted into the arena at all may seem remarkable, if we think of Piranesi's scatological joke against de Chaupy, where the subject of his earnest deliberations is shown as a giant dog-turd lying in a field scattered with disparaging references to the Frenchman's and others' futile

FIG. 6. Allan Ramsay with colour-wash by Jacob More (the title being in Ramsay's hand), *View of Rocca Giovane*. Drawing 185 x 222 mm. National Library of Scotland, Edinburgh, MS 730. *(Reproduced courtesy of the National Library of Scotland.)*

attempts to fix Horace's Villa in a landscape bristling with hazards to entrap the gullible or the unwary.[21]

Horace wrote from the life; and personal inspection of the ground, free from preconception, was the key to the rediscovery of the poet's physical world. De Chaupy had, Ramsay maintained, 'suffered his pencil to be guided rather by his prepossessions than his eyesight'; and he had 'moved heaven and earth in order to make the actual situation of things correspond with what he believed to be Horace's description of them'.[22] By contrast, Ramsay's interpretation of the texts in the light of his own 'attentive inspection of the ground itself' — the 'best commentary' on the poems being found in the actual landscape of the poet as one might study it at the present time — would result in confirmation of the veracity of Horace's poetic descriptions. Ramsay was convinced that his method rendered his

Enquiry of greater value than, say, the theories of Clüver, who possessed the textual knowledge, but was unable to match this with sufficient familiarity with 'the modern face of Italy'. The 'best commentary' lay in the topography. As a long-time Horatian, Ramsay had developed an idea of what such-and-such a natural feature or phenomenon might look like in reality — a notion of what the verse suggested; and so he could look for an actual reflection in the Sabine landscape. An example would be the smooth rocks (*laevia saxa*) of a valley that might echo the sound of the shepherd's pipe. In looking for likely sites, Ramsay explains that he had actually heard an echo 'by one countryman bawling to another, on the other side of the Digentia'. It was little discoveries such as this that convinced him that Horace's 'rural images' were not simply 'drawn from the general face of Nature' but from particular locations. Ramsay, the artist, likened the verse images to 'studies, as the landscape painters call them, taken from [Horace's] own estate'.[23]

In writing to Sir Alexander Dick in 1755 Ramsay indicated that he had early appreciated the importance of maps in archaeological investigation. In his *Enquiry* he explained that he had, in the course of his research, consulted a range of seventeenth- and eighteenth-century maps; and we know that he had made a rough copy from that by Diego de Revillas (1739) when first he began his explorations in 1755.[24] 'To make all this description perfectly intelligible', he wrote in a note to the *Enquiry*, 'I am sensible that a map becomes necessary'.[25] A landscape view of 1777 by Ramsay, taken from a window of the Orsini palace at Licenza, in which topographical accuracy was the prime concern, became the basis for a number of drawings and a detailed landscape view-map by Jacob More. The phrase 'drawn exactly by me A.R. by the aid of pack thread squares' forms part of the minutely detailed description of the physical features included in the view that is inscribed along the top of the sheet.[26] Ramsay seems to have used a drawing-frame incorporating a grid of thread to assist him in achieving the accuracy required for this and other drawings of the landscape of the villa.[27] His drawing (**Fig. 7**) and More's elaboration that was constructed upon it (**Fig. 8**) are remarkable for their date, and together constitute a landmark in archaeological illustration to which little attention has been paid hitherto. More's landscape view-map was in turn superseded by the map that Ramsay was offered by Hackert. The German artist appears, at an opportune moment, to have persuaded Ramsay that he needed his services, and to have produced the map that Ramsay knew his treatise needed, and without which it would be incomplete.[28] Begun in 1782 and appearing on the market in 1784 to accompany a series of engravings of the countryside of Horace's Villa (themselves engraved from 1780 onwards), this map bore in the end no real relation to the *Enquiry*, apart from the legend, which anticipates the expected publication of Ramsay's treatise — of which mention is made as if it were already printed. A second edition of Hackert's map, produced at a date unknown,[29] ironically still refers to the published dissertation of 'Mr de Ramsay' albeit this odd memento of the ill-starred project appeared perhaps anything up to half a century after Ramsay's death, when his contingent treatise had been all but forgotten.

Correct identification of ancient place-names depended upon evidence ranging from documents recording late antique ecclesiastical land donations to the 'lights' (as Ramsay called them) derived from the geography of a particular region. Linguistic and phonetic evidence was important, as, for example, sound changes that rendered the ancient river Digentia of Horace as the modern Licenza, 'a little softened', as Ramsay put it, 'in the pronounciation'; or Varia as the modern Vicovaro. The value of evidence of this kind had been appreciated since the work of the seventeenth-century scholars Clüver and Holstenius. Ramsay was happy to endorse their conclusions and those drawn as a result of work by the perceptive notary of Vicovaro, Giuseppe Petrocchi, whose recent discovery of an inscription had allowed the identification to be made of the modern village of Bardela with Horace's local market town, the ancient Mandela. We should remember Ramsay's own long-standing interest in linguistics, as witnessed by his complex and still unpublished treatise, 'An Enquiry into the Principles of English Versification with some Analogical Remarks upon the Versification of the Ancients'.[30] Ramsay pointed out in the course of his Horace's Villa research the fact that local tradition kept particular land- or place-names in use without any knowledge of their origins; thus the Vigne di San Pietro, as the locals knew the field where, in all probability, the actual ruins of Horace's house stood, was so called without any memory or consciousness of the ancient link with the Constantinian donation of the land to the church of Saints Peter and Marcellinus at Tor Pignattara on the Via Labicana.

Throughout his *Enquiry* Ramsay showed concern for the transmission of the text of Horace. In this context we should note his most interesting and relevant plea for more attention to and better care of finds from Herculaneum, as preserved (if that is the right word) in the Museo Reale Borbonico at Portici. Ramsay was thus endorsing the earlier vigorous attack upon the treatment of the finds — together with their inaccessibility and slow publication — launched by Johann Joachim Winckelmann, and was returning to the theme to which he had drawn the attention of the Royal Society (by way of Paderni's letters) soon after his return to London from his first Italian visit. Others shared his concern, and Father Antonio Piaggio had, of course, already invented a machine for unrolling the papyri.[31] But it is important to record the fact that Ramsay displayed in those years an interest previously unappreciated. As he wrote, sarcastically (in the context of discussion of the authorial integrity of the text of a particular poem):

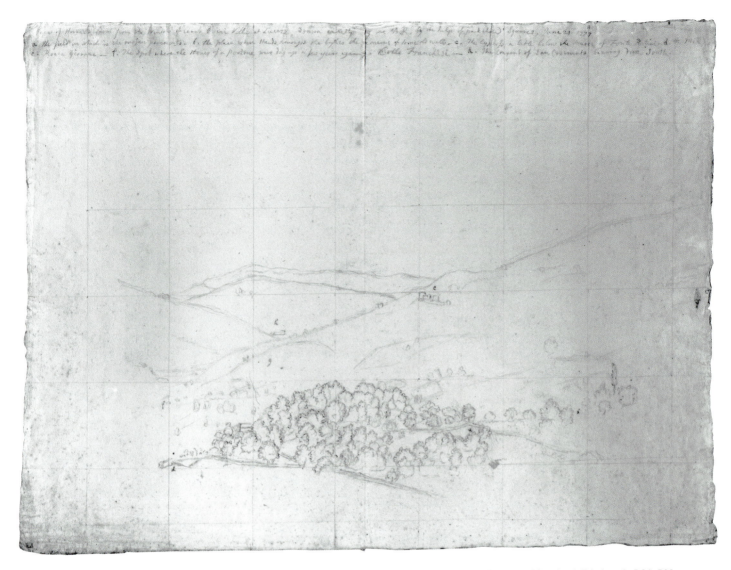

FIG. 7. Allan Ramsay, View-map of the Licenza valley and site of Horace's Villa, 1777. National Gallery of Scotland, Edinburgh, RSA 509. *(Reproduced courtesy of the National Galleries of Scotland.)*

It may some time or other please heaven to inspire the King of Naples or some of his Ministers with a curiosity to know what may be contained in the 800 manuscript volumes found at Herculaneum and now piled up, like lumps of charcoal, in a cupboard at Portici. Perhaps amongst them might be found the works of Horace in his own handwriting, which would clear up this and many other difficulties, in which all the genius and learning of Bentley have not been able to assist us.[32]

As well as published books and printed collections of ecclesiastical documents, Ramsay tells us that he had used a modern unpublished manuscript account of the history of Vicovaro by the local antiquary Petrocchi. Thus he had made the same sort of use of archival evidence as we do. He also was constantly

aware of the value of epigraphic evidence, and recorded all the available inscriptions that had been discovered at Rocca Giovane and Licenza. Not infrequently he made pleas for further epigraphic search and recovery to assist in the interpretation of one site or another, as, for instance, in the case of the Temple of Vacuna or Victory restored by Vespasian. The tablet recording this was preserved in a wall at Rocca Giovane, and Ramsay (who drew the inscription in the manuscripts of his *Enquiry*) had been able to see the missing fragment incorporated in the pavement of a house in the village. This is an instance of Ramsay putting to good use his facility for making contacts with the local inhabitants of the Licenza valley, of which other examples can be highlighted: farmers who showed him mosaic pavements or structures in *opus reticulatum* beneath the vines, or peasants who put him

FIG. 8. Jacob More after Allan Ramsay (Fig. 7), *View-map of the Licenza valley*. National Gallery of Scotland, Edinburgh, D 1415. *(Reproduced courtesy of the National Galleries of Scotland.)*

on the track of alleged Horatian localities or material remains of potential relevance to his search. Only occasionally did the credulity that so famously affected the judgement of eighteenth-century antiquaries as a breed ensnare the circumspect Ramsay. He seems to have believed a garbled story that a 'marble chariot' had been found by peasants, along with two Ionic columns. These the *contadini* had smashed in an idle search for concealed gold. It never occurred to him that the resulting rubble and the improbable chariot were one and the same: 'a cartload of marble'.[33]

Ramsay listened and paid heed to local traditions, and learned from them. He readily applied the knowledge gained in confirming the location of the villa. Horace stated in *Epistles* I.10 that the site of his house was a sheltered one; and the inhabitants of the 1770s confirmed that this was indeed so. Aware of the con-

tinuity in veneration of holy places, whether pagan or Christian, the presence of a chapel seemed to Ramsay to argue for this being the site of the Temple of Vacuna. Its modern name of Madonna delle Case appeared to indicate its relationship to the actual house of the poet. (The notion of continuity — in ways of living, of agricultural exploitation of the land, of religious worship — was indeed one of the distinguishing features of the *Enquiry*.) Ramsay tells us that in the course of his researches he quite literally drank the past: the wine of the modern Licenza valley was compared with Horace's claims as to the modesty of his domestically-produced vintage. (We should note that Ramsay may have been making some sacrifice in the cause of scholarly duty, for he is known to have had a poor stomach and little tolerance for wine![34]) He drank the past in water, too, in order to confirm Horace's praise of the excellence of his supply, and its health-giving properties. But in these researches, as in others more materially connected with his project, he remained ever conscious of how one had to guard against being carried away, as had de Chaupy, by a too 'enthusiastic love of classic ground'. Nevertheless, Ramsay was the son of the poet of *The Gentle Shepherd* and could not resist commenting upon the pastoral idyll he observed in the fields along the banks of the Licenza, a scene surely not much different from that observed by Horace.

One of the most striking features of the *Enquiry* is its author's concern for antiquities at hazard, and for the fragility of ancient ruins in a landscape inhabited by peasants without sensibility to literature or history. Having discussed, for example, the discovery of mosaic pavements assuredly, he felt, too elegant and expensive for the rustic simplicity of Horace — who was forever suggesting that he had no need of such extravagances — and having adduced the evidence of stamped lead pipes in order to assign these decorative features to the more opulent tastes of a later owner of the villa, Ramsay digressed to comment on the fate of the important evidence that the pipes themselves had provided. (He was, in fact, basing his conclusions on a misunderstanding of the chronological evidence offered both by the stamped pipes and the mosaics.) He wrote:

> We are obliged to the Abbé Chaupy for the knowledge of these inscriptions, which would otherwise have been, before his time, consigned to eternal oblivion. For, after selling the bulk of the leaden pipes, the late Arciprete of Licenza preserved the two bits containing the name 'Burrus' and would have transmitted them to his successor, had not, unhappily, a want of shot for killing partridges made it necessary to employ them in that service.[35]

Ramsay, a Fellow of the Society of Antiquaries since 1743, went on to make an appeal for a more far-sighted attitude to conservation and guardianship of the heritage:

> It were to be wished that an Antiquarian Society were established at Rome, similar to that of London, but under the Presidency of the Pope's Antiquary, which having a Secretary, and regular weekly meetings, might receive and register the accounts that might be sent to it of the discoveries daily made in every part of the Pope's dominions. The Pope's Antiquary is gener-

ally a learned and ingenious man, such as Sig. Ridolfo Venuti, the Abbé Winckelmann, and the present Sig. [Giovanni Battista] Visconti, but there are persons who would be willing to write a letter to the Secretary of a public society, where they are sure it would be read and minuted and preserved, who would not take the same pains for the private information of one single Gentleman. Neither, supposing them to be willing to write, is it to be supposed that the Pope's Antiquary would singly take the trouble of reading and recording all their informations in such a manner that the Republic of Letters might, at some future period, receive any benefit from them. The Public is greatly obliged to the present Pope Pius VI, and to some of his immediate predecessors for having preserved so many inscriptions in the Corridors of the Vatican; but they are few in comparison with the number of those which are daily destroyed or neglected.[36]

Elsewhere Ramsay commented, as already noted, on how local people, benighted in prejudice and ignorance, had broken to pieces columns in the hope of finding treasure within. He noted how the Licenza villagers, or the peasants of the surrounding countryside, would instinctively employ as convenient building material any old inscription that was to hand, valuing only the utility of the neatly squared block and 'turning the letters inward, not to deform their wall…'.[37] He related how he had come upon altars in use as chicken-feeding basins, and he explained that he had bought a similar altar for a relatively trifling sum in order to ensure its preservation in the palazzo at Licenza. His hope was that his example might lead to a generally more favourable climate for the preservation of antiquities in the district but also more generally, perchance, in Italy as a whole.

Ramsay cautioned against the drawing of conclusions, or even indulging in too much theorizing until archaeology could show the way securely. His *Enquiry* contains statements that indicate that he himself had dug in pursuit of this hard evidence. On one occasion he had set workers in the Vigne di San Pietro to lay open portions of tessellated floors and so to reveal different mosaic patterns, by the scale and nature of which he deduced both the orientation and something of the extent of the villa buildings. On another he confesses to a desire to have dug to prove or disprove the existence of an alleged 'pavement' or roadway, the fragmentary surface remains of which suggested to him something rather different: his archaeological knowledge of buildings of late Republican and early

Imperial Rome, and of Hadrian's Villa at Tivoli, suggested that what he was shown indicated the presence of *opus reticulatum* walling of similar date, and detailed sketches in his manuscripts prove how he used the archaeological evidence to draw logical conclusions about the likely nature of the ruins below the vines and olive trees. Repeatedly he expressed the hope that more pertinent enquiries might follow from his own investigations: 'but I thought it right to bring forth all I knew or could conjecture concerning the situation of the old Temple, for the sake of promoting farther and more critical enquiry'. Though he was reasonably certain of his method, he remained nevertheless aware that further evidence, epigraphic or documentary, might upset preconceived or fixed notions. Thus he could write: 'Some inscription may be hereafter found, or some charters of the neighbouring lands, able to give us light into this matter; in the mean time it would be shutting the door against future discoveries if we were to mention things as certain, which have no better support than loose conjectures'.[38]

CONCLUSION

Ramsay claimed for himself no monopoly of knowledge in the field or the study. He fairly admitted that he had not illuminated — could not do so — the subject to the fullest possible extent. Repeated pleas were made for further research into the records of local aristocratic families and in ecclesiastical and Vatican archives, and for future excavations. But herein Ramsay, writing with the fullest expression of feeling for the landscape and its peasantry — representing, as they did, the lineal descendants of Horace's people and inhabiting still his countryside —, touched an emotional chord that we discover with some surprise in a treatise so carefully argued and, in parts, so austere in its analysis. He wrote of problems that might be encountered by a would-be archaeologist whose curiosity failed to move in tempo with the superstitions and prejudices of the *contadini*, and in defiance of the pattern of the rustic round.

Much may be still learnt concerning the true situation of the Fanum Vacunae, and other particulars of this interesting valley, if any man of classical curiosity, with 20 or 30 spare seqins [sic] in his pocket would employ the country people to dig upon Colle Franco … But I must caution such a virtuoso either to begin his digging early in the spring, or to defer it till after harvest. For the Country people, who know nothing about Odes or Epistles, believe that all who dig do it from the expectation of finding hidden treasure; and that the Demon who watches over the treasure would raise a wind which might destroy their little crop of corn, wine and oil. Having mentioned the Country people, I should not do them justice if I did not take notice of them amongst the antiquities of the place; for, excepting their Religion (which it is hardly necessary to except) they seem to be of the same stamp with those who, according to the Poets and Historians, inhabited that Country in the days of Numa Pompilius, with the same laborious manner of living, the same contented poverty, and the same innocence: so that when my Wife, my Daughter Amelia, and I took our leave of them upon the 28th of June 1777, we did it with much regret.[39]

NOTES

1. For Ramsay, see A. Smart, *Allan Ramsay: Painter, Essayist and Man of the Enlightenment* (New Haven/London, 1992), and his entry in *The Dictionary of Art* XXV (London, 1996), 881–4. See also Smart's catalogue raisonné of Ramsay's portraits, edited by J. Ingamells and published as *Allan Ramsay. A Complete Catalogue of his Paintings* (New Haven/London, 1999). For the non-artistic side, see I.G. Brown, *Poet and Painter: Allan Ramsay, Father and Son, 1684–1784* (Edinburgh, 1984); I.G. Brown, 'Allan Ramsay's rise and reputation', *The Walpole Society* 50 (1984); and I.G. Brown, 'The pamphlets of Allan Ramsay the Younger', *The Book Collector* 37 (1) (Spring 1988), 55–85. On Ramsay being encouraged to publish his work on the villa, see C.McC. Weis and F.A. Pottle, *Boswell in Extremes* (London, 1971), 253, and J. Boswell, *Life of Johnson* (ed. G. Birkbeck Hill; revised by L.F. Powell, 6 vols) (Oxford, 1934), III, 250.

2. B. Frischer and I.G. Brown (eds), *Allan Ramsay and the Search for Horace's Villa* (Aldershot, 2001), with contributions by P.R. Andrew, J.D. Hunt and M. Goalen. Ramsay's *Enquiry*, printed for the first time in this book, pp. 111–52, was edited by Frischer. In the present essay references to quotations from the treatise are to Frischer's edition. See also J. Holloway, 'Two projects to illustrate Allan Ramsay's treatise on Horace's Sabine Villa', *Master Drawings* 14 (3) (1976), 280–6.

3. Ramsay, *Enquiry* (above, n. 2), 111.

4. Edinburgh University Library, MS La II.212/41,42: A. Ramsay the younger's life of his father is published in A.M. Kinghorn and A. Law (eds), *The Works of Allan Ramsay* (*Scottish Text Society* 4) (Edinburgh, 1970), 71–6.

5. On the Ramsays and Horace, see Brown, *Poet and Painter* (above, n. 1), 24–7.

6. See *DBITI*, 796–8.

7. See C. Pace, 'Pietro Santi Bartoli. Drawings in Glasgow University Library after Roman paintings and mosaics', *PBSR* 47 (1979), 117–55. The connection with Ramsay was first made clear in Brown, 'Ramsay's rise and reputation' (above, n. 1), n. 101 and appendix II, 'Allan Ramsay's purchases for Dr Richard Mead'.

8. See Brown, 'Ramsay's rise and reputation' (above, n. 1), 234–5 and n. 104. The pictures were reprinted in Turnbull's later work, *A Curious Collection of Ancient Paintings* (London, 1741).

9. A. Ramsay, 'Extracts of two letters from Signr Camillo Paderni at Rome to Mr Allan Ramsay, Painter, in Covent-Garden, concerning some antient statues, pictures, and other curiosities, found in a subterraneous town, lately discovered near Naples. Translated from the Italian by Mr Ramsay, and sent by him to Mr Ward, F.R.S.', *Philosophical Transactions* 41 (2) (1740–1), 484–9.

10. Ramsay, 'Extracts of two letters' (above, n. 9), 488–9.

11. This was reissued as one of the four tracts comprising his *The Investigator. Containing the Following Tracts*: I. *On Ridicule*. II. *On Elizabeth Canning*. III. *On Naturalization*. IV. *On Taste* (London, 1762).

12. Ramsay, *The Investigator ... IV. On Taste* (above, n. 11), 45.

13. See B. Frischer, 'Ramsay's 'Enquiry': text and context', in Frischer and Brown (eds), *Allan Ramsay and the Search for Horace's Villa* (above, n. 2). Though it is difficult to come to a definite conclusion, especially when travellers may have left no written records, there seems no evidence to support the contention of P. Levi, *Horace: a Life* (London, 1997), 101 and 195, that Lucas Holstenius took John Milton to visit the villa.

14. National Archives of Scotland, Dick Cunyngham of Prestonfield Muniments, GD 331/5/18: 12 November 1755.

15. National Archives of Scotland, Dick Cunyngham of Prestonfield Muniments, GD 331/5/18: 12 November 1755.

16. Ramsay, *Enquiry* (above, n. 2), 113.

17. Ramsay, *Enquiry* (above, n. 2), 112.

18. Philipp Clüver was the author of a major study of ancient geography, *Italia Antiqua* (Leiden, 1624). His pupil, Lucas Holstenius, sometime librarian of the Vatican, published posthumously notes on his work, *Annotationes in Geographiam Sacram Caroli a S Paulo, Italiam Antiquam Cluverii, et Thesaurum Geographicum Ortelii* (Rome, 1666). The most important recent writings that Ramsay used were Domenico De Sanctis, *Dissertazione sopra la Villa de Orazio Flacco* (Rome/Ravenna, 1761, and two further editions in Ramsay's lifetime), and Bertrand Capmartin de Chaupy, *Découverte de la maison de campagne d'Horace*, 3 vols (Rome, 1767–9). Volpi was the author of *Vetus Latium Profanum* III–X (Rome, 1726–45), which continued the two initial volumes by P.M. Corradini; for the Tivoli area, see vol. X.

19. Ramsay, *Enquiry* (above, n. 2), 113.

20. Ramsay, *Enquiry* (above, n. 2), 150.

21. Piranesi's joke forms the tailpiece to the 'Apologia' prefixed to *Diverse maniere d'adornare i cammini* (Rome, 1769), 35. On this see also J. Scott, *Piranesi* (London, 1975), 177. Informed by me of Piranesi's jibe, Frischer has been able to tease out the full significance of Piranesi's splendid etching with its barbed text and vulgar imagery. See Frischer, 'Ramsay's 'Enquiry'' (above, n. 13), 85–7.

22. Ramsay, *Enquiry* (above, n. 2), 144.

23. Ramsay, *Enquiry* (above, n. 2), 119.

24. The rough map is found on an opening in Ramsay's sketchbook for this expedition (National Gallery of Scotland, D4878/16). Frischer ('Ramsay's 'Enquiry'' (above, n. 13), 78–9) was the first to realize that Ramsay had used the Revillas map as his source, having noticed that Ramsay had included in his rough sketch at least three place-names that occur on no other contemporary map of the area.

25. Ramsay, *Enquiry* (above, n. 2), 145 note.

26. The Ramsay landscape view is in the National Gallery of Scotland, Department of Prints and Drawings, RSA 509; RSA 504–6 and D1415 in the same collection are the Jacob More drawings based upon it.

27. The landscape drawings by Ramsay bound into the National Library of Scotland manuscript of the *Enquiry* also show the use of a drawing grid. I am indebted to Martin Kemp for discussion of Ramsay's likely technique and his possible use of an optical aid such as a camera obscura. He has confirmed

my belief that Ramsay did not use such an aid, in contradiction of some recent suggestions that he did so. Moreover, had Ramsay relied on such a device, he would surely have said so in the inscription on RSA 509, where he tells us everything else of relevance regarding the circumstances of the making of this particular drawing.

28. Patricia Andrew has provided the most likely explanation of a somewhat confused story of a map (and a series of illustrations) being not so much 'commissioned' as offered by an artist practised in opportunism. I am grateful to her for discussion of the likely position: see also her essay 'Illustrating Horace's Villa: Allan Ramsay, Jacob More and Jakob Philipp Hackert', in Frischer and Brown (eds), *Allan Ramsay and the Search for Horace's Villa* (above, n. 2), 51–71.

29. It accompanies a reworked series of the original Hackert engravings by Francesco Morel after Luigi Sabatelli, in which the figures appear transformed into highly theatrical 'classical' dress. The publisher of the rare *Raccolta di no 10 vedute rappresentanti la Villa d'Orazio* was Agapito Franzetti. Patricia Andrew has argued convincingly that the production is likely to date from the 1790s, when Sabatelli was in Rome and Morel active as an engraver (Andrew, 'Illustrating Horace's Villa' (above, n. 28)); but Holloway ('Two projects' (above, n. 2)) has given it a date of ?1840, perhaps following the British Library catalogue.

30. British Library, Add. MS 39999; see Brown, 'The pamphlets' (above, n. 1), 84–5.

31. See, for example, M. Capasso, *Storia fotografica dell'officina dei papiri ercolanesi* (Naples, 1983).

32. Ramsay, *Enquiry* (above, n. 2), 148.

33. I am grateful to Bernard Frischer for pointing out to me the real significance of this insertion in one of the *Enquiry* manuscripts.

34. See Smart, *Ramsay* (above, n. 1), 10, 78.

35. Ramsay, *Enquiry* (above, n. 2), 133, note.

36. Ramsay, *Enquiry* (above, n. 2), 133, note.

37. Ramsay, *Enquiry* (above, n. 2), 135.

38. Cf. Frischer, 'Ramsay's 'Enquiry'' (above, n. 13), 93.

39. Ramsay, *Enquiry* (above, n. 2), 152.

CHARLES TOWNLEY'S COLLECTION OF DRAWINGS AND PAPERS: A SOURCE FOR EIGHTEENTH-CENTURY EXCAVATIONS, THE MARKET AND COLLECTIONS

Brian F. Cook

C harles Townley was born in 1737, and although he lived until 1805 he was essentially a man of the eighteenth century. In 1767, at the age of 30, he set off for Rome on the Grand Tour, and it was in Rome that he began his collection of classical sculptures, which was to become his lifelong passion. He also collected other categories of antiquities, including coins, bronzes, terracottas, seal-stones, vases and jewellery, but it is as a collector of marble sculpture that he is best known.

THE TOWNLEY ARCHIVE

At his death Townley left an enormous quantity of papers concerning his collection, including diaries, bills and account books, correspondence with dealers and other collectors, and a whole series of catalogues, mainly in his own hand. Some of this material is still in the possession of the Towneley family, but a large amount of it, known as the Townley Archive, was acquired by the British Museum in 1992.[1] This has now been checked, arranged, listed and numbered by a professional archivist and a detailed publication is planned.[2] The archive itself has been microfilmed and is available for study by appointment. The purpose of this paper is to survey the kinds of documents in the Townley Archive and elsewhere that are relevant to the marbles, and to illustrate by specific examples the sort of information that can be derived from them about excavations, the market and collections, especially Townley's own.

Soon after Townley's death his marbles were acquired by the British Museum, and the remainder of the collection was to follow in 1814. Unfortunately, no complete list of the collection was made at the time, and the Museum's Register of the marbles was not compiled until about 1848, when the officials involved in the acquisition were long dead. The Register was therefore based on two documents, a catalogue of the collection as exhibited in Townley's house, handwritten by Townley himself in 1804 (to be referred to as 'the 1804 parlour catalogue'),[3] and a supplementary list of objects not included in the 1804 parlour catalogue, which was compiled by Taylor Combe of the British Museum in 1806. This list too can now be shown to have been incomplete, and several of the descriptions are so brief and vague that the objects could not be identified in 1848. Some entries in the Register were therefore marked 'not found'. A few have since been identified from other documents, including the receipt for the collection signed by Taylor Combe on behalf of the Museum.[4]

A new catalogue of Townley's marbles, currently being prepared, will be arranged not by archaeological categories but by the date of acquisition by Townley, and will include objects that did not find a permanent place in his collection. The archive is rich in information about Townley's purchases, including dates, sources and prices paid. Much of this information is new, and some of it contradicts statements previously published, for example in A.H. Smith's catalogue.[5] Smith's errors are sometimes the result of a lack of access to all the evidence or to misinterpretation of what was available, but mistakes are sometimes to be found in papers written in Townley's own hand, and it is not always safe to accept information derived from his later manuscripts unless it is consistent with earlier accounts.

For detailed records of the acquisition of objects, including precise dates of purchase, prices and the names of dealers, Townley's original account books are invaluable. Unfortunately, the series is incomplete. For the earlier part of his first visit to Rome, for example, there is an account book marked 'A' that runs from 25 November 1767 to 4 June 1768.[6] Accounts for the remainder of this journey were no doubt recorded in a comparable book 'B', but unfortunately this has not survived. For this reason, the precise dates of the purchase of objects acquired between 5 June and Townley's departure from Rome in August are not known, although a list of the objects themselves, with dealers' names and prices paid, may be compiled from other sources. The accounts for the whole of his second visit in 1771–2 are preserved,[7] but not those for the third journey in 1777.[8] For the years in London the account books are rather patchy, but they survive for the period from 1780 to 1787,[9] and for parts of 1782[10] and 1804.[11] These account books are supplemented by original bills and receipts from Thomas Jenkins,[12] Gavin Hamilton[13] and James Byres,[14] and by a whole series of receipts for payments by Jenkins on Townley's behalf to Italian dealers, including Giovanni Battista Piranesi, Carlo Albacini, Antonio Vinelli, Giovanni Battista de Domenicis and Laurenzo Cardelli.[15]

In addition to the account books themselves, which are contemporary with expenditure and chronologically arranged, Townley compiled at various times consolidated accounts of expenditure, which may be described as 'transcript accounts' to distinguish them from 'original accounts'. There are several such transcripts in the Townley Archive, including a particularly useful one arranged by dealers and compiled about 1784 (to be referred to as 'the 1784 transcript accounts').[16] A similar transcript, compiled about 1781 with additions to 1785, is now in the possession of Sir Simon Towneley.[17] It seems to have been compiled in part from slips copied by Townley from Jenkins's bills.[18] There are separate lists of purchases for the years 1789 and 1790.[19] There is also a very useful list in an Italian hand of purchases made during Townley's first visit to Italy.[20] The Italian heading, 'Catalogo di tutte le robbe che sono del Sig.e Tonnely acquistate da 24 Xbre 1767', was translated by Townley as 'Catalogue of Different Articles Bought in Italy in 1768'. It does not give specific dates for purchases, but lists objects bought from individual dealers, with the prices paid. It may conveniently be referred to as 'the 1768 Italian catalogue'.

Some rather summary lists of sculptures with the prices paid for them were probably compiled for the purpose of calculating the overall expenditure on the collection. One compiled about 1776 includes esti-mated values, some lower but many higher than the prices paid.[21] Another compiled about 1778 has only prices paid.[22] These two list the sculptures by types (for example, statues, busts, heads, vases), but another compiled about 1784 lists the sculptures under the dealers who supplied them.[23] Another list compiled in stages between 1780 and 1782 gives prices and dealers' names, but lists the sculptures according to the room in which they were kept in Townley's house in Park Street.[24] In another catalogue, compiled about 1781 with additions about 1786, the sculptures are arranged by categories (referred to below as 'the classified catalogue').[25]

The manuscript catalogue used at the hand-over of the collection to the British Museum was the last in a series of 'parlour catalogues' that began before 1790. They were intended for the use of visitors to the house who did not receive a personally-guided tour, and they list most of the objects on view in the order in which they were arranged. Separate volumes could be provided for the ground floor (hall, parlour and dining-room) and the upper floor (drawing-rooms and library). About 1795 and again about 1800 Townley instituted radical rearrangements of the collection, and on each occasion a new version of the parlour catalogue was required. Most are in his own hand, but he sometimes had fair copies made by professional calligraphers.[26] They vary in the amount of detail in the descriptions, but provide much information (not always reliable) on dates of acquisition and provenance. These parlour catalogues are scattered, with several in the archive and others in the British Museum's Department of Greek and Roman Antiquities (the 1804 parlour catalogue), the British Library,[27] Towneley Hall Museum and Art Gallery (Burnley), and in the possession of members of the Towneley family.

Among papers in the hand of the self-styled 'Baron D'Hancarville' is a series of drafts for a catalogue of Townley's marbles as arranged in 1778, when the collector was just moving into the house in Park Street.[28] They are of interest not so much for their rambling commentaries as for the information they provide on the initial arrangement of the collection, antedating Townley's own earliest record of the arrangement by about three years.

Townley's surviving diaries relate mainly to his closing years: there is an almost complete series from August 1797 until July 1804, a few months before his death.[29] These are concerned mainly with his personal affairs, including detailed comments on his state of health, but there are a few scattered references to acquisitions, for example to purchases at the sale of marbles belonging to the Duke of St Albans in June 1798.[30] A relief with two heads, BM GR 1805.7-3.263 (Smith 555), the source of which is not recorded elsewhere, was actually a gift from Sir William Hamilton on 1 May 1801. It had been found in the sea, off Agrigento according to Combe, followed by Smith, but actually off Baiae according to Townley's diary for 12 May 1801.[31] The gift from the Duke of Bedford in May 1804 consisted not only of an Attic votive relief, BM GR 1805.7-3.139 (Smith 776), but also of a circular base with griffins in relief, BM GR 1805.7-3.453 (Smith 2512).[32] The earlier diaries include accounts of his visits to Paestum in 1768[33] and to Calabria in 1772.[34]

Correspondence forms a substantial part of the Townley Archive, the letters from Jenkins, Hamilton and Byres[35] being particularly valuable. Many of Townley's important sculptures were bought not during his trips to Rome but from London, by what we would now call 'mail-order'.

Hamilton's letters to Townley are of two types: current correspondence (running from 1772 to 24 April 1796) and reminiscences.[36] The latter consist of retrospective accounts of his excavations and are well known from Smith's publication of them based on a copy among the Stowe manuscripts in the British Library.[37] There is another copy in the Department of Greek and Roman Antiquities, but the originals are in the archive.[38] In the regular correspondence Hamilton's main topics are current excavations by himself and others, and negotiations on the sale of objects to Townley, sometimes marked by extravagant praise of his offerings, and often followed by the details of packing, shipping and the arrangements for paying bills. The bills themselves were written separately, but are sometimes noted as enclosed in the letters. The tone of the correspondence is usually amicable, but for several months in 1775 there were acrimonious exchanges on the relative quality of sculptures sent by Hamilton to Townley and to his other clients. Hamilton also discussed the restoration of various pieces and his negotiations for export licences with the papal commissioner, Giovanni Battista Visconti.

Jenkins too had much to say in his letters about the progress of excavations and about the objects he was offering to Townley.[39] Negotiations for objects could last for months, with many exchanges of letters, and with Jenkins at first promising and then actually send-ing drawings. Townley evidently kept the drawings separate from the letters, for the drawings came to the Museum with the collection. The possibility of matching drawings to letters was demonstrated some years ago by Gerard Vaughan,[40] and Ian Jenkins has recently done more work along those lines.[41]

A section of the archive containing papers on Townley's purchases for others is not confined to antiquities, but includes anything from English razors and scientific equipment to silk stockings.[42] Antiquities were acquired on behalf of Smith Barry, Col. Claud Martin and Lyde Browne. From time to time Townley visited other collections of classical marbles in England and made notes on them. There is much in the archive about Henry Blundell's marbles at Ince, but other collectors named include Lord Egremont (Petworth), Lord Palmerston, Browne (Wimbledon), Mr Beaumont (Christie's, May 1776), the Duke of Montague and Chase Price.[43]

RELIEF OF A YOUNG MAN WITH A HORSE AND A DOG
(Fig. 1)
BM GR 1805.7-3.121 (Smith 2206)

In Smith's *Catalogue* it is stated for the first time in print that this relief was 'Found in the part of Hadrian's Villa called the Pantanello, by Gavin Hamilton, in 1769'. This detail Smith took from the 1804 parlour catalogue. The 1784 transcript accounts, however, state that Hamilton found the relief in the Pantanello in 1770, adding that it was purchased from Piranesi for 150 scudi, and naming the young man as Castor. The 1782 catalogue and Sir Simon Towneley's transcript accounts confirm the immediate source as Piranesi and the price of 150 scudi, but while the former names the young man as Castor, the latter simply describe the piece as 'A bass relief of a Man stoping a horse early greek stile'. So far we have been dealing entirely with manuscripts from about 1781 or later. When we consult earlier documents, a different picture emerges. Among purchases from Piranesi in the 1768 Italian catalogue we find the following entry — 'Bas relief, about two square feet in size, portraying Alexander the Great and Bucephalus ... 150 Scudi'[44] —, and Townley's daily account book for 1768 records the purchase from Piranesi on 5 May of a 'bas relief of Alexander and Bucephalus'. Even though the supposed identification of the young man changes, the general description of the relief and the continuity of

FIG. 1. *Relief of a young man with a horse and a dog.* BM GR 1805.7-3.121 (Smith 2206). *(Photo: British Museum. Reproduced courtesy of the British Museum.)*

Piranesi's exact price make it clear that the various documents are referring to the same object. Since it was evidently purchased in 1768, Townley's later statements that it was found in 1769 or 1770 must be mistaken.

His further statement that it was Hamilton who found it in the Pantanello at Hadrian's Villa must also be mistaken, since Hamilton's licence to excavate there was not issued until 3 November 1769,[45] the year after Townley acquired the piece. Indeed, Hamilton himself did not mention this relief in the report on his various excavations that he sent to Townley in 1779.[46] It is just possible that the relief was excavated at Hadrian's Villa before 1768 by someone other than Hamilton, but unless some positive evidence is found to support that possibility, it seems safer to doubt the provenance as well, even though it is now deeply embedded in archaeological literature.[47] It begins to look as though Townley in his later manuscripts mistakenly transferred to this piece information that really belongs to another. The same may be true of the following item.

STATUE OF DIANA
(Fig. 2)
BM GR 1805.7-3.12 (Smith 1558)

Smith recorded that this statue was 'Found, in 1771, near La Storta, about eight miles from Rome'. According to the 1804 parlour catalogue it was found there in 1772, and Smith seems to have taken the earlier date from the classified catalogue. In the 1784 transcript accounts the supposed date of discovery is again given as 1772, and the price as £250. In another set of transcript accounts covering the period 1768–73,[48] under a heading 'Bought of Mr Jenkins in 1772 and –73', there is a reference to 'A statue draped of an Atalante' bought for £250. Other documents confirm that the statue originally called Atalante is the same one that was later identified as Diana. The shipping details indicate that the head of the Atalante was packed separately from the body; the head of Diana fits into a socket in the top of the body (and is probably alien). A bill from Jenkins in 1774 states that case 24 contained the Atalante;[49] Townley's entry for that bill in the transcript accounts belonging to Sir Simon Towneley names the statue as Diana. Jenkins continued to refer to the statue as Atalante in letters up to August 1774, but in October of that year agreed that the identification as Diana was probably correct.[50] With the identity of the statue confirmed, we must return to the list of marbles bought from Jenkins in 1772–3, where the description of the piece continues: 'found in May 1773 in a vineyard on the side of the hill betwixt the Villa Pamphili and Saint Peters'.[51] Another manuscript gives the provenance as 'near the Villa Pamphili outside the Porta S. Pancrazio 1773',[52] which is in effect the same thing. Here we have yet a third date for the discovery of the statue, not long before 12 July 1773, when Jenkins sent his bill for it to Townley. Of even greater interest is the discrepancy on the provenance, for in these apparently early documents the statue is said to have been found not at La Storta but in Rome itself. It seems that at some stage Diana acquired the provenance and date of discovery of another sculpture, the group called Bacchus and Ampelus.[53] Papers in the archive now allow us to correct Townley's mistake.

THE SEATED MUSES
BM GR 1805.7-3.37 (Smith 1687)
(Fig. 3)
and BM GR 1805.7-3.240 (Smith 1686)
(Fig. 4)

Another mistake to be found in Smith's *Catalogue* derives from the combination of an error on Townley's part with Smith's own misinterpretation of the documents that were then available to him. There are in the collection two small statues of Muses playing the lyre. Although they differ in many details, especially in the form of the two lyres, the most obvious difference is that one of them is inscribed on the plinth in Greek characters 'Eumousia' (**Fig. 3**). Of this piece Smith stated that it was 'Purchased from the Barberini Palace, 1771'. He was wrong on both counts: it was the other Muse, the one without the inscription (**Fig. 4**),[54] that came from the Barberini Palace, and the date of Townley's purchase was not 1771 but 1768. An examination of the documents that were not available to Smith reveals both the true facts and how Smith came to be misled.

The essential clue is to be found in two earlier versions of the parlour catalogue that were not avail-

FIG. 2. *Statue of Diana.* BM GR 1805.7-3.12 (Smith 1558). *(Photo: British Museum. Reproduced courtesy of the British Museum.)*

able to Smith, one compiled about 1801 and now in the archive, the other in the possession of Sir Simon Towneley and compiled about 1795. The latter contains the earliest reference I have yet found to the inscribed statue. Both statues appear in these catalogues, the Barberini Muse downstairs, 'Eumousia' upstairs. In documents written before about 1795, there is only one Muse; whenever a dealer is named, it is Jenkins; whenever a source is given, it is the Barberini Palace. For example, the 1784 transcript accounts and Sir Simon Towneley's set both credit the sale to Jenkins, the former adds the Barberini Palace as source, the latter gives the date as 1768. The source is confirmed in a list in Townley's hand in the Bodleian Library.[55] Among the purchases from Jenkins listed in the 1768 Italian catalogue is 'A statuette of a Muse with lyre and plectrum. 80 Scudi'.[56] The inescapable conclusion is that it was the uninscribed Muse that came from the Barberini Palace and that Townley acquired it in 1768. All that can yet be said for certain about 'Eumousia' is that she was acquired from an

FIG. 3. *Statue of a seated Muse*, inscribed 'Eumousia'. BM GR 1805.7-3.37 (Smith 1687). *(Photo: British Museum. Reproduced courtesy of the British Museum.)*

FIG. 4. *Statue of a seated Muse.* BM GR 1805.7-3.240 (Smith 1686). *(Photo: British Museum. Reproduced courtesy of the British Museum.)*

unknown source before about 1795. Why then did Smith state that she was acquired from the Barberini Palace in 1771? To answer that question the documents must be examined again.

From the earlier versions of the parlour catalogue it is evident that the Barberini Muse was moved around the ground floor, from room to room, at various times. About 1804 she was again on the move, and in the 1804 parlour catalogue there is a blank page where she might be expected. She had in fact been moved to the space at the foot of the staircase, and Combe noted her presence there on his supplementary list. Unfortunately he described her there only as 'A small female figure. Marble'. In the receipt that was given to the Towneley family a fuller description confirms the identity: 'A small female figure playing upon a lyre'. Combe doubtless remembered which statue he meant, but the lack of detail in his supplementary list led to the statue remaining unidentified

when the Museum's Register was compiled in 1848, and so the relevant entry was annotated 'Not found'. When Smith came to write his *Catalogue*, there was only one seated Muse identified in the Towneley register, namely 'Eumousia'. There was also only one seated Muse listed in the classified catalogue, since 'Eumousia' had not been acquired when that catalogue was compiled. Smith therefore assumed that the two were identical, and transferred to 'Eumousia' Townley's comment on the other Muse in the classified catalogue: that it came from the Barberini Palace and had been acquired in 1771. As demonstrated above, the date was wrong, but Smith's repetition of Townley's mistake on this point confirms the source of his misinformation. Smith's conclusion was reasonable enough on the basis of the documents that were available to him. Other documents in the archive and elsewhere enable us to set the record straight.

RELIEF OF AN 'EQUES SINGULARIS'
(Fig. 5)
BM GR 1973.1-3.17
(Smith 2392)

The archive also makes it possible to confirm that some apparently unprovenanced items in the British Museum actually came from Townley's collection. In an earlier article on the Townley Collection,[57] I listed a number of sculptures that were unrecorded in the Museum before 1835, suggesting that some of them might be Townley pieces exhibited for the first time in that year. In 1977 I doubted whether proof could be found; access to papers in the archive has provided proof for one object, a fragment of the grave-relief of an 'eques singularis' (**Fig. 5**).

FIG. 5. *Relief of an 'eques singularis'.* BM GR 1973.1-3.17 (Smith 2392). *(Photo: British Museum. Reproduced courtesy of the British Museum.)*

In the 1784 transcript accounts Townley recorded the purchase from Piranesi of 'A small Bass relief of a man leading a horse', which is described in greater detail in the 1768 Italian catalogue: 'A bas relief on a base a foot long and ten inches wide, which portrays a horse-trainer who leads by a rope a horse with a cloth over its back'.[58] This description matches the relief with complete accuracy, and, since even the dimensions tally with those given by Smith, the identity seems certain.

STATUE OF A RECLINING NYMPH
(Fig. 6)
BM GR 1805.7-3.456 (Smith 1711)

Another sculpture assigned to the Townley Collection in the same article, on the grounds that Townley had a drawing of it, is a figure of a reclining nymph with a water-jar.[59] Documentary support for the hypothesis is now found in the letters from Hamilton, who had two other versions of the same subject. Writing to Townley on 6 April 1775, he mentioned one from a site on the Via Latina some miles from Rome, then known as Roma Vecchia. The statue was much damaged, lacking the head and other parts, which Hamilton had hopes of finding when he resumed excavations at Roma Vecchia in June. He did not, however, recommend this one to Townley, since he had recently found a larger example of the type at Ostia, which he characterized as 'fine sculpture', promising to send it to Townley.[60] On 21 April he proposed to call the piece 'Egeria', reiterating that it was for Townley. The missing fragments were being sought, since their absence was delaying restoration.[61] In a letter of 27 May Hamilton sent detailed notes on the condition of the statue: the back of the head, the feet and some parts of the drapery and the rock were missing.[62] In a bill of the same date, Hamilton listed 'Egeria or sleeping nymph' at £150.[63] On 17 June Hamilton promised to send a sketch of the fountain nymph,[64] presumably the one now in the Department of Greek and Roman Antiquities, on which Townley copied Hamilton's notes about the condition of the piece, adding that it had been bought by the Duke of Dorset for £200. Townley's comment on the statue's eventual destination must have been added later, for meanwhile Hamilton had it shipped to Townley. By the time he wrote to Townley again on 17 August he had already heard that Townley did not want to acquire the piece since he already had a duplicate, but it was then too late to stop the shipment. Noting that Mr Barry might be interested in it, he asked Townley to see it through customs and to keep a note of the charges.[65] Townley wrote to Hamilton on 30 October and kept a copy of the letter.[66] 'Egeria' was now in Townley's warehouse, and Townley had looked at it by taking two boards from the front of the case. He thought it much the best

FIG. 6. *Statue of a reclining nymph.* British Museum GR 1805.7-3.456 (Smith 1711). *(Photo: British Museum. Reproduced courtesy of the British Museum.)*

example of the type that he had seen, but did not want it for his own collection since he had one already. Hamilton later informed Townley that he had offered it to Charles Greville,[67] apparently in vain, since it was actually acquired by the Duke of Dorset and is now at Knole. Adolf Michaelis noted that it was found by Hamilton at Roma Vecchia,[68] but according to Hamilton's letters it now seems that the version he sent to Townley under the soubriquet of Egeria was actually found at Ostia shortly before 6 April 1775.

The example in the British Museum now seems to be firmly identified as Townley's copy. It is not mentioned in any version of the parlour catalogue nor in any of the transcript accounts compiled by Townley himself. It does, however, seem likely to be the 'Ninfa di fonte', listed in the 1768 Italian catalogue among the purchases from Pietro Pacilli in 1768.

These examples give some idea of the richness of the Townley Archive and of the information it can yield, especially when examined in the light of Townley's other papers and his collection of drawings.

Acknowledgements

My thanks are due to Ilaria Bignamini and Andrew Wallace-Hadrill for inviting me to contribute to the first session of the workshop in Rome, to the British Academy for awarding me an Overseas Conference Grant to enable me to take part, and to the British Museum for permission to publish photographs of sculptures in the Townley Collection and to quote from the Townley Archive.

NOTES

1. The spelling of the family name as Townley, rather than Towneley, was an idiosyncracy of Charles Townley and his brother Edward. Some papers were catalogued separately and dispersed when the Townley Papers were sold at Sotheby's in July 1985. The rest of the archive, having failed to make the reserve price when offered at Sotheby's again in 1992, was later acquired by private treaty.

2. The Calendar of the Townley Archive will appear in the *British Museum Occasional Papers* series.

3. 'Catalogue of Ancient Marbles Collected in Mr Townley's House Park Street Westminster'. This is the manuscript described as 'the second Townley Inventory' by A.H. Smith, 'Gavin Hamilton's letters to Charles Townley', *JHS* 21 (1901), 306 n. 1; and simply as 'Parlour Catalogue' by B.F. Cook, 'The Townley marbles in Westminster and Bloomsbury', *British Museum Yearbook* 2 (1977), 34–78.

4. TY 18/6. The numbers of the papers in the Townley Archive have the prefix TY.

5. A.H. Smith, *A Catalogue of Sculpture in the Department of Greek and Roman Antiquities British Museum*, 3 vols (London, 1890–1904). In the present article, Smith's catalogue numbers follow the British Museum register numbers, the latter being prefixed BM GR.

6. TY 8/2.

7. TY 8/4/1.

8. For details of the journeys, see *DBITI*, 946–8.

9. TY 8/5/1.

10. TY 8/6.

11. TY 8/7.

12. TY 8/74–9.

13. TY 8/109–14.

14. TY 8/115–20.

15. TY 8/83–108.

16. TY 10/3. There is also an almost perfectly accurate copy of the book in the hand of Charles Townley's uncle, John Towneley (TY 20/3).

17. For this and TY 10/3 (above, n. 16), see also B.F. Cook, *The Townley Marbles* (London, 1985), 14.

18. TY 8/75.

19. TY 8/13–14.

20. TY 10/1.

21. TY 10/6. Some items were added in pencil to as late as 1795, but this subsidiary list is far from complete. See Cook, *Marbles* (above, n. 17), 25, 29.

22. TY 10/7; see Cook, *Marbles* (above, n. 17), 32.

23. TY 10/5.

24. TY 12/1; see Cook, *Marbles* (above, n. 17), 33–7, there described as 'the 1782 catalogue'.

25. BM, Department of Greek and Roman Antiquities: 'A Catalogue of the Ancient Marbles in Park Street Westmt The Places Where They Were Found and Where They Were Bought'. This is the manuscript described as 'the first Townley Inventory' by Smith, 'Letters' (above, n. 3), 306 n. 1; and as 'MS Cat 1785–86' by Cook, 'Westminster' (above, n. 3),

34–78. See also Cook, *Marbles* (above, n. 17), 32–3.

26. For example, Dacosta (who wrote TY 12/4–6) and Upcot (payment recorded in Townley's accounts for 20 December 1804: TY 8/7).

27. British Library, Add. MS 34009, copied by John Towneley after 1804 from an earlier version; abbreviated 'MS Cat, John Towneley' by Cook, 'Westminster' (above, n. 3), 34–78.

28. TY 16/27–8. When the Archive arrived at the British Museum the sheets were jumbled. Comparison with the various parlour catalogues has made it possible to arrange them into two incomplete, but complementary, groups.

29. TY 1/8–20.

30. TY 1/10.

31. TY 1/15.

32. TY 1/20.

33. TY 1/3.

34. TY 1/5.

35. TY 7/682–704.

36. TY 7/551–672.

37. Smith, 'Letters' (above, n. 3), 306–21.

38. TY 7/633 and TY 7/638.

39. TY 7/295–550.

40. G. Vaughan, *Charles Townley* (D.Phil. thesis, University of Oxford), publication forthcoming.

41. See A. Wilton and I. Bignamini (eds), *Grand Tour. The Lure of Italy in the Eighteenth Century* (London, 1996), 228–69.

42. TY 11.

43. TY 15.

44. 'Basso rilievo di due piedi quadrati incirca rappresentante Allessandro Magno col Bucefalo … 150 Scudi.'

45. Information kindly provided by Ilaria Bignamini.

46. See Smith, 'Letters' (above, n. 3), 306–21.

47. E.G.H. Winnefeld, *Die Villa des Hadrian bei Tivoli* (*Jahrbuch des Deutschen Archäologischen Instituts, Ergänzungsheft* 3) (Berlin, 1895), 160; A.B. Cook, 'A pre-Persic relief from Cottenham', *JHS* 37 (1917), 123–4, fig. 10; P. Jacobsthal, *Die Melischen Reliefs* (Berlin, 1931), 93; W. Fuchs, *Die Vorbilder der Neuattischen Reliefs* (Berlin, 1959), 135, n. 69; B.F. Cook, *Greek and Roman Art in the British Museum* (London, 1976), 184; Cook, *Marbles* (above, n. 17), 14, fig. 8; M. de Franceschini, *Villa Adriana* (Rome, 1991), 12.

48. TY 10/2.

49. TY 8/74/13.

50. TY 7/339.

51. TY 10/2.

52. TY 10/8.

53. BM GR 1805.7-3.1 (Smith 1636). The source of both statues is given as Tor Angela on the Via Praenestina, Rome, by R. Neudecker, *Die Skulpturenausstattung Römischer Villen in Italien* (Mainz am Rhein, 1988), 213.

54. BM GR 1805.7-3.240 (Smith 1686). Re-registered in error as BM GR 1805.7-3.455 before its true identity was discovered.

55. Bodleian Library, Add. D 71, fol. 63v.

56. 'Una statuetta di una Musa con lira e plectro. 80 Scudi.'

57. Cook, 'Westminster' (above, n. 3), 34–78.

58. 'Un Basso rilievo appartenente ad una Base Lunga un piede, e

larga dieci pollici che rappresenta uno Scozzoni de Cavalli che
tiene colla corda un Cavallo con panno sul dorso.'

59. Cook, 'Westminster' (above, n. 3), 69 no. 4, fig. 53.

60. TY 7/585.

61. TY 7/587.

62. TY 7/589.

63. TY 8/110.

64. TY 7/591.

65. TY 7/593.

66. TY 7/597/2.

67. TY 7/599.

68. A. Michaelis, *Ancient Marbles in Great Britain* (Cambridge, 1882), 419–20, Knole no. 2.

HOW ANTIQUE IS ANTIQUE? THE RESTORATION OF MOSAICS FOR THE VATICAN MUSEUMS

Klaus E. Werner

This essay is a study of the use of ancient mosaics in the Vatican Museums from about 1775 until the late 1860s.[1] It focuses on the actual restoration of the mosaics and their use as decoration in the various rooms of the Museums, and it explores the changing concepts of authentic antiquity. The aim is to demonstrate that the restoration of ancient mosaics can only be understood, and judged, in its specific historical and cultural context.

ANCIENT MOSAICS IN A NEW CONTEXT

The embellishment of the Vatican Museums, notably the Pio-Clementino Museum, followed a concept of stylistic unity that embraced both the objects displayed and the newly-designed building itself. The best-known example is the Sala Rotonda, a circular hall that housed the collection of Roman deities and was based on the design of the Pantheon. Ancient architectural sculptures ideally were to be integrated into the new building. This applies, for instance, to the pair of porphyry tela-mones, the so-called 'Cioci', from Hadrian's Villa at Tivoli, which were placed on either side of the monumental entrance to the Pio-Clementino.[2] A consequence of this concept was the use of ancient mosaics as pavements. The idea was first expounded in a letter of Giovanni Battista Visconti, the founding father of the Museums, dating from 1773/4 and relating to a mosaic found on the Esquiline in 1773 and to another one discovered at Tusculum in 1741.[3] These were the first in a long series of ancient mosaics used to embellish rooms in the Museums.

The use of ancient mosaics inevitably had a series of undesirable consequences. The mosaics had to be lifted from their original find-spots, cut into pieces, carried to the studio of the mosaicist, thor-oughly restored and, finally, reassembled. All this did not help to preserve their specific setting, that is to say the intricate ways in which the individual tesserae had originally been laid out. In most cases not even the original material was preserved. The outcome was the result of a series of circum-stances: the good or poor state of conservation of the mosaics, the method used for their lifting and reassembling, the aesthetic and stylistic influences (*Zeitgeist*) during the period in which they were restored and, finally, their use as pavements in the Museums.

LIFTING AND RESTORATION

To understand fully mosaic restoration, one needs to understand the method used for lifting the pavements from their original site. Although we have no complete description of this procedure, numerous hints can be found in the records left by the mosaicists in charge of the restorations.

Firstly, the mosaic was cleaned and panels of *peperino* (of about 2 x 3 feet) were glued on to its surface, using lime as an adhesive. Deep cuts were made along the edges of each panel, first verti-cally and then beneath, towards the centre, in order to break them off the ground. The single compounds of mosaic and *peperino* were then lifted using pulleys and transported to the workshop in Rome. The destructive nature of the lifting process can be seen by comparing a pavement before it was lifted with the compounds on arrival at the workshop. An example of this is a mosaic from the church of San Rocco, which was found in 1833 but not restored until 1996.[4] A comparison of the present mosaic with the original, as documented in a drawing made by Enrico Calderari, reveals that one-third of the original surface was destroyed as a result of the cutting and lifting and of the manner in which it was transported.

Once in the workshop, the ancient mortar on the back of the compounds, which had become fragmented and degraded, was removed. The compound was placed into a temporary bed of lime, or clay, which prevented the mosaic structure from falling apart. It was only then that the *peperino* panels were taken away. As in most cases the original mosaic was not in perfect condition, often having suffered as the result of the collapse of a roof or from a fire, numerous gaps had to be filled. The process of filling these, and also the strips missing between the various compounds where the cuts had been made, was an arduous task, as it was difficult to find exactly the right materials. Therefore, in order to avoid different colouring between the ancient and modern parts, whole motifs were reset using new materials.

During this phase, the original setting was inevitably lost. How faithfully the new setting mirrored the mosaics' original appearance depended solely on the taste and skill of the restorer. The single compounds were eventually set into a new bed and were then ready to be reassembled in their new location in one of the rooms of the Museums.

PHYSICAL CHANGES

Unfortunately, because of the huge gaps in the mosaics and because many parts had to be patched or replaced, the restoration process usually led to the resetting of the entire composition. In fact, the original parts left untouched rarely amounted to more than 1–5% of the whole pavement once they were placed in the Museums. This has been proved by the technical analysis of the mosaics from the Baths of Caracalla, now in the Gregorian Museum of Pagan Antiquities,[5] and those from the Tenuta di San Cesareo, now in the main hall of the Ingresso Nuovo.[6] In both cases it has been possible to identify the original parts by identifying the few spots in which original tesserae are still preserved. These became evident during modern restoration work, when the mosaics were turned on their backs and the mortar taken off. This revealed that for the figures of the athletes from the Baths of Caracalla (**Figs 1** and **2**) original work amounted to about 5%, while for those of the mosaic from the Tenuta di San Cesareo it was less than 1%.

Sometimes, when the mosaics had broken during the lifting process, it was necessary to start from scratch, normally using sketches made before the lifting. This was the case, for instance, for a mosaic discovered in the Tenuta di Fiorano, which is now located in the Gabinetto delle Stampe of the Vatican Library.[7] Since the few original fragments left after attempts to lift it were not worth the transport costs, the mosaic was entirely reconstructed in the studio on the basis of the sketch that had been made before the lifting had been attempted, and used new materials. Another example is the mosaic that was found under Palazzo Sora in 1845, which is now also in the Ingresso Nuovo. In this case, one of the mosaicists involved in the restoration later revealed that the pavement had been ruined irretrievably when it was lifted and had had to be completely reconstructed.[8] Yet, the official reports do not record any such problems, possibly because no one wished to take responsibility for the failure. The same probably applies to the pavement from Tusculum now in the Sala a Croce Greca.[9] In its present state it is completely modern, although ancient materials (but not the ancient setting) were used in a few of the central parts. The fact that the mosaic had been exposed to humidity, heat, cold and vegetation damage for more than 30 years before it was acquired makes it highly probable that in the meantime the mortar had, in any case, become loose. Furthermore, the mosaicists employed *peperino* panels of 4 x 4 feet. These may have been too big for the purpose, since they would not have been able to guarantee a uniform adhesion of the mosaic to the panel's surface. This is, in fact, the only time that one hears of the use of such large and clumsy panels.

It might even be that the ruinous state of some mosaics was responsible for the decision to lift only specific parts of larger depictions. The panel of a panther from Falerone, now in the Simonetti staircase, originally was part of a larger composition consisting of several octagons. Other depictions in the same pavement, which are known from sketches made by the excavators, were deliberately left *in situ*.[10]

Some mosaics underwent substantial work not just once, but repeatedly, at different times. For example, the depictions of theatre actors from the Tenuta di Porcareccia on the Via Aurelia, now on display in the Ingresso Vecchio, were restored on at least three occasions: after their discovery in or shortly before 1779, after serious damage in 1884, and again in 1935–9. Were a careful analysis made, one might be able to distinguish between these restorations, but the original setting disappeared long ago.

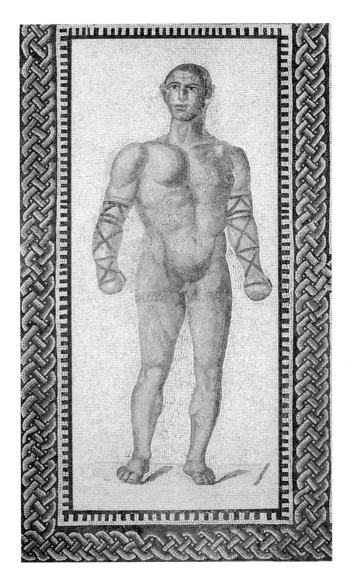

FIG. 1. One of the athletes from the Baths of Caracalla as it is today.

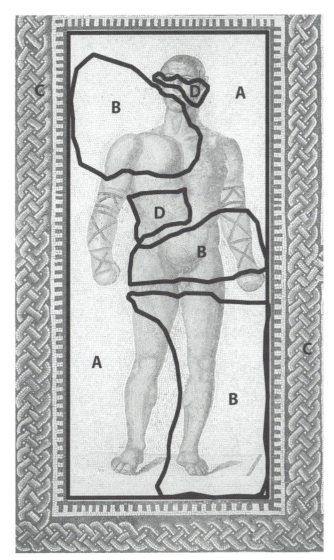

FIG. 2. The same athlete as in Figure 1 with the various interventions marked: (A) restoration of the parts damaged at its lifting; (B) a reconstruction of the gaps that were missing when the mosaic was discovered; (C) parts made anew in 1836–40, and again in 1963–76; (D) the original antique parts.

STYLISTIC CHANGES

The extent to which restorations could vary in their style is illustrated by a comparison of some of the earliest restorations with some of those undertaken at the end of the Papal Government, towards the end of the period in which mosaics were being acquired for the Vatican Museums.

A good example of neoclassical restoration is offered by the famous panels from Hadrian's Villa. These were restored and set into a common frame by the mosaicist Andrea Volpini in 1780–91.[11] At the time of their discovery, in the entrance of the so-called Basilica of the Palazzo Imperiale, three of them were in very poor condition, with only about 10% of the original composition preserved. In contrast, the fourth

panel, which showed four theatre masks and had been found in the antechamber of the basilica (**Figs 3** and **4**), only needed some minor repair at the edges. Despite this, all these panels now make a perfect stylistic match: Volpini restored them in a manner aimed at preserving, or recreating, the original antique work. He did so by imitating the original work in all those parts where it was possible for him to understand the ancient style and decorative motifs; but he refused to 'reinterpret' the larger gaps where there were no hints, and confined himself to filling them with a uniform yellowish golden background.

A mosaic from the Esquiline, formerly in the centre of the Sala delle Muse, demonstrates how faithfully the

FIG. 3. The central panel from the antechamber of the so-called Basilica of the Palazzo Imperiale at Hadrian's Villa as it looks today.

FIG. 4. The same panel as in Figure 3 with the interventions by Andrea Volpini of 1780–91 marked on it. Volpini confined himself to completing the ancient motifs.

mosaicists working in the late eighteenth century tried to emulate antique styles and decorative motifs, even when they had to set whole parts anew.[12] Since, for unknown reasons, it was impossible to lift the whole pavement, the frame — with a motif of undulating lines — was reconstructed in the workshop and, due to the fact that the mosaic had to fit into the middle of the Sala delle Muse, was reshaped into an octagon. This, however, had no serious consequences for the motifs and style of the newly-set frame, which perfectly match the few original fragments (which happened to turn up again in 1931, and are now in the storerooms of the Museo Nazionale Romano). In this example, the frame in the Vatican Museums was effectively recreated *all'antica*.

The mosaic in the middle of the Sala Rotonda, from Otricoli, has puzzled scholars and students of archaeology for a long time.[13] Its quality makes it a remarkable object, especially given that no one has been able to explain its stylistic features, some of which appear to be unique in Roman art. In this case, too, the Vatican mosaicists imitated the original style perfectly, revealing their own work in only a few modern features. For example, the grandiose spatial composition is that of the original Roman mosaic. The fact that the ancient style was preserved and imitated is even more interesting, because about 40% of the original pavement had already been lost by the time the mosaic was dis-

covered, due to the collapse of the vault of the ancient bathing structure it came from. Instead of creating new decorative motifs, the Vatican mosaicists decided that the missing parts should be reconstructed in a symmetrical composition based on the existing groups of Nereids riding marine centaurs. In this case, too, the taste perfectly matched the original style.

Such a subtle and sensitive interpretation of the antique is not to be found in mosaics restored after about 1800. At first it was only the arrangement of the ancient parts that was varied slightly, but around the middle of the century their entire stylistic appearance was subjected to hefty rearrangement and adaptation. A good example is the mosaics from the Tenuta di Tor Marancia (**Figs 5** and **6**), which were placed in the Braccio Nuovo in 1817/18.[14] The principal mosaic, representing Ulysses, originally had an L-shaped form. This was turned into a square, matching the other two mosaics on either side of the gallery in its shape and dimensions. To attain these results, all the scenes inside had to be rearranged. It is obvious that this type of alteration could hardly respect the original setting — indeed, there are no original parts extant. Smaller mosaic panels flank the main one, and these also were set entirely anew, according to a new design.[15]

Two of the panels discovered at Hadrian's Villa in 1779 initially stayed with the excavator; they were

FIG. 5. One of the oblong twin panels complementing the mosaics from Tor Marancia as it looks today.

FIG. 6. The same panel as in Figure 5 in a drawing made at the time of its discovery in 1817.

acquired for the Museums almost a century later, in 1867, and set into walls of the Sala degli Animali.[16] In the intervening period, they had been restored by Michelangelo Barberi, one of the best mosaicists of the day. As the motifs here were identical to those on the mosaics acquired in 1781 and restored by Andrea Volpini, a comparison is possible between the approaches of the two restorers. While Volpini confined himself to filling the gaps with a homogeneous colour, Barberi inserted a fantastic landscape, which he integrated with the few (if any) original parts in an indistinguishable manner. But the most striking difference regards the overall appearance, which in Barberi's panels mirrored his own Romantic taste, and thus contrasts markedly with the original style.[17]

In the latter part of the nineteenth century, the possible range of modifications became even greater. Some of the pavements used for the embellishment of the Stanze di Raffaello were altered substantially according to the taste of the day. This became increasingly problematic as the gap between antique — or rather neoclassical — and contemporary styles was widening constantly. A good example of this is the mosaic pavement from the baths of the so-called Palazzo Imperiale at Ostia, which was discovered in 1857 and put into the Sala dell'Immacolata Concezione. This mosaic was restored by Pietro Palesi in 1859–64, in such a way that the floral motifs reflected the prevailing taste of the day.[18] His alterations went as far as affecting the overall chromatic appearance; indeed, the colours of single motifs were harmonized with the gallery's fresco decorations — one of many changes expressly requested by the papal architect who supervised his work.[19] Some formal changes were also made: the three rows of four squares were cut down to two rows of three squares, and fantastic motifs were added on both sides to make the dimensions of the pavement more balanced within the size of the gallery.

In the late 1860s, the possible rearrangements of an ancient mosaic hardly knew any limits. Since for the embellishment of the Galleria dei Santi e Beati, now the Sala del Sobiesky, no ancient mosaic was available — or the available ones were too costly —, Palesi decided to patch with modern parts the ancient fragments left over from a pavement in the Sala di Costantino. These modern parts were based on the design of an ancient mosaic found, but never lifted, in the Tenuta di Tor de' Schiavi in 1861, and also on the representation of a basket with fruit and flowers that was part of a larger pavement discovered at Ostia in 1863, and which had been kept in a storeroom ever since.[20] Yet, even with these additions, the resulting mosaic did not cover the entire central part of the floor. Palesi had to fill the remaining space with black and white floral motifs of his own invention. Typical of Palesi's attitude towards antique mosaics are his remarks about the missing parts, which he thought could easily be filled by fragments from the excavations at Ostia.[21]

The simple fact that the results were not only accepted but even praised — if only for economic reasons —[22] shows how things had changed dramatically since the restorations carried out by Volpini in the Pio-Clementino Museum. After the mid-nineteenth century, the Vatican mosaicists no longer emulated the ancient style and setting, but they tried, instead, to find new creative solutions that are clearly incompatible with twentieth-century understanding of the purpose of restoration.

THE PROBLEM OF PRESERVATION AND AUTHENTICITY

Why does no one appear to have been aware of these transformations or, at least, why is no mention made of them? A number of possible answers can be given to this question. Firstly, very few people saw the original mosaics before they were restored. In most cases, the excavators are known to have done their best to cover up any sort of damage to the mosaics in order to get as high a price as possible for their finds, and usually contemporary witnesses were reliant on the information given to them by the excavators. Moreover, the Vatican officials, such as the Commissario delle Antichità e Cave and the *assessori* assisting him, who were charged with supervising excavations and the acquisition of objects for the Museums, were also responsible for the lifting and successful restoration of

the mosaics. Therefore they, too, had no personal interest in denouncing irregularities between the original and the restored.[23] Thus, the lifting process was always praised and described as successful, even when the pavement had been broken, as in the case of the mosaic from Palazzo Sora, mentioned above (p. 136).

Secondly, the restoration process was not optional, but necessary. Unlike other media, a mosaic cannot be conserved until it has been restored. Once uncovered, an ancient mosaic is subject to rapid degradation, caused by humidity, temperature and vegetation. Conservation, in the strict sense of the term, would have 'fixed' the state of the pavement as it was at the time of its discovery; this would have meant a fractured mortar bed, an undulating surface and large gaps caused by the collapse of vaults onto the mosaics.

Thirdly, proper restoration was usually regarded as necessary to return a mosaic to its state of ancient grandeur. In fact, the public had followed with great interest the installation of pavements in the Pio-Clementino Museum. Even with cases in which modern changes have heavily undermined authenticity, the excellence of restoration and adaptation turned the mosaics into masterpieces of eighteenth-century mosaic art at least, if not of the genuine antique.

Only a few individuals expressed independent views and were, in fact, particularly interested in the fate of lifted and restored mosaics. This is the case, for instance, for the comments of Eduard Gerhard, who stated that the mosaics of the Braccio Nuovo were 'Kopien' ('copies').[24] He may have obtained such information from the circle of restorers collaborating with the Vatican Museums.[25] In addition, Antonio Nibby criticized the mosaics from the Baths of Caracalla because they were almost entirely reconstructed after they were lifted. Instead of leaving the building bereft of those mosaics, Nibby favoured conservation, or reassembly, *in situ*.[26] The excavator Egidio Girolamo Di Velo also suggested that some specimens of mosaics should be preserved *in situ* and the creation, together with architectural fragments, of a sort of archaeological park.[27] But despite all this criticism, Bartolomeo Nogara's monumental work on the ancient mosaics in the collections of the Vatican and Lateran, published in 1910,[28] did not question the circumstances of their restoration. His work was but the final stage in the monumentalization of the Vatican mosaic collection. This had a long-lasting impact upon future research and scholarship, for it sanctioned the superiority of the Vatican mosaics, which — thanks to their excellent, though modern, execution — overshadowed virtually all the other mosaics found on Italian soil. This proved to be particularly problematic when other mosaics were compared to Vatican examples, which, due to their eminently neoclassical restoration, were usually thought to be of the Hadrianic period.[29]

Evaluating the mosaic collection of the Vatican Museums along modern lines, one must bear in mind that, even though those mosaics can no longer be regarded as authentic, the loss is more than compensated for by the insights they give us into contemporary views of antiquity, especially its restoration and reuse during the eighteenth and nineteenth centuries.

Notes

1. K.E. Werner, 'Zur Restaurierung antiker Mosaikpavimente im 18. und 19. Jahrhundert', *Mitteilungen des Deutschen Archäologischen Instituts. Römische Abteilung* 104 (1997), 477–504; K.E. Werner, *Die Sammlung Antiker Mosaiken in den Vatikanischen Museen* (Vatican City, 1998).

2. H. Beck, P.C. Bol, W. Prinz and H. Von Steuben, *Antikensammlungen im 18. Jahrhundert* (Frankfurt, 1981), 149–65; G.P. Consoli, *Il Museo Pio-Clementino. La scena dell'antico in Vaticano* (Modena, 1996).

3. Werner, *Sammlung* (above, n. 1), 57: 'Se si forma il pavimento in simil guisa, pel pregio dell'antichità, sarà più confacente ad un Museo e si allontanerà dalla somiglianza impropria co' pavimenti delle Capelle' ('Laying out the pavement in this manner, given the merit of antiquity, it will be more fitting for a museum and distance itself from an improper similarity with the pavements of chapels').

4. Werner, *Sammlung* (above, n. 1), 252–9. Also K.E. Werner, 'Il mosaico con scena bacchica da S. Rocco. Contesto e inquadramento', in *Atti del III° congresso nazionale dell'Associazione Italiana per lo Studio e la Conservazione del Mosaico, Bordighera 1995* (Rome, 1996), 525–32.

5. Werner, *Sammlung* (above, n. 1), 217–33.

6. Werner, *Sammlung* (above, n. 1), 279.

7. Cf. the mosaicist's comments in Werner, *Sammlung* (above, n. 1), 194: 'Mentre avendo rinvenuto il masso, che legava le tessere del mosaico, di una qualità fragile, e terrea, ad ontà di tutte le possibili cautele, e mezzi suggeriti dell'arte, non risparmiando veruna spesa per procurare di salvarlo, non gli riuscì; mentre nel muovere i massi con la massima diligenza, quantunque foderati, si crepolavano in varj sensi da non potersi estrarre' ('When laying bare the core of the mosaic binding, which keeps the tesserae together, it was found to be fragile, more resembling earth than mortar. Using the best tools, and acting with diligence, and experience, no matter what the cost, did not help, for whilst moving the mosaic parts with the utmost care, they disintegrated and could not be rescued').

8. See the report by Carlo Garelli (Werner, *Sammlung* (above, n. 1), 288–94): 'È da notarsi che questo prezioso Musaico avea molto sofferto per l'antichità, ed avea molti avvallamenti cagionati dall'enorme peso che sosteneva per l'interramento e scarichi di sassi fatti sul medesimo che da secoli giaceva non curato: nel farne il restauro, e metterlo in opera, è stato riportato quasi al suo piano' ('It is worth noting that this precious mosaic had suffered a lot from its old age, with quite a few bumps in its surface because of the enormous weight of the earth covering it and the stones that had built up on top of it, and because it was uncared for for centuries: during its restoration, and new installation, it has been almost totally remade').

9. Werner, *Sammlung* (above, n. 1), 55–65.

10. C. Barsanti, in Werner, *Sammlung* (above, n. 1), 83–8.

11. See Volpini's contract of 1789 (Werner, *Sammlung* (above, n. 1), 112–41): 'Io Sott.o Musaicista … prometto in virtù de'

Sovrani comandi di Sua S.tà per il lavoro sud.o e mi obligo do collocare nel gabinetto del Museo li quattro Quadri di Musaico antico entro la cornice e riquadro di quel paviment … e di costruire … con musaico novo di pietra l'ornato intermedi … Un tal lavoro deve imitare in tutto la maniera di quello dei Quadri e deve essere eseguito con ogni perfezione secondo le regole dell'arte, e con la magior stabilità' ('I, the undersigned mosaicist … promise by virtue of the sovereign commands of his Holiness, to undertake this work, and oblige myself to set up in the Gabinetto of the Museum the four ancient mosaic squares into the rectangular framing of the pavement … and to fill … with new mosaic tesserae the intermediate spaces … Such a work must imitate fully the style of the existing squares and has to be executed with absolute perfection according to the rules of the art, and with high stability').

12. Werner, *Sammlung* (above, n. 1), 66–72.

13. Werner, *Sammlung* (above, n. 1), 147–71.

14. Werner, *Sammlung* (above, n. 1), 191–210.

15. See the note on one of the plans for the Braccio Nuovo in Werner, *Sammlung* (above, n. 1), 194: 'I sudetti pavimenti devono essere eseguiti secondo i disegni consegnatici' ('The above pavements must be executed according to the layout designs given to us').

16. Werner, *Sammlung* (above, n. 1), 112–27.

17. For Barberi's style, see M. Barberi, *Alcuni musaici usciti dallo studio del Cav.r Michel'Angelo Barberi* (Rome, 1856).

18. Werner, *Sammlung* (above, n. 1), 318–25.

19. Werner, *Sammlung* (above, n. 1), 320 for the full description of the adaptation of the pavement to the gallery by Palesi: 'Quando visitato un'altra volta dal Sig.re Architetto il Pavimento gli fu fatto la questione perché non infilavano tutti i triangoli, et avendo a questo risposto di non essersi parlato punto di ciò nel Contratto, e di avere scrupolosamente adempito a quanto questo gl'ingiungeva, cioè di averlo rimesso in opera come lo aveva levato, e di averlo affilato, e livellato, il Sig.re Martinucci altamente dichiarò, che non avrebbe mai permesso, che un Lavoro di simile entità, collocato in sì magnifica sala dovesse restare imperfetto' (When the [papal] architect visited again the pavement, I was asked why the triangles [of the geometric ornament] did not fit all on the same line, and I answered that this had not been talked about in the contract, and that I had fulfilled scrupulously all that had been requested — that is, to set it up as I had found it, and to make it fit and to level it out. But Mr Martinucci declared, raising his voice, that he would never allow such an important piece, situated in such a magnificent hall, to remain imperfect').

20. Werner, *Sammlung* (above, n. 1), 333–45.

21. From Palesi's report (Werner, *Sammlung* (above, n. 1), 336): 'In caso mancasse qualche fascia si può prendere in Ostia' ('Where some bands are missing, one could always take them from [the mosaics of the excavations at] Ostia').

22. From the report by Luigi Grifi (Werner, *Sammlung* (above, n. 1), 336): 'In tale maniera sono stati con ogni speditezza adempiti i Sovrani comandi del S. Padre, che bramava di vedere al più presto possibile ornata di lastrico di musaico quest'altra Sala del Vaticano, e in pari tempo si è ottenuta una notevole economia poiché fuori della spesa dell'adattamento, e mettitura in opera, nulla è costato il musaico essendovi stato adoperato qualche residuo di quello scavato in Ostia ('In this way, the sovereign wishes of his Holiness have been executed with all speediness for he yearned to see — as soon as possible — another Vatican hall covered with fine mosaic. At the same time, it was possible to keep down the costs because, apart from the price of the [necessary] adaptation and installation, the mosaic itself cost nothing, having used some leftover parts of the one excavated at Ostia').

23. In about 1817–20, Alessandro D'Este sold the mosaic of Diana, now in the central niche of the Braccio Nuovo, to the Reverenda Camera Apostolica; see Werner, *Sammlung* (above, n. 1), 211–16. According to official publications, it had been discovered at Poggio Mirteto, but letters from those involved in the acquisition make clear that it was entirely modern and that Volpini had been commissioned to execute it by D'Este himself, whilst he was employed in the embellishment of the Quirinal Palace.

24. E. Platner, C. Bunsen, E. Gerhard and W. Röstell, *Beschreibung der Stadt Rom* II, 2 (Berlin, 1843), 88–9.

25. He also acquired one of the leftover panels of the mosaic found in the Tenuta di Porcareccia before 1779; see Werner, *Sammlung* (above, n. 1), 102.

26. A. Nibby, *Roma nell'anno MDCCCXXXVIII. Parte II antica* (Rome, 1839), 792.

27. Di Velo, quoted in Werner, *Sammlung* (above, n. 1), 221, wrote: 'Quanto [ai] mosaici … basterebbe servare una piccola porzione, e collocarla nelle nicchie quadrate tuttora esistenti. Fuori dalla rapacità dei curiosi indicherebbero quale sia stato il pavimento della sala, ove furono posti. Capitelli, fregi, basamenti, colonne di granito spezzate aumenterebbero le cognizioni dell'architetto e la delizia dell'Osservatore' ('As for the mosaics, it would be enough to leave only a small part, and set it up in one of the existing rectangular niches. Out of reach of the curious, none the less they would indicate the original nature of the pavement of the room, where they had been placed. Capitals, friezes, plinths, broken granite columns would enhance the perception of the architect and the pleasure of the observer').

28. B. Nogara, *I mosaici antichi nei palazzi pontifici del Vaticano e del Laterano* (Vatican City, 1910).

29. See the remarks by Giovanni Becatti (*Scavi di Ostia* IV. *Mosaici e pavimenti marmorei* (Rome, 1961), 287) about the mosaic in the Sala dell'Immacolata Concezione. Also Werner, *Sammlung* (above, n. 1), 318–25.

Towns and tombs: three-dimensional documentation of archaeological sites in the Kingdom of Naples in the late eighteenth and early nineteenth centuries

Valentin Kockel

INTRODUCTION

MODELS of ruins and of graves have not been objects of importance for either archaeology or art history for a long time. At first glance, they look like children's toys, small-scale imitations of grand originals. Yet their value around the year 1800, when they were first produced, was assessed somewhat differently. The aim of this essay is to restore these models to their rightful position as distinguished records of ancient monuments. As reproductions, they also demonstrate that in their own time the original monuments were perceived in a different light to today. By studying them, therefore, we can increase greatly our understanding of the history of archaeology.[1]

To excavate means to destroy, a well-known fact acknowledged by all archaeologists. Firstly, when searching for even earlier layers, the destruction of later archaeological finds is unavoidable. Secondly, once exposed, ancient remains are robbed of their subterranean protection. The latter problem is nowhere more apparent than in the ruins of Pompeii. Without the layers of pumice stone and the original covering roofs, the fragile architecture and wall-paintings soon begin to suffer, simply because of exposure to sun and rain.[2] For this reason, the 250-year history of the excavations of Pompeii is also the history of great losses of archaeological material. It is estimated that less than ten per cent of all the wall-paintings that were uncovered have survived. But the history of those excavations also tells the story of countless efforts made to preserve and document such a unique monument as Pompeii.

Complaints that excavations were not carried out and documented effectively, that publications were too thin and produced too slowly, and that there was not enough emphasis on the conservation of areas around Vesuvius, are all issues that are fully documented in both travel accounts and the academic literature of the eighteenth and early nineteenth centuries.[3] Since then, we have gradually come to realize that these 'accusations' are only partly true, or that they apply to specific periods. In 1763, when Pompeii had begun to be viewed as a homogeneous whole whose function was not just to provide the Museo Reale in Portici with new objects but also to attract visitors, attention turned to the conservation of the exposed ruins.[4] Protective roofing was built to cover either individual paintings and rooms or entire buildings, such as the Temple of Isis.[5] But even then the most beautiful wall-paintings were still removed and taken to Portici. Karl Weber, who was responsible for excavations until his death in 1764, had already envisaged a comprehensive publication in which architectural remains, paintings and finds would be presented together.[6] Francesco La Vega, director of excavations from 1764 to 1807, took care to write comprehensive reports on the Temple of Isis and the so-called Villa of Diomedes.[7] From 1782, the condition of the most important wall-paintings at the time of their discovery, that is to say, before their central panels were removed, was systematically documented. After 1787, the documentation was available also in colour. The on-site artists who recorded the paintings to scale were always named in La Vega's weekly reports.[8] The final step would have been the publication of complete houses with their plans, sections and wall-paintings;[9] evidence for this is provided by the large number of engravings preserved at the Museo Archeologico Nazionale in Naples. This kind of publication, illustrated with coloured engravings of the discoveries, would have been, in a sense, similar to recent academic works such as *Häuser in Pompeji*.[10] Apparently those publication schemes failed because of the different opinions held by the various members of the Accademia Ercolanese and, particularly, the hostility of the Minister, Bernardo Tanucci, who appears to have been interested only in the actual finds, not in their excavation context.[11]

ALTIERI'S TEMPLE OF ISIS

The question of whether La Vega's lavish graphic documentation would culminate in a suitable publication was still unresolved when the King of Sweden presented him with a different project. This must have come at a rather inconvenient moment.[12] Gustav III visited Pompeii in 1784 and was given permission by his host, Ferdinand IV, to have models made of the two most important buildings that had been excavated by that date, the Temple of Isis and the Villa of Diomedes.[13] We do not know whether this idea was conceived by the King himself, or if it came from one of his travelling companions. His artistic adviser, Francesco Piranesi, obviously comes to mind.[14] In any case, Gustav III had already come into contact with the model-maker Giovanni Altieri in Naples and had acquired numerous cork models of Roman architecture from him, including the Acropolis of Tivoli.[15] Together with Antonio Chichi and Rosa, Altieri belonged to the first generation of model-makers in Rome. Thanks to a close collaboration with the art dealer and excavator Thomas Jenkins and the architect Thomas Hardwick, Altieri had become a craftsman appreciated for his great precision. Since his return to his home town of Naples in 1783, Altieri had not found new employment. The commission from Gustav III opened up new opportunities for him; he enthusiastically undertook the construction of a model of the Temple of Isis on a scale of 1:18 (**Figs 1–2**). The model is a remarkably detailed and accurate reproduction of the temple complex. Altieri did not confine himself to measuring the building; he also documented the condition of the wall-paintings and stuccoes at that time with the utmost care. A comparison with the 'official' documentation of the temple reveals that many pictures and vignettes had already been removed, and Altieri marked the gaps at the appropriate points on his model.[16]

In many respects, Altieri's Temple of Isis presents a new approach to the reproduction of antique architec-

ture. In comparison to models of ruins in Rome, this model depicts the ancient temple not as a solitary monument but in relation to its surroundings. The large scale permitted detailed reproductions of the paintings and the state of conservation of the building. It is, without exaggeration, a three-dimensional record of the entire complex and, as such, it far surpasses any other architectural model made before that date. This was the common feeling even at the time, and it can be seen in the correspondence between members of the Neapolitan authorities concerned with antiquities dating from 1790.[17] Altieri had asked for permission to produce and sell copies of the model. La Vega, who was still hoping that his drawings of the temple would be published, rejected his request for two reasons: firstly, that the model was not accurate enough, and, secondly, that by offering the model for sale, Altieri would be publishing the temple, which he had no authorization to do. The second reason was, in fact, a contradiction of the first.

PADIGLIONE'S POMPEII

The first attempt to produce a three-dimensional record of Pompeii failed because the Neapolitan authorities claimed that the quality of the model was unconvincing. The deciding factor had probably been the fact that the model reproduced an unpublished building, rather than one well known from *vedute* and plans. Fifteen years later, when an *Officina per la costruzione di modelli in sughero* was officially established at Naples, there may still have been some memory of this event.[18] Felice Nicolas, who was the director both of the Real Fabbrica (the royal porcelain factory) and of the authorities concerned with antiquities, took the model-maker Domenico Padiglione and other artists with him to Paestum, and undertook there excavations and restorations. It was here that Padiglione began producing models of the temples, the city gate and other parts of the town at various scales. Indeed, in Paestum excavations and three-dimensional models went hand in hand. Except for the so-called Temple of Neptune, these models have either been lost or have been handed down to us in very poor condition.[19] However, we know them through copies, which are numerous and of good quality. Moreover, these copies are on a scale that enables the onlooker to imagine the actual extent of the buildings and their original dimensions. Padiglione, who had been working as a maker of cork models in the Real Fabbrica since 1802,

FIG. 1.   **Giovanni Altieri, Model of the Temple of Isis in Pompeii, 1784/5. Medelhavsmuseet, Stockholm.** *(Reproduced courtesy of the Statens Konstmuseer, Stockholm.)*

joined the Museo Reale in 1806 to continue his work in the newly-created 'Gallerie dei Modelli'.[20] The very fact that a whole section in the museum had been set up solely for models of ancient architecture shows the great importance that was placed on three-dimensional replicas.[21]

As we know from numerous unpublished documents preserved in the Soprintendenza Archeologica di Napoli and the Archivio di Stato in Naples, Padiglione made models of ancient buildings in the Kingdom of the Two Sicilies until his death in 1832.[22] By the end of his life, about twenty models of Greek and Roman architecture could be admired in the

museum's two model rooms, the favourite rooms of the visitors. The Greek temples of Sicily, however, were missing, and, apart from the temple of Paestum and the theatre of Herculaneum, all his models are now lost.[23]

The same applies to the most demanding project Padiglione was commissioned to undertake, the model of the whole city of Pompeii. By 1810 he had already made a model of the Temple of Isis and one of the theatre quarter.[24] This was followed by other models, including the Odeion by 1819, part of the amphi-theatre in 1818–22, and the Villa of Diomedes in 1821/2. We know a great deal about the latter model;

FIG. 2. Giovanni Altieri, Detail of the east portico from the model of the Temple of Isis in Pompeii, 1784/5. Medelhavsmuseet, Stockholm. *(Reproduced courtesy of the Statens Konstmuseer, Stockholm.)*

Padiglione's calculations and weekly reports allow us to reconstruct the working process exactly.[25] It was envisaged that the reproduction of the villa would be on a scale of 1:48. The plan, probably the one produced by La Vega, was copied on to a large board. Slots were then sawn, into which wooden planks were inserted for the walls. Then, onto these, cork was stuck. The model was transported to Pompeii three times, for a total of 47 days, to record the height and condition of the walls and paintings. The recording of the more important parts of the wall-paintings may have been completed with the help of the extensive graphic documentation from the eighteenth century. The subordinate rooms, on the other hand, had to be examined and recorded on site. Padiglione worked on the model with his son for more than a year.[26] Further tasks, on the same scale, followed this one, up to 1838. From documents we know that models were made of the area around the Forum and Basilica (1822–5), the east section of the Forum (1826/7) and, after

Domenico Padiglione's death, the House of the Faun (1835), the House of Actaeon (now of Sallust) (1833), and finally the House of the Tragic Poet (1837/8), which were produced by Padiglione's son and assistant, Agostino.[27]

Those models are no longer extant. Luckily, however, two copies have survived, which give an idea of the high quality and excellence of Padiglione's Pompeii models. In 1840, Ludwig I of Bavaria was able to have a copy of the House of Sallust made, which was intended for display in his Pompeian house at Aschaffenburg am Main, where it is presently preserved (**Figs 3–4**).[28] It was made by Agostino Padiglione and by the painter Giuseppe Abbate, and was rather expensive, costing 500 ducats. The model shows not only the house itself but also large parts of the insula (IV,1) in which it is situated. Building techniques such as *opus reticulatum* and *opus vittatum* are depicted in it. The exact documentation of plaster work and wall-paintings is of particular interest to

FIG. 3. Agostino Padiglione and Giuseppe Abbate, View of the small peristyle from the model of the House of Sallust in Pompeii, 1840. Schloßmuseum, Aschaffenburg am Main. *(Reproduced courtesy of the Bayerische Verwaltung der Staatlichen Schlösser, Gärten und Seen.)*

archaeologists, since the house has suffered not only due to natural causes, but from damage caused by American bombs during the Second World War. The condition of each room, particularly the side rooms, is recorded meticulously. This becomes clearer when one focuses on a room in which fragments of wall-painting of the third Pompeiian style are preserved on the upper third of the wall (**Fig. 4**); the lower section had been newly distempered during a phase of reconstruction and the rest of the old decoration disappears behind a ceiling that was added at that time. The holes for the ceiling beams can still be made out in the model (**Fig. 4**). This redecoration and structural change cannot be seen today in the actual archaeological record; the model is the only documentation we have of the remodelling of the house.

One plan and numerous watercolours could have been consulted for the making of the model of the House of Sallust.[29] The decoration of each room, the condition of each floor and the state of individual walls, all had to be examined and recorded at the excavation site. In this way, a completely three-dimensional description of the condition of the house was produced, which was remarkably accurate and whose architectural value was priceless. A careful study of the model is still, today, a precondition for any publication relating to this house. It is also worth noting that, unlike other publications of that period, strict attention was paid to documenting the condition of the ruins of Pompeii, rather than presenting a reconstruction of them.

The model at Aschaffenburg, which is not only a

FIG. 4. Agostino Padiglione and Giuseppe Abbate, East wall of room 30 from the model of the House of Sallust in Pompeii, 1840. The third Pompeian style has been left only in the upper part, invisible above a later lower ceiling, marked by beam-holes. Schloßmuseum, Aschaffenburg am Main. *(Reproduced courtesy of the Bayerische Verwaltung der Staatlichen Schlösser, Gärten und Seen.)*

reproduction of a house but of half an insula, leads us to think that models of other houses also reproduced their surrounding areas as well as the actual houses themselves.[30] Thus, it seems that the whole city, not just its individual buildings, was depicted. This idea appears to have developed gradually. It is documented in a letter of 1822, and it was only then that the whole city was divided into five areas that were meant to form the individual units of a model of the city.[31] The suggested scales were 1:48 or 1:96.

The great novelty about this plan was the idea of documenting absolutely everything, not just the most beautiful buildings and paintings. The model, therefore, would be markedly different to both the drawings and watercolours of paintings and to the cork models of ancient temple architecture. It was aimed at giving the visitors to the museum in Naples a vivid picture of the discoveries. Moreover, the model included the faithful reproduction of buildings that, as far as the authorities were concerned, had not yet been published, a privilege that only the king could possibly grant via the Accademia Ercolanese. For this reason, it was out of the question to make copies and sell them to Grand Tour travellers, which was the usual practice with temple models. In 1820, Domenico Padiglione was explicitly forbidden to sell copies without express authorization.[32] The existence of the model of the House of Sallust at Aschaffenburg can only be explained by a king (Ludwig I), who was also a lover of the antique, expressing the desire to have such a model made to a royal colleague. Another copy of the theatre quarter, reduced to half the size, is in Sir John Soane's Museum in London, but it is unclear when and for whom it was made (**Fig. 5**).[33] On the other hand, a drawing executed by the architect Alfred Guesdon in 1849 can be regarded as yet another consequence of this first model of Pompeii; he portrayed Pompeii from a birds' eye view, giving his drawing the appearance of a photograph, which may suggest that he used the model in the Museum.[34]

Padiglione's model probably was destroyed sometime in the 1860s, when his second son, Felice, was commissioned to make a smaller model of the town (which can still be seen in the Museo Nazionale) by the new director of the excavations, Giuseppe Fiorelli.[35] Its scale, 1:100, is not suited particularly well to reproduce such detailed paintings, but even these miniature portrayals document several walls that were lost to rain and frost a long time ago. The value of this model as a valid archaeological document has

FIG. 5. Domenico Padiglione (?), Model of the theatre quarter in Pompeii, c. 1820. Sir John Soane's Museum, London. *(Photo: Jeremy Butler by courtesy of the Trustees of Sir John Soane's Museum.)*

been recognized only recently and has not yet, by any means, been exhausted. Johannes Overbeck praised this model in his 1866 book on Pompeii:

[The model is one of the] most praiseworthy enterprises of the new era [namely Fiorelli's directorship] that anyone who knows the extent to which ruins are faced with decline will admit. That is why the production of a model depicting every structure as it really is, or as it was when excavated, is not only desirable but essential. In addition, when looking at the model as opposed to the original, it is easier to gain an insight into the context and location of all the individual rooms and buildings in relation to each other, into the layout of the streets and the differences of level and other such things; and finally this model of cork, plaster and paper, produced with the greatest accuracy and exactness, where even the paintings on the walls and the mosaics on the floors are of the

finest artistry, is a highly delightful and admirable work of art.[36]

One can hardly think of a better way to describe the quality of those models.

TOMB MODELS

The thorough documentation of the decay threatening archaeological sites was not the only purpose of the city models: vividness was a fundamental goal. With a series of small models produced in Naples at this time, the principal aim was to attain a high standard of didactic vividness. Such were the models of ancient tombs.

In the crypt at Sir John Soane's Museum (an appropriate place, indeed), there are three models of ancient tombs that recently have been returned to display from the museum storerooms (Fig. 6).[37] Soane owned them

FIG. 6. Domenico Padiglione (?), Three models of tombs at Nola, Canosa and Paestum, before 1825. Before restoration. Sir John Soane's Museum, London. *(Photo: V. Kockel by courtesy of the Trustees of Sir John Soane's Museum.)*

by 1825, but their provenance is still uncertain.[38] These cork cases, which are somewhat inconspicuous from the outside, reveal interesting treasures when they are opened. Next to a skeleton there are vases and weapons serving as burial gifts; the vases themselves are painted with detailed art-work. The three tombs differ in their furnishings. Only ceramics are found in the first tomb, the second is painted and contains a wealth of weapons, while the third is equipped with an antechamber, a *cline* in the main chamber and reliefs on the walls.

These models represent a tomb in Nola, one in Paestum and the Monterisi-Rossignoli tomb in Canosa. These tombs were quite famous between 1800 and 1820, and were often illustrated in appropriate publications (**Fig. 7**).[39] So far, I have discovered seventeen copies of the models (eight of Paestum, seven of Nola and two of Canosa). The specimens in Soane's Museum, despite being the best preserved of all, are not the prototypes.[40] Their history is rather complex but it can be reconstructed on the basis of various sources, though only certain critical points will be dealt with here, namely the question of the models' authenticity, of their purpose and, finally, what they represent as far as documentation is concerned.

As a consequence of the peace treaty of Tolentino (1801), the victorious First Consul Bonaparte was given a number of Pompeiian finds, as well as 34 ancient vases, by the King of Naples.[41] They arrived in Paris in the autumn of 1802, and later entered the collection of the Empress Josephine at Malmaison.[42]

Along with the vases, she also owned a model depicting a tomb in Nola at the time of its discovery. It was based upon Heinrich Kniep's famous illustration in Heinrich Tischbein's publication on vases from 1795 (**Fig. 8**).[43] The tomb was also illustrated when the first substantial discourse on ancient vases, dedicated to the Empress, appeared in French.[44] Its author, Aubin Louis Millin, explained the vignette with the following words: 'You see in the vignette of this introduction the depiction of an ordinary tomb found at Nola. In the gallery of Malmaison there is an old model of these tombs'.[45] The model, which was made by Domenico Padiglione in 1802, is now lost. It was produced in the Real Fabbrica, where ancient vases were also restored, under the directorship of Nicolas.[46] The specimen in London (**Fig. 9**) can be regarded as a faithful replica. Unlike Kniep's illustration, the model of the tomb was taken completely out of context. It depicted the stone case alone, as it normally would not have been seen. The miniature vases that were placed inside do not correspond with those in the picture. The themes of the paintings on the vases are, admittedly, all taken from the Sir William Hamilton's collection of vases (**Figs 10–11**), but this collection had sunk at sea, along with the ship Colossus, long before the model was made.[47] So Padiglione not only took all his information about the tomb from the drawing, but also the shapes and paintings of the vases came from the same publication. Kniep already had created a fictitious situation. His drawing does not represent the tomb at Nola, but 'un tombeau ordinaire', an ordinary tomb, and illustrates the excavation context in which ancient

FIG. 7. Different types of Greek tombs in Campania and southern Italy: the 'Nola-Tomb' (upper row), the 'Canosa-Tomb' (middle row, left) and the 'Paestum-Tomb' (middle row, right). From R. Gargiulo, *Cenni sulla maniera di rinvenire i vasi fittili italo-greci* (Naples, 1831), pl. I. *(Photo: V. Kockel.)*

vases usually were discovered. The model is even more abstract. It is taken out of context and represents a typical, rather than specific, tomb, with typical, rather than specific, vases.

In 1805, excavation work in Paestum was not just confined to the temples. A necropolis was uncovered at the city gate, which revealed several tomb chambers dating from the fourth century BC.[48] Two were painted, and the others were richly furnished with burial gifts. Nicolas, the excavator and director of the Real Fabbrica, had Domenico Padiglione with him at the excavation site as a model-maker, and the model

could very well be an authentic record. The paintings, weapons and vases that are reproduced in Soane's model also originate from the excavations of 1805 (Figs 12–16).[49] At that time, however, emphasis was placed on ordering the tombs according to their material genre, rather than on the arrangement of the individual tombs, and they were published according to this priority. This procedure can be traced in the model; it does not reproduce a specific excavated context, but portrays all the finds in order to give an overall impression.[50]

The third model represents a tomb chamber that

FIG. 8. C. Heinrich Kniep, *Sir William and Lady Hamilton observing the finds from a newly-discovered tomb in the forest of Nola.* Drawing. Art market, Rome, 1938. Deutsches Archäologisches Institut, Rome, neg. no. 38.149. *(Reproduced courtesy of the Deutsches Archäologisches Institut, Rome.)*

Fig. 9.   Domenico Padiglione (?), Model of a tomb at Nola, after C. Heinrich Kniep. Sir John Soane's Museum, London. *(Photo: Ole Woldby, by courtesy of the Trustees of Sir John Soane's Museum.)*

was discovered near Canosa in 1813 (**Figs 15, 17–20**).[51] From the outside, the form of the tomb is an even less convincing reproduction than the other models. Padiglione was certainly not at the excavation site on this occasion, and some of the details that were given by Millin in his first publication of the tomb are misinterpreted. The large Apulian vases, which are presently preserved in Munich, were correctly reproduced as far as the scale of reduction allowed (**Figs 19–20**).[52] The original finds were no longer in Naples when work was being done on the model, which meant that only the printed copies were available for reference. In the case of the Canosa tomb, for the very first time a very specific monument was reproduced, but here again we are not dealing with an authentic record as we would understand it today.[53]

In contrast to the model of Pompeii, these tomb

models cannot be regarded today as faithful documentation of actual discoveries, although at the time of their production they would have been seen as such. They represent three general excavation contexts and their typical furnishings; this also applies to the shapes of the vases and the subjects of the pictures, and with that they reached a level of accuracy that fulfilled the expectations of the time. As far as the context of the finds was concerned, they even imparted more information than the usual publications. This didactic expectation of a three-dimensional visual aid, which the models fulfilled at that time, and partly still do — as, for example, in Oxford[54] and in Leiden, where they are still on display—, is for us their most important aspect. The only model that actually was intended to provide an accurate documentation of a necropolis was destroyed a long time ago. In 1812, Padiglione

FIG. 10. **Miniature copy of a vase from Nola, after J.H.W. Tischbein. London, Sir John Soane's Museum.** *(Photo: V. Kockel by courtesy of the Trustees of Sir John Soane's Museum.)*

FIG. 11. **Drawing after a Greek vase from Nola, then in the collection of Sir William Hamilton. From J.H.W. Tischbein,** *Collection of Engravings from Ancient Vases … in the Possession of Sir W. Hamilton* II (Naples, 1796), pl. **53.** *(Photo: V. Kockel.)*

FIG. 12. Wall-paintings in Paestan tombs excavated in 1805. From R. Paolini, *Memorie sui monumenti di antichità ch'esistono in Miseno … ed in Pesto* (Naples, 1812), pl. VI. *(Photo: V. Kockel.)*

FIG. 13. Domenico Padiglione (?), Model of a tomb at Paestum excavated in 1805. Sir John Soane's Museum. *(Photo: Jeremy Butler by courtesy of the Trustees of Sir John Soane's Museum.)*

FIG. 14. Miniature copy of the Asteas-Lekythos found at Paestum in 1805. Sir John Soane's Museum, London. *(Photo: Jeremy Butler by courtesy of the Trustees of Sir John Soane's Museum.)*

FIG. 15. H. Ansted, Drawing of two tomb models in Sir John Soane's collection, dated 8 November 1825. Sir John Soane's Museum, London. *(Photo: Jeremy Butler by courtesy of the Trustees of Sir John Soane's Museum.)*

FIG. 16. Drawing after the Asteas-Lekythos: Herakles in the gardens of the Hesperides. From A.L. Millin, *Peintures des vases antiques vulgairement appelés étrusques* (Paris, 1808), pl. 3. *(Photo: V. Kockel.)*

FIG. 17. Plan and sections of the Monterisi-Rossignoli tomb in Canosa excavated in 1813. From A.L. Millin, *Déscription des tombeaux de Canosa* (Paris, 1816), pl. I. *(Photo: V. Kockel.)*

FIG. 18. Domenico Padiglione (?), Model of the 'Canosa-Tomb'. Sir John Soane's Museum, London. *(Photo: Jeremy Butler by courtesy of the Trustees of Sir John Soane's Museum.)*

FIG. 19. Miniature copy of the 'Underworld-Krater' from Canosa. Sir John Soane's Museum, London. *(Photo: Jeremy Butler by courtesy of the Trustees of Sir John Soane's Museum.)*

FIG. 20. Detail of the 'Underworld-Krater' from Canosa. Staatliche Antikensammlung, Munich. inv. no. 3297 VAS, neg. no. K81. *(Reproduced courtesy of the Staatliche Antikensammlungen und Glyptothek München.)*

copied a Graeco-Roman burial site. This was discovered at the back of the present Museo Nazionale Archeologico in Naples when the old Palazzo degli Studi was extended, and was destroyed during this building work.[55]

CONCLUSION

What conclusions about our perception of excavations do these different depictions allow us to draw? Obviously three-dimensional documentation could only be produced once older traditions of miniature reproductions of monuments and finds had already developed. Models of the ruins of Roman architecture eventually gave rise to adaptations of this technique in Pompeii. Every part of the city was thought to be unique, so it had to be depicted in its entirety. The integral perception of the architecture was not confined to individual houses, house typologies or the iconography of individual paintings; that is, one saw Pompeii as a whole and not as a collection of single houses or walls.[56] On the other hand, the depicted furnishings of the buildings and the tombs were regarded as being exemplary rather than as specific representations of their original contents. They were seen as prototypes, and the different finds combined to create ideal situations that could be understood and depicted as real. It was much easier to understand the context of ancient finds from looking at these models than at a display of vases organized typologically in the archaeological collections of the time.[57]

NOTES

1. For cork models, see A. Büttner, 'Korkmodelle von Antonio Chichi', in *Kataloge der Staatlichen Kunstsammlungen Kassel* VI (Kassel, 1974); P. Gercke (ed.), *Antike Bauten in Modell und Zeichnung um 1800 (Kataloge der Staatlichen Kunstsammlungen Kassel* 14) (Kassel, 1986); P. Gercke (ed.), *Antike Bauten. Korkmodelle von Antonio Chichi, 1777–1782 (Kataloge der Staadtlichen Museen Kassel* 26) (Kassel, 2001); W. Helmberger and V. Kockel (eds), *Rom über die Alpen Tragen* (Landshut, 1993); V. Kockel, *Phelloplastica. Modelli in sughero dell'architettura antica nel XVIII secolo nella collezione di Gustavo III di Svezia* (Rome, 1998).

2. For an early description and discussion of weather damage, see J. Overbeck and A. Mau, *Pompeji* (Leipzig, 1884[4]), 627–9.

3. The complaint by Johann Joachim Winckelmann (*Sendschreiben von den Herculanischen Entdeckungen* (Dresden, 1762), 20) that he saw only eight workers at Pompeii in 1762 is famous. See also S.G. Bruer and M. Kunze (eds), *J.J. Winckelmann. Herkulanische Schriften* I (Mainz, 1997), 79, and note on p. 161. In 1766, Sir William Hamilton, the British Resident at Naples, complained directly to the Minister, Bernardo Tanucci; see I. Jenkins and K. Sloan (eds), *Vases and Volcanoes* (London, 1996), 42–3. In 1769, the Emperor Joseph II blamed his brother-in-law, Ferdinand IV, within earshot of the excavation director, Francesco La Vega, for the fact that excavations were too slow, that too few workmen were employed and so on; see G. Fiorelli (ed.), *Pompeianarum Antiquitatum Historia* (Naples, 1860–2), I, 1, 230.

4. From 1763 the area around the Herculaneum Gate, and later also the Temple of Isis, was visible.

5. The protective roofing over the Temple of Isis was torn down in 1794. Frequently mentioned, it is documented in two drawings by Louis Jean Desprez of 1777/8 and an engraving by Jakob Philipp Hackert of 1793. See *Louis Jean Desprez. Tecknare, Teaterkonstnär, Arkitekt* (Stockholm, 1992), 53 no. 35; Kockel, *Phelloplastica* (above, n. 1), 43 fig. 23; W. Krönig and R. Wegner, *Jakob Philipp Hackert: der Landschaftsmaler der Goethezeit* (Cologne, 1994), fig. 108. For the roof, see also S. De Caro, in *Alla ricerca di Iside: analisi, studi e restauri dell'Iseo pompeiano nel Museo di Napoli* (Rome, 1992), 6.

6. C.C. Parslow, *Rediscovering Antiquity* (Cambridge (Mass.), 1995), 184–98 (with figs 55–9) and 296–319.

7. For reproductions of La Vega's drawings, see *Pompei. Pitture e mosaici. La documentazione nell'opera di disegnatori e pittori dei secoli XVIII e XIX* (Rome, 1995), 36–67 and 138–9 (Temple of Isis), 68–88 and 121–34 (Villa of Diomedes).

8. See I. Bragantini and M. de Vos, 'La documentazione della decorazione pompeiana nel Settecento e Ottocento', in *Pompei 1748–1980: i tempi della documentazione* (Rome, 1981), 34–41; I. Bragantini, V. Sampaolo and L. Martorelli, in *Pompei. Pitture e mosaici* (above, n. 7), 17–28 (for the artists Giovanni Battista Casanova, Filippo Morghen, Giuseppe Chiantarelli and Francesco Morelli); M. Pagano (ed.), *I diari*

di scavo di Pompei, Ercolano e Stabiae di Francesco e Pietro La Vega (1764–1810) (Rome, 1997), 93–4.

9. Actually formulated by La Vega on 20 October 1787; see Pagano, *Diari* (above, n. 8), 92.

10. V.M. Strocka (ed.), *Häuser in Pompeji* (Tübingen/Munich, 1984–), eight volumes published to date.

11. A. Allroggen-Bedel, 'Tanucci e la cultura antiquaria del suo tempo', in R. Ajello and M. d'Addio (eds), *Bernardo Tanucci. Statista, letterato, giurista* (Naples, 1986), 521–36; Parslow, *Rediscovering* (above, n. 6), 196–7 (the Accademia still arguing in favour in 1760), 232 (negative opinion).

12. La Vega frequently reported that his plans appealed to important visitors, for example to Emperor Joseph II on 7 April 1769; see Fiorelli, *Pompeianarum* I, 1 (above, n. 3), 230. In 1778, the architect Thomas Hardwick described La Vega's plans as 'extremely well drawn'; see P. de la Ruffinière du Prey, in J. Lever (ed.), *Catalogue of the Drawings of the Royal Institute of British Architects, G–K* (London, 1973), 91 no. 2. Otherwise, La Vega kept his plans under lock and key. Gustav III was not able to see them on his visit to Pompeii because La Vega was not present and the royal visitor had not been introduced to him before; see Fiorelli, *Pompeianarum* I, 2 (above, n. 3), 165 (13 February 1784).

13. Kockel, *Phelloplastica* (above, n. 1), 72–89.

14. Francesco Piranesi's father, Giovanni Battista, worked with the cork model-maker Agostino Rosa in Paestum in 1777. See M. McCarthy, 'Documents on Greek revival in architecture', *Burlington Magazine* 114 (836) (November 1972), 760–9. Abate Ferdinando Galiani probably had the idea of producing these models; under his instructions, Altieri made a Vesuvius landscape, which Gustav III had seen in the Royal Palace at Portici before he visited Pompeii. See M. Olausson, 'I modelli', in Kockel, *Phelloplastica* (above, n. 1), 27, 41, 43, 48.

15. Kockel, *Phelloplastica* (above, n. 1), 57–63 no. 1.

16. V. Sampaolo, 'La decorazione pittorica', in *Alla ricerca di Iside* (above, n. 5), 23–39.

17. Kockel, *Phelloplastica* (above, n. 1), 37–9.

18. The last we hear of Altieri is in the letter of 1790 mentioned above, n. 17. One might assume that there is some connection with the Real Fabbrica, where he tried to work, but this has not been proved yet.

19. P. Mascilli Migliorini, 'La diffusione di Paestum nei modelli', in J. Raspi Serra (ed.), *La fortuna di Paestum e la memoria moderna del dorico, 1750–1830* I (Florence, 1986), 148–9; T. Lutz, *Die Wiederentdeckung der Tempel von Paestum* (Bamburg, 1991), 90ff.; V. Kockel, 'sog. Poseidontempel, Paestum', in Helmberger and Kockel (eds), *Rom über die Alpen Tragen* (above, n. 1), 323–5 no. 54 (with a list of copies by Padiglione); E. Ruggiero, *Degli scavi di antichità nelle Province di Terraferma dell'antico Regno di Napoli* (Naples, 1888), 462ff.

20. A. Caróla Perrotti, *La porcellana della Real Fabbrica Ferdinandea* (Naples, 1978), 207–8.

21. For the first mention of this department in the museum guides, see L. Giustiniani and F. De Licteriis, *Guida per lo Real Museo Borbonico Napoli / A Guide through the Royal Bourbonic Museum* (Naples, 1822), 54, 202–4.

22. The files on the cork models are summarized in Archivio Storico della Soprintendenza Archeologica di Napoli, XIV, B 8. I am grateful to Enrica Pozzi Paolini, then the Soprintendente, for allowing me to see the documents, and also to Valeria Sampaolo and Andrea Milanese. See A. Milanese, 'Il Museo Reale di Napoli al tempo di Giuseppe Bonaparte e di Gioacchino Murat', *Rivista dell'Istituto Nazionale di Archeologia e Storia dell'Arte* s. III, 19–20 (1996–7), 345–405.

23. Complementary to the Paestum buildings in the Naples museum were the theatre of Herculaneum (1808), the late antique church of Nocera Inferiore (before 1819), the *macellum* of Pozzuoli (before 1819, with changes 1823), the amphitheatre of Capua (from 1827) and a number of Roman buildings from Rome. The model of the theatre of Herculaneum is now preserved in the local museum. The only one in Padiglione's series, it shows a reconstructed building, not a ruin. For a recent illustration, see U. Pappalardo, 'Nuove testimonianze su Marco Nonio Balbo', *Mitteilungen des Deutschen Archäologischen Instituts. Römische Abteilung* 104 (1997), 418–19, fig. 1. Padiglione's work on this model is documented in 1808, but work for a different (?) model of the theatre is mentioned as early as 1764: Parslow, *Rediscovering* (above, n. 6), 255, 367 n. 70. In the 1790s this model was in the museum at Portici; see M. Starke, *Letters from Italy* I (London, 1800), 117.

24. According to Milanese, 'Museo Reale' (above, n. 22), it was mentioned by Michele Arditi, the museum director, in 1810.

25. Archivio Storico della Soprintendenza Archeologica di Napoli, XIV, B 8, 7 and XXI, D 8. For the graphic documentation, see above, n. 7.

26. It is not known who copied the paintings. Francesco Morelli, who was responsible for documenting the wall-paintings in Pompeii until 1829, was named in connection with another model.

27. Agostino Padiglione worked with his father from 1815; from 1818 he was paid as an *aiutante* (assistant) and from 1831 as a *custode* (custodian). He is still mentioned in 1849, but must have died before 1856.

28. Kockel, 'Das Haus des Sallust in Pompeji', in Helmberger and Kockel (eds), *Rom über die Alpen Tragen* (above, n. 1), 134–47, 321–2. A copy of this model was made for the Deutsches Museum in Munich but was destroyed during the War. Only a photo remains: neg. no. *03159. I am grateful to T. Kockel, who drew it to my attention.

29. *Pompei. Pitture e mosaici* (above, n. 7), 92–5, 137.

30. This is attested for the Casa di Campagna (= Villa di Diomede), 'colla prossima strada de' sepolcri ed altri edifici' ('with the next street of tombs and other buildings') and the Calcidico (= Eumachia building) 'con altri molti edifici adiacenti … e il modello del Pantheon' ('with many other adjacent buildings … and the model of the Pantheon') (= Macellum) '… con altri edifici' ('with other buildings'). See V. Sampaolo, 'La realizzazione del plastico di Pompei', *Il Museo. Rivista del*

Sistema Museale Italiano 3 (1993), 82–3.

31. Archivio Storico della Soprintendenza Archeologica di Napoli, XIV, B 8, 27. The idea of reproducing the whole city of Pompeii in model form is somewhat of an enigma. The handwriting of the letter is certainly not that of Domenico Padiglione. One might think of his son Agostino, or the head architect Antonio Bonucci. The actual distances are given approximately (the Villa of Diomedes to the town gate; the town gate to the House of Pansa; the House of Pansa to the Forum; the Forum to the theatre portico), and the surface area of the model. In the light of this, the planned scale must have been about 1:42/3. In the Neapolitan system of measurements (12 *once* = 1 *palmo*), that would mean a ratio of 1 *oncia* to $3\frac{1}{2}$ *palmi*, not a very probable relation. The Aschaffenburg model was produced with the ratio 1:50, which, in turn, would leave us with a round scale of 1 *oncia* to 4 *palmi* = 1:48. Correspondingly, in a letter of 19 February 1823 (Archivio Storico della Soprintendenza Archeologica di Napoli, XIV, B 8, 23) a scale of 4 *palmi*, namely 1:48, was mentioned in connection with the model of the Basilica. Whether the author of the first letter miscalculated the scale or the plan was altered is not clear. More relevant is the closing sentence in that letter: 'Volendosi poi costruire l'intera città di già scavata, si potrà eseguire per metà della scala di pal. sudetta; allora tutti i pezzi sarebbero per metà' ('If one wished then to construct the whole of the city that has been excavated to date, it would be possible to execute it at half the above-mentioned scale of *palmi*; thus all the pieces would be half the size'). This is exactly the idea that Giuseppe Fiorelli took up in 1860, when the new model was made, not to the scale of duodecimal 1:96, but decimal 1:100. See below, n. 35.

32. Archivio Storico della Soprintendenza Archeologica di Napoli, XIV, B 8, 23. There must have been an event that provoked this letter. As far as we know, Padiglione sold a model of the Temple of Poseidon in Paestum to Crown Prince Ludwig of Bavaria (later King Ludwig). This was perhaps the same occasion that the model of the theatre quarter, now in Sir John Soane's Museum, was made. See Kockel, 'sog. Poseidontempel, Paestum' (above, n. 19), 323–5, no. 54.

33. Sir John Soane's Museum, inv. no. MR 1. See V. Kockel, 'Rom über die Alpen tragen. Korkmodelle antiker Architektur im 18. und 19. Jahrhundert', in Helmberger and Kockel (eds), *Rom über die Alpen Tragen* (above, n. 1), 22, fig. 14. Finally, it appears that the Austrian General Koller, the commanding officer of the allied auxiliary troops in the area of Naples in the 1820s, also owned a Pompeii model: see G. Heres, 'Die Erwerbung der Sammlung Koller durch das Berliner Antikenkabinett', *Listy Filologické* 100 (1977), 106. The stationing of these troops, which was necessary for the suppression of internal enemies, had one further consequence; the Engineer Captain Ludwig von Goro Agyagfalva published the first monograph on Pompeii in the German language, *Wanderungen durch Pompeji* (Vienna, 1825).

34. Alfred Guesdon (1808–76) specialized in birds' eye views of cities and may, therefore, have made the design independently. See U. Thieme and F. Becker, *Allgemeines Lexikon der*

Bildenden Künstler XV (Leipzig, 1922), 245. The illustration originates from H. Etiennez, *L'Italie à vol d'oiseau* (Paris, 1849–). See L. Fino, *Ercolano e Pompei. Vedute neoclassiche e romantiche* (Naples, 1988), 29; A. Ciarallo and E. De Carolis (eds), *Lungo le mura di Pompei* (Rome, 1998), cover.

35. In 1860, the east and west sections of the model of the Forum were described as unfinished. At first a model with a ratio of 1:200 was envisaged, but the idea was discarded in 1862. For the Padiglione family and this model in particular, including numerous documents, see Sampaolo, 'Realizzazione' (above, n. 30), 79–95.

36. J. Overbeck, *Pompeji in seinen Gebäuden, Alterthümern und Kunstwerken* I (Leipzig, 1866²), 47 (my translation). A lithograph showing a detail of the Forum model taken from a photograph is reproduced on a fold-out plate. The model-maker is not named. In the fourth edition, with A. Mau (Leipzig, 1884, p. 40), there is a mistake (by Mau?) in the corresponding footnote, whereby the model is attributed to Vincenzo Bramante instead of Felice Padiglione. The older model, superior in quality, was apparently unknown to both authors.

37. I am grateful to Peter Thornton, Margaret Richardson and Helen Dorey for their help with archival material and for allowing me to study and photograph the models.

38. Soane owned four grave models. Three of these (inv. nos. M 1078, 1085, 1088) first appear in drawings dating from 1825. A fourth ('Nola-Grave', inv. no. M 1276) was acquired from the Lord Berwick's Bequest at an auction sale in 1827. All that remains of it today is the covering stone. See P. Thornton and H. Dorey, *A Miscellany of Objects from Sir John Soane's Museum* (London, 1992), 66 no. 64.

39. These types of models of ancient tombs are mostly unpublished. The present writer is preparing an in-depth study of them. **Figure 7** shows the first plate of the somewhat obscure booklet by R. Gargiulo, *Cenni sulla maniera di rinvenire i vasi fittili italo-greci* (Naples, 1831). Raffaele Gargiulo, an art dealer, restored vases in the Museo Borbonico. He also manufactured the small copies of vases for the models, and sold them. For Gargiulo, see R. Donceel and A. Lezzi-Hafter, *Auf Classischem Boden Gesammelt* (*Antike Welt* 10, special issue, 1980).

40. The prototypes of all these models were in the Real Museo Borbonico in Naples and were invariably mentioned in travel guides of the nineteenth century, though often with the wrong names. They were first mentioned in Giustiniani and De Licteriis, *Guida* (above, n. 21), 202–5. The only surviving fragments are of the Nola and Paestum tombs. In addition to those in Soane's Museum, there are copies of the models also in Bern (Donceel and Lezzi-Hafter, *Classischem Boden* (above, n. 39), 32, 73–4), in Cambridge (H.A. Chapman, *Handbook to the Collections of Antiquities and Other Objects Exhibited in the Fitzwilliam Museum* (Cambridge, 1904²), 66), in Leiden (unpublished), at the British Museum (Jenkins and Sloan, *Vases and Volcanoes* (above, n. 3), 145 no. 27), at Malmaison (see below, n. 42) and Oxford (below, n. 53), today partly destroyed.

41. List of gifts (with no mention of the model) in A.L. Millin, 'Monumens', in *Magasin Encyclopédique* 8 tome 3 (Paris, 1802), 535.

42. S. Grandjean, *Inventaire après décès de l'Impératrice Joséphine à Malmaison* (Paris, 1964), 37, 206 no. 1604.

43. J.H.W. Tischbein, *Collection of Engravings from Ancient Vases ... in the Possession of Sir W. Hamilton* I (Naples, 1791), front plate. For the identification of the graves, see Hamilton's preface, p. 24; also Jenkins and Sloan, *Vases and Volcanoes* (above, n. 3), 144, no. 26.

44. A.L. Millin, *Peintures des vases antiques vulgairement appelés étrusques* I (Paris, 1808), p. I (drawing after Tischbein/ Kneip) and p. VI n. 39 (quotation).

45. 'Voyez dans la vignette de cette introduction, la figure d'un tombeau ordinaire trouvé à Nola. Il y a dans la Galerie de Malmaison un modèle antique de ces tombeaux.'

46. Caróla Perrotti, *Porcellana* (above, n. 20), 207–8.

47. Sir John Soane's Museum, inv. no. M 1078 (length 0.72 m; breadth 0.35 m; height 0.21 m). The prototype of four out of the six larger vases in Soane's model can be identified in Tischbein's *Collection* (above, n. 43), pl. 53, here **Fig. 11**.

48. First published in F. Nicolas, *Illustrazione di due vasi fittili ed altri monumenti recentemente trovati in Pesto* (Naples, 1809); most recently in A. Pontrandolfo, 'La conoscenza di Paestum nella storia dell'archeologia', in Raspi Serra (ed.), *La fortuna di Paestum* (above, n. 19), 119–38. See also A. Pontrandolfo and A. Rouveret, *Le tombe dipinte di Paestum* (Modena, 1992), 13–14 fig. 234.

49. Inv. no. M 1088 (length 0.48 m; breadth 0.35 m; height 0.36 m). The wall-painting was first reproduced in R. Paolini, *Memorie sui monumenti di antichità ch'esistono in Miseno ... ed in Pesto* (Naples, 1812), pl. 6. The book was published posthumously by Nicolas, who was probably the author of the long chapter on Paestum. It has been reproduced most recently in Pontrandolfo and Rouveret, *Tombe dipinte* (above, n. 48), 129 fig. 17. See also A. Pontrandolfo, 'Paestum', in *I greci in occidente. La Magna Grecia nelle collezioni del Museo Archeologico di Napoli* (Venice, 1996), 15–16, 22–8. For the identification of the vases from Nicolas's excavations, see A.D. Trendall, *The Red-figured Vases of Paestum* (London, 1987), 4. They are illustrated here as **Figs 14** and **16**: Lekythos signed by Asteas with Heracles in the gardens of the Hesperides. See Nicolas, *Illustrazione* (above, n. 48), pls 2–3; Trendall, *Red-figured Vases*, 86, 99–103, no. 135 pl. 57; Pontrandolfo, 'Paestum', 22 nos. 1–2, 34 colour pl. The weapons lying in the model are also reproductions of grave finds. See Nicolas, *Illustrazione* (above, n. 48), 398–408; Pontrandolfo, 'Paestum', 25–6, nos 1,11–1,20. Our **Fig. 15** shows two of the Soane tomb models (Paestum and Canosa). It was drawn by one of his pupils, H. Ansted, in 1825 and is one of the first documents that demonstrates the existence of such models.

50. The vases were encrusted with lime sinter and were cleaned in Naples. For this reason it is impossible to reconstruct a grave complex with only the first descriptions, written in Paestum, at hand.

51. Inv. no. M 1085 (length 0.66 m; breadth 0.34 m; height 0.32 m). The weapons found at Canosa are missing in the model. It was first published by A.L. Millin, *Déscription des tombeaux de Canosa* (Paris, 1816), and most recently reproduced in M. Mazzei, 'L'ipogeo Monterisi Rossignoli di Canosa', *Istituto Universitario Orientale. Annali Dipartimento di Studi del Mondo Classico e del Mediterraneo Antico. Sezione di Archeologia e Storia Antica* 12 (1990), 125–30 and 161–5; M. Mazzei, 'L'ipogeo Monterisi Rossignoli di Canosa', in R. Cassano (ed.), *Principi — imperatori — vescovi. Duemila anni di storia a Canosa* (Bari, 1992), II, 163–75; R. Cassano, 'Ruvo, Canosa, Egnazia e gli scavi dell'Ottocento', in *I greci* (above, n. 49), 108, 134, 148–50.

52. Queen Caroline Murat took the vases with her in 1815, when she went into exile. In 1826, she sold them to Ludwig I of Bavaria (at the time Crown Prince). Mazzei has written in great detail about this subject: see, Mazzei, 'L'ipogeo' (above, n. 51), 125–30, 161–5. The vases presently are in Munich (Staatliche Antikensammlung 3296 VAS (*Volutenkrater of the Dareios-Painter*); 3297 VAS (*Volutenkrater of the Underworld-Painter*); 3300 VAS (*Loutrophoros*)) and Naples (Museo Nazionale, inv. no. 82383 (Amphora)). All the vases and their drawings were reproduced by Millin, *Déscription* (above, n. 51). See here **Figs 19–20**.

53. The model-maker certainly had not seen the tomb, and repeated the same mistakes as in Millin's publication. The most serious is that the reliefs, which in reality are on two walls, are only shown on one side, above the *cline*, on the model, as in Millin's sketch (**Figs 17–18**).

54. In one of the vase rooms in the Ashmolean Museum there are two small copies of the Nola and Paestum tombs: inv. 1888, 1140 (length 0.265 m; breadth 0.158 m; height 0.09 m); inv. 1888, 1139 (length 0.27 m; breadth 0.16 m; height 0.157 m). The provenance of these models is unknown. I am grateful to Michael Vickers and Arthur MacGregor for the opportunity to study them.

55. M.R. Boriello, A. Greco-Pontrandolfo, M. Lista and G. Prisco, 'La necropolis di Via Santa Teresa', in *Napoli antica* (Naples, 1985–6), 279–82. The model is also mentioned in Giustiniani and De Licteriis, *Guida* (above, n. 21), 56 n. 1.

56. Cf. the comment in *Pompei. Pitture e mosaici* (above, n. 7), 24, where it was stated that the reproduction of paintings alone, not entire walls, was the primary concern during the 1830s and 1840s.

57. For example, the Lamberg collection in Vienna; see A. Laborde, *Collection des vases grecs de M. le Comte de Lamberg* I (Paris, 1813), frontispiece. Similar displays are often seen today in archaeological museums.

THE NINETEENTH CENTURY

GIACOMO BONI'S EXCAVATIONS IN THE ROMAN FORUM AS SEEN IN THE PHOTOGRAPHS OF THOMAS ASHBY

Rita Turchetti

INTRODUCTION

ONLY recently has photography achieved the status of a true and proper medium of archival documentation, even though it has been clear for a long time that photography is at least as important as other types of evidence due to its objective nature. The results of research conducted in the photographic archive of Thomas Ashby confirm this; this research has led to a modification in the reconstruction of several archaeological 'truths' from the excavations of Giacomo Boni in the Roman Forum (1899–1911). Ashby's photographs have made it possible to identify not only the structures excavated and then reburied, but also, and more importantly, it has revealed the destruction caused to a large degree by the archaeological approaches of the period. Monuments were destroyed to investigate earlier levels, and reconstructions were based upon erroneous identification of architectural fragments, which then became topoi in archaeological literature. All these things mean that it is possible to reconstruct a number of monuments in the Forum area in a quite different manner.

It is, perhaps, superfluous to introduce Ashby, who was a significant figure in a generation of great archaeologists that also included Rodolfo Lanciani and Giuseppe Tomassetti, the masters of the school of Roman topography who straddled the nineteenth and twentieth centuries. Ashby's most important work was the archaeological surveys along the great roads radiating from Rome and through the Roman Campagna — a region that is profoundly different today.[1] Less well known, perhaps, is his photographic activity, mostly undertaken to document his research. This produced a collection of over 8,700 images, preserved in the archive of the British School at Rome.[2] Ashby's work 'notes' are also kept there.[3] Since 1986, collaboration between the British School, the Istituto Centrale per il Catalogo e la Documentazione of the Ministero dei Beni Culturali — and more specifically the Gabinetto Fotografico Nazionale, where the negatives are on permanent loan — and, more recently, the Centro di Documentazione dei Beni Culturali of the Regione Lazio has led to the publication of four volumes,[4] and the same number of exhibitions,[5] devoted to the Roman Campagna, to Rome, to Lazio and to the Via Appia. This has meant the publication of photographs (many — 1,500 out of over 3,000 — previously unpublished) of more than 400 monuments. In many cases, this has resulted in a reconsideration of the existence, nature and chronology of entire complexes. Despite this, at the end of each volume one is left with the impression that it has contributed to the rediscovery of only a small part of Ashby's research.

As has been pointed out frequently by others, Ashby's research forms the basis of our current knowledge of the territory around Rome, and often this has not been updated. The fundamental character of his methodology emerges from the mound of photographs and notes and from his maps;[6] he sought to achieve a reading of archaeological topography in its historical context through honest record-making and prompt cartographic recording.[7] Moreover, Ashby combined study of the monument or find with an appropriate use of the literary sources and research in relevant documents. Of his archival work, we have not just his published work,[8] but also the pile of excavation documentation obtained from the Camerale, Camerlengato, Ministero dei Lavori Pubblici and other sources in the Archivio di Stato of Rome, which one finds accurately transcribed amongst his notes. Among these documents also can be found, often on the back of the same page, notes about monuments visited, often with sketches, measurements and indications of the possible use of rooms and even objects, or, as in the case of the Roman Forum, invaluable

Fig. 1. View of the Roman Forum from the Campidoglio after the final demolitions of 1882. The lining of the embankment of the Basilica Aemilia has been constructed from many of the marble fragments recovered during Lanciani's excavations. British School at Rome Archive. *(Photo: d'Alessandri.)*

descriptions of and reflections upon what was being discovered.[9]

With the publication of *Archeologia a Roma nelle fotografie di Thomas Ashby 1891–1930*, including Ashby's photographs of the city of Rome, it has been possible to reunite the documents and obtain interesting results relating, above all, to the area of the Roman Forum in the period between 1892, the date of the first photograph, and 1915. These were the years in which the archaeology of this area was definitively uncovered, initially by Pietro Rosa and Rodolfo Lanciani, and completed by Boni.

Before Boni's excavations, the Forum complex (Fig. 1) seems to have been a fairly homogeneous entity chronologically and looked rather as it had done at the end of antiquity; that is to say, levels and monuments relating to earlier periods had not been explored. Indeed, Lanciani restricted his work to the removal of the heavy fill from Renaissance excavations, which, from the point of view of stratigraphy, had been greatly disturbed.[10] Boni had gained experience as an architect and archaeologist when he was an Ispettore dei Monumenti for the Direzione Generale delle Antichità e Belle Arti. With Boni as the new director of the Forum excavations, 1898 saw the start of an intense period of excavation and study organized within a new programme and in accord with the new research interests embraced by this scholar. However, in the ten years of activity, which changed the appearance and scholarly knowledge of the area, the only published reports are the accounts to be found in *Notizie degli*

Scavi di Antichità and the *Bullettino della Commissione Archeologica Comunale di Roma*, which have few supporting materials.[11] Many scholars know of the manuscripts of Boni and his collaborators in the archive of the Soprintendenza Archeologica di Roma. There are drawings and photographs that support these, although unfortunately they are mostly unpublished even today.[12] Such lacunae can be made up for, even if only in part, by Ashby's images and notes, the result of his frequent visits to the Forum,[13] and by reports that appeared in English newspapers and journals. These reports go beyond simple notification of new discoveries and often contain information invaluable for the study of individual monuments and the history of the excavations, as has been pointed out by Boni's biographer, Eva Tea.[14]

However, one can see a significant omission in these images, that is of the deep excavations that represented Boni's main interest. One might imagine a tacit agreement between the two scholars by which the 'stratigraphic excavations' were out of bounds to Ashby. Ashby limited himself to a prompt summary of the information as it was published by Boni.

The situation was different for the monuments that were being uncovered and for the progression of this work. The transformation of the Forum area into a building site and the relocation of marble finds (Fig. 2) often led to erroneous identification of the location of monuments and to the discovery and, in several cases, to the demolition of structures (most often those attributed to the medieval period). Ashby's position on the

FIG. 2. The piazza of the Roman Forum filled with earth and stones that mostly came from the Basilica Aemilia. British School at Rome Archive, neg. Ashby II,4. *(Photo: British School at Rome.)*

interpretations that became attached to the excavated remains is significant. He always reported them accurately, but expressed doubts or different readings without polemic and often with humour, such as when he called Boni's so-called 'pozzi rituali' (ritual wells) 'not wells'.[15] Moreover, in his reports we always find valuable references to the late antique and medieval phases, whose structures were considered unimportant relative to those of the Imperial age and especially the archaic period.[16]

In effect, one might say that at the beginning of the nineteenth century the condition of the Forum and of its remains was fairly uniform due to historical reasons. After that, changes disturbed many areas, often profoundly, with a peak at the time of Rosa[17] and Boni.[18] This disturbance has had a profound impact on our understanding of topographical issues. Entire structures were dismantled and parts of them reused to satisfy the short-term needs of those engaged in reconstruction; thus they took on the character of unstratified finds. Several monuments were completely obliterated; others were demolished because they were thought to be medieval. A further obstacle concerns the information that has found its way into the archaeological literature over time and has been taken as 'fact'. A thorough analysis shows it to be entirely false, or rather that it could not have been so. Moreover, the density of the monuments in the Forum, both in a horizontal and a vertical sense, is such that the use of ancient sources becomes difficult. They may refer equally to two adjacent, and often similar, monuments, and thus positive

identification is impossible.

One factor that clearly complicated Boni's work was the presence of an enormous quantity of marble finds, often without provenance, cluttering the area.[19] We know that from 1884 he devoted himself to reorganizing this muddle of stone, the consequence of previous excavations, which was scattered over the whole area. This was such a massive task that in 1898, the year in which he became director of the excavations in the Roman Forum, he proposed the creation of a commission made up of Lanciani, Christian Hülsen, Giuseppe Gatti and Giuseppe Sacconi to identify and attribute the marbles to individual monuments.[20] Ashby noted that by 1904 all that had been achieved was the erroneous re-erection of two honorary columns and the reconstruction of the aedicule of Vesta.[21]

Even if it were true that Boni's excavation methodology did not always achieve the desired results, it is important to remember that he used stratigraphic excavation in sample trenches to investigate the earliest phases of Latin civilization,[22] and was one of the first in Europe to do so.[23]

Of the many pieces of evidence preserved in the Ashby archive, only some of the most significant examples will be discussed here. In these, photography, with or without accompanying annotation, is employed as evidence (often unpublished) of demolished monuments, erroneous reconstructions or fantastic interpretations in the area between the Comitium and the Rostra, and between the Temple of Divus Julius and the Basilica Aemilia.

Fig. 3. The Arch of Septimius Severus and the Rostra before the excavations. British School at Rome Archive, neg. Ashby 42. *(Photo: British School at Rome.)*

THE LAPIS NIGER, COMITIUM AND THE AREA IN FRONT OF THE CURIA

One of the first photographs (**Fig. 3**) that the young Ashby took, on 19 April 1892, documents the situation around the Arch of Septimius Severus before Boni's excavations. Among the significant features, basalt paving slabs can be seen, which Ashby initially described in his notes as 'medieval' and then more correctly as 'late'. There is also a square concrete base and blocks of travertine and marble sticking out of the pavement of the Forum that overlay, up to cornice level, the so-called Rostra vandalica. Patrizia Verduchi recently suggested that this base was the base of an equestrian statue of Constantine the Great.[24] In 1835, it had been cut for the installation of a sewer to drain rainwater from the Arch of Septimius Severus[25] and, as can be seen in the photos, later was cut again by Boni to enable his deep excavations. The Decennalia base was placed on top of it.[26]

Comparison of this with the photos taken during the excavations in 1899, just a few months apart from each other (12 January and 17 May 1899), is important.[27] In the first (**Fig. 4**), work appears to be concentrated on the Lapis Niger (which is protected by a wooden screen). Ashby recorded the discovery in this area of heaps of marble fragments and medieval and modern pottery, attributed to the abrupt reshaping of the area in the first years of the nineteenth century,[28] particularly for the installation of the sewer mentioned above.[29] The street near the Arch of Septimius Severus appeared to be

Fig. 4. The Lapis Niger photographed on 12 January 1899, two days after its discovery. British School at Rome Archive, neg. Ashby 987. *(Photo: British School at Rome.)*

FIG. 5. **The Lapis Niger: detail.** British School at Rome Archive, neg. Ashby 991. *(Photo: British School at Rome.)*

FIG. 6. **The Lapis Niger: the progression of the excavations.** British School at Rome Archive, neg. Ashby 1085. *(Photo: British School at Rome.)*

intact still. Entry to the Curia, and to what remained of the Comitium, was made possible at this time by two sets of steps to the sides of the Lapis Niger (**Fig. 4**), especially those on the west side (**Fig. 5**). Apart from the alterations caused by the construction of the sewer, Ashby noted that these western steps had seemed rather ruinous in the plans of Angelini and Fea but now were in good condition and placed against the earth. These factors led him to suppose, correctly, that the steps had been restored by Rosa.[30] After almost a century of use, this restoration is no longer visible

today. Ashby also noted certain facts about the Lapis Niger, such as the breakage of one of the 'enclosure' slabs, probably caused by the pressure of the street paving behind it.

The photograph taken five months later (**Fig. 6**) records the structure and layers relating to the earliest phases, which Ashby described as 'a bewildering confusion of levels and direction'. We see that in the course of widening the excavation towards the edge of the Forum, the base of the equestrian statue of Constantine was damaged. To the side of this, there are

FIG. 7. Curia: removal of the embankment in order to restore the ancient entrance. British School at Rome Archive, neg. Ashby 1199. *(Photo: British School at Rome.)*

cornice blocks from another monument that had been located at the edge of the piazza and was demolished by Boni.[31] He relocated the blocks on the base of the statue where they do not belong. Only the photographic evidence, and a few marks on the pavement, bear witness to this monument, which otherwise has been lost. It permits a glimpse of the situation as it was in antiquity, which today is scarcely comprehensible. Furthermore, in the photos it is possible to see other displacements that have led to erroneous identifications. Lying on the paving of the Curia is the marble pedestal dedicated to Constans II (Fig. 5). It is located near to a brick base, onto which it was raised shortly afterwards. In reality, the pedestal was found near the Arch of Septimius Severus in 1547, with the Decennalia base, which suffered the same fate. Boni arbitrarily placed it onto a brick base that was much older and of a different size,[32] which had been built above the Augustan pavement of the piazza and incorporated into the Severan pavement.[33] Thus, the monument to Constans II that we find mentioned in almost all the guides to the Forum was created and placed *ex novo*, as was the Decennalia base of Diocletian.

THE CURIA

At the same time as the excavation of the Lapis Niger, work was taking place to isolate the façade of the Curia. This work aimed to remove the fill (7.7 m) and to restore the ancient ground level. Ashby (Fig. 7)

distinguished four strata with a corresponding raising of the level of the Curia door.[34] The first related to the Diocletianic phase, and was in use until the fire of 1088. Following this, the pavement was raised two or three metres to about half the height of the door; this led to the construction of a stairway. In 1548 Alfonso Sottomayor raised the door to the level we see today (Fig. 7). Beneath this, a sizeable necropolis was discovered, composed of burial recesses in the walls that held caskets of tufa and terracotta, and a marble sarcophagus with grave-goods datable to the fourth to twelfth centuries. Two ossuaries were identified in the core of the flight of steps.[35] Resting against the eastern corner of the Curia was what Boni described as a poor dry-stone wall, in reality a curtain of alternate bricks and small tufa blocks with a niche in the centre. He partly demolished this, since today it stands to a height of only 0.8 m.

To the south, several marble bases were found — one dedicated to the Emperor Maximianus, one to Constantine and a third to Theodosius. These were reused in the foundation of a wall. To one side was a stairway with three surviving steps, which Ashby attributed to a medieval tower or campanile.[36] We have no other records of a medieval tower in this area, unless we are prepared to identify it in a drawing by Alò Giovannoli that also depicts the remains of a portico. As for the wall to the side of the Curia, it is possible that what remains is part of one of the side entrances to the church in its eleventh-century phase.[37]

FIG. 8. **Comitium: in the foreground are the deep excavations conducted by Boni. British School at Rome Archive, neg. Ashby 1213.** *(Photo: British School at Rome.)*

These structures also are recognizable in another photograph (**Fig. 8**), probably taken on 25 April 1900, when Boni had begun his thirteenth stratigraphic trench in the area of the Comitium. In addition, it records the settings of a fountain basin[38] and the three latest pavings of this judicial area: from top to bottom, the Severan, the Augustan — on which ceramic fragments lay — and the Sullan.[39]

THE 'SCHOLA XANTHA' AND THE MILIARIUM AUREUM

The first photograph (**Fig. 9**), taken at the start of 1900, records the condition of the so-called 'Schola Xantha' before its excavation. Barely recorded structures can be identified, including the remains of the viaduct of Via della Consolazione, which incorporated a brick wall of indeterminate date built on top of a marble pavement. Among Ashby's notes, there is a sketch relating to these structures. Initially, the base of the Miliarium Aureum (Golden Milestone) was identified among them.[40] This had been erected by Augustus during the 'cura viarum' (Cass. Dio LXV.8.4) and was thought by scholars to be located at the southern end of the Rostra hemicycle, forming the pendant of the so-called 'Umbilicus'.

On the basis of this hypothetical identification, a fragmentary circular marble base was placed on top of this structure. This was decorated with palmettes and lotus leaves, and had been found in the Basilica Julia during the excavations of 1852 for the construction of the Via della Consolazione.[41] When the inaccuracy of this hypothesis was recognized, the fragment was moved close to the steps of the Temple of Saturn, together with a column drum that came from the Rostra hemicycle (more specifically, from between the Arch of Septimius Severus and the Rostra).[42]

Boni, working on the basis of evidence provided by the ancient literary sources that recorded that the Miliarium was located 'in Capite Romani fori' (Pliny, *Naturalis Historia* III.66) 'sub aede Saturni' (Tacitus, *Historiae* I.27; Suetonius, *Otho* VI), collected fragments from around the stairway leading to the Temple of Saturn (see below, **Fig. 11**) and reconstructed a hypothetical monument from marble fragments of different provenances. Today the Miliarium is still identified for tourists by a plaque.[43]

One can see other things in the photograph (**Fig. 9**); there is a square room (4 x 5 m) with a marble pavement and concrete wall with marble veneer. Since Hülsen had suggested that the Schola Xantha would be discovered on the southern side of the Rostra, this room inherited the name when it was uncovered. It is impossible to identify here any of the three small porticoed rooms or the architrave with inscriptions described by Bartolomeo Marliano and Pirro Ligorio. Moreover, the Schola was described as a highly decorated building, with silver statues and bronze thrones. Scholars have tried hard to identify traces of these in the floor, but only a channel can be seen.[44] Today, we still lack a study of the functions of the building,

FIG. 9. The so-called Schola Xantha: in the foreground the remains of the viaduct of Via della Consolazione. British School at Rome Archive, neg. Ashby 1215. *(Photo: British School at Rome.)*

construction of which post-dated that of the Arch of Tiberius. Before this time, the area had served as a simple thoroughfare between the Forum and the Clivus Capitolinus above. An important feature, visible in the photograph (**Fig. 9**), is the remains of a staircase with several fragmentary steps. Today these are no longer visible, and thus scholars normally have assumed that this stairway was located on the opposite side, facing the Arch of Septimius Severus. What can be seen is the span of the steps as shown by the two marble covering slabs. These still survive because they were incorporated into the later concrete wall, whose façade faces south.[45]

THE SUBSTRUCTURE OF THE VICUS IUGARIUS

Between November and December 1900, behind the so-called Schola Xantha, there came to light the substructure of the Vicus Iugarius (**Fig. 10**). Ashby described this as a succession of eight small arches constructed in tufa *opus incertum* for a total length of 20.8 m and a height of 2.3 m. The individual rooms are of smaller dimensions: 1.6 m high and 1.7 m wide, varying in depth from 1.5 to 2.15 m, and in a poor state of preservation. Traces of stucco were still visible, present even on the cornice slabs.[46] The pavement was formed of large brick tesserae that were joined to the walls by means of angular edging stones. A parapet forms the boundary on the east side. This heavily restored structure (**Fig. 11**) was interpreted by Boni as

the Rostra of Caesar, on the basis of a hypothetical identification with the well-known coin of Q. Lollius Palikanus. Ashby jokingly called the structure the 'Rostra Boniana'. Considering both the building technique, which was certainly older than the age of Caesar, and that the literary sources recorded the rebuilding of the Clivus Capitolinus in 174 BC, Ashby maintained more correctly that this was the substructure of a road. Possibly, given the type of surface, it could have served a hydraulic function in some way (as a fountain?). The construction of the hemicycle (first century BC), and then of the Schola Xantha and the so-called Arch of Tiberius, led to its disappearance.

THE 'EQUESTRIAN STATUE OF TREMULUS'

The base of the so-called 'equestrian statue of Tremulus' is another monument that, when it was discovered, was identified by Boni on the basis of an examination of the literary sources and vague topographical agreement.

In the spring of 1904, 'spianandosi il terreno tra la fronte del tempio dei Castori e l'*heroon* di Cesare' ('in the course of levelling the ground between the front of the Temple of Castor and Pollux and the heroon of Caesar'), a rectangular base was found (**Fig. 12**). On a wave of enthusiasm aroused by the recent and still discussed identification of the equestrian statue of Domitian, it was easy for the excavator to

FIG. 10. Substructures of the Vicus lugarius during its excavation. British School at Rome Archive, neg. Ashby I,76. *(Photo: British School at Rome.)*

FIG. 11. Substructures of the Vicus lugarius after the restorations. British School at Rome Archive, neg. Ashby I,77. *(Photo: British School at Rome.)*

propose that it be identified with another equestrian base, that of Q. Marcius Tremulus, dedicated in 306 BC. After an initial consensus, this hypothesis was criticized, particularly by Otto Richter and Ettore De Ruggiero, who emphasized the inconsistencies of the identification.[47] Indeed, the structure did not seem to be a monument of the Republican period, and Ashby himself was quite cautious, noting traces of restoration in the concrete, or, more specifically, cuttings for the insertion of travertine blocks during a phase of reuse. In the end, he accepted Hülsen's hypothesis

that dated the plinth to the Augustan age. This ruled out the possibility, amongst other things, that the monument of the 'so comparatively unimportant' Tremulus could be located in an area of prime importance at that time. Even today, the identification of the base is debated (base of a cuirassed statue of Divus Julius?), as is the topography of the area in front of the temple. It is interesting to note the appearance of the monument as Rosa left it after the excavations of 1870–1. In a photograph that dates to 2 April 1898 (**Fig. 13**), one can see a marble block resting on the

FIG. 12. **The area in front of the Temple of Divus Julius during the excavation of the so-called Equus Tremuli. British School at Rome Archive, neg. Ashby 1755.** *(Photo: British School at Rome.)*

FIG. 13. **The area in front of the Temple of Divus Julius before Boni's excavation. British School at Rome Archive, neg. Ashby 768.** *(Photo: British School at Rome.)*

travertine foundations of the equestrian statue base, three further blocks — one of *peperino*, and two of tufa, large,[48] well-connected and *in situ*. These were removed by Boni and today lie in the northwest corner of the area. In the light of what is visible,[49] one might attribute these remains to a monument built with reused materials probably in late antiquity, which made use of a plinth of an earlier period. It was a base with a side 2.4 m long facing the piazza, a side of 1.78 m facing the Basilica Aemilia, and preserved to a height of 1.25 m.[50]

Evidence for the presence of other late antique and medieval remains in this area also is provided by a large concrete conglomeration of square plan, perhaps part of a tower, built with reused material and apparently set on a mortar layer that relates to the foundation of the pavement. Today this structure can be seen on the ground only with difficulty. To the same phase probably can be attributed the paving around the so-called base of Tremulus, which had 'patching and repairs' made from recovered materials.[51]

FIG. 14. Basilica Aemilia: the area of shops and a small part of the hall during Boni's excavation. British School at Rome Archive, neg. Ashby 1200. *(Photo: British School at Rome.)*

FIG. 15. Basilica Aemilia: the shops in the southeast corner. British School at Rome Archive, neg. Ashby 1216. *(Photo: British School at Rome.)*

THE BASILICA AEMILIA

Photographic documentation reveals the different phases of clearing and excavation that started in 1899 (the excavation began on 17 March), carried on without interruption throughout the first decade of the twentieth century, to be completed in 1930 by Alfonso Bartoli. Of particular interest are the descriptions and reports (**Figs 14** and **15**) that Ashby gives relating to the late antique and medieval phases of the building, particularly in the southeastern corner. Here, between

tabernae VII–IX and the eastern entrance of the hall, different buildings can be identified (**Fig. 16**). A first phase, generally attributed to the period after Alaric's Sack of Rome, relates to the restoration (in brick with occasional tufa courses) of several dividing walls of the *tabernae* and of part of the northeastern wall.

The paving of the *tabernae* and of the eastern entrance in polychrome marble *opus sectile* probably can be attributed to a successive phase (sixth century AD),[52] as can the construction using recovered blocks of other rooms that occupied the southern side of the

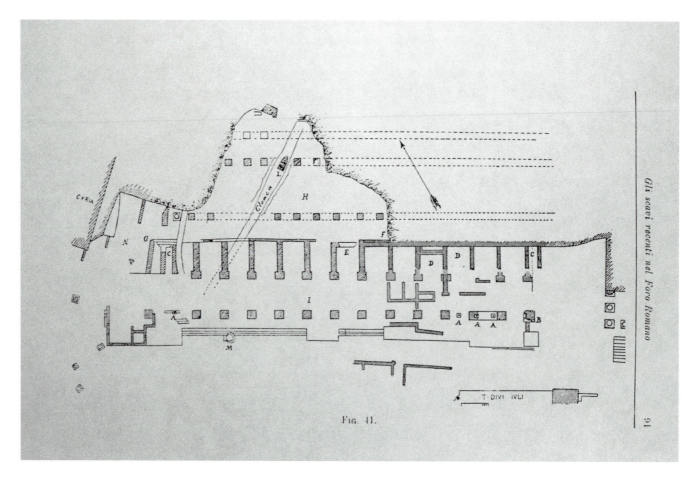

FIG. 16. **Plan of the Basilica Aemilia after Boni's excavation. In darker colours can be seen the structures relating to the late antique and medieval periods, partly demolished between 1910 and 1939.** *(Photo: R. Turchetti.)*

portico. These rooms must have been set on different levels, as can be seen from the stairway still visible in front of *taberna* VIII (**Fig. 16**). On the exterior, Boni inserted reliefs showing figures of animals emerging from acanthus plants (**Fig. 14**). These had been found on the covering of a sewer that ran along the southern side of the Basilica. Ashby also recorded the discovery of many medieval glazed ceramics in this sewer.[53]

Evidence of a final building phase is provided by the reconstruction of this part of the northeastern wall of the *tabernae*, which later collapsed due to disturbances suffered by the building. It was replaced by a structure consisting of marble fragments, bricks and small tufa blocks. Finally, probably between the twelfth and thirteenth centuries, a wall was raised with alternating small tufa blocks and pilasters on both sides (**Fig. 15**).

The interpretation of what was recorded is subject to doubt: Bartoli claimed that most of the structure belonged to the church of San Giovanni in Campo,[54] while Antonio Valeri attributed it to Santa Maria in Foro.[55] Ashby thought that it was a private house built

in a later period on the remains of the Basilica, and that the church of San Giovanni in Campo could be identified possibly in the structures at a higher level (**Fig. 15**),[56] a hypothesis that has been revived recently.[57] Ashby's valuable records report numerous other signs of late antique and medieval occupation, shown by the presence of bricks with stamps of Theodoric in the entrance hall, by wells containing, amongst other things, glazed pottery, by part of the sewer network and by a street that crossed the Basilica itself. One must add to this Romolo Artioli's report on the discovery of burials in the terrace behind the *tabernae*, along with various architectural fragments from the eighth–ninth centuries AD.[58]

Other post-antique structures are visible in photographs of this area (**Fig. 14**). The photographs, and several plans, are the only sources of information for these. These structures seem to have been built, at least in part, with reused materials using techniques similar to those used in the *tabernae*. They are set directly on the ancient level, and cut into part of the basalt street paving. In as far as one can make out the internal layout, one can see a room. One wall (on the northern side) remains, with three slit windows. Adjacent to this is a room with an entrance on the same side (**Figs 2, 14 and 16**). These structures were demolished gradually in order to uncover the earlier phases, together with those described above that were designated as unsafe at the time of their excavation.[59] The final event of this sort occurred in 1939 when, in order to raise the south-eastern wall of the hall that had been found in a state of collapse, the structures that had replaced it were destroyed.

The lack of non-photographic evidence means that a complete study or understanding of the functions and chronology of this complex building phase is impossible. However, it possibly corresponds with the phase between the sixth and seventh centuries in the Forum (when shops were built between the honorary columns, closing the piazza on the side of the Basilica Julia) and around the eighth–ninth centuries (when the large-scale robbing of building materials started, as shown by the numerous workshops discovered).[60] This probably put an end to the Forum being used as a piazza.

It is interesting to compare the late antique and medieval structures in this part of the Basilica Aemilia with the medieval complex recently uncovered in the Forum Transitorium.[61]

In any case, it is interesting to emphasize how the construction of new buildings over the ruins of the Basilica retained the orientation of the Basilica and reused, where possible, its walls, not only in the Middle Ages[62] but also during the Renaissance. This can be seen, for example, in the view of the southern side of the Roman Forum by Martin van Heemskerck where, next to the Temple of Antoninus and Faustina, there seem to be buildings incorporating the remains of ancient structures.[63]

Continuation of the excavation of the Basilica Aemilia, thanks in part to the financial aid of Sir Lionel Phillips, brought to light part of the basilica hall, and in particular its southern perimeter wall. This probably had collapsed in the eighth century, sealing the abandonment phase of the hall, which most likely had been used as a workshop for the salvage and working of building materials — activities that most certainly would have contributed to the collapse of this part of the structure. Such a situation is well documented in the photographs of the excavation of this part of the hall (**Fig. 17**).

Restorations had been undertaken already by the Diocletianic era, following the fire of Carinus.

FIG. 17. Basilica Aemilia: the central hall during the excavation. The collapsed southern perimeter wall that seals the stratigraphy relating to the preceding phases is still *in situ*. British School at Rome Archive, neg. Ashby LIX,24. (*Photo: British School at Rome.*)

Probably one can attribute to this phase the brick curtain-wall designed to reinforce the southern side, the redressing of the marble slabs, and perhaps also the wall with niches placed along the Argiletum. The final collapse seems to have occurred after Alaric's Sack of Rome; since it was impossible to restore the entire building, the *tabernae* alone were restored and used. These were the narrowest rooms and had a columnar façade towards the Forum, establishing a dignified flank between the still monumental piazza of the Forum and the possibly irrecoverable ruins of the Basilica.[64] The stratigraphy relating to its use as a workshop and the consequent collapse of the structure is clearly visible in the photographs, and also described well by Bartoli.[65] In the late medieval period, this area was, according to Lanciani, part of the 'Campo Torrecchiano' until the construction of the Alexandrine quarter in the middle of the sixteenth century.[66]

FIG. 18. Tufa paving of the Republican period and wells between the Comitium and the Basilica Julia. British School at Rome Archive, neg. Ashby I,78. *(Photo: British School at Rome.)*

FIG. 19. Tufa paving of the Republican period and the side of the Cloaca Maxima. British School at Rome Archive, neg. Ashby I,75. *(Photo: British School at Rome.)*

THE PAVEMENT OF THE REPUBLICAN PERIOD

This pavement is one of the many features of the Forum visible at the moment of excavation that, because they lacked monumental character or could not be related to a description in the ancient literary sources, have remained unknown. Such features are quickly hidden by undergrowth;[67] in some cases they have been reburied, and even their physical presence has been lost. The photographs (**Figs 18** and **19**), prob-

ably taken in December 1900, reveal the excavations conducted by Boni under the basalt street paving in front of the Basilica Aemilia. At a depth of around 2.3 m, 60 m² of a pavement made from rectangular tufa blocks came to light. These blocks were laid rather irregularly on a northeast–southwest orientation, like the so-called ritual wells in front of the Comitium. Ashby described them as 'crossing the earliest cloaca at right angles, which runs northward right up to the Comitium, from which it is separated by a raised edging of tufo blocks, a similar edging existing on the

W. side also'.[68] In the western trench (**Fig. 18**), several wells were found of the type already documented in the Comitium, in the Forum and near the Basilica Julia. Close to these we can see piles of pots found during the excavation; on top of this section of the pavement there are lead pipes. The second section of pavement (**Fig. 19**) was cut by a concrete foundation connected with the Cloaca Maxima of the Flavian period. The photograph shows that the pottery found in the excavation was placed upon wooden boards, partly restored already. Among this pottery one can recognize jars and basins of the early Republican period. Ashby identified the pavement as part of the Via Sacra of the Republican period, while Esther van Deman maintained that it related to one of the earlier paving phases of the area.[69] The chronology, at least, of this tract of paving, can be reconsidered in the light of new information about the different phases of paving of the Forum, together with the paving discovered near the Temple of Divus Julius and that found during the dismantling of the street paving facing the Basilica Julia.

VENUS CLOACINA

Ashby indicated in his notes that this small structure, about 2.4 m in diameter, was probably discovered on the 23 April 1900 (**Fig. 20**), in front of the steps of the Basilica Aemilia. The remains were immediately identified as the shrine whose location is recorded by ancient literary sources. Boni pointed to the incident reported by Livy (III.48.5) when the Decemvir, Appius Claudius, sought to take the young Virginia from her father. This account reveals that the shrine was 'ad tabernas quibus nunc novis est nomen' ('near the shops that are now called new'), that is, near to the *tabernae* in front of the Basilica Aemilia. The oldest phases of these shops had been uncovered during the excavation. The foundation of the sanctuary can be dated to an early period,[70] and its etymology and connection to the sewer can be seen in the name of the divinity herself, explained by etymologists as a derivation from 'cluere', to purge, to purify. The appearance of the shrine, attested from the Republican era, can be reconstructed on the basis of a coin of L. Mussidius Longus,[71] where it is portrayed as a roofless circular precinct surrounded by a balustrade, consistent with what remains of the elevation. On the base (**Fig. 20**), one can see holes for the balustrade, while on the side of the block there are traces of the entrance to the small shrine. Inside, there

FIG. 20. Shrine of Venus Cloacina during Boni's excavations. British School at Rome Archive, neg. Ashby I,72. *(Photo: British School at Rome.)*

must have been two female cult statues with, probably to the left, an altar. It is more difficult to read the remains of the shrine uncovered below ground level. Indeed, Boni, continuing the excavation, found a cylindrical structure made of courses of tufa blocks that went down to a depth of *c.* 4 m. Van Deman identified this as three levels relating to different periods and to at least two increases of height,[72] while other scholars have seen it simply as the foundations of the shrine, although this is hard to understand given its small dimensions. The general character of the construction, shown in the photograph (**Fig. 20**), leads one to think, instead, of the exterior of a cylindrical well, covered and monumentalized as a cult place.

CONCLUSIONS

Despite the difficulties caused by the historicization of the excavations carried out by Boni, the results presented here exemplify a method of research that uses an objective form of documentation, such as photography. This has permitted a reconstruction of a number of archaeological realities and may have cleared up several 'ambiguities' about monuments in the Forum, both famous and unknown (or, rather, forgotten). It has also allowed us to consider the attributions about which Ashby already had expressed caution with his common use of the term 'so-called'.

The major contribution is surely that provided by the structures, now largely demolished, that can be attributed to the late antique and medieval periods. The continuity of life in this part of the Roman Forum is shown by the presence of public buildings and houses, of workshops for the working and/or the salvage of building materials, and by areas of burials gathered near Sant'Adriano or in ruined or abandoned public buildings, such as in part of the Basilica Aemilia. Together, these elements provide a picture of an urban landscape in which, as in other parts of the city,[73] areas of habitation alternated, uninterrupted, with other areas that were uninhabited and used as quarries for building materials or occupied by groups of tombs. These lay within a network of streets that, in part at least, must have remained in use.

NOTES

1. F. Castagnoli, 'Thomas Ashby e gli studi sulla Campagna Romana', in *Thomas Ashby. Un archeologo fotografa la Campagna Romana fra '800 e '900* (*British School at Rome Archive* 1) (Rome, 1986), 15–18.

2. The photograph albums recall Ashby's life and are not only pictures relating to his research but also to holidays in different parts of the world (from Switzerland to Spain, Roman Africa, the Philippines, Australia, for example), to interests and hobbies (above all folklore), to his personal and family life (the college at Oxford where he completed his studies, photos of his friends, of his wife, of dogs and cats) and, finally, to the First World War, in which Ashby served in the ranks of the Red Cross on the Italian–Austrian border.

3. The documents, written on sheets of various format, from a book with notes about his countryside reconnaissance to foolscap pages with transcribed archival documents, are preserved in about 20 boxes. Only those relating to the city of Rome have been reorganized and catalogued so far.

4. *Thomas Ashby. Un archeologo fotografa la Campagna Romana fra '800 e '900* (*British School at Rome Archive* 1) (Rome, 1986); *Archeologia a Roma nelle fotografie di Thomas Ashby 1891–1930* (*British School at Rome Archive* 2) (Naples, 1989); *Il Lazio di Thomas Ashby 1891–1930* I (*British School at Rome Archive* 4) (Rome, 1994); *Sulla Via Appia da Roma a Brindisi. Le fotografie di Thomas Ashby 1891–1925* (*British School at Rome Archive* 6) (Rome, 2003).

5. The first, dedicated to the Roman Campagna, was held at the British School (17 April–5 May 1986) and at the Central London Polytechnic (11–20 February 1987); the second, concerning Rome, at Castel Sant'Angelo (16 October–19 November 1989) and at the University of Exeter; the third, on Lazio, at the British School (10 January–2 February 1995), in various towns in Lazio and then, in 1996–7, in Norway (University of Bergen), Sweden (Medelhavsmuseet) and Denmark (University of Ejsberg, University of Aarhus, and Ny Carlsberg Glyptotek, Copenhagen); the fourth, on the Via Appia, at the British School (23 January–21 February 2003) and at the Museo Archeologico in Sperlonga, Museo delle Navi in Nemi and the Museo Archeologico in Minturno.

6. His maps were 'inherited' by Giuseppe Lugli and now can be found in the Archivio Lugli at the Unione Accademica Nazionale. However, several examples are preserved in the archive of the British School. For an index, see R. Turchetti, 'Le carte topografiche', in *Il Lazio* (above, n. 4), 257–60.

7. The term 'Wanderer', used by Franco Cambi and Nicola Terrenato (*Introduzione all'archeologia dei paesaggi* (Rome, 1994), 27) to define Ashby and Lanciani's method of work, is inappropriate and intentionally dismissive.

8. Of major importance, to point out the most well-known, are 'The Bodleian MS. of Pirro Ligorio', *JRS* 9 (1919), 170–201; 'Dessins inédits de Carlo Labruzzi', *Mélanges d'Archeologie et d'Histoire de l'École Française de Rome* 23 (1903), 375–418.

9. In the case of the Roman Forum, we are dealing with real note-books, in which the notes were written, day by day, during visits to the excavations. These have been transcribed almost entirely and published in *Archeologia a Roma* (above, n. 4), 156–88.

10. R. Lanciani, in *NSc* (1882), 216–38; R. Lanciani, *Ruins and Excavations of Ancient Rome* (London, 1897), 104–5, 175–258.

11. Particularly significant are the excavation reports published in those years by G. Gatti, in *NSc* (1899), 10–14, 49–50, 77–8, 128–30, 151, 200, 289–93, 333–8, 384–7, 431–5, 486–92; G. Boni, in *NSc* (1899), 220–3, 265–7, 325–32; R. Lanciani, 'Le escavazioni del Foro', *BullCom* 27 (1899), 169–204; G. Gatti, 'Notizie di recenti trovamenti di antichità', *BullCom* 27 (1899), 126–49, 205–47; G. Boni, in *NSc* (1900), 291–340; G. Gatti, in *NSc* (1900), 11, 48–9, 570; D. Vaglieri, 'Nuove scoperte al Foro Romano', *BullCom* 28 (1900), 57–74, 266–98; R. Lanciani, 'Le escavazioni del Foro', *BullCom* 28 (1900), 3–27, 299–320; G. Boni, in *NSc* (1901), 41–144; R. Lanciani, 'Le escavazioni del Foro', *BullCom* 29 (1901), 20–51; G. Boni, in *NSc* (1902), 96–11; R. Lanciani, 'Le escavazioni del Foro', *BullCom* 30 (1902), 125–33; D. Vaglieri, 'Nuove ricerche al Foro Romano', *BullCom* 30 (1902), 186–91; G. Boni, in *NSc* (1903), 123–70, 375–427; D. Vaglieri, 'Gli scavi recenti nel Foro Romano', *BullCom* 31 (1903), 3–239, 252–73; G. Gatti, 'Scoperte recentissime al Foro Romano', *BullCom* 32 (1904), 75–82, 174–9; G. Tomassetti, 'Il lago Curzio nel Foro Romano', *BullCom* 32 (1904), 181–7; G. Boni, in *NSc* (1905), 143–93; G. Boni, in *NSc* (1906), 5–46, 253–94. Important reports were also published by Boni and his colleagues in the daily newspapers, the most effective way of stimulating public interest and generating lively debate about the Forum excavations. For the comparable reports by Ashby, and signs of the great interest that these excavations aroused in the outside world, see: 'Recent excavations in Rome', *Classical Review* 13 (1899), 184–6, 232–5, 321–2, 464–7; 14 (1900), 236–40; 15 (1901), 85–9, 136–42, 328–30; 16 (1902), 94–6, 284–6; 17 (1903), 135–7, 328–9; 18 (1904), 137–41, 328–31; 19 (1905), 74–9, 328–30; 20 (1906), 132–6, 378–80; 'The recent excavations in the Forum Romanum, 1898–1903', *The Builder* 86 (1904), 2–4, 574–5; 'Recent discoveries in the Roman Forum', *The Builder* 87 (1904), 88, 692; and 'Roman notes', *The Builder* 87 (1904), 178.

12. I have studied this material on a number of occasions, both for research undertaken for the Soprintendenza itself and for work towards a *tesi di laurea* on the Boni archive, supervised by Ferdinando Castagnoli. This is material of undoubted interest, and as a first step one might anticipate the transcription of, a critical commentary on and the publication of the drawings and photographs preserved in the respective archives in a scholarly edition. Unfortunately, this remains unrealized, apart from brief and rare contributions, such as D. Palombi, 'Contributo alla topografia della Via Sacra, dagli appunti inediti di Giacomo Boni', *Quaderni dell'Istituto di Topografia Antica* 10 (1988), 77–97; E. Carnabuci, 'L'angolo sud-orientale del Foro Romano nel manoscritto inedito di Giacomo Boni', *Memorie. Atti dell'Accademia Nazionale dei Lincei, Classe di Scienze Morali, Storiche e Filologiche* serie 9, 1(4) (1991), 249–365. The study of Ashby's photographs leads to different conclusions from those of both Palombi and Carnabuci — cf. *Archeologia a Roma* (above, n. 4), 55–6, 80–5.

13. These began on 12 January 1899 and continued throughout 1900, becoming less frequent in 1901–2 and only occasional after that, until 1906 when the visits were limited to a few excavations being conducted in the piazza. On the chronology of the photographs, notes and excavations, see *Archeologia a Roma* (above, n. 4), 26–9, 156–88.

14. E. Tea, *Giacomo Boni nella vita del suo tempo* II (Milan, 1932), 46–7, in which Ashby is described thus: 'Più assiduo di tutti, lo Ashby ne diede cronaca sulla *Classical Review*. Era un osservatore attento ed imparziale. Non faceva complimenti al Boni, ma nemmeno ne sminuiva il merito. La sua testimonianza è delle più preziose per la storia degli scavi' ('More conscientious than the others, Ashby chronicled it all in the *Classical Review*. He was an attentive and impartial observer. He did not pay compliments to Boni, but neither did he diminish his achievements. His testimony is among the most important for the history of the excavations'). A final sign of the good relations between the two is the presence of photographs by Ashby amongst Boni's documentation in the photographic archive of the Soprintendenza Archeologica di Roma.

15. Ashby used this term in order not to contradict Boni, who insisted on associating the various wells of different shape, size and chronology found in the Forum with ritual activities.

16. Cf. on this subject the things that have come to light in the area in front of the Curia and the Basilica Aemilia, as described below.

17. During the clearances between 1872 and 1874 under the direction of Rosa, the greater part of the Forum piazza was brought to light, but all the medieval structures were destroyed systematically. There was no distinction made between medieval and late antique, and, even worse, all that was not understood was considered to be medieval. This led, for example, to the demolition of part of the Diocletianic Rostra. See C.F. Giuliani and P. Verduchi, *Il Foro Romano* (Florence, 1987), 148–66.

18. When Boni began the definitive clearance of the Roman Forum complex, soundings under monuments such as the Lapis Niger, the Comitium and the paving of the Forum were included in the vast excavation programme. In these cases, too, some damage was caused, even though there was little to demolish. From this viewpoint, in fact, structures entirely of the Roman period were neglected in favour of research into older evidence or monuments cited in the literary sources. During such work, reconstruction also was undertaken, such as the restoration of the paving inside the so-called Aiola of Marsyas and in the northeast corner of the Forum, and of parts of monuments, such as the southern side of the Temple of Divus Julius, using material from different sources; see Giuliani and Verduchi, *Il Foro* (above, n. 17), 11–19, 95–102. For example, Ashby demonstrated, as noted also by Romolo Artioli, that basalt paving-stones from the street in front of the Basilica Aemilia were used to reconstruct that in front of the

Basilica Julia after the excavation of the so-called ritual wells; see *Archeologia a Roma* (above, n. 4), 70 n. 43.

19. Lanciani recorded the demolition of the embankment of earth, 20 m wide and 10 m high, which had been used as a bridge between San Lorenzo in Miranda and Santa Maria Liberatrice, located between the Temple of Romulus and the Arch of Titus, at the finish of the excavation of the Via Sacra in 1879. The clearance work started on 6 February 1882 and ended on 21 April. It required the removal of 10,200 m³ of earth, and led to the discovery of 2,800 m² of ancient soil; on this occasion more than 300 m² of marble was found — some architectural, some inscribed, some with reliefs and broken into tiny pieces. Only some of these were used to build the embankment above the Basilica Aemilia (**Fig. 1**), which a few years later was dismantled by Boni; see Lanciani, in *NSc* (above, n. 10), 216.

20. Tea, *Giacomo Boni* (above, n. 14), 5–9.

21. Ashby, 'The recent excavations in the Forum Romanum' (above, n. 11), 2. For the erroneous re-erection of the columns, see also Giuliani and Verduchi, *Il Foro* (above, n. 17), 166–73.

22. Boni (in *NSc* (1900), 312–40) described the methodology used in the excavation of the Comitium thus: 'Ognuno di questi strati testimonia qualche residuo di vita del periodo al quale appartenne, e spesso reca l'impronta di strumenti e tracce di lavorazione nei materiali manipolati o cotti, i quali hanno percorso determinate e diverse vicende prima di arrivare fino al punto in cui giacciono, ricoperti da altri strati e da altri materiali. Perciò ebbi sempre cura di esaurire, per quanto era materialmente possibile, l'analisi d'ogni singolo strato, entro l'area assegnata a ciascuna esplorazione, e di non passare al taglio di uno strato inferiore senza averne prima diligentemente raschiata e spazzolata la superficie o lavata con una spugna. Di ciascuno strato feci scomporre le zolle e separare i materiali più minuti o caratteristici, avvolgendoli in carta solida e chiudendoli in una speciale cassetta, con tutte le indicazioni topografiche ed altimetriche necessarie. Ogni serie di queste cassette rappresenta un'opera in più volumi, e il complesso delle serie costituisce l'archivio stratigrafico dell'esplorazione compiuta. Oltre ai saggi di materiali contenuti in ciascuno strato mi è parso utile di tenerne un blocco, onde abbia a servire di elemento nel campionario dell'intera sezione, e di lasciare sussistere a posto i testimoni dei diversi scavi, questo ho fatto oltre che per il niger lapis e il comizio, anche per la Regia, e altrettanto reputo necessario di fare, dovunque continuerò ad esplorare terreni non colmati d'un tratto, ma da successive sovrapposizioni, ognuna delle quali appartenne ad età storica diversa ... Nel corso di una esplorazione sarebbe facile e comodo trascurare gli indizi o i residui che rivelano l'esistenza di gravi problemi, e offrono forse il modo di risolverli: ma la scienza non può lasciarsi illudere dalla elegante semplicità o dalla astrusa complicazione di definizioni non mai controllate e troppo spesso difese come assiomi archeologici' ('Each of these layers bears witness to some memory of life from the period to which it belongs, and often bears the mark of tools or of the manufacture of worked or baked materials. These all followed their own paths and were involved in different activities before they came to the place where they lie, covered by other layers and other artefacts. For this reason, as far as was practically possible, I always took care to exhaust the potential for study of each individual layer, within the area designated to each investigation. I didn't move on to the excavation of a lower layer without first having diligently scraped and brushed the surface or washed it with a sponge. I broke up the earth of each layer and separated the smallest or most diagnostic material, wrapping it in paper and placing it in a special box, with all the necessary topographical and altimetric information. Each series of these boxes represents a work of many volumes, and the ensemble of these series constitutes the stratigraphic archive of the complete exploration. As well as samples of the material contained in each layer, it seemed useful to me to keep a block, to serve as a sample of the entire section, and to leave *in situ* evidence of the different excavations undertaken. Moreover, I have done this not only for the Lapis Niger and the Comitium, but also for the Regia, and I consider it necessary to do so wherever I continue to explore terrain consisting not of just one fill, but of successive layers, each of which represents a different historical period ... In the course of an excavation it would be easy and convenient to neglect the signs and residues that reveal the existence of serious problems and perhaps offer the means to resolve them: but science cannot allow itself to be deceived by the elegant simplicity or by the tricky complications of definition that are never controlled and too often defended as archaeological axioms'). In order to understand the excavation data, Boni asked for the collaboration of experts in various disciplines: geologists, naturalists, ethnologists, for example, and had the entire area of the Forum surveyed by the Regia Scuola degli Ingegneri, as well, of course, as the extremely accurate surveys and photographic documentation of his collaborators mentioned above (n. 11).

23. In 1885, Boni already had conducted a stratigraphic sounding of the medieval layers of the campanile of San Marco at Venice. Thus we can date one of the first applications of this methodology, of which Boni can be considered not only a pioneer, but also a theorist; see, for example, *Nuova Antologia* (16 July 1901) and above (n. 22).

24. The description of the anonymous author of the Einsiedeln Itinerary seems to correspond to this monument, located just beyond the Arch of Septimius Severus, opposite the Curia and in front of the Forum itself. For the interpretation of the remains, see Giuliani and Verduchi, *Il Foro* (above, n. 17), 69–73.

25. F.M. Nichols, *Notizie dei Rostri del Foro Romano e dei monumenti contigui* (Rome, 1885), 3, also discussed this sewer, which collected water from the Arch and the Column of Phocas and drained it into the sewer of the Subura. For its construction, the stretch of paving to the side of the Augustan Rostra was also dismantled and rebuilt.

26. The base was found in 1547 and remained near the Arch until 1587, as documented also by the drawings from the period by Giovanni Antonio Dosio and Étienne Du Pérac; see Lanciani, *Storia* (1989–), II, 204–10, figs 132, 135. Then it was taken to

the Orti Farnesiani and brought back here during the excavations and remounted on a brick base built especially for the purpose. It was probably during this last operation that Ashby noted the detaching of several fragments that Boni reused to restore the so-called Rostra vandalica, which were recovered during the restoration of 1983; see P. Verduchi, 'Le tribune rostrate', in *Roma: archeologia nel centro* I (*Lavori e studi di archeologia* 6) (Rome, 1985), 33; *Archeologia a Roma* (above, n. 4), 40, 44, 159.

27. The discovery of the Lapis Niger occurred on 10 January 1899, as reported in the newspapers of the day. Ashby's visit two days later is significant, therefore. On the same occasion, a photograph was taken that immortalized Boni, Welbore St Clair Baddeley and Alfonso Bartoli; see *Archeologia a Roma* (above, n. 4), 31 fig. 1.2.

28. In particular, he pointed to a well in the northwestern corner of the Lapis Niger that contained much medieval kitchen-ware; see *Archeologia a Roma* (above, n. 4), 159–66 *passim*.

29. Evidence for the installation of this sewer is shown by the dismantling of the basalt street paving, and in this case Ashby disagreed with Baddeley, who had believed it to be ancient. Nearby, under the street paving, was found a Napoleonic centime (1811), a *quattrino* of Leo XII (1826) and a porcelain pipe. Unfortunately, the presence of this material convinced Boni that the street paving was medieval or even later, and thus he authorized its dismantling. Its location has since been lost. On the subject, see Ashby, 'Recent excavations in Rome' (1899) (above, n. 11), 233; W. St Clair Baddeley, in *Athenaeum* 3717 (21 January 1899), 90; *Archeologia a Roma* (above, n. 4), 159–60.

30. *Archeologia a Roma* (above, n. 4), 160.

31. Verduchi has suggested that there was previously another monument in this location, something presumably of better workmanship and of the same date as the Severan pavement, which only later came to hold the equestrian statue of Constantine. Moreover, Boni's excavation altered the alignment of the piazza to its edging stones, by moving it backwards; see Giuliani and Verduchi, *Il Foro* (above, n. 17), 69–76.

32. The marble base measures 1.35 x 2.4 m, while the brick one has dimensions more than twice the size, 3.04 x 4.83 m. On the location of the base, see G. Boni, *Esplorazioni e lavori in corso nel Foro Romano ordinati da S.E. Guido Baccelli* (Rome, 1899), 20.

33. Amongst other things, this base must have borne a rather important monument. Its presence was respected not only by the Severan paving but also by the construction of the Arch — the northern supporting arch of the Arch would have been obstructed, at least visually, by the monument.

34. *Archeologia a Roma* (above, n. 4), 162.

35. Boni, *Esplorazioni e lavori in corso* (above, n. 32), 19; Boni, in *NSc* (1900) (above, n. 11), 295–301; *Archeologia a Roma* (above, n. 4), 161–4.

36. Ashby described it as a medieval tower-like structure at the eastern corner of the Curia, constructed in a rough *opus quadratum*, with three inscriptions of the fourth century contained within it, which was removed on 22 December 1899; see *Archeologia a Roma* (above, n. 4), 161–2.

37. For the drawing by Giovannoli, see A. Bartoli, *Cento vedute di Roma antica* (Florence, 1911), tav. IX, while for one by Du Pérac in which can be seen the entrance with a stairway to the church of Sant'Adriano, see Lanciani, *Storia* (1989–), II, 210 fig. 132.

38. According to Lanciani, the fountain can be identified as the granite monolith placed by Pius VI in front of the Quirinal and previously located in front of the three columns of the Temple of Castor and Pollux; see Lanciani, *Storia* (1989–), II, 211–13. The water supply was guaranteed by a pipe that ran in a canal (Fig. 8) parallel to the settings relating to the railings dividing the Curia from the Comitium, discovered for a length of 6.95 m.

39. On the phases of the paving of the Forum and its chronology, see Giuliani and Verduchi, *Il Foro* (above, n. 17), 31–66.

40. *Archeologia a Roma* (above, n. 4), 167.

41. According to some scholars, the marble fragments were found on the floor of the Basilica, while others think they were found closer to the Temple of Saturn; see E. Braun, 'Scoperta della crepidine e del cornicione del militario aureo', in *BullInst* (1852), 81; G. Montiroli, *Osservazioni sulla topografia della parte meridionale del Foro Romano* (Rome, 1859). Nichols noted that these remains, preserved for some time under the arch of the modern Via della Consolazione, were found in 1885 on the pavement of the Basilica Julia and in that year put together near the southern corner of the hemicycle, as in the photograph (Fig. 9); see Nichols, *Notizie dei Rostri* (above, n. 25), 5, 50–1 n. 75. On this subject, see also Lanciani, *Storia* (1989–), II, 204.

42. The fragment (diameter 1.16 m, height 1.42 m) comes from the so-called Umbilicus and was found during work conducted in 1833 to bring to light the ancient level of the Arch of Septimius Severus; the column then was moved near to the Temple of Saturn, as noted by Richter and as can be seen in another of Ashby's photographs (Fig. 4); see O. Richter, *Rekonstruktion und Geschichte der Römischen Rednerbühne* (Berlin, 1884), 35–7.

43. On the assumption (not necessarily valid) that the column drum belonged to the Miliarium, we should note how the shape, size and depth of the marks of numerous unfinished settings (maximum 0.14/0.20 x 0.14 m; minimum 30 x 40 mm) lead one to think more of slots for the attachment of decorative metal pieces or brackets. A similar fragment, but with a different diameter (0.78 m and 0.82 m, in contrast to the 1.16 m of the Forum column) can still be seen today on the slopes of the Argentari, to the side of the enclosure of the Forum of Caesar. See *sub voce* 'Miliarium Aureum', in E.M. Steinby (ed.), *Lexicon Topographicum Urbis Romae* III (Rome, 1996), 250–1.

44. In reality, this is a concrete structure, without any curtain-wall, with external and internal marble veneer and *cocciopesto* edging stones. According to Giuliani, the absence, at ground level, of any doorway makes it a type of basin or pool, a sort of *lacus,* rather than a normal room. The marks on the marble

flooring, although not clearly visible, do not relate to bronze seats but rather to peripheral decoration and small memorial *cippi* or altars in the central part; see C.F. Giuliani and P. Verduchi, *Foro Romano, l'area centrale* (Florence, 1980), 12–13.

45. Verduchi, 'Le tribune' (above, n. 26), 31, with bibliography.

46. For a description of the structure, see *Archeologia a Roma* (above, n. 4), 167–8.

47. O. Richter, *Beitrage zur Römischen Topographie* IV (Berlin, 1910), 23; E. De Ruggiero, *Il Foro Romano* (Rome/Arpino, 1913), 470–1.

48. Dimensions of the blocks: length from 1.73 to 1.77 m; height from 0.89 to 1.27 m; width from 0.70 to 0.48 m.

49. In the foreground of this photograph there is another base (perhaps of an equestrian statue) consisting of cemented rubble with marble slabs on top, probably reused. When it was discovered, it was attributed by Rosa to the equestrian statue of Domitian, then to the equestrian statue of Constantine or Septimius Severus. According to Verduchi, the shape and position of the plinth, which is located in the middle of the piazza, suggest a commemorative monument that was not particularly high in elevation but considerable, given the surface-area of the base. This implies that it probably was built after the Severan paving, and probably before the Rostra of Diocletian. At the time of its discovery many bits of marble were found around it — these are very visible in the photo — and relate to its use as a storage yard for a marble-recovery workshop, active at least as late as the ninth century. Cf. Giuliani and Verduchi, *Il Foro* (above, n. 17), 143–7.

50. The inscription that can be seen leant against the base of the monument was found in the southeastern corner of the Basilica Aemilia, near to the inscription of Lucius Caesar.

51. *Archeologia a Roma* (above, n. 4), 57 fig. 16.2.

52. In this last room the marble veneer of the walls was preserved also. On the decoration, see F. Guidobaldi and A. Guiglia Guidobaldi, *Pavimenti marmorei di Roma dal IV al IX secolo* (Vatican City, 1983), 264–77, 350–3.

53. *Archeologia a Roma* (above, n. 4), 174.

54. A. Bartoli, 'Ultime vicende e trasformazione cristiane della Basilica Emilia', *Rendiconti. Atti dell'Accademia Nazionale dei Lincei, Classe di Scienze Morali, Storiche e Filologiche* 21 (1912), 758–66.

55. A. Valeri, 'I monumenti cristiani del Foro Romano', *Rivista d'Italia* (1900), 711–19.

56. Regarding the raising of the level of the Forum, note that Carlo Fea pointed out a compact stratum near to the base of the Column of Phocas, about 1 m thick, relating to a flood datable to between 1100 and 1200. Other traces of this silt can be seen in the cavities (beam slots, for example) of the walls of the eastern Rostra. Their levels are close to the raised level visible in the Basilica Julia; see C. Fea, *Nuova descrizione de' monumenti antichi ed oggetti d'arte … con le nuove scoperte fatte alle fabbriche più interessanti nel Foro Romano* (Rome, 1919), 267, and Giuliani and Verduchi, *Il Foro* (above, n. 17), 145 fig. 199.

57. See above, n. 52 and related text.

58. *Archeologia a Roma* (above, n. 4), 173–7; R. Artioli, *Giornale di scavo* (unpublished manuscript, held at the Soprintendenza Archeologica di Roma).

59. The demolitions must have occurred before 1910, since the buildings in question are not visible in photographs of that year.

60. This includes a workshop for the recovery of lead from the Diocletianic Rostra, in front of which there was also a marble workshop, and a foundry for the recovery of iron on the north side of the piazza, documented in Giuliani and Verduchi, *Il Foro* (above, n. 17), 188 fig. 264.

61. The information was presented during a conference at the Deutsches Archäologisches Institut Rom by Roberto Meneghini and Riccardo Santangeli Valenzani.

62. Evidence for private houses is also provided by the letter of King Theodoric, amongst the *Varia* of Cassiodorus (4.30), in which a licence is granted to the patrician Albinus (507–11) to build, above the 'porticus curva quae, iuxta domum palmatam posita, forum in modum areae decenter includit' the 'domus palmatam', perhaps the same as that of the Anicii Glabrioni Fausti 'ad palmam', where the Theodosian Code was promulgated (438), as hypothesized by Lanciani, 'Le escavazioni del Foro' (1899) (above, n. 11), 188–9.

63. Similar information is contained in the drawing of the *Codex Escurialensis*; see Lanciani, 'Le escavazioni del Foro' (1899) (above, n. 11), 194–204. Concerning the interpretation of this part of the Forum, see F. Castagnoli, 'Gli Iani nel Foro Romano. Ianus = un arco quadrifronte?', *BullCom* 92 (1987–8), 11–16; also Carnabuci, 'L'angolo sud-orientale' (above, n. 12), 320–1, in which, however, the drawing of the *Codex Escurialensis* is erroneously attributed to van Heemskerck.

64. Inscriptions of the fifth century were found in 1899 amongst the materials used for the buildings that in the fifth–sixth centuries occupied the area of the Basilica; see Gatti, 'Notizie di recenti trovamenti' (above, n. 11), 224–30.

65. Stratum 1: above the marble pavement 60/100 mm of ash mixed with groups of coins, pieces of iron and wood burnt by fire relating to the fire of 410 that destroyed at least the ceiling and the roof. Stratum 2: large stratum 1 m in depth composed of soil mixed with clay and brick. Both within and on top of this were numerous architectural fragments of varied size and several fragments of statuary. These do not have any traces of fire damage and do not lie on the pavement but rather on strata of soil and potsherds of variable depths, which seem to relate to normal robbing out after the hall was abandoned; several seem broken not from having fallen but by hammer blows, an indication that the hall was deliberately destroyed, or rather used as a building site. The fragments of the Basilica lie in complete disorder together with elements that perhaps belonged to other monuments. Stratum 3: brick dividing wall between the hall and the *tabernae* collapsed and placed over stratum 2. See Bartoli, 'Ultime vicende' (above, n. 54), 758–66.

66. Lanciani, 'Le escavazioni del Foro' (1901) (above, n. 11), 20–5. One of the most lively debates between Boni and Lanciani was about the Basilica Aemilia, the excavation of

which was begun by Lanciani. On the basis of the inscription of Gaius and Lucius, he wrote: 'Per le nostre ricerche è essenziale mettere in chiaro se i blocchi iscritti e scolpiti siano stati accatastati presso l'angolo della basilica da coloro che sotto il pontificato di Paolo III, o prima, ricercavano materiali per la fabbrica di S. Pietro, ovvero se rappresentino la rovina di un edificio crollato sul posto, rovina non disturbata ancora dalla mano dell'uomo. Nel primo caso la scoperta direbbe poco o nulla; nel secondo caso direbbe moltissimo per la storia della rovina del Foro. L'indagine è resa difficile da che il geniale direttore degli scavi cav. Giacomo Boni non ha creduto opportuno disturbare in modo alcuno il cumulo dei frammenti preferendo lasciarli come apparvero il giorno della scoperta: di maniera che talune facce dei blocchi sono ancora nascoste, né è possibile accertare la loro relazione rispettiva' ('For our research it is essential to clarify whether the inscribed and sculpted blocks were stacked near the corner of the basilica by those who, under the pontificate of Paul III or before, sought building materials for the construction of Saint Peter's, or whether they represent the ruins of a building that collapsed on the spot, a ruin not disturbed again by human hand. In the first case, the discovery will reveal little or nothing; in the second, it will tell us much about the history of the ruins of the Forum. The excavation is rendered difficult by the fact that the director of the excavations, Cav. Giacomo Boni, did not think it appropriate to disturb in any way the mound of fragments, preferring to leave it the way it appeared on the day of its discovery. They are in such a condition that many of the faces of the blocks are still hidden, nor is it possible to ascertain their respective relationships') (Lanciani, 'Le escavazioni del Foro' (1899) (above, n. 11), 189).

67. For the position of this excavation, see Archivio Storico della Soprintendenza Archeologica di Roma, Palazzo Altemps, Cart. Basilica Emilia no. 493/27; and Vaglieri, 'Gli scavi recenti nel Foro Romano' (above, n. 11), 100 fig. 44.

68. Ashby, 'Recent excavations in Rome' (1901) (above, n. 11), 138; *Archeologia a Roma* (above, n. 4), 68 and 70 n. 44.

69. E.B. van Deman, 'The Sullan Forum', *JRS* 12 (1922), 1–31, esp. pp. 4ff. The author owes to Ashby much of the information both about this pavement and about the substructures of the Vicus Iugarius.

70. On the characteristics of the cult, see F. Coarelli, *Il Foro Romano. Periodo arcaico* (Rome, 1983), 83–9; F. Coarelli, 'Cloacina, Sacrum', in E.M. Steinby (ed.), *Lexicon Topographicum Urbis Romae* I (Rome, 1993), 290–1.

71. M. Crawford, *Roman Republican Coinage* (Cambridge, 1974), 508–10.

72. Van Deman, 'The Sullan Forum' (above, n. 69), 19–21, claimed that the lowest structure was composed of six rows of blocks, while in the photograph at least nine can be seen.

73. R. Meneghini and R. Santangeli Valenzani, 'Sepolture intramuranee e paesaggio urbano a Roma tra V e VII secolo', in L. Paroli and P. Delogu (eds), *La storia economica di Roma nell'alto medioevo alla luce dei recenti scavi archeologici* (Florence, 1993), 89–109.

'Excavations' in the Corso Vittorio Emanuele, 1885–1904: Analysis of the Pre-Existing Medieval Remains under the Palazzo Le Roy

Susanna Le Pera Buranelli

TOPOGRAPHICAL SETTING

THE PALAZZO Le Roy is located in an area that occupies the central part of the ancient Campus Martius (**Fig. I**).[1] During the Roman period, this area was occupied and built over in successive phases, according to a planned urban development. The various zones within this development were defined by their different orientations: the southern zone followed the course of the Circus Flaminius (221 BC); the central zone was oriented according to the cardinal points and followed the course of the Saepta Iulia, redesigned by Julius Caesar (the building complex dedicated by Pompey was built later on the same alignment); finally, at the edges of the area, the orientation followed the course of the Tiber, which at this point is very straight, ending at the Pons Neronianus (down-river from the Ponte Vittorio Emanuele) and the Pons Aelius (Ponte Sant'Angelo). Two important roads, the Via Recta and the Via Triumphalis, crossed the region, and determined a secondary network of streets.[2]

For the centuries following these grand urban developments, we only have records of restoration work that, despite being of impressive dimensions, did not alter substantially the boundaries and orientations set out above. Indeed, on the whole, the axes of orientation were preserved to such an extent that even today it is possible to identify the meeting-point of the different orientations within this roughly triangular area. A new building phase of considerable significance occurred during the sixth century, and is connected with Pope Damasus. He built the large Basilica of San Lorenzo in Damaso, probably within the vast papal property in the area. This is referred to in the medieval literary sources as '*in Prasino*, from the name of the faction of the Circus that had its Stabulum here' ('*in Prasino*, dal nome della fazione del Circo che qui aveva il suo Stabulum'). From this time onwards, the Basilica of San Lorenzo became the most distinctive feature of the area.[3]

Between the eleventh and twelfth centuries, the area of occupation expanded into the Tiber bend, and directly affected the zone controlled by the Cenci and later the Orsini families. The importance of the Basilica was restored and grew greater during these centuries. Urban III was elected Pope in 1186. He had been the incumbent cardinal of the church,[4] which, having been restored once more, gained prominence and became the most importance religious complex within the Tiber bend. The location of the building was extremely fortunate, situated as it was near to the most important medieval axial street, the Via Papae or Maior, which linked the Vatican to the Lateran.

The district, or rather the Rione, known in the thirteenth century as 'Parione e San Lorenzo in Damaso', is mentioned in ceremonials relating to papal processions, such as the *Ordo Romanus* written by Benedetto, Canon in 1140–3, and the later book by Cencio Camerario.[5] It was here that the areas of influence of the most important Roman families, who had their fortified homes in the district, met. One can point to the Orsini family, who built their palazzo-fortress upon the imposing ruins of the Theatre of Pompey. Among other things, it was equipped with two towers, the Arpacata or Arpacasa (today incorporated into the Palazzo Pio-Righetti in Via del Biscione) and the Pertundata.[6] Then there was the Anguillara family, which occupied several groups of houses and towers near the piazza of the Campo de' Fiori.[7] The Savelli family are known in Parione from 1363, the year in which they inherited the majestic palazzo with squared towers that was partly demolished and partly incorporated into the Palazzo Fieschi-Sora. The Amateschi family owned houses in the area between Via del Governo Vecchio and Via Sora. The Della Valle family occupied the area close to the future Palazzo

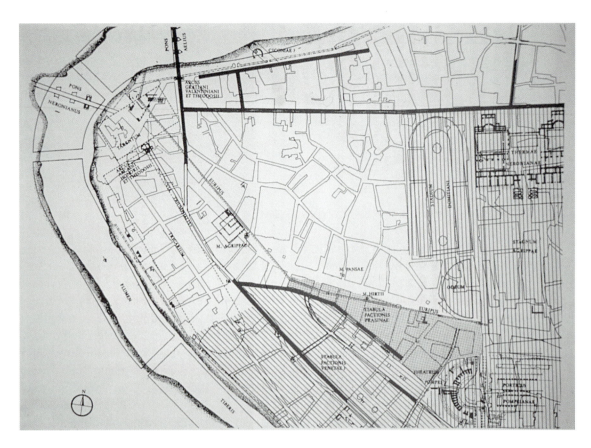

FIG. 1. **The Campus Martius: the orientation of the ancient monumental complexes.** *(Reproduced courtesy of the Sovraintendenza ai Beni Culturali del Comune di Roma.)*

Della Valle from the Middle Ages. Finally, the Massimo family had their houses, fortified with towers, in Piazza San Pantaleo from 1159.[8]

It is recorded in many documents that the area between Piazza San Pantaleo, the Cancelleria and Via dei Baullari was scattered with towers and tower-houses, such as the house of Bartolomeo Giorgio of Novara, near the Palazzo Massimo alle Colonne.[9] Other towers of less important families include those of Oddone Buonfiglio, Niccolò (the so-called *turris de Piscionibus*), Pietro delli Cosciari and, on the site where the Palazzo Braschi would be built in the middle of the fifteenth century, the towered house of Cencio Mosca. Moreover, it appears that the entire zone was populated densely with artisans and merchants, who lived and had their shops there according to a pattern of habitation deriving from antiquity. This pattern consisted of single-storeyed houses with one or two rooms, a portico, a well and, sometimes, a loggia.

From the twelfth century, there was an important wave of immigration, particularly into the Ponte and Parione districts. This was due to a revival of craft and commerce caused by an influx of pilgrims, and to the

existence of two important centres of attraction, one political (the Vatican) and one commercial (the Campo de' Fiori or 'Platea Florea' and, later, the banking-houses). As their economic prosperity gradually grew, 'bourgeois' families built for themselves houses or complexes of houses, often fortified by towers (known as tower-houses).[10] In addition to their defensive value, these conferred greater status upon their owners. The names of the Bussa, Pantaleoni, Muti and Tebalsci families appear frequently in legal documents; by the fourteenth century they already owned small or large properties that they rented to artisans or immigrants.

During the exile of the popes to Avignon, the condition of the area declined; in 1425 the campanile and church of San Lorenzo in Damaso were close to ruin, and the roads and piazzas were uncared for and often occupied by illegal buildings. The return of the popes to Rome and the provisions made for building activity from the time of Nicholas V (1447–55) led to a slow renovation of the urban fabric, particularly in the Ponte and Parione districts. In the Statutes of 1452 relating to construction, the pope provided for the maintenance and improvement of the medieval 'trident' (the Trivio

Messariorum) that began at Ponte Sant'Angelo and consisted of the Via Peregrinorum or Florea 'from the Canale de Ponte up to Santo Agnolo Pescivendolo' ('dallo Canale de Ponte insino a Santo Agnolo Pescivendolo'),[11] the Via Recta 'from the Canale de Ponte ... up to the Magdalena' ('dallo Canale de Ponte ... insino alla Magdalena'),[12] and the Via Papalis 'from the Canale de Ponte ... up to the Campidoglio' ('dallo Canale de' Ponte ... insino allo Campidoglio').[13] The area under examination here was affected, since it was crossed by these two great roads and was intersected throughout by a series of alleys that ran in a disorderly manner between one building and another.[14] Laws were passed to regulate the paving of streets and their maintenance, and to control the use of porticoes, 'mignani' (from 'meniani', meaning small balconies) and 'sporti' (balconies projecting out from a building). Finally, definitive measures were taken to enable the demolition or closure of anything that had been built 'illegally' in streets and piazzas.

An important process of architectural transformation began towards the middle of the fifteenth century, and became evident during the course of the following century. A very different vision of the city and of domestic architecture, particularly the high-flown, gradually took the place of medieval ideas of town planning. This occurred by means of successive adaptations; today, recent stratigraphic investigations undertaken in the most important Renaissance palazzi of the area (the Cancelleria, Palazzo Massimo alle Colonne, Palazzo Altemps, Palazzo della Valle) have rendered these changes even more evident. It seems clear that as the grand Renaissance palazzi were constructed, they swallowed up older houses, towers, and even entire blocks of housing, including the streets (as in the case of the Palazzo Altemps), and exploited, where possible, pre-existing masonry.[15]

The construction of Raffaele Riario's palazzo (today known as the Palazzo della Cancelleria) can be placed within this context. It involved the gradual demolition of the Damasian church between 1497 and 1503, and its reconstruction within the palazzi of the Cancelleria from 1517. This noteworthy construction altered the urban fabric of the zone. It led to a change in the route of Via dei Leutari in 1523 and caused the demolition of the housing block between that part of Via del Pellegrino 'opened' by Sixtus IV and the ancient, unnamed, street towards Piazza San Pantaleo.[16] In 1523, Tommaso Le Roy, having acquired several properties within the block, 'iuxta bona Mazzatostis' ('near to Mazzatosti's properties'), began the construction of a building that later would become known as the Farnesina ai Baullari.[17]

THE PALAZZO LE ROY: CONSTRUCTION HISTORY

This small Renaissance building of great architectural elegance is known by the name of the Farnesina ai Baullari.[18] It was built at the centre of the flourishing Parione district in 1523 by the Breton prelate, Tommaso Le Roy (Fig. 2).[19] The construction date of the palazzo has been established from two inscriptions that were discovered at the base of the ashlar foundations of the southwest and southeast corners during restoration work in August 1900. These inscriptions refer to the purchaser of the building and the moment construction began. One reads:

TOMA REGIS BRITO DE MECZACO REDONENSIS
DIOCESIS CAMERE APLICAE CLERICUS ABBRETOR
DE MAIORI ET SCRIPTOR APLIC
ME FIERI FECIT MDXXIII[20]

Renovation work in the surrounding area has taken place during the last few centuries, in particular the building works of the nineteenth century and the later demolitions carried out to make way for Corso Vittorio Emanuele (Figs 3–4). This has destroyed, or rendered difficult to read, the palazzo's original relationship to the buildings near to it and, more importantly, its ancient position within the urban fabric. Thus, it is useful to examine the written documents relating to the palazzo, together with the drawings, paintings and principal plans of Rome, in order to re-establish in general terms the relationship between the palazzo and its urban context. The aim is also to reconstruct, at least in part, the topography of the housing block that existed in this location in the centuries before the construction of the palazzo.

The strong ties that link the Palazzo Le Roy to the urban fabric often are emphasized in sixteenth-century documents, which echo a situation from many centuries before. In a document of 1523, the palazzo is located:

in the same city in the Parione district, in the parish of Saints Laurence and Damasus, comprising the area between these boundaries; to the front there is a public piazza that looks onto this palazzo, on one side there are some houses that look onto the street where poultry, herbs and other things are sold, and on the other side there is a small street that leads to an enclosed piazza.[21]

FIG. 2. **The Palazzo Le Roy, or the Palazzo della Farnesina ai Baullari.** *(Reproduced courtesy of the Sovraintendenza ai Beni Culturali del Comune di Roma.)*

Thus, the Palazzo Regis has ties with the Cancelleria, which was located along Via del Pellegrino with a piazza in front of its principle façade and which was the main point of reference for the surrounding urban fabric. In fact, according to what can be read in the documents already referred to, the palazzo was located 'in front of the building of the church of Saints Laurence and Damasus' ('in cospectu ejusdem palatii ecclesie sanctorum Laurentii et Damasi'). Today this relationship is completely hidden by nineteenth-century buildings that have been placed between the palazzo and the Cancelleria. The important relationship between the two palazzi, Le Roy and Cancelleria, is underlined both by the abovementioned documents and by plans of Rome, starting with that by Leonardo Bufalini in 1551. This relationship explains the orientation of the palazzo's main axes: indeed, its two main façades, on Vicolo dell'Aquila, constituted a 'public face' and looked onto a 'plateola publica' (a small public square) that connected directly with Piazza della Cancelleria. Another fundamental element was its close relationship with the Via Papalis, the city's most important road from medieval times, revived and improved in the middle of the fifteenth century; the 'Mazzatosti

houses' alone, partly backing onto its northern side, separated the palazzo from the Via Papalis and from Piazza San Pantaleo in particular. Despite this, the piazza was approached from the street (later to become Via dei Baullari) that connected the houses of the Massimo family with Piazza Pollarola.

This chapter now will analyse, as far as possible, the information found in the sixteenth-century plans and in the documents to be found in the Archivio di Stato in Rome that allow us to understand and date the building phases of the medieval housing block upon which the Palazzo Le Roy was imposed. In addition, the ancient and medieval structures that have been discovered during restoration work will be analysed.

In Bufalini's plan (1551), Palazzo Le Roy is depicted schematically with three rectangular structures located on the southwest corner of the block between Piazza San Pantaleo and Vicolo dell'Aquila; the street is drawn as two corridors that join together in a right angle, widening into a small piazza connected with Piazza della Cancelleria. This small piazza is depicted in a similar manner in Mario Cartaro's plan (1576), while the plan by Étienne Du Pérac and Antoine Lafréry (1577) illustrates the palazzo in elevation as part of the block already described, but with a

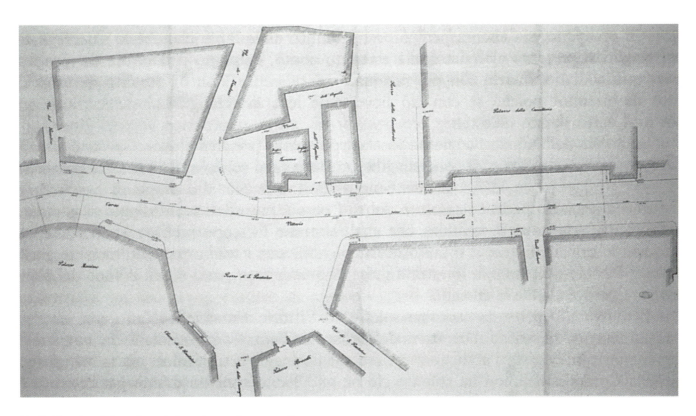

FIG. 3. The site of the palazzo before the work to open Corso Vittorio Emanuele II. Archivio Storico Capitolino, Piano Regolatore, b. 14, fasc. 71A. *(Reproduced courtesy of the Archivio Storico Capitolino.)*

right-angled recess on the southeast side of the palazzo. Thus, the 'plateola' formed by the current Vicolo dell'Aquila has a particular shape caused by these broken lines; it almost forms an S-shape, enhancing the two principal façades that are connected visually to the Cancelleria.

An examination of the plans and drawings from this period relating to the western side of the building is interesting for our study of the pre-existing medieval remains. This is the rear façade, on the current Via dei Baullari, enclosed by a low wall that looks onto a garden belonging to the houses behind. This can be seen in a picture attributed to Du Pérac from 1567, in which a panorama of Rome from the roof of the Palazzo della Cancelleria is drawn:[22] the northeast façades of the Palazzo Le Roy are depicted in the foreground to the left and stand out in relation to the surrounding buildings. The courtyard of the palazzo is enclosed by a wall that is lower than the surrounding buildings; in the direction of the current Via dei Baullari, this wall partly frames a rectangular area (probably the garden). There is a square structure similar to a campanile with a cross at its summit on the roof of the northeast corner of the palazzo. This same struc-

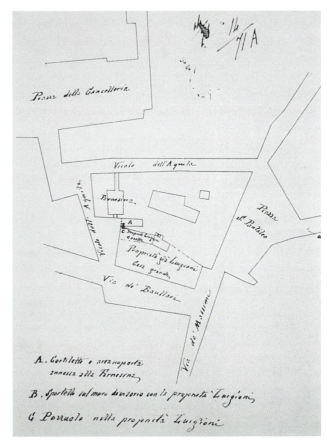

FIG. 4. Plan of the area of the Palazzo Le Roy before the restorations. Archivio Storico Capitolino, Piano Regolatore, b. 14, fasc. 71A. *(Reproduced courtesy of the Archivio Storico Capitolino.)*

ture, but without the cross, is repeated in Antonio Tempesta's plan of 1593, which also reveals the 'S'-shaped piazza seen in the preceding plan. However, here the main façade of the palazzo is depicted with greater accuracy: its rows of windows, the accentuated string-course cornices, and the entrance that juts onto the piazza from which a glimpse of the southern façade also is visible. In the Du Pérac–Lafréry plan, the palazzo is depicted as a square structure that sticks out in respect to the block behind (from which it is clearly separate). It is depicted in the same way in Francesco de Paoli's plan, dating to 1623.[23]

A detailed account of Le Roy's Roman properties has been given by Abbot Mollat, including the legal problems caused by the issue of inheritance that affected the palazzo in the sixteenth to eighteenth centuries. In 1511, Le Roy had bought three houses in the Parione district. One of these (which in 1606 would belong to Annibale Guerra) had a garden, where later an oratory was built by the Confraternity of the Holy Sacrament of San Lorenzo in Damaso. This oratory still exists on Via dei Baullari. The second house was demolished almost completely in 1504, and only a shop, next to another shop owned by Andrea Pollarolo, remains. Mollat also maintained, although without providing documentary evidence, that 'on the same occasion' ('par la même occasion') Le Roy acquired the ground where the palazzo known as the Farnesina would be built.[24]

A document dating to 30 May 1517 is of particular interest. It concerns a house on three floors ('domum terrineam soleratam et tegulatam'),[25] which was built with a ground, first and second floor and described in the document as old and almost in ruins ('antiquam et ruinam minantem'). The document relates to the restitution of this old house to the chapter of San Lorenzo in Damaso by Filippo di Giovan Battista da Orvieto, and to the sale of the house by the chapter to Le Roy for 560 ducats, paid in cash ('in prompta et numerata pecunia'). Filippo da Orvieto had rented the house on 14 March 1512 from the chapter of San Lorenzo for fifteen ducats ('ducatos quindecim de carlenis'), undertaking to 'convert and repair the above-mentioned house within the space of the next four years' ('in aptamine et reparatione domus praedicta infra spatium quattuor annorum tunc proxime futurorum'). However, Filippo 'was prevented from the building of the above-mentioned house by the aforesaid Thomas Regis' ('fuerit impeditus in domo praedicta aedificare per praefatum dominum Thomas

Regis'), and therefore the two parties took their case before the Maestri delle Strade. Filippo gave up the house 'to live quietly, and in peace, and without arguments' ('quiete, et in pace, et sine lite vivere'), returning it to the chapter who sold it to Le Roy. The house bordered 'on one side the property of Angelo Gabrielli, inhabitant of Rome from the Arenula district, and on the other side the property of the heirs of Giovanni Battista Lumelli, and to the rear the property of Giovanni Battista and Lorenzo de Valeriani, and in front partly on the property of Jacopo Regis Bretone and partly by the public street' ('ab uno latere bona Angeli Gabriellis civis Romani de Regione Arenula, et ab alio bona haeredum Joannis Baptista Lumelli, ac retro bona Joannis Baptiste ac Laurentii de Valerianis, ante vero in parte bona domini Jacobi Regis Brittonis, et in partem viam publicam') and 'in the middle the above-mentioned house was located opposite the house in which now lives the Sig. Thomas Regis' ('medietatem terrenam dictae domus ut praemittitur locatae versus domum quam nunc inhabitat dominus Thomas Regis'). Although its neighbours are not recorded in the population censuses of the zone in 1517 and 1526–7, it is clear that the house, in ruins, was located near to other properties owned by Le Roy from at least 1512. Le Roy's desire to own it, so that he could prevent it from being restored by the tenant and force him to leave, leads one to think that the house was located in the block of housing owned by the prelate — the place chosen by him as the site for his palazzo.

In his will of 24 July 1524, Le Roy recorded his palazzo as 'started to be built by me' ('per me aedificari coeptae') and proceeded to leave all of his property 'in the same ground upon which I have constructed and am constructing my buildings' ('tam in eodem fondo quam in desuper aedificis meis per me in ibi constructis, et construendis'), although he concluded by mentioning 'all the other houses that I bought at Rome around the said house that I inhabit' ('omnes aliae domus quas emi Romae, circum circa dictam domum, quam inhabito'), to his nephew, Rodolfo. If this is the palazzo under examination, one might think that in 1524 its construction had reached an advanced stage, sufficient for it to be lived in, despite not being completely finished. It would be left to his nephew, Rodolfo Regis (or Raoul Le Roy), his only heir, to finish the work and endow it with rich furnishings. (The palazzo and its contents were damaged during the Sack of Rome in 1527 and then restored by Raoul.)

Thus, in this period, the first phase of construction of the palazzo was completed, and was strongly influenced by the pre-existing structures. These structures themselves probably had been built with respect to a network of streets and buildings dating to the Roman period, which had been maintained throughout the medieval period up to the start of the Renaissance. (The Roman portico discovered in 1899 under the present-day courtyard is on the same alignment as the rear façade.)

DISCOVERIES UNDER THE PALAZZO LE ROY

In 1885, preliminary work to excavate the course of Corso Vittorio Emanuele (Via Nazionale) through the zone took place. Along with other buildings, the *Comune* of Rome expropriated for public use the palazzo known as the Farnesina ai Baullari, since it was located in an area adjacent to the route of the new road. On the same occasion, a group of houses owned by the Tomarozzi family were expropriated and demolished. These were located between the corner of Via dei Baullari and Vicolo dell'Aquila, opposite the church of San Pantaleo, and occupied a large part of the piazza that today lies at a right angle to Piazza della Cancelleria. Their demolition exposed the northern side of the Farnesina, up to which the demolished houses had backed. The *Comune* of Rome then decided, in April 1887, to announce an international competition for the restoration and completion of the Farnesina ai Baullari, granting absolute freedom to the competitors; the only condition was that none of the pre-existing structures should be touched. The most serious of the difficulties that needed to be overcome was the wall that had been discovered on Corso Vittorio Emanuele; in relation to the other walls of the palazzo it was slanted, and did not run in a straight line from one corner to the other, but formed a recess. On 9 December, the commission given the task of judging the competition chose the project of Enrico Guj. However, lack of funds delayed the start of work by more than ten years.

In 1895 the journal *L'Edilizia Moderna* published an anonymous article (attributed to Guj) in which was written:

the urgent need to smarten up that most central of areas by the restoration of the Farnesina ai Baullari seems ever more necessary for the architectural dignity of Rome. Today, overlooking piazza San Pantaleo and the Corso, it is an unfinished building, ruined, disfigured by shapeless additions and profaned by vandalism. At the time when the improvement of Via Nazionale, from Piazza dei Gesù to the Tiber by the Mausoleum of Hadrian, was decreed, it was decided that, together with the Palazzo Massimo and Palazzo della Cancelleria, the Palazzo della Farnesina needed to be attended to, and the buildings backing onto it were expropriated. However, even though the demolition of these structures has achieved the isolation of this important building, it still remains to be restored and completed.[26]

According to the anonymous writer, the condition of the building before the restorations was one of complete abandonment, and more than three and a half centuries of extensive additions and alterations had heavily disfigured the original architectural harmony that had struck the Renaissance architects who had often drawn plans and elevations of it.

It was only on 15 May 1898 that the work began, and it was completed in 1903–4. After the first few months of work, the remains of important ancient buildings were found during the excavations for the foundations of the new façade along Corso Vittorio Emanuele and beneath the staircase on Via dei Baullari. Another structure (probably datable to the medieval period) also had been brought to light during the demolition of the nineteenth-century accretions. Unfortunately, it escaped the attention of scholars, and was partly demolished and partly covered by the new structures of the restoration.[27] Giuseppe Gatti gave a timely notice of the discovery of Roman structures in his 1899 report for the *Bullettino Comunale*; these consisted of a series of marble columns with reused bases and capitals set out around a peristyle (**Figs 5–6**).

In summary (**Fig. 7**), only a wide area paved with white marble slabs, bordered on the west side by a brick wall, remains of the oldest phase. The presence of a *labrum* might lead one to think that this area was open to the sky, but it is impossible to establish its size and chronology. It is possible that this large open-air area was part of the grounds of the Stabula. Indeed, today the hypothesis is generally accepted that the practice-ground of the four oldest Circus factions was located in this part of the Campus Martius. Even if its layout and size is unknown, it is clear that it occupied a very large area, certainly enough to incorporate entire housing blocks and to have room for extensive housing with service-areas, storerooms and rich entertainment areas, as well as stables and sheds for chariots.

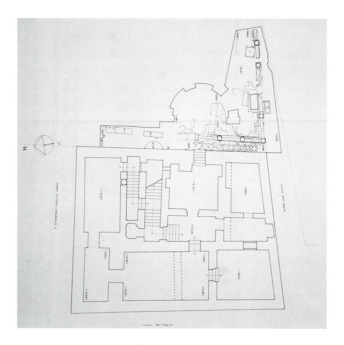

Fig. 5. Plan of the Roman structures and of the ground floor of the Palazzo Le Roy. Museo Barracco, Rome, Archive. *(Reproduced courtesy of the Sovraintendenza ai Beni Culturali del Comune di Roma.)*

Fig. 6. **The Roman structures under the Palazzo Le Roy.** *(Reproduced courtesy of the Sovraintendenza ai Beni Culturali del Comune di Roma.)*

Within this area, in a later period, a peristyle was inserted that used the older paving as the surface for the open-air courtyard;[28] if the pavements of the rooms on the western side are excluded, no traces of the buildings to which this peristyle belonged remain. The construction of the surviving part consists almost entirely of materials salvaged from monuments (*spolia*), mostly from the Augustan period. From the peristyle, one enters the rooms on the western side by means of a single opening, since originally all the intercolumnar gaps were walled up to a height of around a metre. One has the impression of a continuous balcony, richly decorated, from which the upper parts of the columns stand out according to an architectural fashion and concept of space widely documented in the peristyles of late antique *domus*. In this phase, the portico was richly decorated with polychrome marbles and frescoes that, from their style and iconography, can be dated to around the second half of the fourth century AD.

The *opus vittatum* technique, the wide and casual use of materials from different periods, and the reuse of medium-sized tiles of *opus sectile* also support this chronology. This is clearly evidence of a reorganization of the zone. The area, occupied firstly by the Stabula of the *prasina* faction, may have become the property of the father of Pope Damasus. In effect, this Pope (366–84) built his Basilica and the *titulus* connected to it 'near the church of San Lorenzo in Damaso that came to be known by another name in Prasino' ('ad ecclesiam Sancti Laurenti in Damaso quae alio nomine appellatur in Prasino') in the area of the 'stabula factionis prasinae', exploiting the ancient buildings probably contained within his father's vast estate.[29] The perfect similarities and the exact coincidence of the levels of the two examples of *opus sectile* pavements found in the excavations under the Palazzo Le Roy and in the Damasian church under San Lorenzo in Damaso support this hypothesis.

Important structural alterations are not apparent in following phases. Instead, there are small but significant changes: the insertion of a basin, on inappropriate supports, and a *mensa ponderaria* (measuring table), as well as the construction of the enclosure wall in the ambulatory. The final changes need to be put in the context of the probable change of function of the building. This can be seen in the *mensa ponderaria* leant against the second partitioning wall of the southern ambulatory of the portico, as well as by the reorganization of the space in that area by the construction of an *opus vittatum* wall. Today, this wall can be seen to a height of a few centimetres in the modern wall of the crypt. From this time, and in all successive periods, the buildings that were constructed above the Roman structures preserved their orientation. As we shall see,

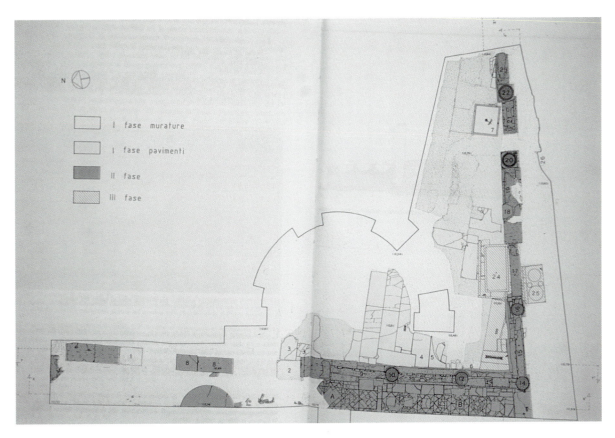

FIG. 7. **Building phases of the Roman structures under the Palazzo Le Roy.** *(G. Cimino and S. Le Pera Buranelli; photo: S. Le Pera Buranelli.)*

the medieval buildings in particular followed the alignment of the Euripus, the canal discovered right in front of the medieval part of the palazzo, but at a depth of more than 7 m from it.

Despite the scanty documentation, it is perhaps possible at this point to offer an analysis of the documented remains and to propose the existence of previously unpublished medieval buildings upon which the Farnesina ai Baullari was built. In this way, a contribution will be made to our knowledge of the reconstruction of that part of the city within the bend of the Tiber during the medieval period.[30]

The plan of the cellars executed during the time of Guj's restorations, and those made about a hundred years later for the restructuring of the Museo Barracco, revealed the presence of a building and, probably, a pre-existing open area under the northeast corner of the palazzo and courtyard. Both were reused by the Renaissance architect in the construction of the building (**Fig. 8**). In addition, a well was found against a wall that was described by the restorers as 'medieval';[31] this was part of a wall in *opus laterizia* made from reused bricks of excellent quality and incorporated into later walling. Moreover, the ground-floor wall that bordered

the staircase facing Corso Vittorio Emanuele had a column embedded in the wall (**Fig. 9**); this rested on two arches built of reused brick connected to a reused column with a capital. On the lower floor, on the same axis as the column on the ground floor, part of another column of the same diameter (**Fig. 10**), was found. There was part of a column drum 2.8 m from this, perhaps *in situ* (**Fig. 11**). It sticks out from the wall and today, unfortunately, is painted white. It appears very worn, particularly lower down, something that leads one to think that it was some type of reinforcement (a cornerstone?), perhaps on the corner of the medieval building. One might hypothesize that the remains described up to this point relate to a portico with a loggia above, contemporary with the room with the well. The brick arches resting on the residual column have been filled in with a wall that dates to a later period. (Benocci referred to a fifteenth-century wall; this might have been built in response to the laws that, starting in this period, caused porticoes and loggias to be closed in.) In the cellars of the palazzo, two pavement levels can be identified, that of the Roman portico and that of the medieval building with portico and well (higher by *c.* 1.5 m). The Renaissance

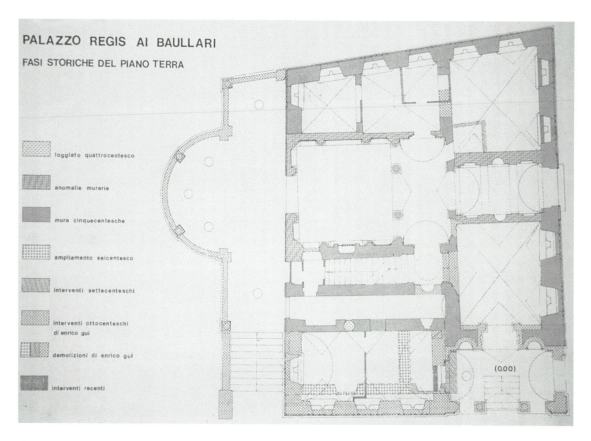

PALAZZO REGIS AI BAULLARI

FASI STORICHE DEL PIANO TERRA

loggiato quattrocentesco

anomalie murarie

mura cinquecentesche

ampliamento seicentesco

interventi settecenteschi

interventi ottocenteschi
di enrico gui

demolizioni di enrico gui

interventi recenti

(0.00)

FIG. 8. **Plan of the ground floor revealing the presence of the medieval structures. Museo Barracco, Rome, Archive.**
(Reproduced courtesy of the Sovraintendenza ai Beni Culturali del Comune di Roma.)

building was on a level a little higher than the medieval one (*c.* 0.5 m).

In addition, examination of the plans made during the course of the nineteenth-century restoration reveals the remains of three sections of wall that can be seen clearly in the plan of the ground and first floors. These walls are revealed in a sketch depicting the ancient structures of the building; between them they form two right angles, but they have a slanted alignment with respect to the two main façades. To judge from the plan, these walls appear to be *c.* 0.9 m wide and are described in Giorgioli's work specifications as 'made from red bricks of poor manufacture' ('realizzati in mattoncini rossi e di rozza fattura'). They appear to be wider and more solid than the fifteenth-century walls, which consisted essentially of simple partitioning and blocking, and were used during Le Roy's work as supports for the walls of the ground-floor courtyard. Proof of the changes suffered by the pre-existing structures can be seen in the resulting irregular perimeter walls of the rear façade, which enclosed the courtyard; the wall of the aedicule that frames the well in the courtyard, which is on the same alignment as the medieval well beneath it; the two

walls that border the hall, also characterized by a different width and dissimilar to the walls beneath; and the wall of the front façade that tapers noticeably towards the corner of Vicolo dell'Aquila.

The section of wall made from reused brick, found in 1991 during work to install water-pipes in Vicolo dell'Aquila, also perhaps can be attributed to the phase that we are gradually identifying. It follows the same orientation as the medieval walls within the building. Only a short tract of this wall was seen, since it mostly had been buried when it collapsed and was lost under the corner of the Palazzo Le Roy. Finally, it should be noted how all these structures on the northern side follow the alignment of the Euripus conduit, which dates to 1,200 years before they were built.[32]

The existence of medieval structures beneath the Palazzo Le Roy also seems to be supported by an examination of the plans and drawings made when the buildings backing onto the palazzo were demolished and also by those made later for the *Comune* of Rome at the time of the restoration and reorganization of the Museo Barracco. The above-mentioned walls that rest on the medieval level of the area relate to these structures, as do the irregularities noticed on the ground floor. These walls probably were part of the 'domum antiquam et ruinam minantem' recorded in 1512; rather than demolish it, the architect employed by Le Roy to construct the palazzo chose to reuse, although not completely, the walls of the preceding period. He inserted a high quality architectural link, that is the central axis with its progression of hall, portico and courtyard, and adjusted as far as possible the pre-existing walls and defined the external image of the renovated palazzo with a new façade. Moreover, the architect created a recurring theme in the rooms of the central axis. It consisted of the niche with aedicule that framed the old well and was repeated on the op-posite side of the courtyard (today altered). This can be seen in the sixteenth-century depictions of the plan of the building that are held in the Kunstbibliothek in Berlin and in the Biblioteca Marciana in Venice — the same theme appears clearly on the walls of the hall,

although of smaller dimensions. However, it must be noted that, in comparison to the main façade, the sixteenth-century drawings relating to the palazzo (those in Berlin and Venice, together with those in Würzburg (Martin von Wagner Museum), the Uffizi (Gabinetto dei Disegni e Stampe, no. 4096, LA 1720v and LA 2698) and by Du Pérac) document less precisely the side of the palazzo on Vicolo dell'Aquila, as if this side were incomplete or less interesting.

A photograph that records the condition of the palazzo after the initial demolitions resulting from the construction of Corso Vittorio Emanuele will help us to complete these observations.[33] This photo was taken immediately after the demolition of the Tomarozzi houses that had backed onto the palazzo. It may be possible to recognize the remains of a tall building within the high square structure in the corner of the palazzo. The lower part of this building is built of brick (as described by Guj and the restorers of

FIG. 9. Reused column incorporated into the masonry, ground floor. *(Photo: S. Le Pera Buranelli.)*

FIG. 10. Reused column incorporated into the masonry, basement level. *(Photo: S. Le Pera Buranelli.)*

FIG. 11. **Fragment of a column drum incorporated into the masonry.** *(Photo: S. Le Pera Buranelli.)*

1982), the upper part of fairly regular tufa blocks (which can be glimpsed where the plaster has flaked off). The putlogs (which can be seen in the lower part of the building) are also regular. A wide plinth in *opus mixtum* made from tufa blocks, bricks, and perhaps also travertine, arranged irregularly, can be seen at the bottom on the outside, similar to that recorded in the intercolumnar blocking walls at Santo Stefano Rotondo;[34] as in that case, it forms a base upon which the structure in tufa blocks rests. In contrast, the remains at the height of the two windows of the third floor relate to the addition of the seventeenth-century rooftop loggia. This is the northeast corner of the palazzo, the point at which the three walls that stand outside the alignments of the Renaissance palazzo can be seen in Guj's plan. It may be that this was a building, perhaps a tower-house, with a courtyard and well on the other side and a portico with loggia above; perhaps this was the 'tower-house on three

floors' ('domum terrineam, solaratam et tegulatam') that the document of 1517 describes as already in ruins. Unfortunately, as can be seen in Guj's plan, these elements were demolished to ground level; only the wall with the columns incorporated and a stretch of brick walling in the basement, today covered by modern bricks to support the current building, remain.

CONCLUSIONS

When, during 1993, the decision was made to study and publish the remains of the Roman buildings under the Museo Barracco, one expected, given the centuries of Roman occupation of the Campus Martius and those immediately afterwards of late antique houses (attributable to the Damasian phase), to draw for the Palazzo Le Roy the same conclusion that André Chastel came to for the Palazzo Farnese: 'during the ten following centuries it appears no longer to have a history' ('pendant le dix siècles suivantes, le site semblait n'avoir plus guère d'histoire'). In fact, just as for all those Renaissance palazzi for which a careful examination of the archival and 'archaeological' documentation has been undertaken, important information has been uncovered for our understanding of the medieval phases of the districts. These phases have been preserved, sealed from above, under a layer of modern plaster and the construction of later buildings.

Provided that necessary precautions are taken (given the impossibility of verifying the types of masonry present in the remains that have since been demolished or covered with plaster or modern brickwork), it is possible at this point to hypothesize the existence of a house — a tower-house — consisting of at least two floors, with a portico with loggia and with a courtyard within which a well was located against one of the walls. It is likely that this house faced onto the street that was destroyed by the creation of Via dei Baullari. The loggia and portico appear to have been blocked in during the fifteenth century, according to the dictates of the Maestri delle Strade, who enforced the closing-up of all loggias that faced the street. The layout of the portico and the loggia next to the courtyard, the height of the building and the strength of the walls suggest that this was a fairly prestigious house. Its lower levels were built of reused brick, with small arches constructed from pieces of brick placed on reused columns (*spolia*) inside, and tufa masonry in the upper parts of the building. It is possible, therefore, to propose that this building be interpreted as one of those houses, or tower-houses, that from the twelfth century, with the increasing economic power of the 'bourgeois' families, neighboured the true defensive towers and fortifications of the grand families of the area. Indeed, it is known that in the Parione district itself, as in the Ponte and Regola districts, there was a growth in population in this period. This was caused by immigration (for example, the German colony), by the economic and commercial activities connected to the passage of pilgrims, by the growth in importance of the Platea Florea and by the establishment of bankers in the area. From the fifteenth century, there were new attitudes towards street arrangements and new ideas about town planning and public architecture, and it is possible to witness progressive changes in the urban layout of the zone, including the creation of wide streets and grand palazzi. All this, however, occurred in later phases and involved the progressive absorption of older buildings.

NOTES

1. For the ancient topography of the area 'in medio campo', see F. Castagnoli, 'Il Campo Marzio', *Memorie. Atti dell'Accademia Nazionale dei Lincei, Classe di Scienze Morali, Storiche e Filologiche* 1 (1984), 93ff.; F. Coarelli, 'Il Campo Marzio occidentale', in K. de Fine Licht (ed.), *Città ed architettura nella Roma imperiale (Analecta Roma Instituti Danici, suppl. X)* (Odense, 1983), 59ff.; E. La Rocca, *La riva a mezzaluna* (Rome, 1984); M.P. Muzzioli, 'Fonti per la topografia della IX regione di Roma: alcune osservazioni', *PBSR* 60 (1992), 179–211; F. Coarelli, *Il Campo Marzio — Dalle origini alla fine della repubblica* (Rome, 1997); P. Sommella and L. Migliorati, 'Corso Vittorio Emanuele II. Storia di una stratificazione urbanistica areale: il periodo antico', in *Corso Vittorio Emanuele II tra urbanistica ed archeologia* (Naples, 1998), 75–120.

2. Until the last decades of the Republic, the area, in which cult places connected to cthonic divinities had existed from most ancient times (Tarentum, Ara Ditis, Trigarium), was used for burials, and the part that we are examining seems to have been used for the tombs of famous men: the tombs of Sulla (Livy, *Epitomae* XC; Plutarch, *Sulla* XXXVIII; Appian, *Bella Civilia* XXXVIII.106–7; Dio Cassius, *Historia Romana* XXXIX.64, LXXVII.53) and Caesar (Livy, *Epitomae* CVI; Suetonius, *Caesar* LXXXIV; Plutarch, *Pompey* LIII, *Caesar* LXXXIII) are recorded 'in medio campo'. The tomb of Aulus Hirtius and the funerary inscription of Pansa were found under the Palazzo della Cancelleria. On his return from the East, Pompey the Great built a grand complex in this area, comprising the Theatre and porticoes, although only going as far as the south-eastern border of the area with this work. Later, the land passed to Agrippa who, as part of Augustus's grand urban project, constructed the Acqua Vergine aqueduct to carry water to the Campus Martius, built the Pantheon and the baths with the attached Stagnum (to the right of Corso del Rinascimento) and excavated the great Euripus canal. The monumental renovation of the *stabula quattuor factionum* along with the Trigarium and the Circus Flaminius may belong to this phase. The ancient boundaries of the area 'in medio campo' were formed by the Stagnum and Euripus to one side, the Stabula to another, and the later Domitianic complex comprising the Stadium and the Odeon.

3. ASR, Notaio A.C. Raydettus, vol. 6149, fols 461v, 465v; cited in U. Gnoli, *Topografia e toponomastica di Roma medievale e moderna* (Rome, 1939), 396. In effect, the ancient *titulus* of Damasus I (366–84), located in an area that was inhabited for the entire Middle Ages, became a focus of restoration during periods of large-scale renovation of the city. The Basilica was restored under Hadrian I (772–95), as part of the general revival of the Carolingian age that witnessed the reaffirmation of the role and authority of the Church. The donative bestowed on the church by Leo III (795–816) in 806–7 confirmed its civic role. Stephen IX's (1057–8) later restoration can be placed within the context of the rebirth of the city in the age of Otto.

4. C.L. Frommel, 'Sotto il cortile del cardinale. Gli scavi della Basilica di S. Lorenzo in Damaso', *Archeo* 47 (1989), 45–6.

5. R. Valentini and G. Zucchetti (eds), *Codice topografico della città di Roma* III (Rome, 1953), 210–22 ('Dal Liber Politicus di Benedetto Canonico'), 223–70 ('Itinerario della seconda feria di pasqua dall'*ordo* di Cencio').

6. For a study of the Orsini houses and the identification of a further three towers belonging to their fortifications, see, most recently, F. Bosman, 'Una torre medievale a Via Monte della Farina: ricerche topografiche ed analisi della struttura', *Archeologia Medievale* 17 (1990), 633–60.

7. Dolce I of the Anguillara family dictated his will, drawn up in 1400, from a house 'in regione Parionis'.

8. Cencio Camerario, for example, referred to the 'domus Maximorum' along the Via Papalis, and in 1532 the Palazzo Massimo alle Colonne was referred to as 'domus antiqua' or 'de' portico'.

9. A. Katermaa-Ottela, 'Le case-torri medievali in Roma', *Commentationes Humanarum Litterarum* 67 (1981), 44–5.

10. On medieval town planning, see F. Castagnoli, C. Cecchelli, G. Giovannoni and M. Zocca, *Topografia e urbanistica di Roma* (Rome, 1958); P. Llewellyn, *Roma nei secoli oscuri* (Rome/Bari, 1975); R. Krautheimer, *Roma, profilo di una città* (Rome, 1981); H. Broise and J.C. Maire Vigueur, 'Strutture famigliari spazio domestico e architettura a Roma alla fine del Medio Evo', in *Storia dell'arte italiana* XII (Turin, 1983); L. Pani Ermini and E. De Minicis (eds), *Archeologia del Medio Evo a Roma. Edilizia storica e territorio* I (Taranto, 1988); J. Heers, 'Les villes d'Italie centrale et l'urbanisme: origines et affirmation d'une politique (environ 1200–1300)', *Mélanges de l'École Française de Rome. Moyen Âges et Temps Modernes* 101 (1) (1989), 76–93; R. Motta, *Note sull'edilizia abitativa medioevale a Roma* (Rome, 1990).

11. The route corresponds to the present-day Via del Banco di Santo Spirito, Via dei Banchi Vecchi, Via del Pellegrino, Campo de' Fiori, Via dei Giubbonari, Piazza Cairoli, Via del Pianto, Via del Portico d'Ottavia and ended in front of the church of Sant'Angelo in Pescheria.

12. The road runs from the bridge to the Piazza del Pantheon. Cf. C. Benocci, *Rione S. Angelo* (Rome, 1980).

13. The most important financial and commercial activities took place on this street; its course followed the modern Via dei Banchi Nuovi, Via del Governo Vecchio, Piazza Pasquino, Via San Pantaleo; it passed in front of the houses of the Massimo family and the church of Sant'Andrea della Valle and then, by means of Via del Sudario and part of Corso Vittorio Emanuele, it reached Via Ara Coeli and the Campidoglio.

14. These were the routes formed gradually during the Middle Ages that, corresponding to ancient roads, often linked the political (Campidoglio), religious (Vatican) and economic (Piazza Navona, Campo de' Fiori, Sant'Angelo in Pescheria) centres of the city to each other.

15. G. Curcio, 'Il Rione Parione durante il pontificato Sistino: analisi di una arca campione — i processi di trasformazione edilizi', in M. Miglio (ed.), *Un pontificato ed una città — Sisto IV (1471–1484)* (Vatican City/Rome, 1986), 706ff.

16. S. Valtieri, *La Basilica di S. Lorenzo in Damaso nel Palazzo della Cancelleria a Roma attraverso il suo archivio ritenuto scomparso con documenti inediti della zona circostante* (Rome, 1984).

17. The other houses of the block were demolished in 1549 to make room for the new Via Farnesiorum, the modern Via dei Baullari.

18. The Palazzo Le Roy has been attributed to various architects. According to G. Mollat (*Thomas Le Roy et le palazzetto della Farnesina à Rome* (Rome, 1902)) it can be attributed to Jeande Thororlès, an architect whose relationship with Le Roy was well-known. G. Giovannoni ('Roma dal Rinascimento al 1870', in *Topografia ed urbanistica di Roma* (Bologna, 1958), 350ff.) and A. Venturi ('L'architettura del '500', in *Storia dell'arte italiana* (Milan, 1901–39), XI (1), 570–90), followed by later scholars, maintained that it was designed by Antonio da Sangallo on account of two drawings preserved in the Uffizi that are attributed to him (nos. 1092 and 960). These drawings relate to the palazzo in general terms and have stylistic similarities with various other Sangallo structures. Another drawing by Aristotele da Sangallo, also in the Uffizi (UA 1720v), has been related to the palazzo by C. De Fabríczy ('La Farnesina ai Baullari', *Rivista dell'Istituto di Archeologia e Storia dell'Arte* (Rome, 1892),141ff.), while vague references to the work of Baldassarre Peruzzi and Raphael have led other authors (such as C. Astolfi, 'Sulla casa abitata da Raffaello e sul più vero architetto della Farnesina ai Baullari', in *Studia Picena* (Rome, 1939), 119–25) to attribute it to them. Recently, L. Frommel ('S. Luigi dei Francesi: das Meister Werk der Jean de Chenevières', in *Il se rendit en Italie. Études offerts à André Chastel* (Rome, 1987), 169–93, esp. pp. 180ff.) has hypothesized that the palazzo was the work of Jean de Chenevières, who was responsible for the church of San Luigi dei Francesi, on the basis of stylistic similarities between this and the Palazzo Le Roy.

19. Over time, the name Le Roy became Latinized as *Regis*. Le Roy arrived in Italy in 1494 in the retinue of Charles VIII. He remained in Rome, where he held high office in the pontifical court. He played an important part in drawing up the concordat of 1516 between Leo X and Francis I, and was ennobled by the sovereign (1522) and allowed to augment his coat of arms with the lilies of France. This part of his coat of arms, frequently found in the architectural decoration of the building next to the ermines of Brittany, Le Roy's homeland, was confused with the well-known emblem of the Farnese lily, which gave rise to its popular name, the Piccola Farnesina. Le Roy's choice of area in which to build his residence seems more than justified by his activities. It was in close proximity to the Via Papale, the road closely connected to international affairs and papal politics, and also it was near the new palazzo of the Cancelleria.

20. With the discovery of this tablet, the hypothesis that the construction began in 1517, suggested by Gnoli (*Topografia* (above, n. 3)), collapsed. This hypothesis had been based on the presence of a Thomasso Regis in the census of the Parione district, published by M. Armellini (*Un censimento della città*

di Roma sotto Leone X (Rome, 1892), 72). The census clearly reveals that Le Roy was in the district, as do the documents cited by Mollat, *Thomas Le Roy* (above, n. 18), from which it appears that he acquired three houses in 1511. One was located between Via dei Baullari and the Cancelleria and had a garden; it was later given to the Confraternity of San Lorenzo in Damaso who built an oratory there that still exists today. Le Roy had his home here. The other two houses were nearby. One, near Piazza Pollarola, was almost completely demolished in 1549 to make way for the new Via Farnesiorum (Via dei Baullari): only a small shop remains. The palazzo, referred to as 'iuxta bona Mazzatostis' ('near to Mazzatosti's properties') in the will drawn up by Le Roy on 24 July 1524, was described as 'domus mea per me aedificari coepta' ('my house, started to be built by me'), while the other houses were designated as 'domus quas emi Romae circum circa domum quam inhabito' ('the houses that I bought at Rome near to the one in which I live'). The information gained from the inscriptions and their positions led Frommel ('S. Luigi dei Francesi' (above, n. 18)) to hypothesize that the plan to construct the building dated to 1520–1 and that work began in 1522 and continued into 1523, when the base where the two inscriptions were located was constructed. These inscriptions can be dated to June 1523, since the offices held by Le Roy up to that date are recorded, that is those before his assumption of the episcopate of Dol, an office assigned to him by Hadrian VI in the Consistory of 29 June 1523. G. Tommasetti ('Scoperte recenti nel Palazzetto della Farnesina', *BullCom* 28 (1900), 321–41) referred to the discovery of the two Renaissance stones on which the name of Thomas Le Roy appears as a purchaser. The first, in the southwest corner of the building, was placed horizontally into the ground on the level of the ashlar, and four silver coins were found under the slab; the other stone, of *giallo antico*, was found in the southeast corner and there were seven silver coins under it (the eleven coins were of Popes Innocent VIII, Alexander VI, Julius II and Leo X). Cf. Comune di Roma, Archivio Storico della Ripartizione X, Registro dei Trovamenti VII, p. 113.

21. 'in hujusmodi urbe ac regione Parionis, in parrochia Sanctorum Laurentii et Damasii, in cospectu ejusdem palatii ecclesie sanctorum Laurentii et Damasi, infra hoc fines, ab uno latere anteriori est plateola pubblica versus dictum palatium respiciens, ab alio sunt domus respicientes versus stratam ubi venduntur pulli herhe et alie res et ab alio latere est parva strata que ducit ad plateam reclaustram.' ASR, Notaio A.C. Raydettus, vol. 6149, fol. 465v (also Gnoli, *Topografia* (above, n. 3), 396), concerning the inheritance left by Raoul Le Roy to his son, Francesco. The proximity to the Basilica of San Lorenzo is underlined also in a document of 25 October 1548 ('Palazzo or large house that came to be called Palazzo or House of Thomas Regis, located in the Parione district near San Lorenzo in Damaso' ('Palatium seu domum magnam que dicitur Palatio o casa de Thomas Regis sitam in regione Parionis et apud sanctum Laurentium in Damaso')) (ASR, Notaio A.C. Raydettus, vol. 6149, fol. 461v) and in another of 30 June 1573 ('Palazzo or large house that came to be called

the Palazzo or House of Thomas Regis, located in the Papione district near San Lorenzo in Damaso' ('Palatium seu domum magnam que dicitur Palatio o casa de Thomas Regis sitam in regione Papionis et apud sanctum Laurentium in Damaso')) (ASR, Notaio A.C. Raydettus, vol. 6149, fol. 465v).

22. Ashby collection; cf. T. Ashby, 'Due vedute di Roma attribuite a Stefano Du Pérac', in *Miscellanea Francesco Ehrle* II (*Studi e testi* 38) (Rome, 1923), tav. 1.

23. These characteristic elements are always present in the plans of the seventeenth to nineteenth centuries. Of interest are the plans by Goffredo Van Schayck (1630) and Giovanni Battista Falda (1676), in which the rooftop loggia is located towards San Pantaleo, by Giovanni Battista Nolli (1748), in which the palazzo is depicted with particular precision, by Giuseppe Vasi (1781), the plans in Pius VII's urban land register (1819–22), by Pietro Ruga (1824), by the Direzione Generale of the census (1829 and 1843), by Augusto Fornari and Luigi Piale (1852) and by the Direzione Generale of the census (1866). For an examination of the position of the palazzo within the urban fabric, see, in addition to the texts indicated in Frommel, 'S. Luigi dei Francesi' (above, n. 18), Francesco Ehrle's introductions to the following: F. Ehrle (ed.), *Pianta topografica della città di Roma divisa in otto Giustizie di Pace* (Rome, 1908); F. Ehrle (ed.), *Roma prima di Sisto V: la pianta di Roma Du Pérac–Lafréry del 1577* (Rome, 1908); F. Ehrle (ed.), *Roma al tempo di Giulio III: la pianta di Roma di Leonardo Bufalini del 1551* (Rome, 1911); F. Ehrle (ed.), *Roma al tempo di Urbano VIII: la pianta di Roma Maggi–Maupin–Losi del 1625* (Rome, 1915); *Roma al tempo di Clemente X: la pianta di Roma di Giovanni Battista Falda del 1676* (Rome, 1931); *Roma al tempo di Clemente VIII: la pianta di Roma di Antonio Tempesta del 1593* (Vatican City, 1932); and the plans in A.P. Frutaz, *Le piante di Roma* (Rome, 1962), tavv. 11, 244, 291, 300, 329, 450, 472, 491, 515, 523.

24. Mollat, *Thomas Le Roy* (above, n. 18), on the basis of documents preserved in the Archive de la Loire-Inférieure, E. de la Tullaye collection.

25. ASV, Capitolo di S. Lorenzo in Damaso, Instrumentum a die 20 sept. 1501 usque ad diem 26 maij 1576, A, n. 19, ce. 91–101; also C. Benocci, 'Thomas Le Roy e l'isola della Farnesina ai Baullari', *Alma Roma* 24 (376) (May–December 1983), 1–6.

26. 'apparirà sempre più evidente, pel decoro edilizio di Roma, l'urgenza di sistemare quella località centralissima mediante il restauro della Farnesina ai Baullari, la quale attualmente si presenta sulla piazza San Pantaleo e sul Corso, come un edificio incompiuto, cadente, deturpato da aggiunte informi e profanato da manomissioni vandaliche. Già fin dall'epoca in cui si decretò la sistemazione della via Nazionale, dalla Piazza dei Gesù fino al Tevere nei pressi della Mole Adriana, fu stabilito di dover mettere in vista, insieme al Palazzo Massimo e a quello della Cancelleria, anche il Palazzetto della Farnesina, espropriando gli stabili che vi erano addossati. Però, se con la demolizione di questi stabili si ottenne di isolare il pregevole edificio, rimane pur sempre da restaurato e completarlo.'

27. In the summary drawn up by the contractor of the work, Benedetto Giorgioli, there is reference to thick masonry in the northwest corner of the palazzo that had to be cut out by chisel since it impeded the work to lay the foundations of the building and the excavations of the Roman structures underneath (ACS, Fondo Ufficio V, Lavori Pubblici, serie Piano Regolatore, B11, fasc. 3).

28. G. Cimino and S. Le Pera, 'Analisi delle strutture ed interpretazione dei resti dell'edificio romano', in *Museo Barracco* (Rome, 1995), 84ff.

29. In the *Liber Pontificalis* (L. Duchesne (ed.), 'Le Liber Pontificalis', *Bibliothèque de l'École Française à Rome* 1 (1981), 212–15) one can read: 'hic constituit titulum in urbe Roma. Basilicam quam ipse construxit, ubi donavit: patena argenteam; domus in circuitu basilicae … balneum iuxta titulum' ('he built a *titulus* in the city of Rome. A basilica that he built himself and to which he gave: a silver patera; a house at the perimeter of the basilica … a bath building near the *titulus*'). On the problem of the correct reading of the Damasian hymn (Sylloge of Lorsch and Sylloge of Verdun), from which derives the hypothesis of the existence of property owned by Damasus's father in this part of the Campus Martius, see A. Ferrua, 'Epigrammata Damasiana', *Rivista di Archeologia Cristiana* 29 (1953), 231–5. On the building activities of Pope Damasus at Rome, see, most recently, C. Pietri, 'Roma Christiana', *Bibliothèque de l'École Française à Rome* 44 (1976), 464ff., and A. Nestori, 'Attività edilizia in Roma di papa Damaso', in *Saecularia Damasiana* I (Vatican City, 1986), 161–72, with bibliography. The couplet is recorded in the Sylloge of Verdun, incised into a baptismal font.

30. Bosman, 'Una torre medievale' (above, n. 6), 633; E. De Minicis, 'Strutture murarie medievali', in Pani Ermini and De Minicis (eds), *Archeologia del Medio Evo* (above, n. 10), 11–33.

31. C. Benocci, 'Il palazzo Regis ai Baullari, sede dei Museo Barracco', in *Museo Barracco* (above, n. 28), 9ff.

32. The Euripus, the large open-air canal that facilitated the flow of water from the 'Stagnum Agrippae', affected the orientation of the buildings in the area; part of it was discovered during Guj's work, but it was not recognized and no mention of it was made in the publications that followed the excavation of the Roman house. The drawings made by Giorgioli — the contractor of the work — in order to support a further request for funds for the excavation were found in the Lanciani codex, BAV, Vat. Lat. IX, 13040, fol. 174v, and published in *Museo Barracco* (above, n. 28), 119ff. See, most recently, F. Coarelli, 'Euripus', in E.M. Steinby (ed.), *Lexicon Topographicum Urbis Romae* II (Rome, 1994), 237–9; M.G. Cimino and S. Le Pera, *Corso Vittorio Emanuele II tra urbanistica ed archeologia* (Naples, 1998), 147ff.

33. The photograph was published in *Nuovo Album Romano*, no. 224. The provenance was given as the Cianfarani–Negro collection, and it is dated 1889.

34. M.E. Avagnina, V. Garibaldi and C. Salterini, 'Strutture murarie degli edifici religiosi di Roma nel XIII secolo', *Rivista dell'Istituto Nazionale d'Archeologia e Storia dell'Arte* 27 (1976–7), 173–256, esp. pp. 197ff.

DISCOVERIES AT THE SCALA SANTA: THE EXCAVATIONS OF 1852–4*

Paolo Liverani

INTRODUCTION

THE SANCTUARY of the Scala Santa is located in Rome at a place of great historical and religious importance. Indeed, together with the *Sancta Sanctorum*, it constitutes the only surviving part of the Lateran Palace, the original seat of the bishop of Rome that was almost completely demolished during the radical urban reorganization ordered by Sixtus V.[1] Despite its importance, our knowledge of the classical and medieval topography of this area unfortunately is limited: in addition to there being more uncertainties than certainties about its present form, there is the problem that studies have not progressed beyond the research of Philippe Lauer in the early twentieth century[2] and the synthesis by Antonio Maria Colini of 1944.[3] Thus it is interesting, where possible, to make the most of several sources that remain unpublished. These records relate to the finds audited between 1852 and 1854 during the construction of the monastery of the Passionist Fathers. Pius IX entrusted the sanctuary to the monastery after he dissolved the ecclesiastical college established by Sixtus V in 1590 (which was no longer up to the pastoral requirements of the time).[4]

EXCAVATIONS AND FINDS

The monastery was built by the architect Giovanni Azzurri. Having acquired the necessary land, he demolished the inn and the houses that had occupied the area immediately to the north of the Sistine building and began excavating for the foundations of the monastery and the enclosure wall of the kitchen garden. In this first phase, numerous fragments of sculpture came to light, which are recorded in the *Nota delle sculture rinvenute nel cavo de' fondamenti fatto per la costruzione del Convento contiguo alla Scala Santa che esistevano nell'abitazione di S.E. R.ma Mons. Castellacci ed ora trasferite nel magazzeno del Museo Lateranense* (Appendix, no. I).[5] I have been able to find the *Nota* in the Archivio Storico of the Vatican Museums. The information contained in it can be integrated with records found in two later lists preserved in the same archive, as well as with the documents of the 'Fondo particolare di Pio IX' and the records of payments made for the restoration of some finds that are preserved in the Archivio Segreto Vaticano.

In particular, the group of Eros on a dolphin (**Fig. 1**), restored between 1855 and 1856 by Massimiliano Laboreur,[6] a headless female bust (**Fig. 2**) from the second half of the second century AD,[7] a herm of Hercules (**Fig. 3**),[8] and a series of architectural fragments (which can not be identified now), are recognizable in the *Nota*. In addition, there were two inscribed fragments: a reused Christian inscription (**Fig. 4**),[9] and a fragment of the upper part of a sarcophagus or cinerary urn (**Fig. 5**).[10] Finally, a fragment of a headless caryatid also was found during the excavation of the foundations of the monastery, and was reused to form Pius IX's coat of arms, located on the sanctuary façade.[11]

A useful but somewhat sparse complement to these lists can be found in the reports published by Pietro Ercole Visconti in a newspaper of the era, the *Giornale di Roma*. In 1853, a mithraic group (**Fig. 6**)[12] and a head of Marcus Aurelius (**Fig. 7**) were found 'during the work for a conduit just a few metres from the Scala Santa towards the south'.[13] The head was restored by Camillo Pistrucci in 1854 and placed on top of a bust from elsewhere, probably found previously.[14]

Also in 1853 a large polychrome mosaic came to light (**Fig. 8**).[15] This was taken up, restored and

FIG. 1. *Eros on a dolphin.* Musei Vaticani, Museo Gregoriano Profano. Archivio Fotografico Musei Vaticani, Vat.-FAK 2438/1. *(Reproduced courtesy of the Vatican Museums.)*

FIG. 2. Headless female bust. Musei Vaticani, Museo Gregoriano Profano. Archivio Fotografico Musei Vaticani, Vat. XXXII-6-481. *(Reproduced courtesy of the Vatican Museums.)*

transferred on to *peperino* slabs, according to the normal technique of that period (cf. Chapter 9), and set in the last of the Stanze di Raffaello, the Sala di Costantino. This work was undertaken between 17 November 1853 and December the following year by the mosaicist Pietro Palesi, in collaboration with Cesare Ruspi and Eugenio Mattia. The mosaic measures 60 × 54 *palmi romani* (13.40 × 12.06 m). In addition, it has a black border that measures 4 *palmi romani* (0.89 m). This perimeter band was reduced in size when it was inserted into the new pavement.[16] In its present location, a bronze inscription has been inserted into the modern perimeter band of the mosaic, which records its provenance: 'This was transferred from the Lateran square near the *Sancta Sanctorum* through the generosity of Pius IX, Pontifex Maximus, in the ninth year of his papacy'.[17] The mosaic had been adjacent to a bath structure: Visconti referred to 'a large bath: a place sumptuously decorated, as can be seen by the remains of columns and Corinthian capitals, by the sculpted friezes and by the fragments of fine marbles'.[18]

The newspaper articles also list a series of numismatic finds made during the work at the Scala Santa, 'near to the place where the large coloured mosaic was found'.[19] These consisted of two coins of Pope Leo IV (847–55) and a lead seal of Celest III (1191–8). Continuation of the work brought to light five silver coins from the mint at Pavia, three of which were of Otto III (983–99) and two of Henry II (1002–24); a bronze coin of the Doge Pietro Gradenigo (1288–1310); a mixed metal coin of Pico II (Duke of Mirandola and Concordia); and one of Sixtus V (1585–90).[20] As can be seen, these finds date to between the ninth and the beginning of the fourteenth centuries in particular, and constitute the only traces we have of the medieval period.

Two lists datable to 1858 include a series of other sculptures, but it is difficult to say when they were found and to which structure they relate. Among them, in addition to a 'fragmentary female figure without arms and head, of good workmanship, taken to the Lateran Museum', which cannot be identified easily today,[21] were found 'three fragments of a well-sculpted balustrade that are in the Lateran Museum'.[22] These may be the two pieces of *transenna* now on display in the new setting of the Gregorian Museum of Pagan Antiquities (**Fig. 9**).[23] They have tritons on one side and on the other decoration including an arched gateway — this side is probably later (late Roman or early medieval). The

FIG. 3. Herm of Hercules. Musei Vaticani, Museo Gregoriano Profano. Archivio Fotografico Musei Vaticani, Vat.-FAK 2178/51. *(Reproduced courtesy of the Vatican Museums.)*

FIG. 4. Reused Christian inscription *ICUR* 1852.5. Musei Vaticani, Lapidario Cristiano ex Lateranense. Archivio Fotografico Musei Vaticani, Vat. XXXIII-38-201. *(Reproduced courtesy of the Vatican Museums.)*

FIG. 5. Fragment of sarcophagus or urn *CIL* VI 17449. Musei Vaticani, Lapidario Profano ex Lateranense. Archivio Fotografico Musei Vaticani, Vat. G.L. 12671. *(Reproduced courtesy of the Vatican Museums.)*

FIG. 6. Sculptural group of Mithras slaying the bull. Musei Vaticani, Museo Gregoriano Profano. Archivio Fotografico Musei Vaticani, Vat.-FAK 2176/51. *(Reproduced courtesy of the Vatican Museums.)*

transenna had been worn by the passage of feet, which shows that it must have been reused as a pavement with the original face buried. Identification is made difficult by the fact that the *transenna* is formed of two groups made up of a total of five fragments, rather than the three that feature in the list, yet there are no other balustrades that have been exhibited at the Lateran Museum. A *labrum* of large dimensions, restored and placed in the second room of the Lateran Museum in 1882, is rather interesting (**Fig. 10**).[24] This is a basin *c.* 1.2 m in diameter, which we can imagine was used in the bath-building described above. Today it is in the storerooms of the Vatican Museums.

A better-known sculptural find is undoubtedly the group consisting of a Satyr and young Dionysus, today in the Galleria dei Candelabri.[25] The main part of the group was found in fragments in the first half of 1854 and made a particular impression on the Commissario delle Antichità, Pietro Ercole Visconti. He wrote to the Ministro dei Lavori Pubblici, who was also responsible for archaeological excavations, in order to obtain the necessary funds to continue the search for the missing fragments, and received 50 scudi.[26] Pietro Galli restored the group from 1855.[27] Finally, we have mention of a series of other fragments, not all of them ancient, which were gathered together in the storerooms of the Lateran Museum.[28]

FIG. 7. Bust of Marcus Aurelius. Musei Vaticani, Museo Gregoriano Profano. Archivio Fotografico Musei Vaticani, Vat.-FAK 2169/61. *(Reproduced courtesy of the Vatican Museums.)*

On the basis of documents and the few unpublished notes, it is quite easy to establish, at least in general terms, the history of these excavations. However, it is much more difficult to give a more precise outline with a topographical interpretation that places the discoveries in their original structures (**Fig. 11**). The most interesting topographical element is obviously the mosaic (**Fig. 8**), which must have been the floor of a room, *c.* 14.30 x 13 m in size,[29] connected to the bath complex that Visconti discussed.[30] The adjacent Claudio-Neronian aqueduct must have supplied this bath complex. Probably we can attribute the *labrum* to

the same bath-building (**Fig. 10**). In this area many bath complexes have been discovered, which is not surprising, given the quite high social status of the area,[31] and the availability of water from the aqueduct. One might mention, for example, the Severan Baths (still partially visible at the crossroads between Via dell'Amba Aradam and Via dei Laterani[32]), the baths found under the Lateran Baptistery, which were most likely private,[33] and those excavated underneath the Folchi ward of the hospital of San Giovanni.[34]

Nevertheless, the baths seen by Visconti do not seem to have been found under the main part of the

FIG. 8. Polychrome mosaic in the Sala di Costantino. From B. Nogara, *I mosaici antichi conservati nei palazzi pontifici del Vaticano e del Laterano* (Milan, 1910). Archivio Fotografico Musei Vaticani, Vat. XXXV-30-101. *(Reproduced courtesy of the Vatican Museums.)*

Fɪɢ. 9. *Fragmentary transenna.* Musei Vaticani, Museo Gregoriano Profano. Archivio Fotografico Musei Vaticani, Vat.-FAK 2370/01. *(Reproduced courtesy of the Vatican Museums.)*

new monastery, between the Scala Santa and the aque-duct, as is usually thought.[35] The mosaic came to light only in 1853, when the excavations for the foundations had already finished.[36] Indeed, these excavations had ended in October 1852, while the most reliable account of the excavation of the mosaic, from November 1853, confirms in general terms that the discovery occurred 'when work was taking place … near the eminent sanctuary', but does not specify whether the mosaic was excavated in the area of the new monastery of the Passionist Fathers or in an adjacent area.[37] Perhaps the discovery can be linked to the excavations that were taking place in the same year for a conduit 'a few metres from the Scala Santa towards the south',[38] or one might consider even the area behind the sanctuary. Perhaps the group of the Satyr with the small Dionysus also can be linked to the bath complex, since, as noted above, they too were found later, in 1854.

At this point, it is useful to recall a series of unpublished or little-known finds that came from the same area. Apart from the discovery in 1857 of the funerary inscription *CIL* VI 12791 in the kitchen garden of the Scala Santa, it is not known what came to light during the work undertaken behind the Scala Santa for the foundations of a new basilica (1925), which was never completed, and for the extension of the chapel of San Lorenzo (1935).[39] It is likely that the discovery of several coins, ranging from the Julio-Claudian era to the modern age, was made during this work.[40]

On the southern side of the Scala Santa the road-works undertaken in 1958 in Piazza San Giovanni and in the tract between this and the northeastern corner of the Lateran Palace (**Fig. 11**, no. 4)[41] brought to light the remains of a structure in *opus mixtum*. This had a poly-chrome mosaic, which had been damaged by fire.

FIG. 10. *Labrum*. Magazzini Musei Vaticani. Archivio Fotografico Musei Vaticani, Vat. XXXIII-40-451.
(Reproduced courtesy of the Vatican Museums.)

Another room further to the west had walls constructed in the same building technique and originally covered with a marble veneer; it was paved with a fine polychrome mosaic depicting a labyrinth enclosed by a wall with battlements.[42] It is possible to hypothesize that this was part of the same complex within which the Vatican mosaic was found. We need more precise details to clear up several chronological problems, for which we must await the definitive publication. For example, the *opus mixtum* technique of the structures points to its construction in the first half of the second century AD, the mosaic with the labyrinth has been dated to the middle of the first century BC, and the Vatican mosaic seems to come from the age of Constantine (AD 306–37).[43]

It can be observed also that the orientation of the walls observed during the work of 1958 is different from that of the walls discovered by Lauer in the foun-dations of the *Sancta Sanctorum* (Fig. 11, no. 2).[44] In addition, they are also on a different orientation from the room beneath the Oratory of the Archiconfraternity of the Holy Sacrament (Fig. 11, no. 3).[45] On this subject, a digression is in order about these finds. In the foundations of the *Sancta Sanctorum* one can still see short tracts of wall that are difficult to understand and that must relate to different phases. It is possible to distinguish clearly at least two main phases: the first in brick (walls U and Y in Lauer's plan; Fig. 12) and the second in *opus listatum* (wall V) that cuts a pre-existing brick wall at a right angle (W_x). The latter phase is dated to the fifth or sixth century by the presence of the famous fresco of Saint Augustine.[46] On the basis of this fresco, the suggestion has been made that one should identify these remains as the first papal archive. As for the room under the oratory, it might be useful to say a

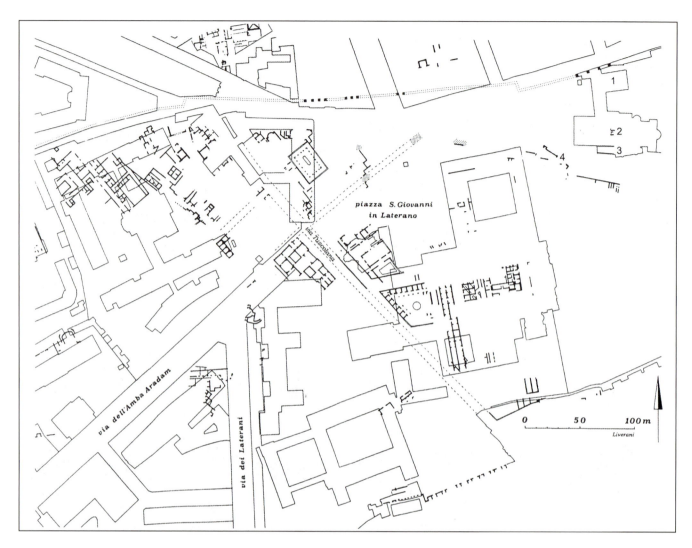

FIG. 11. Ancient topography of the area surrounding the sanctuary of the Scala Santa: 1. Monastery of the Passionist Fathers; 2. Lauer's excavations under the *Sancta Sanctorum*; 3. Structures under the Oratory of the Archiconfraternity of the Holy Sacrament; 4. The 1958 excavations of the Comune of Rome. *(Drawing: Paolo Liverani.)*

little more, since the interesting information published by Bertani has appeared only in a journal with limited circulation. On the southern side of the complex of the *Sancta Sanctorum* and the Scala Santa is the Oratory of the Archiconfraternity of the Holy Sacrament, oriented in an east–west direction. Beneath this, and on the same orientation, is a room still partially buried, roofed with a plastered cross-vault. The plaster preserves a simple polychrome decoration of good quality, consisting of geometric patterns with some vegetal motifs on a white background (**Fig. 13**). At a first and superficial glance, the frescoes seem to be Hadrianic. On the plaster there are traces of numerous drawings and inscriptions from the medieval and modern periods, some of them dating to 1661, 1792 and 1865. The room had been narrowed on its longest sides and closed on its short sides (east and west) by

walling-up carried out in post-antique times (**Figs 14–15**). Despite this, it is clear that the range of rooms must carry on beyond the walling-up.

CONCLUSIONS

I now shall attempt to summarize the information gathered here. The lack of any discoveries relating to the Lateran Palace remains a puzzle, since undoubtedly this was built over excavated Roman structures. This can be explained in part by the fact that Visconti was interested solely in the Roman phases, or rather Roman monuments with figurative art, and did not record medieval walls. It is likely that other objects came to light, given the presence of the medieval coins discussed above. It is less easy to understand

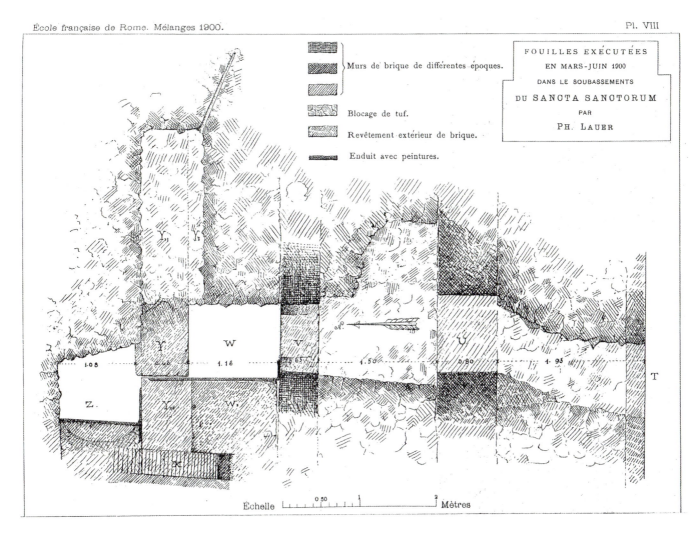

École française de Rome. Mélanges 1900.

Pl. VIII

Murs de brique de différentes époques.

Blocage de tuf.

Revêtement extérieur de brique.

Enduit avec peintures.

FOUILLES EXÉCUTÉES
EN MARS-JUIN 1900
DANS LE SOUBASSEMENTS
DU SANCTA SANCTORUM
PAR
PH. LAUER

Échelle 0 50   1   2 Mètres

FIG. 12. Ancient masonry discovered in the foundations of the *Sancta Sanctorum*. From P. Lauer, 'Les fouilles du Sancta Sanctorum au Lateran', *MEFR* 20 (1900), tav. VIII.

the lack of medieval finds in the excavations of 1958, but in this case too the excavation is virtually unpublished. In contrast, for the Roman phase it is possible to draw several topographical conclusions, as well as being able to restore a context and a provenance to a good number of sculptures. The different orientations of the different structures seen up to this point suggest that the core beneath the sanctuary of the Scala Santa — demonstrated by the walls preserved under the *Sancta Sanctorum* and the Oratory — relate to a different complex to the one uncovered during the excavations of 1958 to the south. The possibility remains that one can associate with this second nucleus the remains of the bath-building seen by Visconti in 1853. Finally, a mithraic cult centre must have been located in the surrounding area, as is shown by the sculptural group of Mithras slaying the bull.

APPENDIX

I.
MUSEI VATICANI, ARCHIVIO STORICO, B. 21, FASC. 2, ANNO 1853[47]

Nota delle sculture rinvenute nel cavo de' fondamenti fatto per la costruzione del Convento contiguo alla Scala Santa che esistevano nell'abitazione di S.E. R.ma Mons. Castellacci ed ora trasferite nel magazzeno del Museo Lateranense

1. Figura in mezza natura giacente sopra un delfino che guazza nelle acque la quale colla destra accarezza un uccello. Essa è frammentata ne' piedi, nelle braccia, e senza testa

2.3.4. Testa più grande del naturale barbata, rotta nel naso e in un orecchio; Testa al naturale mutilata ed altra frammentata di molto

Fɪɢ. 13. Fresco on the vault of the room beneath the Oratory of the Archiconfraternity of the Holy Sacrament. *(Photo: P. Liverani.)*

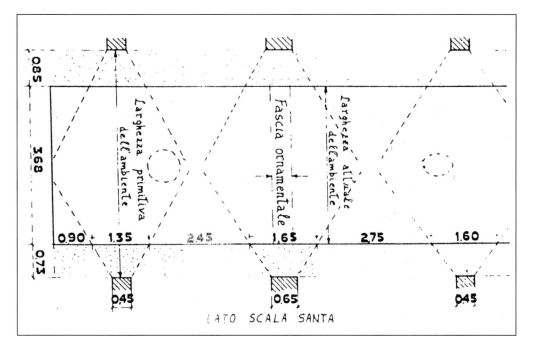

Fɪɢ. 14. Room beneath the Oratory of the Archiconfraternity of the Holy Sacrament, plan. After B. Bertani, 'I sotterranei della sede dell'Archiconfraternita lateranense del SS. Sacramento', *Alma Roma* 27 (3–4) (May–August 1986), fig. 2.

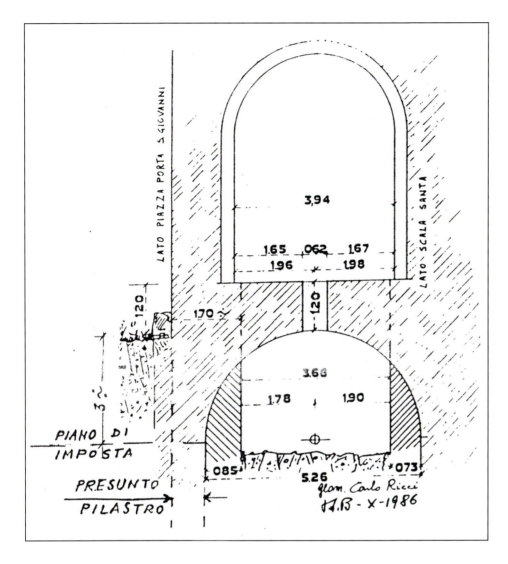

FIG. 15. **Room beneath the Oratory of the Archiconfraternity of the Holy Sacrament, section. After B. Bertani, 'I sotterranei della sede dell'Archiconfraternita lateranense del SS. Sacramento', *Alma Roma* 27 (3–4) (May–August 1986), fig. 1.

5. Busto muliebre al naturale senza testa panneggiato

6. Erme con testa d'Ercole alquanto guasto

7. Capitello d'ordine corintio

8.9. Parti di capitello uno composito, altro corintio

10.11. Parte superiore di capitello di fascia, frammento di fogliame di Capitello parimenti di fascia

12. Piede di sedile con zampa di leone ed ornato

13. Frammento di alto rilievo in cui apparisce una testa ed un vaso

14.15. Frammenti di pieghe

16.17. Piccole basi una delle quali ovale con due piedi di fanciullo, altra quadra con piede di donna e parte della veste

18.19.20.21.22. Piccoli frammenti di bassorilievi

23. Frammento di zampa di leone in granito

24.25. Frammenti di piccole gambe

26. Frammento di braccio

27.28.29.30.31. Frammenti di Cornici con ornato

32.33.34. Piccoli torsi frammentati

35.36. Frammenti di braccio con serpe attortigliato

37. Mascherone in alto rilievo

38. Frammento di piccola cornice angolare con fusarola dentelli fogliame ec

39. Frammento di cinerario rotondo rappresentante una Caccia

40. Parte di un'ala di spogritto [sic!]

41. Piccola base di colonna

42. Piccolo rotondo di marmo con Foglie d'Acanto

43. Frammento di lapide colla seguente iscrizione

NIS LV M II D X D

RT IN PACE

CEM SVAM.A[48]

44. Titoletto frammentato coll'iscrizione seguente

M.S

NI EVTYCHIDES

VALERIANA

FECIT[49]

I suddescritti oggetti furono ricevuti il giorno 18 ottobre 1853

Giovanni Forti P(ri)mo Custode

II.
MUSEI VATICANI, ARCHIVIO STORICO, B. 21, FASC. 2, ANNO 1858[50]

Nota degli oggetti di scultura/ rinvenuti nel cavo de' fondamenti del Convento contiguo alla Scala santa edificato dalla Munificenza della Santità di N.S. Pio Papa IX e ricevuti nel Pontificio Palazzo Lateranense

(1)   Una bellissima Testa di M. Aurelio Antonino il filosofo frammentata nel naso e nelle orecchie la quale restaurata e posta sopra un busto esistente ne' Magazzini Vaticani, ora adorna il Museo Lateranense

(2)   Figurina muliebre frammentata senza braccia, senza testa di buon lavoro collocata nel Museo Lateranense

(3)   Tre frammenti di balaustra di buona scultura esistenti nel Museo Lateranense

(4)   Busto muliebre senza testa collocato nel Museo Lateranense

(5)   Tazza di bellissima breccia antica frammentata e senza piede la quale restaurata ora esiste nel Museo Lateranense

(6)   Graziosissimo Gruppo di un Amore sopra un delfino in atto di scherzare con un'Anitra senza testa e senza braccia e frammentato ne' piedi il quale restaurato esiste nel Museo Lateranense

(7)   Frammento di un Torso di fauno bellissimo avente sulle spalle un frammento di un piccolo Bacco che ora sta restaurandosi per lo scultore Galli

III.
MUSEI VATICANI, ARCHIVIO STORICO, B. 21, FASC. 2, ANNO 1858[51]

Nota de' frammenti rinvenuti nel suddetto luogo/ e depositati nel Magazzeno del Museo Lateranense perché riconosciuti di nessun valore

(1)   Frammento di zampa di sfinge in Granito

(2)   Frammento di zampa di Cane parimenti in Granito[52]

(3)   Una piccola Testa muliebre frammentata[53]

(4)   Due mattoni con bollo

(5)   Frammento di Mascherone ed altri piccoli frammenti di cattiva scultura[54]

(6)   Frammento d'Erma in cattivo stato[55]

(7)   Frammento di Capitello in pessimo stato d'ordine corintio[56]

(8)   Frammento di una Testa di fauno con vaso[57]

(9)   Due Teste incognite molto mutilate

(10) Piccola base[58] e parte di Capitello in cattivo stato[59]

(11) Frammento di piccola colonna a spirale

(12) Frammento di piccola colonna bizantina a spira

(13) Piccolo pilastro quadro bizantino scorniciato

(14) Frammento di pilastrino scorniciato in due pezzi parimenti bizantino

(15) Frammento di ornato bizantino

(16) Frammento di stemma Pontificio colle imprese di Alessandro VI sostenuto da putti parimente frammentati

In fede li 17 Novembre 1858.
Giovanni Forti Custode

Notes

* This article is dedicated to the memory of Fabrizio Mancinelli, friend and work colleague for a decade, and taken from us too soon. After he directed the extremely important restoration of the frescoes and mosaics of the *Sancta Sanctorum*, he proposed to undertake a comprehensive study of this building and asked me to aid him with the problems of topography in the ancient and medieval periods. I hope to fulfil this request in full in the near future, but in the meantime I present here the preliminary results. By chance, the most prestigious find from the excavation considered here is the mosaic that, having been set into the pavement of the Sala di Costantino for almost 150 years, constitutes an integral part of the decoration of the Stanze di Raffaello in the Vatican. This is the complex to which Mancinelli devoted so much consideration and careful scholarship. The present contribution would not have taken shape without the suggestions, encouragement and help of Mario Cempanari, whom I thank sincerely. In particular, Cempanari directed me towards the list of finds to be found in the Appendix, no. I. He had found a copy of this list dating to the 1930s in the Scala Santa archive. Starting from this document, I have been able to rediscover the original in the Archivio Storico of the Vatican Museums and to widen the research to other archives.

1. Cf. M. Delle Rose, 'Il patriarchio: note storico-topografiche', in C. Pietrangeli (ed.), *Il Palazzo Apostolico Lateranense* (Florence, 1991), 19–27, 327–8.

2. P. Lauer, 'Les fouilles du Sancta Sanctorum au Latran', *Mélanges d'Archéologie et d'Histoire de l'École Française de Rome* 20 (1900), 251–87; also *AE* (1989), 75.

3. A.M. Colini, 'Storia e topografia', *MemPontAcc* 7 (1944), 361–4.

4. On these events, cf. M. Cempanari, 'Il collegio sistino delle Scale Sante ad Sancta Sanctorum (1590–1893)', *Mélanges de l'École Française de Rome. Italie et Méditerranée* 103 (1991), 521–71; M. Cempanari, 'Pio IX e il riordinamento del Santuario della Scala Santa', in *Pio IX. Studi e ricerche sulla vita della Chiesa dal Settecento a oggi* XIX (2) (Vatican City, 1990), 109–72. Also L. Donadono, *La Scala Santa a San Giovanni in Laterano* (Rome, 2000), 49–55.

5. 'Note on the sculpture found in the foundation trench made for the construction of the monastery next to the Santa Scala, which lay in the dwelling of His Excellency the Most Reverend Mons. Castellacci and now transferred to the storerooms of the Lateran Museum.'

6. Appendix, nos. I(1), II(6); Musei Vaticani, Gregoriano Profano, inv. 9575. Cf. A. Nibby, *Itinerario di Roma e delle sue vicinanze* (revised by A. Valenti) (Rome, 1861[7]), 157 (with an incorrect date for the excavation, 1854); O. Benndorf and R. Schöne, *Die Antiken Bildwerke des Lateranensischen Museums* (Leipzig, 1867), 240 no. 366. For the restoration, cf. ASV, Palazzo Ap., Computisteria 1838, fasc. 25 (25 August 1855, transportation to Laboreur's atelier at Piazza dell'Oca); fasc. 28 (3 September 1855, start of the restoration); fasc. 52 (7 July 1856, marble for the restoration); 1861, fasc. 23 (17

July 1856, transportation from Laboreur's atelier to the Museum; 18 August 1856, placement on its base at the Museum.

7. Appendix, nos. I(5), II(4); Musei Vaticani, Gregoriano Profano, inv. 10307. Cf. A. Giuliano, *Catalogo dei ritratti romani del Museo Profano Lateranense* (Vatican City, 1957), 85 no. 104, tav. 62. Giuliano's uncertainty about this bust and no. 105 can be resolved in favour of the first, since this one was put on display, as can be seen in the *Nota* of 1858 (Appendix, no. II).

8. Musei Vaticani, Gregoriano Profano, inv. 9806. Cf. C. Vorster, 'Die Herme des fellbekleideten Herakles. Typenwandel und Typenwanderung in hellenistischer und römischer Zeit', *Kölner Jahrbuch für Vor- und Frühgeschichte* 21 (1988), 7–12. Identification is possible thanks to a note in the old inventory register of the Lateran Museum, which gives its provenance as the Scala Santa. The entry date given here (1909) probably refers to its display in the third room of the old museum; before this, it must have been in the storerooms.

9. *ICUR* 1852.5 (Musei Vaticani, Lapidario Cristiano ex Lateranense, inv. 33797). The text is actually more extensive than that given in the *Nota*: [---?]/ [--]+++[--]/ [dep. k]al iun que vix[it]/ [post ob]itum suum annu I[--?]// [-- an]nis LV m. II d. X de[p]/ [-- m]art. in pace/ [--]+cem suam a[--?]/ [---?]. Some clarification is needed in respect of the reading of the *ICUR* entry: l. 1, the first letter could be O, C, or G, as could the second (C in *ICUR*), the third A, M, or less probably X; l. 4, d[ep] *ICUR*; l. 5, [ma]rt *ICUR*. The slab clearly is reused since it has been recut without regard to the text of the inscription.

10. *CIL* VI 17449 (Musei Vaticani, Lapidario Profano ex Lateranense, sett. z, 26v, inv. 26844): [D.] M. S. / [--]ni. Eutychides /[--] Valeriana / [--] fecit. To the right and underneath the table, in pieces, there were unidentifiable remains of the figurative decoration.

11. ASV, Fondo part. Pio IX (cass. no. 16). See Donadono, *La Scala Santa* (above, n. 4), 54.

12. Musei Vaticani, Gregoriano Profano, inv. 9933. Cf. Nibby, *Itinerario* (above, n. 6), 155 and n. 1 (with an incorrect date for the excavation, 1854); Benndorf and Schöne, *Die Antiken Bildwerke* (above, n. 6), 117–18 no. 199; V. Tizzani, *La statua equestre di Marco Aurelio* (Rome, 1880), 20; Colini, 'Storia e topografia' (above, n. 3), 363; M.J. Vermaseren, *Corpus Inscriptionum et Monumentorum Religionis Mithriacae* (The Hague, 1956), 164 no. 370; W. Helbig, *Führer durch die Öffentlichen Sammlungen Klassischer Altertümer in Rom* I (Tübingen, 1963[4]), no. 1036.

13. 'Nel fare una conduttura pochi metri distante dalla Scala Santa verso il sud'. P.E. Visconti, in *Giornale di Roma* 266 (23 November 1853), 1061.

14. Appendix, nos. I(2), II(1); Musei Vaticani, Gregoriano Profano, inv. 10223. Cf. J.J. Bernoulli, *Römische Ikonographie* II (2) (Stuttgart/Berlin/Leipzig, 1891), 168 no. 23; Benndorf and Schöne, *Die Antiken Bildwerke* (above, n. 6), 15; Tizzani, *La statua equestre* (above, n. 12), 20; Giuliano, *Catalogo* (above, n. 7), 57, no. 63, tavv. 39, 61; Vermaseren, *Corpus* (above, n. 12), 164 no. 371; H. von Heintze, in Helbig,

Führer (above, n. 12), no. 1095; M. Wegner, *Die Herrscherbildnisse in Antoninischer Zeit* (Berlin, 1939), 193–4; M. Wegner, 'Verzeichnis der Kaiserbildnisse von Antoninus Pius bis Commodus', *Boreas* 2 (1979), 169. For the restoration, cf. ASV, Palazzo Ap., Computisteria 1816, fasc. 28: 'Busto semicolossale di Marco Aurelio: adattata una testa antica di d° imperatore ad un busto parimenti antico, aggiuntovi porzione del collo e fattoci n. 8 tasselli in marmo; la spina ed il pieduccio nuovo' ('Semicolossal bust of Marcus Aurelius: an ancient head of the said emperor attached to a bust equally ancient, part of the neck added and eight restorations; new support and base'). More than eight restorations can be seen on the bust, but it is possible that some of the folds of the drapery had been restored previously.

15. Visconti, in *Giornale di Roma* 266 (above, n. 13), 1061; G. Melchiorri, *Guida metodica di Roma e suoi contorni* (Rome, 1856), 503; Nibby, *Itinerario* (above, n. 6), 155 and n. 1, and p. 568 (with an incorrect date for the excavation, 1854); Tizzani, *La statua equestre* (above, n. 12), 20 (with an incorrect date for the excavation, 1852, and attributed to the work on the monastery of the Passionist Fathers); G. Stern, *Collezione di pavimenti classici a mosaico* (Turin, 1889), tav. VI (with liberties taken in the drawings); B. Nogara, *I mosaici antichi conservati nei palazzi pontifici del Vaticano e del Laterano* (Milan, 1910), 7–8, tavv. x–xiv; M. Blake, 'Roman mosaics of the second century in Italy', *Memoirs of the American Academy of Rome* 13 (1936), 124, 180, tav. 26.4; G.M.A. Hanfmann, *The Season Sarcophagus in Dumbarton Oaks* II (Cambridge (Mass.), 1951), 156 n. 222; K. Parlasca, in Helbig, *Führer* (above, n. 12), no. 601; L. Abad Casal, *LIMC* V (1990), 523 *sub voce* Kairoi/ Tempora Anni, no. 108, tav. 359; K. Werner, *Mosaiken aus Rom. Polychrome Mosaikpavimente und Emblemata aus Rom und Umgebung* (Würzburg, 1994), 150–2, K 60; G. Canuti, 'I mosaici con raffigurazioni delle stagioni in Italia', in *Atti del 1° Colloquio Associazione Italiana per lo Studio e la Conservazione del Mosaico 1993* (Ravenna, 1994), 95–6 no. 36, 524–5 no. 37; K. Werner, *Die Sammlung Antiker Mosaiken in den Vatikanischen Museen* (Vatican City, 1998), 262–7.

16. ASR, Ministero dei Lavori Pubblici, b. 373, fasc. 2a. The *Giornale di Roma* 98 (30 April 1855), 397, describes it as already in its new location.

17. 'A foro Lateran(ense) prope aedem Sanctiorem / hoc traslat(um) munificentia Pii IX p(ontifici) m(aximi) an(no pontificatus) IX.'

18. 'Un grande bagno: luogo già sontuosamente ornato, come si dimostra dagli avanzi di colonne e di capitelli corinti, dai fregi scolpiti e da frammenti di nobili marmi.' P.E. Visconti, in *Giornale di Roma* 258 (14 November 1853), 1029. Also Colini, 'Storia e topografia' (above, n. 3), 363.

19. 'In prossimità del luogo nel quale s'è scoperto il grande musaico a colori.' Visconti, in *Giornale di Roma* 266 (above, n. 13): 'si sono trovate due monete in argento che hanno pregio di rarità nella numismatica pontificia. Sono due denari di Leone III … Le monete, diverse nel conio, sono uguali nel tipo, che il Vignali prima e poi il Salvaggi pubblicarono cogli altri delle più antiche monete dei Papi. Nel diritto si vede nel centro in nesso di lettere: *Leo Papa*. Nell'esterno è scritto: *Sanctus Petrus*. Sta nel rovescio, similmente nel centro, il nesso … cioè *Hlotarius Imperatori* … all'intorno della moneta hlotarius. Si è pure trovato un piombo di Celestino III, che ha nell'anteriore parte i capi de' Santi Apostoli Pietro e Paolo colle iniziali de' loro nomi, e nell'altra l'iscrizione celestinus pp iii; piombo appeso già a una bolla di quel pontefice, del quale ci presenta ora la memoria' ('Two silver coins were found that have the value of rarity in the papal numismatics. They are two denarii of Leo IV… The coins, from different minting dies, are of the same type, which were published first by Vignali and then by Salvaggi with other examples of the most ancient papal coins. On the reverse in the centre can be seen the joined letters: *Leo Papa*. On the outside is written: *Sanctus Petrus*. On the other side, similarly at the centre, the link … that is, *Hlotarius Imperatori* … on the margin of the coin *hlotarius*. Also found was a seal of Celest III, which has on the front the heads of the Holy Apostles Peter and Paul with the initials of their names, and on the other side the inscription *celestinus pp iii*; the seal was once part of a stamp of that pontiff, of whom it now reminds us').

20. P.E. Visconti, in *Giornale di Roma* 9 (12 January 1854), 35; taken up by G. Moroni, *Dizionario di erudizione storico-ecclesiastica* LXVII (Venice, 1854), 106, *sub voce* Sisto V. The discoveries occurred 'coll'occasione dei lavori, che si proseguono presso l'edificio del Sancta Sanctorum' ('when work was taking place near the Sancta Sanctorum building'). Besides the coins, Visconti also noted the discovery of 'una statuetta di bello stile' ('a beautiful statuette'), not more fully described, which possibly could be identified with that in the Appendix, no. II(2).

21. 'Figurina muliebre frammentata senza braccia, senza testa di buon lavoro collocata nel Museo Lateranense': Appendix, no. II(2). This could be the following statue: inv. 9839 (Benndorf and Schöne, *Die Antiken Bildwerke* (above, n. 6), 139 no. 222; Giuliano, *Catalogo* (above, n. 7), 31 no. 34, tavv. 13, 60; Helbig, *Führer* (above, n. 12), no. 1031), which has an inscription on the base — 'Munificentia Pii IX Pont. Max.'. However, its description as a 'figurine' raises a problem, since this cannot be reconciled with the life-size dimensions of the statue.

22. 'Tre frammenti di balaustra di buona scultura esistenti nel Museo Lateranense.'

23. Appendix, no. II(3); inv. 9605–6. Cf. Benndorf and Schöne, *Die Antiken Bildwerke* (above, n. 6), 47 nos. 73–73a.

24. Appendix, no. II(5); Musei Vaticani, Magazzino ex Ponteggi, inv. 54618. Cf. Nibby, *Itinerario* (above, n. 6), 155 and n. 1 (with an incorrect date for the excavation, 1854). For its location in the Museum, cf. ASV, Palazzo Ap., Computisteria 1882, fasc. 23: 'Dallo Scalpellino Camillo Scagnoli, fu restaurata una Tazza Antica di Africano lumachellato, rinvenuta presso la Scala Santa al Laterano, e collocata nel Museo Gregoriano Lateranense — Lavoro eseguito sotto la direzione del Comm. De Fabris, Direttore. / Detta Tazza era rotta in quattro pezzi che furono riuniti, era mancante di gran parte del

labbro e fu riportato con pezzi tagliati dalla stessa pietra; poi furono applicati n. 3 pezzi di *peperino* attaccati in mistura con sopra i vecchi pezzi di impellicciatura interna ed esterna. / Fatti n. 22 tasselli fra grandi e piccoli e cioè n. 12 nella parte esterna e n. 10 nella parte interna, e fatta la pelle piana e patinati. Incassata la staffa a madrevite di metallo onde ingallettarla al pieduccio, e ricavato il pieduccio fermato con perno di metallo. / Fatto la base con marmo chiaro di carrara per il piedestallo che sorregge la tazza' ('By the sculptor Camillo Scagnoli was restored an ancient basin of African lumachella-type marble, which was found near the Scala Santa at the Lateran, and placed in the Gregorian Lateran Museum — Work was carried out under the direction of Commander De Fabris, Director. / The said basin was broken into four pieces that were joined together again, a large part of the lip was missing and it was repaired with pieces cut from the same stone; then three pieces of *peperino* were attached with glue to the old pieces of the internal and external veneer. / Twenty-two large and small restorations were made, that is twelve on the outside and ten inside, and the surface was smoothed and patinated. Fitted the metal nut thread clip by which it was attached to the base, and secured the base with a metal pivot. / Made the base with white Carrara marble for the pedestal that supports the basin'). Cf. also ASV, Palazzo Ap., Computisteria 1882, fasc. 23, payment of 28 October 1857 for the transportation of the basin and its base to the Museum.

25. Musei Vaticani, Galleria dei Candelabri II.40, inv. 2555. Cf. G. Lippold, *Die Skulpturen des Vaticanischen Museums* III (2) (Berlin, 1956), 262–3, no. 40, tav. 121; C. Pietrangeli, in Lippold, *Die Skulpturen* (above), 547, no. 40. On the plinth is the inscription: 'Munificentia Pii IX P.M. anno XXIII. Effossa e ruderibus ad Sancta Sanctorum' ('A gift of Pius IX, Pontifex Maximus, in the year 23. Dug up from the ruins at the Sancta Sanctorum').

26. ASR, Ministero dei Lavori Pubblici, b. 397, fasc. 11 (P.E. Visconti to the Ministro dei Lavori Pubblici, 2 June 1854): 'Una scoperta ben rilevante si è di recente fatta nel luogo presso la Scala Santa, dove si sta edificando una nuova casa per i PP. Passionisti. Consiste essa scoperta nel ritrovamento della maggior parte d'un gruppo in marmo di notevole grandezza, rappresentante un Fauno, che sostiene sul collo Bacco bambino … / Avendo il Santo Padre assegnato ai PP. Passionisti cospicua somma per la fabrica ed essendo stato di sua munificenza l'acquisto del suolo, hanno i religiosi dato già, e sono per dare, quanto di pregevole e d'antico è avvenuto loro di scoprire per ornamento de' pontifici musei senza pagamento alcuno. Essi però non han mezzi a continuare le ricerche e il profittare dell'occasione per tentare un luogo, che ha già dato tre statue, un grandissimo musaico e molti pregevoli frammenti, parmi di tanta importanza e di tanto utile che ho stimato dovere del mio ufficio farlo presente all'Ecc.enza V.ra Rev.ma. / I religiosi, che in progresso di tempo non vedrebbero volentieri lo scavo, ne sono adesso contenti. La somma da erogarsi da potersi prendere sull'imprevisti, sarebbe dai 50 ai 100 scudi e dove si riuscisse a trovare solo qualcuna delle parti mancanti del gruppo, che

nello stato attuale non può stimarsi meno di scudi 300, il valore sarebbe portato agli scudi 800 e forse ad altro maggiore' ('A particularly important discovery was made recently near the Scala Santa, where a new home for the Passionist Fathers is being built. This discovery consists of the greater part of a marble group of notable size, representing a Faun supporting a baby Bacchus on his shoulders … / Since the Holy Father has given a considerable sum to the Passionist Fathers for the building and since the land was acquired through his munificence, the fathers have given already, and are about to give, free of charge, whatever of value or antiquity that they have happened to discover for the adornment of the papal museums. However, they do not have the means to continue the investigation. Since it seems to me to be of great importance and extremely useful to profit from the opportunity to probe a place that already has given up three statues, a very large mosaic and many valuable fragments, I thought it necessary for my office to draw it to the attention of Your Most Reverend Excellency. / The monks are happy about it, since over the course of time they themselves would not consider willingly an excavation. The amount of money needed to be able to profit from this unforeseen discovery should be between 50 and 100 scudi, and should we succeed in finding even one of the missing parts of the group, which in its present state cannot be valued at less than 300 scudi, the value would rise to 800 scudi or even more').

27. ASV, Palazzo Ap., Computisteria 1838, fasc. 38 (cost estimate, 20 November 1855; copy in Musei Vaticani, Archivio Storico, b. 20a, 1855); fasc. 41 (21 November 1855, transportation to Galli's atelier). The third and last instalment of the payment was in 1869 (Musei Vaticani, Archivio Storico, b. 20).

28. Appendix, no. III; cf. the notice already given dating to 1 June 1854 (ASV, Palazzo Ap., Computisteria 1816, fasc. 21) according to which 'da Gennaro Viola furono presi diversi oggetti dalla Scala Santa e portati al Magazzino al Laterano' ('various objects from the Scala Santa were taken from Gennaro Viola and carried to the Lateran storeroom').

29. Such dimensions can be extracted from the documents cited above relating to the lifting and restoration of the mosaic. According to Visconti, in *Giornale di Roma* 9 (above, n. 20), the dimensions should be, instead, 60.5 × 56 *palmi romani* (c. 13.51 × 14.07 m). Today the dimensions of the mosaic are 12.95 × 10.35 m.

30. Visconti, in *Giornale di Roma* 258 (above, n. 18).

31. P. Liverani, 'Le proprietà private nell'area lateranense fino all'età di Costantino', *Mélanges de l'École Française de Rome. Antiquité* 100 (1988), 891–915.

32. Colini, 'Storia e topografia' (above, n. 3), 334–9.

33. G. Pelliccioni, *Le nuove scoperte sulle origini del Battistero Lateranense* (*MemPontAcc* 12(1)) (Vatican City, 1973); R. Neudecker, *Die Pracht der Latrine* (Munich, 1994), 100–1, fig. 54.

34. V. Santa Maria Scrinari, 'Il Laterano e le fornaci di epoca imperiale', in K. de Fine Licht (ed.), *Città e architettura nella Roma imperiale* (*Analecta Romana Instituti Danici*

Supplementa 10) (Odense, 1983), 203–18; Liverani, 'Le proprietà' (above, n. 31), 895; V. Santa Maria Scrinari, *Il Laterano imperiale* II. *Dagli 'Horti Domitiae' alla cappella cristiana* (Vatican City, 1995), 174–91, who revived the improbable interpretation that it was the furnace of the bath complex.

35. Thus, for example, Colini, 'Storia e topografia' (above, n. 3), 363.

36. Cempanari, 'Pio IX' (above, n. 4), 131–2.

37. 'In occasione dei lavori … presso l'insigne santuario.' Visconti, in *Giornale di Roma* 258 (above, n. 18), 1029.

38. 'Pochi metri distante dalla Scala Santa verso il sud.' Visconti, in *Giornale di Roma* 9 (above, n. 20); Moroni, *Dizionario* LXVII (above, n. 20), 106.

39. A. Petrignani, *Il santuario della Scala Santa nelle sue successive trasformazioni, dalle sue origini ai recenti lavori per l'ampliamento della Cappella di S. Lorenzo* (Vatican City, 1941), 82–6, figs 50–1.

40. I have been able to examine these coins thanks to the kind cooperation of Mario Cempanari. As of Germanicus: H. Mattingly, *Coins of the Roman Empire in the British Museum* I (London, 1976²), 158 nos. 74–8 (AD 40–1). As of Nero: Mattingly, *Coins of the Roman Empire* (above), 247, no. 246. Bronze coin, probably Neronian (REV: profile facing right; OB: winged Victory moving to left with a palm branch and wreath in her hands, greatly damaged surface). Sestertius of Commodus: H. Mattingly, *Coins of the Roman Empire in the British Museum* IV (London, 1968²), 670 no. 1657 (AD 177). Bronze coin of the Tetrarchic era, perhaps similar to C.H.V. Sutherland and R.A.G. Carson, *The Roman Imperial Coinage* VI (London, 1967), 365 no. 125 (Constantius Chlorus), but from a different mint. Bronze coin from Arabia. Seventeenth-century coin (on one side the image of a saint and the legend 'Sanctus Paulus'). Bronze coin with unrecognizable papal coat of arms. Lead seal. Four illegible coins. The coins are preserved now by the Passionist Fathers.

41. M. Nota Santi, 'Attività del Comune per la topografia di Roma e della Campagna Romana. La zona del Laterano', *Archeologia Laziale* 1 (1978), 3–4, fig. 4, tav. I.2. For its location within the general topography, cf. Liverani, 'Le proprietà' (above, n. 31), tav. I; P. Liverani, 'L'ambiente nell'antichità', in C. Pietrangeli (ed.), *S. Giovanni in Laterano* (Florence, 1990), table on pp. 26–7.

42. See the entry on 'Piazza S. Giovanni in Laterano', *BullCom* 83 (1972–3), 53; Werner, *Mosaiken aus Rom* (above, n. 15), 68–9, K 21.

43. Werner, *Die Sammlung* (above, n. 15), 262–7.

44. Lauer, 'Les fouilles' (above, n. 2), fig. 1, tav. VIII.

45. B. Bertani, 'La sede dell'arciconfraternita lateranense del SS. Sacramento', *Alma Roma* 20 (6) (September–December 1979), 15–23; B. Bertani, 'Le fondazioni del 'Sancta Sanctorum'', *Alma Roma* 21 (3–4) (May–August 1980), 29–39; B. Bertani, 'I sotterranei della sede dell'Arci-confraternita lateranense del SS. Sacramento', *Alma Roma* 27 (3–4) (May–August 1986), 79–96; B. Bertani, 'Sulle tracce delle 'Aedes Lateranorum' nei sotterranei dell'Arciconfra-

ternita lateranense del SS. Sacramento', *Alma Roma* 31 (5–6) (September–December 1990), 163–79; B. Bertani, 'Proposte e studi per una più approfondita conoscenza del Patriarchìo Lateranense', *Alma Roma* 33 (3–4) (May–August 1992), 97–107. The essential information can be found in the article of 1986. Some observations also have been made in L. Donadono, 'In margine alle celebrazioni sistine. La Scala Santa (1586–1853): nuove acquisizioni', *Roma Moderna e Contemporanea* 2 (1) (1994), 254–5, n. 23.

46. G. Matthiae and M. Andaloro, *Pittura romana del medioevo. Secoli IV–X* (Rome, 1987), 123–53.

47. Cf. also ASV, Fondo part. Pio IX (cass. no. 16): 'Registro delle carte e documenti diversi', 'Nota degli oggetti rinvenuti nel cavo de' fondamenti', and letter 'g'.

48. *ICUR* 1852.5.

49. Fragment of a sarcophagus cover or cinerary urn, *CIL* VI 17449.

50. The numeration in brackets is not original, but has been added for ease of reference.

51. The numeration in brackets is not original, but has been added for ease of reference.

52. Cf. Appendix, no. I(23).

53. Missing from Appendix, I, unless this refers to no. 2.

54. Cf. Appendix, no. I(37).

55. This does not seem to be identifiable with Appendix, no. I(6).

56. Cf. Appendix, no. I(7 or 9).

57. Cf. Appendix, no. I(13).

58. Cf. Appendix, no. I(12 or 17).

59. Cf. Appendix, no. I(7 or 9).

Records of the Excavations of 1836 in the Sabine Necropolis of Poggio Sommavilla and of the Activities of Melchiade Fossati

Giorgio Filippi

ARCHAEOLOGICAL SITE — DOCUMENTARY SOURCES — MAIN CHARACTERS

Poggio Sommavilla is a small village located in the northern Sabina Tiberina, that is on the eastern bank of the Tiber, in the province of Rieti, about 70 km to the north of Rome. Today it is part of the *Comune* of Collevecchio Sabino (Fig. I).

The essential source of information for the reconstruction of the first excavations in the necropolis of Poggio Sommavilla is a dossier relating to the excavation concessions granted by the papal authorities, firstly to Benedetto Piacentini and later to Melchiade Fossati. This dossier is preserved in the Archivio di Stato di Roma.[1] A reference to the landowner in the Catasto Gregoriano, and the marked location of individual parcels of land on the accompanying map (Fig. 2), makes it possible to identify the precise place of the excavation. The personality and activities of the two principal characters can be reconstructed, not only from the above-mentioned documents, but, for Piacentini, by directly approaching his heirs in Collevecchio Sabino and, for Fossati, from his correspondence and publications along with documents from the archive of the Museo di Parma, the Vatican Museums, the Archivio di Stato in Terni, the Archivio Segreto Vaticano, the Biblioteca Apostolica Vaticana, the Accademia di San Luca, the Deutsches Archäologisches Institut Rom, the Archivio del Vicariato in Rome, the Louvre and the *Comune* of Amelia.

THE ORGANIZATION OF THE PROTECTION OF ARTISTIC HERITAGE IN THE PAPAL STATES

Pope Pius VII's decree of 1 October 1802 gave overall authority in matters of the supervision and preservation of artistic heritage as a whole to the office of the Cardinal-Camerlengo, aided by the Ispettore di Belle Arti and the Commissario delle Antichità. The roles of these officials ranged from granting excavation licences to the supervision of the acquisition of works to be placed in public museums. In 1820, the Pacca Edict created a new and definitive organization dedicated to the protection of the artistic heritage.

Under the authority of the Cardinal-Camerlengo was the Commissione Generale Consultiva di Antichità e Belle Arti di Roma. This was presided over by the Monsignor Uditore of the Camerlengato and comprised the Ispettore delle Pitture Pubbliche in Rome, the Commissario delle Antichità, the Director of the Vatican Museums, the first Professor of Sculpture and a Professor of Architecture from the Accademia di San Luca. Under the above-mentioned Commissione were the Commissioni Ausiliarie di Belle Arti; these were set up in all the provinces of the States, and also had the job of monitoring carefully archaeological excavations and their documentation.[2]

FIG 1. G.D. Campiglia, Detail of the *Tavola generale della Provincia di Sabina*, 1743. *(Photo: G. Filippi.)*

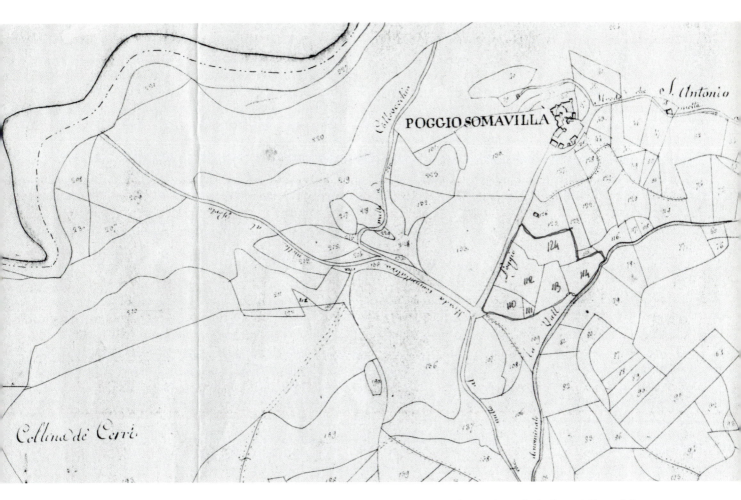

FIG. 2. Plan of the Ara de' Gelsi region where the excavations of 1836 were carried out (area indicated). Archivio di Stato di Roma, Catasto Gregoriano, Poggio Sommavilla; concessione ASR 38/2002. *(Photo: G. Filippi.)*

THE DISCOVERY

On the evening of 22 February 1836, around 11 p.m., Benedetto Piacentini was at his Collevecchio mill. He was advised by a workman that a few hours previously the peasants assigned to working on one of his estates, known as Ara de' Gelsi, had seen the earth collapse under the feet of their oxen. Discovering an underground cavern, they had entered and removed several vases. He went to the place, and observed that all but a few of the vases had been broken, because they had been excavated with pickaxes. He made the peasants stop excavating, forbade them all from entering the cavern and, collecting the fragments, returned to his home town of San Polo. The pouring rain and the bursting banks of the Laia stream prevented him from returning to the place for several days. When his son, Tommaso, in the company of two men, finally was able to reach the site, he found it devastated.[3]

BENEDETTO PIACENTINI

Benedetto Piacentini came from a family of Emilian extraction. He was the son of a doctor who had married Rosa Rinaldi in the Sabine town of San Polo. Rosa was the sister of the vicar of the parish, a Monsignor of a local family of means. Having completed his study of law, Benedetto became a lawyer and practised his profession at Collevecchio from 1808 to 1829. He married Ernestina Felli, who bore him five children: Giuseppe, Pietro, Brigida, Tommaso and Giovanni. He can be considered the progenitor of the complex Sabine family group of the Piacentini, which owned considerable property at San Polo, Collevecchio, Rome and other places.

Giuseppe (1803–77) became his great-uncle Monsignor Rinaldi's heir, on condition that he assumed his uncle's surname, studied law and excelled in it swiftly in the Roman courts. In 1847, he was appointed a member of the Consulta di Stato for finance and administration, created by Pius IX; in 1870 he was elected deputy for the constituency of Poggio Mirteto, and in the same year he was also elected Senator. His line is extinct. From Tommaso can be traced the origins of the so-called Torri in Sabina branch. Giovanni (1825–1901) was the progenitor of the Collevecchio branch, for, in the division of the patrimonial lands, he was assigned the rich estates located in the territory of this area. These included the palazzo built to a Sangallo design by Monsignor Paolo Coperchi, Commissario Generale of the Reverenda Camera Apostolica at the time of Clement VIII (1592–1605), and the fiefdom of Poggio Sommavilla, both once the property of the Orsini family. Palazzo and fiefdom both derived from the endowment of the Collevecchian family by the Marchese Monsignor Pier Francesco De Rossi (1591–1673). De Rossi was a famous judge, Commissario Generale of the Camera Apostolica at the time of Paul V, and considered one of the most learned prelates at the time of Urban VIII. Chamber-tombs similar to those at Ara de' Gelsi were excavated in 1896 elsewhere on Giovanni's Poggio Sommavilla lands. The contents of these were scattered and divided between the museums of Florence, Boston and Copenhagen.[4] After the death of Gualtiero (1896–1977), son of Cesare (1857–1913) and grandson of Giovanni, the Collevecchio branch of the family also died out. Gualtiero was the last member of the Piacentini family dwelling in Collevecchio. At his home, he showed me several relics from old excavations and recounted to me an anecdote about his mother's visit, while pregnant with him, to the tombs that had just been discovered in 1896. In order to enter the tombs, she had had to be carried down in a sack. Following this, the Piacentini family relocated to Terni, and the palazzo was sold in 1982.

THE CONFISCATION OF THE FINDS AND PROSECUTION FOR CLANDESTINE EXCAVATIONS

Following the unexpected discovery of the first two tombs, the recovery of their contents and the visit made in April 1836 by the Commissione Generale Consultiva to see the finds at the house of Piacentini's son in Rome (Via di Santa Chiara 57), a 'licence to carry out excavations for the research of Antiquity' was given by the Camerlengo, Pier Francesco Galleffi.[5] At the end of the same year, the Camerlengo had not received 'the periodic lists of the finds recovered, in open contempt of the Edict of 7 April 1820, which

prescribes the things that must be carried out by those conducting excavations': thus, he brought an action against Piacentini and ordered the governor of Poggio Mirteto, the official responsible for the area, to verify where the finds were kept, to confiscate them and, having prohibited the continuation of any further excavation, to seal the locations where the finds were kept.[6] On 5 January 1837, the governor of Poggio Mirteto went to Collevecchio, where the objects found in the excavations were being kept. Being unable to find Piacentini or any member of his family at the house, he urgently summoned him from his home at San Polo. At 10 a.m., he managed to enter the Piacentini house together with the Uditore Legale, who undertook the role of clerk of the court, and two witnesses.[7]

In a room on the top floor of the palazzo, he identified around twenty bronze objects, fifteen terracotta vases and six figured vases with impressed decoration, six iron objects and 68 terracotta beads. He descended to the ground floor and entered a reception room that was lit by light from a loggia. Here, Piacentini showed him an intact black-glazed crater placed on a marble table. On one side of the crater there was a depiction of the figures of a king and a queen above a chariot pulled by four horses; on the other side there were two human figures. Piacentini declared that he did not have other ancient objects in his Poggio Sommavilla house, apart from a few fragments of little interest. The crater, with the other pieces, was moved to the apartment on the upper floor. This apartment was closed, the key to it confiscated, and it was secured, using a strip of paper and lacquered wax, with a 'seal representing the chariot of the sun' ('sugello rappresentante il carro del sole').

In response to the warning to stop all excavation on his lands, Piacentini promised to obey and declared himself willing to conform to the Camerlengo's directives. It was now 10 p.m. and too late to check the remaining fragmentary material kept at Poggio Sommavilla. Since Piacentini did not have the key to the room with him, the governor returned to his own home in Poggio Mirteto.[8] Thus opened a judicial inquest into the 'clandestine excavations', and eleven people from Greccio, a small village in the Rieti valley, who had worked on the Piacentini estate, were questioned.[9]

The governor of the Sabina presented Piacentini to the Camerlengo as a person of suspect character, and his son Giuseppe, the famous lawyer of the Roman Curia, as a man with influence in every government department. Untrustworthy right from the start, they had cast suspicion on the other son, Tommaso, whom they claimed had undertaken the excavations at night with the intention of hiding the finds of greatest value from the government, and even from his father. Moreover, they had ignored the suspension of work and undertook other excavations in the place where the necropolis was thought to extend. Contradictions had emerged from their declarations concerning the quantity of vases found in the first and second tombs. In conclusion, the governor had not been able to supervise Piacentini's excavations properly. His suggestions had not been listened to — for example, that an expert should be employed both to direct and to carry out the excavations, who could be taken into partnership for a small part of the enterprise where he did not want to venture the expense for the whole; and that adequate notice had to be given of the start of work so as to allow it to be checked by a person entrusted by the government. The previous October, Piacentini had sown grain right in the area of the burials, in order to give the impression that he had no intention of carrying out further excavations. Then, in December, he had sent for some 'mountain roughs' from the far-away village of Greccio to carry out deep excavations right up to Christmas Eve. He had covered with earth not just the areas in which burials had been found, perhaps because he believed that the governor, who has been absent from the province when the work had begun, would not hear of the excavations: the site was hidden and about 13 miles from the governor's home along a bad road, there had been frequent rain, and Piacentini had a close friendship both with the new prior and with the Uditore Legale of Collevecchio.[10]

THE SOCIETÀ PIACENTINI–FOSSATI

The events of the excavations, the visit by the Commissione and the sale of two vases to Giuseppe Baseggio, a merchant at Via del Babuino 42, were re-iterated in a defensive 'memorandum' presented to the Camerlengo at the beginning of February. Its subject was the proceedings brought at the expense of Benedetto Piacentini, which had disturbed his peace of mind and compromised his reputation. A third vase (the best, since it was intact and had unusual subject-matter and various inscriptions) remained unsold in his hands. The document stated Piacentini's innocence concerning the accusations against him and his correct, even wise, behaviour in notifying the discovery and in placing the objects uncovered at the disposal of the

authorities.[11] Ongoing negotiations about the excavations with the archaeologist Melchiade Fossati are mentioned for the first time in this document. These negotiations were completed on 26 February in Rome, at the home of Benedetto's son, Giuseppe Piacentini (in Via di Santa Chiara). The Contract of Association is as follows:[12]

1. Sig. Piacentini, owner of the land of Sommavilla al Tevere and other Sabine estates, concedes and gives to Sig. Melchiade Fossati from today the right to excavate antiquities in the said estates at his own expense, and according to the terms given here.

2. This concession will endure for a period of nine years, up to and including the year 1846.

3. Fossati will be responsible for the entire cost of the excavation, without Sig. Piacentini having to pay or to refund any amount of money.

4. Piacentini will be free to have the work supervised by the person he considers best.

5. Fossati will backfill the excavated earth in such a manner that agricultural work will not suffer.

6. He will not be able to excavate in cultivated fields, except after the harvest, just as he will not be able to excavate in the vicinity of factories, so that no damage is caused, otherwise Fossati will be obliged to rectify the damage.

7. If Fossati causes even involuntary damage to plants, or plantations, he will pay compensation at the end of each season.

8. Every evening he will deposit the finds made in a room of a sufficient size at Sommavilla, which Sig. Piacentini will supply free of charge, and he will make two different keys, one to be held by each of them.

9. Sig. Piacentini will supply free of charge two appropriate rooms for Fossati to live in, and a room suitable for the workmen.

10. Fossati will excavate where, and how, and with however many men he believes best.

11. Sig. Piacentini will permit Fossati to excavate as soon as the Camerlengato allows it, and from today Fossati will petition and obtain the permission for this excavation; and will do so every year, and, moreover, Fossati alone will be responsible to the most Eminent Camerlengo for as long as the present contract lasts, observing fully the laws concerning the matter, and Sig. Piacentini will remain completely free from responsibility.

12. Every three months, and at the end of every season, Fossati will divide the finds into two parts, and Sig. Piacentini will choose one of the two and the other will become the property of Fossati.

13. Excavations may take place even in the site, or sites, but in the following year, and in this Fossati is obliged not only to backfill but to pound the earth, so that it can be used again for threshing.

14. Should one of the parties succeed in gaining permission to excavate in the bordering lands, or near to those of Sig. Piacentini, the contracts will include both parties if it should please the partner who does not have the permission in question, and in this case the expense and the profit will be shared.

15. Having consented to this contract in the presence of qualified and trusted staff, neither Sig. Piacentini nor Sig. Fossati can cede or transfer the rights accorded to him to anyone for whatever reason or cause, otherwise the contract comes to an end; this excludes, however, the event of testate or intestate inheritance.

16. Sig. Fossati undertakes to restore and illustrate the objects, but does so at his own expense and may not make any claim for compensation.

17. Until Sig. Fossati begins the excavation, Sig. Piacentini retains the right to excavate ~~outside the territory of Sommavilla~~ wherever he pleases, and the finds will belong to him.

18. Should Sig. Piacentini find outside the territory of Sommavilla other suitable and profitable places for excavation during his agricultural work or for whatever reason, Fossati may help him to conduct an orderly excavation, and the finds will be divided in half as usual.

19. With the exception of objects of art, which will be divided as specified above, the building materials found in Sig. Fossati's excavations, be they rocks, tufa blocks or terracotta, will become the property of Sig. Piacentini.

20. Should Fossati, having the State's permission, remain inactive for a single season, and not undertake the work, the present contract will lapse as if it had never existed.

MELCHIADE FOSSATI

The family of Melchiade Fossati may have been of Ligurian origin, but it is attested at the beginning of the eighteenth century at Amelia, a small town in southern Umbria, once a diocesan seat. Fossati was born in Rome in 1798,[13] where he lived with his family: his father, Vincenzo, who practised as a lawyer and held the position of Vice-President of the Campo Marzio Rione; his mother, Vittoria Bernardelli, who was a native of

Corneto; his sister Marianna, who was two years older than him; his brother Tito, who was three years younger; and his uncle, Don Filippo, who was a priest.[14] About 1820, Fossati lived in the Trastevere quarter, at Arco de' Tolomei 3, where his father owned property.[15]

From a well-to-do family, Fossati was able to complete his studies of classical philology and antiquity in Rome in order to become an archaeologist. It is likely that the cultural environment and birthplaces of his parents influenced his education and choices. Modern Amelia had developed continuously through time, from the ancient Umbrian centre of Ameria, to become a Roman municipium that coincided topographically with the ancient town. Over the centuries, it had remained substantially unaltered. In quality and quantity of ancient remains, it was unique, particularly for its polygonal city walls (**Fig. 3**). Much the same can be said about Corneto, the birthplace of his mother, which was located at the edge of the high-ground of Monterozzi. Here, during those years, were found the best examples of Etruscan tomb paintings, and the town represented a continuation up to modern times of the Etruscan and Roman city of Tarquinia, which had grown up on the nearby hills of Civita.

THE RELIEFS OF THE COLOSSEUM

The name of Melchiade Fossati appears in the documents of the Camerlengo for the first time in 1821, in association with that of Emiliano Sarti, a fellow scholar. Together, they had asked Cardinal Pacca, the Camerlengo, if they could 'take detailed measurements of the Flavian amphitheatre', remove 'clutter and rubble' and, where needed, 'erect steps and scaffolding'. They were given permission, 'but only under the supervision of the Sig. Cavaliere Ingegner Valadier, adviser to the Commissione Generale Consultiva di Belle Arti and with the assistance of Sig. Ilari, Inspector for the Polizia dei Pubblici Monumenti'.[16] Sarti (1795–1849), his contemporary, a professor of Greek language and philology at the University of Rome, would become famous for his philological, epigraphic and topographical studies. He maintained good relations with Fossati, who procured inscriptions for his collection.[17]

THE EARLIEST EXCAVATIONS IN SOUTHERN ETRURIA

Tarquinia was the testing-ground for his 'freelance' profession. The years 1824–5 saw a period of research in the Monterozzi estates and in the two areas of Mantica and Dognaccia. The excavation permit was issued by Cardinal Pacca in June 1824 on the recommendation of the Commissione Ausiliaria di Belle Arti of Civitavecchia, which was formed of two members, the lawyer Pietro Manzi and Canon Alessandro Bianchi. To begin with, Fossati excavated on behalf of Lord Kinnaird, and later worked in association with other local people, including Carlo Avvolta.[18] In the Louvre, there is an Attic red-figure crater (inv. no. G 482) from the Fossati collection, its provenance given as Corneto.[19] Among the archival documents, there are statements and complaints about the removal of objects. Together with those relating to clandestine excavations, such documents are common in this period, and often relate to the time spent waiting for the issue of a licence (for example, at Vulci in 1828). They provide evidence that the laws in force were transgressed and of the serious difficulties faced by the central authorities, despite the strict legislation and the work of officials dedicated to the protection of the artistic and archaeological heritage.

In 1828, Fossati was given a permit to carry out excavations with the priest Don Carlo Cristofari at Montepizzo, in the territory of Viterbo.[20] In the same year, with the consent of the leaseholder, Bruschi Falgari, he entered into an association with the lawyer, Pietro Manzi, a member of the Commissione Ausiliaria, to excavate in the Civita estate on ground owned by the hospital of Santo Spirito in Sassia. The licence was issued on 17 May 1828. In 1830, four black and white mosaics depicting marine subjects were found, among other things; the drawings of these made *in loco* by Luigi Valadier have been preserved.[21] Fossati participated in the excavations at Vulci, which began in August 1828, in association with Vincenzo Campanari and the Candelori brothers.[22] This collective economic agreement contributed to the establishment of one of the 'most productive and rich' ('più produttive e ricche') campaigns of excavation in the history of archaeology. Campanari remained in association with Fossati alone from 1830 to 1834.[23] Although some items from Campanari's and Candelori's collections were acquired by the Papal Government,[24] there is no record of the place or phases of the sale of Fossati's share of the material. It is likely that part of Fossati's share was ceded to Campanari.[25] Two further excavation permits of 1830 can be connected to Fossati: the first in the territory of Tivoli, in association with Cavaliere Pietro Manzi; the second at Montalto di Castro, in the grounds of the deanery, in

FIG. 3. Wall in polygonal stonework in the ancient Umbrian centre of Ameria, drawn by Melchiade Fossati in 1835. Photo from the beginning of the twentieth century. *(Photo: G. Filippi.)*

association with Manzi, Don Giulio Caratelli and Giuseppe Biasi.[26]

Not all of the investigations into the above-mentioned excavations have met with the same success. At times, there is documentary evidence only of the preliminary proceedings relating to the issue of a licence. We do not always have the excavation reports with records of the objects discovered. In some cases, the lack of information can be made up for by the reports in the *Bullettino dell'Instituto di Corrispondenza Archeologica*, which gave particular attention to new finds.[27]

PARIS: A CONGENIAL PLACE

Fossati had scholarly and commercial relations with the circles of artists and antiquarians in Paris.[28] Here, in about 1832, he married Marguerite Geneviève Bissonnet, who gave birth to Matilde Fossati on 2 May 1833.[29] From this point, his travels and visits to France must have increased, since his family did not accompany him or move to Rome. In the records of marital status of his parish at Rome, he was recorded as a 'bachelor'.[30]

BETWEEN SOUTHERN ETRURIA AND UMBRIA

In 1835, Fossati's interest extended to the territory of Vetralla, at Monte Panese, of Soriano and of Tolfa, at Capannone and Vallescetta.[31] Thus, he returned to his native Amelia with the intention of measuring the polygonal walls and undertaking several soundings to locate the foundations and the gates of the wall.[32] Here, too, we are not able to say whether the work progressed beyond the project stage, or what results were obtained if it actually took place. Other, as yet unexplored, archival sources may be able to resolve these questions.

THE PROJECT TO SURVEY THE ARCHAEOLOGICAL AREAS OF THE PAPAL STATES

By 1835, Fossati had reached almost the mid-point of his life's work and experience, and this date corresponds to his attainment of full maturity. Fossati was inspired by that enthusiasm needed by an archaeologist to progress with research and plan future work, and had faith in the governing bodies. Together with Carlo Piccoli, he proposed a new project to the Camerlengo, that of a topographical description of all the ruins and monuments in the Papal States.[33] The document clearly reveals his thoughts, and demonstrates a profound knowledge of the discipline and, effectively, his vocation as an archaeologist. The scientific advantages of such a topographical survey project, along with accurate archaeological documentation, are revealed, as are the immediate implications for the protection and enhancement of the archaeological heritage. In summary, the aims were:

1) to have an idea of what the Papal States possessed;

2) to establish a reference-point for the future about the state of preservation of this property;

3) to allow the possibility of correcting information about the location of ancient towns, above all by means of inscriptions;

4) to enable greater control by the Camerlengato, through weekly reports, of the state of preservation of the most well-known archaeological areas, with the possibility of preventing further degradation and preparing detailed documentation;

5) to obtain a reference-point to check the description of ruins and the type of terrain when excavation permits were granted, particularly if they were far from Rome;

6) to contribute to the architectural and topographical knowledge of less well known remains;

7) to establish the supremacy and leadership of Rome over other 'Italian capitals' by an initiative of this type;

8) to encourage visitors to travel further afield and to stay in greater numbers in provincial towns, with notable economic consequences;

9) to provide an opportunity for several provincial towns to appreciate and value their antiquities.

The Papal Government would have had to take an analogous initiative to that of the Académie of Paris, which, with the help of private contributions, had undertaken the illustration of the ancient remains in each of the various *départements*. Melchiade Fossati and Carlo Piccoli put themselves forward for this task, the first in his capacity as an archaeologist with a deep understanding of antiquity, the second as an architect who knew how to record things faithfully on paper. They did not ask for payment, only for the reimbursement of their travel expenses, subsistence and an assistant. The project provided for a weekly progress report, with descriptions and drawings of the monuments, from the largest and most accessible to the smallest and most hidden. Lastly, in consideration also of the recent acquisition of a large number of ancient objects by the Vatican Museums, the two participants made particular note of the scholarly need for elevations of the architectural structures from which these finds came, since information about finds and find-spots was reciprocal and inseparable. However, the poverty of the treasury did not allow the project to go ahead, which was a cause of great disappointment for Fossati.

FROM THE EXCAVATIONS AT CHIUSI — A CONTRIBUTION TOWARDS THE FORMATION OF THE GREGORIAN ETRUSCAN MUSEUM

The archaeologist from Amelia remained occupied with the excavation of southern Etruria until 1836, when above all the 'good agreements and fortunate investigations of Vulci' made him famous.[34] In this year, the Papal Government, under the pontificate of Gregory XVI (1831–46), developed the idea of an Etruscan Museum, which was inaugurated on 2 February 1837. The material from Campanari's excavations at Vulci was pre-eminent in this museum. A bronze vase also features in the documents relating to the Museum's formation, acquisitions and records of objects. It was found by Fossati at Chiusi and 'removed from an exceptionally large dolium of most ancient style, in excellent condition, most delicate, with herring-bone relief work over the entire surface'. It was acquired on 11 March 1837 for 60 scudi (**Fig. 4**).[35]

HOME AND WORK PLACE

Fossati's home in Rome was in the Campo Marzio Rione. According to archival documents, he lived and worked at Via della Croce 78A, in the Palazzo Gomez Silj, built in the seventeenth century. In a register dating to 1839, Melchiade Fossati was recorded as a resident on the ground floor, 'dealer, bachelor, 40 years of age':[36] in reality, he had married in Paris and had a six-year old daughter. In Via della Croce, he owned a studio, storeroom, restoration workshop and a shop selling ancient objects. In the courtyard of the palazzo, there is a nineteenth-century neo-Renaissance portico and important Roman archaeological finds can be seen on the walls. The fountain is particularly noteworthy. It is formed of a statuary group representing a married couple lying on a triclinium. At the foot of the group, there is a Roman sarcophagus of white marble, placed on two stone blocks. It is adorned with a rich bas-relief depicting hunting scenes.[37] Several of these finds may have been part of Fossati's collection.

THE RESUMPTION OF EXCAVATIONS AT POGGIO SOMMAVILLA

We have reached the moment in which Fossati's interests shifted to Poggio Sommavilla, the place where we began. The years 1837 and 1838 were dedicated entirely to investigations in the Sabina. 'With the favour of that gentleman, and the fact that I have some experience in such excavation, I have obtained the most grateful job of directing the excavation myself, which most probably will be pronounced one of the most important of its kind.' With these words, Fossati announced the resumption of excavations at Ara de' Gelsi in partnership with Benedetto Piacentini.[38] In March 1837, as soon as the Camerlengo declared that 'every criminal action against Piacentini was ended', and 'all the objects were freed',[39] Fossati began his investigations at Poggio Sommavilla (Fig. 5).[40] We have seven lists of objects that were found up to the month of December.[41]

THE VISIT OF THE COMMISSIONE GENERALE DI BELLE ARTI — THE SALE OF THE OBJECTS — THE END OF THE EXCAVATIONS

The excavated material was taken via the Tiber to the port of Ripetta. It was examined by the Commissione Generale di Belle Arti, which decided to buy two figured craters and an inscribed olla.[42] The excavators asked for 550 scudi, but the Commissione offered them 300; the excavators then replied that they would not accept less than 330. Until July 1838, the two craters remained in Fossati's hands, and only the inscribed olla was acquired for 40 scudi (Fig. 6).[43] This vase was placed in the Etruscan Museum. Over time, knowledge of the provenance of this vase was lost, as

FIG. 4. Bronze vessel from Chiusi, sold by Fossati to the Camerlengato in 1837. Musei Vaticani, Gregoriano Etrusco, inv. no. 12864. From *Monumenti* I (1842), tav. V, 5. *(Photo: G. Filippi.)*

has happened to numerous other objects. This is due to the lack of a systematic inventory of objects, omissions in the archival documentation of the Vatican Museums, and the fact that the original deeds of sale were kept in the archives of the Camerlengato and of the Prefettura dei Sacri Palazzi, that is, outside the Museums. Glancing through the tables of the first catalogue of the Etruscan Museum (1842), I found a vase that may be the one in question (Fig. 7).[44] It is unfortunate that today the inscription on this vase is thought to be 'definitely' false;[45] I hope that the issue will be re-examined, above all in the light of this likely identification. The inscribed olla in question was placed in Room III of the Etruscan Museum.[46]

The negotiations for the sale of the objects between the excavators and the Camerlengato were profitless and exhausting. Fossati was aware of the importance of keeping together the burial goods and of the excavation context in general. He must have found himself up against a Commissione made up of men of authority, but who were ignorant of archaeological learning; they chose pieces solely for their greater historical and artistic interest. For its part, the Papal Government was unable to cope with the demands of excavators and antiquarians who seemed too greedy.

It appears that Piacentini and Fossati did not divide the archaeological material between themselves, but only the proceeds of its sale, contrary to their

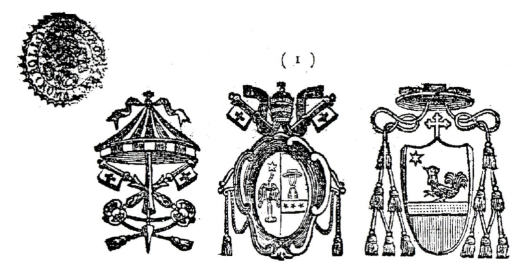

(I)

PIER FRANCESCO per la grazia di Dio Vescovo di Porto, S. Rufina, e Civita Vecchia CARD. GALLEFFI, della S. R. C. Camerlengo

Adesivamente al nostro Editto dei 7 Aprile 1820 con Sovrano espresso ordine publicato sulle Antichità e gli Scavi, e per l'Autorità del nostro ufficio di Camerlengato, in virtù del Rescritto da Noi firmato a favore *del Sr. melchiade Fossati* — — — — — — *sotto il di 7 marzo 1837* — — — — — — — concediamo *al medesimo* licenza di poter fare scavamenti per ricerca di Antichità *nelli Terreni di Proprietà del Sr. Benedetto Bocentini situati in Poggio sommavilla in Sabina* — — — —

mentre ci ha fatto constare dell'adempimento delle condizioni volute dalla citata legge, ed abbiamo preventivamente fatte eseguire le volute verificazioni sopra luogo, inteso non meno il parere della nostra Commissione *generale* Consultiva di Belle Arti. I quali scavamenti dovrà *il med. Sr. Fossati* — — — — — cominciare e perfezionare a suo conto, senza che ad altri possa rivolgersi questa nostra concessione, che in tal caso dichiariamo irrita e nulla, e sotto le pene sanzionate dalla legge contro gli escavatori non autorizzati. Incomberà innoltre all'Intraprendente sotto le medesime pene di non incominciare alcuno scavo, se non abbia avvertito dieci giorni prima la nostra Commissione *generale* Consultiva, la quale invigilerà per se stessa, o farà invigilare l'escavazione, e successivamente riconoscerà gli oggetti rinvenuti per farne relazione. Sarà oltre a ciò in obbligo l'Intraprendente di avvertire la stessa Commissione tanto della sospensione, quanto della cessazione definitiva della opera, che non potrà protrarsi oltre l'anno dalla data della presente senza nuovo permesso. E all'adempimento rigorosamente voluto dalla suddetta legge abbiamo determinato d'inse-

FIG. 5. Licence to carry out excavation in the territory of Poggio Sommavilla, granted in 1837 to Fossati by the Camerlengo. Archivio di Stato di Roma, Camerlengato II (IV), b. 240, fasc. 2466; concessione ASR 38/2002. *(Photo: G. Filippi.)*

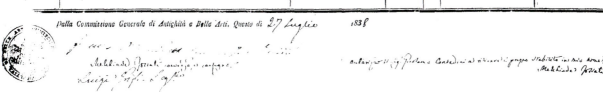

FIG. 6. Contract for the acquisition of a vase with inscriptions from Poggio Sommavilla, sold by Fossati in 1838 to the Camerlengato. Archivio di Stato di Roma, Camerlengato II (IV), b. 240, fasc. 2466; concessione ASR 38/2002. *(Photo: G. Filippi.)*

contract, which provided for division of the goods at the end of every three months. On 31 December 1838, having examined at Piacentini's house in Via di Santa Chiara the objects excavated in that year and recorded in three lists by Fossati, the Commissione di Belle Arti resolved to leave them with their possessors free of charge.[47] In 1839, the excavation probably finished once and for all. In the archival documents for this year, there is only a single list (the eleventh) of the objects found at Poggio Sommavilla, dating to 7 December.[48] On 16 January 1840, Fossati returned to the issue of the two painted craters, and was ready to cede them to the Camerlengo for the price originally offered by the Camerlengato.[49] However, nothing came of the petition presented to the Cavaliere Pietro Ercole Visconti to bring the business to a close,[50] since Cardinal Giustiniani did not think it the right moment to reopen negotiations.[51]

The Attic red-figure kylix G 93 is published in the *Corpus Vasorum Antiquorum*;[52] the provenance is given as Fossati's excavation of 1837 (acquired in 1872) since it corresponds to the description of it given by Emil Braun.[53]

EXCAVATIONS IN THE URBAN AREA OF THE MUNICIPIUM OF AMERIA

The civic administration of Amelia, which had obtained a licence to carry out an excavation within the inhabited parts of the town, on the Via di Sant'Elisabetta, entrusted the direction of this excavation to Fossati in April 1840. In that same year, he published a short description of the finds there.[54] Noteworthy remains of walled structures were discovered, along with numerous architectural pieces and

FIG. 7. Jar with inscription, identified as the vessel seen by Fossati in 1838. Musei Vaticani, Gregoriano Etrusco, Magazzini, inv. 55. From *Monumenti* II (1842), tav. XCIX, 3. *(Photo: G. Filippi.)*

sculptural and epigraphic fragments and some brick stamps.[55] In the same article, Fossati recorded his possession of an altar, 'a monument unpublished and perhaps unique', that he said had been found 'earlier, in a suburb near the ancient road that led from the Cassia to Ameria', where 'there are several ancient inscriptions'. He gave it to the *Comune*, where it is preserved today.[56]

SALE OF ANTIQUITIES TO THE MUSEO DI PARMA

In 1841, the two large red-figure craters from Poggio Sommavilla (**Figs 8–9**) remained unsold in Fossati's shop.[57] Canon Don Luigi Cipelli, a resident in Rome in the Campo Marzio Rione, in Via de' Prefetti 26, proposed to purchase several pieces.[58] He was employed by Michele Lopez, the director of the Museo di Parma, to search out ancient objects on the Roman market to enlarge the collection of that museum. From the list sent to him, Lopez chose six objects, including the two craters, which were bought for 250 scudi.[59] The vases arrived broken at Parma's customs-house, which led to a formal legal warning against Fossati and notice of the devaluation of the

objects, which Fossati would have to go to Parma to restore at his own expense.[60]

Fossati's letters to Lopez include references to his affections, his business affairs, his daily 'cultural' meetings with friends and acquaintances who came to his shop, his research and activities as an antiquarian merchant, his future plans, and happenings in the news and archaeology of Rome.[61]

At the end of 1842, he agreed the sale of ten inscriptions (six Latin and four Greek) to the Museo di Parma.[62] In the same museum, there are a further two Latin inscriptions that Fossati had acquired from the estate of Carlo Fea and sent to Lopez.[63] These were sent perhaps in place of two Etruscan inscriptions that had been chosen by Lopez, thus causing the ill-temper revealed in a subsequent letter.[64] The crate containing these inscriptions bound for the Museo di Parma was stopped at the customs-house because the Commissario delle Antichità, Pietro Ercole Visconti, 'found them to be Christian inscriptions, which our Government does not like to be exported'.[65] The despatch was possible only after Fossati made a written declaration that confirmed that 'the two extremely brief Christian inscriptions' had come to him through his commercial activities and 'for a long time had been fixed to the walls of a vineyard', thus 'ruling out a burial provenance'.[66] In 1844, Lopez wrote to Wilhelm Henzen to ask his opinion about two of the inscriptions bought from Fossati, which he suspected were forgeries; but he was reassured of their authenticity.[67] In contrast, the business of the 250 inscribed pieces of pottery that Fossati told Lopez he had acquired from the estate of Abbot Carlo Fea (1753–1836), and which he planned to sell for 920 francs, was not brought to a successful conclusion.[68] Fossati's collection of brick stamps, comprising around 280 pieces (*CIL* XV), became part of the Campana collection at the Louvre, which before 1861 (the date the collection was acquired) possessed only the 27 brick stamps of the Durand collection.[69]

HIS FATHER'S DEATH — EXCAVATIONS IN THE SABINA

Fossati's father, Vincenzo, died at Amelia at the beginning of 1843.[70] 'I started and conducted excavations, which I briefly reprised at Osteria dei Massacci or Nuova, from which a beautiful monument came to be illustrated, so that it should not be displeasing if I

FIG. 8. Red-figure crater from Poggio Sommavilla, sold by Fossati in 1841 to the Museo di Parma. From *CVA, Italia 46, Parma 2* (Rome, 1970), figs 1–2. *(Photo: G. Filippi.)*

FIG. 9. Red-figure crater from Poggio Sommavilla, sold by Fossati in 1841 to the Museo di Parma. From *CVA, Italia 46, Parma 2* (Rome, 1970), figs 3–4. *(Photo: G. Filippi.)*

dwell upon this subject with our learned readers'.[71] He continued his excavations in the Sabina, at Monteleone and at Montelibretti, until 1844.[72]

THE ROSETTA STONE AND FINAL WORK IN FRANCE

On 11 November 1847, Fossati offered Pius IX one of the three plaster casts of the trilingual Rosetta Stone, 'a source by now incontestably unique in Egyptian studies', which he had made from the original, 'knowing that in matters of epigraphy, mutilated or classical, true scholars must not trust anyone but use their own eyes and intelligence').[73] His memorandum containing the offer also gave a brief summary of his activities: 'The Roman Melchiade Fossati, a scholar, was recently in Paris, and employed in archaeological work by the Count of Clarac, director of the Louvre, by Sig. Ballanche, member of the Institute, and by the Royal Library, where by himself he drew up the catalogue of more than a thousand ancient monuments'.[74] He asked that the plaster cast be placed 'somewhere in the Vatican, which is not off the beaten track or difficult to get to, but an everyday and public place, so that our scholars can study it easily, and benefit from it', and for reimbursement of the nine scudi charged by customs.[75] Father Giuseppe Marchi (1795–1860) was asked by Pius IX's major-domo to form an opinion about the merits of the purchase and he expressed a wholly negative opinion. However, the plaster cast was acquired and placed in the Gregorian Egyptian Museum, where it remained until the refurbishments of 1982.[76] In September 1844, the British Museum had made a gift of a plaster cast of the same stone to Gregory XVI;[77] by 1847, it could not have existed anymore, since Father Marchi omitted it in his report, and it was for this reason that Fossati's offer was taken up.

THE PERSONALITY AND CHARACTER OF MELCHIADE FOSSATI

A sincere, straightforward figure who knew his business emerges from the small number of letters preserved at the Museo di Parma. Fossati did not hesitate to say what he thought, and knew how to do it with style, at times opposing his interlocutors. He knew how to make his ideas heard and he knew what he wanted to achieve. In business he was extremely active, but he was criticized for not completing the tasks he undertook.[78] Although his earnings were not excessive, he was not the type of person to save money; on the contrary, he was always on the look out for new investments, excavations, acquisitions of works of art and collections. He sought to present himself as an archaeologist and scholar, rather than as a merchant of antiquity and fine art. Indeed, he was a man of culture, his knowledge ranging from Latin to Greek mythology, from architecture to physics and the natural sciences. He had gained solid experience during the course of his research and excavation campaigns in Etruria, Lazio, the Sabina and Umbria. He was an excellent illustrator of his finds, and was well-versed in law (which he had learnt from his lawyer father).

The profession of archaeologist was not an official occupation within the Papal Government, except as a university teacher or in the running of a museum. We know the popular opinion of archaeologists from one of Fossati's contemporaries, the French novelist Henry Beyle (1783–1842), known under the pseudonym of Stendhal, who called himself a 'damned antiquarian!':[79] 'In order to be admitted in the however so respectable circles of archaeologists, you have to know Diodorus of Sicily, Pliny and a dozen other historians by heart; in addition you must have abjured all respect for logic. This annoying art is the personified enemy of all systems'.[80] And also there was the distrust that was felt generally towards the scholars of antiquity: 'silly, incompetent, naive, pedantic, vain and ridiculous, boring doctrinaires and imbued by the spirit of the system, detestable scholars devoid of logic and common sense'.[81]

Fossati, like Stendhal, understood the difference between scholar and dealer in antiquities. Thanks to the financial help of his family, he was able to become an archaeologist, supporting himself by means of the two tightly intertwined activities of contractor of excavations and dealer of antiquities. He was one of the most active, although less well-known, protagonists in the antiquities' market in the first half of the nineteenth century. He travelled widely throughout Europe, particularly in France, which, with its capital, Paris, was considered to be an ideal nation, so much so that his young compatriot, the philosopher Augusto Vera (1813–85), moved there:[82] here Fossati was loved and appreciated more than in Italy. From his studies, he learnt the aims and techniques of scholarly research, but in this he was ahead of his time and therefore not understood. Often he was in contention with and in

N. 5244

MINISTERO DEL COMMERCIO, BELLE ARTI, INDUSTRIA E AGRICOLTURA

Acquisto di Oggetti di Antichità e d'Arte ad ornamento dei Pontificj Musei in esecuzione di Ordinanza di S. E. il Sig. Ministro del Commercio ec. in data del 22 novembre 1851, analogo alla deliberazione della Commissione del dì 18 marzo 1851

NUMERO del Protocollo del Ministero	INDICAZIONE DEGLI OGGETTI	COGNOME E NOME DEL VENDITORE	PREZZO CONVENUTO		EPOCHE DEI PAGAMENTI	OSSERVAZIONI
			Scudi	Baj.		
5244	N. 1 e 2 Vasi di Terracotta	Eredità di Melchiade Fossati per la quale il Sig.r Avv.to Tjinetti	50	—	All'atto della consegna degli Oggetti	}
	3. 4. 5 Capitelli, Compositi a canestro jonico angolare					
	6 Frammento con due figurine					
	7 Cinerario con iscrizione					
	8 Basso rilievo con figure frammentato					
	9 Capitello angolare rientrante					
	10. 11 Frammento di antecapitello					
	12 Capitello angolare di cinta					
	13. 14 Figure sedenti panneggiate					
	15 Gamba nuda con suo piede					
	16. 17 Due iscrizioni originali di Raffaele uno di Pavonazzetto, l'altro di Giallo antico					

Dal Ministero del Commercio Belle Arti ec. Questo dì 22 novembre 1851

opposition to the institutions dedicated to the preservation and custodianship of the artistic and archaeological heritage with which he had had dealings from the start of his activities. He was kept at a distance because he was anti-establishment and a dissident. He hated bureaucracy, particularly if it took action without adequate knowledge. He was irritated above all by the ignorance of technical and scholarly problems demonstrated by the Camerlengato, the Ministero del Commercio (Belle Arti, Industria, Agricoltura and Lavori Pubblici), and by the members of the Commissione Generale Consultiva. The Commissione was formed of influential experts from fields different to that of the 'true science of archaeology', in which Fossati considered himself to be a real expert.

His dissent can be seen above all in his last two memoranda of 1848. In the first, dated 20 July, he opposed the proposal of the minister, Don Mario Massimo, the Duke of Rignano (1807–73), to put lightning-conductors inside the columns of Trajan and Marcus Aurelius without first having investigated the technical problems in greater depth and without the approval of the Accademia di San Luca and the Accademia di Archeologia. In a learned technical and scientific report, Fossati revealed a new aspect of his scholarly eclecticism, which switched from archaeology to electricity. In a tone somewhere between ironic and sarcastic, he concluded that 'the Rignano apparatus is a very powerful bomb, which will make both columns explode at the very first strike of lightning'.[83] In the second memorandum, of 15 September, he contested the authority of the Ministro, the Commissario per le Antichità and the Commissione Consultiva to allow the seizure of the Haterii monument, which had been discovered only recently, on public land outside the Porta Maggiore, by private interests of the Capitolo Lateranense.[84] His dissertation dealt with the legal status and the legal consequences of the discovery, which had occurred half on private land and half on public land, and its fate in the future. Fossati's knowledge of the law, which previously had not been well known, emerges from his discussion of the basis of the law concerning the discovery of treasure and excavations. Concluding his pamphlet, he warned the relevant authorities that, should a solution to the problem of the relationship between public and private not be found within the year, he would incite the people to 'claim their public rights before the common courts'.[85] Between the lines of this warning to the Ministro, in fact one can read a prophecy of what would happen in the Papal States three months from then. Indeed, an image dear to him and one that he evoked in a letter of 3 May 1842, was that of Tiresias, who predicted victory only if someone volunteered to die.

ENLISTMENT IN THE CIVIC GUARD AND SACRIFICE FOR THE ROMAN REPUBLIC

Fossati was positivist in thought and action in a monarchic and conservative Rome. In his younger years, he was disappointed in his relationship with the institutions of the Papal Government and his thoughts of rebellion increased. The proclamation of the Roman Republic in 1849 gave him his first opportunity to turn such thoughts to revenge. Fossati played his part in the revolution by volunteering for the Civic Guard.

A democratic majority was established in the elections of January 1849. On 9 February, they proclaimed that the papacy was 'removed in fact and in law from the temporal government of the Roman State' and established 'pure democracy' with the 'glorious name of the Roman Republic'.[86] A triumvirate composed of Giuseppe Mazzini, Aurelio Saffi and Carlo Armellini took over the government. The military defence of the new Republic was entrusted to Giuseppe Garibaldi. On 30 April, convinced that the Roman people did not support the Republic and that there would not be serious resistance, the French army under the command of General Oudinot launched its first assault on the city. In the patrician villas by the Roman walls, such as the Villa Pamphili and the Villa Spada, the 'Vascello', the volunteers of the Roman Republic put up a heroic

resistance and made a glorious and bloody sacrifice: Melchiade Fossati was among them.

'On 3 May, 1849, Melchiade Fossati, son of the late …, on the last day of the last month having repelled the attack of the French at the walls of the city of Rome, was hit by a burning bullet, and died on the spot, at the age of 57 years. His body was recognized and buried.' Thus reads the entry in the book of the dead in San Giacomo in Augusta for 1849.[87]

The impression that one has of Fossati's life is that of a man who lived alone, but not in solitude. He had a great number of interests and much boldness in his actions and human contacts. There are no hints of his affections, beyond that towards his father, revealed in his letters. Upon his death, his daughter Matilde came from Paris especially for the sale of the items in his collection, and remained in Rome. On 15 January 1852, she married Giovanni Francesco Vachez.[88]

THE INHERITANCE OF THE FOSSATI COLLECTION

In 1851, the Papal Government acquired part of Fossati's estate for 70 scudi (Fig. 10).[89] There were seventeen pieces: two inscriptions that had belonged to Raphael and his fiancé Maria Bibiena, later placed in the Pantheon;[90] two bronze vessels with the inscription *SVTINA* now in the Gregorian Etruscan Museum, more specifically a vase (trefoil oinochoe, Magazzino Belvedere, Sala IV, inv. no. 49506) and a plate (thymiaterion bowl, Sala III, inv. no. 12819),[91] two *pondera* (inv. nos. 10466, 10467) and eleven fragments of capitals with bas-relief and statues now in the Lateran Museum (inv. nos. 9554, 9582, 10310, 10529, 9514, 9717, 9642, 9644, 10306, 10309, 9533, although the identification of several pieces remains uncertain).[92]

On 30 April 1891, under the auspices of the Società dei Reduci, a memorial stone with the names of the citizens 'who died for the liberty of their homeland' ('morti per la libertà della patria'), including that of Melchiade Fossati, was placed in Piazza Guglielmo Marconi in Amelia. In 1903, the civic authorities named a street in the historic centre of Amelia after this illustrious archaeologist and courageous fighter.[93]

APPENDIX 1

Documents from the Archivio di Stato di Roma, Camerlengato, Parte II, Titolo IV, Antichità e Belle Arti, busta 240, fasc. 2466, relating to the excavations of Benedetto Piacentini and Melchiade Fossati in Ara de' Gelsi near Poggio Sommavilla, 1836–40

Key:
[ ] Square brackets indicate that the information is not given in the document but has been deduced from the context.
* An asterisk indicates items in the incoming letter-book; those entries that do not have an asterisk are items in the out-going letter-book. Where known, the protocol number of the incoming item in the records relating to the sender is given in the subject column.

Doc.	Nos. written in pencil	Date of arrival	Protocol no.	Place and date of despatch	Sender	Addressee	Subject
1	241–7	18 March 1836*	96485*	Rieti, 14 March 1836	G. Caracciolo, papal delegate	Cardinal-Camerlengo	Prot. no. 1704. Consignment of a copy of the report of the Governor of Poggio Mirteto of 13 March 1836
2	234–40	18 March 1836*	96486*	Poggio Mirteto, 12 March 1836	A. Maricotti, Governor of the district	Cardinal-Camerlengo	Prot. no. 1235. Report of the discovery of a tomb with vases and weapons
3	232–3	18 March 1836*	96487*	San Polo in Sabina	Benedetto Piacentini	Cardinal-Camerlengo	Notification of the discovery of ancient objects and request to carry out excavation to recover further items
4		28 March 1836		Poggio Mirteto	A. Maricotti, Governor of the district	Prior of Collevecchio	Prot. no. 1393. Reprimand for not having sent notification of the discovery and excavation of two tombs
5	242	29 March 1836	96485	Rome	Cardinal P.F. Galleffi, Camerlengo	Papal delegate to Rieti	Thanks for the letter of consignment of 14 March 1836
6	203–4	30 March 1836		Collevecchio	G.B. Floridi, Prior of Collevecchio	Governor of the district of Poggio Mirteto	Prot. no. 85. Reply to letter of 28 March 1836 (above, doc. 4)
7	226–31	30 March 1836*	96676*		Benedetto Piacentini	Cardinal-Camerlengo	Request to be submitted to the Commissione di Belle Arti for authorization to transport excavated objects to Rome
8	219–21	1 April 1836*	96708*	Poggio Mirteto, 29 March 1836	A. Maricotti, Governor of the district	Cardinal-Camerlengo	Prot. no. 1352. Report on the discovery of another tomb with objects
9	222–5	1 April 1836*	96707*	Rieti, 28 March 1836	G. Caracciolo, papal delegate to Rieti	Cardinal-Camerlengo	Prot. no. 1960. Consignment of a copy of the report of the Governor of Poggio Mirteto of 27 March 1836
10	229	5 April 1836	96676	Rome	Cardinal P.F. Galleffi, Camerlengo	Governor of the district of Poggio Mirteto	Request for authorization to transport some excavated objects to the Porta Salara, house of Caretti, in Rome
11	228–30	5 April 1836	96676	Rome	Cardinal P.F. Galleffi, Camerlengo	Tesoriere Generale	Request for authorization from the customs-house of Ripetta for the transport to Rome, to the house of Caretti, of some excavated vases
12	235	7 April 1836	96486	Rome	Cardinal P.F. Galleffi, Camerlengo	Governor of the district of Poggio Mirteto	Thanks for the report (Prot. no. 1235; above, doc. 2) and sending of the excavation licence for Piacentini
13	215–16	8 April 1836*	96797*	Montecitorio, 6 April 1836	A. Forti, Tesoriere Generale	Cardinal-Camerlengo	Prot. no. 83062. Authorization for the collection of the ancient objects at the Ripetta customs-house

Doc.	Nos. written in pencil	Date of arrival	Protocol no.	Place and date of despatch	Sender	Addressee	Subject
14	217–18	8 April 1836*	96793*	Rome, 6 April 1836	L. Grifi, Commissario delle Antichità	Cardinal-Camerlengo	Report of the visit to see the ancient objects at the house of Mr Niccola Caretti in Via di Santa Chiara
15	223	9 April 1836	96707	Rome	Cardinal P.F. Galleffi, Camerlengo	Papal delegate to Rieti	Thanks for the letter of consignment (Prot. no. 1960; above, doc. 9) of 28 March 1836
16	220	19 April 1836	96708	Rome	Cardinal P.F. Galleffi, Camerlengo	Governor of the district of Poggio Mirteto	Acknowledgment of the report (Prot. no. 1352; above, doc. 8) of 29 March 1836
17	213–14	28 April 1836*	97152*	Rome, 18 April 1836	L. Grifi, Commissario delle Antichità	Cardinal-Camerlengo	Report of the visit to see the ancient objects by the Commissione Consultiva di Antichità e Belle Arti
18	211–12	18 May 1836*	97468*	Rome, 5 May 1836	G. Santucci, Uditore del Camerlengato and Presidente della Commissione	Cardinal-Camerlengo	Favourable opinion about granting an excavation permit to Piacentini
19	208–10	16 December 1836	101009	Rome	Cardinal P.F. Galleffi, Camerlengo	Governor of the district of Poggio Mirteto	Complaint about undeclared objects
20	209	20 December 1836	101009	Rome	Cardinal P.F. Galleffi, Camerlengo	Governor of the district of Poggio Mirteto	Legal action against Piacentini
21	168	26 December 1836#		Poggio Mirteto	A. Maricotti, Governor of the district	Cardinal-Camerlengo	'Clandestine excavations for antiquities in Poggio Sommavilla ... Against Benedetto Piacentini' [enclosed sheets 1–49]
22	int. 4	26 December 1836		San Polo	Benedetto Piacentini	Governor of the district of Poggio Mirteto	Initial report of excavations for planting vines and discovery of a second tomb with objects
23	int. 6	5 January 1837		Collevecchio	A. Maricotti, Governor of the district	Cardinal-Camerlengo	Record of inspection of Piacentini's house and confiscation of the ancient objects
24	int. 14, 26	8 January 1837		Poggio Mirteto	A. Maricotti, Governor of the district	Assessore Legale of Rieti	Request to interrogate the workmen from Greccio about the excavations and the objects found
25	206–7	11 January 1837*	101388*		Benedetto Piacentini	Cardinal-Camerlengo	Letter in defence of himself, expressing disappointment at the events
26	202–5	14 January 1837*	101472*	Poggio Mirteto, 8 January 1837	A. Maricotti, Governor of the district	Cardinal-Camerlengo	Prot. no. 2 P.S. Report of the suspicious behaviour of Benedetto Piacentini in the excavations
27	199–201	14 January 1837*	101471*	Poggio Mirteto, 8 January 1837	A. Maricotti, Governor of the district	Cardinal-Camerlengo	Prot. no. 91. Report of the sequestration of 5 January 1837 and backdated letter by Piacentini about the start of excavations
28	200	21 January 1837	101471	Rome	Cardinal P.F. Galleffi, Camerlengo	Governor of the district of Poggio Mirteto	Reply to Prot. nos. 2 and 91 of 8 January 1837 (above, docs 26–7); reminder about the prompt end of the interrogation of Benedetto Piacentini's workmen
29	195–6	27 January 1837		Rieti	A. Colarieti, judge (for) the Assessore Legale	Governor of the district of Poggio Mirteto	Prot. no. 33. Awaiting information from the Prior of Greccio about the workmen who worked for Piacentini
30	int. 15	2 February 1837		Greccio	L. Laureti, Prior of Greccio	Assessore Legale of Rieti	Prot. no. 413. List of the names of Benedetto Piacentini's workmen
31	194–8	6 February 1837*	101822*	Poggio Mirteto, 31 January 1837	A. Maricotti, Governor of the district	Cardinal-Camerlengo	Prot. no. 318. Reasons for the delay in examining the witnesses, to be done in Rieti

#. This is the earliest date of a series of documents bound together and dating to different periods.

Doc.	Nos. written in pencil	Date of arrival	Protocol no.	Place and date of despatch	Sender	Addressee	Subject
32	190–3	6 February 1837*	101832*		Benedetto Piacentini	Cardinal-Camerlengo	Defensive 'memorandum' about the sale of two vases to the antiquarian Baseggio in Via del Babuino 42
33	int. 33, 50	6 February 1837		Poggio Mirteto	A. Maricotti, Governor of the district	Uditore Legale of Torri	Prot. no. 5 PS. Request to question Piacentini's workmen and custodian
34	int. 12	9 February 1837		Rieti	A. Colarieti, judge (for) the Assessore Legale	Governor of the district of Poggio Mirteto	Report of verbal interrogation of eleven people from Greccio who worked with Benedetto Piacentini
35	197	18 February 1837	101822	Rome	Cardinal P.F. Galleffi, Camerlengo	Governor of the district of Poggio Mirteto	Order to recommence the excavations for planting vines and to open the rooms that had been sealed; request for information about the judicial investigations at Rieti and Torri
36	187–8	19 February 1837		Torri	A. Baffi, Uditore Legale of Torri	Governor of the district of Poggio Mirteto	Prot. no. 401. Reference to the questioning of Piacentini's custodian
37	int. 38	22 February 1837		San Polo	Benedetto Piacentini	Uditore Legale of Torri	Clarification about the false testimony given by the custodian, Giuseppe Ottavi
38	184	26 February 1837		Rome	Benedetto Piacentini and Melchiade Fossati		Contract containing agreements and conditions for the undertaking of excavations
39	183–5	4 March 1837*	102233*		Melchiade Fossati	Cardinal-Camerlengo	Request for the issue of an excavation licence, with copy of the contract with Piacentini attached
40	186–9	4 March 1837*	102232*	Poggio Mirteto, 24 February 1837	A. Maricotti, Governor of the district	Cardinal-Camerlengo	Prot. no. 617. Reply to Prot. no. 101822 (above, doc. 35) about the progress of the questioning of the witnesses
41	int. 32	5 March 1837		Torri	A. Baffi, Uditore Legale of Torri	Governor of the district of Poggio Mirteto	Report of the questioning of Piacentini's custodian and workmen
42	102	11 March 1837		Rome	Cardinal P.F. Galleffi, Camerlengo	Melchiade Fossati	'Licence to carry out excavations for the study of Antiquity'
43	166–77	15 March 1837*	102425*	Poggio Mirteto, 10 March 1837	A. Maricotti, Governor of the district	Cardinal-Camerlengo	Prot. no. 835. Reply to Prot. nos. 101009 and 101822 (above, docs 19–20 and 35). Transmission of the dossier on the clandestine excavations. See above, 26 December 1836, doc. 21
44	180–2	15 March 1837*	102452*		Melchiade Fossati	Secretary to the Commissione di Antichità	Notification of the start of excavations
45	181	21 March 1837	102452	Rome	Cardinal P.F. Galleffi, Camerlengo	Governor of the district of Poggio Mirteto	Notification that the transfer of excavations from Piacentini to Fossati would begin soon, and request for supervision
46	167	30 March 1837	102426	Rome	Cardinal P.F. Galleffi, Camerlengo	Governor of the district of Poggio Mirteto	Reply to Prot. no. 835 (above, re. doc. 43). The 'end of any criminal action against Piacentini' is declared and all objects are freed
47	160–2	31 March 1837*	102675*	Poggio Sommavilla, 24 March 1837	Melchiade Fossati	Cardinal-Camerlengo	Letter accompanying the first list of finds
48	161	[31 March 1837*]	[102675] enclosure		[Melchiade Fossati]	[Cardinal-Camerlengo]	First list of objects discovered 21–4 March 1837

Doc.	Nos. written in pencil	Date of arrival	Protocol no.	Place and date of despatch	Sender	Addressee	Subject
49	071–3	1 April 1837*	102690*	[Stimigliano]	Carlo Jorio	Cardinal-Camerlengo	Request for a licence to excavate in the lands near to Piacentini's, with the permission of the private landowners
50	072	[1 April 1837*]	[102690*] enclosure		C. Jorio / F. Canali and C. Jorio / I. Fochetti		Authorization for two private citizens to conduct excavations within their lands
51	077–9	1 April 1837*	102690*		Carlo Jorio	Cardinal-Camerlengo	Request for a licence to excavate
52	164	2 April 1837		Collevecchio	Girolamo Rosati	Governor of the district of Poggio Mirteto	Letter denouncing Fossati's discovery of 'a large and beautiful vase, and various pieces of copper and brass'
53	078	4 April 1837	102690	Rome	Cardinal P.F. Galleffi, Camerlengo	Governor of the district of Poggio Mirteto	To verify the site and whether there are impediments to the granting of a licence to Jorio
54	158–9	5 April 1837*	102750*		Melchiade Fossati	[Cardinal-Camerlengo]	Second list of objects discovered up to 31 March 1837
55	074–5	10 April 1837		Collevecchio	A. Marini, Uditore Legale of Collevecchio	Governor of the district of Poggio Mirteto	Prot. no. 17. Reply to Prot. no. 1086 of 6 April 1837. No impediment to the issue of a licence to Jorio
56	155–6	12 April 1837*	102827*	Poggio Sommavilla	Melchiade Fossati	Cardinal-Camerlengo	Third list of the objects discovered up to 7 April 1837
57	157	13 April 1837	?	Rome	Cardinal P.F. Galleffi, Camerlengo	Melchiade Fossati	Complaint about the lists being too generic in their description of the number and quality of the objects
58	163–5	15 April 1837*	102860*	Poggio Mirteto, 9 April 1837	A. Maricotti, Governor of the district	Cardinal-Camerlengo	Report of new discoveries (forwarding of Rosati's letter of 2 April 1837; above, doc. 52) and suspicious behaviour of Piacentini
59	151	19 April 1837		Collevecchio	A. Marini, Uditore Legale [of Collevecchio]	Benedetto Piacentini and Melchiade Fossati	Order to suspend all excavations and immediate consignment of the objects discovered
60	153–4	19 April 1837*	102950*	Poggio Sommavilla, 15 April 1837	Melchiade Fossati	[Cardinal-Camerlengo]	Fourth list of objects discovered up to 15 April 1837
61	069–76	21 April 1837*	102967*	Poggio Mirteto, 18 April 1837	A. Maricotti, Governor of the district	Cardinal-Camerlengo	Prot. no. 1218. Reply to Prot. no. 102690 (above, doc. 53). Permission given for the issue of a licence to Jorio; sending on of the letter of the Uditore Legale of 10 April 1837 (above, doc. 55)
62	066–7	22 April 1837		[Rome]	Carlo Jorio	Uditore of the Camerlengato	Letter of apology and declaration of the start of work
63	070	27 April 1837	102967	Rome	Cardinal P.F. Galleffi, Camerlengo	Governor of the district of Poggio Mirteto	Consignment of excavation licence for Jorio
64	065–8	29 April 1837*	103101*	Rome, 22 April 1837	Carlo Jorio	Cardinal-Camerlengo	Notification of the date of the start of work, on 1 May
65	062–4	17 May 1837*	103378*	Rome, 15 May 1837	Carlo Jorio	Cardinal-Camerlengo	Consignment of list of objects found
66	063	15 May 1837		Rome	Carlo Jorio	[Cardinal-Camerlengo]	First list of the objects discovered up to 15 May 1837
67	150	6 June 1837		Collevecchio	Prior V. Filippi	Innocenzo Fochetti	Fochetti's declaration that the land where Jorio excavated did not belong to him but to Piacentini
68	149–52	1 July 1837*	103965*	[Rome]	Benedetto Piacentini and Melchiade Fossati	Cardinal-Camerlengo	Exposure of Jorio's fraud to the detriment of Fossati and Piacentini, with Fochetti's declaration of 6 June 1837 (above, doc. 67) attached

Doc.	Nos. written in pencil	Date of arrival	Protocol no.	Place and date of despatch	Sender	Addressee	Subject
69	146–8	12 July 1837*	104099*	[Rome]	Benedetto Piacentini and Melchiade Fossati	Cardinal-Camerlengo	Request for authorization to transport 'via the Tiber to Ripetta' some of the objects discovered
70	147	14 July 1837	104099	Rome	Cardinal P.F. Galleffi, Camerlengo	Tesoriere Generale	Request for authorization to transport the objects via the Tiber to Ripetta
71	142–5	26 July 1837*	104296*	Monte Citorio, 17 July 1837	A. Tosti, Tesoriere Generale	Pro-Camerlengo L. Lambruschini, Segretario di Stato	Prot. no. 13923. Customs authorization
72	138–9	18 October 1837*	98*		Melchiade Fossati and Benedetto Piacentini	Cardinal G. Giustiniani, Camerlengo	Invitation to the Commissione to see the objects at Via della Croce 78A
73	136–7	13 November 1837*	340*		Melchiade Fossati	Cardinal-Camerlengo	Notification of the start of excavations on 15 November
74	140–1	11 December 1837*	628*	Poggio Mirteto, 2 December 1837	A. Maricotti, Governor of the district	Cardinal-Camerlengo	Prot. no. 3973. Reply to Prot. no. 102452 (above, no. 45). Inspection to check excavations: 'several pieces of gold were being brought to light'
75	134–5	11 December 1837*	629*		Melchiade Fossati	[Cardinal-Camerlengo]	Notification of reprisal of excavations on 23 November 1837; fourth list of objects found up to 1 December 1837
76	132–3	18 December 1837*	740*		Melchiade Fossati	[Cardinal-Camerlengo]	Fifth list of objects discovered 2–8 December 1837
77	128–9	20 December 1837*	790*		Melchiade Fossati	[Cardinal-Camerlengo]	Sixth list of objects discovered up to and including the 15 or 18 December 1837
78	042–3	24 December 1837*?	831*????	Rome, 26 November 1837	G. Santucci, Uditore del Camerlengato, Presidente della Commissione	Cardinal-Camerlengo	The Commissione has decided that Fossati should bring the two painted craters and the vase with inscriptions to the secretarial offices
79	130–1	10 January 1838*	1068*	Amelia, 1 January 1838	Melchiade Fossati	Cardinal-Camerlengo	Notification of the suspension of excavations; fourth weekly list of discoveries
80	126–7	26 January 1838*	1379*		Melchiade Fossati	[Cardinal-Camerlengo]	Seventh list of objects discovered 16–22 December 1837
81	115–16	7 February 1838*	1556*	Rieti, 30 January 1838	People of Poggio Sommavilla	Cardinal Gamberini, Segretario Affari Stato Interni	Denunciation of Benedetto Piacentini for excavations and the discovery of objects from antiquity
82	120–4	7 February 1838	1556	Rome	Cardinal G. Giustiniani, Camerlengo	Pietro Battaglia	Pietro Battaglia is given the task of gathering confidential information about what valuable items had been found by Benedetto Piacentini
83	123	8 February 1838			Salvatore Melia		Fossati's lists examined and on 10 February 1838 it is declared that they do not include gold objects, jewellery, etc.
84	121–2	8 March 1838	1556	Rome	Cardinal G. Giustiniani, Camerlengo	Pietro Battaglia	Request for verification about an unnamed memorial, gold objects, jewellery etc. from the Piacentini/Fossati excavation
85	039–41	9 March 1838		Rome	Melchiade Fossati	Cardinal-Camerlengo	Request for 550 scudi for the three vases owned by Piacentini and Fossati

Doc.	Nos. written in pencil	Date of arrival	Protocol no.	Place and date of despatch	Sender	Addressee	Subject
86	040	[9 March 1838]	enclosure		Melchiade Fossati		Drawing of the inscription
87	119–25	26 March 1838*	2258*	Poggio Mirteto, 15 March 1838	Pietro Battaglia	Cardinal-Camerlengo	Acceptance of the task of verifying several ancient objects excavated by Piacentini
88	113–14	19 April 1838		San Polo	A. Sabuzi, Mayor of San Polo	Capitano Battaglia	Declaration in favour of Piacentini
89	112	28 April 1838		Collevecchio	Canonico Agostino, Ciammanelli Vic. For.	[Pietro Battaglia]	Declaration in favour of Piacentini
90	035–6	1 May 1838		San Polo	Benedetto Piacentini	Melchiade Fossati	Disagreement about the sale price of the vases, which is too low
91	061–80	4 May 1838*	2852*		Carlo Jorio	Cardinal-Camerlengo	Request for an extension to allow the reopening of the excavation on the Canali estate [La Collina]
92	101–3	14 May 1838*	3003*	[Rome]	Melchiade Fossati	Cardinal-Camerlengo	Request to continue the excavation on Piacentini's land
93	109–18	19 May 1838*	3064*	Poggio Mirteto, 11 May 1838	Pietro Battaglia	Cardinal-Camerlengo	Reply to Prot. no. 1556 of 8 March 1838 (above, doc. 84). Report on the investigations undertaken of Piacentini's excavations
94	105–6	25 May 1838*	3183*	Rome, 18 May 1838	Carlo Jorio	Cardinal-Camerlengo	Request for licence renewal and notification of the reopening of excavations in the following week
95	110	26 May 1838	3064	Rome	Cardinal G. Giustiniani, Camerlengo	Pietro Battaglia	Thanks for the report on the investigations into the alleged concealment of antiquities by Piacentini
96	038–44	12 June 1838*	3331*		L. Grifi, Secretary to the Commissione di Antichità e Belle Arti	[Cardinal-Camerlengo]	Decision of the Commissione of 27 April 1838 to acquire the vases: 300 scudi offered
97	099–100	8 June 1838*	3424*	Osteria Nuova, 5 June 1838	Melchiade Fossati	Cardinal-Camerlengo	Eighth list of objects discovered 21–9 May 1838
98	097–8	12 June 1838*	3480*		Melchiade Fossati	Cardinal-Camerlengo	Ninth list of objects discovered up to 8 June 1838 and notification of the suspension of excavations
99	107–8	12 June 1838*	3483*	Poggio Mirteto, 4 June 1838	Pietro Battaglia	Cardinal-Camerlengo	Reply to Prot. no. 3064 of 26 May 1838 (above, doc. 95). Refusal to reimburse the costs of the work carried out
100	037–45	27 June 1838*	3765*	[Rome] 25 June 1838	Melchiade Fossati	Cardinal-Camerlengo	Request for 330 scudi for the three vases chosen by the Commissione, which had offered only 300 scudi
101	034–46	4 July 1838*	3866*	Rome, 30 May 1838	L. Grifi, Secretary to the Commissione di Antichità e Belle Arti	[Cardinal-Camerlengo]	The Commissione does not wish to agree to the increase in the price of the vases
102	055–57	6 July 1838*	3912*	[Rome]	Melchiade Fossati	Cardinal-Camerlengo	Collection of two vases from the General Secretary of the Camerlengato; request for contract for 40 scudi for the inscribed vase
103	056	17 July 1838	3912	Rome	Cardinal G. Giustiniani, Camerlengo	Uditore del Camerlengato, Presidente Commissione Medici	Despatch of contract with Melchiade Fossati for the purchase of the inscribed Etruscan vase

Doc.	Nos. written in pencil	Date of arrival	Protocol no.	Place and date of despatch	Sender	Addressee	Subject
104	052–53	27 July 1838		Rome		Cardinal-Camerlengo	Contract for the acquisition of a vase with inscription from Melchiade Fossati
105	050–54	29 July 1838*	4343*	Rome, 28 July 1838	L. Grifi, Secretary to the Commissione Antichità e Belle Arti	Cardinal-Camerlengo	Consignment of the contract signed by the interested parties for the acquisition of the Etruscan vase with inscriptions
106	051	3 August 1838	4343	Rome	Cardinal G. Giustiniani, Camerlengo	Tesoriere Generale	Request for the issue of a money order for 40 scudi drawing on the fund of 500 scudi for Melchiade Fossati
107	051	[3 August 1838]	[4343]	Rome	Cardinal G. Giustiniani, Camerlengo	Major-domo	Request for the collection of a vase from the Secretary of the Camerlengato
108	049–58	18 August 1838*	4641*	Quirinale, 14 August 1838	A. Fieschi, major-domo	Cardinal-Camerlengo	Receipt for the collection of the Etruscan vase with inscriptions
109	096–104	16 November 1838*	5997*	[Rome]	Melchiade Fossati	Cardinal-Camerlengo	Notification of the start of excavations in the following week
110	094–5	28 November 1838*	6193*	[Rome]	Melchiade Fossati	Cardinal-Camerlengo	Tenth list of objects discovered
111	090–3	10 December 1838*	6370*	[Rome]	Melchiade Fossati	Cardinal-Camerlengo	Report that up to Saturday 1 December nothing had been found
112	083–4	15 January 1839*	165*		Benedetto Piacentini and Melchiade Fossati	Cardinal-Camerlengo	Request for a visit by the Commissione Generale Consultiva di Antichità e Belle Arti to see the objects at Piacentini's house, Via Santa Chiara 57
113	086–9	18 January 1839*	209*	[Rome]	Melchiade Fossati	Cardinal-Camerlengo	Report that up to 7 December 1838 nothing was found
114	082–5	4 February 1839*	481*	Rome	L. Grifi, Secretary to the Commissione di Antichità e Belle Arti	[Cardinal-Camerlengo]	The Commissione decides that the vases discovered in 1838 should remain free of charge with their owner
115	059–81	16 March 1839*	1059*	Stimigliano, 3 March 1839	Carlo Jorio	Cardinal-Camerlengo	Notification of the resumption of excavations on 13 March 1839
116	060	25 May 1839	1059	Rome	Cardinal G. Giustiniani, Camerlengo	Governor of the district of Poggio Mirteto	Request for verification that Carlo Jorio is excavating without a licence
117	087–8	18 December 1839		[Rome]	Melchiade Fossati	Cardinal-Camerlengo	Eleventh list of the objects found up to 7 December 1839
118	032–3	16 January 1840*	187*	[Rome]	Melchiade Fossati	Cardinal-Camerlengo	Reiteration of the offer of the two painted craters, which Fossati would sell at the price fixed by the Camerlengo

APPENDIX 2

Documents in the Archivio di Stato di Roma, Camerlengato, Parte I (1816–23) and II (1824–54), Titolo IV, Antichità e Belle Arti, relating to the research and excavation activities of Melchiade Fossati between the years 1821 and 1848, the sale of his collection in 1851, after his death, together with details of publications arising from this work.

Year	Location of research or excavation	Folder/ envelope	Fasc.	Subject
1821	Rome	42	231	Licence to Emiliano Sarti and Melchiade Fossati to measure the Colosseum
1824	Corneto	46	424	Melchiade Fossati — Licence to undertake excavations
1825	Civitavecchia	155	206	Melchiade Fossati and Lord Kinnaird — Excavations at Corneto on the Monterozzi estates — Objects found
1828	Viterbo	181	767	Carlo Cristofari and Melchiade Fossati — Excavation in the territory of Viterbo at Montepizzo
1828a	Corneto-Tarquinia	181	780	Pietro Manzi and Melchiade Fossati — Excavations on the Civita estate — Notes on objects and drawings
1830	Corneto	205	1249	Pietro Manzi and Melchiade Fossati — Licence to undertake excavation in a property known as Gli Archi
1830a	Tivoli	210	1402	Melchiade Fossati and Cav. Pietro Manzi — Permission to excavate in Tivoli
1830b	Montalto	211	1441	Cav. Manzi, D. Giulio Caratelli, Melchiade Fossati, Giuseppe Biasi — Excavations in the grounds of the deanery — Objects found

1831 'Monumenti dell'Etruria: Tarquinii', *Bullettino dell'Instituto di Corrispondenza Archeologica* (1831), 4–7

Year	Location of research or excavation	Folder/ envelope	Fasc.	Subject
1835	Rome	233	2260	Report of the meeting of the Commissione Generale Consultiva di Belle Arti
1835a	Rome	236	2343	Melchiade Fossati — To carry out excavations in the territory of Vetralla, Soriano and Tolfa
1835b	Amelia	238	2385	Melchiade Fossati — To have permission to measure the cyclopean walls of Amelia
1835c	Rome	238	2398	Melchiade Fossati and Carlo Piccoli — To be employed to compile a general topographic description of all the monumental ruins in the Papal States
1836	Poggio Sommavilla	240	2466	Benedetto Piacentini — Excavations in his lands located in the territory of Poggio Sommavilla in Sabina — Objects found
1836a	Rome	245	2570	Major-domo of His Holiness — On the desire of the pope to found an Etruscan Museum — Documents relevant to the formation of this museum, acquisition and records of objects and other matters
1837–40	Rome	249	2620	Commissione Generale Consultiva di Belle Arti — Record of meetings from 1837 to 1854 1) 25 February 1837 The examination of the objects offered for sale by Fossati and others is considered 2) 11 March 1837 Acquisition of the Chiusi vase for 60 scudi 3) 18 November 1837 Examination of vases from Poggio Sommavilla: 2 figured craters and an olla with inscriptions 4) 26 Jannuary 1838 Decision to buy the vases and enquiry to Fossati about the price 5) 27 April 1838 Decision not to buy a vase with the inscription SACESI and restriction of the price to 300 scudi 6) 30 May 1838 Increase of price for Fossati's vases is not accepted, otherwise he becomes free to sell the vases to whoever he likes 7) 31 December 1838 The vases found at Poggio Sommavilla in 1838 are left free of charge to Fossati and Piacentini 8) 11 March 1840 Continuation of the excavations at Amelia in the urban Via di Sant'Elisabetta with several conditions

1837 'Scavi di Sommavilla in Sabina', *Bullettino dell'Instituto di Corrispondenza Archeologica* 5 (May 1837), 65–7

1837 'Scavi di Sabina. Al sig. Luigi Manni ottimo amico', *Bullettino dell'Instituto di Corrispondenza Archeologica* 12 (December 1837), 209–13

Year	Location of research or excavation	Folder/ envelope	Fasc.	Subject
1837a	Rome	254	2696	Melchiade Fossati — To carry out excavations near to the Osteria de' Massacci of Giuseppe Smorti on the road to Rieti and in the lands of Pietro Gamberi in the territory of Monteleone — Objects found
1838				'Escavazioni a Poggio Sommavilla e all'Osteria Nuova in Sabina', *Bullettino dell'Instituto di Corrispondenza Archeologica* 6 (June 1838), 71
1840				'Scavi di Amelia', *Bullettino dell'Instituto di Corrispondenza Archeologica* (1840), 81–7
1842				'Il sepolcro di Priamo liberto presso la via Labicana, nel fondo oggi Delgrande da alcuni creduto un tratto di catacombe', *Dissertazioni della Pontificia Accademia Romana di Archeologia* 10 (1842), 113–22
1844	Montelibretti	295	3369	Anonymous — About an illegal excavation undertaken in that territory by Giovanni Leoni, Bartolomeo Fedeli and Ambrogio Valentini — Melchiade Fossati and the Petricca brothers to carry out excavation in the same territory — Record of the objects found
1847				Through the major-domo, Monsig. Rusconi, Fossati offers Pius IX a plaster cast of the trilingual Rosetta Stone, asking to be reimbursed the 9 scudi paid to the customs-house (Archivio Segreto Vaticano, Titoli 108)
1848				*Le preziose sculture del monumento degli Aterii fortuitamente poco fa discoperte ristorandosi la Via Labicana in tutto o in parti spettanti al publico e possedute dal Capitolo Lateranense per colpa del Sig. Duca Massimi, allora ministro* (Rome, 15 September 1848)
1849, 30 April: Melchiade Fossati falls defending the Roman Republic				
1850–2	Fossati's estate	295	[3369]	22 May 1850: the Commissario delle Antichità requests an inspection of the Fossati collection before it is sold
				27 November 1851: Acquisition by the Ministero del Commercio, Belle Arti, Industria e Agricoltura of seventeen objects chosen by the Commissione di Belle Arti for the Vatican Museums
				14 January 1852: two inscriptions are delivered to the Insigne Artistica Congregazione de' Virtuosi and relocated in the Pantheon

APPENDIX 3

Documents and letters associated with Melchiade Fossati in the archive of the Museo di Parma, Protocollo del Ducale Museo d'Antichità di Parma I (1825–43), II (1844–61), concerning the acquisition of ancient objects in the years 1841–3

Doc.	Protocol no.	Place and date of consignment	Sender	Addressee	Subject
1	1349	Parma, 6 April 1841	Director of the Ducale Museo di Antichità	Canon Don Luigi Cipelli, Rome	Request for objects to enrich the Museo di Parma, with descriptions and cost of these objects
2	1367	Parma, 27 May 1841	Director of the Ducale Museo di Antichità	Canon Don Luigi Cipelli, Rome	Reply to letter of 19 May 1841 with list of five vases to be bought for 326 scudi
3	1374	Parma, 11 June 1841	Director of the Ducale Museo di Antichità	Presidente dell'Interno	Proposal to buy two astronomical vases, one in the form of a duck, one jug with a plate and a sphinx for 301 scudi
4	1375	Parma, 11 June 1841	Director of the Ducale Museo di Antichità	Presidente delle Finanze	Proposal to buy as above
5	1376	Parma, 15 June 1841	Director of the Ducale Museo di Antichità	Canon Don Luigi Cipelli, Rome	Message that the Government will acquire the suggested vases
6	1386	Parma, 8 July 1841	Director of the Ducale Museo di Antichità	Canon Don Luigi Cipelli, Rome	Instructions to send the pieces well-packed so they should not 'arrive broken or damaged'
7		Ischl, 10 July 1841	Maria Luigia	Presidente delle Finanze, V. Mistrali	Acquired for L.1775,90: two Etruscan vases, one in the form of a duck, one jug with a bronze plate, and a sphinx
8	1392	Parma, 24 July 1841	Director of the Ducale Museo di Antichità	Canon Don Luigi Cipelli, Rome	Protest that the sphinx is missing from the objects already chosen and about the increase in price of the vases
9	3029 / 1611	Parma, 24 July 1841	Presidente dell'Interno, M. Pazzoni	Director of the Ducale Museo di Antichità	Reply to letter Prot. no. 1374 of 11 June 1841 (above, doc. 3). Transmission of the royal rescript for the buying of antiquities.
10	1608-1612	Parma, 28 July 1841	Usher of the customs-house	Michele Lopez, Director of the Museo di Parma	Notification of the opening of the chests containing the vases sent by Melchiade Fossati, which are found to be broken
11	1395	Parma, 29 July 1841	Director of the Ducale Museo di Antichità	Canon Don Luigi Cipelli, Rome	Complaint that the vases had not reached the museum intact
12	1396	Parma, 29 July 1841	Director of the Ducale Museo di Antichità	Presidente delle Finanze	Notification of the arrival of 'the two well-known astronomical vases', found broken
13	1397	Parma, 31 July 1841	Director of the Ducale Museo di Antichità	Melchiade Fossati, Via della Croce 78, Rome	Protest that the vases were 'found broken and smashed'
14	1398	Parma, 31 July 1841	Director of the Ducale Museo di Antichità	Don Luigi Cipelli	Notice of the letter of complaint sent to Fossati to reduce the price of the vases that arrived in fragments
15	1399	Parma, 31 July 1841	Director of the Ducale Museo di Antichità	Presidente delle Finanze	Notice of the letter of complaint sent to Fossati to reduce the price of the vases that arrived in fragments
16	1405	Parma, 10 September 1841	Director of the Ducale Museo di Antichità	Canon Don Luigi Cipelli, Rome	Asking for a reply regarding the 'well-known vases' — Via de' Prefetti 26, 2nd floor (cf. doc. 14)
17	1406	Parma, 10 September 1841	Director of the Ducale Museo di Antichità	Melchiade Fossati, Via della Croce 78, Rome	Request for a reply to letter no. 1397 of 31 July 1841 (above, doc. 13)

Doc.	Protocol no.	Place and date of consignment	Sender	Addressee	Subject
18	3052 / 1618	Rome, 13 September 1841	Melchiade Fossati	Michele Lopez, Director of the Museo di Parma	Declaration of experience in the field of consignment and restoration; damage the responsibility of the stagecoaches
19	1409	Parma, 17 September 1841	Director of the Ducale Museo di Antichità	Melchiade Fossati	Reply to letter of 13 September 1841 (above, doc. 18), with conditions of sale: 'price of 250 scudi' and 'excellent state of conservation'
20	3061 / 1623	Rome, 23 September 1841	Melchiade Fossati	Michele Lopez, Director of the Museo di Parma	Clarification of the loss of value of the broken vases; proposal of the Greek inscription from the Fea estate
21	1414	Parma, 2 October 1841	Director of the Ducale Museo di Antichità	Presidente delle Finanze	Request for an audience about the astronomical vases
22	1415	Parma, 6 October 1841	Director of the Ducale Museo di Antichità	Canon Don Luigi Cipelli, Rome	Clarification of the terms of the contract for the purchase of the vases
23	1416	Parma, 6 October 1841	Director of the Ducale Museo di Antichità	Melchiade Fossati	Request for the restoration of the vases
24	1419	Parma, 26 October 1841	Director of the Ducale Museo di Antichità	Canon Don Luigi Cipelli, Rome	Reply to a letter of 21 October 1841
25	1420	Parma, 26 October 1841	Director of the Ducale Museo di Antichità	Melchiade Fossati	Request to halt judicial proceedings against Don Luigi Cipelli
26	1421	Parma, 26 October 1841	Director of the Ducale Museo di Antichità	Emilio Braun, Rome	Invitation to suspend the negotiations with Fossati, since the annulment of the contract has not been announced
27	3074 / 1626	Rome, 30 October 1841	Emilio Braun	Michele Lopez, Director of the Museo di Parma	Reply to the letter of 26 October 1841 (above, doc. 26) — displeasure if the 'famous vases' should be placed in another museum
28	3075 / 1627	Rome, 1 November 1841	Melchiade Fossati	Michele Lopez, Director of the Museo di Parma	Commitment to go to Parma to restore the two craters in person
29	3076 / 1628	Rome, 1 November 1841	Canon Luigi Cipelli	Michele Lopez, Director of the Museo di Parma	Reaffirmation of Fossati's commitment to go to Parma to restore the vases
30	1431	Parma, 18 December 1841	Director of the Ducale Museo di Antichità	Presidente delle Finanze	Request for an audience concerning the arrival of the restorer of the well-known vases
31		Parma, 30 December 1841	Melchiade Fossati	Michele Lopez, Director of the Museo di Parma	Notice of the shipment of two Etruscan vases, one in the form of a duck, one jug with a bronze plate
32	1433	Parma, 30 December 1841	Director of the Ducale Museo di Antichità	Presidente dell'Interno	Request for the issue of a money order for the acquisition of the Fossati objects and chronicle of the events
33	1434	Parma, 30 December 1841	Director of the Ducale Museo di Antichità	Presidente dell'Interno	Accompanying letter (confidential) asking that the following petition be received kindly
34	1435	Parma, 30 December 1841	Director of the Ducale Museo di Antichità	Presidente dell'Interno	Petition that the cost of shipment of the Fossati items be paid with the savings made from the acquisition
35	4006 /1644	Parma, 11 January 1842	Presidente dell'Interno M. Pazzoni	Michele Lopez, Director of the Museo di Parma	Reply to letter no. 1433 of 30 December 1841 (above, doc. 32). Sending of money order for L. 1530 to Melchiade Fossati
36		Parma, 11 January 1842	Melchiade Fossati	Michele Lopez, Director of the Museo di Parma	Money order for L. 1530 received

Doc.	Protocol no.	Place and date of consignment	Sender	Addressee	Subject
37	1440	Parma	14 February 1842	Director of the Ducale Museo di Antichità	Melchiade Fossati	Surprise at the long silence; arrival in Rome of the Count of Montenovo, collector of Roman medals
38	1442	Parma	16 February 1842	Director of the Ducale Museo di Antichità	Melchiade Fossati	Letter of presentation of Count Guglielmo di Montenovo, Commander of the Order of Malta
39	4032 / 1659	Rome	25 February 1842	Melchiade Fossati	Michele Lopez, Director of the Museo di Parma	Apologies for the long silence, father ill at Amelia; inscriptions sent; …
40	1449	Parma	5 March 1842	Director of the Ducale Museo di Antichità	Canon Don Luigi Cipelli	Apologies for the lateness of the reimbursement of the costs incurred for the transportation of the vases
41	4949 / 1668	Rome	18 March 1842	Melchiade Fossati	Michele Lopez, Director of the Museo di Parma	Start of excavations at Monteleone in the first days of April … the anonymous illustrated book of our Etruscan Museum printed
42	1457	Parma	29 March 1842	Director of the Ducale Museo di Antichità	Presidente dell'Interno	Sending on of the letters of Avv. Bernardino Cipelli of Parma and of Melchiade Fossati
43	1467	Parma	16 April 1842	Director of the Ducale Museo di Antichità	Melchiade Fossati	Due to the shortage of funds in the accounts of the museum, the suspension of the shipment of the famous inscriptions is requested
44	4102 / 1693	Rome	3 May 1842	Melchiade Fossati	Michele Lopez, Director of the Museo di Parma	Government acquisition from Gaetani's heirs of a mosaic of coloured stones; start of excavation from 15 cm
45		Parma	8 October 1842	Avv. B(ernardino) Cipelli	Michele Lopez, Director of the Museo di Parma	Money order for L. 87.96 received for expense of shipment, taxes etc.
46		Parma	8 October 1842	Canon Luigi Cipelli	Michele Lopez, Director of the Museo di Parma	L. 93.19 (= scudi 33.54) received for shipment expenses of the Fossati vases
47	1526	Parma	4 November 1842	Director of the Ducale Museo di Antichità	Melchiade Fossati	Thanks for the consignment of fragments of painted vases; request for the shipment of the twelve chosen inscriptions …
48	4223 / 1762	Rome	23 December 1842	Melchiade Fossati	Michele Lopez, Director of the Museo di Parma	Consignment of chest with eight Latin inscriptions, one Greek funerary inscription, one bilingual inscription and other objects; 250 Fea terracottas noted
49	4230 / 1763	Rome	30 December 1842	Melchiade Fossati	Michele Lopez, Director of the Museo di Parma	Inscriptions found … acquisition of marbles from the Amendola vineyard (Capitoline urn) …
50	1538	Parma	30 December 1842	Director of the Ducale Museo di Antichità	Melchiade Fossati	Anger about the missing inscriptions and about the objects sent without having been requested
51	1543	Parma	7 January 1843	Director of the Ducale Museo di Antichità	Melchiade Fossati	List of twelve inscriptions chosen for acquisition and conditions of payment
52	4257 / 1777	Rome	11 February 1843	Melchiade Fossati	Michele Lopez, Director of the Museo di Parma	Apologies for the fact inscriptions were missing from the consignment … loss of father three weeks ago … inscriptions of Serapis and Isis
53	1556	Parma	25 February 1843	Director of the Ducale Museo di Antichità	Melchiade Fossati	Reply to the letter of 11 February 1843 (above, doc. 52) concerning the shipment of the well-known inscriptions
54	4278 / 1790	Rome	27 March 1843	Melchiade Fossati	Michele Lopez, Director of the Museo di Parma	Swift payment and decision about the seal collection …

Doc.	Protocol no.	Place and date of consignment		Sender	Addressee	Subject
55	1564	Parma	17 March 1843	Director of the Ducale Museo di Antichità	Melchiade Fossati	Arrival of ten inscriptions, excluding the two Etruscan inscriptions and other objects outside the contract; doubts about the antiquity of an inscription
56	1566	Parma	1 April 1843	Director of the Ducale Museo di Antichità	Melchiade Fossati	Payment for ten inscriptions and nine gems acquired by the museum; resentment over Fossati's poor behaviour
57	1582	Parma	27 May 1843	Director of the Ducale Museo di Antichità	Melchiade Fossati	Resentment over the long silence and prompt dispatch of the receipt for the sum earned from the sale of the marbles
58		Rome	9 June 1843	Melchiade Fossati	Michele Lopez, Director of the Museo di Parma	Declaration that the consigned inscriptions are 'undoubtedly ancient', also the gems; … other proposals
59	1680	Parma	6 July 1844	Director of the Ducale Museo di Antichità	Guglielmo Henzen, librarian at the Archaeological Institute in Rome	Request for opinion about two inscriptions, one Latin and one Greek, acquired from Fossati
60	4536 / 1938	San Marino	26 September 1844	Guglielmo Henzen	Michele Lopez, Director of the Museo di Parma	The suspicious Latin inscription is authentic and had been seen by Borghesi at the home of the lawyer Fea in Rome

NOTES

1. ASR, Camerlengato II, Antichità e Belle Arti, 1836, busta 240, fasc. 2466; see Appendix I.

2. A.M. Corbo, 'Le Commissioni Ausiliarie di Belle Arti nello Stato Pontificio dal 1821 al 1848', in *Lunario Romano (Ottocento nel Lazio)* (Rome, 1982), 433–46; M. Bencivenni, R. Dalla Negra and P. Grifoni, *Monumenti e istituzioni. Parte I. La nascita del servizio di tutela dei monumenti in Italia 1860–1880* (Florence, 1987), 30–6; M.A. De Angelis, 'Musei e istituzioni di belle arti in Roma. Cronologia del personale direttivo dal 1768 al 1956', *Bollettino dei Musei Vaticani* 17 (1997), 83–103.

3. ASR, Camerlengato II, Antichità e Belle Arti, 1836, busta 240, fasc. 2466; Appendix I, doc. 1.

4. A. Pasqui, 'Poggio Sommavilla (frazione del comune di Collevecchio) — Di un'antica necropoli scoperta a nord dell'abitato', *NSc* (1896), 476–89; most recently, P. Santoro, 'Gli scavi a Poggio Sommavilla nell'Ottocento', in *Miscellanea etrusco-italica* I (*Quaderni di archeologia etrusco-italica* 22) (Rome, 1993), 53–9, with bibliography.

5. A 'licenza di poter fare scavamenti per ricerca di Antichità'. ASR, Camerlengato II, Antichità e Belle Arti, 1836, busta 240, fasc. 2466; Appendix I, docs 12 and 17.

6. 'Le periodiche assegne dei ritrovamenti fatti, in aperto disprezzo dell'Editto dei 7 Aprile 1820, ove prescivonsi le cose d'adempiersi dagli Intraprendenti delle escavazioni.' ASR, Camerlengato II, Antichità e Belle Arti, 1836, busta 240, fasc. 2466; Appendix I, doc. 20.

7. ASR, Camerlengato II, Antichità e Belle Arti, 1836, busta 240, fasc. 2466; Appendix I, doc. 23.

8. ASR, Camerlengato II, Antichità e Belle Arti, 1836, busta 240, fasc. 2466; Appendix I, doc. 23.

9. ASR, Camerlengato II, Antichità e Belle Arti, 1836, busta 240, fasc. 2466; Appendix I, docs 21, 23–4, 30, 33–4, 37, 41.

10. ASR, Camerlengato II, Antichità e Belle Arti, 1836, busta 240, fasc. 2466; Appendix I, doc. 26.

11. ASR, Camerlengato II, Antichità e Belle Arti, 1836, busta 240, fasc. 2466; Appendix I, doc. 32.

12. ASR, Camerlengato II, Antichità e Belle Arti, 1836, busta 240, fasc. 2466; Appendix I, doc. 38.

13. Archivio di Stato di Terni, Notarile di Amelia, 1108, fol. 90v.

14. Archivio del Vicariato, Roma, Stato delle Anime della Parrocchia di San Salvatore della Corte, anni 1821 (nos. 34–9), 1825 (nos. 1278–81), 1827 (nos. 1344–7), 1829 (nos. 2229–33).

15. ASR, Catasto fabbricati, 1824, reg. 36, no. 265: Rione XIII, maps nos. 368–9. The original building has been rebuilt and modified; cf. L. Gigli, *Guide rionali di Roma. Rione XIII. Trastevere* III (Rome, 1982), 96–9.

16. That is, 'predere misure ancora di dettaglio sull'Anfiteatro Flavio … ingombri e calcinacci … provi scale o ponti … ma solo sotto la vigilanza del Sig. Cavaliere Ingegner Valadier, Consigliere della Commissione Generale Consultiva di Belle Arti e coll'assistenza dei Si. Ilari, Ispettore alla Polizia dei Pubblici Monumenti'. ASR, Camerlengato I–II, Antichità e Belle Arti, 1816–54; see Appendix II, 1821.

17. *ICUR* IV, 11202 and 11477 from San Callisto, now in the Vatican Museums, Lapidario Cristiano ex Lateranense, inv. nos. 33598 and 33193; M. Fossati, 'Il sepolcro di Priamo Liberto presso la Via Labicana, nel fondo oggi Delgrande da alcuni creduto un tratto di catacombe', *Dissertazioni della Pontificia Accademia Romana di Archeologia* 10 (1842), 113–22 (dissertation on the inscription *CIL* VI 24926, then held by Emiliano Sarti, now in the Capitoline Museums).

18. ASR, Camerlengato I–II, Antichità e Belle Arti, 1816–54; Appendix II, 1824, 1825; M. Fossati, 'Rapporto intorno le tombe di Tarquinia e di Vulcia', *Annali dell'Instituto di Corrispondenza Archeologica* fasc. 1–2 (1829), 120–31; M. Fossati and P. Manzi, 'Scavi etruschi: Tarquinia', *BullInst* (1829), 197–9.

19. *CVA, France 8, Louvre 5* (Paris, 1928), fig. 30,1–3,7; R. Rochette, *Monuments inédits d'antiquité figurée grecque, étrusque et romaine* (Paris, 1833), 417.

20. ASR, Camerlengato I–II, Antichità e Belle Arti, 1816–54; Appendix II, 1828.

21. ASR, Camerlengato I–II, Antichità e Belle Arti, 1816–54; Appendix II, 1828a, 1830; *Diario di Roma* (2 January 1830), 1–2; M. Fossati and P. Manzi, 'Monumenti dell'Etruria: Tarquinii', *BullInst* (1831), 4–7; P. Manzi, *Stato antico ed attuale del porto, città e provincia di Civitavecchia* (Prato, 1837), 61; G. Moroni, *sub voce* 'Tarquinia', in *Dizionario di erudizione storico-ecclesiastica* LXXII (Venice, 1855), 272.

22. F. Buranelli, *Gli scavi a Vulci della società Vincenzo Campanari–Governo Pontificio (1835–1837)* (*Studia Archaeologica* 58) (Rome, 1991), 7.

23. *Notizie del Giorno* (1 April 1830), 3–4 n. 13; Buranelli, *Gli scavi a Vulci* (above, n. 22), 10.

24. Buranelli, *Gli scavi a Vulci* (above, n. 22).

25. Three vases associated with Fossati's name were pointed out to me by Gianpaolo Nadalini: Louvre, inv. no. F 59 in *CVA, France 5, Louvre 4* (Paris, 1926), figs 30,8 and 31,2,6; inv. no. F 295 in *CVA, France 9, Louvre 6* (Paris, 1929), fig. 70,7; inv. no. G 55 in *CVA, France 1, Louvre 1* (Paris, 1922), figs 6,3–5 and 7,3. I have not yet identified other vases. Cf. H. Giroux, 'Les acquisitions du Louvre aux ventes Canino', in A.J. Clarke, J. Gaunt and B. Gilman (eds), *Essays in Honor of Dietrich von Bothmer* (*Allard Pierson Series* 14) (Amsterdam, 2002), 127–35.

26. ASR, Camerlengato I–II, Antichità e Belle Arti, 1816–54; Appendix II, 1830a, 1830b.

27. O. Gerhard, 'Scavi etruschi', *BullInst* (December, 1830), 231–3, and 'Scavi e monumenti di Tarquinii', *BullInst* (May–June, 1831), 81–3, for example.

28. See, for example, the above-mentioned sale to the Louvre of the Attic crater from Corneto. More generally, see also R. Mariano, *Augusto Vera* (Naples, 1887), 12–13.

29. Archivio del Vicariato, Roma, Ufficio III, Posizioni Matrimoni, 1852, 17992, containing the certificate of baptism from the Parish of Saint-Germain-l'Auxerrois; her godfather was Carlo Campanari, Fossati's associate in the excavations at Vulci.

30. Archivio del Vicariato, Roma, Stato delle Anime del 1839 (see below, n. 36).

31. ASR, Camerlengato I–II, Antichità e Belle Arti, 1816–54; Appendix II, 1835a. This contains the contract of 20 January 1835, detailing the settlement or division of the Manzi–Fossati association: Manzi remained the owner of the excavation of Bieda, Fossati of Vetralla, Soriano and Tolfa 'already explored without gain' ('già sperimentato infruttuoso'). Of particular interest in the document are the references to a number of archaeological finds owned by Manzi and Fossati that were placed in the hands of third parties and to Vincenzo Campanari's outstanding debts; the licence to undertake excavations was issued to Fossati on 8 October 1835. For the excavations at Tolfa, cf. A. Naso, 'Scavi sui Monti della Tolfa del secolo XIX: documenti e materiali', *Archeologia Classica* 45 (1) (1993), 56–7.

32. ASR, Camerlengato I–II, Antichità e Belle Arti, 1816–54; Appendix 1835b.

33. ASR, Camerlengato I–II, Antichità e Belle Arti, 1816–54; Appendix 1835c.

34. The 'bene intese e fortunate investigazioni vulcenti'. E. Braun, 'Sui vasi di Sabina', *BullInst* (May 1837), 70.

35. 'Estratto da un dolio stragrande d'antichissimo stile, conservatissimo, sottilissimo, con lavori di rilievo a spina di pesce per tutta la superficie.' Today it can be found in Sala I, inv. no. 12864. ASR, Camerlengato I–II, Antichità e Belle Arti, 1816–54; Appendix II, 1836a. See also *Monumenti del Museo Etrusco Vaticano acquistati dalla munificenza di Gregorio XVI Pontefice Massimo e per di Lui ordine disegnati e pubblicati* I (Rome, 1842), tav. V, 5 — the caption is quite vague, reading 'Escavazioni di Vulci, Bomarzo ed Orte: dal 1830 al 1839' ('Excavations at Vulci, Bomarzo and Orte: from 1830 to 1839'); G. Pinza, 'Appendice B — Materiali per la etnologia antica toscano-laziale', in G. Pinza and B. Nogara, *Documenti relativi alla formazione ed alle raccolte principali del Museo* (Milan, 1915) (the only copy is held in the library of the Vatican Museums), doc. XX; W. Helbig, *Führer durch die Öffentlichen Sammlungen Klassischer Altertümer in Rom* I (Tübingen, 1963[4]), 520 no. 689; there is a note on the excavations at Chiusi in M. Fossati, 'Scavi di Sabina. Al sig. Luigi Manni ottimo amico', *BullInst* (December 1837), 211.

36. 'Neg(oziante), scap(ol)o, di 40 anni.' Archivio del Vicariato, Roma, Stato delle Anime della Parrocchia di San Giacomo in Augusta (compiled by the parish priest, Giuseppe M. Galligari), vol. 10 (1839), fol. 122; the Stato delle Anime of 1848, fol. 132, and of 1849, fol. 125, record the 'Antiquario Michele Fossati' in Via della Croce 78A.

37. P. Hoffmann, *Guide rionali di Roma. Rione IV, Campo Marzio* IV (Rome, 1993), 49–52.

38. 'La cortesia di quel signore, e l'avere io alcuna esperienza in tali indagini mi procacciarono la gratissima occupazione d'avere a condurre in mio nome lo scavo, che s'annuncia con assai probabilità come de' primari in tal genere.' M. Fossati, 'Scavi di Sommavilla in Sabina', *BullInst* (May 1837), 65.

39. 'Terminata ogni azione criminale verso il Piacentini … al tutto liberi gli oggetti.' ASR, Camerlengato II, Antichità e Belle Arti, 1836, busta 240, fasc. 2466; Appendix I, doc. 46.

40. ASR, Camerlengato II, Antichità e Belle Arti, 1836, busta 240, fasc. 2466; Appendix I, docs 42, 44–5; ASR, Camerlengato I–II, Antichità e Belle Arti, 1816–54; Appendix II, 1837.

41. ASR, Camerlengato II, Antichità e Belle Arti, 1836, busta 240, fasc. 2466; Appendix I, docs 48, 54, 56, 60, 76, 77, 80.

42. ASR, Camerlengato II, Antichità e Belle Arti, 1836, busta 240, fasc. 2466; Appendix I, doc. 78; ASR, Camerlengato I–II, Antichità e Belle Arti, 1816–54; Appendix II, 1837.

43. ASR, Camerlengato II, Antichità e Belle Arti, 1836, busta 240, fasc. 2466; Appendix I, docs 85 and 90 (excavators' request, offer by the Commissione), 100 and 101 (not less than 330 scudi), 103 (acquisition of the olla).

44. *Monumenti del Museo Etrusco* II (above, n. 35), tav. XCIX,3. The caption reads: 'Escavazioni di Cere, Tarquinia, Vulci, Toscanella ed Orte dal 1834 al 1838' ('Excavations at Caere, Tarquinia, Vulci, Toscanella and Orte from 1834 to 1838').

45. *TLE*, 758; *CII*, 2596; *NRIE*, 1196. Also M. Pandolfini Angeletti (ed.), *Thesaurus Linguae Etruscae* I. *Indice lessicale* (Rome, 1978), 36, 411–12.

46. See the photograph (no. 886) dating to about 1900 in the Archivio Fotografico of the Vatican Museums, in which the piece is on a shelf on the left wall; subsequently it was placed in Room V, inv. no. 55 (neg. Musei Vaticani XVIII.24.27).

47. ASR, Camerlengato II, Antichità e Belle Arti, 1836, busta 240, fasc. 2466; Appendix I, docs 97, 98, 110.

48. ASR, Camerlengato II, Antichità e Belle Arti, 1836, busta 240, fasc. 2466; Appendix I, doc. 117.

49. ASR, Camerlengato II, Antichità e Belle Arti, 1836, busta 240, fasc. 2466; Appendix I, doc. 118.

50. BAV, Autografi Ferrajoli, Raccolta Visconti, 2974.

51. ASR, Camerlengato II, Antichità e Belle Arti, 1836, busta 240, fasc. 2466; Appendix I, doc. 118.

52. *CVA, France 28, Louvre 19* (Paris, 1977), figs 53,1–4 and 54,1.

53. Braun, 'Sui vasi di Sabina' (above, n. 34), 73.

54. Archivio Storico del Comune di Amelia, Scavi nella Strada di S. Elisabetta; the file contains fourteen documents datable to February–June 1840 concerning entreaties made for the issue of the excavation licence to the civic magistrature, the approval of the expenditure by the civic council, the appointment of Fossati to the directorship of the excavation by the gonfalonier, Cavaliere Filippo Vannicelli, and several short records of the finds. Cf. M. Fossati, 'Scavi di Amelia', *BullInst* 5 (May 1840), 81–7.

55. Cf. most recently, M. Matteini Chiari, 'Appunti per una storia degli interventi di scavo in Amelia. La formazione della raccolta archeologica comunale', in M. Matteini Chiari and S. Stopponi (eds), *Museo Comunale di Amelia. Raccolta archeologica. Iscrizioni, sculture, elementi architettonici e d'arredo* (Perugia, 1996), 17–36, and the entries in the catalogue.

56. 'Monumento inedito e forse unico … l'età scorsa in un suburbano presso la via antica che dalla Cassia menava ad Ameria … esistono varie iscrizioni antiche.' M. Fossati, 'Escavazioni Amelia', *Notizie del Giorno* (4 February 1830), 3–4, no. 5, and 'Scavi di Amelia' (above, n. 54), 86–7. This is a piece of

notable interest, already known from several drawings by Giovanni Antonio Dosio; cf. H. Blanck, 'Eine Rundara in Amelia', *Bullettino dell'Istituto Archeologico Germanico. Sezione Romana* 75 (1969), 174–82; H.P. Isler, *Acheloos. Eine Monographie* (Berne, 1970), 40, 131–2, no. 53; M. Matteini Chiari, 'Ara circolare', in *Gens Antiquissima Italiae. Antichità dall'Umbria in Vaticano* (Perugia, 1988), 121–2; D. Monacchi, 'Ara neoattica', in Matteini Chiari and Stopponi (eds), *Museo Comunale di Amelia* (above, n. 55), 172–4.

57. E. Braun, 'Il sole e la luna', *Annali dell'Instituto di Corrispondenza Archeologica* (1838), 266–76; *Monumenti dell'Instituto di Corrispondenza Archeologica* (Rome, 1854–6), II, fig. LV; *CVA, Italia 46, Parma 2* (Rome, 1970), figs 1–6.

58. Archivio del Museo di Parma [hereafter MP], Protocollo del Ducale Museo d'Antichità di Parma I (1825–43), II (1844–61); see Appendix III, docs 1 (growth of the collections), 2 (acquisition of pieces).

59. MP, Protocollo del Ducale Museo d'Antichità di Parma I (1825–43), II (1844–61); Appendix III, doc. 3.

60. MP, Protocollo del Ducale Museo d'Antichità di Parma I (1825–43), II (1844–61); Appendix III, docs 13 (broken vessels), 15 (proceedings against Fossati), 28 and 29 (restoration).

61. MP, Protocollo del Ducale Museo d'Antichità di Parma I (1825–43), II (1844–61); Appendix III, docs 41, 44, 49, 52.

62. Latin inscriptions: *CIL* VI 1318 = XI 156*,4; *CIL* VI 1550 = 31678 = XI 156*,5; *CIL* VI 3709 = XI 156*,2; *CIL* VI 8778 = XI 156*,23; *CIL* VI 9443 a = XI 156*,12; *ICUR* VII [1980] 18927, from the 'Coemeterium Cyriacae' = XI 156*,43. Greek inscriptions: *IG* XIV 1005 = G. Sacco, *Iscrizioni greche d'Italia. Porto* (Rome, 1984), 22–4, no. 9; *IG* 1604 = *IGUR* III [1979] 1215; *IG* 2034; G. Bovini, 'Sulla cronologia di due frammenti scultorei paleocristiani conservati nel Museo Nazionale d'Antichità di Parma', *Felix Ravenna*, Series III, 14, LXV (1954), 37–43. MP, Protocollo del Ducale Museo d'Antichità di Parma I (1825–43), II (1844–61); Appendix III, docs 48, 51, 55; M.G. Arrigoni Bertini, 'Regio VIII. Aemilia: Parma', in *Supplementa Italica* 11 (Rome, 1993), 125–6.

63. *CIL* VI 16778 = XI 156*,27; *CIL* VI 5894 = XI 156*,22.

64. MP, Protocollo del Ducale Museo d'Antichità di Parma I (1825–43), II (1844–61); Appendix III, doc. 56.

65. 'Vi rinvenne iscrizioni cristiane, che il nostro Governo non ama che si esportino.' MP, Protocollo del Ducale Museo d'Antichità di Parma I (1825–43), II (1844–61); Appendix III, doc. 52.

66. 'Le due iscrizioni brevissime cristiane … stavano da buon tempo fisse a pareti di vigna … esclude ogni provenienza cemeteriale.' BAV, Autografi Ferrajoli, Raccolta Visconti 2973.

67. *CIL* VI 1318 and *IGUR* III, 1215. For the suspicions of forgery, cf. MP, Protocollo del Ducale Museo d'Antichità di Parma I (1825–43), II (1844–61); Appendix III, doc. 59; for the reassurance, doc. 60.

68. MP, Protocollo del Ducale Museo d'Antichità di Parma I (1825–43), II (1844–61); Appendix III, doc. 48 (notification of acquisition); cf. BAV, Vat. Lat. 10591, fols 1–56 (epigraphic entries: dolia inscriptions); Appendix III, doc. 54 (request for 920 francs).

69. A. Héron de Villefosse, *Sur quelques briques romaines du Louvre* (Paris, 1880), 5–6, n. 4.

70. MP, Protocollo del Ducale Museo d'Antichità di Parma I (1825–43), II (1844–61); Appendix III, doc. 52; Archivio di Stato di Terni, Notarile di Amelia, 1108, fols 90–1.

71. 'Incominciai inoltre e condussi gli scavi, che riprenderò in breve all'Osteria dei Massacci o Nuova, dai quali siccome viene ad essere illustrato un bel monumento, così non sia discaro se ne trattengo diligentemente i nostri eruditi lettori …'; M. Fossati, 'Escavazioni a Poggio Sommavilla e all'Osteria Nuova in Sabina', *BullInst* (June 1838), 71; ASR, Camerlengato I–II, Antichità e Belle Arti, 1816–54; Appendix II, 1837a. The investigations took place on lands owned by Giuseppe Smorsi on Via Reatina and by Baron Pietro Gamberi at Castellano, Valle Trebola, Pantano, Cerri and Gorgo Granato in the territory of Monte Leone.

72. ASR, Camerlengato I–II, Antichità e Belle Arti, 1816–54; Appendix II, 1844.

73. 'Fondamento finora incontestabile unico degli studi egizi … sapendo che in fatto d'epigrafi copiose, mutilate e classiche i veri studiosi non debbon fidarsi ciascuno che de' proprii occhi, e lumi.' He had given another copy as a gift to his friend, Emiliano Sarti, professor of Greek at the Università di Roma, La Sapienza.

74. 'Melchiade Fossati romano, uomo di studi stava di recente a Parigi, ed era adoprato in lavori archeologici dal Conte di Clarac direttore del Louvre, dal sig. Ballanche membro dell'Istituto, e alla Biblioteca Regia, dove solo rediggeva il catalogo di più migliaia di monumenti antichi.' His employment by Ballanche has been mentioned also by Mariano, *Augusto Vera* (above, n. 28), 13.

75. 'In alcun luogo del Vaticano, non già di rado e difficile accesso, ma di quotidiano e pubblico, acciò i nostri studiosi abbiano pieno agio di consultarlo, e profittarne.' M. Fossati, *pro-memoria*, in ASV, Titoli 108 = Musei Vaticani, Archivio Storico, b. 14 g (1847).

76. O. Marucchi, *Il Museo egizio vaticano descritto ed illustrato* (Rome, 1899), 315–16, no. 58 a (IX Sala dei monumenti di imitazione); O. Marucchi, *Guide du Musée égyptien du Vatican* (Rome, 1927), 80, no. 81 (Sala delle imitazioni romane); *Guida breve generale ai Musei e alle Gallerie di pittura del Vaticano, del Laterano e della Biblioteca Vaticana* (Vatican City, 1958), 94, no. 56 (Sala III delle imitazioni); Foto Anderson 23829; Foto Danesi = neg. Musei Vaticani IV.32.14: the piece is within a wooden frame; the last photograph, in Room III, dates to 20 November 1977, no. 28; today the plaster cast, inv. no. 25064, is in the storeroom above the Egyptian Museum.

77. ASV, Titoli 7 = Musei Vaticani, Archivio Storico, b. 20 e (1844), no. 11.

78. MP, Protocollo del Ducale Museo d'Antichità di Parma I (1825–43), II (1844–61); Appendix III, docs 8, 50, 55, 56.

79. An 'antiquaire en diable!'. Letter of 1833 to Romain Colomb,

in H. Martineau and V. Del Litto (eds), *Stendhal, Correspondance* II (Paris, 1967), 502.

80. 'Pour être admis dans le corps d'ailleurs si respectable des archéologues, il faut savoir par coeur Diodore de Sicile, Pline et une douzaine d'autres historiens; de plus, il faut avoir abjuré tout respect pour la logique. Cet art importun est l'ennemi acharné de tous les systèmes.' H. Beyle, 'Les tombeaux de Corneto', *Revue des Deux Mondes* (1 September 1853), 1003.

81. The 'sots, incompétents, crédules, pédants, vaniteux et ridicules, ennuyeux doctrinaires et imbus de l'esprit de système, détestables érudits dépourvus de logique et de sens commun'. A. Hus, 'Stendhal et les Étrusques', in *L'Italie préromaine et la Rome républicaine (Mélanges offerts à Jacques Heurgon)* I (Rome, 1976), 457; S. Nardi (ed.), *Je deviens antiquaire en diable! Io Stendhal, console a Civitavecchia e 'cavatesori' (1831–1842)* (Tarquinia, 1996), 53–4.

82. Mariano, *Augusto Vera* (above, n. 28), 12–13.

83. The 'apparecchio Rignano è una potentissima mina, onde far saltare del tutto le due colonne al primissimo colpo di fulmine'. M. Fossati, *I parafulmini Rignano a conduttore interno, ed a spirale, causa immediata di rovina alle colonne di Trajano e di M. Aurelio. Proemio dell'appendice ministeriale ai lavori famosi del morto ed insepolto Camerlengato* (Rome, 20 July 1848).

84. On the monument, see most recently F. Sinn and K.S. Freyberger, *Vatikanische Museen, Museo Gregoriano Profano ex Lateranense, Katalog der Skulpturen* II. *Die Grabdenkmäler 2, Die Ausstattung des Hateriergrabes* (Mainz, 1996).

85. To 'rivendicare i diritti del Pubblico innanzi i Tribunali ordinari'. M. Fossati, *Le preziose sculture del monumento degli Aterii fortuitamente poco fa discoperte ritrovandosi la Via Labicana in tutto o in parti spettanti al pubblico e possedute dal Capitolo Lateranense per colpa del Sig. Duca Massimi, allora ministro* (Rome, 15 September 1848).

86. 'Decaduto di fatto e di diritto dal governo temporale dello Stato Romano … la democrazia pura …glorioso nome di Repubblica Romana.'

87. 'Die tertia Maji 1849 — Melchiades Fossati qm … postremo die proxime elapsi mensis, cum vim a Gallis in moenia Urbis illatam propulsaret, ignito globulo percussus, illico obiit. Aetatis suae anno octavo post quinquagesimum. Cadaver eius recognitum, inde humo traditum est.' Archivio del Vicariato, Roma, Parrocchia di S. Giacomo in Augusta. Liber Mortuorum [1840–1876], fol. 106; Rivista Militare, *La Repubblica Romana e il suo esercito* (*Quaderno* 4) (Rome, 1987), 103.

88. Archivio del Vicariato, Roma, Ufficio III, Posizioni Matrimoni, 1852, 17992.

89. ASR, Camerlengato I–II, Antichità e Belle Arti, 1816–54; Appendix II, 1850–2; ASV, Titoli 112 (1851), n. 139.

90. V. Golzio, *Raffaello nei documenti, nelle testimonianze dei contemporanei e nella letteratura del suo secolo* (Vatican City, 1936), 119–20.

91. On the bronze vases with the inscription, *suthina*, cf. M.

Pandolfini, 'Rivista di epigrafia etrusca: Volsinii 45–56', *Studi Etruschi* 44 (1976), 243–8.

92. For inv. no. 10529 and inv. no. 9514, cf. F. Sinn and K.S. Freyberger, *Vatikanische Museen, Museo Gregoriano Profano ex Lateranense, Katalog der Skulpturen* I,1. *Die Grabdenkmäler 1, Reliefs, Altäre, Urnen* (Mainz, 1991), 99, no. 79, 25–7, no. 6.

93. F. Della Rosa, 'A proposito delle nuove denominazioni di alcune vie e piazze della città di Amelia', *Archeologia. Gruppo Archeologico Guardeese* 27 (I semestre, 1997), 10.

THE DISCOVERY OF THE ETRUSCANS IN THE EARLY NINETEENTH CENTURY: SOME ARCHIVAL DOCUMENTS

Ronald T. Ridley

INTRODUCTION

WHEN Giuseppe Micali published his epoch-making book *L'Italia avanti il dominio dei Romani* in 1810, in the magnificent volume of illustrations there appeared only the walls and gates at Volterra, some bronzes and gems, and the cinerary urns of the Guarnacci Museum at Volterra. Only two or three of the great underground painted tombs of Tarquinia were known.[1]

In truth, the Tartaglia tomb and the Tomb of the Cardinal had been discovered at Tarquinia in 1699, and excavations at Volterra from the 1720s led to the founding of the Guarnacci Museum in 1750, but one should not forget the even earlier finds at Arezzo: the *Chimaera* (1553), *Minerva* (1554) and *Arringatore* (1566), and from Praeneste the *Ficoroni Cist* (1738). These finds are, however, only one part of the story. The other is the amazing outpouring of scholarship not only describing the collections but also grappling with the most fundamental questions of Etruscan history and culture: Thomas Dempster's *De Etruria Regali Libri Septem* (written 1616–19, published 1723–4, with 93 plates); Antonio Gori's *Musei Guarnacci monumenta etrusca* (1744), *Museum Etruscum* (1737–41) and *Museum Cortonese* (1750); Mario Guarnacci's *Origini italiche* (3 vols; 1767–72); Giovanni Battista Passeri's *Picturae Etruscorum* (the Gualtieri collection) (1767–75); and Luigi Lanzi's *Saggi di lingua etrusca* (1789) and *De' vasi antichi dipinti volgarmente chiamati Etruschi* (1806).

All of this was transformed, however, by the discovery of tombs at Vulci by shepherds in 1827, which for the first time revealed the amazing wealth of the Etruscans. Specialist works on this city usually provide some historical introduction in a few pages on the story of the excavations, but always, it seems, based on published sources. The real account is buried in the Archivio di Stato di Roma.[2]

The discoveries at Vulci made by the shepherds were exploited illegally by the Prussian chargé d'affaires, Wilhelm Dorow. He was pardoned, however, when he gave at least part of his finds to the State.[3] Excited by the spectacular finds, a company was set up in 1828 to excavate with a licence; it consisted of the Candelori (leasers of Camposcala),[4] Vincenzo Campanari (**Fig. 1**)[5] and Melchiade Fossati. The licence was granted on 22 August, and excavations began on 13 October 1828. The result of this first year's work was a collection purchased by the Vatican for 4,500 scudi in January 1829.

These Campanari excavations were to continue for a decade, but the story is one of endless scandal and illegality. The original partners fell out almost immediately over the division of the spoils. The Candelori actually broke into the store at Santa Chiara in Rome, to which only Campanari and Fossati had keys, and removed the collection to their own palace.

The papal minister in charge of antiquities was the Camerlengo, at this time Cardinal Pier Francesco Galleffi (**Fig. 2**). He never trusted Campanari, who had been guilty of 'grave demerits' in the past. There were constant delays in the renewal of his licences. In February 1832, for example, Galleffi refused to renew Campanari's licence because of unauthorized restorations to vases. In June 1833 Campanari was accused of selling finds, especially the best pieces, to foreign collectors, such as Beaufort and Durand. The Commissione Generale Consultiva di Belle Arti, which had been established in 1816 to assist the Camerlengo in the control of excavations, exports and purchases of antiquities, refused to select any material for the museums, because it was unwilling to take only 'leftovers'. When the Commissione visited to view the finds of 1830–1 in the Palazzo Giustiniani,

Fig. 1. *Vincenzo Campanari.* From *Album* (Rome, 1840).

participate in *his* excavation. As for the sharing of the finds, one side was to divide them into two equal parts, and the other party was to have the choice of which half it wanted. The Government still had the right to buy anything of special merit from Campanari's share.

These excavations closed in December 1837. They were marred by scandal. Surveillance must have been minimal, with workers and collectors having a free hand, since in 1836 the supervisor, Artedoro Buontrombone, was dismissed for 'very bad conduct'. It transpires that he had been a soldier, with a list of punishments a page long. All of this, however, was nothing in comparison to the sequel, which broke in 1837.

KING LUDWIG OBTAINS HIS VASES

On 24 November 1837, King Ludwig I of Bavaria (**Fig. 3**) applied directly to Pope Gregory XVI for the right to export his Etruscan collection to Munich. Which collection? Why, the one he had bought from the Candelori, in contravention of Cardinal Galleffi's orders, in 1831.

From the first discoveries, the Candelori had received offers from people like King Ludwig and the Duke de Blacas, French Ambassador and first President of the Deutsches Archäologisches Institut, who were willing to pay up to 25,000 scudi for the 1829 finds that the Commissione valued at 5,000.

Yielding first place to none was King Ludwig. In April 1829 he was in Rome, and what nicer memento of his visit could there have been than three vases from the Candelori collection in the Vatican Museums. Might he even have hinted what would have pleased him most? The Segretario di Stato, Cardinal Giuseppe Albani, told his colleague Galleffi that the King had demonstrated a 'mania' to have some of the newly-found Etruscan vases. There were surely some duplicates that he could have: if possible, those with painted decoration, or some signed by the painter. Pope Pius VIII had personally pointed out how grateful the King would be. He had, moreover, given to the Vatican Museums casts of the Aegina sculptures, so that this

they found total chaos, and some items had been sent off to a restorer called Rosi, who refused to return them. Other finds were lying about in complete disorder on the floor, covered in dust. As well, Fossati decamped in March 1831, taking a 'significant quantity' of the antiquities with him. The year before he had been accused of selling pieces to the Marquis of Northampton.

In 1835, however, the Papal Government incredibly formed a joint company with Campanari to carry on the excavations, relying on the simple logic that it was thus entitled automatically to a share in the finds instead of having to buy them. The contract was signed on 16 January 1835, and laid down that the costs, estimated at 4,000–5,000 scudi per year, were to be shared. As well, the Government was to pay Campanari 1,000 scudi each year for the right to would be simply a return gesture. It was conveniently overlooked that the casts had in fact been given in return for the cession in 1819 of the *Barberini Faun*. It seemed, however, that three vases worthy of the King but that would not deplete the papal collection could not be found. Lucien Bonaparte, Prince of Canino, was therefore asked to produce them from his collection. He chose one mended in antiquity (a fashionable collector's item) and two 'signed' vases by 'Pythia' and Andokides. The Bavarian collection made in this way a modest beginning.[6]

It was in July 1830 that the Candelori asked permission to sell the King sixteen vases for 4,000 scudi. They were admitted to be 'bonded' pieces (that is, reserved by the Commissione for ultimate purchase), but it was promised that they would remain in Rome. The Candelori boldly alluded to the Pacca Edict of 1820, which had aimed to encourage excavations: if this sale were not allowed, that would not happen. Public interest would not be damaged in any way. The King's agent, Johann Martin von Wagner, promised to obey the laws. Moreover, all property rights included that of alienation: if pictures and sculptures could be sold, why not vases? Even bolder reference might be made to such notorious recent episodes as that of Douglas, tenth Duke of Hamilton, who had been allowed to 'extract his share', despite contravention of the law.[7] The Candelori asked less, only that foreigners in Rome might have their share. Galleffi refused permission. The contract was, nevertheless, signed, in June 1831, for 15,000 scudi. The collection included fifteen vases and twelve items in gold. The Candelori later claimed that the Government had declined the offer to buy it. In fact, it had been unable to pay the inflated price asked, but had reserved individual pieces.

The collection was then transferred from the Palazzo Candelori to the Villa Malta. When this was made known, Antonio Candelori was called to court, where he denied on oath that any sale had been made, and claimed that the move was only to make room and save rent. He swore that he was an ardent patriot who would never harm his beloved Rome by alienating such treasures. He even asked the Camerlengo to send agents to seal the bonded pieces. The Candelori were later to use this as the basis of their claim that the Camerlengo

FIG. 2. *Cardinal Pier Francesco Galleffi.*

knew and approved of the transfer to the villa. Out of the collection of 590 items, 332 were bonded. In August 1831, Galleffi wrote to the Segretario di Stato, alarmed at the transfer of the collection to the villa, where it was in the hands of the King's agent, Wagner. He suspected from what he already knew of him that the items would be spirited out of the city in some way. Galleffi recalled with bitterness the case of the *Barberini Faun* and noted the 'bad faith' of the Candelori.

Despite all this, in 1834 the Candelori gave Pope Gregory XVI the famous *Exekias Vase* and as a result, in November 1835, were ennobled as marquises. The story was revealed, as we have seen, in 1837. As a personal favour to King Ludwig, the pope granted the export licence.

Threatened with a fine that might well amount to 50,000 scudi for the vases alone, without taking into

Fig. 3. Joseph Steiler, *Ludwig I in his coronation robes* (detail). *(Reproduced by kind permission of the Bayerische Staatsgemäldssammlungen, Alte Pinakothek, Munich.)*

Minister of Bavaria in Rome intervened with the Segretario di Stato, Cardinal Brunelleschi, to drop the case against the Candelori, on the grounds that it might involve the King. Galleffi replied to Brunelleschi that it concerned only the Candelori. They, in turn, claimed that the whole case was simply a vendetta against them by the secretary of the Commissione Generale Consultiva di Belle Arti, Luigi Grifi, and the new Commissario delle Antichità, Carlo Fea's successor, Pietro Ercole Visconti, who had taken up office in 1836.

THE PRINCE OF CANINO MAKES HIS OWN RULES[8]

In December 1828, Lucien Bonaparte, the 'Principe di Canino' (**Fig. 4**), wrote to Cardinal Galleffi reporting that he had made a few finds in his excavations at Vulci, for which he had been given a licence in September. The objects were mostly broken, but he was bringing them to Rome, to Palazzo Gabrielli, for the Commissione Generale Consultiva di Belle Arti to inspect them. From such modest beginnings arose yet another archaeological scandal.

It transpired that there were 200 vases on show, mostly red-figure ware, in comparison with the predominantly black-figure ware of the Candelori collection. The Commissione agreed that they should be joined with that collection to form a museum. In that way, the museum would then have only to buy special pieces. Prices had in fact been reduced dramatically already by the flooding of the market.

consideration the gold also sold illegally and the criminal deceit involved, which amounted to perjury, the Candelori had the temerity to offer to give up their excavation 'rights' for ten years in place of the fine. This offer was set out in the form of an outrageous calculation of financial gains for the Government, based on the value of the finds that they could expect to make.

The full revelation of the mentality of the Candelori, however, came with the manifesto dated 15 January 1838, in which they announced their plan to continue the excavations. They called on all 'lovers and promoters of antiquity' to join with them in excavating the whole of the ancient city of Vulci. Their address was given as the Palazzo Cavalieri, Via de' Barbieri. They had friends in the highest quarters. In February, the

The vases needed restoration. Much can be learned about this craft in Rome at this time from the reports of the Commissione. There were four experts available: Francesco Depoletti,[9] Rosi, Carlo Ruspi[10] and the mosaicist Bocchigiani. The Commissione devised a neat test: all four were to be given two vases, both needing the same time to restore, and then the results and prices were to be compared. It was suggested by the Commissione, however, that the real experts for this kind of work could be found only in Naples.

There was a special trip to see the collection and the excavations in progress. On 30 May 1829 some six members of the Commissione made the five hours' journey to Civitavecchia, where they were entertained by the Prince and Princess at Musignano. They were amazed at the room upon room full of the most beautiful vases, with another gallery for the bronzes. There followed a visit to Cuccumella, which was being 'completely cleared' (read, ransacked), and there was a show excavation of two tombs, named after Pacca and the Commissione.

The Commissione was interested to note the way in which the Prince was restoring bases, gluing the pieces together and filling in the gaps with a paste made from crushed 'unimportant pieces'. The whole vases numbered 550. The members were alarmed at what criticism there would be if this collection, so much better than that at Naples, were missed, but did not know how to pay for it. The Prince's taxes might be reduced, or he might be offered some state land. This was the clever solution: if he unduly raised the price of the vases, the Commissione could increase the value set on the land.

Then came the not unexpected intervention from on high. In July the Segretario di Stato, Cardinal Albani, wrote to Galleffi on the Prince's behalf. He wished, it seemed, to sell abroad a mere 100 vases. In compensation, he had set aside 25 very precious ones for the Government, 'at a price to be arranged by common agreement'. The Camerlengo's reply of 14 July is memorable, and makes exhilarating reading. The hand behind it must be that of Carlo Fea, the Commissario delle Antichità.

Galleffi began by setting out the laws, emphasizing that the Pacca Edict of 1820 relinquished the State's rights in the matter of antiquities in return for having first choice of any pieces and the right to seal them even for eventual purchase. If the Prince had selected pieces for sale before the Government had exercised its option, he was guilty of contravention of the laws, and was subject to their penalties.

He then proceeded to lecture the Segretario di Stato on antiquities. These Etruscan finds were important not only as art but also as historical sources. The vases would also complement Rome's unrivalled collections of sculpture and painting. And what would be said of a government that allowed such treasures to be exported when 'the learned world from one end to the other' was discussing them? Turning to a more personal level, Galleffi asked how it was possible for the Segretario to countenance such a loss when he came from a family famous for its love of antiquity and its own collections. Such conduct was in contrast to that of the Camerlengo, who was working night and day to enrich

FIG. 4. *Lucien Bonaparte, already (1815) anxious to advertise his intellectual interests.* From *Serie di vite e ritratti di famosi personaggi degli ultimi tempi* (Milan, 1815).

the Museums and prevent the loss of anything worthy to be preserved in them.

If the Prince were allowed to export the best 100 vases, Galleffi continued, how could anyone else be refused the same right, especially the Bavarians. The offer of 25 vases in compensation might be taken as an insult if one did not know the Prince's 'courtesy'. What status as an expert did he have to make the choice? What compensation were 25 for 100, especially when he was anticipating a price of 100,000 scudi for that 100? Under no circumstances, Galleffi concluded, was the licence to be granted. How typical that such people tried to evade the laws and use their influence with other sections of the Government.

The response was astounding. Albani conveyed Galleffi's views to Pius VIII, who demanded that the

Vatican Museums immediately choose what was wanted, so that the Prince could then do what he wanted with the rest, including exporting them.

At the end of August, Francesco Pelagi, the Prince's agent, announced that the collection had arrived at the Palazzo Gabrielli at Monte Giordano. The Commissione Generale Consultiva di Belle Arti was divided into three groups in view of the complexity of the task before them, to classify and choose. The visits began in September and took two weeks in all. The commissioners chose 168 objects of first-class merit valued at 150 scudi each (25,200), 129 of second-class at 75 (9,675), 112 of third-class and five of the fourth, all at 37.50 (4,200 and 187), in all 39,262 scudi. On 12 October the members met to discuss the choices and prices. There was unanimous agreement about everything. A list was to be drawn up of objects not to be exported, which included, of course, the 100 vases that the Prince had set aside and that were at the palazzo of Cardinal Fesch, Napoleon's uncle, living in Rome since the restoration of the Bourbons.

In December, Albani again wrote to Galleffi concerning what he called the Prince's 'very just request' that he be allowed to dispose freely of what the Museums did not want. His appeals were characterized as 'very strong'. Galleffi replied that cataloguing the vases was very complicated; it was in fact finished in February 1830.

Precisely as these legal procedures were completed, on 17 February 1830, the Prince wrote to Galleffi saying that the Commissione had chosen the very best vases, but that he had already been offered 100,000 scudi for the 100 at Fesch's palace by Donato in Florence. He stated bluntly that he would keep these prize vases for himself until either the Government offered him the same price or he were allowed to export them. For all the other objects that the Commissione had chosen, so great was his wish to see them in the Vatican Museums that he was prepared to sacrifice them for 100,000 scudi.

Galleffi's reply was a masterpiece, and very restrained. Certainly the law allowed the Prince to keep whatever he wanted, but they could not be sold abroad and a list had to be provided. He had, however, already contravened the law by transferring some things to the Palazzo Fesch. As for the Government having to pay 100,000 scudi for the 100 vases and the same price again for the rest of what the Commissione had chosen, that was unacceptable. The Government would pay 39,000 scudi for what had been selected. The laws laid down that the price offered be reason-able, in other words as established by the Commissione. Its members, the Prince was reminded, performed their duties without pay, and were 'the most respectable group of experts in Rome'. He himself had accepted their valuation of a collection of sculpture in 1822. In conclusion, Galleffi clearly enunciated higher principles: no private person should complain if the Government wished to buy art for public edification, and even less so when the Government waived its own fiscal rights for the advantage of such private owners.

It was then that the Prince's dishonesty was fully revealed, as if it were not already blatant. In March 1830 he requested the right to export 40 vases to Florence, assuring the Camerlengo that no reserved vases were among them. Three members of the Commissione went to examine them. The list provided gave only numbers, with no description, and they were hidden within the collection. When they were found, no fewer than ten were revealed as reserved. The Prince then had the audacity, after putting the Commissione to such trouble, to ask it to approve 50 vases for export. Galleffi accused him of lying, but amazingly sent the three members of the Commissione again four days later. This time they found only two reserved vases, and so allowed 48 to go. One can only be amazed at their expertise in detecting so many frauds among the chaos deliberately created by the Prince. The value of the vases to be exported was not increased then by the Commissione but remained at a derisory 418 scudi. The exporter thus paid virtually no tax, but clearly counted on vastly inflated prices in Florence. He was in April allowed to send off another 97 vases.

The members of the Commissione had been treated as fools by the Prince, but had operated by the strict letter of the law, and even with considerable generosity. His response revealed much. In May he wrote to Galleffi, declaring roundly that the value set on his collection was unworthy of artists and educated men. It was a 'gratuitous irony', an attempt to impose on the 'religion and fairness' of the Camerlengo. His own valuation was very low compared with the prices such art fetched in Naples and Paris. He was out of patience, and breaking off all negotiations. In a mixture of irony and bluff, he claimed that he would sell them within the Papal States, as the law allowed. In an attempt to give himself credentials as a scholar, rather than a mere trader in antiquities, he was pleased to include copies of his catalogue.[11]

This hardly compared with his letter of 3 June,

which one might describe as that of someone mentally unhinged. He accused Galleffi of not listening to anything he said: he wanted to sell 2,623 pieces, not 329, and their value was 380 scudi each, not 150 (a total of 996,740 scudi). How could the father of a family be deprived of his property? The Government offered him 150 or even 37 scudi for each piece, when he could get 1,000. He announced that he intended to inform public opinion throughout Europe how the Government cheapened Etruscan antiquities. He would ask the pope to allow the export of what the Commissione so scorned. He concluded by accusing the Government of acting like that of Egypt, infamous for its monopolies.

Galleffi's reply calmly asserted that if anyone else had written him such a letter he would not deign to respond. Instead, he most courteously reasserted that the Government's only purpose was 'public ornament and instruction'.

As good as his word, the Prince tried again to go over Galleffi's head. Albani wrote again to Galleffi on his behalf. The Prince was raising, as he described it, a 'clamour' about the price offered to him, and resorting 'energetically' to the pope, who had asked Albani to attempt an accommodation. The Segretario's suggested solution was outrageous: that the existing list of reserved items be divided in two, namely those really reserved, but which were to form the Prince's own museum, and the rest, which could be exported. And for this granting of carte blanche to do as he wanted with everything, Albani suggested that it would be better to choose a new group of experts.

Galleffi's reply was another masterpiece of restraint and logic. First, the Prince had known the conditions when he had applied for the licence (a devastating demolition of his whole case). Second, he could not claim that he was not allowed to export what the Government did not regard as indispensable. He had already exported many items, and the Government chose only 414 pieces out of 2,000. Why did he not export the rest? Third, a new panel of experts would by definition be inferior to the first, because all the best were already members of the Commissione. In conclusion, it was revealed that the Prince had not sold a single vase sent to Florence, because the prices he was asking were thought laughable.

The Etruscan collection of Lucien Bonaparte was in fact dispersed all over Europe, especially to Paris and Munich, but some can be found in the Vatican Museums. Stendhal estimated Canino's profit to 1840 at 1,200,000 francs.[12]

EXCAVATIONS AT BOMARZO

A perfect example of Etruscan excavations in these years, and one on which we have some detail,[13] is at Bomarzo. The owner of the local coffee-shop, Domenico Ruggeri, the head of a large family, began work in October 1830. He is described as an 'uneducated person' and therefore kept no records of interest to an antiquarian. Typical is 65 items, found in four tombs, and mostly called simply *tazzetti* (little cups). The finds were, however, so valuable that by December the ubiquitous Vincenzo Campanari paid 800 scudi to be admitted as an associate. And as early as the beginning of the next year enquiries were being made to see if Ruggeri had been selling anything, but nothing was discovered in Viterbo. His licence was therefore reissued.

In August 1831 Ruggeri reported on the first season (October 1830–June 1831). The excavations had uncovered 'many beautiful' objects — vases, bronzes, funerary urns. Ruggeri confessed that he had received many offers for these, and he admitted that he needed money to continue. He therefore offered the Government all or part of his finds.

A report was also made by the auxiliary (provincial) Commissione Generale Consultiva di Belle Arti at Viterbo in January 1832. It is enough to make one's hair stand on end. One hundred and fifty tombs had been discovered and cleared. The necropolis was on a slope between the Tiber and the stream of the Vezza, some two miles from Mugnano, three from Bomarzo and seven from Ferento. The idea to excavate came when Ruggeri saw some vases found by the Prince of Canino at Vulci. The Commissione stated firmly, however, that his motives were far from vulgar. He found others to finance the work, and cleverly obtained permission from the landowners. (One wonders what the arguments were that were used when these arrangements were made.) The Commissione admitted that it was not sure that all items found had been reported, but if anything had been lost, that was not entirely Ruggeri's fault. The Government inspector, one Michele Piermarini, visited only once or twice, and simply signed 'seen' on the bottom of the lists. What had he seen: the excavations, the objects found, or the lists? It was noted also that after Campanari joined, all objects were deposited in confusion in the store.

Ruggeri may have been without culture, but was not without needs. The Commissione Generale Consultiva di Belle Arti met in Rome in April 1832 to consider his claim for 5,000 scudi for the items chosen by the

Government for purchase. The bronzes were especially impressive. In July 1833 the Vatican Museums acquired three bronze vases, a candelabrum, a strainer and a set of armour for 200 scudi, and in October another set of armour for 400 scudi. It was obviously better not to rush such negotiations.[14]

ETRUSCAN FRAUD ON A LARGE SCALE

Since the late 1820s excavations had proceeded at a feverish pace in every location where one might expect to find traces of the ancient Etruscans. The motives were entirely mercenary, and in the early days there were vast fortunes to be made. The market soon, however, became flooded with vases and prices plummeted. It then became vital to get the material out of Italy, to countries where collectors were still willing to pay vast sums.[15]

In June 1832, the secretary of the Commissione Generale Consultiva di Belle Arti, Grifi, wrote to the President, Monsignor Gropelli, with the first intimations that all was not well. The results of his enquiries were horrifying. The members of the auxiliary Commissione at Civitavecchia, for example, were 'the first to traffic in objects that escape the vigilance of the law'. Names were produced: Feoli, Campanari and the Prince of Canino were not obeying the laws about reporting finds, even for large items, such as a chariot. Pietro Manzi, a judge in the contraband court and a member of the Commissione, 'excavates, discovers, and sells in stealth, betraying the loyalty owed to his post'; he was at that time trying to sell six granite columns found at Tarquinia. The Prince had taken cartloads of finds to the coast, to ship them out. Campanari had sent cases of finds to England and France, making a mockery of the Camerlengo's laws.

Then there were the smaller fry. Avvolta, Querciola, Falzacappa and Mariani all had vast personal collections of Etruscan antiquities, which they offered for sale to foreigners. When painted tombs were discovered, the paintings were removed and the tombs blown up to cover the criminals' tracks. And Depoletti was continually restoring exquisite vases which then totally disappeared. The principal cause of all these difficulties was the fact that there was no one on the spot capable of assessing the finds.

Much of these comments was based on Grifi's own experiences. He had often seen Etruscan material being restored in Roman workshops and the people there refused to tell him who owned it.

Cardinal Galleffi's response was to send copies of this report to both Civitavecchia and Viterbo, asking the local authorities for explanations. The Commissione met on 7 August 1832 to consider the crisis. Those responsible were not, at first, named. It was resolved to send out someone intelligent (sic) to investigate. It was realized that there were no trustworthy people to supervise the excavations. It was known that some tombs had been blown up, and that inspectors did not visit the excavations but simply signed the reports. That was, of course, assuming that a licence had been sought and granted — and in many cases it had not.

In May 1833, Grifi made a further report, to Galleffi. The police investigations had revealed as the only criminals the Prince of Canino and Campanari. They had both excavated in places 'most abundant in discoveries', and had removed vast quantities of material; a local customs-official at Camposcala, one Rufini, had even been corrupted. The Prince was said to have found more than 20,000 items, the majority and best of which he had exported. Even the 100 reserved vases in the Palazzo Fesch were now in Florence. Campanari was known to have discovered fourteen notable bronzes, excellently preserved, some with figures on them, and one weighing 500 lbs, a set of armour inlaid with silver, and gold necklaces. None had been listed in his reports.

At the meeting of the Commissione on 21 June 1833, it was admitted that legal proof was still lacking against Campanari for the illegal sale of Etruscan antiquities, but that it was impossible to tolerate his scorn for the Government. It was decided to send people pretending to be buyers to obtain evidence. The Commissario delle Antichità, Fea, was also investigating in Rome, and would soon know if some objects were hidden near Sant'Ignazio.

In the light of this, it is amazing to find the Commissione in August considering buying a *cista* (cist) from Campanari. Overwhelmed by the proofs of clandestine sales, however, it was decided instead to put seals on his storeroom and to call him to account. The suggestion was approved that pottery from both the Campanari and Feoli collections should be requisitioned, equivalent to the export tax payable.

By the meeting in January 1834, however, Campanari had made a gift of bronzes to the Camerlengo to avoid prosecution. It was decided to wait until the end of the year to take action, depending on his conduct. In November, the Commissione decided not to buy his whole collection, but only certain select pieces. The bronzes given to the Camerlengo were to be valued 'in expiation of his transgressions'. In December, it was agreed to buy only six or seven vases, notably that of Priam, valued at 500 scudi; the bronzes were valued at 800 scudi. These vases and bronzes were then valued together at 2,500 scudi, which was agreed to as a fine. All disputes between the Camerlengo and Campanari were thereupon regarded as settled. Gregory XVI had approved of the joint society for continued excavations. And that is where this retelling of history from the archives began.

CONCLUSION

These episodes reveal how glaringly at variance are the contemporary records in the archives with the anodyne, technical account found in most histories of Etruscology, or the bare notes found in even specialist works on particular sites. For example, the doyen of French Etruscologists at the time, Jacques Heurgon, in 1973 delivered an address to the Académie des Inscriptions on precisely the early nineteenth-century discoveries.[16] It was essentially a literary essay, beginning with Giuseppe Micali and his feud with Desiré Raoul-Rochette, turning to Stendhal and then to the painted tombs at Tarquinia and the argument between Baron von Stackelburg and Raoul-Rochette again, in which Dorow and the 80 years old Goethe also became involved. Heurgon's main source was an article by Fritz Weege.[17] A second example is the admirable study of Vulci by Maria Falconi Amorelli, who provided a most detailed chronology of excavations.[18] With only two archival exceptions, the bibliography is a very comprehensive collection of monographs and journals, notably the *Bullettino dell'Instituto di Corrispondenza Archeologica*, and the later *Notizie degli Scavi di Antichità* and *Studi Etruschi*. One cannot suggest that archival sources for the history of archaeology have not long been prized: one has only to think of Rodolfo Lanciani's *Storia degli scavi*, which began in 1902. And surely the attraction of the archives is obvious: here are the living human documents by the leading participants in the story.

On the other hand, their use does involve much labour, under conditions rather different from those in libraries and the consultation of published sources. There are also fundamental questions that must be addressed. The above account very obviously takes sides in many controversies. It is proper to ask how this can be justified. The answer is simple. In a copious collection of such documents, there is more than enough to allow an experienced historian to form judgements. Statements can be scrutinized internally for consistency and also cross-checked against others. There will be charge, countercharge and defence, and one can assess the evidence. And the major participants provide enough statements of their own for the historian to gain, test and confirm impressions, exactly as one does in real life. It would be impossible for any impartial reader of these documents not to be convinced, for example, that the Prince of Canino habitually lied and that his motives were primarily mercenary. Faced with a choice between the rodomontade and self-incrimination of the Prince and the reason and manners of Galleffi, one does not hesitate for a moment.

Something must also be said, in fairness, of the position of archaeology at this time in the early nineteenth century. It was still very much of a treasure hunt, as far as the excavators were concerned, and would continue to be so until the end of the century — and even beyond. On the other hand, Rome had had laws to protect her cultural patrimony since at least the fifteenth century, if not earlier.[19] The city had also had museums since then: the Capitoline (1471), the Belvedere (1503). Although, therefore, for centuries before the 1820s there had been legislation to protect the cultural patrimony, a new era may be said to have dawned with the appointment of Carlo Fea as Commissario delle Antichità (1800–36), the first lawyer to hold the post, the drafter of a new code (the Chirografo of 1802) and determined to uphold these laws.[20] Major stimulus to this new code had been given by the depredations under the so-called Treaty of Tolentino (1797), but most of these deported works of art were returned in 1815.[21] The next code, the Pacca Edict of 1820, was in turn influenced by that fact and seemed more generous to excavators.[22] The Government, however, still had the right to purchase major pieces for museums at the prices established by the Commissione Generale Consultiva di Belle Arti. There was, on the other hand, no hindrance to the excavator's preferring to retain such pieces, although they could not be exported. It was, it must be stressed, not being laid down that nothing could be exported, that no one elsewhere had the right to admire any of the Italian finds. There was a vast selection for collectors such as Ludwig of Bavaria. The national museums were simply to retain the choicest pieces, and the legal procedures were to be observed for sorting and evalu-ating such items. Any government then or now would insist on as much. The evidence of the archives is incontrovertible: the highest authorities were continu-ally flouted.

Two fundamental principles were, in addition, being stressed by the Government in its difficult dealings with these excavators and collectors: these archaeo-logical discoveries constituted vital evidence for history and art, and had to be treated accordingly; and the requirements of the state should take precedence over private persons' mania for collecting and profit.

There were, however, fortunes to be made, and locals of all classes instantly realized it, from the local aris-tocracy — or parvenus such as Lucien Bonaparte —, wealthy landowners and merchants to the very poor, such as the keeper of the local coffee-house.

These finds in Etruria were, by definition, out of the range of control of the Commissione Generale Consultiva di Belle Arti in Rome. One can have only the highest respect for the professional, unrelenting and unpaid labours of the Camerlengo's men, headed by the Commissario delle Antichità, Carlo Fea. Attempts were made already in 1816 to set up regional equivalents throughout the Papal States. The members perforce were local personalities, ranging from amateur antiquarians and municipal historians to those eminent socially and economically, who had more of an eye to their own profit. With the explosion of Etruscan discoveries, there was no organization cap-able of controlling the excavations or finds in anything like a scientific way.

The Commissione at Rome did its best to bring the criminals to book. It was defeated by a variety of devices. First and foremost, it must be admitted, there was the sheer audacity of the excavators, the dealers and their customers. Not even the pope could deny Ludwig of Bavaria anything he wanted. One would have thought that the Prince of Canino were the descendant of a long-established and most eminent house to hear his arrogant demands. As always, the poor Camerlengo was regarded by such people as a lesser figure in the papal bureaucracy, who could be bypassed. The man in this post in the late 1820s and early 1830s, Galleffi, comes through to us as a deter-mined upholder of the law, undoubtedly fully supported and briefed by the paladin of the protection of the cultural patrimony, Fea. It was men like Albani, Segretario di Stato, who could be appealed to so successfully by the arrogant. And finally, the ultimate paradox: Gregory XVI was prepared to forgive notori-ous criminals like Campanari in order to enter into an agreement with them for joint excavations, reasoning that in this way the state would obtain the best pieces for the Vatican Museums at minimum cost. The major result was, in fact, the creation of the Gregorian Etruscan Museum in 1836. Its contents, however, must represent the mere 'leftovers', as the Commissione itself admitted, from the inestimable riches of those first discoveries.

Notes

1. J. Heurgon, 'La découverte des Etrusques au début du XIX s.', *Comptes-rendus de l'Académie des Inscriptions et Belles-Lettres* (1973), 591–600. See also P. Ducati, 'La ricerca archeologica nell'Etruria. Cenni storici', *Atene e Roma* 16 (1913), 277–305; R. Bloch, 'Le XVIII s. et l'Etrurie', *Latomus* 16 (1957), 128–39; M. Cristofani, *La scoperta degli Etruschi* (Rome, 1983), but only up to the end of the eighteenth century.

2. Specialist studies of the city often give a history of the excavations; for example, A. Hus, *Vulci* (Paris, 1971), 173–80. His chronology is based extensively on F. Messerschmidt, *Nekropolen von Vulci* (Berlin, 1930), 2–12. More detailed is M. Falconi Amorelli, *Vulci* (Rome, 1983), 11–17. The first excavations were in 1783, near Ponte della Badia, by Cardinal Pallotta. (This is, in fact, now to be emended to the Prada excavations, 1776–8: F. Buranelli, 'Si sarebbe potuta chiamare 'vulcente' la cultura villanoviana', *BMusPont* 11 (1991), 5–50.) The first nineteenth-century ones were in 1828, by a company formed by Vincenzo Campanari, the Candelori brothers and Melchiade Fossati, from which the finds are scattered all over Europe. In the same year both Agostino Feoli and Lucien Bonaparte worked at Camposcala and Ponte della Badia, and again the finds were sold all over Europe, not to mention Lucien Bonaparte at Camposcala and Cuccumella, ransacking enormous numbers of tombs. Then came the society formed between the Campanari and the Papal Government working at Camposcala, which Falconi Amorelli dated 1833–8. On this we have now the splendid specialist work by F. Buranelli, *Gli scavi a Vulci della Società Vincenzo Campanari–Governo Pontificio (1835–1837)* (Rome, 1991), which does use the archives. (I am pleased to have found for Buranelli the original contract for the society, which had been very much misplaced in the archives.) The documentation of these finds is among the richest in the archives, with weekly reports of finds in many huge boxes: ASR, Camerlengato II (IV), 160–4.

3. Wilhelm Dorow is an interesting person about whom it is hard to find any information. The following is derived from *Neuer Nekrolog der Deutschen* 23 (1845) (published 1847). He was born at Königsberg in 1790 and was trained as an architect. He then turned to trade with his uncle, but it did not suit him; he meanwhile studied mathematics and philology. In 1811 he went to France, where contacts in the Prussian Embassy opened a diplomatic career, but in 1812 he began military service with the Guards; he served in Poland and France, and became Director of the Allied Military Hospital in Frankfurt. By 1816 he was Secretary of the Legation in Dresden, then in 1817 in Copenhagen. After falling ill, he undertook excavations and was Director of Antiquities in Rhein-Westphalia 1820–2, in which capacity he founded the Bonn Museum. He was briefly in the Ministry of Foreign Affairs in 1822, before being pensioned. In 1827 he journeyed to Italy, where his name is to be remembered for these Etruscan beginnings; his great collection went to Berlin. He died at Halle in 1845. He published much, especially *Etrurien und der Orient* (Berlin, 1829).

4. The Candelori are not to be found in *DBI*, or even in the *Archivio biografico italiano* (microfiche).

5. Campanari cannot be found in either of the above biographical reference works. Not even Buranelli, *Gli scavi a Vulci* (above, n. 2), 45, can offer much beyond his dates of birth and death (1772–1840). His son published an obituary in *Album* (1841), 163. There is now an entry in N. de Grummond (ed.), *An Encyclopedia of the History of Classical Archaeology* I (New York, 1996), 224. Most interesting light is shed on him later by the story of his London exhibition in 1837; see G. Colonna, 'Archeologia dell'età romantica in Etruria', *Studi Etruschi* 46 (1978), 81–117. The exhibition was at 121 Pall Mall, in the form of some eleven reconstructed tombs. The real purpose, however, is revealed to be not educational but commercial: the British Museum bought most of the items. How much of an innovation it was to show tomb interiors is doubtful: Giambattista Belzoni had exhibited models of the tomb of the nineteenth dynasty pharaoh Seti I in Piccadilly in 1821.

6. ASR, Camerlengato II (IV), 197.1058.

7. Hamilton was allowed to export in 1825 two columns illegally extracted from San Giorgio in Velabro. See R.T. Ridley, *The Pope's Archaeologist: the Life and Times of Carlo Fea* (Rome, 2000), 228.

8. For the following events, see ASR, Camerlengato II (IV), 188.

9. Depoletti (1779–1854), a student of Pompeo Batoni, became a mosaicist, then learned ceramic restoration at Naples, for which he became famous all over Europe.

10. On Carlo Ruspi (1786–1863), see de Grummond, *Encyclopedia* (above, n. 5), II, 994.

11. *Catalogo di scelte antichità etrusche trovate negli scavi del Principe di Canino 1828–1829* (Viterbo, 1829). There is a charming history of the excavations on p. 171: two disloyal agents by chance found Etruscan vases early in 1828 near Cuccumella, and sold them to Dorow. The Princess obtained a licence to excavate in October; the Prince himself was at that time totally occupied in his astronomy with the Herschell telescope. By the time he arrived in December, the finds had already been transferred to the palazzo of Cav. Valentini. In four months, more than 2,000 objects had been found.

12. See A. Pietromarchi, *Luciano Bonaparte* (Modena, 1980), 301ff.; for Stendhal, *Correspondance* X (Paris, 1927–), 240–1. Some will notice how much the account of all these events in the archives is completely at variance with the accounts to be found in biographical references on the enlightened aristocrat, so devoted to science. Most notably, in 1995 there appeared a volume, *Luciano Bonaparte, le sue collezioni d'arte, le sue residenze a Roma, nel Lazio, in Italia (1804–1840)* (Rome, 1995), containing a long chapter by F. Buranelli: 'Gli scavi a Vulci 1828–1854 di Luciano ed Alessandrine Bonaparte', 81–218. Buranelli is an archival scholar of great experience, but what he chose to report from these records is completely different from my own findings from the same sources. He reconstructed the excavations, the finds, and their dispersal, but said nothing of the human side of these events, least of all Canino's materialism and ruthlessness, not to say criminal behaviour. The Commissione is mentioned only on pp. 88–92.

Buranelli stressed rather Canino's 'scientific rigour and method' and his fine 'laboratory for reconstruction' (p. 84), the marvellous detail and speed of his catalogues (p. 86). It is even suggested that the Commissione could work with 'greater calm' in the Palazzo Gabrielli (p. 89). Economic motives are only alluded to (p. 82), although it is admitted that the scattering of the finds in so many locations was to facilitate their sale (p. 89) — so were the catalogues. The main motive was in fact to impede as far as possible accurate evaluation by the Commissione.

13. ASR, Camerlengato II (IV), 208.1326.

14. For the excavations at Bomarzo, north of the town in the angle between the Tiber and the Vezza, see *BullInst* (1830), 234; (1832), 195; (1834), 50; G. Dennis, *The Cities and Cemeteries of Etruria* I (London, 1848 and 1907), 258–71 (in the Everyman edition of 1907), who mentioned these finds; A. Testa, *Candelabri e thymiateria* (Rome, 1989), 5 — the acquired candelabra are nos. 53 and 55.

15. ASR, Camerlengato II (IV), 208, 217.1695, 223.1947, 224.1967, 227.2098, 233.2260.

16. Heurgon, 'La découverte des Etrusques' (above, n. 1).

17. F. Weege, 'Etruskische Gräber mit Gemalden in Corneto', *Jahrbuch des Deutschen Archäologischen Instituts* 31 (1916), 105–68.

18. Falconi Amorelli, *Vulci* (above, n. 2).

19. R.T. Ridley, *The Eagle and the Spade. Archaeology in Rome During the Napoleonic Era 1809–1814* (Cambridge, 1992), ch. 1; R.T. Ridley, 'To protect the monuments: the papal antiquarian 1534–1870', *Xenia Antiqua* 1 (1992), 117–54.

20. R.T. Ridley, 'In defence of the cultural patrimony: Carlo Fea goes to court', *Xenia Antiqua* 5 (1996), 143–58.

21. R.T. Ridley, 'An unpleasant bicentenary: the Treaty of Tolentino', *Xenia Antiqua* 6 (1997), 175–94.

22. Ridley, *The Pope's Archaeologist* (above, n. 7), ch. 12.

Excavations in Etruria in the 1880s: the case of Veii[*]

Paolo Liverani

INTRODUCTION

In recent years, much has been written about the archaeology of 'Roma Capitale'. This phrase is a historiographic term alluding to Rome's role as the capital city of unified Italy in the immediate post-Risorgimento period. From the 1870s, important archaeological discoveries were made during a period of rapid and chaotic growth, which transformed Rome into a modern city but also caused irreparable damage to its monuments and countryside. Less well known are the excavations in the Roman Campagna, in which the principal figures of Roman archaeology operated against the more traditional background of the large estates of the landed aristocracy. The case of Veii is particularly interesting, because it illustrates this transition in Italian society and, thus, between two ways of pursuing archaeology. One of the protagonists of the excavations at Veii in the 1880s was Rodolfo Lanciani. His frenetic activities in Rome are well known. Equally known are his excavations and studies on neighbouring sites such as Ostia, Portus, and Hadrian's Villa near Tivoli. But his activities at the Etruscan city of Veii are little known and rarely associated with him. Documents and drawings are preserved in various collections in Rome, and they permit us to obtain a more detailed picture than that which emerges from his own publications. The material is preserved in the Biblioteca dell'Istituto Nazionale di Archeologia e Storia dell'Arte at the Palazzo Venezia, the Archivio Centrale dello Stato, the Biblioteca Apostolica Vaticana and the archive of the Soprintendenza Archeologica per l'Etruria Meridionale at the Villa Giulia. This essay offers a synthesis of the colourful nature of Lanciani's work at Veii, as it emerges from these sources.

RODOLFO LANCIANI AT VEII

Rodolfo Lanciani first worked at Veii in 1878 (**Fig. 1**). In that year, barely 30 years of age, he travelled to nearby Campagnano in his capacity as Direttore dell'Ufficio Tecnico degli Scavi (Director of the Technical Excavation Office). His mission was to examine a bust of Antinous dressed as Bacchus that had been ploughed up on a property situated just north of Veii.[1] The records about the find are thin, consisting of a report written by Lanciani for the Ministero della Pubblica Istruzione (Ministry for Public Instruction) and a short note preserved among his papers. The present whereabouts of the bust is unknown;[2] it may have become the property of the Marchese Ferrajoli, who had perpetual rights over the lands around the city, but more likely it entered the collection of the owner of the land on which it was discovered, that is to say Donna Teresa Cristina di Borbone, Empress of Brazil, to whom we shall return below.

Four years later, following the discovery of a tumulus at Monte Aguzzo,[3] Lanciani became interested once again in excavations in the territory of Veii. The tumulus was built on the top of a hill, a short distance from Formello, and is still visible from the plateau of Veii and the surrounding countryside. It probably was part of a larger necropolis. Sir William Gell noted another tomb nearby, which in his own day had been practically destroyed.[4] Early in the twentieth century, Thomas Ashby recorded that 'two other tombs of the same group, built in the same style, had been located on the summit of the mountain, but they were destroyed by the miners digging for pozzolana'.[5] Between 1901 and 1902, the Benedetti brothers identified various burials in the same area;[6] they excavated a chamber-tomb and a tomb *a cassone*, both of which lacked furnishings.[7]

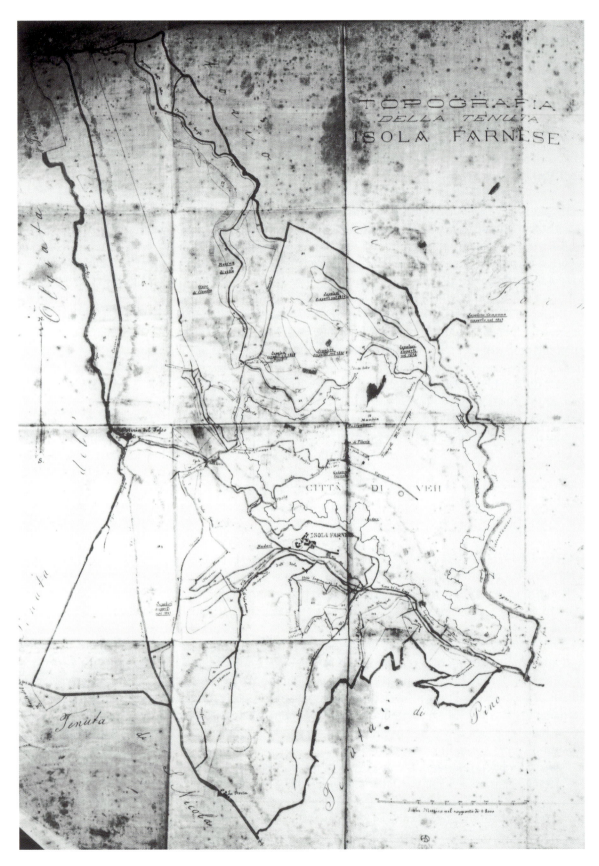

FIG. 1. Map of Veii with the sites of the excavations carried out by Lanciani in 1889 marked on it. Biblioteca dell'Istituto Nazionale di Archeologia e Storia dell'Arte, Palazzo Venezia, Rome, Collezione Lanciani, MS 79. *(Reproduced courtesy of the Istituto Nazionale di Archeologia e Storia dell'Arte, Rome.)*

EXCAVATIONS AT MONTE AGUZZO

In January 1882, Lorenzo Marini discovered a burial chamber, with walls of tufa blocks, while digging for *pozzolana* on Monte Aguzzo (**Fig. 2**). Representatives of the landowner, Prince Mario Chigi, finished his excavations, but only after the tomb had been opened and most of the furnishings removed. Interesting details are given by various sources, including the correspondence published by Lanciani in the British journal *Athenaeum*,[8] notes in Lanciani's personal archive,[9] and two letters he addressed to the Ministro della Pubblica Istruzione.[10] The letters are accompanied by sketches, which illustrate the tomb and some of the finds. These sources permit us to see some of the most colourful aspects of this story, and also to add some important archaeological information to what can be found in the slim publication of this excavation.

Marini, the man responsible for the discovery, was immediately jailed. It was claimed that he was to blame for the disappearance of the bulk of the finds.[11] We do not know how he managed to wriggle out of it, but, perhaps for lack of clear proof, he was set free. Lanciani, who was told of the discovery and had informed Prince Chigi, was invited by the latter to inspect the excavation site. He went there for the first time on 29 and 30 January 1882. The grave consisted of a dromos and three chambers. Four amphorae remained in one of the side rooms opened by Marini (**Figs 2** (letter 'B'), **3** and **4**).[12] Part of an iron tripod was also found.[13] Another small room had already been destroyed by *pozzolana* miners, or *tombaroli*, while in the larger room the vault had collapsed and had buried its rich furnishings, which were found broken into fragments. These included a Nicosthenian amphora of bucchero and, most importantly, the most famous Greek vase found at Veii, the Chigi Olpe.[14] A restorer called Dardano, otherwise unknown, assembled the fragments of this.

The opportunity was taken to make other test trenches in the tomb, as well as in the immediate

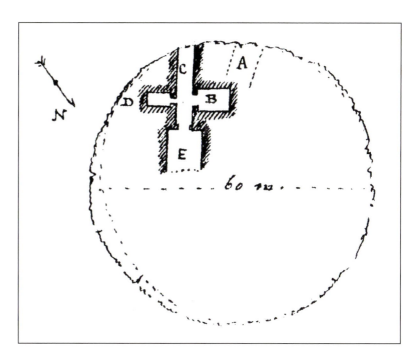

FIG. 2. Rodolfo Lanciani, Plan of the tomb at Monte Aguzzo: letter 'A' marks the pozzolana quarry. Archivio Centrale dello Stato, Rome, Antichità e Belle Arti II vers., I ser., b. 252, fasc. 4376 (R. Lanciani, letter of 31 January 1882).

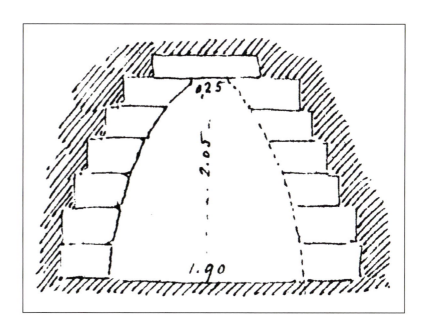

FIG. 3. Rodolfo Lanciani, Section of the side chamber B. Archivio Centrale dello Stato.

vicinity. We do not have a coherent description of this work but, in a short note preserved among his papers, Lanciani recorded the excavation of 'a *montarozzetto* [a little hill] near Monte Acuto', probably a small tumulus.[15] From it came to light '*cassettoni* [coffers] dug into the tufa' and 'many vases, but all black except one [decorated] with a young goose'.

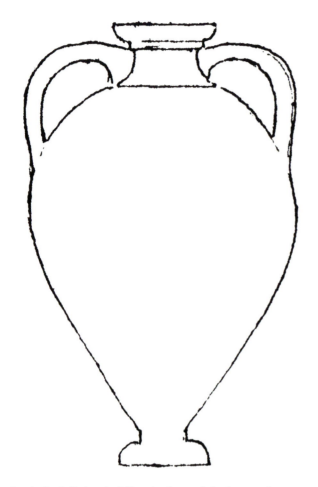

FIG. 4. Rodolfo Lanciani, Sketch of one of the four amphorae.
Archivio Centrale dello Stato.

We may infer that the 'black vases' were of
bucchero, while that decorated with 'the young
goose' leads one to think of an *askos* of a later date.
Included with Lanciani's note are two sketches and
short comments (**Fig. 5**). The first is the plan of a
chamber-tomb dug into the tufa, with a long dromos
and a bed against the right-hand wall, 'supported by
two pilasters', beneath which was found 'a quantity
of black vases'. The second is the plan of three flanking chamber-tombs, all of which had a dromos. The
tomb in the middle had a burial niche in the wall to
the right of the dromos. The tomb on the right had a
bed against the right-hand wall of the chamber. The
tombs were located about 200 m from Monte
Aguzzo. Short notes added that 'in the little grotto'
— probably in the burial niche of the dromos of the
central chamber — there were 'two sherds and two
scarabs', whereas 'an inscribed vase' was found in
the central chamber. While we have lost track of the
two scarabs,[16] the inscribed vase should be identified
with the famous alphabetarium of Formello.[17] This

means that it was not found with the olpe, as was
previously thought on the basis of the brief note that
was published about it.

To complete the story, I must digress a little from
the chronological limits of this essay. In 1903,
Lorenzo Milani obtained permission from Prince
Mario Chigi to remove one of the lateral chambers of
the main tomb and place it in the garden of the Museo
Archeologico of Florence.[18] The reason for doing so
is interesting: the tomb was to be removed 'before the
shepherds, who build a fire there every day, traces of
which remain, may damage it; and also before the
peasants destroy it by taking away its stones to fix up
their huts'.[19] A decade later, in 1913, the Italian State
purchased the olpe and the alphabetarium for 10,000
lire.[20] On the same occasion, the Chigi family
donated 'many other ceramic fragments making up
the furnishings of the same tomb and of three others
discovered on Monte Acuto' to the Villa Giulia
Museum.[21] These last are apparently those recorded
in the second sketch by Lanciani. The remaining finds
were acquired in 1917, when the Italian State
purchased the Palazzo Chigi.[22] The finds are
preserved today in the Villa Giulia Museum; they are
unpublished, and it seems impossible to reconstruct
their original associations.[23] They form an important
collection of orientalizing and archaic vases, though
scattered among them are some pieces that are somewhat later in date. It is not clear, however, if these
pieces were part of a later burial, or whether they
were added to the collection by mistake.[24]

Let us now return to Lanciani and his excavations.
The year 1889 was a critical moment in his career, a
time he was to recall later with pain. He was in
Rome, watching the great excavations on the Caelian
Hill for the construction of the new military hospital,
in the area previously occupied by the Villa Casali.[25]
These excavations were influenced greatly by the
needs of the builders. Moreover, Lanciani had a
peculiar, and rather uncomfortable, double role; he
was secretary of the Commissione Archeologica del
Comune di Roma (Archaeological Commission of
Rome's City Council) and, at the same time, architect of the excavations of the Ministero della
Pubblica Istruzione. At the beginning of 1889, the
situation was still calm, and Lanciani was unable to
foresee the storm that was brewing around him.[26]
Between state and city there was a latent tension,
which was to explode at the end of the year. The
scapegoat was the innocent Lanciani, who was
removed from the administration of the excavations.

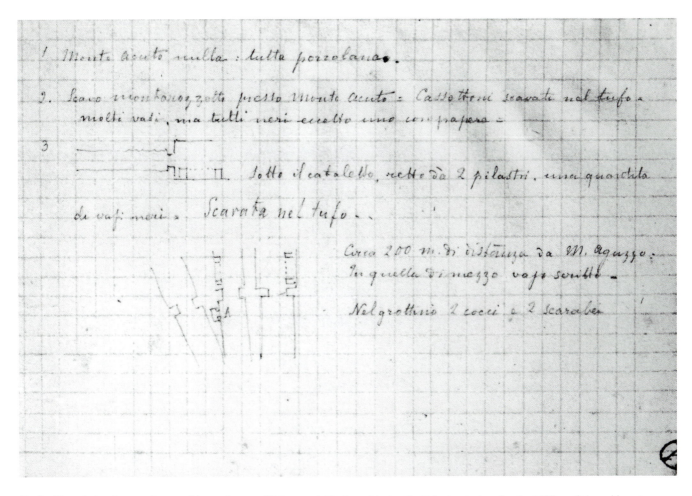

FIG. 5. **Plan of chamber-tombs near Monte Aguzzo. Biblioteca dell'Istituto Nazionale di Archeologia e Storia dell'Arte, Palazzo Venezia, Rome, Collezione Lanciani, MS 79, fol. 9.** *(Reproduced courtesy of the Istituto Nazionale di Archeologia e Storia dell'Arte, Rome.)*

For this reason, too, he left his government position and dedicated himself to research and university teaching (having begun to teach Roman Topography at the Università di Roma in 1882).

DONNA TERESA AT VEII

A rather severe storm was also impending for another protagonist of the excavations at Veii, Donna Teresa Cristina di Borbone, Empress of Brazil. Donna Teresa was the sister of Ferdinand II, King of Naples (**Fig. 6**). In 1843 she had married Dom Pedro II, Emperor of Brazil and a man of great refinement and liberal temperament (at least in so far as an emperor can be a liberal). Despite the emperor's talents, the year 1889 was a critical one for Brazil, for it was in that year that the Republican Revolution broke out. A few years earlier, the empress-archaeologist had sold her estate at Veii to the Marquis Ferrajoli, but she had reserved the right for a few years to undertake excav-

ations on this land and retain ownership of the finds.[27] This was not the first time that Donna Teresa had excavated at Veii. On 15 December 1852 — at the age of 30 — she had been granted a licence to dig on her own properties both inside the town, at Macchia Grande, and outside it, in Oliveto and Poggio del Ponte di Formello. The architect and archaeologist Luigi Canina directed those excavations. The empress's excavations of the necropolis in 1852 stretched over a period of approximately one month. From the documents, it is not clear exactly where she worked. Later, the explorations continued inside the area of the ancient city but, again, the archival documentation is very sketchy.[28]

A few years later, in 1878, the architect Virgilio Vespignani asked on behalf of the empress for a new excavation permit, but nothing came of it because no agreement could be reached with the leaseholders of the land.[29] Finally, in 1889, Donna Teresa revived her old project, perhaps to distract herself from her weighty concerns about the future of Brazil and its

Fig. 6. The members of the Imperial Family Braganza D'Orleans. Photograph of c. 1888. From left to right: Donna Teresa, Prince Antonio, Princess Isabella, Dom Pedro II, Princes Peter August and Louis Gotha-Coburg, Gaston Count of Eu, and Prince Pedro d'Alcantara.

imperial dynasty. A vast excavation campaign got under way, which was to last for six months. In charge of the excavations was Lanciani, who published schematic reports in the *Notizie degli Scavi di Antichità*.[30]

Excavation was undertaken at the necropolis of Picazzano to the north of Veii and also in the cemetery of Vaccareccia to the east.[31] Various trenches were dug in the inhabited part of the site, bringing to light both Etruscan houses and Roman structures. Noteworthy were the discoveries of a Roman villa with a polychrome mosaic (**Fig. 7**) of the fourth century AD[32] and of a large votive deposit on the spur of land known as Piazza d'Armi, which connects the plateau of Veii with the acropolis. These excavations are documented in notes, numerous sketches and some plans preserved in the Lanciani collection. Part of this material was used for the reports published in *Notizie degli Scavi*, but another part of it was presumably intended for a publication that was never finished. So far, very

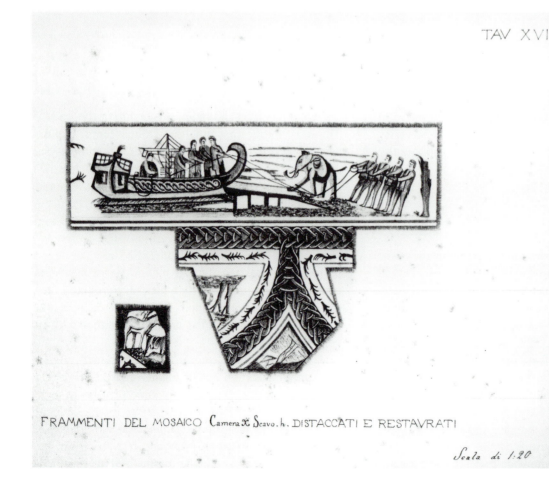

Fig. 7. Mosaic with the shipping of an elephant. Biblioteca dell'Istituto Nazionale di Archeologia e Storia dell'Arte, Palazzo Venezia, Rome, Collezione Lanciani, MS 79, pl. XVI. *(Reproduced courtesy of the Istituto Nazionale di Archeologia e Storia dell'Arte, Rome.)*

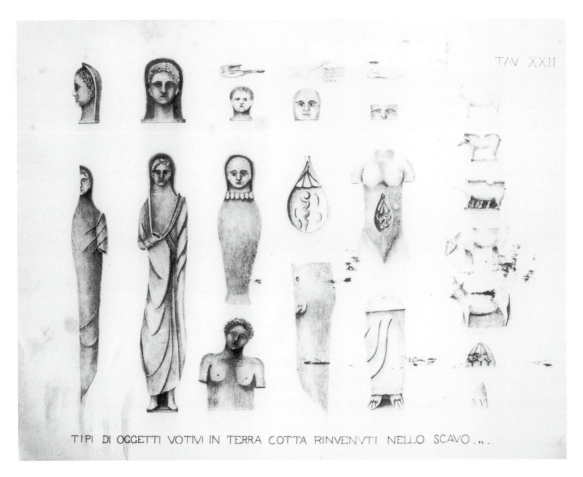

FIG. 8. Votive offerings from Piazza d'Armi. Biblioteca dell'Istituto Nazionale di Archeologia e Storia dell'Arte, Palazzo Venezia, Rome, Collezione Lanciani, MS 79, pl. XXII. *(Reproduced courtesy of the Istituto Nazionale di Archeologia e Storia dell'Arte, Rome.)*

little attention has been devoted to this collection, despite the fact that it includes information of great interest for the topography of the ancient city.[33] In this essay, I shall limit myself to a detailed reconstruction of the excavation of the votives of Piazza d'Armi.

THE VOTIVES OF PIAZZA D'ARMI

During the excavations, a stratum of material about 75 m long and 15 m wide was found, with a variable thickness of between 0.9 and 1.2 m. Very quickly 2,000 objects — perfectly or, at least, well preserved — were found.[34] Twice as many fragmentary pieces were found, occupying many cubic metres. They were reburied where they were found because, in accordance with the standards of the day, they were judged to be of no interest.

As is common with late archaic and mid-Republican votive deposits in central Italy, most of the finds were of terracotta, including male and female

statues, male and female heads and half heads, bodies with exposed intestines, torsos, and the lower half of the body from the navel to the feet. There were also anatomical votives of various types: masks and half masks, babies wrapped in swaddling bands and small animals (**Fig. 8**). Also found were a loom weight, black-glazed ware, little balls made of tufa, a small bronze, one of the so-called 'andirons' of bucchero,[35] and some coins (**Fig. 9**). Lanciani described these as 'a *quadrans* of the type with the hand and two seeds; an *uncia* of the type with a helmeted Minerva and a ship prow with the legend ROMA; an uncial coin of southern Italy; and a piece of *aes rude*'.

The situation in Brazil worsened while Donna Teresa excavated at Veii. Her daughter Isabella (appointed regent while Dom Pedro was in Europe) cut the Gordion knot by finally abolishing slavery through the Golden Law of 13 May 1889. For this courageous gesture Isabella earned the nickname of 'Redentora' and international applause. Yet, this hastened the end of the dynasty. The landowners and

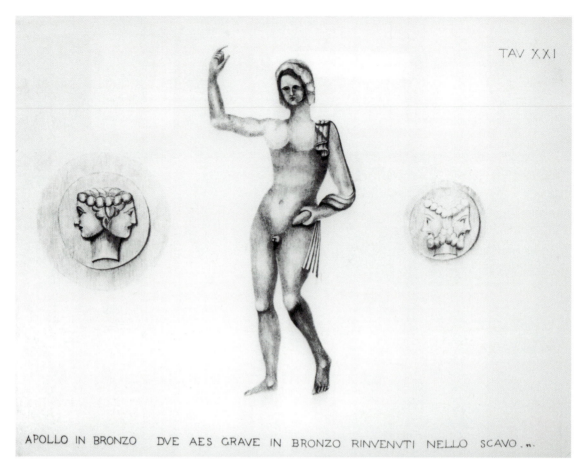

TAV XXI

APOLLO IN BRONZO   DVE AES GRAVE IN BRONZO RINVENVTI NELLO SCAVO.*

FIG. 9. **Coins and a bronze statuette from Veii.** Biblioteca dell'Istituto Nazionale di Archeologia e Storia dell'Arte, Palazzo Venezia, Rome, Collezione Lanciani, MS 79, pl. XXI. *(Reproduced courtesy of the Istituto Nazionale di Archeologia e Storia dell'Arte, Rome.)*

Republicans rose up on 15 November, and two days later the emperor and his family (who had only just returned to their homeland) set sail for Europe, this time for good. The empress died unexpectedly, perhaps of grief, a little after her arrival in Portugal on 28 December 1889. The emperor did not survive her for long; he died in Paris two years later, on 5 December 1891.

It is likely that in this terrible predicament the excavations at Veii were the last things on the mind of the imperial family. Only at the beginning of 1892 was the question raised about where to house the finds. In the meantime, for two years they remained at Isola Farnese. Here the votives awakened great interest and more than half of them were sold to tourists and collectors (we don't know by whom). It is unlikely that the heirs of Donna Teresa were aware of what was going on, and we do not know if Vespignani, the executor of the estate of the deceased empress, knew about these sales. In any event, in those days the finds were widely dispersed, and we are now able to trace only a few pieces, which ended up in private and public collections all over Europe.

Ludwig Stieda, a German physician who published various anatomical studies of them, acquired 21 pieces. It appears that this group later passed to the Museum of Königsberg,[36] today Kaliningrad, but they were probably lost as a result of the terrible destruction suffered by that city during the Second World War. Four other pieces were in the hands of Georg Karo and are to be found today in the Akademisches Kunstmuseum in Bonn.[37] It is likely that nine pieces now in the Muzeul de Istorie at Cluj, Romania, are part of Lanciani's finds.[38] A more substantial nucleus, consisting of busts, heads and a whole statue (**Fig. 10**), is preserved in the Museo Civico of Bologna.[39] The pieces arrived there by way of the collection of a certain Palagi and the collection of the University. Their provenance can be ascertained from a drawing found among Lanciani's notes.[40] This fact, when combined with typological affinities, makes it likely that a good part of the Bologna nucleus may have the same provenance.

Lanciani's drawings are precious for another reason; they permit us to trace a small bronze of the third century BC,[41] which — notwithstanding some differences in the mantel — can be identified with that passed from the Tyskiewicz collection to the Rothschild collection (**Fig. 11**).[42] Its presence among the finds is very interesting. Probably to be identified with Veiovis, it may provide the identity of the divinity of the sanctuary from which the votives came, a subject about which scholars have so far been able to offer only tenuous hypotheses.[43]

Some terracotta tablets showing the abdominal organs were preserved in the Deutsches Archäologisches Institut in Rome.[44] They are very similar to those published by Stieda,[45] and they, too, may be part of the Lanciani finds. Another tablet is preserved in the Museo Civico of Treviso.[46] In 1913 terracotta objects from a location to the southeast of Veii — and thus, perhaps, from Lanciani's excavation — were the property of a physician of Isola Farnese.[47]

In March 1892, Giovanni Nicotera, the Ministro degli Interni, heard rumours that the empress's heirs — Princes Peter August, Leopold and Louis Gotha-Coburg — were planning to sell the archaeological finds. Nicotera immediately informed his colleague, Martini, the Ministro della Pubblica Istruzione, who got in touch with Vespignani. He also created a commission with the task of examining the archaeological material. Its members included Milani, Count Adolfo Cozza, Giuseppe Gatti and two further experts to be designated later. At first, Vespignani replied that the heirs had not yet made up their minds to do anything, but he eventually communicated the news that they had decided to donate all the material to the Museo Preistorico ed Etnografico at the Collegio Romano, nowadays known as the Museo Pigorini at EUR (Rome).[48]

Approximately 800 votives of the 2,000 excavated remained, and these were deposited in the museum. The Director, Luigi Pigorini, was very interested in tombs of the Iron Age but had no interest in the votives. Consequently, he sent 115 pieces to the Museo Civico of Modena in exchange for some ethnological material.[49] He rid himself of the rest by sending it off to the Museum Kircherianum. From here about 40 pieces reached the Museo della Villa Giulia, while one fragment passed in 1952 to the Museo Internazionale della Ceramica at Faenza.[50] Some of the votives remaining in the Roman museums were exhibited in 1898 at an exhibition on the history of medicine held

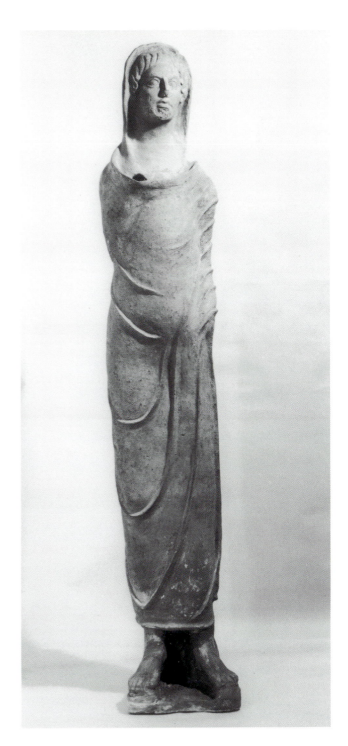

FIG. 10. **Terracotta statue. Museo Civico di Bologna.** *(Reproduced courtesy of the Museo Civico Archeologico, Bologna.)*

in Turin,[51] but in the following years only a few of them were published.[52]

By combining published information and archival data, we can draw a modest conclusion by correcting the commonly held view according to which the archaeological material from Piazza d'Armi dates from the fourth or third century BC.[53] Some pieces — prob-

FIGURINE ETRUSQUE EN BRONZE

FIG. 11. Bronze statuette. Rothschild collection.
From M. Froehner, *La collection Tyskiewicz,
choix des monuments antiques* (Munich, 1892),
29 pl. 32.

ably only a small fraction of the material — lead me to believe that the cult from which the votives come should be dated to an earlier period. Apart from minor details,[54] one can note a bearded head preserved today in Modena that is datable to the fifth century BC.[55] A female head from the same group in Modena probably dates from the end of the same century, and two statuettes of the fifth century are preserved, which have a mould in common with examples discovered at Campetti.[56] One might even consider a date in the sixth century, given the presence of the bucchero 'andiron'

found by Lanciani (**Fig. 12**),[57] and of bucchero sherds, which were found together with fragments of anatomical votives during a recent survey in the same area.[58]

CONCLUSION

In conclusion, the excavations examined in this essay marked the end of an era. With them the tradition of excavations patronized by high-ranking tourists and royalty came to a definitive end, a tradition that had

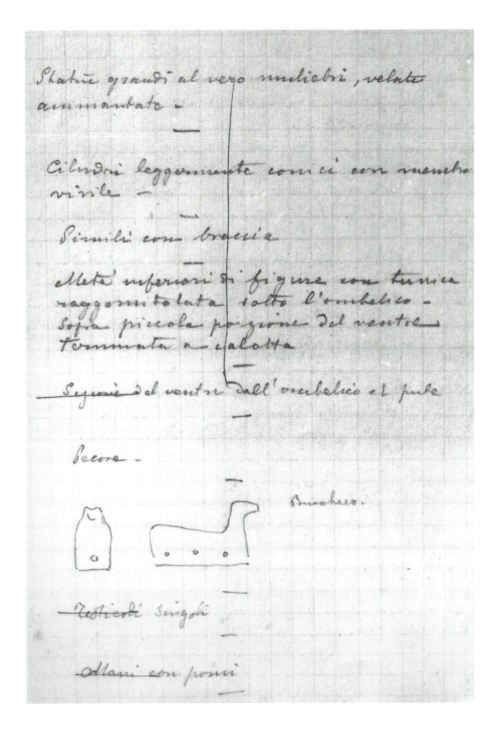

FIG. 12. R. Lanciani, Bucchero andiron. Sketch. Biblioteca dell'Istituto Nazionale di Archeologia e Storia dell'Arte, Palazzo Venezia, Rome, Collezione Lanciani, MS 79, fol. 11v. *(Reproduced courtesy of the Istituto Nazionale di Archeologia e Storia dell'Arte, Rome.)*

had its 'golden age' at the end of the eighteenth century, at the very height of the Grand Tour. With them, also, the history of the imperial family of Orleans Braganza of Brazil also came to an end. And — of lesser importance, perhaps — a particular stage in Lanciani's life came to an end as well.

As far as the finds are concerned, we have observed their great dispersion into collections all over Europe. Even after the donation of 1892 to the Museo Preistorico ed Etnografico, the situation did not improve greatly, as the remaining pieces continued to

be scattered, this time amongst collections of various public museums in many parts of Italy.[59] It is hoped that, thanks to the new vigour presently given to archival research by many scholars, including the contributors to this volume, we shall be able to reconstruct those excavations in a more comprehensive way and bring together again at least the principal finds that are now preserved in Italian museums. This would certainly have pleased that very 'odd couple', Donna Teresa and Rodolfo Lanciani.

Notes

* I am most grateful to Bernie Frischer for translating my text. In this essay most quotations in Italian have been translated into English.

1. The bust was carried to the house of a certain Sili, the tenant of the estate. For the documents, see Archivio Centrale dello Stato, Roma [hereafter ACS], Antichità e Belle Arti, II vers., I ser., b. 252, fasc. 4292 (1888); Biblioteca dell'Istituto Nazionale di Archeologia e Storia dell'Arte, Palazzo Venezia, Roma [hereafter BINASA], Collezione Lanciani, Roma XI, MS 79, fol. 24. The bust was found together with 'il plinto di una statuetta virile di marmo, grande circa 2/5 del vero, con la parte inferiore delle gambe ed alcuni frammenti del busto' ('the plinth of a male statue in marble, about 2/5 life-size, with the lower part of the legs and several fragments of the bust').

2. The bust is not included in H. Mayer, *Antinous* (Munich, 1991).

3. G. Girardini, 'Formello', *NSc* (1882), 291–300.

4. W. Gell, *The Topography of Rome and its Vicinity* I (London, 1834), 19.

5. T. Ashby, 'Il castello d'acqua arcaico del Tuscolo', *BullCom* 57 (1929), 179 n. 2.

6. For the Benedetti excavations, see R. Mengarelli, 'Veio (territorio di Formello)', *NSc* (1901), 238. The excavation assistant R. Finelli mentioned the *cassoni* in a note (Archivio della Soprintendenza Archeologica per l'Etruria Meridionale [hereafter ASAEM], cart. 2, class. II (Scavi)). See also the excavation licence granted to the Benedetti brothers by Prince Chigi (BAV, Archivio Chigi 20060).

7. ASAEM, cart. 2, class. II (Scavi), 28 January–1 February 1910 (Giornale degli scavi che si eseguono a Formello). Tombs excavated illegally by *tombaroli* are evident in aerial photographs of 1977 (Aereofototeca Nazionale, Rome, *strisciata* 8, photo no. 66679); also G. Brunetti Nardi, *Repertorio degli scavi e delle scoperte archeologiche nell'Etruria Meridionale (1971–75)* III (Rome, 1981), 144. In 1980, during a survey of the area, I noted fragments of vases from tombs of the end of the seventh century BC.

8. R. Lanciani, in A.L. Cubberley (ed.), *Notes from Rome by Rodolfo Lanciani* (London, 1988), 107–8.

9. BINASA, Collezione Lanciani, Roma XI, MS 79, fols 9, 28.

10. ACS, Antichità e Belle Arti, II vers., I ser., b. 252, fasc. 4376 (letters of 31 January and 21 February 1882).

11. BINASA, Collezione Lanciani, Roma XI, MS 79, fol. 28 (Pio Gui to Prince Chigi, 20 January 1882).

12. Lanciani described four amphorae painted with horizontal polychrome bands (height 0.77 m, diameter 0.43 m). They probably are of Greek production, Attic type *à la brosse*; see M.A. Rizzo, *Le anfore da trasporto e il commercio etrusco arcaico* I *(Complessi tombali dell'Etruria Meridionale)* (Rome, 1990).

13. The tripod is missing from the Chigi inventory of the finds from Monte Aguzzo (ASAEM, cart. 107, fasc. 1, pos. Formello).

14. L. Banti, *sub voce* in *Enciclopedia dell'arte antica classica e orientale* V (Rome, 1963), 669–70.

15. BINASA, Collezione Lanciani, Roma XI, MS 79, fol. 9.

16. There is no mention of them in the Chigi inventory (above, n. 13).

17. T. Mommsen, 'Alfabeto greco-italico primitivo del vaso Chigi', *BullInst* (1882), 90–6; *TLE* no. 49.

18. BAV, Archivio Chigi 20060.

19. L.A. Milani, *Il Regio Museo Archeologico di Firenze* (Florence, 1912), 70.

20. ASAEM, cart. 260, class. Ia (Collezioni), tit. Formello (Vasi della collezione Chigi).

21. ASAEM, cart. 260, pos. IIa (Collezioni), prot. 865 (G.A. Colini to Ministero della Pubblica Istruzione, 2 November 1912).

22. ASAEM, cart. 260, class. IIa (Collezioni), tit. Formello (Vasi della collezione Chigi); cart. 107, fasc. 1, pos. Formello; BAV, Archivio Chigi (Arte e antichità, fasc. nos. 106, 109) nos. 7474, 7476–7. For the Chigi's inventory of these finds, dated 1881, with the inventory numbers of the Villa Giulia Museum noted in the margins, see ASAEM, cart. 107, fasc. 1, pos. Formello. At a later date somebody renumbered all the finds on a copy of the inventory, using the same numbers but for different objects.

23. In the 1970s M. Di Bisceglie studied them for his thesis in Etruscology (Università di Roma), but he was not aware of all the documentation in the various archives.

24. For instance, an amphora of the third or second century BC, a black-glazed lamp of the third century BC and a plate with a christogram of the fourth century AD.

25. A. Carignani, 'Cent'anni dopo. Antiche scoperte e nuove interpretazioni dagli scavi all'ospedale militare del Celio', *Mélanges de l'École Française de Rome. Antiquité* 105 (1993), 709–46. Also M. Musacchio, *L'archivio della Direzione Generale delle Antichità e Belle Arti (1860–1890), Pubblicazioni degli Archivi di Stato — Strumenti* CXX (Rome, 1994), 45–51.

26. M. Barnabei and F. Delpino, *Le 'memorie di un archeologo' di Felice Barnabei* (Rome, 1991), app. III.

27. Lanciani, in Cubberley (ed.), *Notes* (above, n. 8), 208.

28. ASR, Ministero Lavori Pubblici, b. 397, fasc. 2–3; Biblioteca Civica Berio, Archivio Canina, m.r. XXVII, 262, fols 1, 7–8; C.L. Visconti (?), in *Giornale di Roma* 106 (12 May 1853), 420; L. Canina, 'Notizie sui recenti scavi di Veii', *BullInst* (1853), 109; *CIL* XI 3783.

29. ACS, Antichità e Belle Arti, II vers., I ser., b. 252, fasc. 4292 (1888).

30. R. Lanciani, 'Veio — scoperte nell'area della città e della necropoli veientana', *NSc* (1889), 10–12, 29–31; R. Lanciani, 'Veio', *NSc* (1889), 60–5, 154–8; R. Lanciani, 'Veio — scavi della necropoli', *NSc* (1889), 238–9.

31. J. Palm, 'Veiian tomb groups in the Museo Preistorico, Rome', *Skrifter Utgivna av Svenska Institutet i Rom* 16 (*Opuscula Romana* 7) (1952), 50–86.

32. Lanciani, 'Veio — scoperte' (above, n. 30), 10; F. Baratte, *Catalogue des mosaïques romaines et paléochretiennes du Musée du Louvre* (Paris, 1978), 18–20; P. Liverani,

Municipium Augustum Veiens (Rome, 1987), 162.

33. The documents were used especially by J.B. Ward-Perkins ('Veii: the historical topography of the ancient city', *PBSR* 19 (1961)) and F. Delpino (*Cronache Veientane. Storia delle ricerche archeologiche a Veio* I. *Dal XIV alla metà del XIX secolo* (Rome, 1985); 'I rilievi archeologici di Veio della collezione Lanciani. Appunti su Francesco Caracciolo', *Bollettino d'Arte* 68–9 (1991), 161–76). In recent years they have been studied systematically in research in progress on Veii at the Istituto di Topografia Antica, Università di Roma 'La Sapienza'; the present contribution contains some of the earliest results, but the main part of the collective study is to follow.

34. Lanciani, 'Veio — scoperte' (above, n. 30), 30–1, 63–5; ACS, Antichità e Belle Arti, II vers., I ser., b. 252, fasc. 4292 (1888); R. Lanciani, *Pagan and Christian Rome* (London, 1892), 64–6; Lanciani, in Cubberley (ed.), *Notes* (above, n. 8), 211, correspondence of 28 September 1889; BINASA, Collezione Lanciani, Roma XI, MS 79, pls XXI–XXII, fols 6, 11–12, 15, 29. The figure of 4,000 finds mentioned by Lanciani (*Pagan and Christian Rome*, 64–6) is probably a misprint.

35. It consists of a crouching animal, of a type known at Veii (L. Murray Threipland, 'Excavations beside the North-West Gate at Veii 1957–58. Part II', *PBSR* 31 (1963), 71–3, pls XII–XIII, with a list), published by Lanciani as found during the excavation of the building at Comunità (Lanciani, 'Veio' (above, n. 30), 63). On the contrary, it is recorded among the votive offerings of Piazza d'Armi in his unpublished notes (BINASA, Collezione Lanciani, Roma XI, MS 79, fol. 11v).

36. L. Stieda, *Anatomisch-archäologische Studien* II (Wiesbaden, 1901), 70–2, 82, 84–6, 100–5, 108–9, pls II.1–5, III.9, IV–V.1011, 14–15, 18–28; P. Decouflé, 'La notion d'ex-voto anatomique chez les Etrusco-Romains', *Collection Latomus* 72 (1964), 18–19, fig. 7.

37. Only three of them (inv. D 77, 79–80) were published. See L. Stieda, 'Ueber alt-italische Weihgeschenke', *Mitteilungen des Deutschen Archäologischen Instituts. Römische Abteilung* 14 (1899), 230; Stieda, *Studien* II (above, n. 36), 70, 82–4, pl. III.8; Decouflé, 'La notion' (above, n. 36), 23, figs 10–11; M. Hofter, *Untersuchungen zu Stil und Chronologie der Mittelitalischer Terrakotta-Votivköpfe* (dissertation) (Bonn, 1985), 180–1 no. 89. I have not had the opportunity to consult either the *Verhandlungen der Gesellschaft Deutscher Naturforscher und Aerzte, 71. Versammlung zu München (1899)* II (II) (Leipzig, 1900), 451, nor A. Körte-Greifswald, *Verhandlungen der Gesellschaft Deutscher Naturforscher und Aerzte* (Düsseldorf, 1898), 70, mentioned by Stieda, *Studien* II (above, n. 36). W. Geominy has kindly informed me that the three votive offerings and an unpublished breast (inv. D 78) were presented to the Museum by Karo, but it seems to me unlikely that he acquired them at Veii itself. Karo did not visit Italy before 1896; he probably bought them on the Roman antiquarian market.

38. E. Crisan, 'Ex voto-uri anatomice de la Veii în Muzeul de Istorie Cluj', *Acta Musei Napocensis* 7 (1970), 489–97.

39. S. Tovoli, in *Il Museo Civico di Bologna* (Bologna, 1982),

196, room VIII, showcase 7.

40. BINASA, Collezione Lanciani, Roma XI, MS 79, pl. XXII; its provenance from Veii was suggested by G. Hafner, 'Etruskische togati', *Antike Plastik* 9 (1969), 35–6, pls 13, 22 on the basis of typological arguments. I am indebted to C. Morigi Govi for the photo I publish here.

41. BINASA, Collezione Lanciani, Roma XI, MS 79, pl. XXI (in the middle).

42. M. Froehner, *La collection Tyskiewicz, choix de monuments antiques* (Munich, 1892), 29, pl. 32; M. Froehner, *Collection d'antiquités du comte Michel Tyskiewicz*, sale of 8–10 June 1898, lot 121, pl. X; S. Reinach, 'Une statuette de bronze représentant Alexandre le Grand', *Revue Archéologique* IV, 5(1) (1905), 32–43, pls I–II; S. Reinach, *Répertoire de la statuaire grecque et romaine* (Paris, 1908²) II, 505.6, and III, 274.6; M. Bieber, 'Die Venus Genitrix des Arkesilaos', *Mitteilungen des Deutschen Archäologischen Instituts. Römische Abteilung* 48 (1933), 267, n. 3, who dated the small bronze (height 0.225 m) to the Augustan period. The context and dating of similar bronzes from Etruria suggest that it should rather be dated to the third century BC. For an Etruscan bronze related to the iconography of Alexander the Great, see W. Wohlmayr, 'Alexander in Etrurien', *Jahreshefte des Österreichischen Archäologischen Instituts in Wien* 58 (1988), Beiblatt, 59–70; A.M. Nielsen, 'Alexandroider', *Meddelelser fra Ny Carlsberg Glyptotek* 47 (1991), 30–45.

43. M. Torelli, 'Review of L. Vagnetti's *Il deposito votivo di Campetti a Veio*', *Dialoghi di Archeologia* 7 (1973), 124–5, has attributed this material to a supposed temple *c.* 400 m to the north, partly excavated by Lanciani ('Veio' (above, n. 30), 63); see also Ward-Perkins, 'Veii' (above, n. 33), 31, 69, fig. 19c, pl. IX. More details may be found in Lanciani's unpublished notes (BINASA, Collezione Lanciani, Roma XI, MS 79, fol. 6r). Torelli has recognized in these structures the famous Temple of Juno Regina, but at present there is insufficient evidence to prove it.

44. M. Tabanelli, *Gli ex-voto poliviscerali etruschi e romani* (Florence, 1962), 65 nos. 6–7, fig. 30 and 66–7, nos. 9–11, fig. 31.

45. Stieda, *Studien* II (above, n. 36). The types are well known at Veii thanks to the excavations of the sanctuary near the Caere Gate; see I. Pohl and M. Torelli, 'Veio. Scoperta di un piccolo santuario etrusco in località Campetti', *NSc* (1973), 247–8, k1–6, fig. 126.

46. M. Borda, *Ceramiche e terrecotte greche, magno-greche e italiche del Museo Civico di Treviso* (Treviso, 1974), 188 no. 203. The (misinterpreted) fragment arrived in the museum with the Donà collection. Part of this collection entered the museum between 1883 and 1886, but it is equally possible that other acquisitions are of a later date, before the death of Pietro Donà in 1892 (Borda, p. 7).

47. G. Tomassetti, *La campagna romana* II (Rome, 1913), 93.

48. For the documents relating to the donation, see ACS, Antichità e Belle Arti, II vers., I ser., b. 247, fasc. 4292 (1888). Also L. Pigorini, 'Tombe arcaiche a Veio', *Rendiconti. Atti dell'Accademia Nazionale dei Lincei, Classe di Scienze*

Morali, Storiche e Filologiche 1 (1892), 422; Stieda, *Studien* II (above, n. 36), 124–5; H.R.W. Smith, 'Investigation in the National Museum in Rio de Janeiro, Brazil, of the Etruscan antiquities excavated in Italy for the Empress Dona Teresa Cristina in 1889', *The American Philosophical Society Yearbook* 24 (1960), 572; L. Vagnetti, *Il deposito votivo di Campetti a Veio* (Florence, 1971), 30 no. 5.

49. Pigorini's letters are in ACS, Antichità e Belle Arti, II vers., I ser., b. 247, fasc. 4292 (1888). Also A. Crespellani, *Guida al Museo Civico di Modena* (Modena, 1897), 89 (XXXV); Tabanelli, *Gli ex-voto* (above, n. 44), 40–1, no. 8, fig. 11, p. 69, no. 14, fig. 35, and pp. 69–70, no. 15; Smith, 'Investigation' (above, n. 48); Vagnetti, *Il deposito votivo* (above, n. 48), 30 no. 5. Photographs and drawings of part of the material preserved in Modena are reproduced in E. Govi, *Etruschi 'fra tutti i popoli il più religioso'* (Modena, 1991), cover and figs 14, 17, 21, 23–4; M.G. Bertani, 'Veio e i suoi santuari', in Govi, *Etruschi*, 12, figs pp. 6, 11–18.

50. Tabanelli, *Gli ex-voto* (above, n. 44), 68–9, no. 13, fig. 34.

51. P. Giacosa, *Magistri Salernitani nondum editi: catalogo ragionato della esposizione di storia della medicina aperta a Torino nel 1898* (Turin, 1901), 578–9, atlas pl. 34 (only six of the pieces come from Veii). I could not consult P. Giacosa, *Breve notizia sugli oggetti esposti alla mostra della storia della medicina* (Turin, 1898), 36ff.

52. L. Sambon, 'Donaria of medical interest', *British Medical Journal* 2 (1895), 146; G. Kaschnitz von Weinberg, 'Ritratti fittili etruschi e romani dal secolo III al I av. Cr.', *RendPontAcc* 3 (1924–5), 338; Tabanelli, *Gli ex-voto* (above, n. 44), 73 no. 1, fig. 36; Hafner, 'Etruskische togati' (above, n. 40), 33–5, pls 20–1; G. Bartoloni, 'Review of the exhibition *Enea nel Lazio, archeologia e mito*', *Bollettino d'Arte* 67 (1982), 13, 141, figs 4–6.

53. Bartoloni, 'Review' (above, n. 52). According to Vagnetti, *Il deposito votivo* (above, n. 48), 20, no material is earlier than the third century BC.

54. This nucleus of votive offerings includes 21 heads (Bartoloni, 'Review' (above, n. 52), 52, figs 5–6) comparable with types found at Lavinium of the first half of the fourth century BC. See M. Fenelli's short entries in *Enea nel Lazio, archeologia e mito* (Rome, 1981), 267–8 (D 265–71), 236–8 (D 218–20).

55. Only quoted by M.G. Bertani, 'Veio e i suoi santuari', in Govi, *Etruschi* (above, n. 49), 12; dated to the second half of the fifth century BC and conjecturally attributed to the architectural decoration of a building. It consists of a male face of the late archaic period, with the typical compact and elongated beard.

56. Vagnetti, *Il deposito votivo* (above, n. 48), 75 no. 6, pl. XXXVII (female seated statuette type G XXVII, mid-fifth century BC); p. 82 no. 3, pl. XLIV (warrior type J V, first half of the fifth century). Torelli ('Review' (above, n. 43), 400) preferred a later date, within the fourth century, for both pieces, but his arguments are too weak.

57. See above, n. 35.

58. The survey was undertaken for the Istituto di Topografia Antica, Università di Roma 'La Sapienza'.

59. Material left *in situ*, or not excavated, was frequently robbed.

See ASAEM, pos. 31 (IX Isola Farnese), and pos. 1 (La Storta); A. Sommella Mura (ed.), *Repertorio degli scavi e delle scoperte archeologiche nell'Etruria Meridionale (1939–1965)* I (Rome, 1969), 50; Vagnetti, *Il deposito votivo* (above, n. 48), 18 no. 8; M. Torelli, 'Veio, la città, l'arx e il culto di Giunone Regina', in H. Blanck (ed.), *Miscellanea archaeologica dedicata a Tobias Dohrn* (Rome, 1982), 125.

BIOGRAPHICAL NOTES ON THE CONTRIBUTORS

and

CONTRIBUTORS' ADDRESSES

Biographical Notes on the Contributors

Ilaria Bignamini †, a historian of art and archaeology. Responsible for new archival research for *A Dictionary of British and Irish Travellers in Italy 1701–1800*, edited by J. Ingamells (New Haven/London, 1997). Co-curator and co-editor, with A. Wilton, of *The Grand Tour* exhibition and catalogue (Tate Gallery, London, 1996, and Palazzo delle Esposizioni, Rome, 1997). Leverhulme Trust Research Fellow at the Department of the History of Art, University of Oxford, 1996–9 (*British archaeological excavations in Italy 1764–1801*). Organizer of the workshops on *Archives & Excavations* (British School at Rome and Ashmolean Museum, Oxford, 1997–8). Publications on eighteenth- and nineteenth-century excavations include essays in *The Burlington Magazine* (August 1994), *Bollettino Monumenti Musei e Gallerie Pontificie* (1996), *Journal of Hellenic Studies* (1998), *Papers of the British School at Rome* (1998) (with A. Claridge), *Castelporziano* IV (forthcoming) and *Rendiconti della Pontificia Accademia Romana di Archeologia* (forthcoming). Research projects: *I 'marmi inglesi' nei Musei Vaticani: catalogo generale*; *Correspondence of British excavators and dealers active in Rome during the eighteenth and early nineteenth centuries (with appendices of excavation and export licences, and sales)*.

Iain Gordon Brown (Principal Curator of Manuscripts, National Library of Scotland), historian of British eighteenth- and early nineteenth-century literature, art and taste. Author of many books, essays and articles in these fields, including *The Hobby-Horsical Antiquary* (Edinburgh, 1980), *Poet and Painter: Allan Ramsay, Father and Son* (Edinburgh, 1984) and (as joint editor and contributor) *Allan Ramsay and the Search for Horace's Villa* (Aldershot, 2001). Fellow of both the Royal Society of Edinburgh and the Society of Antiquaries of London.

Ian Campbell (Reader in Architectural History and Theory, Edinburgh College of Art), art historian, specializing in Renaissance architecture in Italy and Scotland. Collaborated on the *Census of Antique Works of Art and Architecture known to the Renaissance* (CD-ROM, Munich, 1998). Principal author of three-volume catalogue of architectural drawings (London, 2004) in *The Paper Museum of Cassiano dal Pozzo* series. Contributor to two volumes of *The Architectural Drawings of Antonio da Sangallo the Younger and his Circle* (New York/Cambridge (Mass.), 1994–).

Amanda Claridge (Reader in Classical Archaeology, Royal Holloway, University of London), archaeologist and historian of Renaissance and seventeenth-century antiquarianism, archaeology and collections. Assistant Director of the British School at Rome for many years. Co-curator and co-author, with J.B. Ward-Perkins, of the exhibition and catalogue *Pompeii AD 79* (Royal Academy of Art, London, 1976, and elsewhere). Editor and author of volumes in the Antiquities Series of the *catalogue raisonné* of the dal Pozzo collection, *The Paper Museum of Cassiano dal Pozzo* (London, 1996–). Co-editor, with A. Gallina Zevi, of *'Roman Ostia' Revisited* (London, 1996) and author of *Rome (An Oxford Archaeological Guide)* (Oxford, 1998).

Brian F. Cook (Former Keeper of Greek and Roman Antiquities, British Museum). Retired archaeologist and historian of eighteenth- and nineteenth-century antiquarianism in Italy, Greece, Turkey and Egypt. Investigated the contents of the so-called 'Soldiers' Tomb', excavated in 1885 near Alexandria (*Inscribed Hadra Vases in The Metropolitan Museum of Art* (New York, 1966)), and the post-classical history of the Mausoleum frieze-blocks (*Relief Sculpture of the Mausoleum at Halicarnassus* (Oxford, 2004)); contributed a paper on 'British archaeologists in the Aegean' to V. Brand (ed.), *The Study of the Past in the Victorian Age* (Oxford, 1998), and also has published on Greek sculpture, pottery and inscriptions. Currently working on *Catalogue of the Townley Marbles* for the British Museum, drawing extensively on papers in the Townley Archive.

Giorgio Filippi (Principal Curator of the Department of Epigraphy, Vatican Museums), archaeologist, epigraphist, historian of archaeology and collections.

Ingo Herklotz (Professor of the History of Italian Art, University of Marburg), historian of medieval, Renaissance and seventeenth-century art, of antiquarianism, archaeology and collections. Author of the book *Cassiano dal Pozzo und die Archäologie des 17. Jahrhunderts* (Munich, 1999). Contributor to volumes on Baronio (Sora, 1985), Cassiano dal Pozzo's *Paper Museum* (Milan, 1992), *Documentary Culture: Florence and Rome* (Bologna, 1992), *Poussin et Rome* (Paris, 1996), *Art History in the Age of Bellori* (Cambridge, 2002). Publications on various aspects of the seventeenth-century antique have appeared in *The Burlington Magazine* (1993, 1995, 1996, 1997, 1998), *Memoirs of the American Academy in Rome* (1995) and *Wolfenbütteler Renaissance Mitteilungen* (1995, 1998, 2001, 2002).

Valentin Kockel (Professor of Classical Archaeology, University of Augsburg), archaeologist and historian of excavations in Pompeii and methods of documenting archaeological finds in the eighteenth and nineteenth centuries. With particular regard to the field of *Archives & Excavations*, has co-curated and co-edited, with W. Helmberger, the exhibition and catalogue *Rom über die Alpen Tragen* (Munich, 1993), and *Ansicht — Plan — Modell. Zur Darstellung Antiker Architektur* (Augsburg/Stendal, 1996–7). Author of the book *Phelloplastica. Modelli in sughero dell'architettura antica nel XVIII secolo nella collezione di Gustavo III di Svezia* (Rome, 1998).

Susanna Le Pera Buranelli (Sovraintendenza Comunale ai Beni Archeologici, Rome), archaeologist, specialist in ancient topography and historian of archaeology. Curator and contributor to books on Ashby's photographs published for the British School at Rome: *Thomas Ashby. Un archeologo fotografa la campagna romana tra '800 e '900* (Rome, 1986), *Archeologia a Roma nelle fotografie di Thomas Ashby 1891–1930* (Naples, 1989), *Il Lazio di Thomas Ashby 1891–1930*, vol. I (Rome, 1994), *Sulla Via Appia da Roma a Brindisi. Le fotografie di Thomas Ashby 1891–1925* (Rome, 2003). Curator of the new series of publications *Quaderni della Carta dell'Agro Romano*. Responsible for the editing of the new *Forma Urbis Romae*.

Paolo Liverani (Keeper of the Department of Classical Antiquities, Vatican Museums), archaeologist, specialist in ancient topography and Roman art of the Imperial period, and historian of archaeology, collections and museums. Since joining the Vatican Museums, has devoted much of his time to research on the excavation and collection provenance of marbles in that collection and has contributed to several of its recent catalogues. Editor of two volumes of the new edition of Rodolfo Lanciani's *Storia degli scavi* (vol. IV, Rome, 1992; vol. VI, Rome, 2000). Author of the books *L'antiquarium di Villa Barberini a Castel Gandolfo* (Vatican City, 1989) and *La topografia antica del Vaticano* (Vatican City, 1999). Contributor to books on *Polykletforschungen* (Berlin, 1993) and *Luciano Bonaparte* (Rome, 1996). Publications on the Lateran include essays in *Mélanges de l'École Française de Rome. Antiquité* (1988), *Rendiconti della Pontificia Accademia Romana di Archeologia* (1992–3), *Bullettino della Commissione Archeologica Comunale di Roma* (1993), *Rivista di Archeologia Cristiana* (1999) and the editing of *Laterano 1. Scavi sotto la Basilica di S. Giovanni. I materiali* (Vatican City, 1998). His work on Veii has appeared in *Papers of the British School at Rome* (1984), *Municipium Augustum Veiens* (Rome, 1987), *Archeologia Classica* (1986–8), *Arva metunt* I. *Materiali per un Museo dell'Agro Veietano* (Rome, 1998).

Ronald T. Ridley (Professor of History, University of Melbourne), historian of nineteenth-century Roman archaeology. Author of *The Eagle and the Spade. Archaeology in Rome during the Napoleonic Era* (Cambridge, 1992) and *The Pope's Archaeologist: the Life and Times of Carlo Fea* (Rome, 2000).

CORNELIS SCHUDDEBOOM (Lecturer, Institute of the History of Art, University of Utrecht), historian of art and of Christian archaeology. Author of the book *Philips van Winghe (1560–1592) en het ontstaan van de christelijke archeologie* (Haren, 1996).

RITA TURCHETTI (Regione Lazio, Direzione Regionale Cultura, Area Valorizzazione del Territorio e del Patrimonio Culturale), archaeologist, specialist on ancient topography and historian of archaeology. Curator of exhibitions of and contributor to books on Ashby's photographs published for the British School at Rome: *Thomas Ashby. Un archeologo fotografa la campagna romana tra '800 e '900* (Rome, 1986), *Archeologia a Roma nelle fotografie di Thomas Ashby 1891–1930* (Naples, 1989), *Il Lazio di Thomas Ashby 1891–1930*, vol. I (Rome, 1994), *Sulla Via Appia da Roma a Brindisi. Le fotografie di Thomas Ashby 1891–1925* (Rome, 2003). Other documentary research includes studies on the area of the Imperial Forum, published in *Curia, Forum Iulium, Forum Transitorium* (*Lavori e studi di archeologia* 14) (Rome, 1989). Studies on ancient topography have been published in *Capena e il suo territorio* (Rome, 1995) and *Monterotondo e il suo territorio* (Rome, 1995).

KLAUS E. WERNER (Rome), a specialist on Roman mosaics and the history of archaeology. Has written *Die Sammlung Antiker Mosaiken in den Vatikanischen Museen* (Vatican City, 1998). His current research is concerned with the digitization of museum collections.

Contributors' Addresses

Dr Iain Gordon Brown
Manuscripts Division, National Library of Scotland,
George IV Bridge, Edinburgh, EH1 1EW, Great Britain.
i.brown@nls.uk

Dr Ian Campbell
Edinburgh College of Art, Lauriston Place, Edinburgh,
EH3 9DF, Great Britain.
i.campbell@eca.ac.uk

Amanda Claridge
Department of Classics, Royal Holloway, University of
London, Egham Hill, Egham, Surrey, TW20 0EX,
Great Britain.
a.claridge@rhul.ac.uk

Brian F. Cook
4 Belmont Avenue, Barnet, Herts, EN4 9LJ, Great
Britain.

Dott. Giorgio Filippi
Monumenti Musei e Gallerie Pontificie, Direzione del
Reparto per le Antichità Classiche, 00120 Vatican City.
3332580173@tim.it

Prof. Dr Ingo Herklotz
Philipps-Universität Marburg, Kunstgeschichtliches
Institut, Biegenstr. 11, 35037 Marburg, Germany.
herklotz@fotomarburg.de

Prof. Valentin Kockel
Klassische Archäologie, Philosophische Fakultät,
Universität Augsburg, Universitätsstr. 10, D-86135
Augsburg, Germany.
Valentin.Kockel@phil.uni-augsburg.de

Dott.ssa Susanna Le Pera Buranelli
Sovraintendenza Comunale ai Beni Archeologici,
Via Teatro di Marcello 5, 00196 Rome, Italy.
susannalepera@tiscali.it

Dott. Paolo Liverani
Musei Vaticani, Direzione del Reparto per le Antichità
Classiche, 00120 Vatican City.
P.Liverani@libero.it

Prof. Ronald T. Ridley
Department of History, University of Melbourne,
Parkville, Victoria 3052, Australia.
r.ridley@unimelb.edu.au

Dr Cornelis Schuddeboom
Universiteit Utrecht, Faculteit der Letteren, Vakgroep
Kunstgeschiedenis, Kromme Nieuwegracht 29, 3512
HD Utrecht, The Netherlands.
muffin@wxs.nl

Dott.ssa Rita Turchetti
Regione Lazio, Direzione Regionale Cultura,
Area Valorizzazione del Territorio e del Patrimonio
Culturale, Via del Caravaggio 99, 00147 Rome, Italy.
r.turchetti@regione.lazio.it

Dr Klaus E. Werner
Rome, Italy.
http://www.collectio.org

INDEX